UNFABLING
THE EAST

UNFABLING THE EAST

The Enlightenment's Encounter with Asia

Jürgen Osterhammel

Translated by Robert Savage

PRINCETON UNIVERSITY PRESS
Princeton and Oxford

Die Entzauberung Asiens: Europa und die asiatischen Reiche im 18. Jahrhundert by Jürgen Osterhammel © Verlag C. H. Beck oHG, München 2013

Published by Princeton University Press,
41 William Street, Princeton, New Jersey 08540

In the United Kingdom: Princeton University Press,
6 Oxford Street, Woodstock, Oxfordshire OX20 1TR

press.princeton.edu

Jacket image: *Portuguese in Burma*, 1730, copper engraving by Jan Caspar Philipps (1690–1775) © akg-images.

Jacket design by Faceout Studio, Charles Brock.

Library of Congress Cataloging-in-Publication Data
Names: Osterhammel, Jürgen, author.
Title: Unfabling the East : the Enlightenment's encounter with Asia / Jürgen Osterhammel ; translated by Robert Savage.
Other titles: Die Entzauberung Asiens. English
Description: Princeton, NJ : Princeton University Press, [2018] | Includes bibliographical references and index.
Identifiers: LCCN 2017039097 | ISBN 9780691172729 (hardcover : alk. paper)
Subjects: LCSH: Asia—Foreign public opinion, European. | Asia—Civilization—Public opinion. | Public opinion—Europe. | Asia—Description and travel. | Asia—Relations—Europe. | Europe—Relations—Asia.
Classification: LCC DS33.4.E85 O7513 2018 | DDC 303.3/8095—dc23
LC record available at https://lccn.loc.gov/2017039097
British Library Cataloging-in-Publication Data is available

The translation of this work was funded by Geisteswissenschaften International—Translation Funding for Humanities and Social Sciences from Germany, a joint initiative of the Fritz Thyssen Foundation, the German Federal Foreign Office, the collecting society VG WORT, and the Börsenverein des Deutschen Buchhandels (German Publishers & Booksellers Association).

This book has been composed in Minion Pro

Printed on acid-free paper. ∞

Printed in the United States of America

10 9 8 7 6 5 4 3 2 1

Contents

Preface

The long eighteenth century, lasting from around 1680 to the 1820s, was a period of intensive European engagement with Asia. This engagement was partly colonial—in South Asia, on Java and the Philippines, in the Russian Empire from the Black Sea to the vast expanses of Siberia. Other regions of the continent were barely touched by European imperial ambitions: the Ottoman Empire, Persia, Afghanistan, China, Japan, and the greater part of Southeast Asia. Whether colonized or not, a steady stream of European adventurers, scholars, explorers, diplomats, soldiers, traders, and priests crisscrossed the continent, reporting back on what they saw to an interested public.

Their writings, often translated into several languages and disseminated across the continent and also to the Americas, laid the foundation for some of the era's most important works of philosophy, social theory, and history. The "big names" and armchair travelers who never left Europe referred to Asia extensively, making it a touchstone for their wide-ranging theories. Asia may have been Europe's "Other," but it figured as a permanent intellectual challenge rather than as an entirely alien and incomprehensible world. Montesquieu, Voltaire, or Turgot in France; Adam Smith, Edmund Burke, or Thomas Robert Malthus in Great Britain; Gottfried Wilhelm Leibniz, Johann Gottfried Herder, or Georg Wilhelm Friedrich Hegel in Germany; last but not least the great historian Edward Gibbon in his self-imposed exile at Lausanne—they all grappled with the broad variety of Asia's societies and civilizations, with its past, present, and future. Together with philosophically-minded travelers on the ground—Engelbert Kaempfer in Japan, John Chardin in Persia, the Jesuits in China, Carsten Niebuhr in Arabia, Sir Stamford Raffles in Java, and many others—they formed a single and seamless class of physically and mentally mobile intellectuals, a *classe curieuse.*

I draw on this large body of travel literature and theoretical comment to challenge the conventional postcolonial wisdom that sees all attempts to understand "the East," including those of an era "before empire," as invariably imperialistic and contaminated by European fantasies of power. On the other hand, the book is no partisan and one-dimensional apology of an Enlightenment whose ambiguities and "dialectic"—see Theodor W. Adorno's and Max Horkheimer's famous book *Dialectic of Enlightenment* (1947)—have been revealed by numerous earlier critics. The main argument of my book is that the Enlightenment's discovery of Asia entailed a more open-minded, less patronizing approach to foreign cultures than suggested by those who see it as a mere incubation period of Orientalism. I also discuss how Enlightenment cosmopolitanism came to be replaced by the aggressive colonialism and sense of superiority so prevalent in the nineteenth century. The end result was a mental "great divergence" in Eurasia that has narrowed again only in our own time. Asia was left an object of scientific inquiry while it disappeared from public debates in the many fields where it had played such an enormous role before: political theory, economics, the philosophy of history, or emergent comparative social science. This development can be conceptualized as a passage from "inclusive" to "exclusive" Eurocentrism.

This book has an unusual history, and readers may want to know a little about it before they decide to spend time on the chapters that follow. It was first published in German in 1998 as *Die Entzauberung Asiens: Europa und die asiatischen Reiche im 18. Jahrhundert*; a second edition of 2010 added a postscript commenting on more recent literature. How the English title *Unfabling the East* came about will be explained at the end of chapter 1. Most of the library research for the book was done in the mid-1980s in dim rare book collections and in front of uncomfortable microfiche readers, in other words, at a time when the prospect of having a profusion of sources available at the click of a mouse was beyond one's wildest imagination. After a long interval caused by other professional commitments, I wrote the bulk of the manuscript in 1996–97 while I had the privilege of spending ten months as a fellow at that pinnacle of the German academic system, the Wissenschaftskolleg (Institute for Advanced Studies) in Berlin. It is a pleasure to renew my thanks to that splendid institution, in particular to its rector at the time, Wolf Lepenies, and to the current rector, Barbara Stollberg-Rilinger. The Wissenschaftskolleg in 2001 also graced the book with its own Anna-Krüger-Preis given to publications that bridge the gap between the world of experts and an educated lay public.

For those readers who are familiar with German academia I should add that the book is not one of the two academic theses that are still required in Germany of budding scholars in the humanities; it is no *Habilitationsschrift*. This proved to be a great advantage. While the book aims at meeting high academic standards it was never constrained by the formal conventions of a research monograph. At the same time, no publisher's commission stood at the beginning of the project. I did not write with a specific "market" in mind and could safely ignore deadlines and even word counts. Thus, I enjoyed the freedom to realize my intentions to the fullest extent. This would have been impossible without the understanding and generosity of my German publishers, C. H. Beck at Munich, a distinguished family firm that has succeeded in carrying over a great tradition of publishing into modern times and provides its authors with an intellectual home.

These intentions also imply limitations that I imposed on myself. Though it should become obvious upon casual acquaintance with the book that it does not aim at encyclopedic completeness, readers may miss chapters on two classical topics: religion and language. These omissions are deliberate. The question of Western views of Asian languages demands a specialized knowledge that I would never have been able to acquire within reasonable time, while religion is such a vast and well-researched topic that there would have been little more to do than summarize the existing literature. Splendid new works such as Urs App's *The Birth of Orientalism* (2010) will satisfy the curious. I also felt that I had nothing original to add to the extended debate about the emergence of racism in the eighteenth century.

The present American edition is a thoroughly revised version of the German original. I went through the text and redrafted numerous passages. Any reference to books and articles published in 1997 or later points to material newly consulted. In the meantime, the works by some of my protagonists came out in excellent new editions: Leibniz (his correspondence with the Jesuits in China), Montesquieu, Voltaire, Engelbert Kaempfer, Edmund Burke, George Bogle, Alexander von Humboldt, and others. Long-awaited biographies of and monographs on a few central characters appeared in print: Lawrence Baack on Carsten Niebuhr, Michael Franklin on Sir William Jones, Isobel Grundy on Lady Mary Wortley Montagu, or Richard Bourke on Edmund Burke. J.G.A. Pocock's six volumes on Edward Gibbon and his contemporaries, one of the great achievements of the humanities in our time, were not yet available when I wrote the book more than twenty years ago. They have proved a constant source of inspiration. The same is true for Karl S. Guthke's wide-ranging studies of German cosmopolitanism in Goethe's Weimar as well as for Sanjay Subrahmanyam's series of profound writings on the European-Asian encounter, though they focus on an earlier period and put a stronger emphasis on real-life connections than I do in this book.

Given that this book aims to resurrect a corpus of Enlightenment travel literature and geographical commentary that is rarely consulted today, it will come as no surprise that extensive use has been made of quotations from primary sources. In the case of works in foreign languages, the original wording has sometimes been included in the notes where the expression is especially felicitous, or where the author employs specific terms that informed readers may wish to access for themselves. Where possible, such sources are quoted in the main text from the earliest existing translations into English, which often preserve something of the original's period flavor. Slight modifications have occasionally been made and duly noted. The abbreviation *ff.* has been used to indicate that the reference continues over more than two pages.

There is no need to repeat my acknowledgements from the first German edition of 1998. Anyway, in German academic culture the habits of sharing and consulting are much less developed than in the United States, and lists of supporting friends and colleagues tend to be significantly shorter. Brigitta van Rheinberg at Princeton University Press made this project possible in the first place. This is the fourth book I am doing with her, and it is a privilege and pleasure to collaborate with her and the superb Princeton team. No less indispensable has been the work of Robert Savage, a master translator. Himself a scholar both of Adorno and Heidegger, he is familiar with some of the most difficult texts in the German language and rose with panache to the challenge of finding a language that we envisaged to be as far removed as possible from the notorious ponderousness—perhaps, though, an undeserved cliché—of German academic writing. The funding for the translation was kindly provided by *Geisteswissenschaften International*, a most worthy program that is run by the Börsenverein des deutschen Buchhandels (German Publishers & Booksellers Association) together with the Fritz Thyssen Foundation, the German Foreign Office, and the VG Wort.

At various stages in preparing the American edition Lawrence J. Baack, Sven Beckert, Alexander Bevilacqua, Franz Leander Fillafer, Garth Fowden, Michael Kempe, Harry S. Liebersohn, and Suzanne L. Marchand provided indispensable encouragement and assistance. At the University of Konstanz, Alexandre Bischofberger became highly accomplished in solving bibliographical riddles and tracing online materials. The Leibniz-Preis, awarded in 2010 by the Deutsche Forschungsgemeinschaft (German Research Foundation), made it possible to acquire the necessary literature for the university library at Konstanz.

The original edition of 1998 was dedicated to my wife Sabine Dabringhaus, herself a historian of eighteenth-century (and later) China. I am happy to present her not just with a recent Chinese translation of the book but also with this Princeton University Press version that brings the study back to life and should now count as its standard edition.

UNFABLING
THE EAST

I

Introduction

Looking to the East

The people of our western hemisphere, in all these discoveries, gave proofs of a great superiority of genius and courage over the eastern nations. We have settled ourselves amongst them, and frequently in spite of their resistance. We have learned their languages, and have taught them some of our arts; but nature hath given them one advantage which overbalances all ours; which is, that they do not want us, but we them.

—Voltaire (1694–1778), *Essai sur les mœurs et l'esprit des nations et sur les principaux faits de l'histoire depuis Charlemagne jusqu'à Louis XIII*[1]

In the first quarter of the twenty-first century, the world is taking back many of the outcomes of the nineteenth. The nineteenth century witnessed the culmination of a historically unparalleled process by which Europeans came to assert their dominance over four continents. One of the consequences was an attitude of arrogant condescension towards all civilizations that had given proof of their deficiency, if not terminal debility, through the ease with which they had been militarily overpowered, economically exploited, and technologically outstripped. The "West"—the European great powers, Britain at the fore, together with a United States of America that increasingly hankered after an empire of its own—savored its triumph over Asia, in particular. It had long been taken for granted that indigenous Americans, black Africans, and the natives of Australia, New Zealand, and the Pacific islands could be subdued, dispossessed, colonized, and if necessary slaughtered in great numbers. Ever since Europeans had first learned of their existence, a sense of their own superiority to these "savages" (as they had been called since ancient times) had gone almost unquestioned.

Asia, by contrast, had always been the great counterweight to Europe, a world of mighty empires and prosperous societies, glorious cultural achievements and venerable religions. For thousands of years, the Eurasian continent had formed a single interconnected field. The emergence and spread of agriculture had already been a process of pan-Eurasian diffusion. Time and again, Asiatic peoples had intervened in the history of the lands surrounding the Mediterranean and to the north of it, assimilating the vast spaces of Russia into their equestrian empires. Although Asia Minor and the Levant had been incorporated into the Imperium Romanum, the norm until well into the early modern period was for Europe to be threatened by Asia, not the other way around. Parthians, Huns, Arabs, Mongols, and Turks had all attacked the Western and Eastern Roman Empires and their various successor states, in some cases maintaining political control over previously Christianized regions for many centuries. Even Gottfried Wilhelm Leibniz, a vigilant and sober observer of contemporary world politics, feared a renewed Mongol onslaught, perhaps recalling Crimean Tatar raids on Transylvania and Moravia between 1657 and 1666.[2] "And if these Tatars were not constantly fighting each other," he wrote in a letter in April 1699, "they might be able to inundate large parts of the world, just as they once did under Genghis Khan."[3]

ASIA'S "DECLINE"—EUROPE'S ARROGANCE

Compared with Leibniz's sincere concerns, which admittedly were grossly exaggerated even at the time, the warnings of late nineteenth-century authors about an alleged "yellow peril" were little more than fearmongering propaganda. By then, Asia's political power seemed to have been broken once and for all, its cultural prestige reduced to a shadow of its former glory. Around 1900, at the zenith of high imperialism, most of Asia was under European colonial rule. Only the boldest of prophets would have predicted an end to this dispensation. Although semicolonial states like China, Siam (later Thailand), or the Ottoman Empire had managed to preserve their territorial integrity, their sovereignty had been drastically curtailed. Only Japan had succeeded through a tremendous effort of will, and under the most favorable external conditions imaginable, in transforming itself from a victim of the European powers and the USA into their junior partner, modernizing at breakneck speed. Everywhere else in Asia, the economic forms of European capitalism had triumphed, predominantly under the aegis of foreigners; only in rare cases had they been appropriated by native forces. All Asia seemed to have lost the historical initiative and been left far behind in the race to modernize. It was no zealous advocate of imperialism but the levelheaded Austrian economist Friedricht von Wieser, who in 1909 gave voice to the general European verdict:

> Asia, the cradle of the human race, is buried under the rubble of enfeebled, degraded nations, which are no longer capable of grasping the opportunities for growth offered them by the technical advances of the age.[4]

In short, history seemed to have passed by Asia and the Asians.

Hardly anyone in Europe would have dared or cared to contest this verdict in the years leading up to the First World War, and few did so in the following decades. A first sign of renewed vitality at Europe's gates was Kemal Atatürk's energetic and successful modernization policy in Turkey, initiated in 1923. Yet it was not until the 1940s that Asia was able to wrest back its historical agency in the eyes of the world: with the Japanese attack on the American Pacific fleet at Pearl Harbor in December 1941 and the surrender of the supposedly impregnable British fortress of Singapore barely two months later, with the Vietnamese revolution in 1945 and the Chinese in 1949, and with the independence of the Philippines, India, Pakistan, Ceylon, Burma, and Indonesia between 1946 and 1949.

During the second half of the twentieth century, particularly in its final quarter, the causes and occasions for European arrogance towards Asia vanished in the face of the extraordinarily dynamic economic growth experienced by several of the continent's regions. For all those millions elsewhere who continued to languish in poverty, a majority of citizens of those economic powerhouses were now able to enjoy decent standards of living. The last rearguard argument used to defend European exceptionalism—Asians were capable merely of imitating the achievements of others, not of creative achievement in their own right—forfeited whatever credibility it might once have possessed. On the Asian side, there emerged an indigenous cultural nationalism that self-consciously rejected Western tutelage, asserted its own "Asian values," repudiated all forms of "cultural imperialism," and even turned on its head the old European cliché of Asia's terminal decadence by prophesying a decline of the West. After the Iranian revolution of 1979, this ideological campaign became a factor of global political importance. In the early 1990s, and in more subdued tones following the great Asian economic crisis of 1997, voices from Japan and China, from Malaysia, Singapore, and South Korea could be heard proclaiming the superiority of their own cultural values and social institutions over those of the West. Western warnings about Islamist aggression and a "new yellow peril" were seen to be confirmed, and alarmist visions of an imminent "clash of civilizations" were not lacking.[5]

In the early twenty-first century, precious little thus remains of *fin de siècle* European hubris. Today it is impossible for Europe to recover its global supremacy, its unchallenged control over processes of economic globalization, and its pretensions to cultural superiority. If the nineteenth century belonged to Europe and the twentieth to the USA, many pundits of today are heralding the twenty-first as the Asian century. The time is ripe for historians to inquire into the origins of European exceptionalism, a vision of the world that for so long, and with such powerful repercussions, asserted European primacy over all other civilizations. This vision drew on ancient and Christian antecedents before crystallizing, in the Age of Enlightenment, into a secular worldview that dispensed with the religious belief in divine election. In the nineteenth century, increasingly discolored by racism, it dictated how Europeans presented themselves abroad before subsiding, in the era of decolonization, into an attitude of smug intellectual condescension.

Returning to the era of its formation, the eighteenth century, does not just mean trawling through the archives to illustrate an argument about the rise and fall of a historical discourse—in this case, that of European exceptionalism—and thus adding to the sometimes overdrawn, denunciatory critiques of European hypocrisies, illusions, and officially sanctioned delusions that have flourished ever since the publication in 1978 of Edward W. Said's highly influential polemic, *Orientalism*. It also means exploring a cultural world that no single thesis can exhaust: the world of European interest in Asia in the Age of Enlightenment.[6]

THE GREAT MAP OF MANKIND

The European intellectual climate in the Age of Enlightenment was cosmopolitan in outlook, even when individual writers did not explicitly subscribe to a cosmopolitan agenda or philosophy.[7] National borders played a less important role than in earlier and, especially, later periods.[8] The eighteenth-century republic of letters was multilingual. Latin was no longer predominant yet was still widely understood. Densely woven networks of communication, maintained through correspondence, visits, and foreign employment, connected savants in Paris and Edinburgh, London and Saint Petersburg, Uppsala and Göttingen, Leiden and Turin.[9] Leibniz and Voltaire sought out like-minded contacts in far-off civilizations who could help them in their great project of adding to the store of knowledge about the world. For a time the Chinese mandarins, a meritocratic elite, seemed ideal interlocutors. Enlightenment was conceived as a universal enterprise.

It has become clearer today than even a few decades ago that this enterprise was equally a polycentric one. The peripheries of Europe did not just reflect the light beamed out from Paris and a handful of other metropolises; "epicenters of reason" were scattered throughout the continent.[10] The British colonies in North America assume central importance in a global view of Enlightenment. Benjamin Franklin, Thomas Jefferson, and James Madison were among the key *philosophes* of the age. Impulses emanating from Europe were taken up and creatively reworked in Lima, Calcutta, Batavia, and Cape Town. In the 1780s the Asiatick Society of Bengal, steered by the brilliant jurist, linguist, and *homme de lettres* Sir William Jones, formed one of the most dynamic clusters of transcultural scholarship found anywhere in the world at the time.[11] The Jesuit missionaries at the imperial court of China, some of whom stayed on after the suppression of their order in Europe in the 1760s, remained what their predecessors had already been in Leibniz's day: valued epistolary partners for the leading European intellectuals.

Through such channels, which in many respects anticipate the dense networks of our own time, knowledge about political and social conditions, mores, customs, and religions in the non-European world was imported into Europe. Like other forms of knowledge, it underwent the procedures identified by Peter Burke: professing, establishing, locating, classifying, controlling, selling, acquiring, trusting, distrusting.[12] In Europe, knowledge about Asia was classified, evaluated, and archived; foreign objects were itemized, catalogued, and put on display.[13] Botany and zoology benefited from the specimens yielded by expeditions and colonial collections. The variety of species in nature was literally and figuratively first brought home to Europeans with increasing knowledge of the tropics; indigenous taxonomies flowed into many of the systems that European scientists now set about developing. Eighteenth-century intellectuals and scholars processed a constant flow of data from all around the world. Knowledge cultures cross-fertilized over vast distances.[14] The European Enlightenment opened outwards to the rest of the world and in turn had an impact far beyond the boundaries of continental Europe.

The interest of an educated public in reports from Asia, America, the Pacific, and Africa was stronger than ever before. It was met by a veritable flood of travel literature. The standard travel works of the time crowded the shelves of almost every scholarly library and princely collection.[15] Thanks to the Jesuits, some even made it as far as China.[16] Towards the end of the era, the enormous private library of the Berlin geographer Carl Ritter contained almost the complete European-language literature on the world beyond Europe's borders.[17] Public interest in events in the Ottoman Empire, for example, was so great that in 1789 the geographer Johann Traugott Plant brought out a weighty lexicon on Turkey for the edification of information-hungry newspaper readers.[18] The horizon of the generation that began to write and publish in the mid-eighteenth century spanned the entire globe. This was without precedent in European intellectual history. In 1777 the parliamentarian, political philosopher, and—as we will see—morally concerned commentator on India, Edmund Burke, wrote to William Robinson to convey his grateful "pleasure" on reading his *History of America*, one of the historiographical masterpieces of the epoch:

> The part which I read with the greatest pleasure is the discussion of the Manners and character of the Inhabitants of that new World. I have always thought with you, that we possess at this time very great advantages towards the knowledge of human Nature. We need no longer to go to History to trace it in all its stages and periods. . . . But now the Great Map of Mankind is unrolld at once; and there is no state or Gradation of barbarism, and no mode of refinement which we have not at the same instant under our View. The very different Civility of Europe and of China; The barbarism of Persia and Abyssinia. The erratick manners of Tartary, and of Arabia. The Savage State of North America, and of New Zealand.[19]

Writing at the same time in a similar vein, Jean-Nicolas Démeunier formulated the following Rousseauian sentence in the introduction to his superb ethnographic encyclopedia, a work that systematically collated knowledge about the customs and rites of every nation scattered on the face of the Earth: "We know nearly all the nations, civilized [*policées*] and savage; now the time has come to compare them."[20] And the Scottish social philosopher Adam Ferguson was able to draw on material from all epochs and cultures when preparing his treatise on universal sociology, first published in 1767. "Late discoveries," he declared even before he could profit from Captain Cook's voyages in the Pacific, "have brought us to the knowledge of almost every situation in which mankind are placed."[21]

At the time he wrote this, the East had long been present in more than just images and texts. Europeans could hardly bear to go without spices from the "East Indies"; they clothed themselves in Indian cotton and Chinese silk; they drank Arabian coffee and sipped Chinese tea.[22] Opium from Turkey and India stimulated the artificial paradises of romantic literature and became, at least in England, a mass-market drug.[23] In the eighteenth century Asia was a tangible, consumable presence in European everyday life. We have all seen porcelain from China, the author of a popular history of Asia addressed his readers in 1735, so why should we not study the country's history as well?[24] At the same time, the potential for the high-performing economies of the East to threaten their Western rivals did not go unheeded. Around 1700, competition from China was already giving French producers headaches.

Between around 1750 and 1820 it seemed far more self-evident than at any time before, and indeed at any time since, that the scholarly and educated public in France and Great Britain, Germany and Italy should keep abreast of conditions and developments overseas. It was not primarily on account of its entertainment value that news from foreign lands was consumed so avidly. Along with the classics of the ancient world and the Bible (commonly read as a work of history), it served as raw material for an empirical science of humankind. This *science de l'homme* was supranational, transcultural, and—as Burke and Démeunier indicated—comparative in scope; authors from the most diverse scientific disciplines and from all over Europe contributed to it. Pierre Bayle, the first Enlightenment author of genuinely European stature, had already sought out examples of human behavior from all four corners of the Earth. Countless others followed in his footsteps.

This global knowledge base collapsed in the nineteenth century—or perhaps it would be more accurate to say that it fragmented. For civilizations outside Europe, experts in the emerging field of oriental studies and in the likewise newly minted discipline of ethnology (or anthropology) were now the responsible authorities.[25] There they fraternized among themselves, leaving scholars in the most prestigious and influential disciplines of academic life to narrow their focus on Europe.[26] One example may serve to illustrate this trend. The leading historians of eighteenth-century Germany, such as August Ludwig Schlözer and Johann Christoph Gatterer at the University of Göttingen, had kept themselves as closely informed about the history of Asiatic nations as their sources of information permitted them to be, and they had been quite prepared to make space for these nations in their grand historical canvases. Leopold von Ranke, by contrast, the most distinguished German historian of the following century, confined his late, idiosyncratic *History of the World* (1881–88) to the peoples of classical antiquity and postclassical Europe, in his eyes the only ones that truly mattered in world-historical terms. Ranke, a man with a pan-European perspective, still showed an interest in the Ottoman Empire; indeed, in Germany he was regarded for that reason as something of an Orientalist.[27] Among the generation of his students, however, an obdurate Euro- or even Germanocentrism prevailed. Around the turn of the twentieth century, only the odd intellectual maverick such as Otto Hintze, Karl Lamprecht, Max Weber, or Kurt Breysig bucked the trend, drawing on the latest research in oriental studies to reconnect with the cosmopolitan outlook of the Enlightenment.

THE POWER OF DISCOURSE, THE BURDEN OF LEARNING

Just how serious was the eighteenth century's cosmopolitanism, how genuine its interest in the non-European world? To what extent did these writers strive to attain an adequate understanding of "the others"? Is this not rather a Eurocentrism in exotic dress, perhaps even the vain illusion of a class of overly ambitious European intellectuals trying on a fashionable mantle of urbanity? Did European observers ever really escape from a hall of self-reflecting mirrors? Did they not simply see what they *wanted* to see? Such questions touch on more than just the problem of subjective effort and personal honesty. These are fundamental questions concerning the social and cultural conditions of knowledge, the epistemological possibilities for people of a particular civilization to form an adequate image of members of another civilization. The literature on this topic tends to skeptical judgments. They appear in two versions.[28]

The first could be called the *model of autistic discourse*. Edward W. Said and many of his followers attributed a blindness to European culture in the age of imperial expansion, an incapacity to enter into dialogue with other cultures, which at best came into question as mute objects of political control and scientific analysis. Said was always cautious enough to confine such a suspicion of blanket ideology to the nineteenth and twentieth centuries. For good reasons, he identified Bonaparte's Egyptian expedition of 1798 as the Big Bang of a form of thought he dubbed "Orientalism."[29] Indeed, the great provocation of this kind of discourse analysis lies in its critique of the objectivist self-understanding of oriental studies in nineteenth-century Europe, its unmasking of the tension between the discipline's claims to truth and its unspoken imperial preconditions.[30]

These preconditions were still largely absent in the eighteenth century. Europeans ventured into Asia more as missionaries, traveling scholars, diplomats, and armed merchants than as colonial overlords. At the time of the French Revolution, European colonies were slivers lodged in the flanks of far-mightier Asiatic kingdoms and empires: minor irritants, perhaps, but hardly threats to their existence. Europe and Asia still maintained a precarious balance of power. It tipped over in the period between the assertion of British overlordship in India in 1818 and the forced opening of the Japanese archipelago in 1853/54. The scholarly world of the

European ancien régime had no need of the nineteenth century's imperial trappings. The nexus between knowledge and power was already established in the state-sponsored research and discovery expeditions mounted by the British, French, and Russians, but it was nowhere near as close as in the full-blown colonialism of the decades around 1900. In eighteenth-century Asia, the historical preconditions for applying the "postcolonial" model of autistic discourse were present only in rudimentary fashion.

This model primarily emerged from a theory-internal dynamic and was transformed with the impetus of that dynamic into a globally influential approach for investigating Europeans perceptions of the non-European world. It reflected a general movement in the social sciences that drew attention to the "constructedness" of cultural phenomena and emphasized how what we call "reality" is always shaped by language (the so-called "linguistic turn"). What had previously appeared as the self-evident facticity of human lifeworlds was now decoded as a figment of the collective imagination. The attempt was made to show how supposedly age-old traditions expressing the romantic spirit of the people were in fact "invented traditions" of relatively recent origin. A nation was not a social fact, still less a biological one, but an "imagined community." Concepts that had hitherto been applied in blithe self-confidence to Asia now stood revealed, under the mistrustful, clinical gaze of critical inquiry, as the creations of Western science: neither the idea of a caste *system* nor the notion of Hinduism as a homogeneous, theologically systematic "world religion" (akin to Christianity or Islam) is known to authentic Indian thought, for example. They are essentially Western "inventions."[31] Much the same could be said of the geographical and cultural construct "Asia." Whether such findings directly invalidate these concepts and theorems is another question. Many of them have proven their usefulness as tools of scientific description and explanation.

It is the merit of postcolonialism and the affiliated method of discourse analysis to have sown doubt about descriptions made by *others*. This distrust, however, does not authorize the opposite conclusion that *self*-descriptions are always and under all conditions more authentic and hence more truthful. Yet to assume the a priori "inauthenticity" of *all* statements that make intentional reference to reality goes too far. On this account, "scientific" statements that purport to say something about the real world only shed light on themselves and their authors. With that, any criteria for correctness and truth fall away.

Under such premises, historical texts about foreign cultures are studied only for the rhetorical strategies and semantic procedures by which text-immanent foreignness or difference ("alterity") is produced. It is no longer asked to what extent specific representations are true to the reality they seek to represent. As little interest is shown in the criteria by which information was once found noteworthy. For example, that the author of a travel report from 1760 was firmly convinced he was observing and reporting what he observed with strict accuracy and impartiality, and that his readers judged him by the same criteria: this is a historical fact that can hardly be ignored. The model of autistic discourse alleges the fictitious, figmentary nature of all representations of foreign cultural and social conditions. Every utterance made by a European about non-European civilizations then appears as a pure phantasm, valuable for what it reveals about European mentalities but unrelated to any external cultural reality. The history of ideas neglects its hermeneutic task of tracking down past meanings when it embraces this model. It becomes instead an exercise in politically motivated denunciation, far more than any reductionist critique of ideology in the Marxist tradition.

The second, more conventional, and less theoretically ambitious type of argumentation could be termed the *model of disillusioned humanism*. It tends in the same direction. Advocates of this model likewise doubt whether the much-lauded cosmopolitanism of the Enlightenment ever involved a genuine openness towards foreign cultures. Unlike the model of autistic discourse developed by Said from the ideas of Michel Foucault, however, the model of disillusioned humanism does not rule out the possibility that Europeans could arrive at an adequate understanding of non-European reality. It presupposes that every culture contains a reservoir of meaning that, given sufficient attention and interpretive effort, could be accessed even by outsiders. Yet such transcultural understanding cannot, as the positivist oriental sciences of the nineteenth century maintained, be secured through methodology. Empathetic interpretation can succeed only under the most favorable conditions and thanks to the border-transcending artistry of extraordinarily gifted virtuosi. It is a near-impossible stroke of good fortune.

Guided by such assumptions, a group of historians who had studied European views of America came to the melancholy conclusion that not a single one of the European visitors who described America in the quarter of a millennium between 1500 and 1750 had succeeded unconditionally in meeting the cognitive challenges posed by this alien world. None had therefore created an *America*-centric view of America. Europe had never been "genuinely" interested in these newfound lands and cultures "for their own sake"; it had only been out to enrich itself materially and intellectually through its contact with them. European knowledge of American remained completely self-referential, and the great opportunity for a truly immersive encounter was squandered.[32] Egocentrism and a failure of intellectual nerve were not the only factors to blame for this; the ancient and Christian mental ballast that Europeans brought with them to the New World was equally at fault. The great project of a transcultural hermeneutics was doomed not by a *lack* of prior knowledge and understanding but by an *excess* of it.

While older scholarship had taken overseas travelers to task for their alleged ignorance, gullibility, and naivety, the new disillusioned humanism lamented the intellectual tyranny of the ancients over early modern observers of foreign climes. It was not because travelers failed to understand what they were seeing that the opportunity for a peaceful, mutually enriching cross-cultural encounter was passed up. Rather, forearmed with the ethnographic ideas of the ancients, the Aristotelian doctrine of slavery and an Augustinian theology, visitors were only too confident that they had understood everything there was to understand, whereas they were actually transferring prefabricated schemata onto their new surroundings. On this view, the new was all-too-readily assimilated to the long familiar.[33] America—or Asia, to which such reflections could be adapted without difficulty—appears as a marginal episode in the history of the formation of the European mind.

This way of looking at things is also unsatisfactory. On the one hand, it measures historical statements against an impossibly high standard: that of an unblinkered, unbiased understanding of authentic foreignness. The reproach of "self-referentiality" targets the conditions of *all* understanding. Getting to know another culture from the inside out, a goal shared by a number of Enlightenment thinkers in their efforts to combat prejudice, turns out to be a chimera. Every hermeneutics presupposes that observers bring their own traditions and pre-judgments (or "prejudices") to bear on what they observe; indeed, this first allows them to come to grips with what would otherwise seem unfathomably alien.[34] On the other hand, it is only to be expected that any semi-educated early modern European would perceive foreign civilizations through the prism of the knowledge and concepts he (or she, in the case of the female travelers to be examined later) had inherited from the ancients. In an era when higher education was based on the study of the Greek and Roman classics, European images of Asia could never be separated from contemporary images of the ancient world.[35]

But the ancients steadily came to forfeit their normative force over the course of the eighteenth century. The Comte de Boulainvilliers, an influential philosopher of the early French Enlightenment, declared the history of the Arabs to be as instructive as that of the Greeks and Romans.[36] Voltaire later took a similar view. The information about the world provided by the ancient authorities was quite insufficient, the Leipzig philologist Johann Christoph Adelung found in 1768; modern travel writers needed to be consulted.[37] Around 1790 the universal authority of Greco-Roman antiquity as a whole stood in question. The encounter with Asian civilizations had shaken it more effectively than the earlier one with the American wilderness and the "savages" who peopled it.

Both interpretive paradigms, the autistic discourse model and the model of disillusioned humanism, arrive at similar results via different paths. Whether perceived as the consequence of an inevitable, discursively homogenizing conspiracy between culture and imperialism[38] or as the product of an incapacity to break the shackles of tradition that inhibited intercultural understanding: European texts on America and Asia from the early modern period, it is claimed, testify to nothing short of an epistemological disaster. The study of texts lacking both truth-value and artistic merit can be justified, at best, by demonstrating how in each case non-European cultures were misrepresented, distorted, and disfigured in the age of European global conquest. Only in the "postcolonial" present, many adherents of both schools contend, has it become possible to get closer to the truth about "the other."

If this kind of agnosticism were to have the final say on descriptions of foreignness in history, then there would be no point devoting any more time to them. Entire libraries of literature on America, Asia, and Africa would then consist of nothing but testaments to European folly and hubris that should best be consigned to oblivion. Are there alternatives?

The most obvious is just as unsatisfactory: returning to a precritical historiography that takes a constant expansion of the Europeans' physical and mental horizons as the occasion to celebrate the modern West's supposedly unique capacity for insight into other civilizations.[39] It is true that no other culture in the modern age surpassed the Europeans in their curiosity about faraway lands or created comparable sciences for studying and understanding foreign cultures.[40] Yet the resulting accumulation of knowledge cannot be isolated from the process of European imperial and colonial expansion. Knowledge of the Other and appropriation of what belonged to the Others went hand in hand. Moreover, standard historical accounts of the progressive European discovery of the world, fixated on the ever more precise measurement and cartographical representation of reality, operate with too narrow a conception of the history of science. Early modern texts on Asia appear only as forerunners to modern oriental studies and ethnology. Sources are placed less in the contemporary context of their genesis than in a chronological sequence culminating in the current state of research. The primary interest in early modern travelers to Asia would then lie in what—by today's standards—they "already" saw correctly. Such an immanent history of knowledge accumulation is of limited usefulness. At best, it is applicable only to cartography, meticulous description of the natural world, and (with some reservations) linguistics.

SENSING AND CONSTRUCTING DIFFERENCE

I want to venture down a different path in this book. What we casually refer to as "images" of Asia are accessed, above all, in texts. We work with texts for want of a better alternative. It is not because "culture" itself can be grasped as a text and the history of culture is therefore consummated in textual interpretation that we immerse ourselves in texts, but because there are no other sources at our disposal that so effectively convey how impressions and fantasies of foreignness are imported into native contexts of thinking and feeling. For historians, texts are the products of individual activity set against a societal framework. They are deeply rooted in human praxis. The genesis of texts claims our initial interest. Each individual text emerges from a field of experience and intention, perception and imagination, seeing and hearing, convention and innovation. The text itself is a relatively late product of complex processes. Chapters 3 to 7 deal with these processes by sketching a kind of logistics for producing images of foreignness. This involves travel and the accumulation of useful knowledge, the mobile observer's concrete encounters and interactions with his or her alien cultural environment, the scholarly world (which has its own interests and standards of judgment), and finally the literary market with its laws of valuation and competition.

European texts on Asia should thus not be read in isolation as static "representations" of reality. We should instead situate them in their always-specific contexts of social praxis, paying careful attention to how they switch between real-world reference and fictionality, instruction and entertainment. Setting up the construction and depiction of foreign cultures as a mutually exclusive opposition, and hence interrogating texts *only* for their ideological content or *only* for their empirical accuracy, misrecognizes the shimmering multifacetedness of the great early modern accounts of Asia. That polyvalence is what constitutes their enduring appeal. They would hardly be worthy of our attention if they either merely mirrored European self-understandings or merely anticipated later and more reliable research findings. The texts discussed in this book are both at the same time: projections of the European imagination *and* attempts to grasp reality with the epistemic toolkit of the time.

A second level of contextualization is found where individual statements provide material for broader arguments. Asia functioned in multiple ways in European debates: debates about savagery and civilization, progress and decadence, governance and justice, the wealth and poverty of nations, the rights and happiness of women, truth and falsehood in religion. The second half of this book is taken up with several of these debates. Not everything could be covered: I lack the linguistic competence to give Asian languages the attention they deserve; and the topic of Asiatic religions is so vast that it would have threatened to overwhelm the book.[41] Less than a history of "images," this book is a history of conceptualizations and their instruments: concepts and the overarching idioms or "languages" (in the sense given the term by the intellectual historian J.G.A. Pocock) of which they form the components.[42]

The object of such conceptualizations were differences. What is remarkable about these differences is not the fact that they existed in the first place. To point out that Asia was Europe's Other is a trivial observation. But what was the nature of these differences in the eyes of individual authors? How were they evaluated? How were comparisons made between individual Asiatic civilizations, which differed from Europe and each other in ever-specific ways? A thinking that operates with simple dichotomies, such as the binary opposition between "native" and "foreign," impedes our understanding of how difference was perceived and posited in a broad spectrum of gradations. "Foreignness" is not an unambiguous and absolute category but a relative and endlessly variable one. Every single statement in seventeenth- or eighteenth-century texts that establishes a link between Europe and Asia charts such cultural differences anew. The historian's task is to reconstruct that process. To what end? In the eighteenth and nineteenth centuries, Europe defined itself in opposition to Asia. What is interesting is not *that* this happened but *how* it happened. The times when one could rest satisfied with the simple template of an "inverted world" were long past. Where was the *differentia specifica* between East and West located in each particular case? Was this difference appraised as a sign of superiority or inferiority? Could it be bridged, or was it viewed as natural and inalterable? What strategies were used to contain the discomfort or even terror that such difference could give rise to in the observer? Did European visitors seek to repudiate and exclude the foreign, or did they attempt to assimilate and incorporate it, to meet it halfway, to domesticate it through colonization and revoke its otherness through Westernizing reforms?[43] Whether the countless individual determinations of difference ultimately add up to a single discernible pattern and fit into a general history of shifts in European mentality is the most difficult question of all. The last chapter of the book will attempt an answer to it.

SPACES

The fact that a broadly European perspective on Asia is adopted here, rather than a German, French, or English one, calls for a word of justification. National differences were certainly not insignificant. The British saw India, where they had growing colonial interests, differently from the Germans, whose lack of imperial power afforded them greater freedom of judgment. In the eighteenth century, however, such national nuances were contained within a pan-European, Enlightenment frame of reference. Even within Europe, intellectual lines of influence were often not drawn bilaterally: the image of England propagated by the Frenchman

Montesquieu had a major impact in Germany, perhaps more so than the British representation of themselves. Debates on Asia likewise played out on a pan-European level. Scholars of the time were multilingual. For those among their contemporaries who were not, the more substantial primary reports on Asiatic countries were soon translated into several languages.

Engelbert Kaempfer for example, who got to know Iran and Japan in the 1690s and wrote scholarly works on both countries that enjoyed an exceptionally high standing among the cognoscenti, was a Westphalian physician in the service of the Dutch East India Company (Verenigde Oostindische Compagnie, VOC). His manuscript on Japan, composed in German (although usually he preferred writing in Latin), was acquired by the English collector and scientific administrator Sir Hans Sloane, brought to London, and presented to the public in 1727 in a fairly free translation by the young Swiss naturalist Johann Caspar Scheuchzer. The French translation of Scheuchzer's English text appeared two years later and was more widely read on the continent—including in Germany, where French was more readily understood than English at the time. Those who only read German had to make do with the back translation from the French (1749), until in 1777–79 Kaempfer's Westphalian compatriot Christian Wilhelm Dohm, later a high-ranking Prussian civil servant and diplomat, finally published the original in two volumes.[44] Dohm smoothed the rough edges of Kaempfer's manuscript and adapted his Baroque German to the sensibilities of the age of Lessing. A critical edition did not see the light of day until 2001.[45]

In the eighteenth-century literary market, so complicated an editorial history was far from unique. This prompts us to ask what was specifically "German" about Engelbert Kaempfer's biography—he had been trained in Danzig (Gdańsk), Thorn (Toruń), Cracow (Kraków), Königsberg (Kaliningrad), and Uppsala[46]—and his public impact. These were far more typical of a Europe-wide republic of letters.[47] Similarly, it makes little sense to claim that the reports on China compiled by the French Jesuits, members of a self-consciously cosmopolitan elite, purvey a specifically French view of China, or that the books written in English by the Swiss-born, German-educated Johann Ludwig Burckhardt, whose travels in the Middle East were sponsored by the British African Association, represent a characteristically Swiss perspective.[48] An overview of the French-, English-, and German-language literature on Asia, at the very least, is therefore called for. Much else appeared in Dutch, Italian, and Russian as well, while Spanish and Portuguese reports played only a marginal role in the eighteenth century.

On the other side, what is meant by "Asia"? It cannot be emphasized enough that "Asia," understood as an umbrella term, was and essentially still is a European idea. In the eighteenth century the individual peoples of Asia did not identify themselves as "Asians"; they felt no solidarity transcending ethnic and religious borders; their elites saw no common path of historical development; nobody spelled out visions of a shared Asian destiny. Societies on the Asian continent were considerably more heterogeneous than their contemporary European counterparts. Whereas a similar political model could be found almost everywhere in Europe, a more or less "absolute" monarchy based on a hereditary aristocracy, the spectrum of systems of government was far wider in Asia. Above all, the bond of a common religion, which still loosely linked together Roman Catholic and Protestant Europe even after the interconfessional conflict of the Thirty Years' War, was lacking in Asia. The European discourse on Asia was therefore unmatched by an Asian discourse about itself.[49]

This discourse operated on three levels: national, local, and continental. First, travelers wrote about clearly defined political entities (China, the Ottoman Empire, the Mughal Empire in India, etc.) or clearly identifiable countries in the modern sense (Persia, Japan, Siam/Thailand, etc.). At a deeper level of generalization, individual ethnicities, cities, or landscapes were discussed. This was the eyewitness point of view: it was possible to see the street life of Peking with one's own eyes, but not "China" as such. Yet the local perspective by no means entailed just a naïve close-up account. The more one already knew (or thought one knew) about a country, the greater was the expectation that travelers pay particular attention to local and regional variations. Thus Carsten Niebuhr, the German-Danish traveler to the Orient, informs a public always eager to learn about foreign judicial customs that "homicide is not even punished in the same way in the small domains of the Imam of Yemen, let alone throughout all Arabia."[50] This tendency to ever-greater detail culminated in the extremely thorough "local surveys" carried out by the British in their newly conquered Indian territories from the late eighteenth century onwards.[51]

Over both these levels, the national and the local, floated a *continental* mode of commentary, concerned with comparing the various Asiatic countries and civilizations and with making generalizations about "Asia" and "Asians," the "Orient" and "the Orientals." Statements of such ultimate abstraction were by no means confined to armchair philosophers. On the frequent occasions when a traveler describes a scene or a behavior as "typically Asiatic," the continental mode of commentary comes into play. All three levels are almost always combined in the era's richer texts. If one wants to capture them all, then "Asia" must be viewed in the all-encompassing sense given the term by contemporaries.[52] While limiting coverage to "Monsoon Asia,"[53] for example, might make for a more streamlined presentation, it would fail to do justice to the perspective of the European eighteenth century. Even K. N. Chaudhuri's comprehensive concept of the "four Indian Ocean civilizations" (Arabo-Persian Islam, India, Southeast Asia, China)[54] is too narrow for my purposes since it still excludes Mediterranean Islam, the Asiatic parts of the tsarist empire, and much of the rest of Central Asia. The Enlightenment's "Asia" encompassed all these vast spaces. That is why I also consider what is today called the Muslim "Near East," extending all the way north to the Ottoman-controlled Balkans and as far west as Egypt or even Morocco. Egypt, in particular, was regarded as an outpost of the Asiatic ecumene just as much as it belonged to North Africa. Edward Gibbon pointed out that the land on the Nile "is accessible only on the side of Asia, whose revolutions, in almost every period of history, Egypt has humbly obeyed."[55] Indeed, might not the Chinese civilization, as some speculated, have originated in Egypt?[56] In the course of the eighteenth century, the Ottoman Empire was increasingly perceived as an "Asiatic," non-European power. Those who spoke of "Asiatics" at the end of the eighteenth century almost always meant Turks, Arabs, and Iranians in addition to Tibetans and Mongols. Even the contemporary metageographical category of "the Asia-Pacific" is sometimes anticipated by eighteenth-century authors. However, given the profusion and excellence of recent literature on the Pacific in the age of Captain Cook and on the European debates about blissful and tragic Tahiti, I will mention the South Seas only in passing.[57]

EPOCHS

The eighteenth century covered in this book is not limited to the years between 1700 and 1799. It is a "long" century, extending from around 1680 to 1830;[58] even the French Revolution, which got underway in 1789, does not provide a convincing end point.[59] Attentiveness to European interpretations of Asia highlights continuities in a period that is usually categorized with labels such as "idealism," "romanticism," or "utilitarianism." Criteria supplied by the history of ideas and periodization conventions need to be tied to the real historical rhythms of European-Asiatic relations.

So far as the starting date is concerned, a convergence is not hard to ascertain. Historians of the European Enlightenment are largely agreed that Enlightenment philosophers (Bayle, Fontenelle, Locke) began making concerted and sustained contributions to public debate in the 1680s.[60] Around the same time, a new type of traveling observer enters the scene: the scientifically well-versed man of science or gentleman, drawn overseas less by a love of adventure and commercial enterprise than by a thirst for knowledge, missionary zeal, or diplomatic objectives.[61] The years between 1680 and around 1730 represent the heroic age of Asian travel. Sophisticated empirical accounts of almost all the countries on the continent appeared around this time, claiming canonical status until well into the nineteenth century. Such travelogues fueled the popular craze for the exotic characteristic of the Baroque and the Rococo. In France, to name one prominent example, there was a vogue for all things oriental, beginning with Racine's tragedy *Bajezet* (1672) and reaching a climax with Antoine Galland's translation of the *Tales from the 1001 Nights* (1704–17).[62] French Jesuits reported from China from the mid-1680s, addressing and reaching an even-wider public than their already successful predecessors. The information they sent back contributed to the artistic and commercial flourishing of chinoiseries from the 1730s onwards.[63]

An important Asian country like Siam was first brought to European attention from the 1680s. The work *Du Royaume de Siam* (1691) by the French diplomat Simon de La Loubère was widely praised and imitated as a model eyewitness account. Its only serious rival was Jean Chardin's report on Iran (published in fragments in 1686 and in full in 1711), one of the most significant travel works of the modern age. India under the Mughals was described in the *Voyages* of the indefatigable overland traveler Jean-Baptiste Tavernier, first published in 1676 and subsequently reissued many times. A little later, the political system and social life of the Ottoman Empire was presented with unprecedented thoroughness by Sir Paul Rycaut, who had served from 1667 to 1678 as English consul in Smyrna (Izmir). From this time on, the relative importance of Dutch literature on Asia suffered a marked decline.[64] French, English, and gradually also German became the leading languages for writing about Asia.

This quantum leap in reporting on Asia was accompanied by important developments on the ground.[65] The end of the century initiated something like a "belated early modern age" for Asia. In the 1680s the Kangxi emperor, who maintained as splendid a court as his contemporary Louis XIV and was easily the more accomplished statesman, completed the internal pacification of China by the new Qing dynasty, putting an end to decades of political turbulence following the Manchu conquest of the Dragon Throne in 1644. For more than a century to come, the Qing Empire would enjoy unchallenged predominance as something like a Eurasian superpower, economically all but self-sufficient, culturally self-assured, and untroubled by the machinations of European imperialists.[66] In Japan the shoguns of the Tokugawa dynasty had expelled Catholic missionaries or had them martyred at the beginning of the seventeenth century and brutally suppressed native Christianity. A policy of isolationism (*sakoku*) was rigorously enforced from 1639: foreigners were forbidden from remaining in the country, and the Japanese from leaving it. Only the Dutch, who had supplied the Prince of Hirado with naval artillery in 1638 to help him put down the Shimabara rebellion, a desperate uprising by Japanese Catholics,[67] were permitted to continue trading under extremely restrictive conditions. On Dejima, an artificial island built in the bay of Nagasaki, VOC representatives were placed under virtual house arrest to keep them segregated from the local community. Contact was limited to the special police branch for resident aliens, state-appointed interpreters, and prostitutes.[68] Japan surpassed even China in its internal stability, external sovereignty, and economic dynamism. Despite economic and ecological problems that began to mount from around 1710 in Japan, and from midcentury in China,[69] both countries were far from lagging behind a preindustrial Europe.

For all of Southeast Asia, as for China, the 1680s marked the threshold to a new era, albeit one in which things generally took a turn for the worse.[70] On Java, the VOC had by 1682 succeeded in subduing their native opponents from their headquarters in Batavia, today's Jakarta.[71] Most of the fertile and populous island now stood under Dutch control, although the colonial administration remained patchy and weak throughout the eighteenth century. In 1688, the year of the Glorious Revolution in England, Siam was rocked by a political upheaval that attracted keen interest in Europe as the "Siamese Revolution." Immediately after the death of the outward-looking King Narai, whom Louis XIV had courted in a series of diplomatic missions as a possible global partner for France, xenophobic counterforces overthrew Narai's prime minister Constantine Phaulkon, a Greek married to a Japanese Christian who maintained a European lifestyle and consorted with French priests and English merchants.[72] Siam proceeded to shut itself off from the rest of the world—not as strictly as

Japan, to be sure, yet still comprehensively enough to disqualify itself as a promising target for missionary work and trade.

Not even the most clear-sighted observers were aware that the mighty Mughal Empire had by the 1690s—perhaps, even more precisely, by 1689[73]—passed the peak of its power. The death of Emperor Aurangzeb in 1707, however, revealed fatal weaknesses in an imperial organization that was far less secure than that of China, its great neighbor to the north. The Mughal Empire crumbled and collapsed within a few years; its core territories lingered on as a middling Indian power, but the empire was a shadow of its former self. These dramatic events rapidly transformed the political map of South Asia, but they did not leave the way clear for the English to impose colonial rule; the British did not control any Indian territorial states until the 1760s. Initially, native political forces were strengthened as the comprehensive Muslim empire of the Mughals evolved into a polycentric, multistate system. The downfall of the Islamic-Shi'ite Safavid dynasty in Iran followed with comparable speed. It reached its drastic conclusion when an invasion of Afghan tribes toppled the legitimate monarch in 1722, ushering in a protracted period of chaos and usurpation. Europeans could derive neither political nor commercial advantage from all this.[74]

Finally, the third of the early modern Islamic "gunpowder empires,"[75] the Ottoman Empire, asserted itself incomparably more effectively than the younger Islamic empires of the time. It had been the preeminent political factor in the Eastern Mediterranean since the conquest of Constantinople in 1453; in the sixteenth century it was even the strongest military power in the world. Its decline from such heights has been much debated and discussed. A comparison with India and Iran, and later with the swift erosion of the Spanish global empire, shows just how slowly and steadily that decline proceeded. At the end of the seventeenth century the Ottoman Empire was still a great power, even if it was no longer the terror of Christendom. The failed conquest of Vienna in 1683 broke the expansionary momentum of the once-invincible Ottoman military machine. Under the terms of the Treaty of Karlowitz (1699) the sultan was forced to cede Hungary, initiating the process by which the Christian powers gradually pushed the Ottomans out of continental Europe. The mood quickly shifted in Christian Europe. The old image of the "devil Turk" was now complemented by the bumbling Turkish buffoon, a type immortalized in the harem overseer Osmin from Wolfgang Amadeus Mozart's opera, *The Abduction from the Seraglio* (1782).

There is thus much to suggest that the years after 1680 marked a time of transition in Asiatic history and a key period in relations between Europe and Asia, even if not all individual lines of development pointed in the same direction. It would be far too simplistic—as well as an anachronistic retrojection of later events—to see here the onset of an inevitable decline of Asia and rise of Europe. Decline was far from people's minds in China; on the contrary, the empire was only just entering the lengthy period of peace and prosperity known as the "High Qing." Japan consolidated the gains it had made in the seventeenth century and slowly created the conditions for its eventual modernization in the second half of the nineteenth century. Where civil war and systemic collapse afflicted Asiatic states, Europeans often saw little benefit: trade suffered, yet military intervention and the imposition of colonial rule would have been prohibitively expensive. Economically and politically, the eighteenth century was a time of fluctuating equilibrium between Europe and Asia.

Real power relations can be gauged with some accuracy from the situations faced by travelers on the ground. It is one of this book's fundamental arguments that many eighteenth-century European travelers to Asia—to the extent that they offered public accounts of their travels—were neither passively registering what they had experienced and witnessed nor telling tall stories in the manner of many an earlier fabulist. They constituted instead a class of roving *philosophes*, itinerant scholars who combined high competence with great intellectual authority. Under imperial conditions, such people would have been shielded from danger by the relevant colonial power. Apart from the tsarist empire and a few areas in India and Southeast Asia, however, this was nowhere the case in eighteenth-century Asia. James Cook and other maritime explorers brought their own defenses with them and were practically invulnerable to attack so long as they stayed on board their ships. Travel was impossible or life-threatening elsewhere. The Chinese interior remained off-limits, while in Japan every move made by Europeans was closely monitored by the state. The imperial and colonial character of the eighteenth century should therefore not be overstated, particularly in Asia. Data was collected and observations made by Europeans traveling outside the asymmetrical framework of imperial structures in West Asia and Arabia, Iran, Afghanistan, Central Asia, Burma, Vietnam, Siam, China, and Japan.

The balance of power between Asia and Europe was matched by an intellectual equilibrium that makes the thinking of this era far more attractive and lastingly significant than later triumphalist ideologies of the all-conquering West. The British historians G. S. Rousseau and Roy Porter put it this way:

> It was also a moment when, because of the power of Enlightenment pens, Europe itself was sufficiently self-critical and free from bigotry to be able to confront other cultures, admittedly not as equals, nor even necessarily on their own terms, but at least as alternative versions of living—for a brief moment before the logic of the white man's mission required they be subordinated, eviscerated and destroyed.[76]

This equilibrium broke down over the first three decades of the nineteenth century. Early industrialization in Europe now caused the economic scales to turn against countries of the later Third World. At the same time, Europe confronted other civilizations with newfound aggressiveness. The British completed their conquest of India and gave their colonial state a form that would endure for over a century. On Java, the second bridgehead of early Asian colonization, the unusually bloody anti-Dutch rebellion of 1825–30 marked the transition to a new form of colonialism that interfered far more directly with native society.[77] The Greek war of liberation, beginning in 1821, was no longer waged purely in terms of power politics, as had still been the case for the Russo-Ottoman wars of the eighteenth century. Anti-Turkish propaganda stylized the conflict as a struggle between a freedom-loving West and oriental barbarism; this presupposed that since the 1770s a previously overlooked resemblance, or even historical continuity, had been discovered between the ancient and the modern Greeks.[78] Likewise in the 1820s the Qing Empire started to be destabilized by the contraband trade in opium from India. The resulting Anglo-Chinese Opium War of 1839–42 rudely stripped China of its remaining mystique. Within the multiethnic tsarist empire, as historian Andreas Kappeler remarks, there emerged at the same time "a pejorative way of distinguishing between the state people, the Russians, who were now in the grip of nationalism, and strangers who belonged to another 'rod,' a foreign clan, lifestyle, and perhaps even race."[79] Again at the same time and in a parallel historical development, the Indian tribes in North America were forcibly deprived of whatever was left of their political agency and even autonomy.

In the period between around 1800 and 1830, the discourse on Asia also underwent changes that amounted to a break with the intellectual past. Older conventions and attitudes persisted into the new century in the literature on non-European nations and civilizations, at least for a time. Alexander von Humboldt's great American travel work, which began appearing in 1805, brought the Enlightenment tradition of encyclopedic coverage of foreign cultures by traveling generalists to a crowning conclusion.[80] In 1818–20 the public was presented with a comprehensive synthesis of all the information that the Jesuits had collected on China since the early seventeenth century.[81] It reads like a memorial to a bygone era. The specialization and professionalization of expertise on Asia now gathered pace. In 1822, the year the Egyptian hieroglyphs were deciphered by Jean-François Champollion, the Société Asiatique was established in Paris. The Royal Asiatic Society was founded in London in 1823, followed in 1845 by the Deutsche Morgenländische Gesellschaft (German Oriental Society), an association of German-speaking Orientalists that initially worked in close partnership with classical philologists.[82]

The professionalization of knowledge about Asia was accompanied by its marginalization in the nineteenth-century education system. Asia suffered a loss of prestige in European eyes. By 1830 the process was complete. Georg Wilhelm Friedrich Hegel struck the new tone in his 1822 Berlin lectures on the philosophy of world history when he confined the world-historical importance of Asiatic civilizations to their distant past. The enthusiasm for a Persian, Indian, or Chinese education—conceived as a supplement or even alternative to the traditional grounding in the classics—that had gripped some in the two decades around 1800 also dissipated around this time. Greek, not Sanskrit or Persian, continued to be taught in German Gymnasiums and English public schools, and Goethe's late endorsement of "world literature" met with little support in the long run.[83] Friedrich Rückert, the poet and great translator, displayed all the arrogance of the professional Orientalist when he ridiculed the amateur Goethe:

> Als der West war durchgekostet,
> hat er jetzt den Ost entmostet.[84]

> Having drunk his fill of the West
> He has now uncorked the East.

Finally, the early modern model of travel became obsolete in these years. Alongside the Chardins and Humboldts, intrepid scholar-explorers who industriously traversed, investigated, observed, and measured the Earth from pole to pole, there now appeared a new type: that of the commercially organized globetrotter or tourist.[85] A tourist, informs the Brockhaus *Conversationslexicon*, the leading encyclopedia for the German middle class,

> is the name given to someone who travels not for any fixed purpose, such as in pursuit of a scientific objective, but only to have made the journey and then be able to describe it. He should be a man of cosmopolitan manners, habits and opinions, while otherwise as far as possible giving free rein to his subjectivity in everything he depicts.[86]

Until this point in time unrestrained subjectivism had been the worst offense a travel writer could commit, besides out-and-out fabrication.

Thomas Cook invented the package holiday in 1841. Tours from France to Turkey were organized from as early as 1833—surely an arduous and hazardous undertaking in those early days.[87] Travel guides to oriental countries made their first appearance in 1839: a utilitarian genre that had little in common with older travel reports, which had been written more for the benefit of stay-at-home fellow scholars. Journeying in 1840 in Upper Egyptian Thebes, Prince Hermann von Pückler-Muskau noted the "horrendous . . . devastastion inflicted by art-lovers."[88] The currently fashionable tourist destinations, we read in the 1847 edition of the Brockhaus *Conversationslexicon*, are Scandinavia, Spain, Portugal, "and especially the Orient as far as India."[89] More than two decades before the opening of the Suez Canal, India already lay within reach of the venturesome holiday-maker. News transmission and transportation began accelerating from the 1820s. Even before the invention of the telegraph, contemporaries felt that the world was shrinking before their eyes.[90]

The end of the era may be summed up in an image from October 1829: that of the sixty-year-old Alexander von Humboldt, the erstwhile conqueror of tropical jungles and icy Andean peaks, crossing the Caspian Sea in the safety and comfort of a modern passenger steamship.[91]

Finally, the original German version of this book was called *Die Entzauberung Asiens*. The keyword "Entzauberung"—the most common translation, though a problematic one, is "disenchantment"—will remind informed readers of Max Weber, and a Dutch reviewer of the book complained that this concept was neither defined with sufficient precision nor strictly adhered to in the presentation. Yet in a work of intellectual and cultural history such as this, I did not wish to plow the thorny field of Weber exegesis, culling from various passages in the great sociologist's work a theory of the disenchantment "of the world" as a long-term process. It is partly to avoid awakening such expectations that I have chosen the English title *Unfabling the East*—a title that, in its very neologistic strangeness, draws attention to the way Enlightenment travelers and writers set about defamiliarizing and dismantling the long-cherished construct of "the fabled East." In European eyes, the civilizations of Asia departed from the realm of fairytale over the course of the long eighteenth century. To be sure, images of the fabled East continued to tickle the fancy of Western consumers, from Antoine Galland's translation of the *Tales from the 1001 Nights* (1704) to William Beckford's Gothic novel *Vathek* (1786). Yet alongside such literary confections, attempts were increasingly made to demonstrate by means of rational description and analysis how these societies, their political systems, and their religious practices actually "functioned." The countries of non-Christian Eurasia were by no means subsumed under an overarching concept of "Asia" or the "Orient" and placed in opposition to a similarly monolithic "Europe" or the "Occident." Instead, they were presented comparatively and discussed in their idiosyncrasies. Stark East-West dichotomies were generally avoided, as was the finding that the entire continent had spent centuries languishing in an ahistorical coma or stuck up a backwater of world history.

When Max Weber, in a text from 1920, characterizes the disenchantment of the world as "its transformation into a causal mechanism" through "rational, empirical cognition,"[92] this precisely sums up the goal of enlightened European travelers and writers in the second half of the eighteenth century. There was no concerted effort on their part to exoticize the "foreign" (here an anachronistic category) into an inscrutable Asiatic Other. Rather, writers subjected what they saw in Asia to the same standards of rational analysis and judgment that they applied to political and social conditions in Europe. Asia was demystified and made comprehensible within a single cognitive continuum.

The postmodern critique of European representations of other civilizations has constructed an artificial dilemma: either European observers of Asia, blinded by their universalist assumptions, are reproached with ignoring differences, or they are accused of falling into the opposite trap and exaggerating differences through "othering"—"Orientalism," in other words. Both these simplistic and extreme positions are belied by the complexity of the historical situation. The unfabling of the East in the late eighteenth century was bound up with its reevaluation. Whereas many Europeans in the mid-1700s had found much to admire or even emulate in Asia, especially in China and Japan but sometimes in the Arab desert tribes as well, by the end of the century Asia had been firmly assigned a place below Europe in the hierarchy of world civilizations.

Barriers to the use of force in Asia were removed one by one; the entire continent, deprived of the blessings of civilization and order, seemed to be crying out for European intervention, and Europeans increasingly felt willing and able to answer the call. Colonialism had been largely confined to the Americas until around 1760, but now it became both conceivable and achievable in Asia. The unfabled East became the lectured, harried, and ultimately vanquished East. Needless to say, this momentous change cannot be explained solely in intellectual terms. From the mid-eighteenth century onwards, the geopolitical and economic scales within Eurasia tilted towards the Western end of the continent.

Asia has never since been refabled or reenchanted in dominant European perceptions. The (early) nineteenth-century movement of romanticism showed relatively little interest in Asia, less than in the eighteenth century, despite Friedrich Rückert, the Schlegel brothers, and Samuel Taylor Coleridge, despite Orientalist painting in France, and despite Turks and Arabs in the operas of Gioachino Rossini and Carl Maria von Weber. Two facets of an irrationalist view of Asia emerged more strongly towards the end of the nineteenth century: on the one hand, the threatening, demonic Asia conjured up by the fear of a "yellow peril"; on the other, an Asia of timeless wisdom that could be studied in the holy books of the East—the origin of later New Age fads for Tibetan Buddhism and the I Ching. Both variants remained niche phenomena. The condescending realism of men of commerce and colonial administration set the tone. Asia as a whole or its individual civilizations rarely awakened the kind of enthusiasm that had gripped leading eighteenth-century intellectuals from Leibniz and Voltaire to William Jones and Stamford Raffles.

The eighteenth century has acquired fresh relevance. In many respects, global power relations are shifting back to where they stood before the era of Western arrogance and supremacy. In today's multipolar world, the Eurocentric attitudes sketched in the last chapter of this book have lost all footing in reality. Europeans will need to exercise their powers of discrimination. They have no reason to sacrifice the values of their moral, legal, and political traditions to an indifferent cultural relativism. On the other hand, mental maps oriented to (Western) Europe and the North Atlantic will not provide them with the best guidance for the future. There is no escaping the fact that Europe cannot always do everything better.[93] When we recall the Eurasian equilibrium of the eighteenth century, it should come as no surprise that China understands its (re)ascension to a leading position in the global economy and global politics as a return to historical normality, not as a miracle. Recognizing Asia as a partner of equal standing should not cause Europeans any problems (the USA may find it more difficult). After all, Europe has done it before.

PATHWAYS OF KNOWLEDGE

II

Asia and Europe

Borders, Hierarchies, Equilibria

> The first time I set foot on Asian soil, I threw myself to the ground upon alighting from the kayak and kissed the earth as my spiritual homeland.
>
> —Joseph von Hammer-Purgstall (1774–1856), *Erinnerungen aus meinem Leben*[1]

Joseph von Hammer-Purgstall, one of the three or four most distinguished Orientalists of his time, is looking back from old age on one of the great moments of his youth. Hammer's "Asia" is several things at once. First of all, it is a geographical location. Hammer is crossing the Bosphorus. He has already spent some time traveling through the sultan's territories as an interpreter in the Austrian diplomatic service. But in September 1799, the twenty-five-year-old does not just disembark at a place called Hunkiar-Iskelesi; he lands in "Asia." Hammer appears to have been deeply moved by this experience of passing from one continent, one world, to another. Later, such pathos would become something of a cliché. It is easy to see why, for no two continents meet so picturesquely as at the Golden Horn. Hammer's "Asia" is also a "spiritual homeland," an ideal sphere. What Hammer finds here is the fulfillment of the literary studies he had pursued so ardently at home. He is invoking an ancient tradition: Asia as the motherland of civilization.

ASIA AND EUROPE IN THE TSARIST EMPIRE

Where does Europe end? Where does Asia begin? It has often been seen as an expression of Europe's flexibility and vitality that these questions permit no definitive answer.[2] Since the collapse of the Soviet Union in 1991, and the rise of a Russian great power nationalism supported by ideologies of the country's special "Eurasian" position athwart two continents, the problem of Europe's eastern limit has been posed anew: one of the most daunting political and perhaps also cultural challenges to beset the Eurasian continent since the turn of the millennium.[3]

It has long been common knowledge that "Europe" is a cultural construct. The history of the idea of Europe and European self-awareness reveals a long series of highly diverse attempts to define Europe's "identity," ranging from repudiation and exclusion of the "non-European" to the search for common distinguishing features. "Asia" itself is a European concept. Before the mid-nineteenth century, when European ideas first became widely diffused, there was simply no precedent in any civilization between the Bosphorus and the Sea of Japan for the idea of an overarching unity embracing all the great world religions—for Christianity, too, has "Asiatic" roots—as well as ethnic groups of the utmost anthropological variety. "The Orient," "the East" ("Far," "Near," and "Middle"), "the East Indies": these are all arbitrary ascriptions that can be traced back to specifically European needs to classify, categorize, and delimit what was perceived as alien. Even the division of the Eurasian land mass into two separate continents, which we tend to take for granted today, is a geographical convention that bears no compelling relation to the Earth's physical features. There is, after all, no logical reason why an utterly distinct geographical entity should be taken to begin just east of the Urals and on the other side of the Bosphorus.[4]

Surprising answers to the question of Europe's borders have always been possible: cultural space does not necessarily fit neatly inside the lines drawn by cartographers. Take Cape Town, for instance, founded by Dutch colonists, permanently ceded to the British in 1806, a resting place for the fleets passing to and from Asia: was it even situated in Africa? One skeptic among many records his travel impressions in 1816: "Cape Town itself is so completely European that it excites little interest, at least to those coming from the West."[5] The same was frequently said of Batavia, established by the VOC in 1619 as their Asian headquarters and progressively built up over the following years: despite having a majority of non-white (especially Chinese and Malay) inhabitants, this was a Dutch city in the tropics, so magnificent and elegant "that Batavia bears comparison with the most important, wealthy and beautiful places in Europe, even surpassing them in some respects."[6] Wherever it builds, colonialism sets boundary markers in stone, exporting Europe's borders into its outposts and enclaves. Asia begins where the bridgehead ends.

For those traveling by boat, the transition between the continents is rarely a problem of perception. Between departure and arrival lies the fluid interval of the sea. In stepping off board, they set foot in Asia. For those traveling by land, the matter is more complicated. Where political borders are invisible, other signals are required. For many, "Asia" begins where steeples give way to minarets and the muezzin's call to prayer replaces the tolling of church bells. For others, their arrival in Asia is signaled by the first winding caravan to cross their path.[7] Conversely, the English diplomat James Justinian Morier immediately notices that he has arrived in Europe, not just in Russia, when he crosses the frontier river Araxes on October 5, 1812: instead of camels and mules, he now sees carts and carriages.[8] Europe is the world of wheels.[9]

The land route to Asia passes via the Balkans or through Russia. Ever since the conquest and economic development of Siberia, beginning in the early seventeenth century, the multiethnic kingdom of the tsars had spanned both continents. In the eighteenth century, Russia alone encompassed Edmund Burke's "Great Map of Mankind" with its countless sociocultural nuances, extending all the way from the Western-leaning urban societies of Saint Petersburg, Tallinn, Riga, and (later) Minsk to the hunter-gatherer tribes of Siberia, with innumerable variations and gradations in social conditions in between.[10] For the traveler, which of the many internal cultural borders he crossed marked the great continental fault line between Europe and Asia remained a question of minor practical importance. Asia visibly began at the political border of the empire. Throughout the eighteenth and nineteenth centuries, this was a shifting military frontier, defended—and increasingly pushed outward—in three directions: against the Islamic powers of Iran and the Ottoman Empire, against the nomadic horsemen of the Kazakh and Kyrgyz Steppes, and against the mountain tribes of the Caucasus.

In August 1829, Alexander von Humboldt, traveling as the personal guest of the tsar, inspected the fortified "line" in the steppe lands bordering the Middle Horde of the Kyrgyz.[11] He had earlier set eyes on an altogether different type of border: that with the Chinese Empire or, as he himself notes, the "first post of Chinese Mongolia."[12] In the treaties of Nerchinsk (1689) and Kyakhta (1727), which codified a real balance of power, Saint Petersburg and Peking had agreed on a common border and rules to regulate traffic across that border. Guarded with equal vigilance on both sides, this line remained until the 1850s perhaps the most peaceful and stable border between two major powers anywhere in the world.[13] Western European travelers breathed a sigh of relief upon passing into Qing territory: "for on this side of the markers [i.e., the flags indicating the border] stretched a vast desolate wasteland, while on the other, the Chinese lived in villages and hamlets and had cultivated the countryside."[14] Arrival in the most important transit point, the twin towns of Kyakhta-Maimaicheng, promised a return to civilization on the Chinese side; streets and internal courtyards there were "kept in a state of such tidiness as is otherwise found only in the towns of Holland."[15] To be sure, Kyakhta lay on the Mongolian fringes of the Qing Empire and was not the outer limit of a continuously settled territory. Only upon reaching the Great Wall, built centuries before as a bulwark against the "barbarians" of Inner Asia, could exhausted travelers look forward to reentering a civilized *space*—an especially welcome prospect, given that the Gobi Desert still had to be traversed in the final stage of the journey. On November 2, 1720, thirteen months after setting out from Saint Petersburg, the Russian embassy under Count Leon Vassilevich Ismailov caught sight of the Great Wall from a distance of around forty English miles: "One of our people cried out LAND, as if we had been all this while at sea."[16]

The Scottish doctor John Bell, a member of the count's delegation, leaves those reading his detailed account of the remaining journey in no doubt that the country beyond the Great Wall had nothing to fear from comparison with Western Europe. Even the reception given by the Sino-Manchurian border officials was extraordinary: "I must confess, I was never better pleased with any entertainment."[17] Bell was not a witness typically given to such outbursts of enthusiasm. For him, as for most trans-Siberian travelers of the eighteenth century, arriving in China did not mean entering a foreign, exotic world. Rather, it meant regaining civilized ground after enduring all the strain and discomfort of the world's longest overland journey. The contrast with the Iranian border was especially striking. Following the first Russo-Persian War of 1804–13, Iran's earliest collision with the Christian powers of Europe, which led to the incorporation of the khanate of northern Azerbaijan into the Russian empire, the borderlands were described as devastated and deserted.[18]

The attempts made by geographers to split the Eurasian continent into two parts differed greatly from the liminal experiences of travelers. Behind such cartographical and terminological endeavors stood more than just advances in geographical knowledge. As instruments for measuring and representing space grew ever more precise over the course of the eighteenth century, they proved conducive to the projection of political visions. All the imperial powers of the modern age—from Spain to the Sino-Manchurian Qing dynasty—placed cartography in the service of the state: as much to provide exact descriptions of the territories to be ruled and exploited as to project imperial dreams of the future.[19] Russia was no exception. The Janus-faced nature of its empire, turned at once towards Europe and Asia, offered tremendous scope for imaginative construction.

Peter the Great had set up a cartography department in 1719. In 1721, following victory over Sweden in the Great Northern War, he proclaimed the Muscovite tsarist state an empire on the model of the Western European powers. From now on, Siberia no longer figured as a land ripe for settlement by intrepid pioneers but as an integral, indeed symmetrical, part of the empire. As such, it needed to be assigned a role in the imperial context. Ascertaining the line of demarcation between the Asian and European parts of the empire now emerged, for the first time, as a geographical *and* political problem. According to an ancient tradition that remained influential until the early modern period, the Don River—the "Tanais" of ancient geographers—and the Sea of Azov formed the boundary between Europe and Asia.[20] The map of Europe produced by the illustrious French geographer, Guillaume Delisle, still adhered to the Don border as a far-western dividing line between "Moscovie Europe" and "Moscovie Asiatique."[21] It was not until the 1730s that Philipp von Strahlenberg, a Swedish officer who spent thirteen years in Russia as a prisoner-of-war, and Vassily Nikitich Tatishchev, geographical adviser to Tsar Peter and leading advocate of his Westernization strategy, pushed the boundary far eastward, relocating it in the Ural Mountains.[22] Some time was to pass, however, before their proposal met with widespread acceptance among their Western European colleagues. Having studied the relevant literature, Voltaire came to the conclusion "that the borders of Europe and Asia continue to be blurred."[23] He was writing in 1759; but by 1771, when Peter Simon Pallas, one of the foremost geographers and natural historians of the late eighteenth century, defined and described the Urals as a physical and ecological boundary zone,[24] the Ural solution had begun to prevail in the literature of the West as well. There still remained the question of where the border continued south of the Urals. The matter was eventually decided by geographical convention: the continental limit was declared to follow the Ural River down to the Caspian Sea.[25]

This internal borderline loomed large in the Russian imperial mind, coming to acquire enormous ideological significance.[26] Beginning with Peter the Great, Siberia was "Asianized" and stylized as a colonial supplement to a "European" Russia that now looked to the West for its identity, refashioning its administrative structures, ruling ideology, and elite culture along occidental guidelines. In keeping with this "Asianization" of Siberia, the notion of a "Great Tartary" was borrowed from the Western geographical lexicon. Descriptions of the empire's northern territories sought to conjure up the image of a Russian Mexico or Peru. At the same time, official tsarist ideology emphasized Europe's superiority over Asia, thereby imitating the imperial mindset of the Western colonial powers. Great commercial hopes were pinned on the untapped potential of this vast colonial hinterland, and at times it even seemed that these hopes were being realized.

But when the fur trade that had temporarily fueled North Asian prosperity collapsed in the early nineteenth century, Siberia's prestige sank along with it. What had once, under the reign of Catherine the Great, gleamed as the brightest jewel in the tsarist imperial crown rapidly lost its luster; in the eyes of the Russian public, Siberia now seemed little more than a worthless, barbaric appendage. The union of Europe and Asia under the aegis of the Romanovs had turned out to be a *mésalliance* between a dynamically progressive West and a primitive, stagnating East, fit only as a dumping ground for convicts. Then, from the mid-1820s onward, the tide turned once again. New voices were heard singing the praises of Siberia's uncorrupted simplicity, which—depending on taste and political inclination—promised either radical reform or the conservative renewal of Russian society and civilization. At the same time, following the suppression of the 1830 November Uprising in Poland, liberal opinion-makers in England, France, and Germany instilled fear in the public with the image of an expansionary "oriental despotism" embodied in the person of the tsar. Even in the late eighteenth century, an isolated few had preached caution against the "natural enemy of the Occident,"[27] or at least urged skepticism about the renovation of the empire's despotic façade undertaken by Peter the Great and his successors. In 1748, Montesquieu lamented the absence of a civil society in the tsarist empire and predicted that, in a country where peasants were "slaves chained to the soil" (*ésclaves attachés aux terres*) and trade was held in disrepute, the yoke of despotism would prove impossible to shake off.[28] In his view, the Petrine reforms barely scratched the surface. Even the European part of the tsarist empire remained a quasi-oriental country. This great theme of Russia defining herself—or being defined from abroad—as an "Asiatic" or "semi-Asiatic" culture was reprised with considerable vehemence in the second quarter of the nineteenth century.[29]

THE OTTOMAN EMPIRE: EUROPEAN GREAT POWER OR BARBARIAN AT THE GATES?

The Ottoman Empire's relationship with Europe had previously been debated in similar terms. Cartographically speaking, the situation here is rather more straightforward: just as Europe ends in the southwest at the Straits of Gibraltar, so it terminates in the southeast at the Bosphorus and Hellespont. As in the case of Russia, different continents were brought together in a single imperial embrace. As well as straddling Europe and Asia, the Ottoman Empire held sway over Northern Africa all the way to Algeria, albeit with fluctuating degrees of intensity. This made it a tricontinental empire with a multiethnic ruling elite, recruited in large measure from the Christian Balkans and the Black Sea. Edward Gibbon, the great historian of the Mediterranean in late antiquity and the Middle Ages, was not alone in recognizing that the Ottoman Empire could therefore by no means be classified as a "Turkish" state.[30] Nonetheless, the distinction between "Turquie europe" and "Turquie asiatique" became established as a cartographic convention. Geographical handbooks frequently dealt with Asian and European Turkey in separate volumes.

Did the presence of a "European Turkey" on maps mean that the Ottoman Empire was one of the Great Powers of Europe? Ever since the idea—and, little by little, the reality—of a European system of sovereign states had emerged from the carnage and destruction of the Thirty Years' War, a growing number of commentators had been prepared to perceive elements of this system in the Ottoman Empire. The shift in power relations between the Christian states and the Ottomans following the devastating defeats inflicted on the latter on the outskirts of Vienna in 1683 and on the battlefield of Mohács in 1687, not far from where Suleiman the Magnificent had wrested control over much of Hungary in 1526, helped defuse the "Turkish peril," normalized the image of the "fiendish Turk," and bequeathed to European art the long-lasting motif of triumph over the former archenemy. In 1671–72, the young Leibniz had already recognized the geopolitical weakness of the Ottoman Empire. Seeking to drum up support for the idea of a French annexation of Egypt, he had traveled to Paris on a special mission to win the minister, Colbert, for his cause.[31] A few years later, the protracted, arduous, and fitful process of driving the Ottomans from the Balkans got underway. This time, however, there was no need to dress up the fight in the colors of crusading ideology, as the Vatican attempted to do one last time in 1684 by enlisting the great powers in a "Holy League." From the 1670s, "Europe" rather than "Christendom" figures in political discourse as the counterweight to the Ottoman Empire. The "Turks" were seen less as religious enemies than as practitioners and proponents of civilizational values that were at odds with those of their European neighbors.[32]

Because the European great power system in the eighteenth century was understood purely as a mechanism for recalibrating balances of power,[33] very little political significance was now accorded the fact that the Ottomans were infidels. Religion and ideology never played so minor a role in international politics as in the eighteenth century. So long as the Sublime Porte conducted its foreign policy according to the same principles of rational—that is to say: self-interested and amoral—power politics applied by the Christian states,[34] there was no need to regard the Turks as the Other of European politics. Edmund Burke gave voice to a widely shared viewpoint in 1765 when he called the Ottoman Empire "a great power of Europe."[35] In numerous statistical and historiographical works from the second half of the century, the Ottoman Empire appeared as a part of Europe. Johann Christoph Gatterer, for example, treated it as a world power in his *Allgemeine Weltstatistik* (*Universal World Statistics*, 1773), a systematic description of the state of every nation known to people the Earth at the time.[36] Ludwig Timotheus Spittler, a colleague of Gatterer's at the then-avant-garde university of Göttingen, likewise included the Ottomans in his history of Europe.[37]

Around the same time, new tendencies were emerging that defined membership in the European community of nations by allegiance to a shared set of values. In 1774, Ottoman statesmen were criticized for lacking any understanding of international law.[38] In 1791, overturning his previous verdict, Edmund Burke declared the Ottoman Empire to be a part of Asia after all by virtue of its distinctive religious and civilizational ethos. It did not belong in the European system, he maintained, since this was not just a mechanism for maintaining a balance of power but a community of values with roots stretching all the way back to the Migration Period.[39] Writing at the same time in his *Ideen zu einer Philosophie der Geschichte der Menschheit* (*Outlines of a Philosophy of the History of Man*, 1785–91), Johann Gottfried Herder, the clergyman, poet, and philosopher in Goethe's Weimar, dealt with the Turks under the heading, "Foreign Nations in Europe." The Turks, he argued, could not be counted among the "ancient aborigines of Europe, who have resided in it from time immemorial."[40] His explanation is worth quoting at some length:

> The Turks, a people from Turkistan, notwithstanding they have resided in Europe for more than three centuries, are still strangers in it. They put an end to the eastern empire, which had been a burden to itself and to the world for above a thousand years; and thus unintentionally and unconsciously drove the arts westward into Europe. By their attacks on the European powers they have kept their valour alert for some centuries, and thus preserved them from falling under any foreign dominion: a slight compensation for the incomparably greater evil of having reduced the finest lands of Europe to a desert, and the once most ingenious Greeks to faithless slaves, to dissolute barbarians. How many works of art have these ignorant people destroyed! Their empire is one vast prison for all the Europeans that dwell in it; but it will fall, when its time arrives: for what have foreigners to do in Europe, who, after the lapse of a thousand years, are still resolute to remain Asiatic barbarians?[41]

Here it is not their religion that is held against the Turks—tellingly, Herder uses their ethnic name, not the political and dynastic title of the

Ottomans. Nor do considerations of ethnic hygiene lie behind the demand that they be driven out of Europe. Herder is no nativist. On the contrary, he considers the "intermingling of nations" to be a positive feature of European development: "In no one quarter of the globe have nations been so intermingled as in Europe; in no one have they so often and so completely changed their abodes, and with them their way of life and manners."[42] What makes the Turks an unwanted alien presence on European soil, in Herder's eyes, is instead their unwillingness and evident inability to assimilate to a "higher" culture. They stand aloof from the "general spirit of Europe."[43] Conversely, the people of Greece and the Balkans, who have been languishing for centuries under the tyranny of Turkish rule, qualify as "European." In both Asia Minor and Greece, so says the associated aspersion, the Ottomans had destroyed or wantonly neglected the sites of classical antiquity and laid waste to the fertile landscapes they had seized from their betters. By so flagrantry maladministering what Europe, as represented by the Roman Empire, had left behind in Asia Minor, the Turks appeared only to confirm their foreignness.[44]

Now that the Ottomans could no longer be accused of pursuing a belligerent foreign policy—indeed, an unusually sympathetic observer like Thomas Thornton, resident for fourteen years as merchant at the British factory in Constantinople, could claim with some justice that the Ottoman Empire had been transformed from a ruthless imperialist power into the object of machinations by other ruthless imperialist powers (notably Russia)[45]—criticism turned instead to focus on the un-European nature of Ottoman governance and, ultimately, Turkish civilization. The conservative French political theorist Louis de Bonald summed up this position when he asserted that the Turks had never been at home in the Balkans. They were only camping in Europe.[46]

In such an intellectual climate, the idea that a coalition of European states might intervene in the Balkans to bring about regime change became ever more conceivable. In 1795, the Göttingen scholar Christoph Meiners, displaying the penchant for strongly worded statements that had made him a prominent public figure in Germany, posed the following rhetorical question:

> Why have the greater powers in our part of the world . . . never even considered lifting the barbarous yoke of the Mahommedans at least from the Greek isles, before they are wholly deserted and desolate? A nation . . . that has conquered and ruled in the manner of the Turks has no right to lands on which it has conferred not the least happiness, but rather has plunged into direst misery from the first, and continues to make ever more miserable.[47]

Such an argument would surely have been looked on with suspicion by colonial powers of all stripes, given that here, the right of foreigners to intervene in the internal affairs of a great power was derived from the degree to which it showered blessings on its subject peoples. An English author, writing with one eye on the latest British military successes in India or perhaps the situation in Ireland, hastened to make clear that not every foreign dominion won by the sword is for that reason illegitimate, only a regime that bends its subjects' necks under "the benumbing yoke of ignorance and slavery" and refuses them an enlightening, mutually advantageous "intercourse of knowledge and benevolence."[48]

Needless to say, a grand pan-European campaign to liberate the Balkans from Ottoman rule never came into being. Yet the Ottoman Empire also played no part in the Congress of Vienna (1814–15), as by rights it should have as the sixth Great Power of Europe, nor was it involved in the broad normative consensus for establishing and maintaining peace within Europe's borders that superseded the purely mechanical eighteenth-century principle of equilibrium.[49] This meant that, in the case of an emergency, greater leeway would be granted at Europe's periphery than within the European system itself. On the other hand, the Ottoman Empire had become a reliable and predictable force for order over the course of the eighteenth century, and no European power apart from Russia had a political interest in seeing it destabilized, let alone destroyed. When anti-Ottoman national uprisings broke out from 1804 onward, first in the Pashalik of Belgrade, then in the Danube principalities, and finally in the Peloponnes, European governments were confronted with a dilemma that the Greek rebellion finally brought to a head. Should they lend their support to a popular insurrection against one of Europe's oldest dynasties, the House of Osman, and thereby contravene the counterrevolutionary principles that lay at the foundation of the post-Napoleonic order? Or should they yield to the pressure of public opinion, which sided with the freedom-loving Hellenes in their heroic struggle against Turkish tyranny, painting Turkish atrocities in the most garish of colors while simultaneously downplaying or ignoring those perpetrated by the Greeks?

In the end, the Greek War of Independence that erupted in 1821 could be ideologically neutralized by being interpreted, not as a revolutionary nationalist movement with the potential to spill over into Europe, but as a fundamentally conservative push to restore ancient rights that had been suppressed through long centuries of Turkish usurpation. The Turkish massacre of around thirty thousand Christians on the island of Chios in April 1822, compounded by subsequent Ottoman depredations in the Peloponnes, confirmed the worst anti-Turkish prejudices and unleashed such a storm of indignation that an intervention could no longer be avoided. In 1827, Great Britain, France, and Russia flouted the rules of international law and the Vienna "System of Peace" to launch a joint action against the foes of Greek liberty. Their destruction of a Turko-Egyptian fleet at Navarino saved the rebels from almost certain defeat.

The image of Ottoman rule as barbaric and essentially un-European was nothing new. It had been cultivated for years by sections of the European intelligentsia, but the wave of philhellenism that swept across Europe in the 1820s gave it broader appeal. With the Greeks now taking up arms to win their freedom, the image acquired political significance for the first time. Volunteers from abroad like Lord Byron flocked to join the cause, which could be understood—by analogy to the resistance of the Classical Hellenes to the Great King of Persia—as the revolt of an entire continent against Asiatic darkness. A note of uncertainty nonetheless crept into the ideological campaign to make Greece the frontline of Western civilization. Had the Greeks of the early nineteenth century really been able to preserve their ancient Hellenic identity intact through the vicissitudes of two millennia? Might they not have succumbed to the oriental ways to which they had for so long been exposed? Were they really one of us?[50]

Turkey would not be geographically confined to Asia until 1920, when it was forced to relinquish its last territories on the European mainland (excluding Istanbul and its surroundings). Yet even in the early nineteenth century, the "Asiatic" character of the Ottoman Empire in Europe, along with that of Turkish civilization in general, was scarcely in dispute. Ethnic cleansing of the Turkish population in the territories lost by the Ottoman Empire could be justified without difficulty. Most of his contemporaries would have disagreed with the young Joseph Hammer that "Asia" began at the Bosphorus. For them, it started wherever the Balkan border of the Ottoman Empire happened to be found at the time.

ASIA: THE PREEMINENT CONTINENT?

Joseph von Hammer-Purgstall was perhaps deliberately targeting the anti-Turkish hysteria of the philhellenes when, in his masterful sociological survey of the populace of Constantinople (1822), he included the Greeks among the "Orientals"—"in consideration of their origins in the East, already sufficiently proven by the affinity of their language with the oriental tongues."[51] Drawing on his intimate firsthand knowledge of the country, the great Orientalist shone a critical light on attempts to represent the Greeks of his own time as the direct descendants of the Classical Hellenes and inheritors of an authentically "occidental" identity. At the same time, Hammer-Purgstall cited a tradition that saw ancient Greece as a cultural offshoot of the ancient Orient. This idea was commonplace in late-eighteenth-century scholarship, albeit not universally accepted.[52] There was broad consensus, though, that Europe should be viewed within the larger context of Eurasia.[53] Shortly after the First World War, Paul Valéry described Europe as a western appendix to

Asia ("un petit cap du continent asiatique"), asking what this geographical reality signified for Europe's cultural self-awareness.[54] Such a notion was entirely unremarkable in the seventeenth and eighteenth century.[55] As late as 1808, Alexander von Humboldt could still liken Europe's (climatic) relationship with Asia to that of Brittany with the rest of France.[56]

The influence of militantly expansionary Asiatic tribespeople—Huns, Arabs, Mongols, and Turks—on the history of the Mediterranean, in particular, was a central, much-discussed topic in early modern universal history writing.[57] An awareness that Europe did not develop in splendid isolation, evolving instead through constant cross-cultural exchange with Asia, temporarily submerged from view in the nineteenth century, only to be rediscovered in our own time by a new generation of historians.[58] To this was added the oft-repeated topos of Asia as the source of all civilization. Of the three main parts of the ancient world, late-seventeenth-century authors contended, Asia was the most fertile and possessed the most genial climate. The birthplace of religion, the arts, laws, urban society, and monarchic government,[59] it was also a theologically privileged place in the universe, the setting of mankind's creation in the Garden of Eden and scene of Christ's earthly sojourn. By the end of the eighteenth century, faith in the physical localizability of the Garden of Eden had all but vanished, yet Asia's prestige had largely withstood the skeptical onslaught of a disbelieving age. Study of the continent was still highly recommended, for it represented "the ancestral homeland of the entire human race," the wellspring of all civilization,[60] and the "fatherland of the most rational among the enduring positive religions."[61] In addition, Asia had bestowed more tangible benefits on Europe in the form of its viticulture and much of its agriculture, including "its noblest fruit trees."[62] In 1793, the Göttingen historian Arnold Herrmann Ludwig Heeren, summarized the early modern judgment of Asia in his important work, *Ideen über die Politik, den Verkehr und den Handel der vornehmsten Völker der alten Welt* (*Historical Researches into the Politics, Intercourse and Trade of the Principal Nations of Antiquity*, 1833). Heeren arrived at the conclusion:

> Of the three divisions of the ancient world there is none which more attracts and rewards the attention of the philosophical historian, engaged not in the investigation of individual nations but of the human race, than Asia.[63]

Heeren was writing during the French Revolution, at a time when Europeans tended to see their own civilizational preeminence confirmed chiefly in the field of scientific endeavor. He therefore continued:

> Even when we trace the progress of the arts and sciences, notwithstanding the pains which the nations of the West have bestowed in cultivating such pursuits and conferring upon them, as it were, an impress of their own, we find ourselves uniformly recalled to the East as the place of their origin; and it is there that we discover the native seat not only of our own religion, but of all other modes of belief which have become at any time predominant in the world.[64]

Although Heeren was mainly interested in Asia's past, he advised studying its present as well. The devaluation of modern Asia in favor of a remote classical past, accessible only in ancient texts and architectural monuments, has rightly been identified by Edward Said as a key characteristic of Western "Orientalism."[65] It was a view shared by neither Heeren nor his contemporary, Joseph von Hammer-Purgstall, who adroitly combined antiquarian research with commentary on the current state of the Ottoman Empire.

While the reputation of *ancient* Asia remained consistently high throughout the eighteenth century, representative judgments on how Asia was faring in the *present* were markedly more critical around 1800 than they had been a century before. One indication of this was the precipitous decline in the continent's perceived economic standing. In 1673, John Ogilby was not courting ridicule when he claimed in his handsomely produced compendium, *Asia*, that the world's greatest empires and trading powers lay in Asia, a continent "ennobled with several grand Prerogatives over the rest." All the bullion pouring in from the newly exploited gold mines of the Americas could not outweigh the fabulous treasures of the East.[66] Wyndham Beawes, in his very well-informed merchant's manual from 1754, drew on the latest travelers' reports concerning the world beyond Europe's borders to paint the picture of a dynamic and flourishing economy. In his account, Asia was not simply passively awaiting the arrival of a band of colonial adventurers to plunder its riches at will; on the contrary, it was a vibrant economic powerhouse that tolerated European merchants and trading houses only within specially allocated niches, a finding that has since been amply confirmed by historical scholarship.[67]

By 1800, however, Asia as a whole strikes a majority of observers as economically backward and in need of revitalization through European commercial enterprise. Whereas Heeren, writing at the end of an era, sought to reaffirm Asia's dignity as the preeminent continent, a widely read English author, William Guthrie, had in 1771 already arrived at a very different judgment, one that was to be pronounced ever more frequently and stridently in years to come:

> Asia next claims our attention; which however, though in some respects the most famous quarter of the world, offers, when compared to Europe, extremely little for our entertainment or instruction. In Asia, a strong attachment to ancient customs, and the weight of tyrannical power, bears down the active genius of man, and prevents that variety in manners and character, which distinguishes the European nations.[68]

Comparing Europe with Asia was nothing new at the time. Indeed, the privileged position formerly reserved for Asia in the history of the world resulted precisely from the contrast drawn with Europe. What was new, in a writer like Guthrie, was the idea that Europe and Asia were engaged in a developmental contest that Asia had already lost. Many saw grounds for triumph in this. "For a long time Asia played a leading role in the world," we read in a French encyclopedia from 1796, "little is left of this but memories."[69] A more sophisticated thinker, the French revolutionary politician Volney, registered his dismay at the lack of freedom and primitive conditions he encountered on his travels in the East: "All Asia is buried in the most profound darkness."[70] But was this unique to Asia? Volney avoided such a crude dichotomy between East and West. He found equally deplorable the oppressive conditions in European nations where serfdom had yet to be abolished.[71] For Volney, Asia might no longer be the preeminent continent but at least it still had a future.

CHARACTER AND ENCYCLOPEDIA

In the sixteenth and seventeenth century, Europe left its mark on the New World while still lingering in the shadows cast by an older world. The cultural prestige of a bygone Asia, which was above all an Asia of the Old Testament, remained undimmed. News reports from China, eagerly devoured by European savants, seemed to suggest that the Orient was still capable of enormous cultural productivity. Yet hopes for intercultural dialogue, such as those raised by Leibniz around 1700,[72] were to be disappointed. Over the course of the second half of the eighteenth century, European thought freed itself from what now, from an appalled distance, was perceived to be a debilitating and oppressive tradition that continued to weigh down on Asia. That tradition included Europe's *own* fixation on Asia.

While there may have been areas of cultural convergence in the past, such as the chivalric orders of the Christian and Islamic Middle Ages,[73] the relationship between Europe and Asia was now increasingly construed in antagonistic terms. Situations of dramatic conflict were particularly well-suited to expressing this. Enlightenment historians had almost invariably blamed the Crusades on Christian fanaticism and misguided worldly ambition. William Robertson, a historian not usually prone to severity in judgment, pronounced them "a singular monument of human folly,"[74] depicting Saladin, the sultan who spearheaded the reconquest of Jerusalem, in a far more sympathetic light than the Christian invaders of Palestine. Jean-Baptiste Mailly's history of the First Crusade (1780) struck an altogether different note. Now, for the first time, emphasis is placed on the clash of civilizations: "It is Europe against Asia."[75] Interpretive templates are simplified. "Europe" and "Asia" become more clear-cut in their differences, moving apart and taking up positions on opposite sides of an unbridgeable chasm. Not by chance, it was precisely a late bastion of the Enlightenment in Heeren who warned against overly sweeping generalizations on the subject of Asia and drew attention to the continent's cultural diversity.[76] In the introduction to his historical and ethnographic overview of Asia, he strikes a balance between generalizations of the most cautious kind and sensitivity to the specific complexion of particular landscapes, nations, and cultures. Heeren's contemporary Conrad Malte-Brun, the doyen of French geography and Napoleon's favorite geographer, expressed himself with far less restraint—but also far more in keeping with the zeitgeist—when pontificating in 1812 on "the moral character of the Asiatic peoples." Its essential trait: "immobility."[77]

At the time he wrote these words, the stereotypes of "Asia" and "the Asiatic" that would go on to dominate the nineteenth century were already gaining ground. Conceptual homogenization went hand in hand with dichotomization. A narrower view of Asia was emerging, one that identified the Orient with Islam and left no room for the non-Islamic inhabitants of Egypt (such as the Copts) and the Levant, for example. Around the turn of the century, a new intellectual claim became increasingly prominent: the idea that it is possible to reach through the veil of exotic appearances to grasp the timeless essence of Asia and its people. Hippocrates had already spoken in general terms of the debility and torpor of the "Asiatics."[78] "The Asiatic differs from us in morality and psychology," reads the programmatic introduction to a new Orientalist journal established in 1806.[79] Knowledge that makes claim to such apodictic certitude has the advantage of providing ready orientation. The particular is quickly reduced to the universal. The Ottomans are "perfected Asiatics": one only needs to know Asiatics to know the Ottomans, too.[80] Prejudices and preconceptions are confirmed even when they appear to be falsified. Someone who believes that "the Oriental is a liar," for example, will be all the more impressed when he encounters truthfulness among the Javanese and Malays, since it contradicts the "general deficiency of oriental nations in this quality."[81] The exception proves the rule.

In the end, an entire continent contracts into a literary type. In 1824 James Justinian Morier, a retired English diplomat widely traveled in Iran, initiated the genre of the ethnographic novel with *The Adventures of Hajji Baba*. It became an instant bestseller. Morier set out to present "manners and customs" in a format that held no surprises for a public familiar with the narrative conventions of the European picaresque novel. The novel deploys local color with considerable plausibility and skill, and is thus far removed from the fantasies of cruel despots, conspiring court eunuchs, and scantily clad harem girls penned by his peers. It is also not the anti-Persian diatribe it was taken to be in Iran shortly after its appearance. Hajji Baba, a small-time swindler from a poor artisanal background, is depicted as a charming rogue. He muddles along from day to day, getting by with the help of tall tales and outright lies, and rises to high office before suffering a fall from grace. He lacks the rational mind, fixity of purpose, and high seriousness that distinguish the modern European. Life here is cheerfully endured fatality. Hajji Baba combines all the qualities that his creator wishes to ascribe to the Persian national character. More than that: Hajji Baba *is* the Oriental, the Orient made flesh and blood.[82] At the same time, the picaresque figure of Hajji Baba was by no means rejected in Iran as a degrading Orientalist cliché. Mirza Habib Isfahani's Persian translation of 1886 became an inspiration for Iranian liberals and revolutionaries.[83]

The concentration in a single character of everything that typifies the continent at the end of our epoch stands opposed to a very different organization of knowledge about the Other from the dawn of the eighteenth century. In 1697, Barthélemi d'Herbelot published a folio volume with the imposing title, *Bibliothèque orientale ou dictionnaire universal contenant généralement tout ce qui regarde la connaissance des peoples de l'Orient*

(*Oriental Library, or, Universal Dictionary Containing Every Thing Requisite to the Knowledge of the Eastern Nations*).[84] D'Herbelot's work gathered together the fruits of half a century's research—mostly French—into the Near and Middle East. At the initiative of Cardinal Mazarin, then Colbert, French scholars had been commissioned to collect Greek manuscripts, Roman coins, and anything else connected with classical antiquity, including manuscripts in oriental languages.[85] The Royal Library in Paris thereby became home to the greatest trove of oriental manuscripts in all Europe. D'Herbelot, who could read Latin, Greek, Hebrew, Aramaic, Syriac, Arabic, Persian, and Turkish[86] and in 1692 was made professor of oriental languages at the Collège de France, was probably better acquainted with this material than anyone else. His great work was based almost entirely on earlier publications and original manuscripts in the various regional languages. Following his death, it was furnished with a programmatic introduction and ushered into print by his friend, Antoine Galland, the translator of the *Thousand and One Nights*. Encyclopedic in scope, it became the eighteenth century's unsurpassed authority on the geography, history, and culture of the Near and Middle East.[87] Edward Gibbon, for instance, acknowledged it as one of his chief sources on the history of the Arabs and Turks.[88]

D'Herbelot and Galland's "Orient" is not the world of an Islam diametrically opposed to the West. Both men—Galland even more so than d'Herbelot—understand the Orient as a space for intercultural encounter and exchange, and they devote extensive coverage to Christian and Jewish minorities in the Islamic sphere. Furthermore, both discern an overarching continuity extending from the world of the Old Testament and Greco-Roman antiquity to the Byzantine Empire and reaching all the way down to the present. Rather than emphasizing the contrast and clash of civilizations, the two authors are more interested in showing their complementarity and mutual influence. The *Bibliothèque Orientale* consists of over eight thousand alphabetically arranged short articles.[89] By eschewing any systematic ordering of his own and dispensing with a master narrative, d'Herbelot leaves the discursive field as wide open as possible.[90] Generalizations about the Orient are studiously avoided. Such thematic breadth and dispersion conveys the impression of an immense, infinitely varied civilization that militates against any reduction to its supposed "essence." The world evoked in the work's more than one thousand pages has the inexhaustible variety of *Tales from the Thousand and One Nights*, which in Galland's translation was directed at the same contemporary readership. Numerous entries on place communicate a sense of the Orient's vast extent and size. D'Herbelot's work stands for a perception of non-European cultures that resists the urge to essentialize the foreign, to boil it down to a few easily recognizable features.

EUROPEAN PRIMACY AND PROVINCIALISM

Even in periods when Asia was still viewed with respect, voices proclaiming Europe to be the most valuable part of the world were never lacking. Just a few years after Vasco da Gama's discovery of the sea route to India, Portuguese authors were disputing Asia's superiority.[91] By the second half of the eighteenth century, the idea of European primacy had become commonplace. The geographer, Johann Georg Hager, made the point succinctly: "Europe may be the smallest part of the world, but it is the best."[92] In 1783, the far-from-parochial-minded voyager, polymath, and natural historian, Johann Reinhold Forster, father of the more famous Georg Forster, saw Europe as having attained an "ultimate peak of perfection"; ten years later, the English philosopher and founding theorist of anarchism, William Godwin, called it "the most civilized and favored quarter of the world."[93] In 1785, Anton Friedrich Büsching, more a collator and well-informed synthesizer than an original thinker in his own right, summarized the arguments of his contemporaries:

> Europe may be the smallest of the Earth's four continents, but it should be considered the most important: 1) because none is better farmed; 2) because it is mightier than the other three combined; 3) because Europeans have subjected to their dominion the greater

> part of the rest of the Earth's surface, or made themselves fruitful therein, just as they alone have connected the Earth's main parts with each other through their seafaring, travel and trade; 4) because Europe has for many centuries been the principal seat of the arts and sciences; and 5) because Europeans have brought knowledge of the world's true Lord and Savior to the four corners of the Earth.[94]

Büsching wrote these words at a time when the first signs of industrialization had not yet given Europe an edge over commercially advanced economies and exporters of manufactured goods such as India and China.[95] Europe's economic advantages were still to be found in agriculture, in the excellence of its farming practices, while its political precedence could not yet—four years before the end of the ancien régime—be said to lie in the higher level of freedom enjoyed by its people. Europe's true superiority was shown in the dynamism of its expansion: in the spread of its rule through force of arms, in its thriving settler colonies, in its ability to create a modern global system through "seafaring, travel and trade," in its propagation of Christianity through missionary activity. In the late eighteenth century, almost nobody believed that European predominance might have a biological or racial foundation. The Göttingen professor, Christoph Meiners, was an exception: in 1793, he anticipated later race theories in seeing "the stock of light and fair . . . nations" as destined to attain a position of world-historical supremacy.[96]

Even if Asia, in the judgment of the eighteenth century, was the place where the arts and sciences had originated, Europe *later* became their "principal seat," as Büsching puts it. The abbé Dubos, taking up an idea from Fontenelle,[97] found a striking image for the same thought in 1719: the fine arts and sciences had never strayed far from Europe except to take an occasional turn on southern shores, so to speak ("pour se promener, s'il est permis de parler ainsi, sur les côtes de l'Asie et de l'Afrique").[98] Dubos included warfare among the sciences, and Edward Gibbon considered the rational perfection attained by the Greeks and Romans in this field to have been instrumental in allowing the West to outmatch and overpower the East.[99] The science of politics, according to Dubos, had also suffered comparative neglect in Asia. To be sure, there was more to this than a simple opposition between European liberty and Asiatic despotism.[100] Henry Brougham, the liberal reformer and later British Lord Chancellor, found "[a] perfect knowledge of the arts of administration" only in Europe,[101] detecting slow progress toward greater civic freedoms and public oversight of monarchies even in absolutist states. Brougham attributed this progress in part to the civilizing effects of trade, but also to the general dissemination of knowledge and education brought about by the printing press. Barely a few years after the French Revolution had cut a deep ideological cleft through Europe, he calmly and confidently predicted the spread of a "modern system" of rational politics across the continent. Even under nonconstitutional monarchies, the excesses of princely passions could still be curbed through "the indirect influence of a numerous and enlightened people."[102] Violent passions were, of course, the hallmark of barbaric despotism.

The further the eighteenth century advanced, the more it seemed obvious to European commentators that Europe had outstripped Asia in the natural sciences, above all. Yet it was not until the early nineteenth century that the idea became widespread that in Europe—and only in Europe—knowledge of nature acquired through the sciences could successfully be converted into control of nature. The geographer Malte-Brun was one of the first to state this directly, ascribing the triumph of European civilization chiefly to its technological prowess: "We alone subject even the most fearsome powers of nature to our will."[103] The epoch of the great colonial engineering projects looms on the horizon.

Büsching's third argument for the superiority of modern Europe—that it is the only civilization to have created communication and trade networks crisscrossing the globe—is undoubtedly correct. It should not, however, be read as blatant justification for imperialist and colonialist practices. Eighteenth-century authors were more sensitive than nineteenth-century theorists of imperialism to the process of globalization playing out before their eyes. To witness the emergence of a world society, all they needed to do was visit one of the many port cities strung out along the coastlines of Europe. Their astonishment at the dramatic nature of this development is often palpable in their writings. None expressed this astonishment with greater wit or artistry than Edward Gibbon, the foremost European historian of the age and one of its best prose stylists, who discerned the beginnings of globalization in the impact of Genghis Khan's campaigns on the fishmonger trade in England. "It is whimsical enough," writes Gibbon, "that the orders of a Mogul khan, who reigned on the borders of China, should have lowered the price of herrings in the English market."[104]

Others commented just as perceptively, albeit less cleverly, on the worldwide connections emerging at the time. According to Jean-Jacques Rousseau, trade, travel, and conquest brought nations closer together, gradually blurring the distinctions between different ways of life.[105] To many of his contemporaries, the economic links being forged between continents were plain to see. Europe had organized trans-Atlantic trade routes with African slaves and sugar,[106] and it consumed vast quantities of goods from India and China, paying for them with silver shipped from the mines of Mexico and Peru.[107] In 1754, Wyndham Beawes made a further observation that historians would not rediscover until the 1970s: global trade had not begun with European expansion into overseas markets; Arab merchant vessels had long plied the seas between Asia, Africa, and Europe.[108]

Several authors hyperbolically or prophetically celebrated Europe's rise to global dominance. In 1801, three quarters of a century before the dawn of the age of imperialism, the abbé de Pradt, a prolific writer with particularly sharp antennae for international developments, noted that Europe was something like the capital of the world: it had discovered the secret of making others work for its own profit and filling state coffers with "tribute from around the world."[109] Others, less cynically, felt the need to preach the virtues of enlightenment, emphasizing the worldwide dissemination of European knowledge and good morals: cutting-edge scientific research was already being carried out in Calcutta and Lima;[110] ideas and fashion trends shuttled back and forth between continents; long sea voyages were becoming safer and more comfortable thanks to better ships, the successful campaign against the terrible mariners' disease, scurvy, and the establishment of seafarers' lodges in Asia; educational standards were improving all around the world.[111] Johann Reinhold Forster, who knew a thing or two about travel, having sailed with his son Georg on Captain Cook's second circumnavigation of the globe from 1772 to 1775, saw seafaring—whether for purposes of trade or scientific inquiry—as a "bond" uniting the entire human race in fellowship and amity:

> The bond of conviviality and love, which from time to time may slacken among the children of men, is often strengthened and tightened by travel at sea. Once compelled by dire necessity to set aside the proud spirit of indifference, and to accept the help and solicitude of strangers, one learns to see that a man and a nation do not exist for their own sake, but rather to provide mutual assistance and support.[112]

Yet travel, especially when ventured solely "for the satisfaction of curiosity," was something only "civilized nations" undertook, and Europe alone had turned it into a global industry. Immanuel Kant likewise saw the continents growing ever more closely interlinked through trade, but he judged the consequences of this new wave of commercial activity far more skeptically—and also far more realistically—than Johann Reinhold Forster, normally an irascible character but here subject to a rare fit of Panglossian enthusiasm. Kant had observed the frequency with which trade in Asia paved the way for full-blown conquest and colonization. In his late text, *Zum ewigen Frieden: Ein Philosophischer Entwurf* (*Perpetual Peace: A Philosophical Sketch*, 1795), he showed an understanding for why the Japanese and Chinese restricted rights of access to their countries, even if that meant obstructing the free movement of people, ideas, and goods. Like Montesquieu, Johann Reinhold Forster, and many others, Kant foresaw that "continents distant from each other can enter into peaceful mutual relations which may eventually be regulated by public laws."[113] Yet the philosopher sounded a note of caution:

> If we compare with this ultimate end the *inhospitable* conduct of the civilized states of our continent, especially the commercial states, the injustice which they display in *visiting* foreign countries and peoples (which in their case is the same as *conquering* them) seems appallingly great. America, the Negro countries, the Spice Islands, the Cape, etc. were looked upon at the time of their discovery as ownerless territories; for the native inhabitants were counted as nothing. In East India (Hindustan), foreign troops were brought in under the pretext of merely setting up trading posts. This led to oppression of the natives, incitement of the various Indian states to widespread wars, famine, insurrection, treachery and the whole litany of evils which can afflict the human race.
>
> China and Japan (Nippon), having had experience of such guests, have wisely placed restrictions on them. China permits contact with her territories, but not entrance into them, while Japan only allows contact with a single European people, the Dutch, although they are still segregated from the native community like prisoners.[114]

Kant, who kept himself well-informed in remote Königsberg, was acutely aware of the globalizing tendencies of the age. Sensing the ambivalence of enlightenment and power politics, he sought legal means to ensure that the increasing integration of the world, while driven by European interests, would prove beneficial to all concerned. Europeans should not be permitted to ride roughshod over the rights of natives in their bid to conquer new markets and territories. Kant therefore proposed a "Weltbürgerrecht" or cosmopolitan right. What he understood by this was not so much untrammeled freedom of movement as the right to travel abroad and visit other countries without let or hindrance. He wanted to outlaw colonialism, a demand so radical that even the revolutionaries in France refused to support it. None of his contemporaries thought through the dilemma of early globalization and European predominance as deeply as Kant.

August Ludwig Schlözer in Göttingen, at once the least elegant writer and most astute synthesizer among the European historians of the Enlightenment, was similarly exercised by the emergence of a network of relations spanning the entire globe. Unlike Kant, however, he did not view the problem from a normative standpoint but was more interested in its implications for the writing of history. Schlözer was far from advocating a historiography that celebrated Europe's rise over other civilizations. Alongside the Romans and medieval Germans, he included the Chinese, Arabs, Mongols, and Turks in his list of the "major races" of history, the leading nations that had built up a world empire, whereas the Greeks and Egyptians ranked only among the "merely significant races."[115] Grounded in late-eighteenth-century cosmopolitanism, Schlözer's world history abstains from the kind of teleological narrative that sees history culminating in the Europeanization of the world. It seeks out "concatenations spanning countries and centuries"[116] in earlier epochs, and it employs "apt comparison"[117] between historical phenomena in different civilizations—or, as Schlözer neutrally states, different parts of the world—to discover points of convergence and divergence between developmental stages. Echoing Francis Bacon, Schlözer identifies modern Europe's achievements less in its rise to global hegemony, the line taken by Büsching and especially the abbé de Pradt, than in technical breakthroughs such as the "compass, gunpowder, paper, print, spectacles, clocks and the post."[118] "With the help of these inventions, we discovered three new worlds and proceeded to subjugate, plunder, cultivate or lay waste to them."[119] Although formulated within the intellectual horizon of the late Enlightenment, Schlözer's far-reaching reflections on what a non-Eurocentric history of the world might look like still bear thinking about today. If, for all that, Schlözer was still swayed in his judgment by the civilizational advances made in Europe over the previous three centuries, then this is hardly surprising: no author claimed the complete equality of all lands and nations at the time.

In the eighteenth century, there were those who were convinced of modern Europe's world-historical superiority.[120] They attributed to people like themselves—that is, Europeans in countries like France, Great Britain, Germany, Italy, or the Netherlands—"a degree of culture that raises us far above our contemporaries in the other parts of the world as well as the most enlightened people of antiquity" (Schlözer).[121] Yet they did not have to assert this by rejecting and denigrating other civilizations. To Schlözer we owe the important insight that the creation of a worldwide trade and communications network—the modern global system initiated by the European powers—first made possible a global historiography that went beyond a disconnected summation of national and regional histories. European expansion first created a global epistemic framework within which a wide array of historical subprocesses could be ordered. Like the earlier *Universal History from the Earliest Account of Time*, a monumental work produced by a team of British authors that appeared in sixty-six volumes between 1736 and 1766 and sought to give non-European history its due,[122] Schlözer allows us to glimpse the possibility of an *inclusive* Eurocentrism.

For the philosopher of history Johann Gottfried Herder, modern Europe's primacy also proved compatible with a conception of universal history that respected what was unique to other civilizations.[123] The same holds true for Sir William Jones, one of the Orient's most energetic and successful advocates in Europe, who translated and promoted research on the literature, law, and history of almost every Asiatic culture.[124] Jones never for a moment doubted Europe's superiority. But while he praised its achievements as "transcendently majestick"[125] and upheld the aesthetic normativity of Greco-Roman literature throughout his life, he still treasured Persian poetry and the Indian Sanskrit epics. Such inclusive Eurocentrism characterized the Enlightenment from first to last. Not until the nineteenth century, when intellectual horizons narrowed to reflect the cultural preferences and prejudices of white male imperialists, did it give way to an *exclusive* Eurocentrism.

III

Changing Perspectives

Der Amerikaner, der den Kolumbus zuerst entdeckte,
machte eine böse Entdeckung.
(The American who first discovered Columbus made a bad discovery.)
—Georg Christoph Lichtenberg (1742–99), *Sudelbücher*[1]

CULTURAL TRANSFER AND COLONIALISM

At first, the process of global integration that made such an impression on late-eighteenth-century authors was largely confined to port cities and their immediate hinterlands; the vast interior spaces of the continents remained all but untouched by outside forces. In this way, as in many others, it differed from the strain of globalization that emerged during the last decades of the nineteenth century. At this stage, there were still no signs of widespread "Westernization" in Asian societies that had escaped colonial control. John Richards, editor of the first Persian-Arabic-English dictionary and a comparative cultural historian of sorts, made the point with all forcefulness in 1778:

> With a wonderful predilection for their own ancient manners, they [the peoples of Asia] have a peculiar and invincible antipathy to those of Europe. They are so opposite to their genius, to their hereditary prejudices, and to every idea political and religious, that no instance can be produced, perhaps, of one single custom originally European ever been adopted by the Asiatic nations.[2]

European mores and manners, to the extent that they were known at all in Asia, did not invite imitation. At this stage, Western cultural influence was spread mainly by missionaries scattered unevenly across the world outside Europe, and it left a permanent mark on large swathes of the population only under quite exceptional circumstances. The Philippines alone were subject to effective Catholic missionary activity and evangelization from the sixteenth century onward. In Japan, the great hope of the Jesuit order in the last decades of the sixteenth century, the start of the seventeenth century saw the Catholic mission disbanded and Christianity as a whole criminalized under the new dynasty of the Tokugawa Shogunate. In China, more than two centuries of intensive missionary work had by 1800 failed to convert significant sections of the general populace or make inroads into the administrative elite, the culturally Confucian class of bureaucrat-scholars. The Muslim world remained as resistant as ever to Christian proselytizing. Even in the colonial outposts run by the British and Dutch, Christianity made little progress. The East India Company (EIC) forbade missionary activity in its territories until 1813 in order to avoid causing unnecessary disturbance to the Indian population. And visitors to Batavia were constantly registering their surprise and dismay that the VOC's colored subjects in Batavia and its surroundings were spared Christian instruction.[3] Protestant missionaries only invested time and effort into areas where they faced direct competition from Catholicism.[4]

During the early modern phase of Europe's expansion, then, the immediately apparent influence of European culture on Asia remained primarily (and necessarily) confined to the field of religion, and even here the impact was fairly limited. Cultural transfer, still on a small scale, took place along other pathways: through the magnetic attraction exerted by colonial cities on their environs; through the uptake of Western technologies (particularly those with military applications) and artistic techniques; in China, through the practical—astronomical, cartographical, and architectural—influence of the Jesuits; in Japan, through the uniquely purposeful institutionalization of "Dutch learning" (*rangaku*), which opened the floodgates to Western knowledge of all kinds.[5]

Europe arrived in Asia predominantly in commodity form. European wares quickly filtered through to the furthest reaches of the continent, although the manufacturing capacity of Asian economies remained far superior to that of Europe, and Asian textiles defended their entrenched position in European markets well beyond the middle of the eighteenth century.[6] The traveling English merchant, Jonas Hanway, observed in the 1720s that fully a third of the army of the Iranian conqueror, Nadir (Nader) Shah, was clad in European cloth.[7] Shortly before 1800, coats and vests in the almost completely secluded kingdom of Burma were made of European wool, while the military was armed with mostly French and British rifles.[8] At the same time a visiting diplomat, Samuel Turner, noted with amazement the widespread presence of English brocade in the remote mountain fastnesses of Tibet, where few Europeans had set foot before him.[9] In Bhutan he had earlier delighted the raja and his court with Bordeaux wine and strawberry jam, single-handedly creating a potential export market for European delicacies.[10] Of all the influences emanating from Europe, commodities penetrated the furthest. European imports were circulated by indigenous trade networks in regions where no white man had ever been seen. For most people, then, the encounter between Europe and Asia chiefly came in the form of tradable goods.[11]

Several authors already foresaw the profoundly transformative effect of an expansion that went far beyond the activities of European merchants, soldiers, missionaries, and traveling scholars. In 1769 the French journalist and later academy secretary, Jean-Louis Castilhon, warned in his perceptive *Considérations sur les causes physiques et morales de la diversité du génie, des mœurs, et du gouvernement des nations* of the "corruption" of morals threatened by overseas trade. In an age of flourishing international travel and trade, few parts of the world had escaped Europe's corrosive touch; authentic national character types were fast disappearing from view; few modern peoples had retained the stability and constancy of their ancient forebears.[12] A few years later the assiduous collector of ethnological material, Jean-Nicolas Démeunier , saw the human race growing ever more uniform and recommended, partly for this reason, that the ethnography of ancient and modern nations be studied.[13]

Yet even as European goods were infiltrating the most far-flung corners of Asia, Asian products were conquering European markets. Coffee, silk, fine cotton cloth, and china ware—a name that recalls the Far East's former monopoly in porcelain production—were all in high demand.[14] At the beginning of the eighteenth century, the economic and cultural impact of Asian trade on Europe was greater than the other way around. The scales began to tip in Europe's favor only toward the end of the century.[15]

The relationship between cultural transfer from Europe to Asia and colonial rule of Asians by Europeans was not a fixed one. Paradoxically, cultural transfer was at its greatest where Europeans were afforded the fewest opportunities for colonial expansion: in Japan. Before the idea of a Western civilizing mission in the Orient took root around 1800, allowing colonial rule to be stylized as a benevolent instrument for propagating superior cultural norms, every step to advance European rule in Asia had been dogged by vocal public criticism. The past colonial practices of the Spanish and Portuguese were roundly condemned, particularly from the Protestant side of the confessional divide. So too, unsurprisingly, was the present-day conduct of rival imperial powers; thus the British, for example, waxed indignant over Dutch administration of the East Indies. Yet the version of colonialism pursued by one's own nation was not spared criticism, either. While German commentators such as Immanuel Kant, Johann Gottfried Herder, Georg Forster, Johann Gottlieb Fichte, or Alexander von Humboldt could adopt an air of skeptical but cool detachment, given they were not directly affected by national imperial projects, British and French critics attacked the policies of their own governments with unbridled vehemence.

They could be motivated by quite different considerations. The economist Adam Smith soberly analyzed the irrationality of many aspects of colonialism, especially the monopoly on trade.[16] The "conservative" (by today's standards) parliamentary politician, Edmund Burke, instigated a years-long campaign to impeach Warren Hastings, the first governor-general of India, whom he accused of orchestrating or condoning violent attacks and injustices against the peaceful Indian population, particularly the aristocracy. Burke feared that such barbaric misconduct, if left unchecked, would have repercussions for the political culture of the motherland.[17] The abbé Raynal, a radical man of letters in the twilight of the ancien régime, coauthored with Denis Diderot and others one of the top international bestsellers of the age: the *Histoire philosophique et politique des établissements et du commerce des Européens dans les deux Indes* (1770). In the guise of an unusually detailed denunciation of the misdeeds perpetrated by European conquerors and colonists in both hemispheres, replete with scenes of terror and wide-ranging analysis, they offered a philosophical conception of history that for the first time drew attention to the paramount importance of overseas expansion for modern Europe's self-understanding.

In the Age of Enlightenment, unlike in the nineteenth century, the European takeover of the world was not assumed to be inevitable. A work of the same condemnatory force as Raynal and Diderot's *Histoire philosophique* would never again be written in Europe. Even those among their contemporaries who accepted the fundamental legitimacy of European expansion, and were thus prepared to tolerate a kind of "soft" colonialism, still kept watch for violations of justice in the certainty that the same standards of right and wrong applied to the entire human race. No accusation hit Warren Hastings harder than Burke's claim that he adhered to a relativist "geographical morality" in his dealings with the Indians, treating them in ways that would be proscribed in Europe as tyrannical and criminally reprehensible.[18] The Enlightened critique of colonialism, as formulated perhaps most trenchantly by Diderot,[19] gives the lie to the claim that European intellectuals were capable of nothing other than autistic self-reflection and had, from the very beginning of the age of expansion, been hopelessly compromised by their complicity with power. Self-relativization in a period of increasingly asymmetrical contact between civilizations may not have been the norm, yet it was a far from negligible element in the repertoire of European strategies for coming to terms with the world beyond its borders.

The great Scottish historian William Robertson, a pioneer of empirical global history in an age fond of philosophical histories of mankind, was still expressing this attitude in 1791, in his lengthy *Historical Disquisition Concerning the Knowledge Which the Ancients Had of India*.[20] In his *History of America* from 1777, Robertson had weighed up the costs and benefits of Spanish and Portuguese colonization, as much for the Iberian powers and societies as for the American natives. In doing so, he had depicted European atrocities in the New World rather less colorfully than had Raynal and Diderot in their contemporaneous account. He had also largely absolved both the Spanish state and the Catholic church of direct responsibility for the brutalities of the Conquista. Nonetheless, readers were left in no doubt that the encounter of two societies at such different stages of social evolution had led to catastrophe. This outcome was not the regrettable result of excesses committed by a few rogue individuals operating beyond the reach of the law; rather, it was the necessary consequence of enormous social disparity, coupled with an inability on the part of the Spaniards to perceive the gulf that separated them from their new subjects. The golden opportunity for the discoveries in the New World to lead to progress *for all* had been squandered. While Robertson was well aware that the India of his day did not bear comparison with sixteenth-century America in every respect, he still felt compelled to warn against the newly aggressive stance adopted by his British compatriots in South Asia. He did so, not by polemicizing against the latest wrongdoings in the colonies, but by presenting a highly respectful account of Hindu India's long record of cultural excellence.

The septuagenarian Robertson was by no means swept away by enthusiasm for all things Indian. Unlike several of the German Romantics a few years later, including Friedrich Schlegel in his treatise *Über die Sprache und Weisheit der Indier* (*On the Language and Wisdom of the Indians*, 1808),[21] Robertson was not one to go fishing for age-old truths in the murky depths of the Ganges. He had no interest in the sacred origins of mythology. In common with his younger contemporary Johann Gottfried Herder, a more influential figure in paving the way for the romantic idealization of Brahmanical wisdom,[22] Robertson approached Indian civilization with sympathetic interest and a tolerant acceptance of its differences and peculiarities. Robertson denied neither his Christian beliefs nor his enthusiasm for the achievements of modern Europe, particularly in the field of science. At the same time, however, he refused to elevate religion or progressive values into absolute standards against which other cultures could be judged and found wanting.[23] Robertson and Herder, like Immanuel Kant in his late text *Zum ewigen Frieden: Ein Philosophischer Entwurf* (*Perpetual Peace: A Philosophical Sketch*, 1795), defend a position in the 1790s that soon after becomes increasingly rare before dying out altogether with Alexander von Humboldt, the last bastion of the European Enlightenment: an informed cosmopolitanism, critical both of itself and the colonial enterprise, that takes the non-European world too seriously to patronize and exoticize it.

THEORIES OF ETHNOCENTRISM

In 1717 Charles-Louis de Montesquieu, Baron de la Brède, a twenty-eight-year-old lawyer, vineyard owner, and newly appointed judge at the provincial court or *parlement* of Bordeaux, began writing his *Lettres persanes*. The book appeared anonymously four years later as a series of 161 letters addressed to their friends and wives by Iranians traveling in France. The author was exploiting the fascination with the Orient that had gripped France during the reign of the Sun King. The Orient that the book sets out to illuminate is not purely a figment of the imagination. Montesquieu had read a great deal of the relevant travel literature, above all John Chardin's substantial report on Iran and Sir Paul Rycaut's work on the Ottoman Empire; he was familiar with d'Herbelot's *Bibliothèque Oriental* and Galland's *1001 Nuits*.[24] Much of this literature was also known to his readers. When Montesquieu has the Persian Rica mock the latest fashion crazes of the French, for example, many readers would have been aware that the Orient is represented in that literature as a static realm unaffected by changing tastes in dress; Rica's astonishment is inexplicable otherwise. Montesquieu's Persians act and judge in ways that are anything but unpredictable and randomly motivated. They behave more or less how educated readers of the early eighteenth century expected Orientals to behave. Whereas less talented imitators of the "letters from abroad" genre cloaked opinions that might otherwise have met with censorship or censure in the most threadbare of non-Western guises, Montesquieu succeeds both in creating a plausible counterworld—the sphere of the harem with its bitter power struggles—and in exploiting to the full the opportunities for satire offered by the outsider's fictitious point of view.

Montesquieu is not writing primarily about the Orient or Iran. Yet that is *also* his theme, for the famous theory of oriental despotism presented in his 1748 masterpiece, *De l'esprit des lois*, is already prefigured in the *Lettres* from 1721. An Orient that had to strike contemporary readers as minimally plausible became the backdrop for a virtuosic role play. No great interpretive ingenuity was required to realize that conditions in Regency France were being satirized here, nor would the great seriousness of many of the book's statements—such as the critique of colonialism in Letter 121, where the voice of Montesquieu the political philosopher can already be heard—have been lost on the public. The literary technique of contextual alienation proved so appealing that dozens of imitators tried their hands at it in the following years. While Montesquieu did not invent the format of a report on the state of the nation presented from the exotic and estranging perspective of foreign visitors, the *Lettres persanes* became the model for an entire genre.[25] It was skillfully continued in Oliver Goldsmith's *Citizen of the World, or Letters from a Chinese Philosopher Residing in London to His Friends in the East* (1762) and José Cadalso's *Cartas Marruecas* (written in 1768–74 but not published until 1793), if not with the same prismatic, polyvocal artistry that shimmers through the *Lettres persanes*, where the letters are distributed among no fewer than twenty-one correspondents. In no other work of this kind, moreover, is the Orient sketched so deftly or with such sharply defined strokes as in Montesquieu.

Montesquieu adopts a distancing "ethnographic" gaze that allows aspects of his own culture that had long since been taken for granted to be seen with fresh eyes. One such aspect was an ethnocentric view of the world. All things foreign, Rica writes from Paris to his countryman Rhedi in Venice, appear ridiculous to the French.[26] In the forty-fourth letter, Usbek—who is here likely speaking for Montesquieu himself—refers to a travel report, presumably Froger's *Relation d'un voyage aux côtes d'Afrique* (1698), that depicts the encounter between French sailors and a king in Guinea

> who was dispensing justice to his subjects beneath a tree. He was sitting on his throne, that is, on a log of wood, as proudly as if it were the throne of the Grand Mogul. . . . . This prince, with a vanity which exceeded even his poverty, asked the strangers whether he was much spoken of in France. He thought that his name should be conveyed from pole to pole, and unlike the conqueror of whom it has been said that he had put the whole world to silence, this man believed that the whole universe should be talking about him.[27]

Drawing on popular clichés about rule by "savages," Montesquieu is partly allowing himself a cheap joke at the African's expense. Conditions in Europe are turned on their head: the African king holds court in the sun but is nothing like the Sun King, still less the Grand Mughal, who for the oriental letter-writer—we recognize the care that has gone into Montesquieu's method—clearly represents the apogee of civilization. Yet according to the rules of satirical *subversion*, which here potentially undermine the effect of the ethnographic *inversion*, the two sun kings have indeed swapped roles. For had not Louis XIV, carried away by vanity and vainglory, sent out diplomats and missionaries as far away as Siam and China?

In the black king's ethnocentrism, Montesquieu mirrors that of his white colleagues, a literary procedure that from the end of the eighteenth century came to be driven out in favor of the thinking in binary categories later given immortal expression by Kipling: "O, East is East and West is West, and never the twain shall meet." In the 1790s, for example, we see such thinking in the unfeigned outrage of Western diplomats at the grandiloquent rhetoric, symbolically assumed superiority, and claims to world dominance asserted by the Qianlong emperor in Peking, notwithstanding the fact that the power he wielded at the time entitled him to be every bit as arrogant as the Sun King.[28] Ethnocentrism, it appears, had now become the exclusive possession of bigots elsewhere. At the same time, the crass Gallocentrism and increasingly smug, self-satisfied insular nationalism that were emerging in France and Great Britain, respectively, refused to countenance any form of relativizing self-criticism. Someone who, around the turn of the century, responded to public indignation over the alleged ethnocentrism of the Turks by asking how the Turks would be treated in Europe could expect the question to fall on deaf ears.[29]

In the eighteenth century, by contrast, the possibility of a general critique of ethnocentrism—not just in Montesquieu—still lay on the horizon of European thought. For Johann Christian Adelung, who pioneered the writing of cultural history in Germany, the ethnocentrism of the Chinese, Japanese, or Egyptians paled in comparison with that of the ancient Greeks, who felt themselves to be the gold standard against which the rest of the world should be judged.[30] That was in 1768; a decade later, Antoine Court de Gébelin, royal censor and author of a multivolume work on the universal history of religion, decried the habitual insularity of almost *all* nations as "one of the greatest causes of the misery of mankind."[31] Adam Ferguson, long-standing professor of moral philosophy at the University of Edinburgh and, with Adam Smith, the most important social theorist of the Scottish Enlightenment, reached the dispassionate conclusion that societies at all stages of development could only establish their identity by cutting themselves off from neighboring "barbarians" and dividing the world into opposing camps. In order to form exclusive attachments strong enough for people to set aside their naturally unsociable, quarrelsome inclinations, societies needed to create a "foreign" adversary by attacking another "troop" or nation, for example.[32] This basic law of sociology did not prevent Ferguson from speaking out in his "moral essay"[33] of 1767 against ethnocentrism, particularly in its modern European form. In contrast to the "naïve" ethnocentrism found almost everywhere else, Europe, like China, had theorized a ladder of civilizational progress that in practice proved extremely difficult for other nations to ascend. It therefore functioned as a kind of self-fulfilling prophecy: "We are ourselves the supposed standards of politeness and civilization; and where our own features do not appear, we apprehend, that there is nothing which deserves to be known."[34]

James Dunbar, Ferguson's Scottish contemporary and professor of moral philosophy in Aberdeen, was even more emphatic in denouncing the claims to superiority that effectively denied other cultures their very right to exist. Europe today, he wrote in the 1770s, "affects to move in another orbit from the rest of the species."[35] The remark was occasioned by doubts that had recently surfaced over whether human beings shared a common origin, as suggested by the biblical account of creation. Those who maintained, on the contrary, that they belonged to distinct races not only broke with the "unity of the system" of all living things; they also called into question the natural rights of whichever races they happened to deem inferior. In pointing out the practical consequences of European pretensions to superiority, Dunbar's prophetic warning surpasses the concerns of all his contemporaries in its clear-eyed prescience:

> According to this theory, the oppression or extermination of a meaner race will no longer be shocking to humanity. Their distress will not call upon us so loudly for relief. And public morality, and the laws of nations, will be confined to a few regions peopled with this more exalted species of mankind.[36]

In his essay *Of Heroic Virtue* (1692), the statesman, diplomat, and philosophical essayist, Sir William Temple, had already taken issue with the Europeans' tendency to regard "the laws of nature and nations" as valid for themselves alone.[37] James Dunbar goes a step further and speculates on the foreseeable consequences of such a divided universalism.

COMPETITION AND COMPARISON

Criticism of European ethnocentrism could lead in different directions. Normative standards could be reversed and foreign civilizations held up as superior or even exemplary. This occurred time and again in the eighteenth century. Jesuit missionaries had kept the European public well-informed about the Chinese Empire, which seemed to offer particularly valuable lessons for Europe. Whether the claims made about China could withstand critical scrutiny, then or now, is a less important question. The foreign ideal played a key rhetorical role in the domestic controversies of the era.

Drawing on the favorable reports of the Jesuits, a number of authors projected their own political ideal onto far-off China, then reimported it as a yardstick for gauging the shortcomings of present-day Europe. One such author was the multifaceted political philosopher and economist, Johann Heinrich Gottlob von Justi. Sadly neglected today, Justi was a writer of considerable originality who attempted to bring discussions about society and the state down from the lofty realm of natural law to the firmer ground of empirical historical analysis; in this he resembled his near-contemporary, Adam Ferguson. Justi judged state institutions from the pragmatic viewpoint of justice, freedom, and usefulness.[38] He was by no means the only author of the time to confront his own society with foreign models. What sets apart his tome, *Vergleichungen der europäischen mit den asiatischen and andern vermeintlich barbarischen Regierungen* (*Comparisons of the European with the Asiatic and Other Supposedly Barbaric Governments*, 1762), is its fundamental critique of Eurocentrism. Justi understood that an oriental utopia would carry little conviction unless Europeans were prepared to take seriously social and political arrangements that differed from their own. Any comparison between Europe and Asia therefore had to be preceded by a rationale for their comparability. Justi could no longer rely on the older motif of Asian superiority over "young" Europe. As far back as 1750, the prolific English author and historian, John Campbell, had already concluded from recent "happy" developments that Europe was so far superior to the rest of the world as to render all comparison meaningless:

> That Europe is, beyond all Comparison, the most happy and valuable Quarter of the Globe, is a Thing so much taken for granted, that perhaps few would think a Man much in the wrong who should conceive himself under no Obligation to prove it.[39]

Justi briskly dispatches with such complacency:

> So highly do we esteem our reason, our knowledge, our understanding, that we look down on all other nations that do people the Earth as on so many miserable creeping worms; and in truth, we treat them no better. We consider ourselves lords of the Earth; we seize without compunction the lands belonging to all those that inhabit the three other parts of the world; we dictate them the laws of their lands, appear before them as their masters; and, if they dare put up the least resistance, we exterminate them utterly.[40]

In the chapters of his book, Justi goes on to provide a systematic demonstration of how alternatives to the political order and especially the practice of politics in Europe might be conceived. As a seasoned pragmatist, he was far from blind to the different cultural conditions that would doom any attempt to replicate, say, the Chinese civil service examination system on European soil. When pointing out what is praiseworthy about other nations' institutions, his overriding concern is to train readers in the habit of changing their perspective. A good example of this—and one highly characteristic of his procedure in general—is provided by his discussion of justice.[41]

Justi proceeds from general principles that are the product of rational insight. Above all, the freedom of the individual must be held inviolable;

the laws should be "certain and indubitable"; and justice must be administered "with the strictest impartiality, without regard for person and interest."[42] He next points out that the law can be differently administered under different political systems, "and yet be equally good."[43] The third step involves reviewing how problems have been dealt with empirically. Here Justi finds more grounds for suspicion than for emulation in the brevity of trials in China. In this instance, at least, he warms more to Hottentot justice, the system presided over by Montesquieu's African king. In the early modern period, a great deal was known about the Hottentots (or Khoikhoi, to give them their correct name); it was not uncommon for travelers stopping off at the Cape of Good Hope to make an excursion to see them.[44] Justi could thus draw on a series of travelers' reports and had no need to resort to fantasy.[45]

Following a description of Hottentot justice, he examines the extent to which it accords with the universal principles set out at the beginning of the chapter, concluding that it is of a quality that "places it far above anything to be found in Europe."[46] Anyone who considers it beneath his dignity to be compared with the "savages" of Africa, Justi continues, might still allow the comparison with the culturally more advanced Siamese, "who practice commerce and the arts and are therefore more similar to us, however much we may declare them to be barbarians."[47] Upon testing this case, partly by referring to the very precise report on Siam compiled by Simon de La Loubère, Justi pronounces himself satisfied that the Siamese justice system may be no better than the European, "yet [it is] at least as good."[48]

After these detailed case studies, what remains of European exceptionalism? Only whatever can be rationally demonstrated as *relative* superiority. "For it does not suffice," Justi says, "for a nation to pass itself off as reasonable and civilized; it must furnish the requisite testimony and proof."[49] In many instances, Europeans simply cannot provide such evidence.

> If the European administration of justice is, if not worse, then at least no better than that of the Hottentots and Siamese, my God!,

> what cause do we have for our vain pride in supposing ourselves to be the most reasonable and civilized nations on Earth? I raise this question here once and for all, although it would be necessary to ask it for almost every comparison. If these people are barbarians, then surely we are no less so.[50]

Justi's literary method is in many respects comparable to that of Montesquieu's *Lettres persanes*. Despite passages where he has his Iranian correspondents ventriloquize the ideas of a French philosopher, Montesquieu never adopts a standpoint of omniscient infallibility. When Rica and Usbek cast judgment on Europe, the voice of reason is speaking through foreign observers who may never fully grasp what it is they are seeing. Europe appears from an ethnographically distanced perspective, but there are no grounds for supposing that such an outsider's point of view must always and under all circumstances be privileged over an insider's. Montesquieu thus plays a game with the multiplicity of possible perspectives for viewing and judging the world, while at the same time taking care to avoid falling into the trap of uninhibited relativism.

Johann Heinrich Gottlob von Justi is pursuing the same strategy. The principles that ought to guide public policy can be deduced from natural law and knowledge of human nature. Yet they are never purely manifested in reality, only in culturally specific institutions of human making. No culture on Earth, including that of modern Europe, enjoys more privileged access to rationality than any other. Rational social and political institutions are possible in any culture, regardless of its level of material refinement. This brings with it the great advantage that cultures are able to learn from each other.

Justi wrote his book with no other goal in mind than to make such learning both conceivable and profitable for Europe. For him, shifts in perspective rotate around the fixed axis of the rational. Yet reason is an ethnological as well as anthropological universal. It is something that is not just innate to every human being but distributed among peoples and societies all around the world. Together with Adam Ferguson and Montesquieu, Justi is not yet willing to advance the claim that modern Europe enjoys an exclusive monopoly on reason. He is therefore equally disinclined to attribute the opposite, a lack of reason, to other cultures. A "savage ethnography" (Pierre Clastres) has no relevance for these paragons of enlightened thought, since ethnography as they understand it has an inherently civilizing effect. The Enlightenment contributes to the study of Edmund Burke's "Great Map of Mankind," not by establishing a mental distance between the European ethnographer and an exoticized Orient, but by overcoming that distance in the rational convergence of their experiences.

DISCURSIVE JUSTICE

Justi was not the only European writer to advert to the relativity of intercultural perceptions. The geographer Bernhard Varenius noted in 1649 that the Japanese found the Europeans less ridiculous than the other way around.[51] The philosopher David Hume took issue with an aesthetic ethnocentrism that dismisses everything unfamiliar as barbaric; according to Hume, salutary self-doubts should arise when, "amidst such a contest of sentiment," *all* sides adhere with equal justification to their own preferences.[52] Jean-François Marmontel, later secretary of the Académie Française, pointed out in the *Encyclopédie* that the sense of humor varies from culture to culture.[53] And Jean-Nicolas Démeunier invited his readers to imagine encountering European rituals and customs among the natives of Africa. That thought experiment is likely to show us that many of the cultural usages we take for granted at home would strike us as absurd if we were to see them practiced abroad.[54]

Démeunier , the industrious collator of ethnographic material, did not confine his researches to the world beyond Europe's borders. The purpose of his ethnography—like Adam Ferguson's—was not to gather information about alien cultures but to understand human society everywhere in all its formal variety. In 1798, Charles-Athanase Walckenaer—an ambitious young man at the time, later one of the mandarins of learned France—followed in Démeunier 's footsteps by seeking to correlate levels of social evolution with habits of perception. Sedentary agrarian societies invariably regard pastoral people as barbarians while looking down on more advanced mercantile and trader societies for having been softened and corrupted by luxury.[55] The idea is imperfectly executed but not without interest. It points to the possibility of a sociology of knowledge applied to the apperception of foreignness.

Yet it was one thing to call for a change in perspective; it was quite another to write descriptive texts that implemented it in practice. Authors of fiction had it easier in this regard. Indeed, they frequently made things *too* easy for themselves by merely dressing up their traveling Turks or Chinese in carnivalesque costume without granting them, like Montesquieu, the authenticity of their own cultural background. That is why so much of the literature written in the wake of the *Lettres persanes* reveals next to nothing about how the author viewed the Orient: many a fictitious "Turk" behaves no differently than the average European libertine.

Those who purported to depict reality in works of history or travel reports had to resort to other representational devices. Historians, for example, could incorporate foreign-origin sources and historiographical texts into their accounts. Joseph von Hammer-Purgstall was not the first European historian to do just that, but he succeeded more often than others in artfully combining different perspectives on the same events. Thus, rather than blending the disparate viewpoints of Byzantine and Ottoman historians into a smoothly homogeneous narrative, he juxtaposed them to bring out their incongruities and inconsistencies.[56] Somewhat later, in his great *Geschichte des Osmanischen Reiches* (*History of the Ottoman Empire*, 1827–35), he shows how differently Europeans and Ottomans viewed the Egypt of the Pharaohs.[57] Hammer also clearly marked the—to some extent unavoidable—limits to any European or imperial account of people who inhabit an alien cultural sphere:

> Xenophon and Caesar, Thucydides and Tacitus recorded the history of their own time . . . for posterity, yet to arrive at a correct estimation of their veracity we want the tales of Persian imperial historiographers, the sagas of British bards and Gallic druids.[58]

Historians and authors of travel literature could also attempt to reach a balanced judgment by weighing the supposedly negative characteristics of the Other against comparable qualities on the European side. Alexander Hamilton was a Scottish sea captain who between 1688 and 1723 plied the oceans between East Africa and China in a series of trading missions, leaving behind vividly descriptive accounts of the lands he visited. What was so mystical about the Orient, he ventured to ask, when in Rome, the right arm of a saint was displayed for public veneration: surely that surpassed all the superstition of the East?[59] Around the same time, it was recalled that the much-feared Muslim corsairs who roved the Mediterranean were no crueler than the (nominally) Christian pirates, including the notoriously brutal Knights of Malta.[60] In 1762, Justi reminds those of his readers who regard the Arabs as barbarians that only recently twenty-five unfortunate wretches had fallen victim to a "frenzy of religious enthusiasm" and been burned alive in an auto-da-fé in Portugal.[61] Balancing judgments is a stylistic device much favored by Edward Gibbon, who delights in recounting how crusaders and their Muslim opponents denounced each other as barbarians. Gibbon likes to refer to "Western barbarians" and depicts early Islam in an unusually positive light, partly in order to oppose it polemically to early medieval Christianity.[62] Joseph von Hammer-Purgstall's unflagging commitment to justice for Asia does not lead him to conceal the "flood of horrors" unleashed by Genghis Khan's Mongols at the conquest of Bukhara, yet instead of launching into a diatribe against oriental bloodthirstiness, he judiciously adds: "All the atrocities reported by Byzantine historians when Constantinople was conquered by the Franks [in 1204] were renewed when Bukhara was taken."[63]

CHINESE INTERVIEWS, INDIAN LETTERS

Changes in perspective can also become apparent on the rare occasions when European authors allow real Asians to speak for themselves. Montesquieu had good reason to heap scorn on an attitude that placed greater trust in the reports of travelers to the Orient than in the testimony of people who actually lived there. While mixing in Parisian high society, Rica meets "a man who was extremely satisfied with himself" and has an opinion at his disposal about everyone and everything, including Iran. Rica, a native of Isfahan, immediately finds himself "refuted" by the writings of the French travelers, Chardin and Tavernier, who apparently know Iran better than the Iranians themselves.[64] Not that Asiatics were simply ignored—every traveler and scholar, including Chardin and Tavernier, relied on informants on the ground. Yet they are rarely given a hearing in European texts, and almost never allowed the final say.

Authentic voices are most likely to be heard where Europeans approached an Asian civilization with an attitude of almost deferential respectfulness. Such is the case for some of the reports on China prepared by the Jesuits. The results are fairly meager, however. While the reports quote copiously from Chinese texts in translation, the sense of living discourse is largely absent. One remarkable exception is the interview granted in 1773 by the Qianlong emperor, then at the height of his power and fame, to the Jesuit priest, Michel Benoist, while at the same time having his portrait taken by the French painter and fellow Jesuit, Guiseppe Panzi. Pater Benoist was an experienced missionary and, far more importantly, a distinguished courtier. Resident in China since 1744, he had served the emperor as court mathematician, astronomer, cartographer, and constructor of fountains in the newly built Summer Palace; his universally praised engineering skills were entirely self-taught. Benoist acted as a kind of all-round factotum for the Qianlong emperor, who entrusted him with a wide range of tasks.[65] While we have no means of gauging the authenticity of the transcript, the interview is too plausible for it to be dismissed as the mere fabrication of Jesuit propaganda. Qianlong's grandfather, the Kangxi emperor, had held similar audiences with missionaries, although they are nowhere near so well documented. What is unique about the situation in 1773 is the reversal in roles: the questions are posed by the emperor, the answers provided by the missionary.

Qianlong, one of the wiliest and most successful power politicians of his age, a figure comparable in stature to such contemporaries as Frederick II and Catherine II, presses the missionary for detailed information about the political situation in Europe. Among the copperplate prints you have brought with you from Europe, the emperor asks, there are some that celebrate your sovereigns' victories: which enemies did they vanquish?[66] Were none of these princes powerful enough to enforce a lasting peace? What are the chances that one European state could rise to supremacy over the rest? Why do interdynastic marriages among the crowned heads of Europe not prevent them making war on each other? What is the current state of relations between France and Russia? Are there any French savants residing at the court in Saint Petersburg? And so on. Asia's mightiest monarch later becomes more familiar, quizzing the French padre on whether the Jesuits could order wine from Europe to Peking, whether they brewed their own alcohol in China, whether brandy distilled from grapes was healthier than rice wine, and so forth.[67]

Pater Benoist's text, no doubt subjected to energetic redaction when it arrived at Jesuit headquarters in Paris, sketches the portrait of a highly rational, good-humored statesman who may not know much about Europe (even if he is at least as well-informed as European rulers about China), yet asks exactly the right questions to find out what he needs to know. The text makes no attempt to present the Chinese court setting in an alien or exotic light. Qianlong says nothing to hint at the cultural limits to his understanding of the world. The emperor instead radiates a cultivated, tolerant urbanity. There is nothing "typically Chinese" about what he says. No anthropological barrier separates the Chinese emperor, chatting cordially with one of his court Jesuits, from European readers of the *Lettres édifiantes et curieuses*, the publication where the text first appeared (something like the in-house foreign affairs journal of the Jesuits).

The effect is nonetheless similar to that achieved with different means by Montesquieu and Justi: exposed to the half-bemused, half-critical gaze of an outsider, European ways suddenly no longer appear quite so self-evident. For—the reader might and perhaps should react—is it not entirely reasonable to ask why Europeans find themselves in a permanent state of war while internal peace prevails in China? Had not the great Leibniz asked the same question?

The only other eighteenth-century text on Asia that rivals the Qianlong interview in its directness of address is the *Malabarische Korrespondenz* (*Malabar Correspondence*), brought to European attention by the Protestant missionary, Bartholomäus Ziegenbalg.[68] Ziegenbalg was based from 1706 to 1719 in the small Danish colony of Tranquebar on the southwest coast of India. The Danish colony had been established in 1620 through a treaty between Denmark and a local prince, the Nayak of Tanjore. Its maximum extent was about fifty square kilometers. In spite of its limited size, the colony was an important point of commercial contact between India and Europe. At the time when the *Malabarische Korrespondenz* was compiled, Tranquebar and its environs had about eighteen thousand inhabitants, around two hundred of them Europeans of various nationalities, including up to five missionaries.[69] The vast majority of the Indian population were Hindus who belonged to more than ninety castes. Very few of them had converted to Protestant Christianity.

Ziegenbalg's work consists of ninety-nine letters written by local correspondents in southern India. They were composed between 1712 and 1714 in response to the missionary's written questions; the original manuscripts have never been found. The letters were then translated from the Tamil and provided with commentary by Ziegenbalg's colleague, Johann Ernst Gründler. Finally, after being sent to the headquarters of the Pietist mission in Halle and undergoing a process of revision (now impossible to reconstruct), they were published in two installments in the *Hallesche Berichte* (*Halle Reports*): the first in 1714, the second in 1717. As early as 1717, some of the letters were translated in paraphrase and began to circulate in the English-speaking world. Most of the letters appear to have been written by Aleppa, chief interpreter of the Danish EIC and Bartholomäus Ziegenbalg's Tamil tutor. Aleppa probably put the missionary's questions to his circle of acquaintance and then edited a kind of collective response.[70] All efforts to convert Aleppa to Christianity were in vain. The authentic voice of Hindu "heathenism" thus filters through to us from his letters.

The letters were primarily taken up with religious questions and only secondarily with life in Tamil society. The missionaries sought to gain a clearer picture of Tamil gods, their creation myths and ideas about history, their rituals, everyday life, and views on Christianity. On this last question—to cite only one example from the wealth of material—the correspondent overcomes his initial reserve to express himself with all desirable frankness. In the fifteenth letter of the second installment, after praising aspects of Christian teaching, he responds critically to the question: "What do the Heathens think of the Christians' law, teachings and way of life?":

> You [Christians] ought to renounce the evil practices that you have introduced, such as failing to clean your teeth, not using water to wash after relieving yourselves, not purifying yourselves in holy ponds, your women's failure to observe a period of purification, and ignoring the impurity of your saliva. After contact with the people of despised castes, you do not purify yourselves. You swear and curse about everything. When you give the sacrament, you say that the bread is the holy body and that you drink the holy blood of Christ. Such things are beyond my comprehension. Additionally, in many other respects you lack purity as well, including your eating of beef. It would be much better if you stopped doing such things, for if you Christians abandoned these evil practices all the Tamils would embrace your religion.[71]

In another letter the correspondent goes to the heart of the mission project. His sense of outrage is palpable as he relates what the Danish missionaries find "ridiculous and despicable" about Tamil customs. Then he launches a counterattack:

> It is indeed true that our people do commit several things that are wrong and that should be condemned. Among us, all kinds of sin and unrighteousness thrive that should not. At the same time, one should not reject everything. Had we been heathens and our way of worshipping God was totally false, one would not find virtue or good works among us. But in fact there are many virtues among us, good works are performed on all side by many people: there are even those among us who live such a holy life that one cannot convict them of any sin. Can a *Vētam* ["sacred knowledge" or "law"] that renounces all sin and urges people to do good be viewed as false and unfit to confer salvation? Each and every nation has its own dress, customs and rites that look odd to others, and so it is with religion too. God is manifold in his creatures and diverse in his works; that is why he wants us to worship him in a variety of ways. . . .
>
> At the same time, we have many reasons to fault the Christians who have come here to our country from Europe. Were we to judge the Christian religion by the deeds of these Europeans, we would hardly find any good in it at all. We notice that justice and chastity are hardly found among them. They do very few good works; they give almost nothing away as alms. They do not practice penitential exercises. They accept bribes. They get drunk on heavy liquor. They torture and kill living animals and consume their flesh. They give almost no thought to physical purity. They despise all other people except themselves and are greedy, proud, and angry.[72]

Ziegenbalg and Gründler, along with their mission heads in Halle and their political patrons in Copenhagen, did not study such texts with the dispassionate interest of professional ethnographers. The letters were at once a useful source of information, intended to make work easier for missionaries on the Malabar Coast, and advertising material for the still fairly young mission (it had been founded in 1706), designed to familiarize the public back home with its prospects and difficulties in the hope of attracting financial support. To that end, the master propagandists Ziegenbalg and Gründler gave more space to countervailing native voices than any of their Catholic colleagues in China, India, or Canada. No traveler's report showed the same generosity.

NIEBUHR'S MONKEY

In eighteenth-century European texts on Asia, changes in perspective most commonly appear in the form of reports on European impressions of how Asians see Europe. The European public was always grateful for stories about dim-witted Orientals who entertained absurd ideas about Europe, the exact opposite of the intellectually assured Qianlong emperor or the earnest Tamil letter-writers. Regardless of whether these events actually occurred or were anecdotes invented or embellished by the writer: when a Cochinchinese (South Vietnamese) minister asked a French diplomat on September 30, 1749, if there were any women in Europe (and was satisfied when his question was mischievously answered in the negative);[73] when Chinese mandarins traveled from afar to Peking in fall 1793 to inspect a fabled British hen, reputed to gobble up fifty pounds of coal a day, that had been brought along by the Macartney embassy;[74] or when in December 1762 the emir of Loheia on the Red Sea was unable to contain his delight at being shown a louse under the microscope, and had to admit "that he had never seen so big an Arab louse and that the beast under the glass had to be a European louse"[75]—on each occasion, the reader's laughter came at the expense of the credulous Orientals, who appeared to be incapable of forming an accurate image of Europe, the Europeans, and their technical tricks. Ridiculous, hostile, or both: their ignorance of Europe or their distorted picture of it was—it seemed to many Europeans—entirely characteristic of Asiatic civilizations.

Not all travelers peddled this trite cliché, however. The same voyager who told the story of the louse, Carsten Niebuhr, constantly strove to understand the hidden meaning behind alien modes of perception and behavior. Niebuhr was a member of the Danish expedition to Arabia that left Copenhagen on January 7, 1761, passing through Egypt, Sinai, and the Red Sea before reaching its planned destination, Yemen, in mid-December 1762. After all five of his travel companions had died en route, Niebuhr continued to India on his own. In November 1767 he arrived back in Copenhagen, having returned by way of Iran, Mesopotamia, and Syria.[76]

Niebuhr's extensive report is refreshingly free of self-regard. There are repeated episodes where he not only studies his alien cultural environs and judges them by his lights, but is aware—or is made aware—of the fact that he himself is a foreigner and is rightly regarded as such by locals. His sensitivity to situations in which such perceptual interplay can arise is characteristic of Niebuhr. In Cairo, where the six travelers are treated with far greater animosity than later on in Arabia, Niebuhr sees the monkeys of Egyptian street performers:

> The long Eastern garments are not very suitable for monkeys, as they go around on all fours most of the time. Monkeys trained to dance are therefore often clothed in the European manner. This leads the common Mohammedan to compare us with animals, especially when he sees a well-dressed, bare-headed European with a horizontally hanging sword sticking out from behind him like a monkey's tail.[77]

In Niebuhr's eyes, the monkeys' European costume does not confirm a previously suspected hostility to Europe on the part of recalcitrant Orientals. Instead, he finds a functional explanation for the costume that would strike any impartial observer as sensible: the impracticality of Turkish trousers for dancing monkeys. Niebuhr also refuses to take offense at the less-than-flattering simian simile made by "common" Egyptians; they are not to blame for having had little exposure to foreigners and even less education.

Many other travelers likewise avoided tarring all Asians with the brush of bigotry and xenophobia, as would happen all too often in the nineteenth century. They searched instead for reasons why some people might nurse feelings of animosity towards Westerners. When Europeans complain about Chinese deceitfulness, asks a Jesuit report from 1777, do they not often fail to mention who deceived whom in the first place?[78] Henry Burney, a much-traveled diplomat in the service of the EIC, speculated in 1826 that the Siamese may have gleaned their notions about Europe from their experiences with their own subjects of Portuguese origin, who occupied a lowly position in Siamese society. All other Europeans were then assimilated to this stereotype; time and again, the rowdy behavior of English sailors on shore leave only confirmed the worst Siamese prejudices.[79] Even the far-from-Turcophilic Prussian lieutenant and later field marshal, Helmuth von Moltke, who served from 1835 as military adviser to the Ottoman Empire, was forced to admit that the Turks were right to hold Europeans in low esteem, given that most Europeans they encountered were scoundrels and swindlers.[80] Everywhere in Asian and North African port cities, European consuls and other representatives were busy keeping unruly sailors of their own nationality under control. Drunken mariners were a special nuisance in Muslim countries, where liquor was taboo.[81]

The Swedish physician and naturalist, Carl Peter Thunberg, arrived in 1775 in Nagasaki, the only harbor in the country that was open to foreigners. He noted how the Japanese were horrified at "the frequent unfriendliness and impoliteness shown by Europeans even in their intercourse with each other, and the barbarism with which their sailors are cursed, flogged and treated in sundry other cruel ways."[82] The disdain in which the Japanese held the Europeans was therefore neither incomprehensible nor undeserved, particularly since the Dutch representatives in Nagasaki, including the chief factor himself, threw themselves passionately into the smuggling trade. Shortly before Thunberg's arrival, news had emerged that these "Opperhoofds" and captains had for decades been carrying contraband goods concealed in specially prepared tunics. Now the Japanese were surprised to see the stout Dutch gentlemen slimmed down to the size of ordinary men.[83] On one occasion, a parrot smuggled inside a pair of Dutch trousers revealed its existence by talking aloud.[84] Thunberg, a renowned scholar and author of one of the eighteenth century's two most authoritative reports on Japan—the other being Engelbert Kaempfer's classic *History of Japan*—never thought to accuse his hosts of xenophobia. He found their attitude entirely understandable.

Carsten Niebuhr, to return to him, repeatedly attempts to dissolve rigid East-West dichotomies and treat other people's viewpoints with respect. In an historic note, Niebuhr points out that during the bombardment of the Yemeni port city of Mocha (Mokka) by French warships in 1738, the native population was by no means gripped by anti-European hysteria. English and Dutch residents were allowed to continue living in the city undisturbed; there was no sign of the general hostility towards "farangi" or "Franks" that was commonly attributed to all Muslims.[85] Further evidence of Niebuhr's de-Orientalizing common sense: Dr. John Crawfurd, who led a British diplomatic mission to Burma in 1826, encountered there the opinion that England must owe its wealth to alchemy—a belief that immediately struck him as ridiculous and absurd.[86] Crawfurd's judgment was in keeping with the time; Great Britain, after all, had just won its first war against Burma. By contrast, in March 1763 Niebuhr was told by Yemenites that the local population credited the Danish-German traveling scholars with the ability to make gold. Quite understandably, says Niebuhr; for having previously only met European merchants, the Arabs must have found it puzzling "that we had come such a long way without having any goods to trade."[87] The foreigners appeared to spend a lot of money while earning none. That needed explaining, and the conclusion that they were making gold to finance their expenditure was far from ridiculous. Indeed, in the Yemenite cultural context this must have been a natural and even rational hypothesis.

In his unceasing efforts to use their own way of thinking to understand how the non-Europeans he encountered made sense of the world, Carsten Niebuhr was atypical for his time. But he was not alone. The German circumnavigators, Johann Reinhold Forster and Georg Forster; the British roving diplomats, Michael Symes (posted to Burma in 1795), Samuel

Turner (1783–84 to South Tibet), and Mountstuart Elphinstone (1808 to Afghanistan); the Swede Carl Peter Thunberg (1775–76 to Japan); and Alexander von Humboldt in his voyage to the Americas (1799–1804): these and others like them advocated a dialogic relation to the Other that did not take it as axiomatic that Europeans were always in the right.

They also showed respect for what other nations knew about Europe. While some travelers—perhaps most—mocked Asians for their ignorance of Europe, a part of the world they had never visited, in this countertradition someone like Samuel Turner could still be amazed at the Tibetans' good knowledge of geography: monks in the Tashilhunpo monastery had a rough idea of the relative size of the larger countries in Europe.[88] Their understanding, although basic by European scientific standards, was respectable enough in view of their extremely limited access to information and the absence of any practical need for them to concern themselves with European geography.

Yet recognition of the native point of view did not necessarily go hand in hand with a deeper cultural sympathy. John Barrow, who visited the Chinese Empire in 1793 as comptroller to the Macartney embassy, and would later rise to great influence in London as second secretary to the Admiralty, showed considerable understanding when the Chinese made fun of their guests' tight-fitting clothing and powdered heads:

> If they could not refrain from bursting into fits of laughter on examining the grease and powder with which our hair was disfigured; and if they sometimes lamented that so much oil and flour had unnecessarily been wasted, we might perhaps, in the vanity of self-importance, affect to pity their taste; but setting custom and prejudice apart, we had certainly no great reason to despise and ridicule the Chinese, or indeed any other nation, merely because they differ from us in the little points of dress and manners, seeing how very nearly we can match them with similar follies and absurdities of our own.[89]

Yet Barrow was not the generous cultural relativist this passage makes him out to be. His words need to be read with the correct emphasis: it did not bother him in the slightest that his hosts deviated from the Europeans "in the little points" because he regarded their civilization as inferior in the big ones.

In the end, there was a glaring asymmetry of perception that no European author could fail to notice. While many Europeans traveled to Asia, very few Asians moved in the opposite direction to report back on their experiences in Europe. When Europeans ventured abroad, did they demonstrate a more comprehensive understanding of the cultures they encountered? Were they better able to reconstruct the logic underlying the behaviors they witnessed? Did they immerse themselves more fully in their new surroundings? And if so, did their hermeneutic advantage over the East, their surplus in the intellectual balance of trade between the continents, entitle them to colonial mastery? These were all still open questions at the end of the long eighteenth century, even if more and more writers now treated them as closed.

IV

Traveling

On the other side of the range were tribes and places, of which we had never heard the names; while those we had learned from our maps, were equally new to our informants. All we could learn was, that beyond the hills was something wild, strange, and new, which we might hope one day to explore.

—Mountstuart Elphinstone (1779–1859),
An Account of the Kingdom of Caubul (1815)[1]

Mountstuart Elphinstone is no Marco Polo, Columbus, or James Bruce, no discoverer of unknown worlds.[2] Writing during the Napoleonic Wars, he stands at the end of an era of European overseas travel. He is ten years younger than Alexander von Humboldt, the last and the greatest of the Enlightenment travelers, and he dies in the same year as the Prussian polymath. In 1808, the governor-general of India sends the Persian-speaking officer and diplomat with a small staff on a mission to Afghanistan. Elphinstone, plainly, is an agent of empire. But his mission fails. The emir of Afghanistan, Shah Shuja, stops the embassy at the border town of Peshawar and refuses to make concessions. British India is unable to impose terms on Afghanistan. Elphinstone moves within the world of Asiatic power politics. He does not penetrate into the unknown. Still, knowledge comes in many shades of completeness and reliability, and even a learned agent of the mightiest empire on earth is hampered by some degree of ignorance. His maps fail him, his indigenous informants give vague or contradictory advice. He gazes at the horizon and has no idea what to expect. In his account, composed after his return from the journey, Elphinstone provides a confident description and analysis of Afghanistan as he saw it and as he was able to envisage it from oral and written testimony by others. His work, published in 1815, is a masterpiece of ethnography and political geography. Still, when he tells the story of his advance towards Kabul, he strikes the pose of the clueless traveler heading for "something wild, strange, and new," a traveler who hopes to win higher laurels—those of the explorer.

SIR JOHN MALCOLM'S DINNER PARTY

On June 18, 1825, a dinner was held at the residence of the British ambassador in Paris, the Duke of Northumberland.[3] The host was Sir John Malcolm, who had traveled to France as a curious spectator to the coronation of King Charles X in Reims and was now taking a few weeks' holiday in the metropolis. Sir John, fifty-six years old, had lived in India and Iran from 1783 to 1822 as a servant of the EIC, interrupted by short periods of home leave. One of the EIC's most experienced military commanders, he was also a distinguished scholar in his own right. At the time of his stay in Paris, he held the rank of major-general in retirement; in 1827, he would be recalled to India to serve as the governor of Bombay for a further two years.[4] As a general, diplomat, administrator, imperial strategist, and scholar, Sir John Malcolm was one of the most successful empire-builders of his day; a highly proficient amateur historiographer, he collected many of his sources himself, understood the necessary languages, and, no less gifted a conversationalist than Humboldt, had gathered much of his information by speaking with natives whenever the opportunity arose.[5]

The evening's guest of honor was Alexander von Humboldt, the world's most famous naturalist and traveler. Baron Julius von Klaproth and Sir George Thomas Staunton were seated at the same table. Klaproth, an intensely driven linguistic genius of extraordinary thematic range and fearsome polemical combativeness,[6] had taught himself classical Chinese and Manchu at the Royal Library in Berlin and advised Goethe in his

Chinese studies since 1802.[7] While not endowed with private means, he managed to eke out a living as an independent geographer, cartographer, and oriental scholar. Alexander von Humboldt held him in high regard, procured modest grants for him, and often mentioned him in his letters.[8] Following trips to Mongolia, Georgia, and the Caucasus, Klaproth published numerous works on Asian geography, history, and linguistics. Despite making his career in Paris and Russia, in 1823 Klaproth had relabeled the new "Indo-European" language group as "Indo-Germanic" in a semantic *coup de main* that was to have fateful consequences.[9] Some thought him a Prussian spy, so there was considerable surprise when he tried to name the archipelago he had "discovered" on a Chinese map after his late mentor, the legendary Polish adventurer and novelist, Count Jan Potocki.[10]

Sir George Thomas Staunton, finally, was the first Briton (his family was of Irish descent) ever to converse with a Chinese emperor in Chinese. His father, Sir George Leonard Staunton, was appointed secretary to Lord Macartney's mission to the Peking court in 1793–94. Thomas, twelve years old at the time, had been taught the rudiments of the language by two Chinese priests traveling in the entourage—enough, at any rate, to impress the elderly Qianlong emperor during their audience on September 14, 1793. Staunton Junior went on to represent the EIC in Canton for many years. Upon returning to England in 1817, he was elected to Parliament and was frequently consulted on Chinese affairs by the government of the day. In 1823 he joined Henry Thomas Colebrooke, the great Indologist, in founding the Royal Asiatic Society.[11]

On the evening in question, as on almost all social occasions he attended, Humboldt appears to have dominated the conversation. The talk was of Mexico and Peru and especially Humboldt's chief preoccupation at the time, the distribution of temperature over the earth's surface. What is particularly intriguing is the biographical constellation of the illustrious quartet. All four had undertaken extended overland journeys. Not one of them was an "explorer" of previously uncharted terrain, in the manner of Captain Cook, yet their expeditions—whether undertaken at their own initiative or organized by others—had brought important new information to light about the lands they visited. All four were respected authorities in their field. Alexander von Humboldt probably knew Latin America better than any living Latin American, and had recently published the centerpiece of his vast American travel work: the three-volume *Relation historique du voyage aux regions équinoxiales du Nouveau Continent* (1814–25), a monument of world literature. Sir John Malcolm was intimately familiar with India, having traversed it from end to end and penned a number of works about its modern history. In 1815 he had brought out his *History of Persia*, earning him an honorary doctorate from Oxford University. As a comprehensive overview of Iranian history, it remained unsurpassed for almost a century. Julius von Klaproth was regularly cited and consulted as an expert on Central Asia. And Sir George Thomas Staunton was the leading China specialist in the British Empire, his scholarly reputation built on his translation of the most important legal texts of the Qing dynasty.[12]

One thing all four luminaries had in common was that their knowledge of the world beyond Europe stood in imperial contexts. Admittedly, this was less obviously the case for Humboldt than for the others. Between 1799 and 1804, he had privately traveled the length and breadth of the Spanish colonial empire at his own expense, and he had not held back in his criticism of Spanish rule. Yet even he relied in his travels on the goodwill of the colonial authorities. In 1829 he found no other way to explore Russia and Siberia than to accept an official invitation from the tsar.[13] Klaproth was a Russian imperial privy councilor (a purely honorific title), in which capacity he inspected the expanding borders of the tsarist empire to the east and southeast. Staunton had traveled in British state service since childhood. And Sir John Malcolm, as already mentioned, was one of the preeminent empire-builders of his day.

Sir John's dinner party is informative in many respects. In the early nineteenth century, as already in the second half of the eighteenth, travelers could rise to fame on the strength of their writing. These men were intrepid scholars and at the same time gentlemen, members of a social elite. They traveled not for love of adventure but in pursuit of scientific goals and under state patronage. The knowledge they acquired was useful for empires; even Humboldt's proposals for reform would have benefited the Spanish authorities had they been willing to lend them an ear. Travel at this level was not something that could be left to chance or undertaken at a whim. It demanded the most painstaking organization. "High travel" of this kind had become unexceptional by around 1800. Writing anonymously in the *Edinburgh Review* in 1815, one author distinguished it from "low travel" and welcomed the quality of reporting produced by a new breed of expeditionary scholar. At the same time, he regretted that no region visited by such consummate professionals "was to their imagination surrounded by the dignity of mystery and darkness," whereas the scribbling "physicians and jewelers" of the seventeenth century—he has the likes of Chardin and Tavernier in mind—had boldly plunged into the unknown and come into more frequent contact with "the body of the people."[14]

But what did "traveling" beyond Europe mean in the long eighteenth century? It was not necessarily a geographical extension of traveling to or around England, Germany, France, or Italy.[15] Such voyages were never undertaken simply for pleasure; even with the most careful preparation, they were "hard and dangerous work," as one veteran traveler put it.[16] This was already true of journeys east of Prague. Travelers who ventured outside Europe were expected—far more so than those who journeyed within its borders—to write up their travels upon their return. Patrons and the public were less keen to read about on-the-road adventures and the traveler's shifting mood than to receive detailed reports about the countries visited en route. After all, was it not the empirical knowledge won through scientific experiment and travel that gave modern Europe a leading edge over both the ancient world and other civilizations?[17]

Above all else, traveling outside Europe was a time-consuming affair. A more or less thorough tour of the Near East might take two years, even longer for more remote regions. Many Europeans departed for a posting in Asia knowing they were likely never to return, or at best only at a much later stage in their lives. This should be taken into account when considering what travel meant at the time. The Jesuit missionaries sent to China, for example, could expect never to see Europe again. Pater Antoine Gaubil, a scholar with a European reputation and perhaps the most accomplished Sinologist among eighteenth-century Jesuits, arrived in Peking in April 1723 and died there in July 1759, having left the capital on only a handful of occasions in all that time.[18] Pater Niccolò Longobardi, a learned pillar of the China mission a century before, had spent even longer in the Celestial Empire, a full fifty-eight years. Gaubil was notorious for his deteriorating French and Latin prose style, a consequence of his total immersion in his Chinese environment.[19] Gaubil was no more a traveler in the intra-European sense than was the Moldavian prince, Demetrius Cantemir, author of an influential history of the Ottoman Empire (1734), who arrived in Istanbul as a fifteen-year-old in 1687 and stayed on, with only brief intermissions, until 1710.[20] The merchant and manufacturer Jean-Claude Flachat lived in Constantinople between 1740 and 1755, enjoying such excellent relations with the court that he became the first European to be granted access to the inner quarters of the sultan's harem.[21] In what sense might he be called a traveler?

Of course, Sir John Malcolm traveled up and down India on imperial business, and other Jesuit Fathers were less sedentary than Pater Gaubil. Several were dispatched to remote parts of the empire by Chinese emperors: Jean-François Gerbillon for example, one of the Kangxi emperor's top diplomats, undertook the dangerous journey to Mongolia on no fewer than eight occasions between 1688 and 1698.[22] Such people set out on their travels not from Europe, however, but from regional centers such as Calcutta or Peking. As Europeans more or less permanently stationed abroad, they were "travelers" only in a very broad sense. At any rate, a large part of the era's standard literature on Asia was composed under such conditions of quasi-permanent contact. This was not travel writing, strictly speaking, but it was still first-hand reporting on Asia.

Until the middle of the nineteenth century, very few Asians had the opportunity to practice this kind of participant observation in the lands of the West. One of them was Mirza Abu Taleb, an Indian Muslim, who proved a careful and perceptive analyst of English society during his stay in the United Kingdom from 1799 to 1803.[23] His account, in the words of two modern historians, "provided a view that was not always flattering to the English, but congenial enough, in that it contrasted Albion's vigour to Indian decadence."[24] At the end of the period covered in this book, the young imam Rifā'a al-Tahtāwi was dispatched by the modernizing pasha of Egypt, Muhammad Ali, on a study mission to France that lasted from 1826 to 1831. His report, circulated in manuscript from 1834 onwards but published only in 1849 (in Arabic), easily matches the sophistication of the best Western descriptions of Asian or North African countries.[25] In general, the asymmetries of imperialism and the small number of literate and educated Asians and Maghrebis who sojourned in Europe meant that Europeans came across non-Western views mostly when they arrived as diplomats or conquerors in the countries of South and East Asia. Thus, we have precious documents on Chinese perspectives of the Macartney embassy of 1793–94, on the British military campaigns in India under Lord Wellesley through South Asian eyes, or on the ways in which Egyptian and Algerian dignitaries and savants responded to the French invasion of their countries.[26] These texts were rarely known to European contemporaries. The myriad physical encounters between Asians and Europeans during the long eighteenth century were only in exceptional cases raised to the level of an intercultural dialogue of genuine reciprocity that can be reconstructed from literary sources.

A WEEPING MANDARIN

Our image of overseas travel in the eighteenth century is justifiably influenced by the great Pacific crossings of Captains Wallis, Cook, Bougainville, and Lapérouse, the most spectacular expeditionary voyages of their time.[27] They began during the Seven Years' War and marked an enormous and sudden extension of Europe's geographical vision and imperial reach.[28] Tahiti, more than any other place on earth, was the emblematic discovery of the eighteenth century. Asia, by contrast, was yesterday's news: frequently visited and described, it seemed to have long since yielded its most important secrets. James Cook avoided Asia. After rounding the Cape of Good Hope on his second voyage of 1772–75, the longest he ever made, he sailed due east in Antarctic latitudes, steering well south of the Indian Ocean. Earlier still, in the 1720s, Captain Shelvocke showed scant interest in the continent, "as the Asiatick seas and countries are well known to us."[29] "Countries hitherto unknown," remarked one visitor to China, "have now been so often visited and comprehensively described by curious Europeans that they are almost as familiar to us as our own fatherland."[30] The Germans know all about the East Indies, we read in 1730,[31] while a glut of descriptions meant that Istanbul and the coast of Asia Minor had become "pretty trite subjects."[32] Around 1800 it can be said—not without cause—"that few countries have been visited more frequently than Persia,"[33] that widow burning in India has been so often described that it would be tiresome to do so again,[34] and that the sea voyage from Europe to India and China, although not without risk, is now "a beaten track," no longer a challenge for the ambitious mariner.[35] In 1816 the English captain, Henry Ellis, sailed to China in the firm conviction that there was nothing new to be seen there—and accordingly saw very little.[36]

That was one side of the coin. On the other, there were certainly new societies and ways of life waiting to be discovered and explored. In particular, there were Siberia, the Caucasus, and the lands bordering the Caspian Sea—a vast ethnological field that remained terra incognita until the eighteenth century. In India many ethnic groups, religious communities, and political entities, such as the Sikhs and Marathas, first came to European attention with the decline of the Mughal Empire.[37] Countries like Yemen, previously known only in broad outline, were now intensively traveled and described in detail by men like Carsten Niebuhr. Travelers who ventured beyond the coastal zones frequently found that the people they encountered had never before set eyes on Europeans:

for them, truly a Columbian discovery in reverse. The less there remained to be discovered by sea, following the epochal exploits of a Columbus, Magellan, or Cook, the higher rose the prestige of travel by land. There is no great art, remarked the adventure-loving Alexander Hamilton, in traveling to Bombay or Batavia and from there, as a self-styled "East Indies hand," claiming expertise on more distant countries and customs.[38] The difference between conditions on the coast and in the interior, a Jesuit observes in a letter, is sometimes as great as that between Europe and the rest of the world.[39]

Something like a genuine first encounter was nonetheless still possible, even at the doorstep of the Chinese Empire. Korea was the most closed-off country in Asia in the eighteenth century, even more so than Tibet. Everything known to Europeans about this Sinicized empire at the periphery of China came from two sources. On the one hand, Chinese knowledge of Korea, the most important tributary state within the Sinocentric world order, filtered through to Europe via Jesuit encyclopedias.[40] In the opposite direction, first reports about Christianity were brought back to the Joseon kingdom before 1623 by Korean ambassadors who had come into contact with Jesuit missionaries in Peking. By 1790, the number of Koreans who called themselves Catholics had risen to around a thousand. They had been converted by studying Christian texts written in Chinese, not through direct proselytization by missionaries, and they suffered severe persecution in the following years.[41] Secular knowledge of the West reached Korea shortly after 1600, when an ambassador from Peking presented the court with a map of Europe. In 1631 another diplomat came back from Peking with a musket, a telescope, a clock, a world map, and books on astronomy. At the same time, a Chinese edition of Frater Giulìo Aleni's *World Geography* was closely studied in Korea and subjected to critical commentary.[42] Although missionaries and European traders were forbidden entry into the kingdom, early nineteenth-century Koreans were not entirely in the dark about the West. The second source Europeans could consult for information about Korea was the journal of Hendrik Hamel, who had spent thirteen years in Korea following a shipwreck in 1653. Doubts were cast on his testimony, however, and its authenticity was not confirmed until the early nineteenth century.[43]

When therefore in September 1816 the two British ships, *Alceste* and *Lyra*, part of the squadron that escorted Lord Amherst on his abortive mission to China (Milord found no opportunity to open serious negotiations), spent ten days scouting the west coast of Korea, something akin to a South Pacific first encounter finally took place. Up to this point, there had been no direct contact between Koreans and Europeans; no European ethnographic documentation had ever depicted Koreans, their customs, and their dress. This precious moment was recorded for posterity from the European side by Basil Hall, captain of the *Lyra*, and Dr. John M'Leod, ship's surgeon aboard the *Alceste*.[44] The travelers were not exactly gripped by Bougainvillean euphoria: Korea was no second Tahiti. While Captain Hall did not arrive as a conquistador, he was no well-prepared ethnologist, either. Needless to say, none of the sailors spoke a word of Korean, while a Chinese servant they had brought along with them turned out to be illiterate and thus proved unable to decipher the Chinese characters written down for him by the Koreans. Hall and M'Leod struggled awkwardly to establish minimal communication with the Korean villagers, who at first were unwilling to come out and meet the foreigners. Gifts, including dollar bills, were to no avail. To the unwelcome visitors' surprise, the Koreans neither panicked nor showed the kind of joyfully childish enthusiasm expected of "savages": "These people have a proud sort of carriage, with an air of composure and indifference about them, and an absence of curiosity which struck us as being very remarkable."[45] Nevertheless, they made no secret of their expectations:

> One man expressed the general wish for our departure by holding up a piece of paper like a sail, and then blowing upon it in the direction of the wind, at the same time pointing to the ships, thereby denoting that the wind was fair, and that we only had to set sail and leave the island.[46]

When Captain Hall and his men wanted to set their boats ashore at another point, the signals from the Korean side were similarly blunt, albeit this time more puzzling:

> They drew their fans across their own throats, and sometimes across ours, as if to signify that our going on would lead to heads being cut off; but whether they or we were to be the sufferers was not apparent.[47]

Tensions abated somewhat when a grizzled old dignitary, possibly even a learned mandarin, appeared on the scene and could be enlisted for negotiations on board the *Lyra*. The worthy gentleman—Captain Hall dubbed him the "Chief"—first needed to verify that the foreigners spoke no Korean, then that they were incapable even of reading Chinese characters: unbelievable proof of their utter barbarism.[48] Writing with wit and empathy, and without any hint of mockery toward the Koreans, Basil Hall sketches the subsequent diplomatic pantomime between the honorable mandarin and the British naval officers, culminating in their shared enjoyment of cherry brandy. The Chief is one of the most moving Asiatic figures in all early nineteenth-century literature, the scene in which he appears one of the finest set pieces on mute communication between representatives of different cultures.

It dawned on the British that they were not dealing with primitive savages, at the very latest, when they discovered that the mandarin's escorts had rapidly measured the entire ship and taken notes on its rigging and weaponry.[49] After appearing to befriend each other over several exchange visits, the Koreans' initial feelings of mistrust gave way to a determination to try out Western cultural techniques. While breakfasting on the *Lyra*, the old Chief demonstrated his enterprising spirit:

> He ate heartily of our hashes, and of everything else that was put before him, using a knife, fork, and spoon, which he now saw, probably, for the first time in his life, not only without awkwardness, but to such good purpose that he declined exchanging them for Chinese

chop-sticks, which were provided for him. In fact, he was so determined to adopt our customs in every respect, that when tea was offered to him in the Chinese way, he looked to the right and left, and seeing ours differently prepared, held up his cup to the servant, for milk and sugar, which being given to him, the old gentleman remained perfectly satisfied.

The politeness and ease with which he accommodated himself to the habits of people so different from himself, were truly admirable; and when it is considered that hitherto in all probability, he was ignorant even of our existence, his propriety of manners should seem to point, not only to high rank in society, but to imply also a degree of civilization in that society, not confirmed by other circumstances.

Be this as it may, the incident is curious, as shewing, that however different the state of society may be in different countries, the forms of politeness are much alike in all. This polished character was very well sustained by the old Chief; as he was pleased with our attempts to oblige him, and whatever he seemed to care about, he immediately took an interest in. He was very inquisitive, and was always highly gratified when he discovered the use of any thing which had puzzled him at first. But there was no idle surprise, no extravagant bursts of admiration, and he certainly would be considered a man of good breeding, and keen observation, in any part of the world.[50]

Basil Hall makes no attempt to conceal the visitors' astonishment at the Chief's mastery of proceedings. Far from gawking in stupefied admiration at the West's totemic civilizational achievements—from breakfast tea to the ship's artillery—he displays an interest in them that is at once coolly objective and pragmatic. He is sufficiently in command of the situation to experiment with role changes without ever betraying his own culture. At the end of the encounter, he politely yet energetically requests that the British leave his land forthwith. When they show no signs of doing so, he bursts into tears and loud lamentations, protesting that he is in danger of losing his head:

> The Chief now began crying violently, and turning towards the village walked away, leaning his head on the shoulder of one of his people. As he went along, he not only sobbed and wept, but every now and then bellowed aloud.[51]

Both ships eventually set sail and continued on their course.

This sudden turn of events presents Captain Hall with a serious problem of interpretation. Having initially seen in the Chief the model for an alternative mode of civility, and having paid him the ultimate compliment that could be bestowed on anyone—even a European—who had the misfortune not to have been born British: that of being a "gentleman," the Chief now poses a riddle through his loss of emotional control, his tearful breakdown in the face of British noncompliance.[52] Civility itself, the familiarity of a supraculturally recognized, smoothly polished code of elite conduct, gives way to a shocking, completely alien outburst of emotion. Incomprehensible feelings lurk behind the conventional "forms of politeness." Basil Hall leaves the Korean coast with decidedly mixed impressions, impressions that do not fit neatly into the usual schematic contrast between civilization and barbarism. It says much for the honesty of his report that he makes no attempt to conceal his discomfort by striking a pose of superiority or by taking refuge in clichés of Asiatic weakness of character:

> We quitted this bay without much regret. The old Chief, indeed, with his flowing beard and pompous array and engaging manners, had made a strong impression upon us all; but his pitiable and childish distress, whatever might have been the cause, took away from the respect with which we were otherwise disposed to regard him. Yet, this circumstance, though it makes the picture less finished,

> serves to give it additional interest, whilst every thing ridiculous in the old man's character is lost in the painful uncertainty which hangs over his fate.[53]

Following his retirement from the Royal Navy, Hall launched a second career as a professional travel writer and went on to cofound the Royal Geographical Society. Here, in just a few pages, he has captured scenes that provide the closest equivalent to a prototypical first encounter in eighteenth- and early nineteenth-century Asia. *Alceste* and *Lyra* sailed on to the Ryûkyû (Liuqiu) Islands, where they came across an intelligent, friendly, and peace-loving people who likewise seemed untouched by the West: at long last, Tahiti in the East China Sea![54] Once again, the situation on the ground resembled that of a pure first contact. Yet in this case, once again, what the voyagers discovered was not entirely unknown back in Europe: Spanish reports had briefly mentioned the islands, and Pater Antoine Gaubil, the emissary of European science at the court in Peking, had published a description based on Chinese sources along with a detailed map in his *Lettres édifiantes et curieuses*.[55]

One of the main reasons why Korea—the "hermit kingdom," as it soon came to be known—could remain undisturbed by the West until 1816 was that it offered few prospects for trade. The famous Korean ginseng root, whose miraculous healing powers had been praised by the seventeenth-century polymath, Athanasius Kircher, and expatiated on more fully by Pater Jartoux in 1711,[56] could be procured in sufficient quantities by way of China. For the time being, at least, the visit paid by the British fleet changed nothing. It was not until 1876 that Korea's closed doors cracked open under sustained battering from the Japanese. Only then did more comprehensive reports about Korea reach the West. Ethnographically speaking, the brief accounts provided by Hall and M'Leod were of limited value and were no substitute for Hendrik Hamel's older text.

SEA AND LAND

Over the course of the century, the sea passage to India and the lands located east of the subcontinent became safer and more comfortable. The most important technological breakthrough was the invention of a chronometer that made it possible for longitude to be determined accurately at sea. A solution to this problem had long been sought, and in 1714 a high-profile Board of Longitude, initially chaired by Sir Isaac Newton, had been established in Great Britain to that end, offering cash rewards for scientific results. After decades of attempts, in 1770 the brilliant self-educated clock-maker, John Harrison, finally constructed an instrument that met the practical needs of mariners: an invention that immensely reduced the loss of human life at sea, helped ships maintain their course, and played a key role in the worldwide expansion of British naval power.[57] Similarly crucial were the improvements in naval hygiene and diet recommended in 1753 by the Scottish physician, James Lind, in a bid to prevent scurvy, a dreadful vitamin deficiency disease. During his circumnavigation of the globe from 1740 to 1744, Admiral Anson had lost a total of 1,410 men in his fleet (73 percent of the entire crew), 997 to scurvy alone.[58] From Cook onwards, the disease was almost entirely eradicated from the high seas. Not a single sailor succumbed to it during Otto von Kotzebue's second voyage around the world, which lasted three and a half years (1815–18).[59] In addition, navigational charts—for Britain as for France an imperial project of the first order—could only be perfected and used as a matter of course once steering by the senses had been replaced by scientific methods of navigation.[60]

Notwithstanding this "nautical revolution," the average passage on a merchant vessel operated by one of the European EICs could not be compared with the perfectly equipped, nationally prestigious marine expeditions of a Cook, Lapérouse, or Krusenstern (an Estonian captain in Russian service). The East Indiamen of the EIC, most of which carried between 500 and 1,200 tons, were relatively comfortable ships. Yet even decades after it was formulated, the advice given future sea passengers in

1716 by Johann Wilhelm Vogel, a German mining expert who worked for the VOC until 1688 and was subsequently a civil servant in the small residential city of Coburg, still held good: pray fervently to God and avoid bad company. Take your own supplies on board, including lots of garlic and also brandy, although this should be reserved for storms. Drinking too much is dangerous as you risk falling overboard. Seek out a place to sleep in the middle of the ship.[61] Even the process of boarding ship was generally chaotic, and travelers could count themselves lucky if they set sail with all their possessions still intact. Many were reminded of the old saying: "The man who strikes dead his mother and father is still too good to sail for the East Indies."[62] Life on board ship depended largely on the passenger's station and duties. Naturally enough, sailors had it worst. Subject to strict discipline, they performed hard physical labor, slept in hammocks in steerage, and received the most meager rations. Soldiers and craftsmen were better off. Germans who had signed up with the VOC as experts tended to distance themselves in their travel reports from the "blasphemous" and permanently inebriated "race" of seamen.[63] They clung to their own middle-class values.

Gentry and grandees were accommodated in the quarterdeck cabins as paying passengers or senior company officials. They were no less threatened by maritime disaster than their shipmates but otherwise traveled in this floating class society with far greater ease. Their complaints—as set out in an impassioned diatribe against sea travel written in the late 1740s by the much-traveled botanist, economist, and colonial agent, Pierre Poivre, still a young man at the time—concerned the stench of shipboard animals, the noise and vulgarity of the sailors with whom they lived in such unwelcome proximity, the arrogance and stupidity of the officers, and the stultifying boredom of life at sea.[64] August Ludwig Schlözer, more an armchair traveler than a veteran mariner, placed greater emphasis on the experience of forced companionship in his Göttingen lectures on the art of travel: "People nowhere become better acquainted with each other than at sea. They are practically married."[65] Higher-class passengers were not spared the infectious diseases that spread rapidly in such a confined space, nor could they avoid smelling the putrid waste that accumulated at the ship's side after only a few days of calm weather. If the stench became too much, the ship had to be towed by rowboat to a different location.[66] Pirates and corsairs were a constant danger on the high seas. Each encounter with another ship was an anxiously anticipated adventure. The threat of shipwreck and catastrophe hung suspended over every long-haul passage like the sword of Damocles.[67]

While overseas travel overall became faster, safer, and less onerous, no technological innovation produced a similar effect for transport *overland* until the gradual introduction of the railroad into Asia in the second half of the nineteenth century. By 1825 the voyage out from London around the cape to Calcutta, traveling on the best ships and with optimal winds, had been cut from eight months to five.[68] In 1800, by contrast, travel by land occurred in much the same manner and at much the same pace as in the age of Alexander the Great or Marco Polo. In Iran, Sir Harford Jones' British embassy of 1808/9 (in which James Justinian Morier, author of *Hajji Baba of Ispahan*, took part) crept along at a rate of just nineteen miles a day. Native camel caravans managed thirty-five miles, on average; an army traveling without baggage could cover up to seventy.[69] It took the regular caravan from Aleppo sixty days to get to Baghdad. Europeans had to make do with whatever means of transport were available on the ground. There was thus no land-based equivalent to the technological advantages their modern sailing ships gave them over native vessels operating in Asian waters.

Unlike travel by sea, which was undertaken in company, journeys by land could be individual enterprises fraught with hardship and privation. In the early seventeenth century, Henry Blount had logged some six thousand miles in his peregrinations between England and Egypt, so earning him the byname, "the great traveler."[70] The Portuguese Jesuit, Bento Goës, was the first European to tackle the extremely taxing overland route from India through Afghanistan, over the Pamir Mountains to Turkestan and on to Suzhou in East China, where he died in 1605.[71] In April 1661 his fellow Jesuit from Linz, Johann Grueber, set out for India from Peking, where he had served as mathematician at the imperial observatory. On October 8 of the same year he became the first European ever to set eyes on the holy city of Lhasa—without later committing to paper an account of what he saw. Continuing by way of the Transhimalaya (which he was also the first European to cross), the Mughal capital of Agra, Iran, and Asia Minor, he eventually returned to Rome, arriving there in February 1664.[72] Individual feats of this magnitude became increasingly rare in the eighteenth century; Ippolito Desideri S. J. was the only one to follow in Grueber's footsteps, between 1712 and 1728.[73] The most remarkable quasi-solo enterprise from the second half of the century was the African journey undertaken by the Scot, James Bruce, between 1763 and 1773. It took him and the Italian draughtsman Luigi Balugani via North Africa, Syria, Egypt, and the Red Sea to the court of the Ethiopian emperor in Gondar; in October 1770 he reached the source of the Blue Nile.[74] He had, Bruce wrote in the dedication of his travel report to King George III, traversed a region "which . . . contained all that is terrible to the feelings, prejudicial to the health, or fatal to the life of man," and visited places "so unhappily cut off from the rest of mankind, that even Your Majesty's name and virtues had never yet been known or heard of there."[75]

The great overland journeys in eighteenth-century Asia were no longer the initiative of individuals, even if one still finds the odd footslogger like Joseph Tieffenthaler, a Jesuit from Bolzano, who spent three decades trudging through vast tracts of the Indian subcontinent.[76] In the 1690s the Society of Jesus, supported among others by Leibniz, sought to extricate its Chinese mission from the logistics of the EICs by opening up a land route from Rome to Peking. Yet in winter 1690/91, letters of protection issued by the king of Poland and the Chinese emperor proved of little avail to Pater Claudio Filippo Grimaldi when he was denied transit by the tsar. Attempts to create an overland route for missionaries had to be abandoned in 1712.[77] There were two important long-distance routes across Eurasia. The first led from Saint Petersburg through Siberia and the Mongol grasslands to Peking and was mainly used by diplomatic missions and trade caravans. Long sections of it involved waterborne transport on rivers and lakes. Depending on the availability of a means of transport and the smoothness of the journey, it took between twelve and twenty months to cover the huge distance between the two capital cities.[78] The second route connected the Mediterranean to India and was chiefly used by EIC staff. Its most frequented stretch—the 760-mile-long Great Desert Route—ran from Aleppo in Syria across Mesopotamia to Basra on the Persian Gulf. It was recommended by a 1791 travel guide as a less tedious alternative to the sea route, provided travelers were willing to overcome their distrust of Turks and Arabs and make do without English food.[79] It attained the height of its popularity between 1751 and 1798[80] and acquired a certain political sensation value in the years when speculation was rife about a possible Napoleonic invasion of India.[81]

EAST ASIA: WALLED EMPIRES

The extent and quality of information about the various parts of Asia largely depended on their accessibility to Europeans. In the eighteenth century, unlike in the second half of the nineteenth, many Asiatic governments were still in a position to regulate the entry and movements of foreigners.

This was especially the case in East Asia. Korea was exceptional in its total isolation, but Japan came a close second. Throughout the eighteenth century, the country had been ruthlessly effective in keeping itself closed off from the outside world. Only the Dutch were allowed to maintain their tiny trading post on the artificial island of Dejima.[82] In 1708, sixty years after the suppression of Christianity, the Italian priest, Giovanni Battista Sidotti, became the last Christian missionary before Japan's opening in 1853/54 to make the suicidal attempt to set foot on Japanese soil. He was arrested on the spot and died—possibly of hunger—in the underground cell to which he was eventually confined.[83] The British showed little interest in Japan, fully aware that any foray into the country would founder on the combined resistance of the Japanese and Dutch. When Great Britain occupied the Dutch colony of Java during the Napoleonic

Wars, two ships were sent in 1813 to Nagasaki to break the VOC's trading monopoly. They were forced to return, their mission unaccomplished, bringing back with them the most valuable of the gifts intended for the shogun: a live elephant. It had been thoroughly inspected by the Japanese officials who came on board to parley with the foreigners, and it left a deep impression in Japan as only the fourth example of the species ever to have been seen there.[84]

In the course of the eighteenth century, the Russian Empire emerged as the most active naval power in the North Pacific. The Japanese refused to be intimidated by this development, however. While mapping the southern Kuril Islands in July 1811, Captain Vasily Mikhailovich Golovnin was taken prisoner along with six of his crew and held captive for twenty-six months by the vigilant Japanese authorities, who had been alarmed by brutal attacks against Kurile civilians perpetrated by Russian individuals. The Russians were treated well and subjected to weeks of in-depth interrogation. Although Captain Golovnin and his commander Rikord published informative accounts of their ordeal, the episode probably contributed more to *Japanese* understanding of Europe than to European understanding of Asia.[85] The first Russian expedition to circumnavigate the globe under Captain Adam Johann Krusenstern had already met with a less-than-warm reception in 1804/5. Krusenstern was free to explore and hydrographically chart the seas around Japan but, like almost all other Europeans, he was permitted to dock only at Nagasaki. He was not alone in complaining about "the insulting jealousy which is observed towards strangers in Japan."[86] The sole opportunity to catch a glimpse of the interior was as an official VOC representative on one of the three-month long court journeys to the shogun in Edo, which the Dutch were regularly obliged to perform in their status as quasi-vassals. The route they followed never varied. It became well known in Europe thanks mainly to Engelbert Kaempfer's masterly report from 1691–92 (first published in 1727), as well as to Carl Peter Thunberg's less impressive account of the 1776 court journey.[87]

In China, the situation was at once similar and quite different. There, too, limits were imposed on Westerners' freedom of movement, but there were far more options available for traveling and hence for gathering information. These fell into three broad categories. First, overseas maritime trade in the Qing Empire was not as strictly regimented as it was in Japan. Chinese authorities were fundamentally indifferent to which foreigners visited Portuguese-administered Macau and the European factories in Canton. A sketchy description of Canton was the least readers could expect from any documented trip to China.[88] Travelers wishing to hide their embarrassment at not having ventured beyond Canton could always resort to the curious hypothesis that, wherever you went in China, it all looked the same, anyway.[89]

Secondly, the Jesuits continued reporting back from China in the eighteenth century. The position of the Fathers at court, their standing among the bureaucrat-scholars, and their scientific caliber may all have declined since the previous century. And several excellent descriptions of the country, drawing on extensive travel through a number of provinces, had been produced earlier, notably the books by Alvarez Semedo (1642) and Gabriel de Magalhães (1688).[90] Yet it was not until the arrival of the first French Jesuits in Peking in February 1688 that literature on China began to flood the European market.[91] Around the mid-eighteenth century, the public in France or Germany was better informed about China than about many countries on Europe's periphery. In 1696 Louis Le Comte, scientifically a lesser light than many of his fellow priests but a talented writer nonetheless, published an introduction to the land and its people that was soon much cited as an authority in the field.[92] From 1702, the *Lettres édifiantes et curieuses* appeared periodically in Paris as collections of epistolary reports filed by missionary correspondents based in Peking and Southeast Asia. In a lively and skillfully edited selection, the European public was treated to everything from technical and botanical descriptions to moving stories about miracles and conversions. By way of translations the volumes were disseminated far beyond the circles of

French-reading friends of the Jesuit order, although English editors took care to excise what they took to be "Popish superstition."[93] Following the dissolution of the Jesuit order in 1773, the letters were superseded by the *Mémoires concernant l'histoire, les sciences, les arts, les mœurs, les usages des Chinois*, appearing in sixteen volumes from 1776 to 1814. In 1735 the available material on China was already so abundant that Jean-Baptiste Du Halde, a Jesuit living in Paris, was able to collate it into an encyclopedia in four hefty quarto volumes. Translated soon after into English, German, and Russian, it became the standard reference work on the Middle Kingdom.[94] This massive work, lavishly illustrated with maps and engravings, served the additional purpose of enhancing the reputation of the learned Fathers in Peking in the eyes of the European intellectual elite. However, it took the literary experience of a Paris-based author and editor to produce a systematic and readable account of the Celestial Empire. His co-pères in China supplied the raw materials.[95]

By 1742 the savant and writer, Lenglet-Dufresnoy, could declare "that China is known to us today in as much detail and precision as France and other states in Europe."[96] Fifty years later the abbé Grosier brought this information up to date with the latest research. Later still, between 1818 and 1820, he published a final summation of Jesuitical knowledge concerning China.[97] Yet from around 1710 the position of the Jesuits in Peking, where they were wholly dependent on court patronage, had begun to deteriorate; by the 1730s they were little more than technical personnel in the Forbidden City. Upon the death in 1722 of their most liberal-minded protector, the Kangxi emperor, Christianity itself came under threat in China. The mission in the inland provinces became more and more difficult to sustain. It soon became apparent from their reports that opportunities to roam the country were growing scarce. Restricted to the capital city, the Jesuits came to rely less on their own experiences than on their interpretation of Chinese texts.[98]

The third form of travel in China was the diplomatic embassy. For nonmissionaries there was simply no other way to get to know the country's interior. Between 1692 and 1795, three Russian, two Portuguese, one

British, and one Dutch embassy made their way to China.[99] Each is well-documented, best of all the Macartney Mission of 1792–94.[100] In 1805/06 a further Russian embassy under Count Yuri A. Golovkin—the retinue included Sir John Malcolm's future dinner companion, Julius von Klaproth—turned back at the Chinese border when agreement could not be reached on questions of protocol.[101] The second British mission under Lord Amherst broke down for similar reasons in 1816, although at least the embassy made it as far as Peking and tangentially resulted in Captain Basil Hall's excursion to Korea and the Ryûkyû islands. Unlike the standardized Japanese court journey, the delegations traveled along different routes; the regions mentioned in their accounts thus vary accordingly. For all that, transport and accommodation were still arranged by the Chinese authorities, meaning that the Western diplomats essentially saw only what their hosts wanted them to see. Even though the path to the country was relatively well-trodden and frequently described by 1830, the claim made in that year that many parts of China were "almost unvisited by modern travelers" was not inaccurate.[102] Travelers' reports from *all* of the country's provinces were only available by around 1900.

SOUTH ASIA AND SOUTHEAST ASIA: POROUS BORDERS

No other Asian states practiced so inflexible a foreign policy as Japan, Korea, and China. Interest among Europeans in the lands of Southeast Asia and their access to these lands depended on domestic political developments and economic factors.[103] Seen as a whole, the eighteenth century was on both sides more a time of retrenchment than of expansion. At the end of the eighteenth century, European knowledge of Siam still rested to a large extent on the numerous and sometimes very detailed reports produced during the brief diplomatic flirtation (1673–88) between Louis XIV and King Narai; there had been few travel contacts since then. In Vietnam, which since the 1610s had been divided into Tonkin, the northern kingdom ruled by the Trinh lords, and Cochinchina, the southern secessionist state over which the Nguyen lords held sway, the Catholic mission had been unusually strong and successful, although it also had to endure periodic bouts of hostility. Alexandre de Rhodes, a Jesuit priest from Avignon, had built it up since 1624, and in 1650 he published the first ethnohistorical treatise on Tonkin, soon to be followed by many other missionary texts.[104] Chinese reports, particularly from the culturally Sinicized tributary state of Tonkin, provided a second source of information; they became known in Europe through the Jesuits.[105] Vietnam only began to be visited more frequently by Western merchants toward the end of the century. The Macartney Mission stopped off in the bay of Turon (Da Nang) on its way to China and produced several accounts, albeit from a narrowly coastal perspective. Burma, Laos, and Cambodia, squeezed uncomfortably between Siam and Vietnam, were visited even more rarely than the other states in Indochina. For a long time, probably the most cited source on the land of the Khmer was the 1727 report by that most intrepid of adventurers, Alexander Hamilton.

For obvious reasons, the entire Himalayan region was among the least traveled parts of all Asia.[106] Individual itinerant missionaries—above all the Jesuit Ippolito Desideri, the first European to describe the holy mountain of Kailash—were the most important informants until mounting tensions between the Nepalese Gurkha state and the Chinese Empire attracted the interest of the British. Reports by two political agents of the EIC—William Kirkpatrick and especially Francis Hamilton-Buchanan—then did much to shape the nineteenth century's view of Nepal.[107] Next to nothing was known in the seventeenth century about "the great Switzerland Tibet,"[108] a kind of Qing Chinese protectorate; a century later, Desideri's report remained unpublished and the picture was still essentially unchanged. Once again, Chinese sources were the most reliable.[109] Buddhist subjects of the tsar returning from a pilgrimage brought back rumors to Russia.[110] Warren Hastings, the governor-general of British India, sent George Bogle (in 1774) and Samuel Turner (in 1783) on diplomatic missions to Tibet. Both set down lively, detailed accounts; Turner's appeared in 1800, while Bogle's was edited from the manuscript and published posthumously in 1876.[111] Since there are so few texts, the handful that were written stand out all the more. But Bogle's and Turner's deserve their good reputation. The same holds true for the *Account of the Kingdom of Caubul* (1815) by Mountstuart Elphinstone, a friend and colleague of Sir John Malcolm, written following his return from the embassy of 1808. The Afghans had already drawn European attention to themselves in 1722 by invading Iran, but Elphinstone was the first to report directly from Afghanistan, a country that tenaciously preserved its independence in the imperial age and was never easy for Europeans to access.

By contrast, no Asian land was more easily accessible than India and none so widely and frequently traveled, even in the seventeenth century. The Mughal dynasty had allowed Europeans complete freedom of movement, that is to say: the foreigners were ignored.[112] In a multiethnic empire they were far less conspicuous than in an ethnically homogeneous country like Japan, and they were of little account anyway. Europeans had taken part in succession disputes fought between various pretenders to the throne, entered court service, and pursued opportunities for trade. In the eighteenth century, many had hired themselves out to Indian princes and potentates as officers or artillery experts. Compared with China and Vietnam, the missionary element played a lesser role; the literature on India was not dominated by mission reports. There were still heroic individuals traipsing around eighteenth-century India as well. None better embodies this type than Abraham-Hyacinthe Anquetil-Duperron, an eccentric dreamer and linguistic genius who pioneered the study of ancient Persian language and literature, but also a precise geographer and clear-headed analyst of the contemporary political scene.[113] Anquetil was behind the times in his inveterate hatred of England: even in old age he was imploring Napoleon to liberate India from British colonial rule, offering to take personal charge of the expedition.[114] British supremacy in India was already unassailable by that stage, the literature on India long since established as a British domain.

Wherever the British conquered territories and brought them under their imperial control, the character of travel changed fundamentally. It was transformed from an adventure into an administrative routine. Under conditions of *Pax Britannica*, hostile natives no longer posed a vital threat. Instead, danger now came only from the heat, the tropical diseases, and the tigers that occasionally disturbed art-loving travelers during their inspection of Hindu temples and picturesque landscapes.[115] Travel within India in the period between around 1770 and 1830 was overwhelmingly the prerogative of EIC officials. It came in two forms. Behind the newly established military borderlines marched a legion of administrators and tax-collectors, land surveyors and cartographers, but also historians, who now set about writing the history of subject peoples and victorious British arms *sine ira et studio*. Great works ensued: James Rennell's historical and contemporary geography of the Mughal Empire; James Grant Duff's history of the Marathas, the most formidable Indian opponents to British power; or the socioecological microdescription of southern Indian village life by Dr. Francis Buchanan,[116] respectfully dubbed "the sharp sighted Pausanias of India."[117] The second form of travel involved venturing beyond the empire's secure borders into regions that could turn out to be either potential candidates for later annexation or nothing more than unruly neighbor states. Sikhs in the Punjab, the Baloch people, and many others were visited and described accordingly. A frontier literature thus arose alongside the empire.

THE NEAR EAST: A PILGRIMAGE TO ANTIQUITY

Iran offers a further case study for the power of political relations. Of all Asiatic empires, it was said with some justification in 1783, Iran was the best researched.[118] The shahs of the Safavid dynasty (1501–1722) practiced an open-border policy that European travelers exploited to the full. It is hard to determine why Iran attracted so many learned travelers. In the late Renaissance, a time of burgeoning travel, Iran, the eastern enemy of the Ottoman Empire, was a country that welcomed Europeans more openly than Turkey, the perennial adversary. A century before Peter the Great and two and a half centuries before the Japanese Meiji emperor,

Shah Abbas I (bynamed the Great, reigned 1588–1626) was the first eastern monarch who seemed to open his land to the West, implementing a process of political modernization comparable to that taking place in Tudor England or France under Henry IV. Through his reforms, he became the architect of the modern Iranian state. When Safavid glory began to fade in the seventeenth century and several of Abbas I's successors incarnated the type of the bloodthirsty "oriental despot," other attractions remained: Iran's geographical position as the gateway to the Indian Ocean (by sea) and to the Indian subcontinent (by land), its reputation as an ancient center of civilization, and its genial climate, not to mention the ruins of Persepolis—in the words of one travel guide from 1754, "the most magnificent on the face of the earth."[119]

If the number of literary voyagers to Iran declined in the eighteenth century and not a single new account of the country and its sights matched the high scientific and literary standards of the seventeenth century,[120] then this was not due to a policy of strict isolationism (as in Japan) but rather to a catastrophic breakdown in all forms of political order during and after the Afghan invasion of 1722. Apart from the odd visitor to Persepolis, Iran—unlike Asia Minor, Egypt, and increasingly India—was now completely bypassed by scholarly travelers and tourists. This state of affairs lasted until the turn of the century. In no Asiatic country was travel so hazardous a prospect as in lawless Iran, and few countries had less to offer in terms of trade or strategic advantage. It was not until the era of the Napoleonic Wars and the ensuing "Great Game" between Britain and Russia that Iran gained renewed importance as an ally or buffer state in the imperial conflict. On three occasions—in 1800/01, 1808 (a signal failure), and 1809/10—the governor-general of India dispatched Sir John Malcolm at the head of diplomatic missions to Iran.[121] These experiences flowed into the later chapters of Malcolm's magisterial *History of Persia*. Early nineteenth-century trips to Iran thus became increasingly politicized.

It is impossible to make generalized statements about travel in the Ottoman Empire, so diverse were its constituent provinces. In the eighteenth century, many thousands of Europeans still gained unwanted first-hand experience of Barbary, the corsair state of Algeria, as victims of abduction or extortion. This gave rise to an entire literary genre detailing the trials and tribulations of captivity, along the Mozartean lines of "In Moorish lands imprisoned . . ." (an aria from *The Abduction from the Seraglio*, 1782), although it was supplemented by the works of diplomats, priests, and traveling naturalists.[122] Egypt, ever-present in the European imagination as the land of the pharaohs thanks to Herodotus, hosted barely more visitors in the seventeenth and early eighteenth century than Iran, notwithstanding its proximity to Europe. There was no question of there being any political impediments to travel. The harbor city of Alexandria was occasionally inspected, perhaps also Cairo with its nearby pyramids, Suez by those traveling to India via the Red Sea, and a few hardy pilgrims might pay their obeisances at Saint Catherine's monastery at Mount Sinai.

There had been a first modern wave of scholarly trips to Egypt from around 1585. Its most significant yield was the *Pyramidographia* (1646) by John Greaves, professor of astronomy and mathematics at Oxford. The book maintained its standing as the most scientifically accurate description of the pyramids until the nineteenth century.[123] At almost exactly the same time, Henry Blount was warning his readers against neglecting modern Egypt in their enthusiasm for all things pharaonic: Egypt was still a great and vibrant land.[124] A second wave followed in the 1730s, when two inveterate travelers—the English clergyman, Richard Pococke, as learned a man as he was courageous, famed equally for his Greek scholarship and his investigations into glaciers, and the Danish captain, Frederik Norden—made their way independently of each other to Upper Egypt and described their travels in voluminous, lavishly illustrated works.[125] Neither they nor those who followed in their footsteps took Blount's advice to heart, however. With a few notable exceptions, such as the notes made by Johann Michael Wansleb, who twice visited Egypt in the seventeenth century, the Islamic (and also partially Coptic Christian) Egypt of the present remained all but invisible.[126] Modern-day Egyptians had to wait for Savary's *Lettres sur l'Égypte* (1785–86) and Volney's epochal account of his travels through the country (1787) to be brought to European public awareness.

Until then there had been good reasons for the prevalence of an antiquarian perspective in European views of Egypt.[127] Egypt lacked the contemporary relevance provided elsewhere by Christian missionary work (China and Vietnam), trade (Japan), diplomacy (Siam, Iran), or colonialism (India, Java). Those with an interest in Islam felt they could study its Sunni version more comfortably in Istanbul. Once again, it was the global conflict between Britain and France that shifted the parameters. With his invasion of Egypt in 1798, Napoleon Bonaparte not only pulled off a stunning military coup; he simultaneously ushered in a new era in oriental studies as a state-sponsored collective imperial enterprise, undertaken on a scale that overshadowed even British research activity in India. When Champollion went on to solve the riddle of the hieroglyphs in 1822, a new science was born: Egyptology.

Asia Minor—Turkey in the narrower sense—was by far the most frequented region in Asia. Even in the hottest phases of the ongoing conflict between the Christian powers, it was still theoretically possible to travel through Asia Minor.[128] Istanbul was the best-known city in Asia or, as it could also be viewed, "the greatest city in Europe," incomparable in its grandeur and beauty: "We have nothing in France to rival it."[129] As in Rome, Paris, or Vienna, observers traveled and wrote "in each other's footsteps,"[130] and wholly original achievements became ever more difficult; most descriptions came from French visitors.

Despite the considerable amount of literature devoted to the Ottoman Empire, several genres of travel writing and reporting were poorly represented. Like everywhere else in the Islamic world, there were almost no Catholic and Protestant missionaries. Reports from traveling embassies—so important for China, Siam, Tibet, Iran, and Mughal India—barely played a role, since the European powers had permanent ambassadors stationed in Istanbul (and nowhere else in Asia). It was therefore unnecessary to set foot outside the capital. Several of these representatives or ambassadors were themselves noted scholars, or at least supported the scientific projects of others.[131] Only a few had the competence and interest to write books themselves: Sir James Porter, for example, ambassador to the Sublime Porte from 1747 to 1762, an outspoken Turkophile, friend of Benjamin Franklin and Sir William Jones, and probably the leading British authority on Turkey in the eighteenth century,[132] or the French ambassador, Count Antoine-François Andréossy, author of a work on the physical geography of the Bosphorus and Istanbul's water supply system. Extraordinarily important scholarship was carried out by lower-ranking diplomats, however. The superbly well-educated Sir Paul Rycaut transformed his experiences as English consul in Smyrna from 1667 to 1678 into a historical chronicle of the Ottoman Empire.[133] The versatile, immensely industrious Joseph von Hammer-Purgstall was sent on various Austrian diplomatic postings in the Levant between 1799 and 1807. In the generation between Porter and Hammer-Purgstall, Ignatius Mouradgea d'Ohsson, an Armenian by birth, was reputed to know the Ottoman Empire better than any other European, particularly its legal system and culture. After serving for many years as a dragoman (interpreter), he was appointed Swedish chargé d'affaires (1782–84), then ambassador (1795–99) to the Sublime Porte. His magisterial *Tableau générale de l'Empire Othoman* (1787–1820), based on critical analysis of the available source material, was still considered "indispensable" by early twentieth-century students of the Ottoman Empire.[134]

Large tracts of the empire were seldom or never visited by Europeans: inner Anatolia, several of the Black Sea provinces, the area bordering Iran, Libya, Mesopotamia (apart from the caravan route), or Yemen, which Carsten Niebuhr was the first to explore in any depth. Greece and the coast of Asia Minor were far more popular destinations. Istanbul, where hotels could now be found in abundance, became the eastern terminus of the aristocratic grand tour: from Vienna, one proceeded via Budapest, Belgrade, Sofia, and Adrianople (Edirne) to the Bosphorus and from there by ship to Italy or Marseille.[135] Attica, the Peloponnese, and the ruins of classical antiquity on the Asia Minor coast could all be reached by detouring from this route. Classical Hellas was rediscovered or reconstructed *twice*: from 1755 in the imagination and in artistic theory by Johann Joachim Winckelmann, and already in 1751 by two young English architects, James Stuart and Nicholas Revett, sent out by the Society of Dilettanti to put their expert draftsmanship to use in measuring and sketching the Greek antiquities. Hordes of tourists followed in their wake. Not all were pursuing the lofty goals of education and edification. Many went out to loot and plunder. Thomas Bruce, seventh Earl of Elgin, who notoriously took possession of parts of the Parthenon frieze in 1801–3 (and sold them to the British nation in 1816), embodied an entire species. Whereas members of diplomatic missions to China surreptitiously pocketed stones from the Great Wall and filled their bottles with water from the Yellow River,[136] the Ottoman government was too weak, or too unconcerned, to block large-scale private digs on the field of classical antiquity. The ransacking of ancient sites by well-heeled English tourists was more than offset, however, by the achievements of numerous learned visitors to Greece and the coast of Asia Minor. Together, they pioneered the descriptive scientific study of these regions at the beginning of the nineteenth century. Working around the same time that Dr. Francis Buchanan was researching southern India and employing similar methods, the British artillery officer, William Martin Leake, compiled a comprehensive geographical description of the regions of the Ottoman Empire that had stood under Hellenic influence.[137]

Such scientific rigor, which in Leake as in Buchanan also served the political and strategic interests of empire, was not to everyone's taste. A new type of literary traveler, initially confined to the Mediterranean, responded by flaunting the subjectivity of their impressions. The most influential was the poet Chateaubriand, who in 1806 set out on a round trip from Paris via Venice, Athens, Istanbul, Jerusalem, Alexandria, and Tunis. He too was not above systematically looting the sites he visited—"I have always purloined something from monuments where I happened to pass by"[138]—yet his chief purpose was to drink directly from the fount of classical culture and (in the Holy Land) Christian religion. This was experience on a higher emotional plane than the more studious interest taken by a traveler like Pococke, who journeyed to Egypt and Palestine in the hope of arriving at a better understanding of the Bible stories.[139] Chateaubriand ridicules the mania for antiquity exhibited by his fellow travelers,[140] yet in Palestine he shows no sign of the strain that his near-permanent state of religious ecstasy must have placed him under.[141]

All these travelers, it would be fair to say, showed less interest in the present state of the lands through which they passed than in ancient ruins and biblical reminiscences. Turks and Arabs were nuisances or had to be put up with as hired help; even fanatical philhellenes rarely had the imagination to see a Greek shepherd as the descendant of their Periclean idols. Such pilgrims to antiquity were to be found only in the Ottoman Empire: they may have been traveling in the Orient but they never truly arrived there.

ADVENTURERS AND RENEGADES

The regions targeted by travelers, their aims in traveling, and the various types of travel they undertook can be linked together in certain contexts. Unlike in the politically and culturally relatively homogeneous space of Europe (west of the Russian border, at least), not all forms of travel were possible everywhere in eighteenth-century Asia. There were no mission trips to Japan, no educational tourists in Siam or China, no embassies roaming the Ottoman Empire.

This broad framework of excluded and realized possibilities would need to be filled in by a nuanced sociocultural history of travel. Among the travelers to Asia who documented their journey in their own reports, itinerant adventurers and free agents were less prominent in the eighteenth century than in earlier times. Growth in trade with Asia and the expansion of colonialism in Java and India attracted soldiers of fortune. Yet very few came home as wealthy nabobs, and hardly any published a memoir of note.[142] The accounts of their experiences written by Germans who traveled to the East Indies in the service of the VOC, mostly simple sailors, soldiers, and minor functionaries, play a role within the German literature on Asia only up to around 1730; they are not as informative as the contemporary Dutch literature.[143] Many a journey inadvertently turned into an adventure: following a storm at sea, the eighteen-year-old Robert Knox was shipwrecked on the coast of Ceylon (Sri Lanka) along with his father, the ship's captain, and sixteen crew members and there taken captive by the king of Kandy, Rajasinha II. It took him twenty years to escape to a Dutch fort on the coast. In September 1680 he arrived back in England with an unfinished manuscript in his possession. With help from the Royal Society, this then became the basis for his remarkable *Historical Relation of the Island Ceylon* (1681).[144]

The type of the enterprising private globetrotter who funds his travels from his own pocket and subsequently writes up his adventures in book form had its heyday beyond the Mediterranean Near East in the second half of the seventeenth century. It first reemerges in the early nineteenth century with India's gradual opening to tourism.[145] Around the turn of the eighteenth century, the type is impressively represented by the Calabrian judge, Giovanni Francesco Gemelli Careri, who was driven by frustrations with his judicial office, family strife, and wanderlust to undertake a journey around the world from 1693 to 1698. Gemelli Careri must have been a man of extraordinary charisma. He had the ability to reach places that remained off limits to other travelers and the gift of finding generous benefactors at every turn. His travels took him to Egypt, Palestine, Asia Minor, Iran, India (where he visited the camp of the Mughal emperor, Aurangzeb), and Malacca. During his eight-month stay in China, he not only toured the south of the country but was also one of very few nonmissionaries and nondiplomats to gain admission to Peking. Although some Jesuits intrigued against him, taking him for a secret agent of the Pope, in 1695 he pulled off the unprecedented coup of an audience with the Kangxi emperor. He thereafter crossed the Pacific in one of the famous Manila galleons and spent eleven months in Mexico. His *Giro del mondo* (1699–1700) was highly regarded in Italy, not least because it was so well written, and became something of a bestseller. Long held in suspicion as a braggart and defended by few,[146] the accuracy of many of his descriptions was recognized only later.[147] Gemelli Careri's odyssey remained unparalleled. So far as we know, he was the first person to travel around the world by using the scheduled transportation services available at the time, particularly the great trans-Asiatic caravans (which ran at fairly regular intervals) and the annual round trip across the Pacific on the Manila galleons.[148] At best Alexander Hamilton, already mentioned several times in these pages, cuts a comparable figure: a Scot who first turns up in the records in 1688 as a captain and trader in the Far East and spends the next thirty-five years plying the seas between Mocha and Amoy (Xiamen). But his sober report, written for the practical benefit of fellow seafarers and traders, conceals the adventurousness of his existence.[149]

That is emphatically not the case for Maurice, Count de Benyovsky, a swashbuckling Hungarian nobleman who died in 1786 during a failed attempt to conquer Madagascar for Austria. His travel journal relates his exploits and experiences between 1770 and 1772, primarily in Siberia, Kamchatka, and Japan; it appeared posthumously in English translation in 1790 and went through numerous editions in several languages. Critical readers pointed out glaring inconsistencies in his account, and Benyovsky's good name as a truthful chronicler suffered lasting damage, but this did little to dent his popularity with the wider public: in Germany alone, his book ran through nine editions in eight years.[150] The German translator of the book, no less a personage than the great circumnavigator, Johann Reinhold Forster, who had taken on the project for financial reasons, likewise soon came to harbor doubts about its veracity and simply omitted anything from his German version that struck him as unbelievable, exaggerated, or sensationalized.[151]

The age of the great Asian adventures, whether real or invented, was already over by then. With James Bruce, who published his account in 1790, those looking for tales of action and adventure set in exotic locales shifted their attention to Africa. Far from the public eye, an assortment of oddities and eccentrics continued to be drawn to the East: Giovanni

Ghirardini, a cheerful Italian painter (and irrepressible rhymester) who was recruited for service at the Chinese court by Pater Bouvet, providing a ray of sunshine amidst the gloom of Jesuit piety;[152] Charles-François Tombe, a French officer who was demobilized following the Peace of Amiens of 1802 and who, driven by necessity and despair, set sail for the East Indies, later writing an informative description of Batavia;[153] or John Dundas Cochrane, who trudged through half of Siberia as a private traveler.[154] The travel report of a certain Alexander Drummond is especially curious. He spent much of the 1740s on the road as a grumpy tourist rather than an intrepid adventurer (and he was certainly no objective scientist). In Frankfurt am Main and Aleppo he finds nothing whatsoever to arouse his interest; he grumbles about the lack of hotels in the Orient, seeing only filth and decay wherever he goes. All his expectations are bitterly disappointed; not even oriental bandits find him worth robbing.[155] The poor man arrives home without a single decent traveler's tale to show for his troubles.

At the opposite end of the spectrum were cultural renegades, people who appeared from a European point of view to have crossed the existential border to another civilization. The most radical step of this kind was conversion to Islam. This could be motivated by expediency and practical considerations. In Algiers there were more than a few Christian renegades: some of them converted prisoners who had acquired their freedom in this way, others criminal refugees from Christian countries. If they were snapped up by European ships, a particularly cruel fate lay in store for them.[156] For European sailors to convert to Islam was not uncommon and attracted relatively little comment.[157] It caused a bigger stir when members of the elite took this step. Following the assassination of General Kléber in June 1800, command of the French expeditionary forces remaining in Egypt fell to General Jacques Abdullah Menou. His much-derided conversion to Islam was motivated partly by political considerations, partly by the wish to marry an Egyptian: a descendant of the Prophet, no less.[158] In the early nineteenth century several European converts entered the service of Egypt's modernizing ruler, Muhammad Ali.[159] Only one scientifically distinguished traveler appears to have become a Muslim, however: Johann Ludwig Burckhardt. Carsten Niebuhr was told the story of a French doctor and naturalist named Simon who traveled to Aleppo to conduct his investigations. Unpleasant experiences with Europeans pushed him to the "desperate decision" (as the far-from-Islamophobic Niebuhr calls it) to become a Mohammedan. The Turks advised him against the move and showed him no favors in return. While patients continued to call on him, Monsieur Simon was "despised as a man who had betrayed his religion and his fatherland."[160] Here the convert appears not as a mediator between civilizations but as a wanderer lost between them.

There were many stages leading up to a change in religion. Scholars could express their sympathy for the foreign culture they had studied in outward signs. In 1680 Sir John Chardin, a French Huguenot emigrant returned from his travels in Iran, appeared in London dressed in oriental robes, and when the young Joseph Hammer saw the revered Mouradgea d'Ohsson for the first time in Vienna in 1792, the learned Swede was wearing Turkish robes with a Mozart-style powdered wig.[161] Bedwin Sands, the "elegant dandy and Eastern traveler" in William Makepeace Thackeray's novel *Vanity Fair* (1848, set around 1815), could have been a figure from real life—not implausible for an author who was born in Calcutta as the son of a colonial administrator:

> An Eastern traveller was somebody in those days, and the adventurous Bedwin, who had published his quarto, and passed some months under the tents in the desert, was a personage of no small importance. In his volume there were several pictures of Sands in various oriental costumes; and he travelled about with a black attendant of most unprepossessing appearance.[162]

The Jesuits at the court in Peking, several of whom were high-ranking officials (especially in the seventeenth century), went about clad in the robes of Chinese mandarins. Their opponents within the church, who felt that their theological and philosophical accommodation with Confucianism had gone too far anyway, took this as further proof of their deplorable heterodoxy.

In many respects, the Jesuits who were active in China embodied a distinctively modern type of European living abroad. These were not private travelers; rather, they led a kind of official double life: on the one hand, as members of a large supranational organization, on the other, as experts in the service of a non-European power. In addition, several could regard themselves as diplomatic representatives of the French crown. A number of Asian states employed European experts, mostly in the military, without expecting them to break with their cultural and religious heritage. Indian princes had taken Europeans into their service ever since two Milanese gunsmiths had deserted from the Portuguese army to the Zamorin (King) of Calicut, casting three hundred cannons and field guns for him in three years.[163] In the mid-seventeenth century, François Bernier observed that the great mughal's artillery was operated by highly paid Europeans. Their market value had already slipped, however, since Mughal troops had become more skilled in working with gunnery.[164] French advisers armed the enemies of Britain, above all the Marathas and the sultans of Mysore. Between 1750 and 1803 there were 179 European mercenaries in Indian service, almost half of them French.[165] The Ottoman Empire also engaged European military experts from the early eighteenth century onwards. Such jobs came with no cultural strings attached. Whereas Baron de Tott, for example, a French officer of Hungarian origin who from 1773 set about modernizing the Ottoman artillery, improving military training, and building fortifications on the Danube border and in the Dardanelles, was a rabid Turcophobe, his Scottish colleague Campbell had switched cultural allegiance and taken on a new identity as a renegade ("Ingiliz Mustafa").[166]

SCHOLARS AND ADMINISTRATORS

Considerable misunderstandings arise when conventional ideas about intra-European travel in its various forms are applied to eighteenth-century Asia, especially beyond the Mediterranean basin. The documentary evidence suggests that travel in Asia, unlike in Europe, was not typically an individual project. It became ever less so. The number of institutionally unattached, self-financing travelers can be tallied without difficulty. Of these, the only first-rate travel writers were Gemelli Careri, Volney, Bruce, and Alexander von Humboldt—and the last two traveled mainly in Africa and America, respectively. The wealthy amateur Joseph Banks took part in Captain Cook's first circumnavigation of the globe at his own expense; his diaries long remained unpublished and he never wrote up a full account of his trip. All other travelers were functionaries of large organizations: governmental bodies, quasi-state chartered companies, religious orders, and other church organizations. Several were also sponsored by privately funded learned societies—Johann Ludwig Burckhardt was the agent of the African Association, founded in 1788 by Joseph Banks and others—or one of the academies in London, Paris, and Saint Petersburg. This transformation of travel into an instrument of public or private officialdom is one of the most important developments in the history of transit in the eighteenth century. One anecdote illustrates this nicely: following the dissolution in 1773 of the Jesuit order in France, the missionaries left in Peking—now downgraded from *Père* to *Monsieur*—continued to be paid from the coffers of the French state.[167]

Over the course of the eighteenth century, voyages of discovery and research became increasingly bound up with national prestige and imperial rivalry. At sea, the Pacific was the most important setting of an Anglo-French competition for discovery and nautical success, with Russia later joining in to make it a three-way contest. On land, the era's greatest Asiatic travel projects were carried out within the tsarist empire at state initiative. In the 1760s the interests of politics and science intersected in a series of internationally coordinated mega-projects.

The most important occasion was the expectation of an extraordinary astronomical event: the transit of Venus across the solar disk. This would make it possible to measure the exact distance from the Earth to the Sun. In 1716 the English astronomer, Edmund Halley, had predicted the event for 1761 and again for 1769: it would not be repeated until 1872. The Seven Years' War meant that European astronomers were unable to agree to a joint action plan in time for the 1761 transit, and only a French initiative met with any success. By 1769, however, European governments, academies, and learned societies—the Royal Society in England was particularly active—were in a position to coordinate their efforts to an unprecedented degree.[168] Numerous scientific expeditions were sent out to observe the phenomenon from different points of the Earth's surface: Cook and Bougainville in the South Sea, the abbé Chappe d'Auteroche (who had witnessed the 1761 transit of Venus in Tobolsk, the capital of West Siberia) in California. Le Gentil had already missed the previous planetary passage in the Indian Ocean and had been waiting there ever since for a second opportunity—which, as bad luck would have it, he reportedly missed again. The scientifically trained private traveler, James Bruce, made astronomical observations from Upper Egypt in June 1769. Peter Simon Pallas took up position in Siberia.

Pallas was one of several German scientists commissioned by the Russian government to investigate the Asiatic parts of the empire. Like other research trips taking place at the time, these endeavors were Janus-faced, at once scholarly and imperial in outlook. Scientists worked in the field to gather data in the various natural sciences (geography, geology, astronomy, botany, zoology), but they also collected ethnographical and economic information that could make it easier to govern, develop, and exploit the vast non-European territories of the tsarist empire. Pallas was the most famous but by no means the first or only such traveler.

At Peter the Great's behest, the scientific exploration of Siberia[169] had entered a new phase between 1721 and 1727 with the modestly conceived research expedition mounted by Daniel Gottlieb Messerschmidt, a doctor from Danzig who had received his medical training at the prestigious university of Halle. For fourteen months, Messerschmidt was accompanied by the recently released Swedish prisoner-of-war, Philipp Johann Tabbert, who went by the name of Philipp von Strahlenberg and later published a valuable geographical overview of North Asia.[170] Only isolated fragments of Messerschmidt's journal were published in the eighteenth century. The author died in poverty and disillusionment in Saint Petersburg in 1735. The easternmost part of the Russian Empire, the

Kamchatka peninsula, stood at the center of imperial interest even then. The First Kamchatka expedition of 1725–30, personally initiated and planned by Peter the Great near the end of his reign, was a far bigger undertaking than Messerschmidt's pioneering mission. Part of its brief was to fix Asia's eastern border and search for a land bridge between Asia and America. It was led by the Danish sea captain, Vitus Bering. Upon his return, Bering began planning the Second Kamchatka expedition. This enterprise, better known as the Great Northern Expedition (1733–43), involved a total of 570 men split among three regional groups. It was by far the most ambitious Asian travel project of the century. The Saint Petersburg Academy of Sciences (founded in 1725), one of the greatest scholarly institutions in Europe at the time, assumed responsibility for the scientific aspects. For the Siberian expeditionary group, it set up an academic division that included two young professors: the chemist Johann Georg Gmelin, scion of a long line of scholars from Tübingen, and the historian and ethnographer, Gerhard Friedrich Müller. They were assisted, among others, by the historian Johann Eberhard Fischer, the naturalist Georg Wilhelm Steller, and the student Stepan Petrovich Krasheninnikov.[171] Only the last two made it all the way to Kamchatka. Gmelin and Müller nonetheless logged over thirty-three thousand kilometers in what was probably the longest overland journey made by Europeans during the first half of the eighteenth century.[172]

Pallas's activities fall in the next phase of tsarist exploration policy, dominated by the so-called academy expeditions from 1768 to 1774. The external motivating factor was Empress Catherine II's determination to show the rest of the world what Russian science could achieve when the next transit of Venus occurred in 1769. At the same time, and above all, the expeditions were again intended to serve the economic interests of the empire. They were organized on a smaller scale than the Great Northern Expedition; almost all involved travel by land alone. Russian scientists shared tasks with German specialists recruited by the academy. The German participants were Johann Anton Güldenstädt, who crossed the (then-) imperial border to traverse the Caucasus and Georgia; Samuel

Gottlieb Gmelin, a nephew of Johann Georg Gmelin, who explored the shores of the Caspian Sea; and Peter Simon Pallas himself, the head of the expeditions, who was also in charge of analyzing their findings. Pallas visited the middle Volga and the Urals and traveled as far east as Irkutsk and the Lake Baikal area. The writings of the German scientists, like those of their Russian colleagues Ivan Ivanovich Lepyokhin and Nikolai Petrovich Rychkov (in German translation), were quickly made available to the Western European public.

These journeys were imperial research trips. Their occasionally fatal "adventurousness"—both Bering and Steller died en route—was an unwanted side-effect rather than a guiding principle. Those who took part in them were not thirsting for thrilling escapades and epic quests, nor were they impelled by naïve curiosity, nor did they long to put behind them the stale comforts of modern Europe. Indeed, an important impulse behind the scientific travels of the Enlightenment era was a determination *not* to leave the earth's discovery and investigation in the careless hands of adventurers. For the young German scholars, the tsarist expeditions opened up extraordinary career prospects denied them in the small states of their homeland: J. G. Gmelin was offered a full professorship in Saint Petersburg with attractive conditions at just twenty-two years of age, Pallas at twenty-five. After unhappy experiences in Russian state service, the former went on to become rector of Tübingen University, while the latter retired as one of Europe's most celebrated naturalists to an estate in the Crimea bestowed on him by the tsarina.

A methodical approach to travel had already started to be developed in humanist circles in sixteenth-century Italy, France, and the Upper Rhine.[173] What the traveler would observe was now mapped out in advance in carefully planned itineraries rather than left to his passing fancy. In Asia, scholarly travelers had observed and described their surroundings in precise detail before Gmelin and G. F. Müller: Engelbert Kaempfer in Iran and Japan, for instance, and Pater Gerbillon around the same time in Mongolia. But the eighteenth-century Russian expeditions combined six key elements for the first time:

(1) a detailed work program;
(2) logistical planning on a military scale;
(3) meticulous scientific preparation;
(4) routinized and schematized daily documentation of results;
(5) systematic analysis under the auspices of academic institutions; and
(6) a scientific (and secondarily political) rationale.

Almost concurrently with the Great Northern Expedition, something similar was attempted—albeit in colonies controlled by foreign powers—in La Condamine's journeys to Peru and the Amazon.[174] In theory at least, since the execution often left much to be desired, all the essential elements of a research trip were now in place. Such trips did not have to take the form of an expedition, a kind of mobile colony already partially realized in the circumnavigations and Pacific voyages of yesteryear. The Danish mission to Arabia set out in 1761 as a small expedition but was single-handedly continued by Carsten Niebuhr following the death of his travel companions. Thanks to his diligent preparation he was able to attain many of their research objectives on his own, returning to Copenhagen as a duty-bound servant of the Danish crown rather than as a footloose vagabond.[175] James Bruce and Alexander von Humboldt on his American odyssey relied almost entirely on their own resources. But their cost and public significance almost inevitably turned research trips outside of Europe into affairs of state, with travelers enlisted as functionaries or recipients of patronage—much to the annoyance of a free and fiery spirit like Johann Reinhold Forster.[176]

The Russo-German North Asian voyages of 1733–43 and 1768–74 were unequalled in Asia in their time. Europe's leading geographers and cartographers were based in France, but France lacked colonial possibilities in Asia. Bonaparte's occupation of Egypt in 1798, which was also an invasion of the Orient by the French scholarly world, opened the floodgates to long pent-up energies.[177] It established a tradition of having military interventions accompanied by large state-sponsored scientific research operations.[178] Great Britain's official travel ambitions in the eighteenth century flowed predominantly into the three near-perfectly organized circumnavigations of the globe captained by James Cook. German and Swedish scientists also took part in these voyages, even if they were assigned positions of lesser responsibility than those entrusted to Bering and Pallas in Russia. From 1775, the year of George Bogle's mission to Tibet, to 1815, when Napoleon's downfall brought the empire temporary relief from Great-Power competition in the East, Britain sent out diplomatic embassies from India to almost all the surrounding countries in Asia. All these embassies carried out scientific work in some form or other, but none came even close to matching the level of professionalism shown by the travelers to Siberia.

We turn finally to the areas under direct British control. During the years when the British occupied Dutch-colonized Java (1811–16), their most senior representative, lieutenant-governor Sir Stamford Raffles, collected materials that flowed into his great description of the country, his *History of Java* (1817). Once again we see a typically British discursive model at work, loosely adapted from Julius Caesar: the conqueror as historian and ethnographer. We have encountered it before in Sir John Malcolm. British India itself was subjected to thorough scientific examination not long after its various provinces had been subdued by force of arms.[179] It began in 1765, when Robert Clive, conqueror of Bengal, commissioned the young marine officer and surveyor, James Rennell, to investigate and map the newly won territories as surveyor-general.[180] Like Catherine the Great or—as we will see in the next chapter from Volney's example—France under the Directory, from the late eighteenth century the British colonial state pursued the vision of a comprehensive, systematic, and accurate archive of scientific information about the newly acquired imperial possessions. The most precise instruments that late Enlightenment Europe had to offer for such a task were statistics and survey-based cartography.[181] In a frenzy of measurement and quantification, "philosophically" minded Europeans persuaded themselves that rational processes of description would lead to accurate and incontrovertible representations of territories and the material culture borne by them. A century of more or less regional and uncoordinated data collection in India culminated in the creation in 1878 of a central information bureau, the Survey of India. By that time, all the British territories on the subcontinent were enmeshed in a finely spun web of descriptive detail. The country had been exactly surveyed and mapped from the end of the eighteenth century onwards. From the late eighteenth century, teams of administrator-scholars streamed out from the colonial centers to gather data on the conquered territories' geology, botany, zoology, ethnography, economy (including its capacity for taxation), sociology, and history. A vast stockpile of texts and maps, quantitative data, local gazetteers, and encyclopedias was thus amassed. Enormous collections of manuscripts, coins, works of art, and artifacts of material culture were assembled thanks to the tireless efforts of manic collectors like Colin Mackenzie, who was also a pioneer geodesist and mapmaker and in 1815 was appointed the inaugural surveyor-general of India.[182]

Many of the objects harvested on official research trips were eventually incorporated into the great imperial archives and museums. This type of travel would not have been possible without the prior pacification and organization of peripheral regions. In turn, it not only contributed to the disinterested accumulation of scientific knowledge; it also made Asia's subject lands and peoples easier to govern and exploit.

V

Encounters

The Ameen-ad-Dowlah then got up, and invited the Ambassador and the other guests to follow him into another apartment, where we found that an attempt had been made to lay out a dinner in the European manner. On a number of rude unpainted tables, some high, some low, arranged in the horse-shoe fashion, were heaped all the various dishes which compose a Persian entertainment, not in symmetrical order, for their numbers made that impossible, but positively piled one upon the other, so that stewed fowl lay under roasted lamb, omelet under stewed fowl, eggs under omelet, and rice under all, and so on. Every European was provided with a knife, fork, napkin, and plate; but the poor Persians, alas! made but rueful work of it.

—James Justinian Morier (1780–1849), *A Second Journey through Persia, Armenia and Asia Minor to Constantinopel between the Years 1810 and 1816* (1818)[1]

James Justinian Morier, the Smyrna-born secretary of the embassy who accompanied Sir Gore Ouseley, a speaker of Arabic and Persian, on a mission to the court of Persia, had a deep sympathy for the Iranian people and was far from mocking them as bumbling barbarians. The scene is relished in its potential for farce, fitting for a major comic writer whose *Adventures of Hajji Baba of Ispahan* (1824) was destined to become a model for Orientalizing novelists throughout Europe. The "poor Persians" are eager to be good hosts, they want to please their guests from Britain by making them feel at home. There is little deference to a world power in this encounter. But the Persians get lost halfway in their attempted self-Westernization and almost fall victim to the imported cutlery, which they fail to master with the necessary skill and grace, while their visitors are at a loss confronting the piled-up delicacies. In the end, everybody struggles in this chaotic game played out in a cultural no-man's-land between two different civilizations.

Morier basically describes a scene from a movie. The lesson is that it needs the cinematographer or, in earlier centuries, the resourceful writer to capture the nuances of "cross-cultural" encounters. And nothing could replace the lived experience. The Other had to be seen and heard, smelled and touched. We believe Morier that he was present and that he finally got his roasted lamb.

Observing Asia required going there first. A second-best alternative was to inspect Asians traveling abroad. These were few on the ground in eighteenth-century Europe. Africans, forcibly removed from their homeland by the slave trade, were a more common sight than people from Asia. Africans were employed at court or in private service as manservants ("Moors" or "blackamoors"), soldiers, or musicians. Asians, by contrast, turned up in Europe only in isolated cases. They always had a special story behind them. The few embassies sent by eastern states caused a stir wherever they arrived in Europe: two Siamese embassies in France (1684/85, 1686/87), Persian embassies in England (1626, 1809/10, 1819/20) and France (1715), Ottoman embassies in France (1533, 1571, 1581, 1601, 1607, 1669/70, 1720/21[2], 1741), in Vienna (1665, 1740), and in Prussia (1763/64).[3]

Otherwise individuals made their own way to Europe. To mention only some of the Chinese who have left traces in archives and libraries: Zheng Manu, the first Chinese Jesuit, who traveled to Rome to commence priestly training in 1650; a doctor called "Tibitsia," who followed the ambassador Van Hoorn from Peking to Holland;[4] the unfortunate Jean Hu, who came to Europe in 1722 and has been immortalized by the great historian Jonathan Spence;[5] the five Chinese educated by the Jesuits from 1750–54 at the Collège Louis-Le-Grand; two young sons of Christian families, Aloys Ko and Étienne Yang, invited to France in the early 1760s by the minister Bertin to train for the priesthood.[6] Then there is the Kalmuck boy, "Fyodor Ivanovich": the crown princess of Baden had him schooled and sent to Rome as a talented draftsman after receiving him as a gift from the Russian empress.[7] The only place in Europe where one stood a good chance of encountering well-educated Chinese was at the Chinese College (Collegio dei Cinesi) in Naples, set up in 1732 by the secular priest, Matteo Ripa, for the training of Chinese missionaries. In 1851 people from China were still such a rare sight in London that a Chinese woman could be exhibited with her children at a cost of two shillings.[8] Only a trickle of Asians entered Europe—perhaps twenty thousand South Asians reached British shores between 1600 and 1857[9]—in comparison to the flood of Europeans flowing in the opposite direction. Between 1602 and 1795, it is estimated that around 973,000 people journeyed out to Asia on VOC ships alone.[10]

Given that Asia so infrequently came to Europe, European impressions could only be formed through travel and long stays in Asia itself. How did that come about? After our bird's-eye view of the reasons people traveled and the places they visited, it is time to inspect the experience of travel close-up as a stage toward the published travel account. The transformation of observations into texts is a very complicated process that can be difficult to reconstruct in individual cases. It is not enough to investigate what texts have to say about foreign people and places, the "images" they paint of them. We have to pay equal attention to the specific situations in which observations are made as part of a traveler's practice. Since one traveler seldom observed another and wrote about it, and since natives even more rarely recorded their impressions of foreigners, all we have to go on are the texts themselves. But these are a rich source if read against the grain.

ORDEALS, DISAPPOINTMENTS, CATASTROPHES

For much of the time, travelers were concerned chiefly with themselves. Transport and accommodation had to be arranged, problems with authorities sorted out. In a pre-imperialist age, when Europeans traveling abroad generally enjoyed no special privileges that placed them above the law of the land and were not yet backed up by gunboats and the threat of intervention, overland travel could be a hazardous and even lethal undertaking. Of the twenty students dispatched from Uppsala on research trips around the world by the great natural historian Carl Linnaeus, eight lost their lives and one his sanity.[11] The famous death of Captain Cook in the Sandwich Islands (Hawai'i) on February 14, 1779, can stand in for a host of cases. On July 27, 1774, Samuel Gottlieb Gmelin, having ventured beyond the tsarina's dominions into the still-independent small states on the Caspian Sea, perished in one of the khan of Derbent's dungeons at the age of twenty-nine. William George Browne, who had previously spent three years in captivity in the South Sudan, fell victim to a bandit attack in late summer 1813 while traveling from Tabriz to Tehran.[12] Sir Alexander Burnes, a dashing young protégé of Sir John Malcolm, geographic field researcher and author of the stylish *Travels into Bochara* (1834), met a death to befit the new imperial era: on November 2, 1841, he was lynched in the streets of Kabul as the Afghan people rose up against a hated British occupation that had imposed on them a puppet king.[13] Christian missionaries were occasionally threatened with persecution. While the atrocities committed in early seventeenth-century Japan and at the martyr's stake in Canada were not repeated in such dimensions in the eighteenth century, Tonkin, the northern state of Vietnam, was still a very dangerous place for Christian evangelists.

Losses to illness were significantly higher. In 1667 Jean de Thévenot, who wrote a number of valuable travel reports and was also responsible for introducing coffee to France, died of exhaustion in Armenia on the return leg from India to Europe. The Danish expedition to Arabia was almost wiped out by malaria in 1763/64. In November 1746 Georg Wilhelm Steller succumbed to fever in Tyumen, Siberia. Another traveler to Siberia, Johann Peter Falck, who had studied under Linnaeus and was a professor of medicine and botany in Saint Petersburg, took his own life in 1774 upon failing to receive medical assistance.[14] The veterinarian and expert horse breeder William Moorcroft died of fever and exhaustion in

North Afghanistan on August 27, 1825, after escaping the clutches of Murad Beg, a local tyrant and slave trader on the upper reaches of the Amu Darya.[15] Some regions were especially dangerous. Batavia, initially known as a salubrious and civilized city, became notorious following the first malaria epidemic of 1733 as one of the deadliest places in the tropics, feared by the crew of any ship that could not avoid putting in there.[16] Nature likewise struck back in Bengal. Between 1707 and 1775, more than half of the civil servants sent out from Britain by the EIC went to their graves there.[17] When in June 1688 Engelbert Kaempfer was finally able to set sail from the scorchingly hot Persian Gulf port of Gombroon (Bandar Abbas), he noted: "Heaven be thanked for preserving me in life, limb and property in this house of sickness and death."[18] Thousands no doubt had similar feelings in comparable situations.

Whether less fatal ordeals were mentioned in travel reports depended on the author's temperament and literary aims. Peter Simon Pallas, who traveled further by land than almost anyone else in the eighteenth century, dispenses almost entirely with information about the circumstances of his travel, fixating instead with almost manic objectivity on what he observed. His predecessor as a long-distance traveler in Siberia, Johann Georg Gmelin, cultivated a less austere style. He would like nothing better, he remarks at one point, than to entertain sensation-hungry readers with tales of mishap and adventure, but he feels himself unable to satisfy their appetite for icy terrors:

> They will find that I was often able to arrange my travels with great convenience, even in the remotest areas. I have therefore found it impossible to give an account of hardships where none were to be found, and to breathe new life into old complaints about the wild and barren wastes of Siberia.[19]

Yet although Gmelin's journey benefited from the logistics of a well-organized, state-sponsored expedition, it was anything but a pleasure trip. Even before it got underway, a student, a surveyor, and a scientific-instrument maker were killed in an accident on August 8, 1733. There followed a chain of smaller catastrophes, which Gmelin mentions in passing: their coach burns down because an axle had not been properly greased; their ship runs aground on a sandbank; they lose their way for want of accurate maps; they are constantly tormented by fleas and mosquitoes; they are forced to sleep out in the bitter cold or lodge in smoke-filled "black rooms" (as Samuel Turner will later do in Tibet).[20] Gmelin twice loses notes, books, instruments, and cash to fire—just as Stamford Raffles sees his irreplaceable Java collection go down in a shipwreck.[21] Even under optimal circumstances, getting material to safe custody at home is a risky business. When in 1805 Ulrich Jasper Seetzen dispatches a crate of books from Damascus to the ducal library at Gotha in Thuringia, he has a muleteer take them to the port of Tripoli (in today's Lebanon). From there a French merchant sends them to his Italian business partner in Cyprus who in turn entrusts them to a ship bound for Venice.[22]

In theory at least, the fact that Gmelin, the young scholar from the University of Tübingen, and his companion, Gerhard Friedrich Müller, were traveling in Her Majesty's service with a military escort entitled them to be billeted by local authorities and to requisition horses en route. Indeed, on his official tour of 1829 Alexander von Humboldt had need of some 12,244 horses at 568 posting houses over a twenty-three week period![23] In practice, Gmelin and his party were constantly plagued by problems with lazy boatmen, money-grubbing innkeepers, and uncooperative village elders. Things became more serious when peasants resisted having their horses requisitioned.[24] The further away they moved from the centers of Russian power, the less effective were the royal letters of protection they flourished at each stop. In the empire's Wild East, Gmelin encountered lawlessness and banditry.[25] Where no boatmen were to be found, even diplomatic missions could not avoid having to swim across the occasional river, as Ismailov's embassy to China learned in 1719.[26]

Those traveling on their own found the going even tougher. The hospitality for which the Orient was renowned among Westerners could not always be relied on. It was most likely to be refused travelers who gave off an air of prosperity.[27] Anyone who did not deliberately shun the company of fellow Europeans, like Niebuhr or Anquetil-Duperron, first sought shelter with European consuls, merchants, or missionaries before trusting to the friendliness or business acumen of locals. There were few inns in Asia. Travelers could count themselves lucky to come across well-maintained caravanserais, where they could almost always replenish their water supplies (although there was often no food to be had).[28] Caravanserais needed to be kept in good condition. Where this failed to occur, as in parts of Iran in the eighteenth century, they soon fell into disrepair.[29] Asia did not always come a poor second to the West. At a time when paved roads were still the exception in much of Europe, travelers were impressed by the high standard of the highways in China, which they found to be superior to those in the Near and Middle East as well.[30] The Grand Canal linking Peking with the Yangzi region in east-central China was long described as a near-miraculous feat of civil engineering, unparalleled by anything in Europe.[31]

Finding honest and reliable local servants was perhaps the most pressing problem faced by travelers, closely followed by the need to be periodically resupplied with fresh horses. Donkeys performed good service in Arabia, yaks in the Himalaya. Georg Wilhelm Steller wrote a heartfelt homage to the sled dog.[32] In the Mughal Empire only the imperial court, the aristocracy, and the military rode by elephant. All things considered, horses were probably the most important means of transport for Europeans in South Asia. Wealthier travelers sometimes also opted to be conveyed by palanquin. Bullock carts were the most popular means of long-distance transport for the masses and were not infrequently used by foreign "low" travelers as well; oxen caravans of up to twenty thousand animals regularly plied the route between Surat and Agra.[33] The abbé Perrin, who traveled a great deal in India between 1777 and 1784, hailed the ox as "the first and most useful quadruped in India."[34] The animal's dependability and endurance provided some consolation for its plodding pace.

Travelers almost always felt a sense of relief upon entering camel country. The literature is full of praise for the camel as the most undemanding, biologically stable, and even-tempered of all riding and pack animals. Camel caravans offered no guarantees of safety, however. Dr. Thomas Shaw, an experienced traveler in the Orient who began his career as chaplain in the English factory in Algiers and ended it as regius professor of Greek in Oxford, learned this the hard way. In 1722 he was traveling with a six-thousand-strong caravan from Rama to Jerusalem, escorted by four hundred soldiers under the command of an Ottoman general, when they were raided by Arab tribal warriors. Shaw himself was taken hostage, "very barbarously used and insulted all that night," and was freed in the end only by a rapid task force sent out by the aga of Jerusalem.[35] In general, though, caravans were the most pleasant form of transport (relatively speaking) in the Near and Middle East as well as in Central Asia.[36] Horses often took part in them alongside camels. Caravans posed considerable organizational challenges and could only defend themselves against attack by robbers or the forces of nature through "order, vigilance and solidarity."[37] Missing a caravan could mean having to wait several months for the next one to arrive. One traveler placed in this situation spent the time fretting about his problems back home: greedy relatives, he feared, were helping themselves to the worldly goods of this absent Odysseus.[38]

Europeans traveling to Asia on state business enjoyed the benefits of free oriental hospitality (in the best case scenario) but had to abide by the conditions set by their hosts. The members of the Dutch "Titisingh embassy" who visited China in 1794/95, for example, were treated with far less courtesy and diplomatic politesse than had been shown the Macartney Mission just a few months before. They were unceremoniously assigned to damp, leaky hovels or even left out overnight in their bamboo litters. Far from being entertained with gourmet banquets, all they received on the way from local Mandarins were eggs, apples, biscuits, and raw meat.[39] The "least disgusting" food available was the plain rice on which they largely subsisted.[40] They were so badly fed that the corpulent Andreas Everardus van Braam Houckgeest, accustomed to a lavish lifestyle in Batavia, arrived at the Chinese capital "as thin as a shotten herring."[41] To tell the full story, however, it has to be said that the Dutch ambassadors enjoyed a far more comfortable journey back to Canton when they traveled with the blessing of the emperor.[42] In 1752 the learned Pater Amiot was subjected to a form of harrassment that must have been especially hard for an inquisitive European to bear: the Chinese authorities had him borne at a snail's pace in a closed and windowless litter from Nanchang (the capital of Jiangxi province) to Peking. Amiot crawled on for forty-five days before finally reaching the capital.[43]

From the physical privations of travel there was but a small step to its associated mental hardships. The most harmless of these were dashed hopes and disappointed expectations. European diplomats were well advised to forget the finer points of ranking and protocol. The tsarist embassy to China in 1805 failed, among other things, because the Chinese side cared little for the subtle hierarchies within the Russian delegation, thereby causing great offense.[44] Veteran travelers and perceptive writers of the caliber of a Niebuhr, Gmelin, or Pallas chose not to share their private disappointments with their readers, understanding that all expectations are inherently precarious. They rarely make confessions such as we find in René Caillié, whose mounting excitement at being one of the first Europeans to enter the legendary desert city of Timbuktu (in today's Mali) gave way to disillusionment when he finally set eyes on his dream destination on April 20, 1828:

> I looked around and found that the sight before me did not answer my expectations. I had formed a totally different idea of the grandeur and wealth of Timbuctoo. The city presented, at first sight, nothing but a mass of ill-looking houses, built of earth. Nothing was to be seen in all directions but immense plains of quicksand of a yellowish white colour.[45]

Other travelers lost their illusions about the Orient of fame and fable when they first beheld Baghdad, Kabul, or Peking in all its dusty, grimy squalor, or when they were forced to acknowledge that there was more to

China than just picturesquely terraced landscapes. Some adopted the role of the jaded globetrotter, informing their readers that the Great Wall of China was not nearly as impressive as people claim, and so on.[46] A small number of texts give voice to an unostentatious, deeply felt sense of disappointment—not so much with the touristic shortcomings of the East as with life in the colonies. Joseph Schrödter for example, a Saxon craftsman, happened to be in Egypt when Napoleon's troops came marching in. Schrödter tried his luck in India, "but without success."[47] While fighting for the EIC as a footsoldier against Tipu Sultan of Mysore, he grew increasingly disillusioned with the arrogance shown by the wealthy English in Madras and the lack of opportunities for personal enrichment in India:

> Without capital it is now all but impossible to make one's fortune in the formerly much-praised lands of India. Most leave as poor as they came; one can seldom set anything aside from one's regular wages.[48]

His advice to potential adventurers is that they would be better off staying at home.

Travelers rarely confess to an emotion that must have been felt by many but which sat uneasily with the culturally approved image of the hyperactive, constantly alert European and was regarded instead as typical of savages: boredom.[49] Samuel Turner knew what he was talking about when he identified patience—along with the art of improvisation—as the traveler's cardinal virtue. In 1783, like his predecessor George Bogle in 1774, he struggled to find ways to while away the time in Tibetan monasteries.[50] A journey on the Tigris could also be extremely monotonous,[51] and at least one Siberian traveler voiced a truth to which many more would have given tacit agreement:

> I must confess that the journey through the endless steppe makes for dreary reading, and I can only console the reader by assuring him that it was far drearier in reality: here he can read through in an hour what took us two months and nine days to accomplish.[52]

THE MYSTERIOUS MISTER MANNING

As Johann Georg Gmelin rightly pointed out, readers were keenly interested in the accidents, dangers, and spiritual crises that befell travelers en route. In the end, though, they wanted to find out how travelers overcame such travails. Open expressions of frustration are therefore to be found only in jottings not intended for public view. Such notes were made by Alexander von Humboldt. Yet perhaps no document is more revealing than the journal kept by the mysterious Thomas Manning.

Until the end of the nineteenth century, Manning was the only Englishman ever to have set foot in the holy city of Lhasa.[53] Born in 1772, the vicar's son from Norfolk had broken off a promising career as a mathematician to study Chinese in Paris: at first with Joseph Hager, then under the tuition of a native speaker. Initially motivated by an interest in comparing the language with Greek, he became ever more fascinated by Chinese culture as his studies progressed. His friend, the famous essayist Charles Lamb, advised him: "Read no more books of voyages; they are nothing but lies." But Manning was determined to travel to China and Independent Tartary. On the recommendation of Sir Joseph Banks, the president of the Royal Society, the EIC gave Manning the opportunity to sail by company ship to Canton and reside in their factory from 1807 to 1810. In November 1807 he applied to the viceroy of Canton for the position of court astronomer and physician in Peking. When the Chinese authorities turned him down, he decided to make his way instead to the Chinese protectorate of Tibet.

In August 1811, Manning set off without official authority, papers, or financial support from Calcutta to Bhutan, accompanied by a single Chinese servant. Proceeding via Giansu he reached Lhasa, whose celebrated attraction, the Potala Palace, was known in Europe only through a picture based on Grueber that had appeared in Athanasius Kircher's *China Illustrata* (1667). On December 17, Manning was received by the ninth Dalai Lama, a seven-year-old boy. Manning gave him a piece of brocade, two brass candlesticks, and a flask of lavender water—not out of disrespect but for lack of more valuable gifts—and requested Tibetan books in return. On April 19, 1812, he was pressured by representatives of the Sino-Manchurian protectorate to leave Lhasa. In India he refused to share his experiences with anyone. He then returned to Canton to resume his Chinese studies. In 1817 he joined the embassy of Lord Amherst as an interpreter. On July 1 of the same year we suddenly find him conversing with Napoleon on Saint Helena. The extravagantly bearded Manning was considered something of a buffoon and an eccentric. In 1829 he finally returned to England and retired to a cottage near Dartford, surrounded by his huge collection of Chinese books. He died in 1840 without having published a single line. His travel notes did not see the light of day until 1879, when they were edited from his surviving papers.

Thomas Manning's journal shows him to be an exact observer, acerbic commentator, and free spirit who never allows his perspective to be clouded by partisan British concerns. Manning has no interest in gathering the kind of "useful" information that official India expected of its emissaries and spies. Tibet's geopolitical significance in the imperial "Great Game" then getting underway is a matter of complete indifference to him. One of his recurring themes is the overbearing manner of the Chinese in Tibet, which he often compares with the no-less-distasteful posturing of the British colonial overlords in India. Manning displays an immunity to the era's clichés about Asia (both positive and negative) that was shared by none of his contemporaries except Anquetil-Duperron, who was a generation older. He is equally insusceptible to the mood of dumbstruck awe that seemed to grip other travelers when confronted with exotic spectacles. His first sighting of the Potala Palace has a very different effect on him: the swampy ground at the base of the castle reminds him unpleasantly of the Pontine Marshes in Rome. The palace meets with his passing approval ("it seemed perfect enough")[54] but the architecture strikes him as neither exotically alien nor immediately comprehensible: "[it] eluded my attempts at analysis."[55] The following chapter begins, not with the expected description of the city of Lhasa, but with a lengthy discourse on Tibetan hats.[56]

Manning was one of the better writers in his generation of British travelers to Asia, perhaps the best. When he complains about the barren slopes of southern Tibet, he does so without resorting to a prose style that is equally barren in its abstraction. Instead: "A pot of young growing onions at one corner of the room was the greenest thing I had seen for a long time."[57] His writing is affected neither by lachrymose self-pity nor by the self-aggrandizing vanity that leads the romantic Chateaubriand, traveling around the same time, to push himself to the forefront of each scene. Manning describes his sorrows with unique psychological insight and unfeigned anguish: loneliness, extreme temperatures (including the difficulty of writing with fingers that are frozen half stiff), the consequences of unsuitable clothing, the torments of rheumatic illness, the creeping loss of faith in his own vision, his shame at having to pick off the fleas that infest his body, his need to finance his trip once his money runs out by selling off his belongings piece by piece, and his emotions on encountering others, from hatred of his treacherous environs to deep wonderment at the holy child on the Potala throne. On September 18, 1811, for example, a little way behind the Bhutanese border, he records this expressive entry:

> The snow! Where am I? How can I be come here? Not a soul to speak to. I wept almost through excess of sensation, not from grief. A spaniel would be better company than my Chinese servant. Plenty of priests and monks like those in Europe.[58]

Manning was one of the most honest Europeans in Asia and also one of the least prejudiced. He neither believed in European superiority nor sought to put Asia on a pedestal. Perhaps he never shared his experiences because he sensed they would not be understood. One would give a great deal to know what he discussed with Napoleon.

INTERPRETERS AND DIALOGUES

Thomas Manning's journal has a lot to teach us about how travelers communicated. How did they prepare themselves? How could they make themselves understood by natives?

Manning was one of the leading Sinologists of his age, yet in his audience with the Dalai Lama he tactfully avoided speaking the language of the protectoral power. The Dalai Lama spoke in Tibetan to a Chinese interpreter, who translated it for Manning's Chinese servant (the Munshi), who in turn passed on the message to Manning in Latin:

> I gave answer in Latin, which was converted and conveyed back in the same manner. I had been long accustomed to speak Latin with my Munshi. There was no sentiment or shade of sentiment we could not exchange. Thus, though the route was circuitous, the communication was quick, and the questions and answers delivered with an accuracy which I have reason to believe seldom happens in Asia when interpreters are employed.[59]

It seems that no European could speak fluent Tibetan at the time, although the Jesuit Ippolito Desideri had written four apologetic works in Tibetan during his stay in the country between 1715 and 1721—a feat that earns him the admiration of present-day Tibetologists.[60] This was not for lack of gifted polyglots. A distinction needs to be made between the theoretical knowledge of a language and fluency in speaking it. The latter often outran the former. When both linguistic understanding and practical command of the language came together, works of lasting importance could result: Pater Joseph de Prémare's Chinese grammar was not published until 1831, almost a century after the author's death, but even then it long remained unsurpassed.[61] The Jesuit missionaries were accomplished linguists almost to a man. Joachim Bouvet, to name just one example, was fluent in Latin, Greek, Syriac, Italian, Spanish, and Portuguese as well as Chinese. Besides his mother tongue, the Moldavian prince and historian of the Ottoman Empire, Demetrius (Dimitrie) Cantemir, could speak and write Turkish, Persian, Arabic, Latin, Modern Greek, Italian, and Russian; he also had a reading knowledge of Ancient Greek, Old Church Slavonic, and French. This latter-day renaissance man was immersed in at least three different cultures: Greek Orthodoxy, Western European humanism, and Islamic learning in its broad variety. He was also in a unique position to practice his linguistic skills at the Ottoman court in Constantinople, where he mingled with Western diplomats during his long sojourn there from 1687 to 1710, and was in contact with savants from all over Europe.[62] John Leyden, one of the first scholars of Africa and a close collaborator of Sir Stamford Raffles on Java until his early death from "Batavian fever," was said to have mastered forty-five languages, while Johann Reinhold Forster managed a respectable seventeen.[63] At the age of twenty-five, Joseph Hammer could effortlessly translate from Turkish or Arabic into French, Italian, or English and spoke Turkish like a native.[64] Sir William Jones, the founder of Indology, may have stumbled in the Slavic languages but he felt himself at home in almost every other European tongue. He was also a master of Persian and by the end of his short life had picked up enough Sanskrit to express himself freely in this rich language.[65] Strangely, the impressive efforts of British scholars in Bengal to revive and master the classical language of India did not engender an immediate "transfer of knowledge" back to Europe. The experts either died in India or returned to Britain at an advanced age. The teaching of Sanskrit in Great Britain remained institutionally weak for a long time, and the French and Germans virtually had to start from scratch—with the important help of Alexander Hamilton, a British army officer from Bengal who got stuck in Paris following the breakdown of the Treaty of Amiens in 1803.[66]

Most of the world depended on interpreters. They were deployed everywhere. Their most conspicuous role was in foreign policy. In 1721 the French state began training boys to become interpreters in Turkish and Arabic, sending them to the École des Jeunes de Langues from around the age of eight. The Oriental Academy in Vienna, established in 1754, was more successful in preparing its students for consular and diplomatic service in the Ottoman Empire.[67] This did little to diminish the importance of native translators, however. In the Ottoman Empire, the so-called dragomans (from the Turkish *tercüman*) functioned as specialists in intercultural relations. From 1669 to 1821 the post of grand dragoman of the Sublime Porte lay in the hands of the Phanariots, wealthy Greek or culturally Hellenized families residing in Phanar, the chief Greek quarter of Constantinople. The office-holders enjoyed privileges rarely extended to non-Muslims, particularly symbolic self-representation through clothing, coaches, and luxurious housing. The grand dragoman interpreted during the grand vizier's discussions with foreign ambassadors and at audiences given by the sultan. He translated diplomatic correspondence and wrote memoranda about his own conversations with diplomats. The foreign embassies viewed him as the second-in-charge at the Ottoman Ministry of Foreign Affairs, someone whose visits were to be received with due ceremony.[68] Since the chain of responsibility and command in Ottoman diplomacy was weakly articulated until the 1820s, dragomans sometimes had wide room for maneuver.[69]

The European embassies employed their own dragomans as polyglot guides to an alien environment. They too were more than just interpreters: they were experts on their country, collectors of gossip, spies, advisers, and confidants as well. Recruited from the empire's non-Turkish minorities (for two centuries the British employed dragomans from the originally Italian Pisani family), they generally remained the sultan's subjects; their loyalty could not always be taken for granted. The dragoman system was unique in Asia and was frequently regarded with hostility. The dragomans were suspected of abusing their position as intermediaries to betray confidences and jockey for power. They were also accused of toadying to the Turks. It is quite unseemly, one British diplomat huffed in 1820, for the chief dragoman of the British embassy to kiss the hem of an Ottoman minister's robe.[70] As "local staff," moreover, it was claimed that they understood too little of Europe.[71] There may have been some truth in this, considering that the two dragomans employed by the English consulate in Syrian Aleppo were Greeks who had learned no other European languages apart from Italian.[72] Frequently, however, individual dragomans were enmeshed in cosmopolitan Phanariot networks that channeled news and goods across vast distances. The dragoman's function was tied to the institution of permanent diplomatic and consular missions that were nowhere to be found in Asia outside the Ottoman Empire.

The distrustful governments of East Asia did not expect foreigners to bring with them their own interpreters and linguistic skills. They sought to impose a kind of monopoly on translation. In sixteenth- and early seventeenth-century Japan, a few foreigners—Portuguese missionaries, the Englishman Will Adams, and the Dutchman François Caron—had spoken fluent Japanese. That began to change once the closed-door policy came into effect. A bureaucracy of professional translators was established in Nagasaki to regulate contact with the Dutch on Dejima. Its existence made life easier for the Dutch by sparing them the effort of having to learn Japanese themselves.[73] From around 1808 a number of Japanese also studied English, French, and Russian.[74] The Russian ambassador Nikolai Rezanov, the joint leader of the expedition more commonly associated with the name of Captain Krusenstern, found that his preparations were wasted on his Japanese hosts; in winter 1804/5 they barely gave him an opportunity to practice his laboriously acquired Japanese, conversing with him in Russian instead.[75]

The Chinese court relied on its Jesuits, whose goodwill and readiness to impart information could prove immensely useful to foreign diplomats. The learned Pater Parennin, active in China from 1698 until his death in 1741, an especially close confidant of the Kangxi emperor and much-sought-after correspondent of European scholars, interpreted on many diplomatic occasions. Renowned for his impeccable knowledge of both Chinese and Manchurian, the mother tongue of the imperial clan, he could communicate in Latin, French, Portuguese, and Italian as well. The Jesuits played an important role in negotiating the Treaty of Nerchinsk between Russia and the Qing Empire (1689); one of the official copies of the document is written in Latin.[76] At the height of their influence, when some of the Fathers had risen to occupy senior positions in the imperial bureaucracy, they acted as official representatives of the Chinese state. Thus, the Chinese official who initially received and interrogated the first Dutch embassy when it arrived in Peking in 1655 was the missionary Adam Schall von Bell, a native of Cologne.[77] Japanese diplomacy also made occasional use of European go-betweens until the period of national isolation. In Iran, Raphaël Du Mans, superior of the Capuchin mission in Isfahan and something like an unofficial French ambassador, served for decades as a middleman between the government of the shah and the European EICs.[78]

The missionaries in Peking were indispensable as interpreters even when ambassadors brought along one or two Chinese speakers in their retinue. Prior to his departure Lord Macartney had secured the services of the translator Jacobus Li, who had recently completed his priestly training at the Chinese College of Propaganda Fide in Naples and was now grateful for a free berth back to his homeland.[79] Li appears to have acquitted himself well, even if he was occasionally left tongue-tied by his fear of the court mandarins. Yet only the (ex-)Jesuits had the ability to move with ease between the elevated *written* forms of classical Chinese bureaucratese and the language of European diplomacy. Unlike earlier Portuguese missions, the Macartney embassy of 1793/94 was confronted with the additional problem that none of its interpreters—neither Jacobus Li nor the missionaries—understood English. Official Chinese texts first had to be translated into Latin before they were reworked into English by Johann Christian Hüttner, a tutor from Saxony who was traveling with the embassy.[80] A lack of means or opportunity for direct communication was a general handicap for European missions to China. Lord Macartney himself, one of the most sharp-sighted and objective observers of the country, was only able to break through the barriers to mutual understanding on a single occasion. During the delegation's return journey by boat along the Grand Canal from Peking to Hangzhou, he conducted a series of long and apparently open and respectful exchanges with Song Yun, one of the empire's top officials. Because Macartney had been ambassador to Saint Petersburg from 1764 to 1767 and Song Yun, a native of Mongolia, had served for a time as military governor on the Russian-Chinese border, the two men were able to bypass the need for interpreters by talking in Russian.[81]

On the coast of China, as in all other Asian port cities, communication was less difficult. European merchants rarely bothered learning the local languages. On the Levantine coast, those who spoke neither Arabic nor Turkish used Italian as a lingua franca, even though English and French commercial interests had long outstripped those of the Italian cities.[82] Until the early nineteenth century, Portuguese was still widely spoken in the area between the Persian Gulf and Macau. The widely traveled Alexander Hamilton appears to have successfully navigated the entire East Indies while communicating entirely in Portuguese. Those with a working knowledge of Asia's second most important language for travelers, Persian, had even fewer difficulties. Many a European merchant in India got by with a simplified pidgin version of Hindustani or "Moors."[83] Until the mid-eighteenth century, hardly any of the British stationed in India could speak one of the country's languages. From around 1760 the EIC, now transforming itself into the territorial ruler of Bengal, encouraged its employees to study Persian as the principal language of Indian politics, and later also the Indian regional languages. British officials in India were, in theory, expected to be able to communicate with their subjects without interpreters.[84] Only a minority achieved this goal in the eighteenth century.

The likelihood of finding Asians who could express themselves in European languages was far greater than the chance of meeting with a good knowledge of Asian languages among Europeans. Visiting Canton in 1750, the Swedish chaplain and naturalist, Peter Osbeck, met Chinese people who spoke at least rudimentary Portuguese, French, English, or Swedish.[85] A few years later, Carsten Niebuhr ascertained that very few foreigners in the western Indian seaport of Surat learned native languages because so many Indians spoke Portuguese or English; the regional languages remained indispensable only for training and commanding Indian soldiers. As British ambassador in Cochinchina in 1822, John Crawfurd communicated in Portuguese and hoped to find natives who could do the same. When his delegation moved on to Siam it met a local who spoke fluent Latin.[86] An anecdote reported by Captain Michael Symes, the British emissary to Rangoon, shows just how complicated communication could become in an extreme case. In 1795 Symes encountered a delegation from China at the court of the king of Burma (Ava):

> I spoke in the language of Hindostan to a Mussulman who understood Birman, he delivered it to a Birman who spoke Chinese, this Birman gave it to the first domestic, who repeated it to his master in the Chinese tongue.[87]

It is unclear whether Symes was as satisfied with this game of Chinese whispers as Thomas Manning in Lhasa. Note that the Chinese diplomat considered it beneath his dignity to be addressed by a low-ranked foreigner in the noble language of the Celestial Empire.

A study by Christopher Bayly, finally, conveys a sense of just how much importance was attached to insider sources in India. The great English historian shows how the British successfully tapped into native hierarchies of information transmission in the late eighteenth century.[88] Of particular importance were the "newswriters" at the various Indian courts who penned widely (and half-clandestinely) circulated reports in Persian, the official language of the Mughal Empire and many of its successor states. These correspondents-cum-espionage agents were sent out by rival rulers to gather intelligence on the host state while at the same time disseminating both true and misleading information. They also embodied the political reach of their patron: the more correspondents a prince could place in other capitals without having to make reciprocal arrangements, the greater (at least symbolically) was his political power.[89] The EIC, which mixed in the internal affairs of Indian states with increasing skill and ruthlessness from the 1770s onwards, made use of such informants without relying on them exclusively. They could not be managed, however, without some knowledge of Persian. By the end of the eighteenth century many of the company's higher functionaries had acquired this basic understanding.

It will be recalled that Thomas Manning traveled to Tibet with his "Munshi." In a narrow sense, the term referred to a scribe, secretary, or translator, but it could also be applied to "any respectable, well-educated native gentleman."[90] Munshis were the Indian colonial equivalent to the dragomans in the Ottoman Empire and the court Jesuits in China. However, they played a far more important role in their own society than those two groups, which were both concentrated in their respective capitals. Before the arrival of the British, the Munshis had been able to build up an independent power base through their prowess with the quill and expertise in Indian interstate diplomacy. There had already emerged among them an abstract idea of state service as transcending loyalty to any particular prince.[91] The British first encountered Munshis as teachers of Persian. They then took on a more prominent role as secretaries in the company's administrative apparatus. Even British officials who had a good working knowledge of Persian or Hindustani rarely mastered the subtleties of the formal language spoken at court. Yet in the realm of Islam, as in China and culturally Sinicized Vietnam, successful diplomacy was inconceivable without linguistic correctness. Munshis were therefore indispensable, and those who proved competent and trustworthy commanded both respect and good wages from their employers.[92] For a brief historical moment, the most sophisticated Munshis may even have hoped that, under their tuition, their new masters would come to appreciate the poetically ornate court Persian that was so cherished by the Indian princes. But the Western drive for efficiency soon rationalized away its rhetorical flourishes, reduced it to a prosaic medium of communication, and finally abolished it altogether as an official language in British India.[93]

LANGUAGE BARRIERS

Even if the travel literature has preserved only a few scenes of pantomime such as those that played out between British crews and the Korean coast dwellers in 1816,[94] it is clear that many travelers—including the well-educated—absorbed little of what was going on around them and understood even less for want of linguistic proficiency. The genre tends to brush over this critical point, and travelers are often tempted to lay implicit or even explicit claim to capabilities they could not possibly have possessed. How many of the conversations recorded in the literature were really conducted with such fluency and facility? Thus Sir John Barrow, a member of Lord Macartney's entourage in China, hints in several passages of his much-cited account that he may perhaps have spoken Chinese (he did not). In Vietnam however, where interpreters were even harder to come by than in China and the language perhaps even more difficult to acquire, the awkward truth could not be avoided: "As from our mutual ignorance of each others' language there could be no exchange of conversation, we found little inducement for sitting long at table."[95]

Nonetheless, Barrow observes that it was easier to convey one's meaning through mute pantomime in Vietnam than it was in China. Unlike their Chinese counterparts, Vietnamese officials did not consider it beneath their dignity to communicate by gesture.[96] In general, personal relations in Southeast Asia were less fraught with difficulty than in haughty, protocol-conscious China. In 1822 Dr. Crawfurd was greeted with a warm handshake by a Siamese governor and invited to a banquet bedecked with European silverware.[97] This would have been unthinkable in China, where as late as 1816 the English ambassador, Lord Amherst, had been expected to kowtow nine times before the emperor.

By the second half of the eighteenth century, at the latest, high-minded notions about what it meant to experience a foreign environment required that serious travelers endeavor to learn even difficult languages. There were now no excuses for linguistic ignorance, least of all when illiterate travelers prided themselves on their local knowledge. Not everyone would have agreed with Sir William Jones that, by proceeding methodically, "almost any language may be learned in six months with ease and pleasure."[98] Yet, with a few exceptions that will be discussed later, most travelers would have concurred with his principle "that no satisfactory account can be given of any nation with whose language we are not perfectly acquainted."[99]

There was less agreement concerning the more onerous stipulation that a very long stay, if possible even a government position in the country in question, was a further precondition for arriving at a deep understanding of a non-European country and its language.[100] Many examples could be adduced for fallacies that came about through insufficient or inadequate knowledge of the language in question. It was rightly pointed out that anyone who was incapable of entering into alien worlds of meaning could easily be deceived into taking as bizarre or exotic what in fact bore a rational explanation.[101] Without linguistic knowledge it was barely even possible for travelers in more remote and poorly mapped regions to identify place names. The Danish traveler Frederik Norden encountered this problem in Egypt in 1737: ignorant of Arabic, he frequently had no idea where he was at any given time.[102] The prudent and well-prepared Carsten Niebuhr, by contrast, placed great value on finding out the local toponyms from natives. Niebuhr also draws attention to a deficiency common to almost all native interpreters in the Orient: these people had no knowledge of scientific (e.g., astronomical) terminology.[103] As a good pragmatist, Niebuhr understands that those who fail to learn the local language are restricted in their contacts and informants to the few natives who can express themselves in a European tongue. Yet these are not always the most intelligent, best informed, and most scrupulous members of the society; on the contrary, all too often they are people "who seek out the company of foreigners for their own selfish interests"[104] and take pleasure in pulling the wool over their eyes. In this way, they peddle the most ludicrous ideas to their unsuspecting listeners, who then pass them on to their European readers as established truths.

In addition, Niebuhr shows that while good travel planning is imperative, it is not enough to guarantee successful communication. The academic qualifications of European Orientalists did not necessarily translate to conversational fluency. Recognizing this, Denmark had sent Professor Frederik Christian von Haven, the appointed *philologus* of the Danish expedition to Arabia, to the Maronites in Rome to be taught conversational Arabic—with limited success, unfortunately.[105] Niebuhr himself was no professor, scholar, or high dignitary but a mere surveyor brought along on account of his technical expertise. Although he had learned some Arabic before the expedition, it was only during the voyage that he picked up the Arabic he actually needed to make himself understood by the locals. He seems to have coped quite well, despite struggling with the stylized court language spoken at Sanaa in Yemen, for example.[106] Professor von Haven had pored over the relevant literature back in Europe and now wove some of the phrases he had found there into his conversation. On one occasion, wanting to express himself with exquisite politeness, he had approached some Arabs with the question: "Are your camels faring well?" The inquiry was met with bemusement, and Niebuhr, a farmer's son from Friesland, drew on his healthy common sense to explain the limits of book learning:

> The Orientals have no newspapers. When they meet, they therefore have less to say about politics than we Europeans. The weather is less changeable than it is in Europe, so here too they have less to talk about than we do. Itinerant Arabs like to discuss their trade. Therefore when two Bedouins who know each other's camels or other animals ask each other this question, that is no more out of the ordinary than when farmers in Europe ask each other how their crops are growing, whether their cattle are growing fat, and so on.[107]

Learning a language was a matter of experience.

MIMESIS AND DECEPTION

A traveler's ability to understand the people he talks to in the countries he visits, and preferably to read their texts as well, is—as Sir William Jones and Carsten Niebuhr both emphasize in their own way—the essential condition for any cross-cultural encounter worthy of the name. Linguistic knowledge, however, is rarely distributed evenly. Like all forms of capital, communicative capital is subject to accumulation. Whoever has more of it derives advantages and perhaps even power from the imbalance. Those who can switch effortlessly between languages may consider themselves superior. They live in two worlds, enjoying the benefits that accrue to them by virtue of their deliberate shifts in role and fascinated by their own duplicitious performance. As a secret agent, Alexander Burnes had great fun manipulating the guileless Uzbeks: "Simple people! They believe a spy must measure their forts and walls; they have no idea of the value of conversation."[108]

Language is here a form of disguise. It has become part of a costume, an example of "appropriative mimesis," that is, "imitation in the interest of acquisition," which Stephen Greenblatt sees as an obstacle to any true understanding of the Other.[109] Should one dress like a local when traveling in Asia? This problem of sartorial adaptation to one's surroundings presents itself neither in Europe nor among the "naked savages" of Africa. It is unique to travelers in Asia. The thrill of impersonating natives can only be fully dramatized once the gap separating the two civilizations is perceived to have widened into an unbridgeable chasm. That was not yet the case in the eighteenth century.

Not until the nineteeth century does the image of the dynamic and enterprising Westerner traveling against a static oriental backdrop begin to emerge. European visitors to Asia in the seventeenth and eighteenth century, on the other hand, repeatedly remark on the bustling hubbub of activity on the streets of India, China, or Japan. These societies were extremely mobile. The extended tours of the realm that had almost died out in Europe were still undertaken in grand style by monarchs like the Mughal and Qing emperors. Among the traders, pilgrims, and farmers thronging to the market, a European, particularly if inconspicuously dressed, was only one traveler among many. The community of the transient, since Chaucer a popular setting for works of literature, could be described with appreciation.

In the first place, those who adopted oriental dress were acting pragmatically. It was mainly for this reason that almost all French merchants in the Levant dressed *à la Turque*, albeit often with a powdered wig under their hat or turban.[110] A European *culotte* of the ancien régime was not necessarily the most appropriate garment under tropical conditions. There was much evidence to the contrary, and some doctors blamed the high mortality rate of Europeans in some regions of Asia on their unsuitable apparel. By wearing native clothing, visitors could shield themselves from unwanted curiosity and intrusion, even if they had no wish to give up their own identity as a foreigner in situations of close contact. Sometimes natives also expected foreigners to adapt to their new surroundings in this way. Adaptation did not necessarily entail complete assimilation. Since the Persians kept their heads covered at mealtimes, English ambassadorial staff in the Napoleonic age likewise left their cocked hats on their heads while dining.[111]

Niebuhr went further in this regard than most. He adopted Arabic dress, not just because he recognized the practical advantages it offered but also because he tried in general to adhere as far as possible to local custom.[112] Yet in Iran, where the language was unfamiliar to him, he refrained from wearing the local costume for fear of coming across as an imposter—at the cost of limiting his freedom of movement.[113] It was no mean feat to masquerade convincingly in foreign clothing. Foreigners had to observe the sumptuary laws of their host society and abide by the hierarchy visibly encoded in dress. Where the distribution of sartorial status symbols was dictated by central authority, outsiders had little room for initiative. It could be very useful to be incorporated into the system, though. For the first American delegation to visit Vietnam, it proved highly advantageous that they had been granted the robes of civil mandarins of the second rank.[114]

What appeared in the eighteenth century, in Niebuhr's case, as a sign of particular thoroughness on the traveler's part came in the nineteenth and early twentieth century to indicate either masterful espionage technique (Sir Richard Burton, Charles Doughty, T. E. Lawrence) or eccentric cultural chameleonism. By the 1830s, roughly, no self-respecting missionary would have contemplated following the example of the Jesuits, who had spent some two hundred years clad in the robes of Chinese literati.[115] In India "a cultural imperative of wearing European dress" held sway from the onset of colonial rule in the 1760s.[116] The wearing of Indian clothing on public occasions by EIC officials was prohibited in 1830. This decree was originally directed against Frederick John Shore, a provincial judge who sat in court in Indian robes and spoke out against the institutional bias that saw qualified Indians regularly passed over for promotion in colonial state service.[117] The change in costume foisted on the rebellious judge made the hierarchical relations clear for all to see.

Linguistic proficiency and sartorial adaptation were both ambiguous. They could reduce cultural distance, but they could also increase it. In European travel literature, genuine closeness to the Other is rarely expressed in an unaffected way. Giving the Other an equal voice was problematic. The most beautiful moments in the texts are those when the entanglements of semantics and power are loosened, freeing up space for personal sympathy and the transcultural regularity of play. One of the most touching "discoverer's friendships"[118] was that between George Bogle and the Teshoo (Tashi) Lama (or Panchen Lama), aged around forty at the time. The pair first met at an audience on November 8, 1774, and from then until December 7 kept each other company on numerous informal occasions. They conversed in the Hindustani that the Tashi Lama had learned from his mother, a relative of the raja of Ladakh.[119] Over games of chess, Bogle reached a good understanding with Tibetans who had never before set eyes on a European. The rules of chess transcended cultural differences, likewise helping Samuel Turner, the second British emissary to Tibet, to create an unexpectedly friendly atmosphere in his encounters with the lamas.[120] Everyone was equal at the chessboard, and the lamas provided stiff competition.

A SOCIOLOGY OF PERCEPTION

In what situations and under which conditions did European travelers interact with people in Asia, allowing perceptions of "the Asiatic" to arise? What were they able to see and experience? This question must be posed on a case-by-case, text-by-text basis, and only a few generalizations are possible. Asian countries differed from each other, not only through their accessibility and restrictions on entry, but also through the varying opportunities they afforded visitors to engage with locals. One could imagine a comparative sociology of visibility.

The position held by the guest in his home society was a matter of secondary importance. People in the host nations could infer the status symbols of European societies only imperfectly, if at all. A traveler's social standing therefore tells us little about how he could be expected to be perceived in his new environment; at most, it says something about his educational background. Markers of social status were sloughed off when traveling abroad. Unless he was visiting the colonies, the traveler's social identity became blurred. Gradations in rank were left back home. From the perspective of the natives, the traveler was at first little more than a stranger of indeterminate status.

While colonial societies such as that in British India or the most magnificent European city in Asia, Batavia, appeared to offer more status security, they were not copied directly from a European template. Far from reproducing European hierarchies unchanged, these were societies where many who felt constrained by relations in the home country could rise to a new station in life. A strikingly large proportion of those who embarked on a career in the EIC were unpropertied and untitled lesser scions of the aristocracy and young people from the periphery of the British Isles (that is, Scotland and Ireland).[121] Travelers encountered social fluidity in Asia, not invariance.

Anyone who ventured beyond these relatively small colonial enclaves could not simply expect natives to recognize the rank ascribed to them in their home societies. There may have been the odd exception. James Bruce had broken off his legal studies in Edinburgh and acquired wealth by marrying the daughter (who died soon thereafter) of a wine merchant. He attributed his survival and success on an unusually arduous journey—Volney, who knew a thing or two about travel, called it "the most audacious trip of our century"[122]—to the fact that he always acted the gentleman and therefore everywhere attracted the attention of rulers and aristocrats.[123] Real aristocrats tended to overplay their part at times and were interested almost exclusively in the native nobility: in India they only called on princes.

When foreigners were themselves courtiers, their field of vision narrowed considerably. This was the case for the Jesuits in China during the eighteenth century. The fewer opportunities they were given to pursue mission work in the provinces and the more infrequently they were sent out by the emperor on diplomatic or cartographic missions, the more difficult it became for them to gather first-hand information on everyday life in China. "The very gravity of their character," says the literary critic and Sinophile Thomas Percy, prevented them from entering Chinese private dwellings.[124] It was somewhat easier for merchants and passing travelers to gain insight into how ordinary people lived in Canton and Macau; but the very different image that resulted was no less one-sided than the high-cultural elite perspective of the later Jesuits. Ambassadorial travelers were especially restricted in what they could observe. They were permanently accompanied by military escorts and designated native attendants who could serve them as informants, and they had audiences with dignitaries at various levels of the native hierarchy. Officials rarely dropped the mask of inscrutability in their company, scholars showed little interest in them, and of the urban middle and lower classes—not to mention the peasant majority—they perceived little more than an amorphous crowd.[125]

Being gawked at by such a crowd "as if we had been some strange Africk monsters,"[126] being jostled by curious onlookers, or even having their wigs pulled at or their stockings examined,[127] was a source of constant irritation and outrage to traveling emissaries. As particular objects of public spectacle, they clung to their dignity all the more tenaciously. Few were prepared to concede that an Asian delegation to Europe would attract just as much attention.[128] But several saw advantages in being observed: it facilitated their own observations. "The general desire to see us," remarked Mountstuart Elphinstone in Afghanistan in 1809, "gave us opportunities of observing almost all descriptions of men."[129] And George Bogle, the most well-meaning traveler of them all, maintained that curiosity was a sign of civility that acquired polish only through practice; the Tibetans were therefore not to blame for mobbing the first European they came across in the initial onrush of their enthusiasm.[130]

There was one role that allowed travelers to get especially close to the host population: that of doctor. The most illustrious position was as personal physician to the ruler, an appointment that brought access to the inner court and sometimes even to the strictly segregated harem. François Bernier served the great mughal Aurangzeb in this capacity for eight years, accompanying him on his many campaigns in India. Bernier also relates how his expertise as a healer allowed him to avoid being taken captive by the marauding Koullys.[131] The tale was often told of how ladies of the harem who had fallen ill could not even have their pulse taken by the court physician. They remained fully veiled throughout the examination under the watchful eye of the eunuchs.[132] In all parts of Asia, locals frequently came to European travelers requesting medical advice and assistance. For inquisitive natural scientists like Johann Georg Gmelin, this was a welcome opportunity for pathological and epidemological inquiry.[133] Thomas Manning began his medical studies in England with the intention of making himself welcome and useful as a doctor in Asia. In Tibet he grew tired of the crush of patients; by charging a small fee he was able to regulate demand for his services.[134] The veterinarian and sometime director of the EIC stud, William Moorcroft, was so appalled by the health of the civilian population in Ladakh and Afghanistan that he delayed his journey considerably to perform hundreds of cataract operations.[135] In many places it was clearly believed that Europeans were endowed with healing powers. Failure to possess such powers could be compensated in part through pantomime.[136] The botanist Adelbert von Chamisso, who took part from 1815 to 1818 in Otto von Kotzebue's Russian voyage of discovery, advised the prospective traveler:

> wherever human beings are to be found, the name and reputation of a doctor will be his surest passport and writ of safe conduct, and will secure him the most reliable and bountiful income.[137]

The traveler-physician had extraordinarily good prospects for observation in societies that looked to Western medicine for help (something that appears to have been the case only rarely in China and Japan). It was easy for him to collect natural specimens without drawing undue attention to himself.[138] His social role was quickly determined wherever he went. Here was an observer who not only looked and acted as he traveled but lent a helping hand as well. An element of reciprocity thus entered into the relationship between the passing or resident foreigner and the native environment. The traveler-physician, unlike the globetrotter, botanist, or collector of antiquities, was directly and demonstrably useful. Where others merely took, he gave as well.

VI

Eyewitnesses—Earwitnesses

Experiencing Asia

But I had reason to believe, that all the nations of the South Seas were formerly cannibals, even in the most happy and fertile climates, where they still live upon almost spontaneous fruits, though their population be extremely great. The natives of Tanna gave us more than once to understand, that if we penetrated far into the country against their will, and without their permission, they would kill us, cut our bodies up, and eat them: when we purposely affected to misunderstand this last part of their story, and interpreted it, as if they were going to give us something good to eat, they convinced us by signs which could not be misinterpreted, that they would tear with their teeth the flesh from our arms and legs.

—Johann Reinhold Forster (1729–98), *Bemerkungen über Gegenstände der physischen Erdbeschreibung, Naturgeschichte und sittlichen Philosophie, auf seiner Reise um die Welt gesammlet*[1]

A typical situation from a famous travel account: what is here described for the South Seas could have taken place anywhere in Asia or Africa. The writer is a respected scientist, anything but gullible, and spends his days measuring, observing, drawing, and collecting all sorts of natural and man-made objects. But there is a powerful rumor, so strong that even the scientist believes it in the absence of any evidence. No eyewitness is available to corroborate what hearsay suggests. The rumor gives rise to a scene of speechless pantomime. The natives have their own interests and they know how to defend them rationally, albeit with irrational means. Whether or not they are cannibals, myth is on their side in this game of deterrence and psychological warfare.

GIANTS AND UNICORNS

During the eighteenth century, Asia became for educated Europeans ever less a realm of fantasy and ever more a vast quarry of materials for studying the human race and the history of human civilization. Like all other sciences of the time, this field of inquiry fell under the imperative of empiricism. Empiricism also left its mark on fictional literature. The more authors learned from travelers' reports about faraway lands, the greater was the temptation for them to choose exotic settings for their literary works. At the same time, the demand for verisimilitude was voiced with growing insistence. The literary Orient could never be true, but it should at least be presented truthfully. In researching his tragedy *Bajazet* (1672), set in a Turkish court milieu, Racine had already consulted the recent French translation of Sir Paul Rycaut's *Present State of the Ottoman Empire.*[2] Montesquieu did not simply "invent" the Iran of his traveling Persians, Rica and Usbek; he drew on news reports that had been brought back by travelers from the Islamic world. Decades later, Johann Wolfgang von Goethe, the leading poet of his age, studied the works of Adam Olearius, Sir William Jones, Joseph von Hammer-Purgstall, Jean-Pierre Abel-Rémusat, and other Orientalists in order to give the poems of the *West-East Divan* (1819/1827) as authentically Persian, Indian, or Chinese a coloring as possible. He considered these comprehensive studies important enough to have them published alongside the poems. Readers were invited to familiarize themselves with the unknown poetic worlds of the East while following Goethe in the footsteps of his own recent literary and historical discoveries.[3] Other early nineteenth-century authors liberally sprinkled their literary works set in Asia with footnotes directing readers to the relevant scholarly literature. Examples include Lord Byron's *Childe Harold's Pilgrimage* (1812–18), Thomas Moore's *Lalla Rookh: An Oriental Romance* (1817), and Alexander Pushkin's *Kavkazkij plennik* (*The Prisoner of the Caucasus*, 1822).[4] This literature seeks a status poised indeterminately between fact and fiction. It toys with the ambivalence of the imaginary and the authentic without ever assimilating science to art. Descriptive literature's claim to say something about the "real" Orient is endorsed to the extent that it is recognized as an autonomous sphere of knowledge. The poets can no longer invent Asia because the geographers and Orientalists purport to have already found it.

Since the great circumnavigations had laid to rest old hopes of a great southern land or *Terra australis*, the geographical worldview had become finite. The continents were now definitively known in their outlines and spatial distribution. There were still many niches of foreignness in this finite world, many unmapped spaces: ethnography and fantasy flowed together in the island utopias, those great articulations of eighteenth-century longing. Yet the same natural laws obtained everywhere on Earth, compelling even writers of fiction to conform to the rules of plausibility and acknowledge the persuasive force of hard factual evidence.

Many examples could be cited in support of this. In an anonymous text from 1679, the Chinese are said to "push their children's noses flat."[5] None of the seventeenth-century Jesuit reports contain such an absurdity. In 1768, anyone who still believed that people with tails existed on Formosa and the Philippines (as reported by older travel writers) did so primarily to shore up the theological notion of an uninterrupted "Great Chain of Being."[6] Another case was notorious: ever since the first circumnavigations of South America, one traveler after another claimed to have seen or even spoken with giants of superhuman stature in Patagonia. In the 1760s these "giants" were finally measured and cut down to normal human size.[7] With that, the fable of the giants came crashing down to earth. The case of that famous creature of medieval legend, the unicorn, was more complicated. Since nobody had ever seen a unicorn or unearthed a skeleton, the hypothesis of its existence proved impossible to refute. Perhaps it was simply good at hiding. In 1780 Eberhardt August von Zimmermann, a privy councilor from Brunswick and pioneer of animal geography (and certainly no fantasist), discussed the problem at length, cautioning readers not to regard the case as closed until Central Asia and Africa had been thoroughly explored.[8] Samuel Turner almost tracked down the elusive animal in 1783. The raja of Bhutan claimed to own a specimen. While this might have prompted many sixteenth-century travelers to report back to Europe that there were unicorns roaming the Himalayas, Turner limited himself to a laconic negative finding: the raja made much of his precious animal, "but I never had a sight of it."[9] Further speculation was thereby ruled out. The traveler's sober gaze now rested on a disenchanted world, one from which the last unicorn had fled.

In the second half of the eighteenth century, at the latest, the only news from Asiatic countries that counted was that which had been confirmed by direct experience of reality. Such experience had, as Joseph von Hammer-Purgstall succinctly puts it, two legitimate sources: "eyewitness testimony and book learning."[10] How could even the most erudite interpreter of a foreign country produce valuable work when his procedures as a traveler left much to be desired; when he—as Sir James Porter, the British ambassador in Istanbul, complained in 1755—offered "descriptions" of parts of a country that he had demonstrably traversed at night?[11]

PREJUDICES AND PRECONCEPTIONS

In the eighteenth century there was something like a relatively coherent "grand theory" of overseas travel, a norm that the period's most ambitious travelers kept at the forefront of their attention. It was no longer enough to be impelled by sheer curiosity. Travelers could now be classified into two broad camps according to whether their motives were base or noble.[12] The former category—the "low" travelers—encompasses all those who leave their native shores for selfish reasons such as thirst for adventure, frivolity, boredom, avarice, wanderlust, or heartache. The "high" travelers, on the other hand, those "with more elevated outlooks and firmer principles,"[13] are prepared to undergo any sacrifice and endure any hardship in their pursuit of idealistic and altruistic goals. They set out with the intention of "conquering" new realms for European science, drawing moral lessons from their observations of foreign climes, spreading the Christian religion, and promoting the "improvement of manners" by carrying the torch of Enlightenment wherever they go. From around 1800 these apostles of progress then increasingly make it their mission to serve their nation and the public good. Several travelers go beyond this frequently repeated canon of pious intentions. As widely traveled and well-read experts on the East, they see themselves as "spokesmen for the Orientals among us."[14] In their view, the traveler's task is to defend distant peoples against European prejudice,[15] and more generally to overcome cultural hubris and remove obstacles to intercultural understanding.[16] At the start of his *Lettres sur l'Égypte* (1785–86), Claude Étienne Savary declares travel to be "the most instructive school of mankind" (*l'école la plus instructive de l'homme*): it helps voyagers shed their prejudices, gain critical distance from their homeland, and burst the bonds "that keep reason fettered to custom." Any traveler in whom the right attitude is backed up by meticulous preparation—Savary himself spoke excellent Arabic—is qualified to be a "world citizen," a *citoyen de l'univers*.[17]

A pen portrait of the "high" traveler was provided in 1789 by Anquetil-Duperron, who on his travels in India himself combined lofty motives with a "low," down-to-earth traveling style:

> The true traveler is someone who loves all men as his brothers and who, untouched by pleasures and needs, beyond grandeur and baseness, praise and blame, riches and poverty, passes through the world without striking root in any particular place, witnessing good and evil without regard to who caused it and the causes peculiar to each nation: this traveler, if he is well-educated and sound in judgment, will instantly grasp what is ridiculous and untrue in any given procedure, custom, or opinion.[18]

Anquetil-Duperron is sketching an idealized image here: that of the well-prepared, linguistically assured traveler who constantly seeks out contact with locals, disregards consideration of his own person, and watchfully immerses himself in his surroundings without suspending his critical faculties. Precisely by purging himself of his own base motives and refusing to ascribe the behavior he observes in others to their "cultural background," the ideal traveler gains a spontaneous, quasi-naïve capacity for discrimination. In this view, the traveler proceeds in three steps: first he must free himself from prejudice and any other factors that blinker his perception; then he must make his own observations; finally he has earned the right to pronounce judgment on what he sees, no longer speaking as a culturally conditioned European but with the voice of reason itself.

The first step sets apart the high traveler from the low. The former makes an effort to put his own interests to one side. Liberated from the petty concerns of the self, he looks out into the world with a clinically dispassionate gaze. We find one of the earliest formulations of this epistemo-anthropological ideal in the introduction written by Robert Hooke, secretary of the Royal Society, to the report on Ceylon by the shipwrecked captain's son, Robert Knox (1681). Not only lovers of adventure will profit from Knox's account, Hooke argues, but also serious friends of truth:

> I believe at least all that love Truth will be pleas'd; for from that little Conversation I had with him I conceive him to be in no way prejudiced or byassed by Interest, affection or hatred, fear or hopes, or the vain-glory of telling Strange Things, so as to make him swerve from the truth of Matter of Fact.[19]

The opposite of such objectivity is prejudice, most blatantly expressed in judgments based on inflated subjective experience rather than on universally valid rational insight. One reviewer remarks ironically of a traveler who had set out for China resolved to find nothing there to his liking: "if the people happen to be noisy, it is the character of the nation."[20] The traveler predisposed to negativity will be confirmed in his outlook by every unpleasant encounter he makes along the way.

Among eighteenth-century travelers, freedom from prejudice is equated with fairness toward foreign manners and an impartial detachment from one's own. Above all, it entails a determination not to force the Other into naïve, pre-"philosophical" European categories.[21] Pushed to its logical conclusion, this idea would make comparison invalid. "In representing foreign manners," the unfashionably Turcophile Thomas Thornton observes in 1809, "I have divested myself of national prejudices: in describing foreign religions I have not confronted them with the opinions and practices of other sects or persuasions."[22] Thornton joins Anquetil-Duperron in emphasizing the effort such a feat of cognitive self-overcoming demands:

> To describe with impartiality a people among whom every thing is contradictory to our usages, though not perhaps more repugnant to reason, requires a superiority to prejudice, a sobriety of observation, and a patience of inquiry, which few travelers possess.[23]

The supreme form of this effort, openly attempted by very few travelers, is self-correction from prejudice: a greater moral accomplishment than the dubious exercise of attaining freedom from prejudice *a priori*. Samuel Turner was one such self-critical traveler. The diplomat admits that "a rash and hasty inference" led him to cast overly harsh judgment on the Bhutanese, although he changed his mind as he continued on his Himalayan journey. In another passage, Turner regrets that, despite the best will in the world, he could not bring himself to enjoy the taste of raw meat. He made several attempts but to no avail.[24] And Carsten Niebuhr no doubt aimed at exerting a pedagogical influence on a public still wedded to crude stereotypes when he confessed: "I too entertained such horrible ideas about the Mohammedans when I first stayed in Constantinople," but these were soon rectified.[25]

There was need for such impartiality elsewhere than in the relationship between East and West. It would be wrong to assume that only

Europe and foreign civilizations were placed at opposite ends of a spectrum of values. Within Europe itself, sharply delineated and normatively freighted national stereotypes arose in tandem with the developing dynastic nation-states. Before Enlightenment cosmopolitanism could work its mollifying touch, for example, many English authors heaped greater scorn on the "Papist" French than on the Turks, and a man like Alexander Hamilton, not exactly a champion of Asians, was far more passionate in his hatred of the Portuguese, the Jesuits, and the EIC.

Impartiality extended beyond the observer's relationship to the object of knowledge. It could also mean something else: criticism of the real or imagined shortcomings of *other* observers. Writers demonstrated their own superior vision by exposing the blind spots, misperceptions, and illusions of their precursors and rivals. By drawing attention to the mind-forged manacles that held others captive, they hoped to free themselves from such constraints and bolster the credibility of their own, supposedly more clear-eyed perspective. This argumentative strategy worked less by exposing the factual errors made by others than by discrediting their motives.

The Jesuits in China had begun early on to call into question the reliability of mariners' and merchants' reports, not entirely without reason.[26] They themselves came in the firing line in the second half of the eighteenth century. At first even their Protestant opponents were reluctantly prepared to concede the Jesuits' superiority to all other commentators on the Middle Kingdom.[27] In 1773 the Dutch ex-priest Cornelius de Pauw launched a spirited attack on the Jesuits' credibility, although this did not stop him from using their findings when they supported his negative view of China. De Pauw attacked the Jesuits at the point where their "prejudice" must have seemed most glaringly obvious to an enlightened public: their Catholic faith naturally inclined them to take miracle stories at face value.[28] His polemic did indeed strike the Fathers at a number of vulnerable places, particularly their weakness for embellishment and an erudition that all too often came across as leaden and pedantic rather than elegantly up-to-date. But his plan to give an unvarnished account of

China "as it is" (*suivant les faits*) ultimately fell short of its objective. The Jesuit counterattack rebutted his criticisms with relative ease, although its effectiveness was limited by a lack of publicity.[29] De Pauw's reputation only began to decline shortly before his death in 1799, when reports sent back by the Macartney Mission—by no means favorably predisposed towards China and the Jesuits—partially confirmed the Jesuit account. For example, whereas de Pauw had estimated the Chinese population at an absurdly low eighty-two million, Macartney and his retinue accepted the figure four times higher (and far closer to today's best estimates), which Pater Amiot had calculated on the basis of Chinese sources.[30]

The French naturalist and naval commander, Pierre Sonnerat, was another author who prided himself on his freedom from prejudice. Unlike de Pauw, he had at least seen Canton firsthand before he pilloried the Jesuits, alleging that their show of Christian selflessness was merely a front for their scheme to subject the world to theocratic rule. Their idealized China, he maintained, represented the utopia of a soft despotism over a people kept permanently befuddled by clouds of incense.[31] The most vociferous critic of China among those who took part in the Macartney Mission, John Barrow, accused the Jesuits of tactics and opportunism: while they may not have consciously peddled falsehoods, they suppressed many (although not all) negative reports in a bid to avoid jeopardizing their good relations with the imperial household. The Jesuits had been taken in by the Chinese self-interpretation—in other words, they had adopted their hosts' own prejudices about themselves. The clear-sighted commentator, by contrast, regards foreigners "not as their own moral maxims would represent them, but as they really are."[32] With that, epistemological space had been cleared for the "philosophical" observer, perched in his watchtower far above the fray of competing cultures and beholden only to his own rationality.

To eliminate prior *judgments* is not the same as to dispense with prior *knowledge*, however. Here a dilemma comes into play that was never quite resolved in theory, even if many authors managed to find a way around it in their literary practice. On the one hand, an inordinate amount of mental baggage (in the form of excessive book learning) could make it more difficult for travelers to pick up fresh insights. On the other hand, true understanding could not be had without prior knowledge. Those who set out into the world uninformed (and thus also undeformed) risked seeing much and grasping little.

Declarations of impartiality could also serve as a façade for plagiarism. François Leguat, a French Protestant who somehow ended up island-hopping in the Indian Ocean, asserts in his fairly racy report that he deliberately avoided reading earlier descriptions that might interfere with his immediate impressions. It eventually came to light that precisely the opposite was true: Leguat, celebrated for his depictions of nature, had shown unusual audacity—as well as considerable literary skill—in stealing from earlier authors.[33] The abbé Jean-Antoine Dubois presents a rather different case. Fleeing the French Revolution, the cleric spent more than seventeen years living in southern India, mainly in Mysore. In 1808 he sold a lengthy manuscript to the EIC in Madras describing Hindu manners and customs in unprecedented detail. In 1817 the manuscript appeared in English translation at company expense; seven years later, an extended French edition was published by the Royal Printing Office in Paris. This in turn formed the basis for the new English translation of 1898. An ethnological classic, it has since been reprinted many times—not least in India, where the abbé enjoys lasting esteem thanks to the empathy of his descriptions. The abbé claimed to have immersed himself in his Indian surroundings without the least impediment from book learning. He had brought only his Bible with him into exile and professed to have known very little about India and its people before the voyage out. Having arrived there, "I made it my constant rule to live as they did, conforming exactly in all things to their manners, to their style of living and clothing, and even to most of their prejudices."[34] The EIC directors recognized the value of so extended and intensive a practice of participant observation, something they clearly deemed the British incapable of emulating. They purchased the manuscript chiefly because "the absolute retirement of the Author from European society, for a series of years, well qualified him for penetrating into the dark and unexplored recesses of the Indian character."[35] Unprejudiced observation seemed to plumb depths inaccessible to those who came to India forearmed with knowledge. As late as 1898 Professor Max Müller, the doyen of English Indology, praised Dubois as an all-but-unrivaled witness of Indian customs, better equipped than almost any other foreigner "to enter into the views of the natives."[36] No further obstacle stood between the abbé and immortal fame. Not until the 1980s was it discovered that Dubois had passed off as his own a manuscript written by Pater Gaston-Laurent Cœurdoux, a Jesuit active in India between 1734 and 1779.[37]

While few went so far as to extol the virtues of ignorance, there were frequent complaints that preparatory study of the regions to be visited could dull perception. The following statement by Ulrich Jasper Seetzen, a German traveler to the Orient, is typical:

> By previously acquiring a fairly clear notion through descriptions, copperplates, etc. of the sights we will come across at some point or other on our travels, the first impression they make on us loses a great deal of its force, and our manner of writing on them will be found to be less lively; in short, our description will necessarily forfeit something of its spontaneity.[38]

In keeping with the consensus of the time, Seetzen nonetheless insists on the need "to become acquainted through prior reading with what is most characteristic of a region or country and thereby attain a state of heightened attentiveness."[39] Anyone who neglected to do so had to face the consequences. These were grave indeed in the case of Count Yury Golovkin, leader of the Russian embassy to China in 1805. Having deliberately kept himself in the dark about China in order to experience the country free of any preconceptions, he promptly fell into a series of traps regarding questions of protocol from which even his learned advisers were powerless to extricate him.[40] Golovkin's willful refusal to do his homework was one of the main reasons why his diplomatic mission ended in failure. In 1794 the catastrophic Dutch embassy to the court in Peking met a similar fate. Its second-in-command prided himself on not having read a single book on China in twenty years, with predictable results for the success of the mission.[41] By and large, eighteenth-century travelers who stylized themselves as naïve commanded scant respect from the public and vanished into the netherworld of colportage publications. The "high" traveler was expected to be erudite, well-prepared, *and* free of prejudice.

AUTOPSY

In the second step in Anquetil-Duperron's three-stage model of "high" travel, the purified traveler finds himself confronted with reality, which he is now charged with observing and describing with the utmost precision. His self-imposed task is "to see distinctly and accurately, to describe plainly, dispassionately and truly."[42] There had been sharp-eyed observers with far-reaching pretensions to factual accuracy ever since Europeans first began sending reports from overseas. The *will* to realism was not invented in the Age of Enlightenment; it can already be found in many early seventeenth-century travelers[43]—even before the appearance of the great empiricists at the end of the century: Kaempfer, La Loubère, de Bruin, William Dampier, Tavernier. Nobody, Hammer-Purgstall maintains in 1822, has ever written a more demonstrably accurate description of Constantinople than that furnished by Gylles in 1632.[44] From around 1670, an empiricist approach to knowledge is all but unchallenged: the authority of the classical sources and the modern *érudits* is to be tested against the yardstick of experience.[45] William Milburn's monumental work, *Oriental Commerce* (1813), represents a high point of empiricism. On the basis of seven journeys through numerous parts of Asia between Bombay and Canton as well as a decades-long pursuit of materials, the great cities of Asia are described here with painstaking attention to detail and without the slightest hint of the exotic or the judgmental.[46]

The key to high travel, as domesticated by science, was method. Autopsy—Hammer-Purgstall's *Selbstansicht*—was crucial here. Ever since Herodotus, travelers had placed importance on firsthand observation.

Only what the visitor had seen with his own eyes appeared at least to be *capable* of being true, even if the mere fact of its having been observed did not necessarily *make* it true: whether the observer exaggerated, misunderstood, or lied about what he saw was a different matter. "Sightseeing" was supposed to be a pathway to truth, not an end in itself. The separation between sight-seeing and truth-seeking was first made by Chateaubriand in 1811: "I looked out for pictures, nothing more."[47]

In the eighteenth century, the superiority of eyewitness evidence over hearsay and book learning stood beyond dispute. Great travelers like Niebuhr, Volney, and the Persian scholar James Baillie Fraser were unanimous on this point.[48] To be sure, merely claiming to have seen something with one's own eyes was not enough to satisfy a post-rhetorical age. Critics were only too ready to express their doubts. Gemelli Careri's deserved posthumous fame took a battering on this score. He was simply following a time-honored convention when he assured his readers: "I never take things to be true which I have not seen."[49] But it was not difficult to identify passages he had copied verbatim from other travelers, and someone who, around 1700, had probably traveled more widely than anyone else on Earth was accounted a fraud on the basis of this one lie. James Bruce, an uncommonly honest and educated traveler, spent years defending his reputation following his return from Ethiopia and the Sudan in 1773, as influential contemporaries and sections of the English press attacked the plausibility of many of his depictions of African customs. These were eventually confirmed by later visitors to the same areas, leading to his rehabilitation as one of the most significant overland travelers of his time.[50]

If the old rhetorical procedures for authenticating the truth were no longer accepted, new ways had to be found. Authors frequently sought to demonstrate their truthfulness by acknowledging the limits of their optical horizon. During his circumnavigation of the world, Captain Shelvocke lay sick in his cabin in Canton Harbor and therefore saw nothing of China; he thought it more advisable to admit this openly rather than relay secondhand information.[51] Henry Ellis, a diplomat who visited

China in 1816, even adverts to a problem that must have been widespread and opens up a hair-raising perspective on the entire genre of travel writing: he was short-sighted and had trouble with his spectacles.[52] Travelers more often mention what they would like to have seen but never got around to seeing: the inside of a Turkish harem, a divine judgment in Siam, the rhinoceros on Java "about which many authors have written."[53] Some authors, although not many, pondered more fundamental epistemological questions. William Hodges, a reflective painter, asked himself whether too long a stay in the Orient, far from deepening insight, might be detrimental to the soul, robbing earlier impressions of their freshness while intensifying a tendency to vacuous profundity.[54] In 1769 Louis Castilhon voiced a radically skeptical suspicion: what if the people of Asia were staging a gigantic theatrical performance for their European audience? Indeed, what if "oriental despotism" were nothing more than an act put on for the titillation of sensation-seeking foreigners?[55]

Still others were honest enough to admit that they did not *understand* what they were witnessing and describing. Thomas Manning, it will be recalled, stood nonplussed before the Potala Palace in Lhasa. Frère Jean-Denis Attiret had been engaged through the Jesuits as court painter in Peking. In 1754, shortly after arriving in China, he was commissioned to paint a procession of the Qianlong emperor. What the poor man saw was not the dignified and orderly ceremony he had surely been expecting but instead a mass of people rushing about in no apparent order: "Everything he perceived appeared to him as tumult, confusion, chaos. . . . He saw everything yet he saw nothing."[56] In the end, though, the emperor was not entirely displeased with Attiret's picture. Why? Qianlong had already had some experience with Western painting and its alien techniques for representing reality. As the chief actor in the events depicted, the emperor could thus put down any inaccuracies in their portrayal to cultural differences.

Johann Georg Gmelin, for his part, shows great relish in describing the ritual slaughter of a ram in a Siberian Tatar village but freely admits having failed to grasp its meaning: "It would be good to describe the ceremony with some inkling of its religious significance. Since I have received no information on that head, I will simply relate what I saw."[57] Gmelin neither dismisses the rite as primitive nonsense ("superstition") nor imposes his own theory on it by force. He abstains from judgment and sticks to registering what happened without embellishment. As we can see, not all Europeans explained away foreign customs with high-handed "philosophical" commentary that purported to reach through the veil of appearances to the very heart of things. The autopsy is nowhere more honest than where the author lavishes descriptive attention even on what strikes him as incomprehensible.

BEFORE THE TRIBUNAL OF PHILOSOPHY

In Anquetil-Duperron's portrait of the "true traveler," a third stage follows self-purification from prejudice and eyewitness observation: that of judgment. The scientific observer becomes a philosophical traveler by applying his critical faculties. This involves evaluating what he has seen by measuring it against the yardstick of reason. The professional traveler cannot rest content with merely registering reality as if it were a sharply defined object caught in his lens; ultimately, the restraint shown by Gmelin in the Tatar village does not go far enough. Contemporary readers expected travelers to provide substantiated criticism of foreign conditions and, where possible, to identify lessons to be learned for Europe. Of course, this did not mean adopting a schoolmasterly tone and applying European normative standards to foreign lands. But nor did it mean remaining neutral under all circumstances. Travelers should call improprieties and injustices by name, denounce native tyrants, and not gloss over misdeeds committed by fellow Europeans. This ideal of rational judgment based on informed observation is a product of the *late* Enlightenment. Some travelers—we will meet them again in subsequent chapters—were praised for closely approximating to such an ideal of the "philosophical" observer: Anquetil-Duperron himself; Volney, who traveled through Syria and Egypt; the intrepid voyager to Arabia, Carsten Niebuhr; the Forsters (father and son), who sailed to the South Pacific with Captain Cook on the *Resolution*; William Marsden, author of a report on Sumatra; or Alexander von Humboldt.

Only a few came so close to attaining this high ideal. The whole program of Europeans going forth into the world to submit all they surveyed to the tribunal of reason rested on shaky ground. Anyone who misunderstood or misused it could draw the conclusion that Anquetil-Duperron's first and second stages—purification from prejudice and eyewitness testimony—were optional: all that mattered was the final verdict. An author like John Barrow, for example, who had accompanied Lord Macartney to China in 1793/94, allowed description to be overshadowed by evaluation. In his account, judgment does not follow from a presentation of the facts, it precedes it. Material inspected in the field often served no other purpose than to illustrate apodictic judgments about the degree to which the Chinese satisfied (or failed to satisfy) European criteria for civilized behavior. An openly judgmental attitude was discredited by the practice of "philosophical" salon travelers, such as the aforementioned Cornelius de Pauw. Undeterred by having seen almost nothing of the world, he took delight in casting drastic (and oft-cited) judgment on the Chinese and indigenous Americans. In general, verdicts of this kind tended to be more favored by armchair travelers than by itinerant scholars. Examples of the former include the Göttingen anthropologist, Christoph Meiners, and especially the Anglo-Scottish historian James Mill.

In 1817 Mill, father of the philosopher and economist John Stuart Mill and himself a political theorist of note, published a *History of British India* in three volumes. It was destined to become the nineteenth century's most influential British book on India. For decades to come, aspiring EIC administrators were introduced to subcontinental history and politics with the aid of Mill's work. His literary achievement helped the author secure a career in the London headquarters of the EIC. Eventually he was appointed chief examiner, a kind of state secretary for Indian affairs.

James Mill's *History* is more than a historical narrative in the manner of later nineteenth-century historicism. Its first five hundred pages provide a systematic exposition of precolonial Hindu civilization in India. To this day, Mill is notorious in India for his frontal attack on Indian civilization, which he sees in large part as worthless and incapable of reform. The very complicated background to this verdict need not concern us here.[58] At issue instead is the remarkable way he evaluates his sources. Like Edmund Burke, the great expert on India from the previous generation, Mill never set foot in India. Indian languages and Persian—indispensable for the study of Mughal sources—were equally unknown to him. He was, however, intimately familiar with both the Western literature on India and the EIC's administrative records, which were voluminous even at the time. He also profited from the research findings of the circle of scholars around Sir William Jones, who since 1788 had edited the *Asiatick Researches* from Calcutta. In addition, he had read widely on other Asian countries, allowing him to pepper his *History* with comparative remarks. In short, James Mill was a well-informed and cultivated author.

The fact that his knowledge of India was acquired second- or thirdhand ought to have given Mill cause for caution and modesty. He was, after all, lacking all the prerequisites for judging an alien civilization stipulated by Anquetil-Duperron (and, more generally, the travel theory of the late Enlightenment). Far from acknowledging his limitations, however, Mill turned the tables by challenging the fitness to judge of travelers and Orientalists alike. Travelers and eyewitnesses, along with translators of oriental chronicles and manuscripts, were afflicted by a kind of blindness born of excessive proximity. Having glimpsed only small excerpts of reality, they seemed only too eager to leap to general conclusions. Even a skilled observer who had spent half a lifetime in India studying the native languages and collecting information was by no means thereby qualified to occupy the higher seat of judgment:

> But the mental habits which are acquired in mere observing, and in the acquisition of languages, are almost as different as any mental

> habits can be, from the powers of combination, discrimination, classification, judgment, comparison, weighing, inferring, inducting, philosophizing in short; which are the powers of most importance for extracting the precious ore from a great mine of rude historical materials.[59]

The historian, as conceived by James Mill, is a judge who summons eye- and earwitnesses before his tribunal to provide, from their limited perspectives, the "fragments of information," which he then fits piece by piece into his grand mosaic.[60] Only the "philosophically" oriented historian, privileged through his spatial and intellectual distance from the objects he contemplates, can gain a sovereign overview. He alone has sufficient insight—through his understanding of human nature, politics, and society, his knowledge of causes, effects, and anthropological laws—to impart meaning to the pieces of evidence brought before him.

With James Mill's self-conscious rejection of the senses, the claim to a "philosophical" evaluation of civilizations becomes unmoored from its basis in experience. At the close of the Enlightenment era, the enlightened reasoning that Mill still claimed to espouse loses contact with reality. Mill's unorthodox methodology was not widely emulated. Even at the time, the ideal of a theory-free empiricism that collects facts and lets them speak for themselves was already gaining ground. This was the approach taken by Mountstuart Elphinstone in his important report on Afghanistan, which appeared two years before Mill's *History of India*.[61] The advantage of this approach was that it prevented lesser minds than Mill's from indulging in the kind of empty bombast that could only lead to embarrassment. One such example is Dr. John Crawfurd. This learned and far-from-closed-minded diplomat divided his book on Siam (published in 1828) into two parts: a report on his travels and a systematic account of the country. The report paints a generally friendly picture of the Siamese people. Crawfurd's relations with them were mostly pleasant and he made some effort to engage with their cultural practices and traditions. In the systematic part, by contrast, he arrives at extremely negative judgments that are rooted in nothing more solid than his own tendentious "philosophizing." The unity of the Enlightenment ideal of the "true traveler" had been torn asunder.

METHODS OF THE INQUISITIVE CLASS

Observations are ephemeral, memories deceptive. Who would trust a traveler who committed his impressions to paper years after the event, even claiming to recall the exact wording of his conversations? The greater the public demand for empirical evidence, the more willing travelers were to share *how* they recorded their observations.[62] James Bruce wrote up everything he had seen as soon as he possibly could. Whenever he returned home from a walk through Istanbul, Hammer-Purgstall would betake himself directly to his writing desk. In China, Osbeck allegedly scribbled notes in his pocket to avoid being taken for a spy. Niebuhr greatly regretted not having made notes on mores and customs during the first phase of the Danish expedition to Arabia, when Professor von Haven, the member responsible for ethnography, was still alive.[63] In the early nineteenth century the genres of travel writing then gradually become more differentiated. In the 1830s, Andrew Smith brought back with him from his expedition into the South African interior a diary with field notes, a fleshed-out "journal," and a summary report.[64]

Optimizing the success of observations made in the field was something not entirely left to the discretion and perspicacity of individual travelers. From early on, an apodemics—a methodization of academic travel—had begun to be elaborated in Europe. Addressed to the young gentlemen sent off on the obligatory grand tour, it sought to awaken in them a sense of the seriousness of travel, proposing advice on how they could derive the greatest possible educational benefit from their trip.[65] Prescriptions that had initially been devised for conditions within Europe could equally be applied to transcivilizational journeys. On a tour of the Orient from 1620 to 1625 that took him via Asia Minor and Iran all the way to the interior of southern India, the Silesian nobleman Heinrich von Poser strictly adhered to the apodemic instructions set out in the literature of the time.[66] Questionnaires offered a tried-and-tested means for systematizing perceptions from abroad. In the thirteenth century, Pope Innocent IV provided his informants with lists of questions in an effort to find out as much as possible about the Mongol invaders who were threatening Christendom. "Modern ethnology," comments one historian, "would be hard put to come up with more precise or more comprehensive questions; the essential criteria for grasping a large social unit have here been formulated."[67] In the seventeenth century the VOC instructed several of its employees to fill out questionnaires about different countries in Asia. François Caron, who spent twenty-two years working for the VOC in Japan, was inspired by thirty-one questions sent to him by Philip Lucas, general director of the VOC in Batavia, to write the seventeenth century's most instructive report on Japan by a nonmissionary author (written after 1636, published in 1645).[68] Lucas's questions are those of a man who knows nothing whatsoever about the country he is asking about. He is interested, for example, in "how big the land of Japan is, and whether it is an island," how crimes are punished and inheritances regulated, and which goods the country imports and exports. The very generality of such questions gave Caron ample scope for extended descriptive responses.

From the 1660s onwards, members of the English Royal Society supplied similar questionnaires to compatriots who were traveling or residing abroad, such as Consul Paul Rycaut in Smyrna.[69] This tradition was maintained throughout the eighteenth century, cultivated above all by the long-serving president of the Royal Society (1778–1820), Sir Joseph Banks, himself a veteran globetrotter from his involvement in Cook's first circumnavigation of the globe. In 1689 Gottfried Wilhelm Leibniz sent thirty questions to the missionary Claudio Filippo Grimaldi, mainly about Chinese science and technology, and received verbal answers from him in Rome.[70] In 1766 the French statesman, economist, and social philosopher Turgot composed a survey of fifty-two questions, some going into considerable detail, for Ko and Yang, the two young Chinese recruits who had been sent to France by the Jesuits. The questions dealt largely with economic matters, barely touched on in the routine reports sent back by the Jesuits. Turgot inquired about the property market, the cost of rice, interest rates, and wages in the various provinces of the Chinese Empire.[71]

The questions put to the Danish expeditioners to Arabia by Johann David Michaelis, the Göttingen Orientalist and theologian, filled an entire volume; a separate catalog of questions submitted by the Académie des Inscriptions et des Belles Lettres in Paris was enclosed. Michaelis was hopeful, above all, that the expedition would shed geographical and ethnographical light on the Bible. For each of his questions Michaelis summarized the current state of research. For some, he even formulated hypotheses he wished the travelers to confirm or refute. The scholars in Paris were more interested in Islam and in Arabic political institutions and customs. They wanted to know whether "science had vanished from those lands" since the flowering of Arabic high culture in the Middle Ages.[72] Niebuhr and his colleagues had no opportunity to respond, however. When in 1764 Michaelis's package finally reached its addressee in Bombay, Niebuhr was the last surviving member of the expedition, and he was already preparing for his departure.[73] The same postal delay also prevented them receiving the instructions sent them by the Danish king. These directed them each to keep a journal and regularly send transcripts to Copenhagen. The king additionally instructed them to make natural history collections and purchase any Arabic manuscripts that could be had at a reasonable price—although not the Koran, numerous copies of which were circulating in Europe following the Turkish wars. The king was particularly interested in Arabic demography. For the sake of their own safety, but also from considerations of tact, the expeditioners were enjoined not to go about their work with the élan of scientific conquistadors but with the unassuming modesty appropriate to guests:

> All travelers are to conduct themselves with the utmost courtesy towards the inhabitants of Arabia. They should not impugn their religion, still less cast it in contempt, be it even implicitly. They

> should avoid doing anything that is vexatious to them: those parts of their activity that awaken suspicion among unknowing Mohammedans, as seeming to unearth buried treasure, perform sorcery, or bring aught that is ill to the land, should be carried out as discreetly as possible; and they should clothe themselves as pleasingly as they can.[74]

Such sensitivity is conspicuously absent from the imperial directions given the expeditions sent out to explore the Asiatic regions of the tsarist empire. Emerging from a series of state-run planning conferences, these directions were conceived as large-scale research projects, with particular emphasis being placed on the collection of economic data. Information was to be gathered on the composition of the soil, its suitability for farming and livestock, the state of the rural and nomadic economies, conditions for hunting, fishing, and honey production, the presence of manufacturing and trade, and any available mineral deposits.[75] No less imperially motivated were the similar instructions that the governor-general of British India, Lord Wellesley, gave the naturalist Dr. Francis Buchanan before he set out to survey recently conquered territories in southern India. Wellesley specified not just the objects he wanted Buchanan to inspect but also the questions he expected him to resolve.[76]

The methodological guidance of the "fundamentally inquisitive class"[77] of travelers reached a high point with the French Idéologues, a group of intellectuals active around 1800 who drew on classical Enlightenment themes and sought to integrate them into an empirical science of man. One of the Idéologues was Constantin-François Chassebœuf, who became famous under the pseudonym Volney, a name chosen in homage to his hero Voltaire. Volney had traveled the Near East from 1783 to 1785 as a young man of independent means, all the while serving the minister Vergennes as a secret agent. In 1787 he published his *Voyage en Égypte et en Syrie*, widely acknowledged as a masterpiece for its combination of empirical observation, philosophical commentary, and sophisticated scene-setting. Decades later, Alexander von Humboldt singled out Volney as "the philosophical traveler who knows best how to depict human beings under different climatic conditions."[78] Volney was not just one of the pioneers of sociography, a skilled painter of impressive social tableaux. He was also the scholar who most consequentially translated the old guidelines of apodemics into the scientific methodology of empirical social research. In the report on the Near East he published at the age of thirty, he proposed that a country be divided into *état physique* and *état politique*. By "physical state" he meant mainly geography and climate, while the "political state" encompassed not only the political arrangements of a country, which were partly influenced by those factors, but also ethnic, social, and economic conditions. In contrast to earlier, empirically oriented travelers, Volney avoided making any observations about botany and zoology (areas where he pleaded ignorance), except insofar as they were directly relevant to agriculture. The natural world was of interest to him solely as the conditioning framework—the environment—for human social life.

The traveling gentleman's quest for self-realization—his determination to improve himself by absorbing as much knowledge as possible—no longer plays a role for Volney as a rationale for venturing abroad. Subjective opinions that fail to scale the heights of "philosophical" assertion have been expunged from his report. In this respect Volney differs from an earlier "objective" traveler like Niebuhr. The traveler collects as much exact data as he can and then subjects it to "philosophical" analysis on strictly scientific principles. This analysis leads to clear judgments, indispensable if the labor of travel (as Volney understands it) is to be put to patriotic use. Volney nonetheless recognizes the relativity of these judgments. He does not ascribe universal validity to his own evaluations, acknowledging that judgments of taste and other relativizing factors leave their mark even on scientific judgments.[79] Volney's manner of judging philosophically, especially on the "moral character" of foreign nations, differs greatly from the deductive and apodictic approach favored by James Mill. Forming such a judgment calls for a considerable degree of empathetic identification:

> Such a study requires communicating with the people one seeks to fathom, embracing their situation in order to get a feeling for the factors that influence them and the predilections that result; it requires living in their country, learning their language, practicing their customs.[80]

Readers and travelers alike must learn to combat the prejudices they bring along with them as well as those they are confronted by:

> The heart is partisan, habit powerful, facts are deceptive and illusion lies all around. The observer must therefore be circumspect without growing timorous; and the reader, obliged to see through a different pair of eyes, must at the same time keep watch over the reason of his guide and his own reason.[81]

The systematic approach to his materials that Volney had already employed in his journey to the Orient was subsequently elaborated, at the invitation of the French Directory, into a catalog of 135 precisely worded questions. This was published in 1795 under the title *Questions d'économie publique*; upon being reissued in 1813 it was given the clearer title, *Questions de statistique à l'usage des voyageurs*. The questions were devised for French diplomats, consuls, and traveling agents. In contrast to Michaelis's book-length questionnaire, written specifically for the Danish expedition to Arabia, Volney's questions were conceived as a universally applicable system for collecting data about any country on Earth. Not only was the individual traveler's perception to be trained: Volney's proposal was made in the context of ambitious plans on the part of revolutionary and Napoleonic France to accumulate as comprehensive a store of knowledge about as many countries as possible in an orderly, comparable, and—ultimately—politically useful form: an archive for an increasingly integrated globe.

Napoleon's invasion of Egypt in 1798 offered a unique opportunity for such intelligence gathering on a grand scale. Napoleon had taken 167 scholars and artists with him to Egypt, where they collected the materials later worked into the enormous *Description de l'Égypte*. It appeared between 1809 and 1823 in nine volumes of text and fourteen of plates. Wherever French troops intervened in the following decades, similar mass data-collection projects followed on their heels: in the Peloponnes (1829–31), in Algeria (1839–42), in Mexico (1865–67).[82] Even when travelers had no assigned role in such projects and were left to their own devices, Volney still intended for them to contribute to the success of the undertaking by sticking to his systematic guidelines. Whereas the *ars apodemica* had once sought to educate the independent traveler, now he had been reduced to a cog in a politically operationalized information machine. The traveler has forfeited his autonomy.[83]

Volney's 135 questions were not conceived as an open-ended list and stimulus for further questioning. They were meant to be a closed system that the correspondent was unauthorized to expand or modify at will. In a foreword to the first edition, the French government made abundantly clear that it did not expect expansive, free-flowing responses (*mémoires*) to the questions provided but precisely targeted answers (*notes*) to all of them.[84] Volney's ground plan looked like this:[85]

A. Physical state of the country
  1. Geographical situation
  2. Climate, i.e., state of the sky
  3. State of the ground
  4. Natural products
B. Political state
  1. Populations
  2. Agriculture
  3. Industry
  4. Commerce
  5. Government and administration

Clarifications were occasionally added to questions to make them more precise. In the section on agriculture, for example, Volney recommended that travelers make an in-depth study of an exemplary farming operation while also picking out two or three different types of villages for further examination: a wine-growing village, say, and a crop-farming one.

Not all questions of this nature could be answered with evidence provided by eyesight, the most reliable of the senses. The official preface to Volney's catalog of questions explicitly encouraged users of the booklet to be guided by the questions in their conversations with natives, with which they were advised to fill their leisure time in the absence of other social engagements (*privés de société*). Accordingly, the questions were to be passed on in the form of inquiries.[86] Volney has nothing to say about how the information thus acquired by word of mouth was to be checked for accuracy. At any rate, it was quite clear to experienced correspondents that those who claimed to be *exclusively* recording their visual impressions were following a rhetorical convention rather than describing their actual modus operandi. William Marsden, for example, directly expresses just such an awareness.

As a sixteen-year-old, the Irishman Marsden had followed in his brother's footsteps by signing up to serve with the EIC in their presidency at Bencoolen (Fort Marlborough) in West Sumatra.[87] He had lived there for eight years, acquiring a comprehensive knowledge of the country and its languages. Stimulated by the publications following Cook's first circumnavigation of the globe and relieved of his administrative duties by patronage from the influential Joseph Banks, whose famous "breakfast" he was invited to attend from 1780, Marsden began working on a description of Sumatra, one of the least known parts of Asia at the time. It appeared as a *History of Sumatra* in 1783, just four years after Marsden's return to England. In the same year, Marsden was named a fellow of the Royal Society at the tender age of twenty-eight. Between 1795 and 1807 he occupied the highest posts in the Admiralty, rising to become something akin to a permanent secretary of state for the Royal Navy. In retirement he wrote numerous works, including a Malay grammar and dictionary that were held in high regard by both Wilhelm and Alexander von Humboldt. He was also one of the leading comparative linguists of his age. In many respects, Marsden was Volney's British counterpart: a self-made man who rose to high office from a middle-class background without ever playing party politics; an enterprising youth who made his name through an account of an exotic country that achieved lasting fame as a model of objectivity and precision; and a pioneer and tireless promoter of oriental studies.

Marsden assures his readers at the start of his *History of Sumatra* that everything he has to report is incontestably authentic:

> The greatest portion of what I have described has fallen within the scope of my own immediate observation; the remainder is either matter of common notoriety to every person residing in the island, or received upon the concurring authority of gentlemen, whose situation in the East India Company's service, long acquaintance with the natives, extensive knowledge of their languages, ideas, and manners, and respectability of character, render them worthy of the most implicit faith that can be given to human testimony.[88]

"Immediate observation" refers to the optical impression that Marsden, who never penetrated into the interior of the jungle-covered island, could form in his own field of vision. Unlike Volney, who could always follow in the well-worn tracks of earlier travelers to Egypt and Syria, Marsden was dependent on others' reports if he did not wish to abandon his goal of encyclopedic comprehensiveness. Some—but far from all—of these oral sources are mentioned in his book.[89] Towards his English informants, he can only apply the same methods of verification that the general public was forced to rely on when reading his own report. When empirical confirmation proves impossible and the plausibility test has been passed, all that remains is "faith."[90]

HEARING AND HEARSAY

It is characteristic of the finest travel literature that the reader not only sees with the author's *yeux intermédiaires* (Volney) but hears with his ears as well. The resulting impression of Asia is contradictory. On the one hand, sounds can be heard to which European ears are unaccustomed: a Babylonian confusion of tongues in the great metropolises; a perpetual hum of activity (as in Uzbeki Bukhara); a din of drumming, banging, and rattling on Chinese and Vietnamese streets. Specific noises noted by vistors include the honking of elephant horns in Saigon, gonging on Chinese tugs to direct towing operations, and in Persia, the sound of neighbors gathering on their rooftops on summer nights to escape the stifling heat.[91]

On the other hand—and this is the stronger impression—there is silence. For Alexander Hamilton, there was nothing more acoustically disturbing on his extensive travels in Asia than the bells that tolled through the night in Portuguese Goa.[92] Asian cities are quieter than European ones because they have hardly any paved roads and there are few, if any, carriages with iron fittings. Festive banquets are marked by an absence of polite conversation because the hosts are too busy tucking into their food to bother with such niceties.[93] Court ceremonies generally unfold in an atmosphere that strikes Europeans as eerily hushed. Few words are exchanged during Siamese and Tibetan audiences. All is calm around the Chinese emperor too, as courtiers and mandarins glide to and fro in felt-lined slippers. At the court of Kandy in central Ceylon, everyone whispers in order to preserve state secrets, according to one English visitor.[94] And at the court of Murad IV (reigned 1623/32–1640), a bloodthirsty tyrant, even foreigners had to communicate behind the monarch's back in an elaborate sign language if they wished to survive.[95] The solemn silence attending the sultan's diplomatic receptions—"that more than Pythagorean silence in the Sultan's court," as Cantemir puts it[96]—was often described. Europeans were fascinated by the deaf mutes at court, with whom even the sultan communicated by gesture. They were said to be much in demand for "executions requiring the utmost discretion."[97] Allegedly, Sultan Mehmed III, at his accession in 1595, had his nineteen brothers and twenty sisters murdered by deaf-mute servants.[98] Nobody in the palace dared speak without permission, and conversations between courtiers in the presence of their overlord were unthinkable;

"neither doth any person dare so much as to sneeze or cough, whatever occasion he may have."[99]

The evocation of an acoustic atmosphere and ambient noise needs to be distinguished from news reports originating in oral sources, the communicative aspect of hearing. Marsden was typical of correspondents in the second half of the eighteenth century in providing references for any information he was unable to confirm with his own eyes. Travelers like Tavernier and Gemelli Careri, who freely mixed up what they had witnessed themselves with what they had been told by others, were now held up as examples of how not to proceed. In 1716 Johann Wilhelm Vogel relaxed the normally strict pledge of autopsy on the title page of his East Indies book by adding: "All from my own experience as well as from numerous discussions held in India."[100]

Such discussions were mainly conducted with other Europeans and were usually most successful "when a Bottle or two had opened their Breasts."[101] Merchants felt themselves qualified to discourse on the "moral character" of Asian people, and many a traveler to China, in particular, appears to have internalized the judgments with which he was confronted in the counting houses and taverns of Canton and Macao as the truth about the Middle Kingdom.[102] More independent travelers like Thomas Shaw in the Near East still trusted in the geographical and meteorological information provided them by European residents.[103] The most serious European informants were usually missionaries. Emissaries in China owed them a great deal. Of course, the Jesuits in China had no difficulties transmitting their insights directly to the public through their own media channels. The case was different for the Capuchin monk, Raphaël Du Mans. He spent decades observing events in Iran from Isfahan and, owing to his incomparable expertise on the country, was an important, discreet, and not always acknowledged source of information for the great seventeenth-century travelers to Iran: Thévenot, Chardin, Kaempfer. His own report on Iran, written around 1660, was intended only for the eyes of Colbert, minister under Louis XIV, and remained unedited until 1890. It allows us to draw a number of revealing comparisons with contemporary publications on Iran.[104] The shakier their grasp of the language, the more fleeting their stay in the country, the more forbidding their surroundings, the more visitors were inclined to rely on the information passed on to them by European expatriates. Travelers visiting the Ottoman Empire on an extended grand tour were particularly apt to succumb to this temptation.[105]

There was usually no lack of willingness to quiz *native* informants. Sometimes there was no alternative: by their own account, everything travelers like Tavernier and Bernier could find out about the strictly secret harems kept by the sultan and grand mughal they learned from eunuchs, while Paul Rycaut relied for inside information on a court musician, originally from Poland, who had spent nineteen years serving in Constantinople.[106] Despite all their distortions, the European texts are the most detailed sources we have on this topic.[107] When an entire country cloaked itself in darkness, curiosity had to find indirect means of shedding light on its affairs. While accompanying Peter Simon Pallas on the Russian academy expedition in 1772, Johann Gottlieb Georgi met and interviewed at length a number of shipwrecked Japanese sailors who were teaching at the state-run Japanese school in Irkutsk, founded there in 1753. Georgi's report on Siberia from 1775 thus contained information about Japan—information that the renowned Orientalist, Louis Mathieu Langlès, thought important enough to include as an appendix to the French edition of Thunberg's book on Japan.[108]

Good intentions were no guarantee of success, though. A Dutch captain notes that when in Bengal, he questioned Brahmans about their religion "with the aid of an interpreter," "but I cannot claim to have ever drawn anything specific from them."[109] He suspects that his interlocutors were unwilling to give anything away. In Istanbul, the sober-minded art lover, James Dallaway, found both Greeks and Turks "equally incapable of liberal intercourse."[110] Those traveling in uncharted territory depended in a very practical sense on the local knowledge of their native guides. They should be trusted, Samuel Turner advised in the account he wrote of his Himalayan journey, even if their suggestions seem dubious at first.[111] While performing daring and taboo-breaking exploits, such as ascending holy mountains, Europeans could find themselves temporarily deserted by their hired hands. Carsten Niebuhr found that many Arabs were reluctant to tell him the proper names of places and mountains: "for they could not comprehend the reasons why we would concern ourselves with such things."[112] Small gifts and other friendly overtures helped loosen their tongues. But not every native was a credible authority. Residents of Asian cities often gave the most far-fetched estimates of the city's population.[113] Carsten Niebuhr speaks with the voice of experience when he urges travelers to find out, if at all possible, the source of the informant's information.[114] The most forthcoming conversational partners were merchants, already accustomed to dealing with foreigners, and penurious scholars, who could be rewarded with tips for their services. Needless to say, it was vital that they be approached in a spirit of amity:

> If only the Arabs are treated with forbearance, as much civility may be expected from these Mohammedans, as in Europe reasonable Christians show the Jews.[115]

Niebuhr, who must have been an unusually sensitive interviewer, found it difficult to approach truly learned men. He felt for them: after all, why should they take pleasure "in being assailed with questions by a stranger?"[116] In any event, he counseled, a good deal of patience was required; questions should be posed indirectly and rephrased in a number of ways. If Orientals occasionally veer from the path of truth, then this is not from any moral deficiency on their part but for quite understandable reasons: distrust of foreigners, for example, or the vanity of not wanting to reveal gaps in their own knowledge. In each case, the traveling geographer and social researcher should take the precaution of asking as many people as possible about the matter in question—a strategy earlier recommended by Johann Georg Gmelin, the Siberian expeditioner.[117] The relative importance of oral testimony also varied from one culture to the next, as John Crawfurd astutely observed. In Siam, an oral culture, more was to be learned by the ear than in Chinese-influenced Vietnam, a culture of writing and eyesight.[118]

While the chronic mendacity of his oriental surroundings could occasionally drive an overly anxious European to despair (as Pierre Poivre, further enervated by unending rainfall, experienced while French ambassador to Cochinchina in 1749),[119] the consummate traveler was faced with the ongoing problem of gauging the accuracy of information received by word of mouth. He owed this to his readers as well, who were ever less satisfied with "hearsay relations," as Edward Gibbon remarks.[120] In their contacts with natives, travelers were unable to mobilize the faith in gentlemanly character that allowed William Marsden to assume the trustworthiness of reports from inner Sumatra. Often they could do no more than speculate on the plausibility of their sources. Robert Percival, author of an important report on Ceylon, only included information "that no one could hesitate to believe."[121] François Bernier tells of a widow burning in India that he had only heard about, but which was no more unlikely than many other "improbabilities" he had seen with his own eyes. What is more, the story was "universally credited" by Indians.[122] And Johann Georg Gmelin assures his readers that every statement in his book that is not supported by eyewitness evidence has been assessed on its likelihood, "though I well know that a matter can very well appear to be true without being it."[123]

LOCAL KNOWLEDGE: ASIATIC SCHOLARSHIP IN EUROPEAN TEXTS

Given that many travel reports contain a great deal of information from native sources (however well or poorly understood that information may be), oriental studies could never have gotten off the ground in Europe without local knowledge. Here too, word-of-mouth reporting was of great importance, if only because Europeans were unable to read linguistically demanding texts without assistance from local experts. The Jesuits in China relied on Chinese scholars to help them make sense of challenging texts. More important, however, were the textual sources themselves. Just as the late eighteenth-century theory of high travel no longer so easily forgave the visitor to Asia his linguistic ignorance, so too the historian was expected to draw on Asian historical works and preferably even documents as well. Sir William Jones, president of the Asiatick Society of Bengal (founded in 1784) and himself an effortless polylinguist, expressed this idea in a typically pithy maxim: "All the Asiatick nations must be far better acquainted with their several countries than mere European scholars and travelers."[124]

In practice, this principle of Euro-Asiatic scientific cooperation had long been observed. A good example is Chinese cartography. The *Novus Atlas Sinensis* (1655) by the South Tyrolian Jesuit, Martin Martini, was based in large part on Chinese preliminary studies. Between 1708 and 1717 around a dozen Jesuits, split into smaller surveying teams, put together a comprehensive cartographical record of the empire at the behest of the Kangxi emperor. Needless to say, Chinese assistants were involved throughout; the maps of Tibet, in particular, drew on information provided by officials who knew the country well or were sent there under the pretense of an embassy.[125] Between 1717 and 1726 four different versions of the Jesuit Atlas were printed on wooden or copper plates. The results of this undertaking, which also gave rise to several Chinese editions,[126] went into the fifteen maps that Jean-Baptiste d'Anville, probably the finest European cartographer of the age, created for Du Halde's China encyclopedia of 1735.[127] They remained unsurpassed for over a century. This so-called Jesuit atlas was produced by combining local knowledge from China, as recorded in numerous geographical handbooks, with European surveying techniques and forms of cartographical representation.[128] The cartographical conquest of India followed a different template. Here the needs of British armed forces provided the impetus for the great mapmaking projects; conversely, the wars themselves offered an ideal opportunity for gathering topographical data.[129] Pandits were indispensable helpers in this regard, particularly in surveying areas not yet under British control.[130]

The best historians among the Jesuits in China—Martin Martini in the seventeenth century, for example, or Antoine Gaubil in the eighteenth—built on the achievements of Chinese historiography. The Jesuits were always prepared to fend off doubts about the reliability of their Chinese authorities. Gaubil, "a man who knew China as well as his own fatherland,"[131] rightly pointed out that the methods of source criticism developed in the Chinese historiographical tradition were every bit as advanced as those in Europe.[132] Scholars outside the Societas Jesu including Joseph de Guignes, a man who enjoyed a Europe-wide reputation as one of the most significant historians and Orientalists of the Enlightenment era, confirmed the high standing of Chinese sources, their accuracy and rhetorically restrained closeness to reality, and they unabashedly drew on them in their own writings.[133]

Simon Ockley was a poor country vicar and, from 1711 until his imprisonment for debt in 1717, professor of Arabic at Cambridge. In the important foreword to his two-volume *History of the Saracens*, a history of the Islamic Arabs up to 705, he left his readers in no doubt as to the primacy of Arab sources. Despite complaining bitterly of his struggles with the Arabic manuscripts he found in Oxford's Bodleian Library—"dusty Manuscripts, without Translation, without Index; destitute altogether of those Helps which facilitate other Studies"[134]—he took them to be the sure foundation for any European historiography on the Near and Middle East. He also believed the historian had a responsibility to import only as much narrative and interpretive order into the Arabic material as was needed to allow the voices of the old historians to be heard. His professed aim was to let the Arabs tell their history in their own way.[135] Several years later, George Sale reaffirmed the primacy of indigenous sources in his translation with commentary of the Koran. Sale almost completely ignored the European polemics against Islam that had raged fitfully since the eleventh century, instead basing his elucidations of the Koran in large part on Islamic exegetical traditions.[136]

Pushed a little further, the high esteem in which native texts were held could give rise to the view that it was not the task of European Orientalists to discourse *on* Asiatic cultures but rather, through translation, to allow these cultures to speak for themselves to a European readership. One proponent of this view was Isaac Titsingh, the foremost European expert on Japan around 1800. He considered translations from the Japanese to be more valuable than even the most accomplished descriptions of Japan by a European hand, and he consequently refused to write a description of his own that might supersede Kaempfer's classic.[137] He would have been uniquely qualified for the task. Sir William Jones concurred. In a lecture he gave to the Asiatick Society of Bengal in 1794, *On the Philosophy of the Asiaticks*, he declared "that one correct version of any celebrated Hindu book would be of greater value than all the dissertations and essays, that could be composed on the same subject."[138]

The degree to which a translation should cling faithfully to the text or deviate from it was a perennial subject of debate. In this dilemma between fidelity to the original and deference to European aesthetic sensibilities, some (including Simon Ockley) opted for mimesis, while others plumped for a Westernized style. Francis Gladwin, who was commissioned by Governor-General Warren Hastings to translate the *Ayin Akbery* (A'in-i Akbari) by Abu 'l-Fadl 'Allami, one of the key sources on the rule of the grand mughal Akbar, consciously set out in his translation to make the Persian-speaking author appear to have been writing in English.[139] What Goethe admired about Sir William Jones's translations was that they cautiously sought to bring the foreignness of Asiatic texts closer to readers by clothing them in classical verse forms.[140] Of course, the liberties allowed by translators spanned a broad spectrum, ranging all the way from pedantic adherence to the letter of the text through streamlining, restructuring, and paraphrase of the original to tacit incorporation of commentary. Ideally, every translation would be preceded and informed by textual criticism of the source.[141]

Tongjian gangmu ("Outlines and Details of the Comprehensive Mirror"), the twelfth-century abridgement of a historical work by the famous Sima Guang (1019–86), was translated into French by Pater de Mailla from a Manchu version of the original. In 1737 his manuscript arrived in France, where it was published between 1777 and 1780 in twelve quarto volumes by the abbé Grosier.[142] On its appearance, the translation was roundly condemned for being riddled with errors and all but unreadable. While unrivalled in its annalistic monotony, the work at least gave European readers a first authentic glimpse of the continuity of Chinese history. Because its emphasis on static immobility was strong even by Chinese standards, it helped popularize the idea in Europe that Chinese history essentially boiled down to the eternal return of the same. The Manchu emperors promoted its canonization, meaning that, in effect, de Mailla had chosen to translate the officially authorized version of Chinese history.[143] De Mailla followed his source in broad outline; indeed, he was repeatedly criticized for not having corrected and improved it.

Three decades later, the EIC officer and first British historian of Islamic India, Alexander Dow, took a very different approach. Dow recognized that the history of the Mughal Empire and its Islamic predecessor states could only be written in earnest on the basis of native (Persian-language) material. He accordingly set to work translating *Gulshan-i Ibrahimi*, the historical work by Firishta (1606/7). As he progressed, however, he found himself moving further and further away from his source until eventually, in the work he published under the title *History of Hindostan* (1768–72), the modern Western author's "philosophical" remarks had seeped almost imperceptibly into the text of the translation.[144] Edward Gibbon, the era's most discerning connoisseur of historical literature, also suspected that in Dow's hands, "the style of Ferishta has been improved by that of Ossian"—in other words, Dow had borrowed his tone from the recently "discovered" bardic poetry.[145] Dow himself assured the reader that he had curbed the romantic excesses of the original by emulating the "concise and manly" diction that had prevailed in European historiography ever since the Greco-Roman classics.[146]

It was not uncommon for translations from Persian or Arabic to be produced with the help of scholars from that culture. Where native knowledge was utterly indispensable, however, was in the discovery of Hindu Indian culture. Bernier had occasionally consulted a pandit in order to find out more about the conditions outside the courtly Mughal world in which he mostly moved.[147] In his book *De Open Deure tot het verborgen heydendom* (1651), Abraham Rogerius, a Dutch missionary with ten years' experience in southwest India, for the first time gave Europe a view of Indian religious ideas that was undistorted by religious propaganda. Rogerius owed much of his knowledge to Padmanaba, a Brahman refugee from Portuguese Goa, who introduced him to the Vedic and Puranic literature and translated some of it for him word for word. The two men communicated in Portuguese.[148] The 1780s saw the beginnings of the scientific study of Sanskrit by Western scholars in the circle around Sir William Jones and the Asiatick Society of Bengal he founded in 1784.[149] In 1785 Charles Wilkins, the first European to acquire a sure knowledge of Sanskrit, drew attention in Europe with his translation of the *Bhagavadgita*. Sir William Jones made an even bigger splash four years later with his translation of Kalidasa's fourth-to-fifth-century drama, *Sakuntala*.

With Henry Thomas Colebrooke—a senior judge in India like Jones—Sanskrit philology was placed on a systematic footing.[150] What became known as the "Oriental Renaissance" could never have occurred without the pandits, whose services as transmitters of information proved indispensable to their European masters. The collaboration between knowledge-hungry English and knowledgeable Indians was marked from the outset by mutual apprehension. Mistrust on both sides never disappeared completely. Jones had begun studying Sanskrit for an eminently practical purpose: as a judge, he wanted to be able to superintend the pandits at the Supreme Court and break their monopoly on translation. In his mind, exercising effective control over the colonial judicial system required establishing oversight of courtroom communications as well as setting down Indian common law in writing, systematizing it along Western guidelines, and publishing it in English translation. Over the course of his studies, Jones developed close personal relations with several Indian scholars, especially the venerable Jagannatha Tarkapanchanan. Yet these friendships always remained marked by the ambivalence that, while Jones as a *scholar* was a student of the pandits, as an *official* he was a senior representative of the colonial ruling class. Even Jones, who was more willing than most to acknowledge how much he owed the pandits, still thought it desirable that British scholars and colonial office holders remain as independent as possible from native scholars and translators.

British supremacy in Sanskrit studies did not last long. In the latter part of the nineteenth century, the greatest strides were made by desk-bound German scholars who had never set foot on Indian soil or parleyed with a pandit. Uninterested in learning the language as an instrument of power, they were instead long preoccupied with theoretical questions concerning the origin of language and comparative linguistics.[151] Paradoxically, their very distance from colonialism entailed a detachment from India and hence a devaluation of indigenous knowledge. Scientific Orientalism, which assumed intellectual responsibility for an entire civilization, achieved its greatest feats in a country that had no colonial interests. Yet the autonomy of European (especially German) Indology was a chimera. As Ernst Windisch pointed out as early as 1917, the discipline stood on the shoulders of generations of Indian grammarians.[152]

Asians did not just play a pivotal role in the emergence of the *cultural* disciplines of oriental studies. A brief acquaintance with the civilizations of the Far East was all it took to convince some of the wiser heads in Europe that the empirical study of nature was at least as advanced in India, China, or Japan as it was in contemporary Europe. In a letter to Leibniz from 1699, Pater Joachim Bouvet S. J. expressed a goal held in common by both men: "to extract from this nation [China] everything that can serve to perfect our sciences and our arts."[153] Bouvet even put forward a plan to establish in China an Apostolic Academy for the study of culture, religion, and writing, a kind of theological-cum-Sinological research institute that could one day share its findings with the Academy of Sciences in Paris.[154] Leibniz was more interested than Bouvet in mathematics and the natural sciences. He urged haste, perceiving what the Jesuits on the ground often failed to recognize: that the missionaries' favorable political situation in China depended entirely on the person of the Kangxi emperor and was unlikely to survive his reign. It was therefore imperative that they extract as much knowledge as possible from China before the door was slammed shut in their faces.[155] Leibniz conceived this not as a process of scientific parasitism but as the coming together of complementary advantages: while European scholarship was strong on *raisonnement*, the Chinese had an edge in practical experience and ethical reflection; European knowledge tended to be disseminated in the public sphere, whereas Chinese learning was largely handed down in small scholarly circles.[156]

Leibniz was still guided by the idea of mutually beneficial cooperation between two coequal scientific worlds. By the end of the eighteenth century, however, a one-sidedly imperial outlook had come to prevail. Respect for the scientific achievements of other civilizations was fast disappearing. For a powerful administrator of knowledge like Sir Joseph Banks, all that mattered was getting the Indians or Chinese to surrender—whether through fair means or foul—the few remaining technologies where they were still ahead of their European competitors, such as textile weaving or porcelain manufacture.[157]

Asiatic involvement in the production of European knowledge is particularly evident in botany. Isolationist Japan, of all places, was of special importance here. In 1662 Andreas Cleyer had disembarked in Batavia to take up a position in the VOC. From 1682 to 1686, with occasional interruptions, he was Dutch *Opperhoofd* or headman in Nagasaki. The botanical studies he pursued during his stay there bore fruit in the more than thirty essays he had published in Germany. Cleyer also sent 1,360 illustrations of plants by Japanese artists to the Berlin scholar Christian Mentzel, who used them for an unpublished *Botanica Iaponica*.[158] What appeared instead was Engelbert Kaempfer's *Flora Japonica* (1712), a comprehensive work in Latin about the vegetation native to the Japanese islands. It was valuable not least because Kaempfer was able to profit from the accomplishments of Japanese botany, which in the 1690s, the period when the work was composed, were probably more advanced than European efforts in the same field.[159] In India, too, alert naturalists recognized the extraordinarily high quality of indigenous botanical knowledge. Hendrik Adriaan van Reede tot Drakenstein, a senior officer and administrator in the VOC, spent much of his spare time in the 1670s studying tropical plants on the Malabar Coast in southwest India, a region that lay partly under Dutch control at the time. In his attempts to describe and classify what he saw, he found himself moving ever closer to native taxonomies, which he gradually came to appreciate for their advantages over the Arabic and European systems. In producing his immense *Hortus Malabaricus* (twelve volumes, Amsterdam 1678–93), he relied on several Brahman advisers and, to an even greater extent, on the horticultural expertise and experience of gardeners from low castes, especially the Ezhava caste. For want of any other documentary evidence, their extraordinary knowledge has come down to us solely in the Euro-Asiatic collaborative project that is the *Hortus Malabaricus*.[160] The works of van Reede and Kaempfer were greeted with critical acclaim by the luminaries of the European scholarly world, with Linnaeus leading the chorus of praise. Through their mediation, knowledge originally cultivated in the jungles and forests of Asia was transplanted into the carefully laid out parklands of European nature writing.

VII

Reporting, Editing, Reading

From Lived Experience to Printed Text

It may, I think, be justly observed that few books disappoint their readers more than the narrations of travelers.
—Samuel Johnson (1709–84), *The Idler*, no. 97, February 23, 1760[1]

Except under laboratory conditions, it is impossible for us to observe or reconstruct the processes of seeing and hearing. It was equally impossible for eighteenth-century Europeans with an interest in Asia to bypass the media of the day. Before the invention of photography and technologies for recording sound and movement, travel reports—particularly if illustrated—enjoyed a monopoly on communications. There were simply no rival media for them to contend with. European "images" of Asiatic civilizations were textual evocations supported by engravings or etchings and—more rarely—by watercolors or oil paintings. Compared with the twentieth century, when the world beyond Europe's borders was presented to Europeans as one of images, eighteenth-century Asia was a literary project, a world constructed of language. Today, even people who have never read a book about Asia and routinely ignore foreign news reports still feel they know the continent from television, films, photographs, and the Internet. In the early modern period, those who read nothing, knew nothing.

Visual impressions generally played a subordinate role. But they were still important in many cases. The woodcuts in Sebastian Münster's *Kos-*

mographia (1554) and the copperplate engravings in Theodor de Bry's travel collections (1590–1634), especially the constantly reproduced scenes of cannibalism, influenced the early modern image of America almost to the same extent as texts. Similarly sensational depictions were lacking for Asia. But a few frequently recycled images from a vast stockpile of visual material, reproduced mainly in anthologies, must have made a lasting impression on European observers: the camp of the all-conquering Turks and the minarette-adorned silhouettes of Muslim cities, the splendor of the grand mughal's court with its sumptuously bejewelled parading elephants, the many-armed, animal-headed Indian deities, self-torturing fakirs, the likeness of the venerable Confucius, the Chinese emperor shown ritually plowing the first furrow of the spring sowing season, the Great Wall of China and the Porcelain Pagoda of Nanjing, the Dalai Lama's Potala Palace, the tropical, palm-shaded European city of Batavia, Japanese Buddhist temples, and Siberian shamans.

Eighteenth-century Asian iconography still owed much to older illustrated works such as the *China Illustrata* (1667) by the Jesuit polymath Athanasius Kircher, the report on his Chinese travels by Johan Nieuhof (1665), the Persian voyage of Adam Olearius (1647/56), Abraham Rogerius's description of India (1651), and the great compilations of Olfert Dapper and Arnoldus Montanus, which appeared between 1669 and 1681. Later, the artist Cornelis de Bruijn (or de Bruyn, de Bruin) returned from his two extended journeys (1674–84, 1701–8) with an ample trove of his own paintings and drawings: most spectacularly, the first European representations of the ruins of Persepolis; he was also a pioneer of color printing.[2] Rich collections of visual sources, such as the abbé Prévost's *Histoire générale des voyages* (1746–61) or Thomas Salmon's *The Universal Traveller* (1752–53), drew freely from this stockpile, occasionally adding a piece or two of their own. Asia only began to appear in full color once talented painters and watercolorists were able to join in the great state-sponsored voyages of the late eighteenth century. Realistically observed landscapes and scenes from common life now took center stage. William Alexander, who accompanied Lord Macartney to China, and William Hodges, who, in addition to taking part in Cook's second circumnavigation of the globe (alongside Forster *père* and *fils*), lived in India from 1780 to 1783, pioneered a new way of seeing Asia in their art.[3] A few years after Hodges, between 1786 and 1793, the landscape painters Thomas and William Daniell, uncle and nephew, traveled through vast tracts of India, creating a substantial oeuvre along the way.[4] Apart from India, however, no region in Asia before 1800 was depicted as often or as powerfully as the South Pacific.[5]

While images may have gripped the popular imagination, it was texts that promised to give the eighteenth-century public what they expected more than anything else: information.

THE TRAVEL ACCOUNT AS A TOOL OF INQUIRY

The eighteenth century's famous and influential travelers and travel writers, from Engelbert Kaempfer and John Chardin to Carsten Niebuhr, Constantin de Volney, and Alexander von Humboldt, were no victims of "Orientalist" delusion and peddlars of fantasies and lies about the Other, whose authenticity and truth remained a closed book to them. From Western European humanism, they inherited a role model of the "philosophical traveler"—an ambulatory scholar who, not yet bound by the constraints of strictly defined academic disciplines such as geography or ethnology, contributed to universal knowledge in accordance with the most advanced methodological standards of the day.[6] Together with hundreds if not thousands of curious and often learned armchair travelers at home, they formed a philosophical class with unprecedented cosmopolitan ambitions and pretensions.[7] In this intellectual world, travel accounts enjoyed enormous prestige. Customers and collectors were prepared to spend a lot of money on them. Critics took great pains to gauge their veracity and assess their literary merits. But how did such travel books come to be written?

We should not imagine that all travelers began working up their notes into a coherent, book-length format before they had even returned home, or as soon as they reached their native shores. They were far more likely to take up their quills only once whoever had commissioned the report put pressure on them to deliver, or when they wanted to mobilize the book-buying public as quickly as possible—sometimes in competition with companions from the same voyage or expedition. Participants in state-sponsored expeditions were often expected to hand over their private notes to the expedition leader or his literary amanuensis, who would then collate them in the official account.[8] Reminiscences of a more personal or subjective nature would appear later on, if at all. Official reports were therefore often joint ventures, syntheses from a wide range of documents masquerading as the work of a single author. Only a few writers—Mountstuart Elphinstone, for example—were candid and generous enough to acknowledge the contributions made by their fellow travelers to the final report, signalling it as a collective product.[9] Following particularly spectacular journeys, such as Captain Cook's three circumnavigations of the world or the Macartney embassy to China, struggles for precedence on the book market and for priority and originality would sometimes break out among the journey's chroniclers.[10] It is worth noting, incidentally, that the most intellectually stimulating product of the China mission from 1793–94, Lord Macartney's own notes, remained unpublished until fairly recently. Many reports were never intended for publication: sometimes for reasons of diplomatic confidentiality, sometimes because nothing more was envisaged than "the exotic equivalent of a family chronicle."[11]

Information about Asia arrived in Europe along numerous channels. One of the most important was correspondence. Considered as a well-organized group of knowledge brokers, the Jesuits were unmatched in their epistolary industry. An unceasing flow of letters poured forth from their tireless quills. In the hands of the padres in China, Vietnam, or India, the letter was at once a propaganda tool for enhancing the order's image in Europe, an instrument for strengthening international contacts among members of the order, and a means for transmitting scientific knowledge. The best scholars among the Jesuit missionaries did not just conduct their routine correspondence with the order's headquarters in Paris and Rome, they were also much-sought-after correspondents for the scholarly world outside the church. Conversely, it only helped burnish the reputation of a man like Pater Joachim Bouvet when he was seen in quasi-public correspondence with the great Leibniz, who himself cultivated contacts wherever any kind of mail service was able to deliver his letters. Other epistolary networks radiated out from Leibniz's contemporary, Nicolaas Witsen in Amsterdam: from Voltaire wherever he happened to be at the time; from the academy secretary Nicolas Fréret and the minister Henri-Léonard Bertin in Paris; from Robert Hooke, John Ray, Joseph Banks, and other members of the Royal Society in London; from Peter Simon Pallas and the astronomer Jean-Nicolas Delisle in Saint Petersburg; from Johann David Michaelis and August Ludwig Schlözer in Göttingen; and in the early nineteenth century from Carl Ritter in Berlin. Manuscripts were exchanged as well as letters. Voltaire sent a rough draft of his history of Russia under Peter the Great to Saint Petersburg, asking scholars there for commentary and additional material, particularly on the tribes of Siberia.[12] Much that was of importance went unread: the treatise on Chinese chronology by the great scholar, Antoine Gaubil S. J., arrived in Berlin in 1749 from Peking—and remained unpublished until 1814, when the debate on this topic had long since ebbed away.

Such crypto-public avenues of communication notwithstanding, the travel report remained easily the most important medium for representing Asia. Some reports were written for narrow and specific purposes, such as to instruct fellow mariners and travelers.[13] By and large, however, authors addressed a broad, educated public. What the general reader expected from them, above all, was an objective depiction of a distant reality. Travel reports were assigned to the old category of *Historia*, the genre of descriptive literature as such.[14] This did not just encompass history in today's sense of the word, but all ways of presenting empirical subject matter in a nonspeculative manner. When Engelbert Kaempfer wrote a *Historia Palmae Dactyliferae*, for example, what lay behind this title was a botanical and economic monograph on the date palm.[15] Until the end of the century, ambitious travel reports were expected to give equal coverage to both *historia civilis*—the description of the human world—and *historia naturalis.* Travelers lacking the requisite knowledge of the natural sciences would often apologize for their shortcomings in the foreword. Thomas Shaw, the highly regarded voyager to the Near East, abridged the botanical section in the second edition of his *Travels* due to scientific advances made in the interim.[16]

STYLE AND TRUTH

The authors of travel accounts—or at the very least their publishers—knew the generic conventions they had to abide by. The report should contribute to the growth of European knowledge by presenting as much new information as systematically as possible, without overly subjective impressions getting in the way. First-person narration, if used at all, was to be handled with the kind of unassuming tact and discretion demonstrated in exemplary fashion by Carsten Niebuhr or Samuel Turner. Above all, the report should offer readers an undistorted view of its subject matter. Linnaeus could offer no higher praise of a travel book than to say that it gave him the impression he had been there himself.[17] To be sure, a modicum of information about the course and circumstances of the journey was needed to lend the report authenticity.[18] Yet not all authors cultivated the coolly scholarly style recommended by theorists like Linneaus and Schlözer, and refined to a fault by authors like Pallas and Volney. Niebuhr's fine sense of humor frequently leavens his otherwise dry and objective tone.

British and French authors strayed far less from the ideals of elegance and complaisance than their German colleagues. Some, however, tried to pass off their own lackluster prose as an index of their truthfulness. "All too often," Pierre Sonnerat, the traveling naturalist and superb draftsman, pointed out, "the pleasing only serves to camouflage the untrue."[19] By contrast, Thomas Shaw, a travel writer frequently praised for his precision, feared that his years spent immersed in oriental languages might have spoiled his English. He accordingly sought to remedy his book's stylistic defects when revising it for a second edition.[20] John Chardin had his report on the coronation of Suleyman Shah proofread for linguistic infelicities by a member of the Académie Française before publishing it in 1671.[21] But felicitous expression and vivid description should also not be allowed to degenerate into what Johann Salomo Semler, a connoisseur of overseas travel literature, denounced as "a pointless prolixity that irritates the reader through a profusion of minutiae, fables and unhelpful anecdotes."[22] Minutiae were to be welcomed, on the other hand, when they concerned previously unknown, nontrivial facts: place names, meteorological data, linguistic observations.[23]

Around 1800 there was widespread consensus about which alternative was preferred in a hypothetical choice between truth and stylishness. "Mere faults of style," states Mountstuart Elphinstone, "would be of little consequence if the substance of my account were free from error."[24] But Elphinstone's goal was to prevent the dilemma from arising in the first place. Scientific rigor and literary excellence were combined at the end of the epoch in a number of authors whose mastery was acknowledged throughout Europe: above all, James Bruce, Georg Forster, and his friend and pupil in the art of travel writing, Alexander von Humboldt, who stood at least as much in the French narrative tradition as in the German one with his *Relation historique du voyage aux régions équinoxiales du Nouveau Continent* (1814–25).

Within the generic framework of the *historia* tradition there were numerous possibilities for literary organization. One option was a strict itinerary in logbook format, where even the tedium of long days passed uneventfully at sea or in the steppe and desert would be punctiliously noted;[25] another was a "daily register" for setting down all observations in chronological order, as required of participants in the Russian state and academy expeditions and as kept with particular strictness by one such participant, Samuel Gottlieb Gmelin. "I abide by the chosen scheme of naming all natural bodies in the sequence in which I viewed them," he explained during one of his journeys, "for that is the obligation imposed by a daily register."[26] Happily, Gmelin was gifted enough not to be tyrannized by such pedantry, coming close in many of his "thick" descriptions of nature and human customs to the Goethean ideal of the naturalist who is "capable of presenting and describing the strangest and most exotic things in their local environment, in their own element with all that surrounds them."[27] Several authors arranged their material systematically or grouped it into larger geographical units, regardless of the actual route they had taken on their travels. Chardin adopted this method in the seventeenth century with his famous Persian journey; Volney mastered it in the late eighteenth century. Thomas Shaw, who crammed the account of his journey into a brief foreword, had kept a systematic diary while traveling rather than a daily register, later transposing it into his report in the same order.[28]

At the opposite, more subjective end of the spectrum stood collections of travelers' letters. The most famous were those posted from Turkey between 1716 and 1718 by Lady Mary Wortley Montagu.[29] The letters from India of Mrs. Kindersley lagged far behind them in terms of their literary quality but are of comparable historical value.[30] Letters from the Far East could also serve as a medium of scholarly communication, and not just in the form of the countless published letters by Jesuits. In his journal *Fundgruben des Orients* (*Oriental Repositories*, 1809–18), Joseph von Hammer-Purgstall printed numerous letters dispatched from Asian lands by European residents or visitors. Pitton de Tournefort's authoritative description of Turkey from 1717 was presented in epistolary form, while the letters of the Swedish librarian Jacob Jonas Björnstahl and Savary's Egyptian letters, for example, were also a valuable source of information.

Needless to say, the learned travel report stood under the imperative of firsthand observation or autopsy. Writers nonetheless copied from each other with such frequency that there were constant complaints about the practice. Apropos of reports about China, the French Sinologist Abel-Rémusat expressed his wry bemusement at seeing the same old accounts constantly being rejuvenated.[31] Over the course of the eighteenth century, however, a willingness to tolerate plagiarism all but disappeared. William Tennant, an Anglican priest who nursed a vitriolic hatred of Indians, could only expect a hearing in the future from his ideological bedfellows, not from "philosophers," after the anonymous reviewer of the reputable *Edinburgh Review* ascertained that in his *Indian Recreations* (1803) there was "not one single fact of any consequence which is not taken from some other person."[32] It was an altogether different matter if the intermingling of fact and fiction was openly avowed and aesthetically justified, as was the case in Montesquieu's *Lettres persanes* or the Baron de Lahontan's report on North America from 1703.[33] Direct reference to earlier travelers was also permissible. While it is true that, as Harry Liebersohn has suggested, we comprehend the writers of travel accounts "most fullly when we view them not as isolated authors with full control over their written words but as actors in a global system of intellectual production,"[34] it is equally important to understand that, in an age that held "critique" in the highest regard, the knowledge thus gained and processed was subjected to rigorous scrutiny.

To the extent that the accumulation of European knowledge about Asiatic lands and peoples was conceived as a supranational, collective undertaking, all but the most individualistic travelers (such as Thomas Manning) submitted to the general process of increasing and critically assessing the common store of knowledge. When visiting more frequented regions such as Asia Minor, the Levant, or parts of India, some researchers adopted a specialized role. Assuming that their readers were already familiar with previous travel descriptions, they sought to add to their predecessors' findings and, where necessary, to correct them. The learned traveler was expected to have the older literature stretching all the way back to classical antiquity at his fingertips, yet to approach it in a spirit of critical inquiry rather than one of unquestioning deference. At the beginning of the century Desideri, the voyager to Tibet, still felt obliged to justify himself at length for calling into question the authority of such notables as Athanasius Kircher and Jean-Baptiste Tavernier.[35] By the century's end, no such apologia was required. "Facing the tribunal of the public,"[36] Volney made a virtuosically staged literary dispute with Savary, whose book on Egypt had appeared shortly beforehand, one of the key elements in his report on the Near East. Chateaubriand was continually referring—sometimes with an almost exaggerated display of erudition—to the older literature on Greece and the Orient, although he clung to it more closely than a Volneyan empiricism would allow; given the speed at which he traveled, he had no other option. The first edition (1811) of his *Itinéraire de Paris à Jérusalem* still bristled with footnotes. In a bid to enhance the book's aesthetic appeal, he reduced their number the following year and banished them to an appendix for the third edition.[37]

A traveler attained classic status if his findings could be confirmed or empirically verified by later colleagues. Thomas Shaw's or Carsten Niebuhr's reputation was built largely on the strength of their verifiably accurate topographical descriptions.[38] Later travelers had nothing to correct and little to add. François Bernier owed his enduring fame in France not just to the literary quality of his gripping depiction of power struggles in seventeenth-century India but also to the accuracy of numerous historical details.[39] At least one author was canonized despite or perhaps even because of his copious errors: James Mill's *History of British India* from 1817, subsequently set as a textbook for aspiring colonial officials, was reissued in 1858 in an unorthodox new edition by the India expert, Horace Hayman Wilson, who took issue with the author in a series of lengthy footnotes. Wilson had almost nothing positive to say about his distinguished predecessor. While his countertext left Mill's original utilitarian polemic intact, it also discredited much of its empirical content and in so doing consigned Mill's version to the historiographical archives.[40]

Unlike observations of nature, descriptions of buildings or copies of inscriptions, claims made about *historia civilis* were difficult to confirm or correct empirically. Here old prejudices proved stubbornly resistant to criticism, as the abbé Grosier found to his frustration in 1818. With considerable effort and patience, he had corrected what he saw as the false claims about China made by M. de Guignes (Junior), only to have de Guignes neither respond to his objections nor refrain from repeating his errors in future.[41] More serious was the systematic misunderstanding brought about by the continuing hold of certain "big ideas." The most powerful of these was undoubtedly that of "oriental despotism." Even reporters with a strongly empirical bent took its existence for granted and then looked about for post hoc confirmatory evidence. There will be more to say about this in chapter 10.

ANTHOLOGIES, COLLAGES, MEGA-NARRATIVES

Between the reporting observer and his readers stood all the activity of the literary world: editors, publishers, redactors, translators. By the time they reached the reader, the eyewitness's original perceptions had already passed through a succession of filters. European images of Asia were not simply direct transcriptions of sensory impressions into a textual medium, nor were they even representations once removed. The representation itself was transformed by being processed in different media.

We must start with the most extreme cases. Some of the most significant works on Asia remained unwritten. Alexander von Humboldt was never given the opportunity to undertake the great Asian voyage that he had been planning—and the public expecting—for years. When the sexagenarian toured Siberia and Russian Central Asia in 1829, rather than writing the report himself he entrusted it to his collaborator Gustav Rose, whose execution of the task left much to be desired. Pater Claude Sicard S. J., who traveled in Egypt from 1712 until his death from the plague in 1726, discovered Thebes and had an unrivaled knowledge of the country and its monuments yet left few scholarly traces. "The true measure of Sicard's accomplishments," concludes a modern historian of Egyptology, "will never be known because most of his manuscripts, sketches, and maps were lost after his death."[42] Other works went missing. Thomas Manning's extensive report on his trip to Lhasa has never been found.[43] John Briggs's monumental history of Muslim India, said to have totaled eleven manuscript volumes in folio, was destroyed when the British Residency in Pune was looted in 1817.[44] Some travelers lacked an opportunity to work up their notes into a proper report. Upon returning from Tibet and the Himalayas in 1664, Pater Johannes Grueber was interviewed by many scholars about what he had seen but committed virtually nothing to paper himself.[45]

Editors intruded, partly by necessity, between the traveler and his texts. William Moorcroft's notes were posthumously edited by Horace Hayman Wilson, the critical commentator of James Mill, in careless and piecemeal fashion. The life of this fascinating traveler to Central Asia and passionate horse breeder was first reconstructed by the English historian Garry Alder.[46] Several authors who had never visited the lands they were writing about drew on the papers of anonymous travelers, compiling accounts that were long regarded as definitive.[47] Learned wordsmiths refined the manuscripts of inept writers, just as Jean-Baptiste Du Halde in Paris adapted the reports sent from the Far East by his fellow friars to the stylistic tastes and religious and political sensibilities of his French contemporaries. The English reading public came to know the Jesuit letters only in ideologically expurgated form. As their editor explained, they had been purified of all Jesuitical influence, "such appearing quite insipid or ridiculous to most English Readers, and indeed to all Persons of Understanding and Taste."[48] Besides, the English public preferred the vehemently anti-Jesuit report on China written by the Dominican Domingo Navarette in 1676, which could be read in English translation from 1704.

Not every travel report was presented from the outset in a form that was faithful to the original text. Sir John Chardin's description of Iran was not even close to properly edited until 1735, twelve years after the author's death; a completely reliable edition first appeared in 1811. The Italian merchant Nicolò Manuzzi (sometimes: Manucci), who lived in India from 1656 until his death in 1720 and, despite lacking any formal medical education, served for a time as a physician at the Mughal court, wrote a digressively anecdotal history of the Mughal Empire in Italian, French, and Portuguese that ended with the author's memoirs. Even today, it is still cited by some experts as a half-credible source.[49] In 1700 Manuzzi sent off parts of the manuscript to Paris. There the Jesuit François Catrou carelessly and irresponsibly used it as the basis for his anything-but-rigorous Mughal history, first published in 1705. Even in Great Britain, where literature on India was hardly in short supply, it maintained a presence on the book market until the early nineteenth century.[50] Manuzzi's complete manuscript was later acquired by the Venetian Signoria but then left to moulder away in the archives, mainly for reasons of cost. A fairly faithful English translation was produced by an official in the Indian Civil Service, appearing between 1906 and 1908.[51] The original has never been published. There were other cases where the urtext remained inaccessible. Demetrius Cantemir's history of the Ottoman Empire, written in 1716, was brought to England as a Latin manuscript by his son Antiochus, the then-Russian ambassador in London, where it was translated and published (in 1735) by the editor and historian Nicholas Tindal. This version provided the textual foundation for the subsequent French (1743) and German (1745) editions.[52]

Travel descriptions, particularly voluminous and expensive ones, were not infrequently offered in cheap abridgments. Often these were most readily available in so-called travel miscellanies, wholly or largely devoted to reports from the non-European world. Such anthologies—often in multivolume format—started appearing during the early stages of European expansion into countries engaged in overseas trade.[53] Around 1600, editors like Richard Eden and Richard Hakluyt were already setting high editorial standards. The travel miscellanies brought together widely dispersed materials, made foreign-language texts accessible in English translation, and, ideally, presented unpublished manuscripts as well. They covered a wide spectrum, ranging all the way from slapdash compilations lacking any kind of internal consistency, via ragbag anthologies, where the line between text and editorial commentary was often blurred, to meticulously produced mega-projects that met the highest philological standards of the day.

This last category included the nearly thousand-page compendium, *Noord en Oost Tartarye* (1692), the fruit of a quarter-century's labor by Nicolaas Witsen, thirteen-time mayor of Amsterdam and an even longer-standing member of the VOC's board of directors. Witsen never ventured further east than Moscow on his travels. Yet through his formative experiences as a student of the famous Leiden Orientalist, Jacob Grolius, as well as his zeal for collecting and his excellent contacts among travelers and scholars all around the world, he became one of the foremost experts on North and East Asia. These qualifications equipped him to present a vast array of previously unknown information in his magnum opus. Thanks to his contacts in Moscow, Russian informants who visited him in Holland, and the VOC's internal correspondence, he was privy to information to which nobody else had access.[54] Compilation had been a reputable literary procedure since Pierre Bayle's recently published dictionary, at the very latest; in Witsen, it became a method for showcasing the newly discovered geographical and ethnological diversity of Siberia and East Asia. Like his contemporary Barthélemi d'Herbelot, who arranged his *Bibliothèque Orientale* in alphabetic order, the mayor of Amsterdam eschewed any systematic organization of his material. He preferred to orchestrate a rich and surprising polyphony rather than forcing the voices he had so painstakingly assembled to sing in unison.

A somewhat different approach was taken by his compatriot François Valentyn, a highly educated priest who had lived in the Moluccas and on Java from 1686–94 and 1705–14 while working for the VOC.[55] In the five folio volumes of his *Oud en Nieuw Oost-Indien* (1724–26), at almost five thousand pages the most comprehensive European work on Asia prior to Carl Ritter's *Erdkunde*, he struggled to arrange his material systematically as the sheer abundance of his sources threatened at times to overwhelm him. On other occasions he faced the opposite problem, compelled to uncharacteristic brevity by a shortage of information about countries on the fringes of the Dutch Empire. The conditions under which the work was composed and printed also meant that the finished product—despite the author's best intentions—turned out to be a compilation rather than an architectonically balanced description.[56] Its open-ended character was further underscored by the fact that Valentyn interpolated dozens of official papers, letters, diplomatic instructions, memoranda, and other original documents, many of them previously unpublished. It has rightly been called "a kind of archive," even though the author's guiding hand can be sensed throughout.[57]

Witsen's and Valentyn's methods for producing a collage of miscellaneous materials were applied less frequently by editors of later monumental anthologies. The most original work of the early eighteenth century, a *Collection of Voyages and Travels* in four folio volumes by the brothers Awnsham and John Churchill, still stayed relatively close to the sources. Published in 1704 and expanded in three subsequent editions, it mostly featured material that was new to English readers, edited from manuscipts, or translated from other European languages. The texts were lightly abridged and generally accurately reproduced, albeit haphazardly arranged.[58] In the following year, a competitor product appeared on a hotly contested market: a collection edited by Dr. John Harris. It contained little that was new, however, and it made deep cuts to the texts. The second edition of the Harris collection (1744–48) was curated by the multifaceted writer Dr. John Campbell, whose name did not appear on the title page. He introduced the method of presenting long sections of the texts in editorial paraphrase rather than printing them verbatim. Combined with long essays on history and trade, there resulted a continuous geographical description of the world that anticipated in parts another mega-project in which John Campbell would play a leading role, the English *Universal History*.[59]

In 1745–47 John Green, editor of an immense collection that became known by the name of its publisher, Thomas Astley, went a step further.[60] Green did not reproduce a single original text in his *New General Collection*; he did not even bother "castrat[ing]" his sources, as he put it in his preface.[61] Instead, he recast all the narrative passages in third person and separated the material into travel journals and general remarks about the country. The latter were culled from various reports and worked into so-called "digests," chapters offering summarized information. In this way readers were spared repetition and had no need to leaf backwards and forwards to compare passages: "instead of a great many imperfect Accounts, which the Authors separately afford, he will be furnished with one complete Description, compiled from them all."[62] The raw material was thus more intensively processed than in earlier anthologies as the collection of voyages evolved into a kind of textbook for descriptive geography.[63] At the same time, the all-powerful editor now intervened between the voice of the describing witness and the reader. The immediacy of the original texts was lost. Only occasional page references pointed back to the sources. Indeed, when Green himself relied on another compiler—frequently Du Halde in the case of China[64]—layer upon layer built up between the eyewitness and the final consumer of his information.

The "Astley Collection" was widely emulated on the continent, inspiring the century's two most substantial travel collections. The *Histoire générale des voyages* (1746–59), produced by the abbé Prévost in fifteen lavishly illustrated quarto volumes of more than six hundred pages each,[65] began as a translation of Astley but was continued by Prévost on his own from the eighth volume after the English publisher had to cancel the project due to a lack of subscribers. The abbé translated the English version fairly faithfully but failed to consult the mainly Portuguese, Spanish, and Dutch texts that formed the basis of the Astley/Green collection. Once he no longer had the English template to guide him, he retained its methodology while cutting and splicing the original documents in even more drastic fashion. For obvious reasons, he also gave more space to French travelers. In the entire work—most consistently in volumes twelve through fifteen—the rewritten travelers' texts flowed together into a powerful narrative stream that Prévost, one of the best novelists of his time, knew how to navigate with elegance and unflagging momentum. "Pointless verbosity and tedious repetition" were to be avoided at all costs.[66]

Prévost handled his sources more critically than Astley/Green, weeding out anything that struck him as particularly far-fetched or miraculous.

Nonetheless, he saw his task even less than his English precursors in mere documentation but rather in the synthesizing achievement of the narrative historian.[67] For him, *histoire des voyages* meant two things: the history of travel and that of the lands traveled. Prévost's most ambitious goal was "a complete system of modern history and geography that represents the present state of all nations."[68] That extended to the "philosophical" evaluation of conditions outside Europe and, still more, the activities of Europeans abroad. Prévost's interest was far from antiquarian. In the later volumes produced under his personal control, he sought out the best and most recent sources he could find to convey as up-to-date an image as possible of their respective countries. In this he differed from those less reflective and ambitious compilers who blithely trotted out the same old warhorses from the early days of the Age of Discovery, without giving less educated readers a sense of the age and historicity of their sources.[69]

The greatest German project of this kind was the *Allgemeine Historie aller merckwürdigen Reisen* (*General History of All Curious Journeys*), a monumental work in twenty-one folio volumes edited between 1747 and 1774 by a circle of scholars in Leipzig gathered around Johann Joachim Schwabe. It likewise began as a translation of the Astley/Green collection, although its editors added a good deal of their own material along the way. At first Schwabe's team had sought to emulate Prévost's "graceful style,"[70] only to discover that the abbé had made a number of mistakes and arbitrary changes. They then went back to the English original and a French-language edition that had appeared in Holland. Later, of course, they had no choice but to return to the Paris edition. Unlike the Churchill brothers, Schwabe and his colleagues did not generally take the trouble to translate texts written in languages other than English, French, and German directly from the source. They made more of a concerted effort than Prévost, though, to gauge and critically discuss the authenticity of the material. They also prided themselves on having done a better job at selecting the right "terminos technicos or artificial terms." An extensive apparatus of footnotes was provided partly for this reason. Inconsistencies between statements made by different travelers were to be settled and fabrications eliminated. Like Astley/Green and Prévost before them, the editors paraphrased, streamlined, summarized, and systematized. Reflective remarks in the original were mostly cut. For all its colossal dimensions, the work was meant to be read from start to finish rather than dipped into at leisure. Schwabe was not merely advertising future volumes when he explained in his foreword:

> The work itself is so constituted that the further into it one reads, the more delightful and pleasing it will become: and while much may seem perfectly obscure at the beginning, on account of the unknown lands and places mentioned therein, in the reports that follow they will be elucidated in such a way as to remove all traces of doubt from the reader's mind. Thus ever more light will be shed, and at every moment the desire to gain further insight into this history will increase.[71]

By the century's end, standards had shifted. On the one hand, Prévost was now criticized for being too ponderous and pedantic, too bland—lacking in "painterly force" (*une peinture énergique*)—and too timid in his "philosophical" pronouncements.[72] His work was shortened and revised to suit current public tastes. The price fetched by his great work on the book market had plunged, we are told in 1808, and its only value now lay in the illustrations.[73] On the other hand, compilers with a scientific interest returned to the same ideal of unembellished, faithful documentation that Richard Hakluyt had already realized (by the standards of Renaissance erudition) in his collection from 1589. In 1807 one of the top connoisseurs of the literature expressed the prevailing norm in the following way: "The most useful collections would be those in which every original text is reproduced in full, with critical exactness and, where necessary, with elucidations for obscure passages." But he was forced to concede: "Only it is unlikely there would be enough purchasers even to cover the cost of publication."[74]

Not by chance, Hakluyt's *Principall Navigations* was now reissued for the first time since 1600, albeit in an expensive deluxe edition of only 325 copies.[75] The last of the great British travel collections was planned more along the lines of Astley/Green than of Prévost. The collection edited between 1808 and 1814 by the Scottish geographer John Pinkerton was universal in scope and ambition. Unusually, a significant proportion of the whole was allocated to Europe: some six of seventeen volumes.[76] Pinkerton had nothing new to offer,[77] but he showed keen discernment in selecting texts that he regarded as having already attained classic status. In the four volumes on Asia, these ranged from Marco Polo and William of Rubruck, in the thirteenth century, to the most recent *Survey of South India* by Dr. Francis Buchanan. In Prévost, he took issue with the choice of excerpts, the destruction of the text in its original form through the paraphrasing intervention of an omniscient narrator, and "the easy parade of learned notes"[78]—a charge that might have been leveled against Schwabe as well, and with even better reason. Annotations were not there to correct older authors from the supposedly more enlightened standpoint of the present day. Their sole function was "to illustrate obscure passages, . . . and in such a collection as the present there are happily few obscurities to illustrate." Pinkerton took his own advice and limited himself to printing longer extracts, accompanying them with a minimum of commentary. His own geographical description of the world appeared separately.[79]

With Pinkerton, the compiler's self-assigned role as the most ambitious of all *Historia* authors had been played out, at first in Great Britain and then elsewhere. The different goals that encyclopedically minded authors such as Green and Prévost had sought to bring together in a single work now drifted apart. The geographer no longer aspired to be a universal historian. Travel literature now gradually lost its role as a privileged locus of geographical and ethnographical knowledge. Increasingly, it represented only itself. Charles-Athanase Walckenaer's immensely rich collection of reports on Africa (1826–31) had virtually no other purpose than to illustrate a history of travel and to impart geographical information; it never made the Prévostian claim to be a history of Africa.[80] Older travelogues slowly receded into the auratic distance of museum exhibits, allowing them to be savored more than ever for their purely literary qualities. William Marsden's edition of Marco Polo from 1818 was of epochal significance in this regard. The great Orientalist translated the text afresh and then did precisely what Pinkerton had rejected shortly before. He supplied very detailed notes, "calculated to bring the matter of the text into comparison with the information contained in subsequent accounts of travels and other well-authenticated writings."[81] Marsden—like Goethe at the same time in a different way—aimed to remove the stain of fraudulence from Marco Polo's reputation and demonstrate just how astonishingly accurate his findings were. Unlike the footnotes liberally sprinkled throughout eighteenth-century collections, this successful rehabilitation was not designed to bring an old body of knowledge up-to-date by correcting flaws in the data, but rather to contextualize and historicize an author now elevated to the status of a classic. Only through Marsden's influence did Marco Polo become what he has remained for readers ever since: a medieval writer. It was henceforth impossible to read him naïvely, and it now seemed ridiculous to hold him to the same standards of accountability applied to present-day authors.

Where compilers from the Renaissance up to Prévost and Schwabe had been grateful for every new text from abroad, the genre of the travel collection eventually collapsed under the ever-increasing weight of new information. In the final third of the eighteenth century, the international geographical literature had grown so vast that several journals were kept busy reviewing the latest publications in the field.[82] Pinkerton got around the problem by selecting a canon. That was of little use to science, however, nor was it enticing enough for the general public. Other solutions had to be found.

Conrad Malte-Brun's *Annales de Voyage* (1807–14), a mixture of travel collection and yearbook that initially appeared in periodic installments, represented a remarkable attempt to make available the most recent material from all over the world. The *Annales* were the antipodes to Pinkerton's collection of geographical classics. Whereas Pinkerton printed Engelbert Kaempfer's century-old report as the definitive, still current text on Japan, thereby ignoring Thunberg's more recent voyage,[83] Malte-Brun began by instructing his readers about the collection of Japanese books, manuscripts, drawings, and coins left behind by the recently deceased Isaac Titsingh.[84]

The increased demand for information concerning foreign and especially Asiatic countries, coinciding with an increased supply of such information, was met by several specialist journals. They had their archetype in the *Asiatick Researches*, edited since 1788 by Sir William Jones's Asiatick Society of Bengal. Many of the contributions that appeared there were quickly translated into other European languages. Notable journals in Germany included the *Asiatische Magazin* (1806–11), overseen by Johann Adam Bergk and others, and the *Magazin für die Kunde und neueste Geschichte der außer-europäischen Länder und Völker* (*Magazine for the Study and Recent History of Non-European Lands and Nations*, 1817–18), jointly edited by the Indologist Friedrich Herrmann and an expert on the Americas. The German public had the Forster family to thank for the finest publications in the field: father Johann Reinhold Forster, son Georg, and son-in-law Matthias Christian Sprengel, a student of Schlözer's and, from 1779, professor of history and librarian of the university in Halle, at that time an important center of learning. In 1790 Johann Reinhold Forster established the *Magazin von merkwürdigen neuen Reisebeschreibungen* (*Magazine of Curious New Travel Descriptions*); it continued well beyond his death in 1798, ending only with the publication of the thirty-seventh volume in 1828. The first sixteen volumes, edited by Forster himself, mostly offered new material about Africa and the Pacific, with contributions from the Asiatic region concerning India, in the main. The uniformly lengthy texts, in each case accompanied by copious explanatory and supplementary notes, often appeared at the same time or shortly thereafter in book form as well. Sprengel, who offered his father-in-law editorial assistance on the magazine, also published alongside it his own *Auswahl der besten ausländischen geographischen und statistischen Nachrichten zur Aufklärung der*

Völker- und Länderkunde (*Selection of the Best Foreign Geographical and Statistical Information for Illuminating the Study of Nations and Lands*, 1794–1800). *Völkerkunde*, the study of (other) nations, here did not yet carry the restricted meaning of ethnology as the science of so-called "uncivilized" or "natural" peoples. Sprengel had originally conceived the journal with his brother-in-law Georg Forster, who died shortly afterwards following his ill-fated involvement in the Mainz Republic. Like Malte-Brun a little later, the superlatively well-informed Sprengel (who never traveled outside the German lands) printed only the most recent work in the field. Unlike his counterpart in Paris, however, he did not hold back from adding his own schoolmasterly, all-knowing commentary. In 1798 he published extensive extracts from Sir George L. Staunton's report on Lord Macartney's trip to China, which had appeared in London only the previous year.[85] The limits of the report were critically discussed, and Sprengel could not refrain from observing that Sir George had evidently taken Georg Forster's *Reise um die Welt* (*Journey around the World*) as his stylistic model without, however, even remotely matching it.[86]

Travel collections were compendia of information about the world. They gave readers access to knowledge they would otherwise have been denied. At the same time, editors created images of the world in the way they selected, coordinated, and commented on texts. The individual text never stood on its own. It was always part of a purposefully arranged whole that bore little relation to the original context of observation. While decomposing the travel collection into less compact, less monumental media meant that information was now processed in a more scientific, up-to-the-minute manner, it also entailed the disintegration of Edmund Burke's "Great Map of Mankind" into discrete cartographical projects. Once the encyclopedic order and the voice of the all-guiding historical narrator à la Prévost had disappeared, there was nothing left to replace them as frameworks of knowledge.

THE TASK OF THE TRANSLATOR

It was not just for the great travel collections that reports were translated in such volume. Almost no other literary genre could claim more widespread appeal beyond the authors' homelands than travel descriptions from exotic parts of the world. The translator's principal task, obviously enough, was to transmit texts to readers who did not understand the originals or were unable to access them. Whereas languages like Swedish or Russian were read by few in the core countries of Europe, knowledge of curricular languages—Latin, French, Italian, English, and German—was extensive among the scholarly and educated public. All the same, languages went through phases of popularity. Around 1800, Latin was a less important tool for scholarly communication than a century before, while English, at least in Germany, had risen during the same period from a position of relative insignificance to become utterly indispensable.[87] The reason why all the authoritative travel reports were generally translated into the major European languages was not just so that a less linguistically proficient middle-class public could be supplied with commercially promising literary fodder. The translation of nonfictional texts fulfilled a secondary function it has since lost: improving critique. Originals were not sacrosanct; authors enjoyed no legal right to have their texts translated faithfully. The translator saw his relationship to the translated text as one of mastery, not servitude.

Such freedom could be used in different ways. Very few eighteenth-century translators felt duty-bound to cling slavishly to the text.[88] It was far from exceptional for translators to tamper with their material in the belief—mistaken or otherwise—that they knew better. In 1791 a certain E. W. Cuhn condensed James Bruce's *Travels* into a two-volume "extract"—not, as he explained, because he was not up to the task, but because the Scottish author had squandered words in needless profusion, and "lacked much of the prerequisite knowledge and especially the spirit of philosophical observation needed for such a journey."[89] Not everyone in Germany shared his opinion, given that a five-volume complete translation of the monumental work had appeared shortly before.[90] Both German editions were fitted out with annotations and appendices by noted scholars. Such an approach had become commonplace by the end of the century, particularly in Germany. Fiction, too, inspired translators and editors to enhance its appreciation by attentive readers. The first Chinese novel to appear in English, in 1761, came with extensive footnotes by Thomas Percy describing the world of Chinese elite culture and citing a broad range of references.[91] In the early nineteeth century, Robert Southey and other romantic writers were then to launch a new lyrical genre: the annotated oriental poem.[92]

It was sometimes the case that even a translator who was quite willing to tinker with the original text could find nothing to tinker with. Friedrich Rühs for example, who on another occasion had taken the liberty "to excise the excrescences of the original and curtail its intolerable verbosity,"[93] dared not touch Mountstuart Elphinstone's report on Afghanistan and made do with a few respectful explanations. In other cases the translator's restraint owed more to the dictates of the market. Johann Christian Hüttner, who in 1804, the same year that the original appeared, published his German translation of Sir John Barrow's report on the Macartney expedition to China, complained: "In order to make readable annotations to a journey, a translator must have more leisure than is granted him by German book fairs and the alacrity of competing translators."[94] Hüttner limited himself to providing his German readers with concise explanations of British references. He thus annotates the Smithfield Market in London,[95] which Barrow mentions in passing, but has nothing to say about Barrow's highly controversial statements on China. No one would have been better qualified to comment on this than Hüttner himself, who had been the sole German participant in the Macartney embassy and had already published his own report on the mission in 1798.[96] Based in London as a mediator between the great metropolis and the German cultural scene, he later became an important cultural broker who supplied Goethe and many other German contemporaries with news and texts from all parts of the overseas world.[97]

In the ideal view of the Enlightenment, the comments and corrections made by the translator were supposed to transform the original into a superior work tool. Whether such ambitious claims were recognized was a theme of scholarly criticism. Thus, geographical experts rated Johann Tobias Köhler's achievements as a translator of travel literature more highly than his superficial commentaries, whereas Johann Reinhold Forster was renowned above all for the learned improvements he made to the literature he introduced to a German-speaking public. Both Forsters, father and son, traveled to England in 1766 and initially made a name for themselves as fastidious translators of travel works into English. Georg Forster assisted his father with commercial translations from the age of twelve, at first from Russian into English. His *Reise um die Welt*, a landmark of eighteenth-century German literature, was written in English to allow him to compete on the book market as soon as possible with other accounts of Captain Cook's second circumnavigation of the globe. He did not get around to preparing a German edition until 1778–80. Financial need forced the Forsters to take on almost every translation project that came their way. Johann Reinhold even excused himself at times for having his name associated with second-rate products.[98] More illustrious—and more characteristic for his oeuvre[99]—were projects that gave him the opportunity to bring his immense knowledge to bear on scientifically worthwhile texts. In extreme cases a new work could arise as a result. Thomas Pennant's *Indian Zoology* (1769), a study of Ceylonese and Javanese ornithology, was so expanded and improved in Forster's hands that Pennant himself, one of the foremost zoologists of his time, acknowledged the superiority of Forster's *Indische Zoologie*, a bilingual German-Latin edition that appeared in Halle in 1781. Indeed, he admired it so much that he had Forster's text translated for the second English edition (1790).[100] The editorial work carried out by a scholar of Forster's standing was often carried over into subsequent translations. In his 1798 translation of one of the most important non-British descriptions of India, Fra Paolino da San Bartolomeo's *Viaggio alle Indie Orientali* (Rome 1796), Forster added 190 extensive annotations that were subsequently retained in the Danish (1799) and English (1800) editions. In the Age of Enlightenment, such a transnational cumulative effect was more the rule than the exception.

A further example is provided by Carl Peter Thunberg's travel report on South Africa, Java, and Japan, which first appeared in Swedish in four volumes between 1788 and 1793.[101] By 1792, two German translations of the first three volumes were competing against each other on the market: one, translated by the young Kurt Sprengel under the editorial oversight of Johann Reinhold Forster, cut the original by around a half; the second, undertaken by the Stralsund headmaster Christian Heinrich Groskurd and authorized by Thunberg himself, performed some light cosmetic surgery on the occasionally bulging material. The biggest international impact was made by the lavishly presented French edition of 1796, translated by the well-known Orientalist and keeper of oriental manuscripts at the Bibliothèque Nationale, Louis Mathieu Langlès. Drawing on Groskurd's text as his principal source, he also appears to have consulted the original and borrowed several of the cuts and many of the annotations from the Forster-Sprengel edition. Langlès added his own notes, approaching the famous Lamarck for advice on the sections dealing with the natural world. Thunberg's report became known in Japan in the early twentieth century through a partial translation of the French edition. Thunberg's text was therefore widely circulated in Europe in a translation twice removed from the original—thrice removed, once it arrived in Japan.

The literary middlemen who came between the author and his readers thus only rarely conceived of their role as guardians of textual authenticity. What the public was given to read at the end was often a polygraphic aggregate resulting from deletion and insertion, rearrangement and paraphrase, commentary, translation, and incorporation of supplementary matter. Editors of travel collections obviously used all these techniques, but an individual work could equally be the final stage in a long production chain. A further stage was added when a compilation such as Prévost's *Histoire générale des voyages* was cherry-picked by a second-order compiler like the abbé Raynal, editor-in-chief of the *Histoire philosophique et politique des deux Indes* (1770).[102] At each stage of revision, information was filtered out, perspectives were shifted, and judgments modified. Merely through the mechanisms of the literary market, whatever immediate reality an eyewitness report may once have contained became diluted and fictionalized. But that is only one side of the coin. On the other side, in the hands of critical scholars such as the two Forsters, Matthias Christian Sprengel, Langlès, Pallas, Walckenaer, or Horace Hayman Wilson, editorial intervention and critical commentary could scientifically undergird a primary text, subject it to comparative scrutiny, and qualitatively transform it, thereby increasing its use value. Assuming they were not motivated by blind opportunism, editors could be the most careful readers of these texts. They could chase up much that had escaped the author's notice: inaccuracies in geographical terminology or nomenclature, for example. In the best case scenario, such *reécriture* resulted from a creative reading that filled in gaps and connected the text with relevant contextual information. So long as travel texts could still be useful, this was a justifiable procedure. It no longer made sense once they were read only for pleasure.

TOPICALITY AND CANONICITY

Towards the end of the eighteenth century, a need for more current information made itself felt in sciences with an interest in Asia, a growing awareness that news about other civilizations was rapidly becoming obsolete. The great travel collections were no longer found satisfactory, and editors took considerable liberties with their source texts in an effort to keep pace with the latest scholarly developments. Yet in many areas, an antiquated knowledge base persisted.

In several cases this was due to a lack of up-to-date information. Robert Knox's description of Ceylon from 1681 maintained its standing for around three generations, surpassed in its descriptive detail only by François Valentyn's lesser-known Dutch work (1724–26).[103] A later German visitor reported mainly on his personal experiences.[104] Much the same held true of Japan. The Tokugawa dynasty held fast to its policy of strict isolation throughout the entire eighteenth century. Unlike its British counterpart, the EIC, in the period after Warren Hastings, the VOC did not see itself as a patron of scholarship. Jealously guarding its monopoly on contacts with Japan, it did little to encourage study of the country. Engelbert Kaempfer's report, based on observations made between 1690 to 1692, therefore remained the most important European source on Japan for more than a century after its belated publication (in English) in 1727, although later universal histories and travel collections sometimes presented new material from VOC documents and other minor sources.[105] Thunberg had added to the Westphalian physician's description following his visit in the 1770s without superseding and replacing it as a whole. As late as 1844, James Cowles Prichard, an assiduous scholar, could find no other authority to cite on the physical appearance of the Japanese than Kaempfer.[106] Matthew C. Perry, the commander of the American squadron that "opened" Japan in 1853/54, consulted an 1853 abridgment of Kaempfer's old report before his second voyage.[107] Such anachronism was sometimes understandable. Even older works than Kaempfer's, such as reports by Jesuit missionaries from Portugal, retained their value in the case of Japan, given that vast stretches of the country's interior had not been visited by foreigners since the silk curtain had come swishing down in the 1630s.

Yet even when there was no shortage of recent reports, images of the country conveyed by earlier accounts could still prove remarkably persistent. In 1670 François Bernier had described Kashmir as a terrestrial paradise. Johann Gottfried Herder in the late eighteenth century and Friedrich Schlegel in the early nineteenth were still recycling this vision of the French physician and philosopher, while as late as 1810 Joseph Goerres was making the bizarre claim that Kashmir had been the political center and "earth navel" of antiquity.[108] In several cases, the impression of a timeless Orient was deliberately fostered. Thus, in 1744 there appeared in London an edition of the letters sent from Turkey two centuries earlier by the imperial ambassador Busbecq (Busbequius), with no information given about the context in which they were written.[109] All the year numbers were omitted from the appended author biography, taken from Pierre Bayle's *Dictionnaire*. It was thus made to appear that Busbeck, whose uncommonly lively correspondence was considered of outstanding documentary value by no less an authority than Hammer-Purgstall,[110] was describing the *current* Ottoman Empire.

Students of Asia who did not want to make things too difficult for themselves continued to reach for the same familiar, superannuated standard works. Until around 1730, the *Geographia generalis* (1650) of Bernhard Varenius was considered the definitive textbook on Asian geography.[111] A popular work on China published in 1679 was written as if the Ming dynasty, toppled in 1644, were still in power. More surprisingly still, even the learned abbé Grosier spoke in 1818 of the fifteen provinces of the Chinese Empire, notwithstanding the fact that the Qing dynasty had long ago reorganized the empire into eighteen provinces.[112] Around 1800, other authors were still citing Paul Rycaut, the leading English authority of the seventeenth century, or even Richard Knolles, the late-Elizabethan author of the perennially popular *Generall Historie of the Turkes* (1603), as the most reliable sources on the Ottoman Empire.[113] Hammer-Purgstall knew what he was talking about when he lamented in 1815 that most geographical statistics in Western literature on Turkey were a couple of centuries out of date, "more noteworthy to the historian than to the statistician and politician."[114] Against this background, the fact that Lord Byron read Knolles's stirringly eloquent historical narrative for *pleasure* attested to a new way of approaching old texts.[115]

The sheer prestige of a traveler was often what secured him the public's loyalty. Marco Polo, for example, enjoyed great respect in the eighteenth century. Having long been dismissed as a fantasist, the early Jesuit reports from China were able to confirm many statements of his that had previously been disbelieved.[116] Even the Berlin geographer Carl Ritter, perhaps the greatest expert on old European travel literature there has ever been, and anything but an uncritical reader, praised Marco Polo for his "in many parts deficient yet otherwise classic and unique work."[117] Repeated attempts were made to put together a canon of exemplary travel texts. There were four categories: excellent, good, suspect, and make-believe, declared the geographer Bruzen de la Martinière in 1768. In his opinion, the "excellent" descriptions of Asia included books by Pietro della Valle, Adam Olearius, John Chardin, Simon de La Loubère, Martin Martini, Cornelis de Bruin, Nicolas Gervaise, Joseph Pitton de Tournefort, Louis Le Comte, and Nicolaas de Graaf—a list that has stood the test of time surprisingly well.[118] By around 1800 this hit parade had by general consensus expanded to take in Pococke, Shaw, Kaempfer, and Steller as well as the more recent reports by Niebuhr, Pallas, Marsden, and Volney, in addition to James Cook's and Georg Forster's books on the South Seas. Chardin's voyage to Iran, reissued in a meticulous new edition by Langlès in 1811, occupied for many a position at the "apex of all travel descriptions,"[119] eventually ceding this place to Alexander von Humboldt's journey to the Americas. Far from being the exclusive preserve of experts, these were classics that formed part of Europe's common cultural capital. They were, as one reviewer somewhat ponderously opined in 1812, "books which men pretending to general knowledge will not well be excused from reading, at some period of their lives, in an unabridged form."[120]

Humboldt was not the first to discover that the fame accrued through his travels translated into social recognition. Johann Reinhold Forster was received by no less a personage than King George III, although the monarch spoke only of England during the audience and neglected to mention Forster's recently completed journey around the world.[121] The young Barthold Georg Niebuhr, not yet the great historian he would later become, found that all doors stood open to him in learned England and Scotland. "You can scarcely imagine," he wrote from Edinburgh in March 1799, "the universal interest and esteem with which people ask after Father and speak of him."[122] The name of the traveler to Arabia later became almost proverbial, as when Leopold von Ranke invoked the intrepid spirit of a Carsten Niebuhr in making a trip—to the archives.[123]

For Volney, his voyage to Egypt and Syria in 1783–85 was a stepping stone to fame, royalties, and a political career.[124] The success of his travel book exceeded even his expectations. It was widely read not just in Europe but also in North America.[125] Yet when touring the United States between 1796 and 1798, he passed up the chance to become a forerunner of Tocqueville. Instead, he contented himself with a task he held to be "more serious, more scientific" than his comprehensive account of the Orient: a monograph on the USA's climate and soil conditions.[126] By that time his name had already been made.

TRACES OF READING

It is difficult to gauge the extent to which the "great" reports on Asia and their countless lesser satellites were actually read and utilized. Descriptions of overseas travel undoubtedly made up an important section in the major state and princely libraries, in many lending libraries and reading societies, and in numerous private collections. John Locke owned 195 titles in the genre—a considerable figure for the late seventeenth century.[127] Johann Wolfgang Goethe first encountered travel literature as a child, while rummaging through the collections of his father Johann Caspar and his maternal grandfather Johann Wolfgang Textor.[128] Johann Reinhold Forster's professional interest in the field was reflected in the roughly 1,500 travel descriptions in his possession, while Carl Ritter held around 1,200 works on Asiatic countries alone in his enormous private library in Berlin, not counting all the major travel collections.[129] More representative was the scholar's library assembled in the same city by Johann Bernoulli, which featured 159 bibliographical entries in the division "Exotic History and Travel Description; Universal Travel Collections." Bernoulli estimated that in the 1780s, over fifty private individuals owned similar collections in the Prussian capital alone.[130]

It is easier to say which of the well-known eighteenth-century scholars and writers drew to any significant extent on material from travel descriptions, historical works on Asia, and translations of Asiatic texts in their own work. Montesquieu's and Herder's intimate familiarity with this literature has been established beyond doubt. An entire volume of the standard edition of Montesquieu's works is devoted to his excerpts from and reading notes on the literature about Asia; he had a special confidence in the mundane writings of itinerant merchants who could not afford to indulge in fantasies and wishful thinking about other peoples and countries.[131] Edward Gibbon documents his own omnivorous reading habits—not just restricted to works on antiquity—in countless footnotes.[132] Voltaire, Turgot, Buffon, Rousseau, and Raynal in France; William Temple, John Locke, Samuel Johnson, Edmund Burke, Adam Smith, Adam Ferguson, and Thomas R. Malthus in the British Isles; Schlözer, Gatterer, Meiners, Blumenbach, Goethe, Heeren, Kant, Hegel, and the Humboldt brothers in the German-speaking world were all outstandingly well-versed in this literature.

The interest in Asia displayed by these authors was in each case bound up with specific motives and purposes. None of them was interested in Asia for its own sake, nor did they seek to make specialized contributions to regional geography or oriental studies. What they had in common was that they all sought to give their ideas universal scope rather than confining them to Europe. This was rather to be expected from natural scientists such as Buffon, Linnaeus, or Alexander von Humboldt than from interpreters of social and cultural life. All the same, Voltaire, Gibbon, Schlözer, Herder, or Heeren sought out new ways of writing history as world history, or at least as Eurasian history. A peculiarity of Gibbon in this regard was his use of recent travelogues to add descriptive detail to scenes from late antique and medieval history. In showing how Asiatic peoples had influenced European history throughout the ages, he sought out all the translations from Asiatic languages he could find. Wilhelm von Humboldt, who learned a few such languages, found linguistic raw material for a global comparative theory of language in travel works such as those of Marsden or Pallas. Both these authors also provided Kant with grist for his anthropological observations. Samuel Johnson, for decades a central figure—if not *the* central figure—on the London literary scene, had "a truly imperial range of geographical interests," devouring and commenting on almost all the new travel literature that came his way.[133]

Economic theory, a discipline which today has been almost totally emptied of cultural content, also drew on data from overseas. It was established by Adam Smith as the historically informed, theoretical study of the creation and distribution of wealth. As such, it did not confine itself to European developments but sought to explain Asia's relative backwardness as well.[134] With each new edition of his *Essay on the Principle of Population*, Thomas Robert Malthus worked in ever more ethnographical material concerning "checks on population" in known civilizations.[135] Numerous political and historical authors also thought in universal terms. Writing about India in successive editions of his *Ideas* (1793, 1804, 1815), Heeren gradually weaned himself off the ancient authorities and turned increasingly to more recent travel literature. Edmund Burke was among the first to recognize the immense importance of the conquest of India for English domestic politics. Through voracious reading, he soon acquired a wealth of knowledge that made him one of the best-informed British experts on India of the mid-1780s.[136] Montesquieu developed in his *De l'esprit des lois* (1748) a globally conceived system of the interrelations between social forms, political orders, and environmental conditions. Lesser-known authors followed in his footsteps: the English physician William Falconer, for example, who in 1781 published an intelligent book on universal environmental history, or Christian Cayus Lorenz Hirschfeld, significant as a theorist of gardening, who shortly before had sketched a world history of hospitality.[137]

ARTS OF READING

Just as no author of informative travel literature could escape the dilemma of having somehow to demonstrate his trustworthiness, so too his readers found themselves faced with the difficulty of having to verify his claims. Only the universally admired celebrity travelers were exempted from this obligation. In all other cases, readers were left to form their own judgment about a text's credibility. The more that European thought aspired to cosmopolitan openness, and the more important information sourced from overseas became as the basis for a universal science of mankind, the greater was the need for what we would now call critical literacy.[138]

To be sure, not all readers brought a critical awareness to the printed page. Some—Buffon, Meiners, and even Montesquieu, to name a few—were known for indiscriminately ransacking texts of all levels of quality for whatever happened to suit their requirements at the time.[139] The same reproach was leveled against Arnold Hermann Ludwig Heeren towards the end of our era. Although Heeren was a far more conscientious reader, he failed to meet the entirely novel criteria of scientific source criticism developed by the so-called Historical School in Germany, as Barthold Georg Niebuhr demonstrated to devastating effect.[140] In the second half of the nineteenth century, most readers tended to take a position midway between these two extremes of blind faith in the author's word and methodically disciplined skepticism.

The examples of geography and cartography provide clear evidence for the extraordinary achievements source criticism could attain even in the early eighteenth century. Despite rarely leaving Paris, Jean-Baptiste d'Anville was able to compare and collate the information that came his way to draw detailed maps of China, the tsarist empire, the Ottoman Empire, and other parts of the world. The maps were so accurate that even decades later, despite all the new data that had been gathered in the meantime, they were still being used with profit and regarded with amazement.[141] Such impressive results were harder to attain when evaluating historical sources on Asia. Critical examination of sources was difficult enough even when limited to Europe, although a serviceable methodology had been in place since the sixteenth century. Nonetheless, there was a perceived need to arrive somehow at an evaluation of Asiatic sources as well. But how was that even possible when two or more historians flagrantly contradicted each other in their accounts of the exact same incident? Who could be trusted? Who was in the right? The first priority was to find out as much as possible about the background to the texts: the dates when they were written, their authors, and their varying points of view. These were difficult tasks in the infancy of oriental studies.[142]

The same problem was identified by Siegmund Jacob Baumgarten, Johann Salomo Semler, and the team of scholars they gathered around them to work on their seventy-five volume *Allgemeine Welthistorie* (*General World History*, 1744–1804), based on the English *Universal History* (fifty-one volumes, 1736–66).[143] This project, which eclipsed even Schwabe's *Allgemeine Historie* in the sheer industry required to produce it, attempted to apply at least a minimum of critical source evaluation in the numerous volumes devoted to non-European history. In his foreword from 1744, Baumgarten barely went beyond such generic requirements as multiple documentation, cross-checking of sources, and "attentiveness to other people's experiences."[144] The task had to be tackled on a case-by-case basis. When weighing up several Persian chronicles on the history of Genghis Khan, for example, the editorial team favored those that showed the greatest degree of convergence with Chinese sources (as translated by Pater Gaubil).[145] The Jesuits had always praised Chinese historiography.[146] For a time it was considered the most reliable in all Asia, particularly once Chinese accounts of the advanced age of their own culture gradually came to be accepted. Edward Gibbon went considerably further in his source criticism. When considering how Sultan Bayezid I was treated following his capture in 1402 by the conqueror Timur (or Tamerlane), he extensively discussed his half-dozen sources from the vantage point of the chroniclers' possible bias and their distance or proximity to the events in question.[147] Marshalling all the evidence at his disposal, he did not hesitate to reach a conclusion on the matter. What was new in Gibbon, compared to Baumgarten, was the idea that no single source could be trusted completely, since they were all to some extent subject to perspectival distortion. The indispensability of source criticism had, however, become widely accepted by the mid-eighteenth century. Not only scholars of Graeco-Roman antiquity came to be judged by this humanist standard; it was applied to oriental studies as well. Increasingly, later historians took to criticizing their predecessors for their cavalier treatment of the sources.[148]

Travel reports and historical sources were closely related. The acceleration of temporal perception in the late eighteenth century went hand in hand with an increasing awareness of the historicity of travel descriptions. Travelogues could rapidly fade into obsolescence, as we have already seen in the case of travel collections. In 1799, impressed by Bonaparte's invasion of Egypt, the suspicion dawned on the German theologian Heinrich Eberhard Gottlob Paulus

> that we will soon have need of previous descriptions as our sole possible source for distinguishing the authentically oriental elements [of Egyptian life], which for so long were handed down unchanged, from those affected by modernization and Europeanization.[149]

Over time, there emerged something like a critical methodology for evaluating travel reports. It oscillated between literary discussion centered on aesthetic questions and scientific source analysis—with a pronounced tendency to the latter, given that travel reports were primarily valued for their empirical descriptive content. The underlying impulse was mistrust. It could extend very far indeed: Jean-Jacques Rousseau, for instance, excluded only a handful of classic texts—for Asia, Chardin, Kaempfer, and some of the Jesuit reports—from his generalized suspicion. Writing in 1754, he failed to see a "Great Map of Mankind" but was impressed by the enormity of European ignorance about the greater part of the world. He deplored the fact that the greatest minds preferred to stay at home, leaving the public to be deceived by a plethora of "unsophisticated travelers." "The entire earth," exclaimed the exasperated philosopher, "is covered with nations of which we know only the names, and we dabble in judging the human race!"[150] De Pauw, admittedly a dubious authority given his bizarre prejudices against Americans, thought that only ten out of a hundred travelers spoke the truth: sixty lied from stupidity and thirty from self-interest or sheer willfulness.[151] More cautious readers such as Voltaire, Gibbon, or Schlözer did not go quite so far. They were prepared to judge each case on its own merits. Several critical strategies helped them to do so.

Firstly, a detailed knowledge of the older literature was the indispensable foundation for critique. In its absence, cases of plagiarism would go undetected and time would be wasted on texts "which purport to describe the author's travels yet only ever copy the work of previous authors."[152] Those with a good working knowledge of the genre could trace the filiations of particular statements and images along a chain of texts. A second criterion was the trustworthiness implied by the reporter's social status. This was admittedly a fairly blunt instrument, for by the eighteenth century, at the latest, almost all travelers involved in public discussion were scholars and gentleman,[153] and as such felt committed—at least in theory—to the ideal of accurately descriptive, unbiased eyewitness. "In any travel writer," the world traveler Georg Heinrich von Langsdorff observed on behalf of many, "strict love of the truth is not a virtue; it is a solemn duty."[154]

Trustworthiness was thus a moral, legal, or epistemological problem, not a social one. Sir John Barrow makes this clear when criticizing the report of Æneas Anderson, a fellow traveler to the Far East in the Macartney Mission. Anderson is not to be blamed, Barrow is gracious enough to concede, for having only been Lord Macartney's valet; his fault lies solely in allowing his memoirs to be defiled by a vulgar "hack writer."[155] In a lengthy review of Pater Du Halde's China compendium, Samuel Johnson had already posed the question in such a way as to preclude consideration of the author's person:

> When, therefore, Accounts are produced of equal Authority with Regard of the Reputation of the Writers, yet manifestly contradictory, and which therefore cannot both be true, are we to conclude that either of the Relaters drew up his Narrative with a fixed intention of deceiving Mankind?[156]

Dr. Johnson found that discrepancies between different accounts of the same thing were not the result of malice or ideologically skewed vision.

Instead, they could be traced back to simple human error—understandably enough, given the traveler's often-limited range of observational possibilities. They should be regarded "rather as Errors than Falsehoods."[157]

If this was the case—and it seems likely that Johnson's view was widely shared—there remained a third critical strategy: the search for noncontradiction. It was simplest when several mutually independent, demonstrably nonplagiarizing authors concurred in their description of events. Then there could be no room for reasonable doubt. If two of them differed markedly, then domestic readers, unable to inspect the situation on the ground for themselves, had to look out for signs that one text might be more trustworthy than the other. The fact that Mr. Francklin liked the landscape around Shiraz in Persia, whereas Mr. Scott Waring did not, could be dismissed as a mere matter of taste. But when one claimed that the summer temperature in Shiraz never rose above seventy-three degrees Fahrenheit, while the other maintained that it never fell below ninety, who was right? The eagle-eyed reviewer, noticing a number of minor inconsistencies in Scott Waring (a ninety-degree night was said to be "disagreeably cold"), came down on the side of Francklin.[158] He was therefore *in general* the more trustworthy of the two authors. A distinction thus needed to be made between intratextual and intertextual consistency.

To be sure, freedom from internal contradiction was in itself no guarantee for the empirical value of a report. In the summer of 1703, a young, presumably French-born adventurer—tall, blond, speaking fluent Latin—presented himself to the British public as an inhabitant of Formosa called "George Psalmanazar." At the beginning of his picaresque career he had passed himself off as a Japanese. He claimed to have been proselytized by the Church of England, although this did not prevent him from eating raw meat in front of gaping London crowds, allegedly a custom of his savage homeland. That Formosa, under the name of Taiwan, had recently been incorporated into the Qing empire was known only to a handful of English savants and proved immaterial to the unfolding hoax. "Formosa" sounded suitably exotic and remote. The visitor from outer space proved to be ingenious in fending off skeptical inquiries. The light complexion of his skin was accounted for by the gruesome assertion that the members of the Formosan upper class spent their entire lives underground.[159]

Psalmanazar's *Historical and Geographical Description of Formosa*, published in 1704, was pure fiction, but it was a fiction so plausible, so artfully contrived and so entertaining to read that for a while it reaped its author unwarranted fame as an eminent ethnographic authority. French, Dutch, and German translations were not long in waiting. Psalmanazar's book is a masterly parody of a contemporary travel description. The story reveals, incidentally, just how seriously the eighteenth century took the criterion of truthfulness in such texts, for the prank, once discovered, was roundly condemned as a scam.[160]

The fourth critical strategy—comparison between texts—was also the most frequently employed. The Scottish social scientist John Millar, for example, saw the analysis of agreement and disagreement between texts as a reliable method for determining a work's trustworthiness without the need to question "the veracity of the relater." Millar described the procedure with characteristic lucidity, starting with the observation that the sheer number of travel accounts facilitates critical reading:

> From the number, however, and the variety of those relations, they acquire, in many cases, a degree of authority, upon which we may depend with security. . . . When illiterate men, ignorant of the writings of each other, and who, unless upon religious subjects, have no speculative systems to warp their opinions, have, in distant ages and countries, described the manner of peoples in similar circumstances, the reader has an opportunity of comparing their several descriptions, and from their agreement or disagreement is enabled to ascertain the credit that is due to them. . . . We cannot refuse our assent to such evidence, without falling into a degree of scepticism by which the credibility of all historical testimony would be in a great measure destroyed.[161]

Alternatives were not always so easy to resolve as the contradiction between the two English travelers regarding the climate in Shiraz. Were children exposed at birth in China, and if so, how widespread was the practice? Cornelius de Pauw, the stay-at-home anti-Chinese polemicist, was generally shy of citing his sources. In 1773, writing in the spirit of Enlightenment humanitarianism, he had forged a pointed argument for Chinese barbarism from the supposed prevalence of infanticide.[162] Almost every new book on China now dealt with the topic. Staunton estimated that in Peking, two thousand infants were exposed by their poverty-stricken parents every year. Barrow somehow inflated this figure to nine thousand, deploying his uniquely powerful rhetorical arsenal to renew de Pauw's attack on the Chinese.[163] Yet neither Staunton nor Barrow claimed to have seen any of these cruelly abandoned children during their trip to China with Lord Macartney in 1793/94. Two other habitually careful observers on the mission, neither prone to pro-Chinese sentiments, testified some years later that they had not seen a single victim during their several months in the country.[164] Pierre Sonnerat, ordinarily quite prepared to think the worst of the Chinese, accepted the fact of infant exposure but turned the tables on China's critics, accusing them of hypocrisy and challenging them to contemplate the miserable conditions in French foundling homes.[165] And Voltaire, who held the treatment of children in China to be the darkest blot on the country's reputation, did not forget to add that even London had not had a home for foundlings until a few years previously (1741, to be exact).[166]

In the end, the matter proved impossible to clarify since even the Jesuits, usually the most reliable informants in cases of doubt, became tangled up in contradictions. All the reports of infant exposure ultimately led back to them. On the one hand, they had been condemning the practice for decades as perhaps the greatest stain on Chinese society; on the other hand, in the absence of other converts, they had welcomed the chance to baptize dying children.[167] After de Pauw discovered the polemical potential of this theme, the startled fathers went into damage control mode: earlier generations of Jesuit priests had misunderstood Chinese customs; they had been misled by their own catechists; most of the victims had been suffering from incurable illnesses anyway; the European editors of the Jesuit letters had doctored their reports to make conversion figures look more impressive. In short, the rate of infanticide in China was no higher than in other parts of the world.[168]

This astonishing and all-but-unprecedented burst of Jesuit self-criticism, which cast doubt on the testimony of even such highly regarded scholars as Parennin and Gaubil, left nothing but confusion in its wake. Everyone spoke of "Chinese infanticide" and nobody admitted to having seen it. When Thomas R. Malthus, the first economist to propose a systematic theory of population, attempted to gain an overview of Chinese demography, the methods for critically comparing texts recommended by Millar and others were thus of little use to him. His solution was a sensible one under the circumstances. He first determined the *Chinese* descriptions he had found translated in the Jesuits' *Lettres édifiantes et curieuses* to be the most authentic documents relating to this question. Setting the fraught matter of empirical evidence to one side, he then discussed the functionality (and hence the functional plausibility) of infanticide within the broader context of sociology and Chinese reproductive behavior.[169] The solution resided here in the theory.

Comparison presupposed that a certain quantum of observational data was available to be compared. Psalmanazaar was believed for so long because he had chosen in Formosa a country that was completely closed off to Europeans, even to Jesuit missionaries. And how could the comparative method be applied to Kaempfer in the absence of contending reports on Japan from the same era? European ideas about Chinese landscape gardens rested entirely on the testimony of a single alleged witness, Sir William Chambers.[170] It is impossible to say what he actually saw in China for want of comparable descriptions in other European sources. An astute contemporary, Christian Cayus Lorenz Hirschfeld, was quick to voice his doubts. Why had no earlier travelers left behind descriptions of these famous gardens? Had not Du Halde expressly claimed that the Chinese understood little about gardening? And did they even have sufficient mathematical knowledge to plan a landscape? Hirschfeld did not accuse Chambers of lying. Besides, whether Chambers had correctly described the reality of what he saw was a secondary matter. Chambers, as convincingly interpreted by Hirschfeld, was an original thinker and sincere lover of horticulture who had nursed the vision of a new, more natural type of garden "in his intellect and in his imagination":

> He was clever enough to admix to these ideas elements that were native to the Chinese view of nature. In sum, he planted British ideas on Chinese soil to give them a more striking appearance and greater penetrative power.[171]

If it was therefore frequently impossible to go beyond plausible hunches and speculation on the likelihood of a piece of information, this necessity could still be transformed into a virtue by men of genius. Edward Gibbon was no conjectural historian but a solid empiricist, always careful to indicate the status of an assertion. He could never have written his magnum opus without trusting in the "probability" of the extant sources. James Bruce has a nice anecdote about where this could lead. Dr. Thomas Shaw, the celebrated traveler to the Orient, observed members of a North African Arab tribe feasting on lions. This was something that transcended the bounds of probability: Europeans he told about it "took it as a subversion of the natural order of things that a man should eat a lion, when it had long passed as almost the peculiar province of the lion to eat man."[172] The circumspect doctor therefore omitted to mention this particular episode in his report. Nobody would have believed him. Decades were to pass before James Bruce saw something similar—and tasted lion meat himself.

FRACTURED REPRESENTATION

In the eighteenth century, we can say in summary, description of overseas travel was understood, not as a genre of fictional literature, but as an instrument for empirically apprehending the world in the service of the natural sciences and a transcultural "science of mankind." Nonetheless, it was and remained a literary artifact rather than an impersonal, quasi-photographic protocol of events. Numerous intermediary steps lay between the direct sensory impressions of the traveling observer and the bound volume the European reader eventually fetched from his bookshelf: *always* the act of writing, with generic literary conventions, assumed public expectations and market requirements all playing on the author's mind; then the book's design, production, and distribution by publishers, illustrators, printers, and booksellers. *Often* the text passed through further hands: those of editors, redactors, and translators, who felt no compunction about interfering with it, or those of compilers and anthologists, some of whom opted for the open form of collage, others of whom—the abbé Prévost springs to mind—freely reworked their source material.

The representation of foreignness was consequently not a process by which reality came to be depicted in any direct, unmediated way. On the other hand, it would be an exaggeration to deny eighteenth-century texts on Asia all relation to empirical reality and regard them purely as figments of the imagination. Contemporary readers were cleverer here than many later theorists. Hungry for knowledge of other cultures, they chomped through forests of literature on Asia in order to give European historical, anthropological, economic, and sociological discourses as universal an evidential basis as possible. They knew that there was no alternative to the literature produced by traveling eye- and earwitnesses and to translations from oriental languages. That is why they developed a critical methodology for reading these texts. Applying its strategies, they assigned a text its place in the literary tradition, kept an eye out for plagiarism, checked the text for internal logical consistency, compared it with other reports, and finally considered it from the viewpoint of plausibility and probability. An assessment of the traveler's personal credibility was also important: a reputable scholar, gentleman, or *honnête homme* was considered more trustworthy than an unknown outsider. Yet this aspect of biographical appraisal should not be rated so highly as tends to occur today by those who advocate a "social history of truth."[173] Critical investigation of texts and assessment of their truth claims was, in the first instance, a matter of reasoned argument and debate within an egalitarian republic of scholars. In this cosmopolitan public sphere, social distinctions took second place.

THE PRESENT AND THE PAST

VIII

The Raw Forces of History

Apocalyptic Horsemen, Conquerors, Usurpers

The sequel of these treatises will show how important it is to a correct knowledge, not only of Asiatic history, but also of the human race at large, to possess clear views respecting the manners and institutions of the nomad tribes. It was among them that the greatest revolutions in the history of mankind, which not only determined the fate of Asia, but shook Europe and Africa to the core, had their origin. It would almost appear to have been the design of Providence to continue these nations in a state more true to nature, and nearer in some degrees to their original condition, in order to renovate by their means (as history proves to have been often the case) the more civilized races of the world, which had prepared, by degeneracy and luxury, the way for their own destruction.

—Arnold Herrmann Ludwig Heeren (1760–1842), *Ideen über Politik, den Verkehr und den Handel der vornehmsten Völker der Alten Welt*[1] [Historical Researches into the Politics, Intercourse and Trade of the Principal Nations of Antiquity]

This is how Arnold Herrmann Ludwig Heeren, one of the last European historians working within the intellectual framework of Enlightenment historiography, highlights the significance of his own detailed analysis of a nomadic way of life and its political consequences. Writing in 1793, at exactly the same time that an unprecedented revolution was unfolding in France, the professor in provincial Göttingen reverts to an older concept of "revolution," in some ways outdated in the early 1790s, but keeping alive the idea that "premodern" history was by no means a tale of immobility and unchanging tradition.

TRIBAL ASIA: ATTILA AND THE CONSEQUENCES

One of the enduring geopolitical conflicts of the nineteenth century was the "Great Game," a cold war fought between the era's two most aggressive empires, the British and the Russian, in Afghanistan, Central Asia, and the Himalayas. The British were seeking to protect their sea route to India and to surround their colonial crown jewel with a cordon of dependent buffer states from Iran to Tibet. In pursuing their economic interests in China following its forced opening in 1842, they needed as large an area as possible in which to develop. The tsarist empire, for its part, extended its hegemony through colonial conquests in Islamic Central Asia. Towards the end of the century it had opened up Siberia through railroads and made a start on the *pénétration pacifique* of Manchuria, the three northeastern provinces of China. In all these imperial maneuvers, the continental center of Asia was little more than a chessboard, its people the unwilling pawns of the imperial powers. Only the Afghans refused to be pushed around. In the long run, they could neither be ruled directly nor reliably controlled through indirect means.

The Anglo-Russian conflict in Asia was finally settled in 1907 when the two powers agreed to carve out separate spheres of interest. A restructuring of alliances within Europe, together with Japan's rise to great power status, sealed by its stunning victory over Russia at the Battle of Tsushima in 1905, had made this inevitable. All this did little to change Central Asia's passive role. On the contrary, the end of the Great Game eliminated the last possibilities for playing one side off against the other. Central Asia found itself more firmly than ever in the grip of the empires. Having long figured in the daydreams of geopolitical strategists, Asia's "heartland" only regained a measure of autonomy following the breakdown of the

Soviet Union in 1991 and the emergence of new states in the Islamic regions of Central Asia.[2] Yet the last great empire in Asia, the Chinese, emerged strengthened from the global crisis of 1990/91. It continues to control vast swathes of Central Asia: Tibet, East Turkestan (Xinjiang), and parts of historical Mongolia. Peripheral powers like Iran and Turkey are also stepping up their influence in the region. China's response has been to push the ambitious project of a new Silk Road in collaboration with the European Union.[3]

Central Asia's former significance for the politics and worldview of Europe can hardly be inferred from today's radically altered situation. For many centuries, European dreams about Central Asia had taken the form of nightmares. Ever since Attila and his Huns, the mere thought of Central Asian horsemen thundering down from the steppes had filled with dread all those living on Europe's eastern marches. Hegel spoke in this connection of the "elemental-historical" (*das Elementarhistorische*): as if spilling out of a black hole, wave upon wave of seemingly prehistoric barbarian hordes would periodically intervene in the history of states to vastly destructive—and transformative—effect.[4] As late as 1700, only a few Europeans dared to predict that the danger from the East had been banished once and for all.[5] Time and again, it was recalled that once-mighty empires had been overwhelmed by steppeland warriors: the West Roman Empire, the Caliphate of Baghdad, the Russian principalities, Byzantium, the Song dynasty in China, and later the Ming dynasty as well.[6]

With the takeover of China by the Manchus, who in 1629 had breached the Great Wall from the forested regions to the north and in November 1644 installed their own dynasty on the Dragon Throne, the series of North and Central Asian conquests had by no means come to an end.[7] Around 1710, Afghan tribal warriors began to move against the Muslim empires. In 1722 they destroyed the empire of the Safavid dynasty, plunging much of Iran into chaos. The Iranian emperor Nadir Shah, whose power rested on support from Iranian and Turkoman tribal warriors, sacked Delhi in 1739. In doing so, he delivered the death blow to the

Mughal Empire, which only a few decades before had been basking in its very own Indian summer. In 1747 and again from 1759 to 1761, Afghans pushed into northern India. These invasions unloosed several hundred thousand roving tribal horsemen. Some groups established their own states while others, penetrating as far as southern India, annexed land for themselves, entering into a parasitic relationship with the local populace as a tax-collecting military elite.[8] Until well into the 1790s, the threat of Afghan attack loomed large over northern India, although the British and their Indian allies mostly succeeded in staving it off. A crucial episode was the war launched in 1774 against the Rohilla Afghans by the EIC and the Nawab of Oudh, Shuja ud-Daula.[9] Around the same time, the tribally based religious movement of Wahhabism had grown strong enough in Arabia to achieve the unprecedented feat of rallying the Arabs against their Ottoman overlords. In 1773 the Wahhabis took the city of Riyadh, and later the sacred sites of Islam, to establish themselves as the primary religious and political force in the Arabian Peninsula.[10] It was not until 1818 that Egyptian troops in the pay of the sultan were at last able to bring down the first Wahhabi state.

This revival of tribal dynamism was far from being the prevalent trend in Asia as a whole. None other than the Manchurian Qing dynasty, which itself hailed from the fringes of the Chinese Empire, finally succeeded through a combination of inclusion and destruction in neutralizing the restless Mongolian tribes, their old rivals and allies. The danger of a renewed Mongol assault on Europe invoked by Leibniz in 1699 was banished for good in 1757 with the virtual genocide of the Dzungar people, the last surviving independent federation of Mongolian tribes.[11] In Asia, too, the historical force of the steppe peoples appeared to have been broken once and for all. The Marquis de Condorcet, a well-informed mathematician and philosopher, pondered the prospect of "a new invasion of Asia by the Tartars" only to conclude that it was unrealistic.[12] Shortly after the Sino-Manchu extermination of the Dzungars, nomadic pastoralists began being driven from their traditional rangelands on the steppe frontiers of the tsarist empire.[13] The pinch grip of Russian and

Sino-Manchurian military control and agricultural colonization showed that even a preindustrial imperialism was capable of breaking the political spine of the Central Asian mounted nomads.

At the same time, tribal breakouts in the Indo-Afghan region recalled the ongoing virulence of a mobile warrior force that had always been metaphorically characterized by Europeans as a "deluge" or "swarm." Even the normally unflappable Alexander von Humboldt, the very opposite of a hysterical demagogue and Asiaphobe, condemned Genghis Khan's Mongols as a "pestilential gust of wind."[14] Volney, in a grotesque vision of turmoil and destruction, spoke of ants and locusts inflicting doom on the civilized world.[15] And Edward Gibbon, never one to miss a chance for irony and unexpected historical justice, joined in the usual talk of aggressive Northern invaders and Asian hordes while pointing out that during the Fourth Crusade the victimized—although not entirely innocent—Christian citizens of Byzantium might be forgiven for thinking that the Latin crusaders and their Venetian accomplices, with all their greed and "savage fanaticism," were an especially voracious force of nature.[16] Marveling at the enormous number of warriors mobilized during the period of the Crusades, he too conjured up "the image of locusts."[17]

When eighteenth-century European historians attached signal importance to the motif of barbarian invasion, they did so for reasons that partly reflected contemporary concerns. Up to the time when they were writing, or at least until shortly before it, Asia had been racked by considerable turmoil, and this turmoil had serious repercussions for Europe and its colonies. The European system of states had only recently achieved such a degree of stability that a flamboyant conqueror and rule-breaker such as Charles XII of Sweden was almost doomed to failure. In 1731, Voltaire devoted his first full-scale historiographical monograph to the rise and fall of that reckless imitator of Alexander the Great, advising the crowned heads of Europe that peaceful rule would be worth far more than any amount of military glory.[18] The importance of conquest and coercion in establishing empires throughout Asia became all the more apparent when seen in the light of the pacification of Europe, itself far more a utopian goal than a reality. Conquests seemed to flow naturally from the mobility of a nomadic way of life. Among the tribes of the Asian steppes, remarked August Ferdinand Lueder, a senior public servant in the Duchy of Brunswick, "the military campaign is nothing but a perpetuation of everyday life."[19] The chronic, seething restlessness of herding societies was practically the counterprinciple to European stability, "since the Tatar tribes who live there [in North Asia] roam freely, and their Khans' residences remain unattached to any one place."[20] Sir William Temple pursued this line of argument furthest in his essay *Of Heroic Virtue* (1692). He identified a region of the world lying north of the Caspian and Black Seas, and bordered to the west and east by the Danube and Oxus Rivers, respectively, as the engine room of historical dynamism since ancient times, and he followed ancient cosmographers in calling this region "Scythia."[21] Temple also asserted that conquests, as a rule, move from north to south, the only exception being the expansion of the early Islamic Arabs.[22]

In eighteenth-century thought, we find very few value judgments contrasting a civilized Europe with the "Asiatic hordes" surging at its gates. Such dichotomizing simplifications only became commonplace in the nineteenth century, when Ranke, for example, formulated the historical principle that the "civilized world" (*Culturwelt*) finds itself incessantly attacked and endangered by outsiders. In his *Weltgeschichte* (*History of the World*), Ranke by no means ignores the Huns and Mongols, but unlike Edward Gibbon a century earlier, he makes no attempt to understand their internal dynamics. In Ranke's view, societies existing beyond the religiously and socially regulated pale of "civilization" have always shown "a barbaric hostility towards the civilized world." Consequently, their interventions in history have typically taken the form of "inundation."[23] Mechanical metaphors of pressure and counterpressure pile up, as when Ranke, nearing the end of his work, arrives at a fundamental principle of ancient and medieval history: "Thus the brute force of Asia poured destructively into Europe. Fortunately it met with resistance."[24] The "struggle of the various systems of nations" that determines the course of world history is regarded solely from the perspective of "universal development," which in the post-classical world has found expression only among the Germanic and Latin peoples.[25] They are the standard-bearers of civilization in Ranke's day, so it is only fitting that they should now "rule the world."[26] Ranke was quite prepared to grant the barbarians a modicum of historical justice. He recognized, for instance, that the state-building achievements of Attila the Hun were superior to those of his West Roman opponents. For Ranke, however, the Battle of the Catalaunian Plains is yet another "struggle of the ideal opposition" between civilization and barbarism.[27]

By contrast, Ignaz Aurelius Fessler, known in his lifetime above all as a theorist of Freemasonry and author of a history of Hungary, treated such attacks on the "civilized world" with far greater understanding in his brilliantly written history of the Huns under Attila (1794). In this work, which observed all the aesthetic strictures concerning historiographical presentation that had been introduced into Germany since Schiller, Fessler took issue with a stereotype that had held sway since the earliest Roman reports: that of the Huns' untamed, animalistic savagery.[28] Attila, he argued, was an eminently intelligent and rational ruler. He had lifted his culturally debased people out of a subsistence existence by setting them a new, lofty goal of honor and renown. The excesses of the Hunnic conquests were caused by marauding soldiers running amok; in no way did they reflect the national character of the Huns, nor were they the result of deliberate policy. Ultimately, Attila and his warriors were motivated, not by an atavistic yearning to rape and pillage, but by a long-standing, entirely understandable hatred for the Romans:

> National pride was conjoined with courage, and henceforth the sword became, in the hands of the Huns, the terrible instrument of revenge against a people that cursed them as barbarians simply because, more honest, more just and freer than the Romans, they abhorred the chains of vice and tyranny.[29]

The great Scottish historian William Robertson had earlier warned of playing off the "European" Germans against the "Asiatic" Huns: they had all been savage barbarians, they had all known the freedom of nomads, and there were no fundamental differences in social organization between the two.[30] Edward Gibbon, while unwilling to gloss over the Huns' cruelty, still paid tribute to Attila's qualities as a clever strategist and good religious legislator, pointing out that slaves were better treated by the Huns than by Romans.[31] The Iranist John Richardson, one of the founders of comparative linguistics, admired Attila for having shattered "the chains of Roman servitude."[32] Three decades before, Montesquieu had praised Attila as "one of the greatest monarchs history has ever known."[33] Montesquieu was not concerned with Attila's alleged "barbarism" and the morality or immorality of his deeds, rating him instead as a calculating statesman and strategist no different from the "civilized" monarchs of his time.[34]

Typically for his age, Ranke adopted the perspective of "civilized" Europe and showed scant interest in examining the causes and dynamics of the uncivilized and chaotic world beyond. All that interested him about Asian history was its impact on Europe; only their brute hostility towards culture made the uncultured people of the East worth studying. In 1824 Isaac Jacob Schmidt, an expert on Central Asia, was already lamenting that Europeans only ever perceived the consequences of Asiatic breakouts, not their root causes. That had not always been the case.[35] Two broad schools of thought can be discerned in the eighteenth century. One proposed that historical change in the Eurasian continent, or even in general, results from mass migrations and other such large-scale demographic phenomena; from this perspective, conquests appear as a temporary intensification of mobile normality.[36] The other school inquired into the specific causes of "barbarian invasions" in history. Not everyone made things so simple for themselves as Volney, who with uncharacteristic shallowness ascribed the nomads' aggressiveness to greed and envy.[37] Charles de Peyssonnel, a learned French consul in Smyrna (İzmir), analyzed the interdependence of imperial border policy and "barbarian" behavior. Rejecting the simple opposition of offensive barbarians and defensive civilizations, he anticipated many of the findings of modern research by showing how their mutual influences cut across borders.[38]

And Edward Gibbon developed an elaborate political sociology of nomadism, to be discussed in the next chapter.

A CONTINENT OF REVOLUTIONS

Not only Arnold Hermann Ludwig Heeren, quoted at the beginning of this chapter, but many other eighteenth-century European authors repeatedly applied the concept of revolution to events in Asia. The term was used to refer to political upheavals of all kinds.[39] These were so general a phenomenon that Gottfried Achenwall, a political scientist *avant la lettre*, could decree: "The history of constitutional changes or revolutions in a kingdom or republic should be the first item on the agenda for the historical study of any polity."[40] In 1792 Heeren's senior colleague at the University of Göttingen, the historian Johann Christoph Gatterer, declared world history itself to be "the history of major events, of revolutions."[41] In the year of the French Revolution, however, Anquetil-Duperron was already warning historians against adopting a notion of revolution too narrowly fixated on events, advising them to study longer processes and historical constants as well.[42] He could have cited Edward Gibbon, who, in the preface to the first volume of his *Decline and Fall of the Roman Empire* (1776), defined his topic as "the memorable series of revolutions which, in the course of about thirteen centuries, gradually undermined, and at length destroyed, the solid fabric of Roman greatness."[43] Among these revolutions were the rise of Christianity and the emergence of feudalism in Western Europe.

A number of events in seventeenth- and eighteenth-century Asia were portrayed in European texts as "revolutions":

- coups in the Ottoman Empire, such as the murder of the reforming sultan Osman II by the military in 1622 or the execution of the incompetent sultan Ibrâhîm in 1648;
- the ousting of the pro-European prime minister Phaulkon in Siam in 1688;

- the fall of the sultanate of Golkonda to the grand mughal Aurangzeb in the same year;
- the Afghan invasion of Iran in 1722;
- the destruction of the Siamese kingdom of Ayudhya through a brutal Burmese intervention in 1767;
- the bid for supreme power in Egypt, previously ruled quasi-collegially under Ottoman suzerainty, launched by the Mamluk Ali Bey in 1768;
- the restructuring of the Siamese state by King Rama I from 1782.

In the eighteenth century there was, however, nothing quite so dramatic and violent as the conquest of China by the Manchus in 1644 and the pacification of the Middle Kingdom in the following years. The memory of the "Great Revolution" in China was kept alive by Pater Martin Martini's *De bello tartarico* (1654), quickly translated into seven European languages: a thrilling piece of eyewitness reporting and, along with François Bernier's account of Aurangzeb's rise to the position of grand mughal, one of the most impressive historical works of the seventeenth century.[44] Travel collections seldom failed to include this hair-raising cavalcade of horrors.

European observers asked what these modern "revolutions" in Asia had in common and how they related to the systemic crises facing Europe around the same time—a question that still preoccupies researchers today.[45] They appeared to involve greater bloodshed than similar upheavals in Europe as well as those in Asiatic antiquity. When it was not simply a matter of palace revolutions (as was typical for the Ottoman Empire), internal crises often coincided with invasions from outside. For that reason, the various overthrows had an almost therapeutic, purgative effect. As a comparison between the Manchu conquest of China and the contemporaneous Puritan revolution in England showed, widespread tumult in Asia tended not to do away with the old political system but to rebuild it on the same foundations.[46] The most spectacular "revolution" in eighteenth-century Asia proved an exception to the rule: the gradual rise to power of the British in India from 1757 onwards.[47] Whether speaking in praise or blame, commentators sensed that this development broke with the eternal cycle of Asiatic politics. Edmund Burke remarked that Arabs, Tatars (i.e., Mughals), and Persians had bloodily invaded India and then quickly assimilated, whereas the British turned everything upside down: "The Tartar invasion was mischievous; but it is our protection that destroys India."[48]

Thomas Maurice, on the other hand, looked to the future in striking the more positive tone of imperial apologetics. In his *Modern History of Hindostan* (1802–10), he charted the rise and fall of the Mughal dynasty from an unsympathetic distance: Asian history, particularly under Islamic influence, was nothing but a "dark and dreadful" litany of "perfidy, spoliation and murder." What a contrast strikes the reflective mind when, having beheld such horrors, it "contemplates the blessings enjoyed under a government immutably founded on the adamantine basis of virtue and liberty, possessing the noblest code of equity, and irradiated by the beams of the purest religion."[49] With that, the historical mission of the new overlords was set out: India had been freed from itself by British colonialism and blessed with the strict but just rule of law.

TIMUR: STATESMAN AND MONSTER

From the nineteenth century, at the latest, Genghis Khan, the early thirteenth-century founder of the Mongol world empire, and Timur (Tamerlaine), who from 1380 until his death in 1405 subjected most of western Asia to his rule, pushed through to India, and prepared for an assault on China, were seen as the twin paragons of Asiatic destructiveness and bloodlust.

Was Genghis Khan really, as Baron de Tott contended, "the Madman who overran Asia to enslave the world he had laid waste?"[50] The authors of the *Algemeine Welthistorie* (*General World History*) found that, on the contrary, Genghis may "rightly be considered the greatest prince ever to have occupied the Oriental throne."[51] Although cruel and ruthless, he had also shown immense courage, wisdom, and judgment. He had introduced the principle of promotion by merit into his army, and on questions of religion he was no primitive idol-worshiper but practically a deist in the Enlightenment mold.[52] Edward Gibbon viewed Genghis as a lawgiver who had guided his people wisely and well. "A singular conformity may be found," we read in one of Gibbon's priceless footnotes, "between the religious laws of Zingis Khan and of Mr. Locke."[53]

Timur exerted a more powerful hold on the eighteenth-century imagination than Genghis Khan, about whom far less was known. It did much to help their posthumous fame in Europe that both rulers had campaigned against Christendom's archenemy, Islam. Centuries later, that had not yet been forgotten.[54] The earliest humanists had been Timur's near-contemporaries and left behind a flattering portrait of the conqueror. They saw him as an ambitious self-made man who had compelled luck (*fortuna*) onto his side and combined personal charisma with the utmost rationality in his ruthless exploitation of whatever means lay at hand. In an age without heroes, a figure had arisen whose military exploits had equaled or even bettered those of Alexander the Great.[55] Christopher Marlowe was almost alone in placing the main emphasis on the ruler's brutality and bloodthirstiness in his drama *Tamburlaine the Great*, first performed in 1587 and published three years later.

By the eighteenth century, freshly translated Persian and Arab sources were available, allowing oriental perspectives on the conqueror to flow into European literature. As the historical perspective lengthened, Timur also came to be seen as the ancestor of the Mughal dynasty. Although his own empire did not survive him, his direct descendant Babur succeeded in carving out a Muslim imperium in South Asia.[56] In 1697 Barthélemi d'Herbelot painted a dignified, unrhetorical portrait of Timur in his *Bibliothèque Orientale*. Writing with the sober objectivity that was his hallmark, he insists that reports of the conqueror's cruelty had been overstated in Europe.[57] Although d'Herbelot confined himself to biographies of princes and potentates, readers could still find a brief structural analysis of the Mongol empire in the fourth volume of his work. This allowed them to draw analogies to how the Timurid empire was organized and administered.[58]

Evaluations of Timur were shaped both by value judgments suggested in the sources and by present-day interpretive needs. Until Jean-Baptiste d'Anville characterized him in 1772 as "the scourge of Asia,"[59] Timur was almost universally held up as the very model of a benevolent and beneficent ruler. From the perspective of the early Enlightenment, what spoke in his favor was that he owed his ascent to world domination solely to his personal abilities. Neither inheriting nor usurping kingship and lacking a teacher like Aristotle, he was the maker of his own fortune (*l'artisan de sa fortune*) and as such could be excused the occasional outburst of brutality.[60] Timur's charisma fascinated eighteenth-century authors: his leadership psychology, his capacity to inspire loyality and enthusiasm among his followers, his unerring decisiveness, but also his artfulness and cunning.[61] His constructive legacy seemed to outweigh the devastation his armies left in their wake.[62] As a lawgiver, too, he proved a wise statesman and uniter of nations.[63]

The only dissenting voices were those of Enlightment radicals like Johann Heinrich Gottlob von Justi, who refused to worship at the shrine of the conqueror and saw military heroes as nothing more than contemptible mass murderers.[64] But here, too, Timur was not condemned for anything specifically "Asiatic" in his character. He corresponded instead to a type of leader bound to neither time nor place: the "conqueror." At bottom, his mistakes, sins, and crimes were no different from those of an Alexander, the warlord with whom he was most often compared. As late as 1783, it was still said of him that ambition, "the infirmity of noble minds," was his only flaw; whenever he committed what looked like an atrocity, his hand had always been forced by his enemies' treachery.[65] This largely ahistorical image of the constructive statesman survived well into the nineteenth century.[66] But it could come into conflict with the political correctness of the age. In 1810 a British admirer of

Timur found himself faced with the difficulty of appearing to praise Napoleon (in many respects Timur's modern-day counterpart) alongside his hero—and thought better of it.[67]

A critical view of Timur does not begin, as one might suspect, with Voltaire, whose interest in the conqueror was spurred by reading Cantemir's history of the Ottoman Empire. Voltaire places him in the usual gallery of great revolutionaries and wreckers, seeing that, unlike Alexander, who at least founded cities wherever he went, Timur's legacy was almost wholly destructive. At the same time, he questions some of the reports of Timur's more outrageous atrocities and believes him to have been no more hot-tempered than Alexander, the only European military leader (in Voltaire's eyes) ever to have made an impact on Asia. He even regards Timur—the biggest compliment—as a tolerant deist, with no trace of "superstition" and "believing in a single God, just as the Chinese literati do."[68] Timur's story is no longer a moral tale of virtue or vice but a case study in historical dynamics.

It was Joseph de Guignes, writing around the same time, who brought out Timur's darker qualities more strongly than any other author since the demonizing Christopher Marlowe. In his monumental *Histoire générale des Huns, des Turcs, des Mogols et des autres Tartares Occidentaux* (1756–58), based on source studies in several Asiatic languages, De Guignes dispenses with the reductive character portrait of Timur that was typical of his time. He never utters an explicit judgment. The investigation of historical causes for which he was renowned (and which earned him the admiration of Gibbon, its greatest master among Enlightenment historians[69]) also proved of no use to him here: for how could an appeal to causality possibly explain the meteoric rise to world domination of this "vagrant and outlaw," this near-nobody from the windswept steppelands of Central Asia?[70]

In retelling the story of Timur's life, de Guignes reels off a grim catalogue of mass executions, destroyed cities, and devastated landscapes. He can barely conceal his bewilderment at the phenomenon of the nomad emperor who did everything for his troops and spared his opponents nothing. Where the older tradition admired—with some justification—the purposeful rationality with which Timur, in this view the most modern of the medieval monarchs, had implemented his plans, de Guignes applies the normative criterion of reasonableness to his rule. While Timur's rise until 1380 may have conformed to the usual pattern by which rulers build up a regional power base, his attack on Iran the following year signalled that his ambition now knew no bounds: "Tamerlan lacked a rational motive in starting this war; the dream of universal monarchy was the only guiding star of his actions."[71] De Guignes is clearly horrified to perceive an untrammeled, all-consuming violence at work in Timur's later actions, impelled by the vision of a world where peace was to be secured by crushing all resistance.[72] Needless to say, the period's leading historian of Asia makes no mention of "Asiatic cruelty." De Guignes was writing during an interlude in the history of ideas. While he no longer joined older historians in penning panegyrics for princes, he was also not yet infected by the emerging mindset of East-West antagonism. His lucid description of Timurid power politics squares up to Hegel's "elemental-historical" with great directness and honesty.

Edward Gibbon, who devotes almost a whole, brilliantly researched chapter to Timur, found rich possibilities for paradox in this contradictory situation. His Timur is at once an unscrupulous mass murderer and a cultivated chessplayer who befriended scholars,[73] fortune's favorite and the victim of his own success: "after devoting fifty years to the attainment of empire, the only happy period of his life were the two months in which he ceased to exercise his power."[74] Timur appeared in Asia at a time of chaos and at first seemed to promise a return to order. Far from being a barbaric force of nature, he was a statesman with a keen sense of what was needed. But the means outweighed the ends, "whole nations were crushed under the footsteps of the reformer," and his conquests were never followed by reconstruction.[75] Gibbon's Timur, who on balance did far more harm than good, is finely portrayed, yet one cannot help feeling that de Guignes's sparse documentation does more justice than Gibbon's elegant reasoning to the excessiveness of a man who not only talked about ruling the world but made a concerted effort to do so. Sir John Malcolm was still following Gibbon's interpretation in his *History of Persia* (1815). His Timur is likewise no Asiatic monster but rather a misguided genius who offers proof that empires cannot be founded on violence and charisma alone.[76] With Timur—and this is also how Joseph von Hammer-Purgstall defines his place in history—the era of open borders and world-conquering cavalry comes to an end in Eurasia. The post-Timurid future belongs to territorial states.[77]

NADIR SHAH: COMET OF WAR AND PATRIOT

A century and a half after his death, he was still sending shivers down people's spines. In 1894 George Nathaniel Curzon, later viceroy of India and British foreign secretary, saw him and Genghis Khan as "the most terrible phenomena by which humanity has ever been scourged."[78] What was so horrifying about Nadir Shah, "this notorious eighteenth-century ravager of the countryside, who leapt straight from the dust to the throne"?[79] Nadir was one of the last permanently mobile rulers in history, a nomad who spent most of his time on the warpath with his army and held court from his military camp.[80] Born in 1688 in the Iranian province of Khorasan to simple parents from the Turkmeni tribe of the Afshars, he never denied his humble origins. Throughout his entire career, which he modeled from an early stage on Timur's romantic example, he proudly proclaimed himself a "son of the sword."[81] In the situation of political turmoil following the invasion of Iran by the Ghilzai Afghans, which began in 1709 with the taking of Kandahar and ended in 1722 with the conquest of Isfahan and the fall of the Safavid dynasty, new opportunities were opening up to warlords. The Afghans proved incapable of providing stable government in Iran and protecting the land from Ottoman and Russian depredations. Nadir, a man of the lawless frontier, inexorably built up his power base by either eliminating rivals or winning them over to his side. In 1726 he entered the service of the Safavid pretender and self-nominated shah Tahmasp II, receiving the name by which he first became known in Europe, Tahmasp Quli Khan. It was largely thanks to Nadir that in 1729 the Afghans were driven out and the Safavid dynasty restored, albeit as a shadow of its former self.

Nadir now turned against Iran's internal enemies. He attacked the Ottomans in Baghdad and the Russians in Azerbaijan, correcting the borders in Iran's favor. In 1732 he launched a coup to replace the weak shah Tahmasp with his son Abbas (III), only eight years old at the time; it came as no surprise when Nadir took on the regency. In March 1736 the warlord had himself crowned shah and proclaimed a new Afsharid dynasty. Anyone even suspected of opposing the regime was shown no mercy. In 1737 Nadir began his long-planned Indian campaign. His brutal sack of Delhi and massacre of tens of thousands of citizens in March and April 1739 were its tragic high points.[82] The figure of 225,000 fatalities was regularly cited in the contemporary European literature.[83] Nadir also confiscated the Mughal emperor's famous Peacock Throne and Koh-i-Noor diamond (which in 1849 was to end up in Queen Victoria's possession).[84] Uninterested in extending his scepter over large parts of India, Nadir returned to Iran and spent the next years expanding and securing Iran's borders on the Persian Gulf and in Mesopotamia, all the while ruthlessly plundering his own subjects. Revolts against his tax-collectors became ever more frequent and were suppressed with ever-greater savagery as Nadir, increasingly described as insane, gave free rein to his sadistic impulses. An English traveler was surprised that the Persians, unlike other Muslims, left their ears uncovered by turbans or other headwear: the reason was that anyone whose ears had not been cut off was proud to display theirs intact.[85] Finally, Nadir adopted Timur's practice of stacking the skulls of his victims into towers; in Nadir's case, however, the heads were those of his own people. On the night of July 1, 1747, the tyrant was assassinated in his tent by Iranian conspirators. Nadir had long since loosened his ties to his Iranian power base and there was a strong feeling that he relied too much on Afghan and Uzbek forces.

Along with the Kangxi emperor, whose renown had been spread by the Jesuits even before his death in 1722, Nadir Shah was for mid-eighteenth-century Europeans the best-known personality in recent Asiatic history, at any rate east of the Ottoman Empire. His rise and fall were followed with keen interest. They were cited as an example of how instructive an engagement with current events in faraway countries could be.[86] Thanks to the great travel reports of Chardin, Tavernier, Kaempfer, and others, interest in Safavid Iran had never waned.[87] When the dynasty was toppled by Afghan horsemen from the wild and mountainous north, the news was sure to attract attention. In contemplating such a sad spectacle, Voltaire felt reminded of the fate of Germany in the Thirty Years' War, France during the Fronde, or Russia when laid waste by the Mongols.[88]

Newspaper correspondents in Istanbul and Moscow ensured that European readers were kept informed of events as they unfolded.[89] A detailed account and analysis of the Iranian troubles appeared in 1728: the *Histoire de la dernière revolution de Perse* by the Jesuit father Tadeusz Juda Krusínski, who had experienced events from 1707 to 1725 at close hand; in 1722 he made a narrow escape from Isfahan as it was being starved into submission by Afghan besiegers.[90] Krusínski's evidently somewhat-rambling Latin report was translated into French before being tidied up by another Jesuit, Jean-Antoine du Certeau, and recast as a thrilling narrative. The Ottoman government had such a strong interest in the Iranian "revolution" that it had the text translated into Turkish and this version then translated back into Latin.[91]

Krusínski (or Certeau) opens the work with a long investigation into the demise of the Safavids. This had already begun around the middle of the previous century, allowing the Afghans to gain a foothold in Iran. Until then, the Afghans had been all but unknown even in Asia. Described as ugly, dirty, and coarse, their favorite pastime was to steal from strangers and each other.[92] On the other hand, they treated their captives and slaves far better than was usually the case in Asia. They had been lucky enough to find a leader of genius, Mir Vais, to direct their martial energies to a worthwhile goal. Krunsínski now plays skillfully with the narrative expectations of his readers. Surely they would immediately recall Timur and think that Iran had been overwhelmed "by a terrible flood of barbarians"?[93] Not a bit of it: the decadent Safavids had been overthrown by a relatively small troop of tactically superior mountain warriors. The parallels to the small number of Manchus who had conquered Ming China in 1644 were obvious. Krusínski, who completed his manuscript in 1725, thought he had observed the new rulers in Iran quickly assimilating and acclimatizing to their surroundings. Recently, they had even started pursuing a policy of reconciliation with the native elite. The Iranian Revolution, in his view, could serve as a shining light to the rest of Asia, which had succumbed to stagnation and decadence.[94] The barbarian invasion took on a providential meaning, civilizing the intruders while at the same time reviving a once-great civilization that had grown enfeebled and enervated.

Nadir's rise as a "comet of war" and "the most daring soldier of the age"[95] gave the lie to Krusínski's prognosis. There were other lessons to be learned from Nadir. He first came to public attention in Europe following his 1732 coup and his attack on the Ottoman Empire.[96] Soon there was so much news about him that by 1738 the industrious David Fassmann could publish a 770-page volume on the *Herkunft, Leben und Thaten des Persianischen Monarchens Schach Nadyr* (*Origins, Life and Deeds of the Persian Monarch Shah Nader*), padded out with elaborate setpieces from Iranian history.[97] Nadir appears here as the virtuous, divinely ordained savior of his nation, an Iranian messiah who chastened his "barbarous" enemies, "the Turks, Mongols [Mughals] and Afghans," and restored Iran to great power status. One of the secrets to his success was Westernization: the introduction of European-style military discipline was what first gave Nadir's troops the upper hand over their opponents.[98] Apparently there were even rumors swirling around Europe between 1734 and 1736 that Nadir was of French, German, or Dutch descent.[99]

James Fraser told the hero's tale of Nadir's rise from social banditry à la Robin Hood to supreme command in his *History of Nadir Shah* (1742).

Much of it was based on information received orally from William Cockell, a representative of the EIC in Iran whom Fraser, likewise employed by the EIC, had met in India.[100] Fraser and Cockell's Nadir is a charismatic leader who presented himself as a servant of the state and benefactor of his people, but whose chief concern was to ensure that his troops remained ever loyal and ready for battle. The Indian campaign was also launched mainly to acquire fame and booty.[101] Fraser provides an unvarnished account of the outrages committed during the sack of Delhi. He gives a figure of 120,000 slain citizens as well as precise statistics about the loot carted away from India: enormous quantities of gemstones, gold, and silver, one thousand elephants, seven thousand horses, ten thousand camels, one hundred eunuchs, three hundred masons, one hundred stonemasons, and so on.[102] A character sketch of Nadir Shah, taken directly from Cockell, has him emerging from this bloodbath with his heroic stature practically undiminished. He is depicted as a military leader who shared the privations of his men, a harsh but fair judge, blessed with a perfect memory, and skilled at pursuing several objectives at once[103]—in short, a born genius who disrupted the routine course of history and sent a salutary shock through a moribund Orient. Nadir bears more than a little resemblance to Cromwell here, and his characterization also anticipates a good many features of that later conqueror, Napoleon. The shah's admirers remained long undismayed by their idol's misdeeds. The opinion was even heard that Nadir had done the global economy a favor by returning the grand mughal's hoarded treasures to circulation.[104] His attitude of indifferent pragmatism towards religion and his mistrust of its official representatives also won him the approval of Enlightenment freethinkers.

Nadir's European reputation darkened only after his death. Comparisons with Alexander the Great, by no means an uncontroversial hero in Enlightenment Europe, fell ever less frequently in the Iranian usurper's favor.[105] While the English merchant Jonas Hanway, unlike William Cockell, may not have known Nadir personally, he was able to witness the devastating effects of his rule on Iran when he traveled there in 1743/44.

He reported extensively on what he saw, denouncing the shah as "a monster of cruelty and oppression" and "[a] scourge of the eastern world."[106] Hanway took pains not to explain the descent of the shah's regime into boundless greed and bloody tyranny solely with recourse to psychology (such as the perversion of heroic passions). He detected a certain logic in Nadir's system of rule. The military machine, corrupted by the spoils of victory in India, had become an unstoppable juggernaut. Nadir's original charisma had been eaten away by his distrust and the constant need to control and spy on his own people. In the end, his indisputable virtues as a general and strategist, including his caution, were not enough to make him a wise legislator and administrator.[107]

Hanway's relatively nuanced portrait depicted Iran's tragedy without mystifying its causes. With the passage of time, however, the image was simplified. The temper tantrums that seized Nadir towards the end of his life, recalling the worst of the Roman emperors, were remembered in the Persian chronicle of Mirza Mahdi, the shah's former court historian. The Danish king commissioned the young William Jones to translate this work, which Carsten Niebuhr had acquired in manuscript in Shiraz in 1765 and brought back with him to Denmark.[108] Not least on the basis of this chronicle, Nadir Shah became stylized as an archetypal monster. Crime and terror, wrote Jones, accompanied him wherever he went.[109] The Göttingen professor Christoph Meiners, ever fond of pronouncing judgment from on high, relished the primitive criminality of the regime and indulged in his own violent fantasies:

> Shah Nadir and his generals constantly roved around the countryside with hordes of savage warriors whose sole entertainment was robbery, mutilation and murder, and who filled with blood and destruction all the provinces, cities and villages they visited. . . . The tigerish Turkoman hordes never spawned a more vicious monster than Shah Nadir.[110]

In addition, many Christian authors could warm to Nadir's claim to have been God's punishing rod[111] and so draw providential meaning from his monstrosity. The Jesuit Joseph Tieffenthaler found that Delhi, this Babylon of iniquity, richly deserved the treatment it had received at Nadir's hands:

> It [the city of Delhi] was a cesspit of vice, fornication and filth. It was therefore visited with the fire of war, just as burning sulfur rained down on Sodom and Gomorrah, so that the hellfire of wickedness might be doused in rivers of blood. And for this God had need of Nader Shah to unleash His wrath at the sinners of Delhi.[112]

The evangelical Charles Grant, one of the top EIC officials in the 1790s, regarded all the Muslim conquerors of India up to Nadir Shah as tools of divine retribution against the dissolute Hindus.[113]

The lengthy critical apprisal of Nadir Shah offered by Sir John Malcolm in his *History of Persia* (1815) stands at odds with his demonization as a raving Asiatic monster. Malcolm, who was partially familiar with the Iranian sources, saw Nadir much as Gibbon had seen Attila the Hun: as a king who had used excessively harsh means to revive his ailing fatherland. The difference was that, whereas Attila had been a barbarian wounded in his pride, Nadir had liberated a civilized people from the worst barbarian regime of the eighteenth century.[114] Malcolm believed reports of the atrocities committed during the sack of Delhi to have been greatly exaggerated[115] and tended to forgive the arbitrary (mis)rule of the shah's last years; a good deal could be explained by mental illness. In Malcolm, the immediate shock of travelers such as Hanway and Otter (who traversed Iran in 1738) can barely be felt anymore.[116] The extent to which he ignores their testimony on violence and anarchy in the country is astonishing. Nadir's towering achievement was to have freed Iran from the Afghan yoke and rekindled a sense of national pride, and the esteem in which his compatriots hold him to this day is the best proof of his historical stature.[117] Malcolm, a general by profession, is full of admiration for Nadir's military skills, which put him on a par with the great European commanders of the modern age. Returning in some respects to the judgments of Nadir's European contemporaries, he draws the line between civilization and barbarism not between "us" and the monstrous Nadir but between Persians and the barbarians of Asia—that is, the Afghans and even (albeit to a lesser extent) the decadent Indians of the Mughal court. As an agent of modernization and national renewal, Nadir emancipated himself from his Asiatic background and broke through the eternal cycle of oriental politics. Having conquered parts of Afghanistan, he renounced taking bloody revenge and made the Afghans his loyal vassals. So far as the Indian campaign is concerned, the conduct of his conquering troops struck Malcolm as relatively mild by the standards of Asian history.[118]

Malcolm's encomium was not enough to offset Nadir's vilification.[119] But it was still influential as the verdict of the most respected nineteenth-century British historian of Iran. Malcolm spoke from the elevated platform of an all-conquering British Empire. In the year of Waterloo, he saw Nadir less as an oriental Napoleon than as the forerunner of British heroism on the field of battle. How could he have possibly condemned the conqueror? The British were successful in India because they too introduced their native troops to strict military discipline; their campaigns were also no walks in the park; they too had usurped leadership roles in Asia and heedlessly toppled long-established ancien régimes the length and breadth of the subcontinent, much to Edmund Burke's protestation. From an Asiatic viewpoint—and often in the social context of the British Isles as well—the generals and administrators of the EIC were no less "comets of war" and parvenus than Nadir Shah. It was therefore only fitting that Nadir should be revered as a charismatic renewer rather than reviled as an "elemental-historical" demon who came from nowhere to blaze across the oriental firmament. To be sure, he lacked the very quality on which the British plumed themselves the most: the ability to stabilize their conquests by founding something like a raj. This benign assessment by a contemporary imperialist rings true in an ironic way: by plunging India into chaos, Nadir Shah, more than any other single individual, paved the way for Britain's ascendancy over the subcontinent.[120]

HAIDAR ALI: TYRANT AND ENLIGHTENED REFORMER

The British indeed had every reason to be thankful to Nadir, whose destruction of Mughal rule had greatly facilitated their own later triumphal march through the subcontinent. When that march got underway in 1757 with Robert Clive's victory at the Battle of Plassey, Nadir Shah was long gone but by no means forgotten. As late as 1770, Sir William Jones remarked that events of the Nadir Shah years had not yet cooled down ("perdu leur degré de chaleur").[121]

It was easy for the British to praise someone who had never opposed them on the battlefield. The same could not be said of the Indian powers in the second half of the eighteenth century. A series of new splinter states had emerged following the rapid collapse of Mughal supremacy. In clear contrast to the political stability of China and Japan, or even the heartlands of the Ottoman Empire, South Asia was a laboratory of new state formations. The breakdown of imperial authority released forces that, following the death of the emperor Aurangzeb in 1707, could no longer be contained by a higher power.[122] These included the Sikhs in the Punjab, who evolved over the course of the eighteenth century from a religious community into a fully fledged political state, and above all the Marathas in the South Indian Deccan. In the mid-seventeenth century Shivaji, one of the great state-builders of the early modern period, had forged a new political elite from members of the warrior and Brahmin administrative castes, building up a new Hindu rebel state within the Islamic Mughal Empire.[123] When the unitary state he had founded collapsed, the Marathas entered into looser, constantly shifting configurations that defied the categories of European political theory. Commentators resorted to analogy instead: some were reminded of feudal vassalage, others felt they were witnessing something akin to a federation of Germanic tribes. Yet the best-informed were forced to concede that the Marathi system was unique and incomparable: a "barbarian" but nonetheless remarkably successful form of organization, at least for a time.[124] The Marathas went on to become the EIC's most formidable military adversaries. In 1803 they suffered decisive defeat; in 1818 the remnants of their state were absorbed by the British.

None of the Indian regional states attracted greater interest in Europe than Mysore under its leaders Haidar Ali and his son Tipu Sultan.[125] Between 1767 and 1799, the British and Mysore went to war against each other four times. In 1767–69 Haidar threatened the British colonial metropolis of Madras and was able to negotiate peace on favorable terms. In the Second Anglo-Mysore War (1780–84), Mysore, now allied with France, inflicted several defeats on the British and took a large number of British prisoners. In 1784 Mysore stood at the peak of its power as the strongest state in southern India. Five years later, Tipu Sultan attacked the raja of Travancore, an EIC ally. The British responded to the provocation by launching a massive counterattack in early 1790. It took them until 1792 to secure victory in this third war. Saddled with high war damages, Tipu forfeited a large amount of territory and was forced to hand over two of his sons to the EIC as security for keeping the terms of the peace. When a tiny French auxiliary force turned up in Mysore in 1799, the governor-general, Lord Wellesley—the most aggressive of the British empire-builders in India—interpreted this as a welcome *casus belli* and proceeded to destroy the sultanate. Tipu himself was killed while defending his capital, Seringapatam.

Unlike in the case of Nadir Shah, where Europeans played the passive role of onlookers to the unfolding drama, the conflict with Mysore unleashed a torrent of British war propaganda. The Third and especially the Fourth Mysore War, waged with great brutality on both sides, were presented to the public as a struggle between the forces of good and the dark powers of oriental despotism. In eyewitness reports and contemporary historical accounts, on stage and in iconography, Haidar and Tipu were depicted as the archenemies, not just of the freedom-loving British, but of their own people as well. Whereas earlier English wars in India had been largely unideological affairs conducted with a less-than-clean conscience with regard to their legitimacy, the Fourth Anglo-Mysore War occasioned no such qualms. The destruction of the sultanate was praised as a glorious national deed: not as a conquest (which is what it was in the first instance) but as a blow struck against Muslim tyranny on behalf of the oppressed citizens of Mysore. Tipu's death was hailed as a triumph of justice.[126]

In the early 1790s, Mysore was for the British something like public enemy number two after revolutionary France. Haidar Ali's negative image as a bloodthirsty tyrant crystallized following his death in 1782, when reports emerged of the degrading and cruel treatment suffered by British captives of the Second Mysore War.[127] Britons had endured the greatest imaginable indignity at his hands: they had been forced to convert to Islam.[128] This was countered by a more positive image of Haidar. While he was still alive, one of his earliest biographers, Maistre de la Tour, extolled him as the greatest conqueror India had seen since Nadir Shah, whom he far excelled in the extent of his genius and his civilized conduct.[129] Writing with pronounced antipathy toward the English, the French eyewitness depicts Haidar's life and conditions at court. In his opinion, it was not Haidar who was tyrannizing India but the same EIC that accused him of tyranny.[130]

This view was promptly contested by Francis Robson, who had spent twenty years in India and claimed to have been present at most of the encounters between the British and Mysore. Still, Robson abstained from the kind of overblown rhetoric that would come to dominate anti-Tipu propaganda a few years later. He underscores Haidar's cruelty (while acknowledging it to have been no greater than that of other Indian potentates) yet cannot avoid paying him a certain grudging respect: after Haidar had gained supremacy over a number of regional rajas between 1761 and 1763 and then driven out his more powerful neighbors, the Marathas, in the following years,[131] peace and moderate prosperity finally returned to the land. Without his domestic reconstruction policy, Haidar would have been unable to build up an elite army in so short a time.[132] Robson also shows some sympathy for the sultan's ultimate aim of "ridding the Indian subcontinent of all Europeans."[133]

Colonel William Fullarton, who stood close to Edmund Burke and his critical view of British expansion in India, portrays Haidar Ali in an even more positive light. He praises the military apparatus the sultan built up on European guidelines and with European (especially French) assistance, and he depicts how Haidar, showing all the ambition and tenacity of a Peter the Great, transformed his land into a model state during the period of peace between 1769 and 1780:

> Under his masterly control, they [his countries] attained a perfection never heard of under any Indian sovereign; the husbandman and the manufacturer prospered in every part of his dominions; cultivation increased, new manufactures were established, and wealth flowed into the kingdom.[134]

Haidar clamped down on sloppy practices and corruption, concerned himself with the smallest details, constantly toured his realm carrying out inspections and had documents read to him (he was illiterate), and always made himself available to his people.[135] Put differently, while Haidar was much like Nadir Shah in being a military strongman who had usurped his way to power, he was more than that: he was an effective reformer and brilliant civil administrator to boot. Fullarton repeats several stories already found in Maistre de la Tour, and it is unclear whether his testimony is based on firsthand observation. What is remarkable is that here, for the first time since the Mughal emperor Akbar, an Indian ruler is presented in a way that brings him closer to the model of European enlightened absolutism than that of oriental despotism.

In 1801 the topic was taken up in Halle by Matthias Christian Sprengel, the tireless disseminator of news from overseas; we have met him before as the son-in-law and colleague of Johann Reinhold Forster. Ten years earlier he had already published an extensive history of the Marathas, based largely on British official publications. What interested him in the Marathas was their dramatic rise from a "barbarous tribe of mountain-dwelling bandits" to the strongest political counterweight to the British in India.[136] The available sources did not yet allow him to paint a picture of Maharashtri society. But he was able to name the conditions for the Marathas' success: the visionary foundational achievement of Shivaji; the systematic attention they paid to cavalry and their perfection of tactics for mounted warfare; the lessons they learned from European mercenaries and from their archenemies, the Mughals; their development of plunder as a way of life; and finally their disdain for pomp and luxury and their attachment to their traditional customs.

Whereas the Marathas represented the raw forces of history as a collective, the same forces were embodied in a single individual in Haidar. Mysore's fate "provide[s] us with a fitting image of a typical Indian revolution, showing how a small and insignificant province can quickly advance to become a mighty nation."[137] Like Nadir Shah, Haidar began as a "brigand" or simple troop leader in the service of his lord, whom he ousted in a 1761 coup and permitted to remain on the throne a little longer as a puppet. Unlike Nadir, however, the warlord turned out to be a canny legislator who achieved great success, not least by recognizing the importance of economic growth.[138] If limits were nonetheless placed on his expansionary policies, then this was not due to any shortcomings on Haidar's part but rather to the aggressiveness and ill will of his more powerful neighbors, the Marathas and the British. In contrast to the British and French authors who wrote about Mysore, Sprengel stood at a remove from colonial controversies and international rivalries. So far as his British sources allowed him, he tried to tell Mysore's history from the inside, from Haidar and Tipu's perspective, without polemical exaggeration. Tipu comes off second best when compared to his father: megalomania and a militant Islamism that alienated many of his Hindu subjects ultimately undermined his position.[139]

A decade after the catastrophe of Seringapatam, the history of Mysore under Haidar and Tipu found its definitive historian in Colonel Mark Wilks, who had lived for seven years in Mysore and devoted himself to in-depth studies of Marathi and Persian manuscripts as well as inscriptions, coins, and other sources.[140] Wilks avoids the braggadocio of the triumphant victor. Schooled in the Olympian tones of Edward Gibbon, he looks back with nostalgia on the rise and fall of the Muslim state. His portrait of Haidar Ali, while not downplaying his brutality and duplicity, leaves no doubt in readers' minds that the British as well as most other Indian princes were his equals in both. Wilks is incomparably better informed than Sprengel, writing half a world away in his Halle study, and Haidar's leadership qualities shine through in his report: Haidar was a second, purified Nadir Shah, a patriotic commander-in-chief who waged war more in defense than in offense, a bandit who transformed himself into a promoter of agriculture, trade, and industry. The only thing that was "elemental-historical" about Haidar now was his nondynastic background. His modern, European-inspired policies made him an example of an overwhelmingly successful state-builder. He could have become the Peter the Great of all India if only, as James Mill argued in 1817, he had not come up against a nation that was superior to every Indian power in statecraft, warfare, and understanding.[141] Whereas even Malcolm's skills as a historian were not sufficient to dispel Nadir's reputation as a bloodthirsty monster, British propaganda had to take great pains, conversely, to impugn the good name of Haidar and Tipu. Haidar, in particular, was ill suited to confirming the customary clichés about the barbarism of Asiatic politics. This is precisely what made him suspect and dangerous: a native modernizer who—in a manner similar to Muhammad Ali Pasha decades later in Egypt—threatened to deprive the European civilizing mission of its cherished assumptions and pretexts.

THE MODERNIZATION OF POLITICAL VULCANISM

Anyone who reads the reports sent from China to Europe by the Jesuit missionaries during the first four decades of the seventeenth century, and then again from around 1690 to 1760, would gain the impression of a timeless and unchanging order. This image was not characteristic for Asia as a whole and the European perception of Asia in general. On the contrary, Asia looked more like a continent perennially racked by political turmoil or "revolutions," in the language of the time. Even China was not spared their harrowing touch. Between the Manchu conquest of Peking in 1644 and the final pacification of the kingdom around four decades later, China was the setting for events that dwarfed the violence of the English Revolution, inviting comparison with the Thirty Years' War. All this was well known in Europe.

Once again, as so often in Asian history, the raw forces of history seemed to erupt with explosive force, releasing a tidal wave of primordial, quasi-natural violence that threatened to inundate the centers of civilization. European authors paid a great deal of attention to the opposition between steppeland and farmland, herding societies and agrarian societies, mobility and stability—with good reason, for there can be no doubt that this is one of the fundamental contrasts of world history. But in European texts of the early modern period, matters are not so clear-cut as they would become in the polarizing intellectual climate of the nineteenth century. Authors do not simply take the part of "civilization" against "barbarism." This can be seen in their ambivalent appraisal of the two great medieval empire-builders, Genghis Khan and Timur. Up to a respected early nineteenth-century historian like Sir John Malcolm, both are not yet crudely stereotyped as paragons of "Asiatic cruelty." Their legislative achievements are praised no less than the extraordinary rationality of their policies.

In eighteenth-century Asia, the meteoric rise to power of usurpers and warlords drew an interest similar to that of such comparable European figures as Wallenstein, Cromwell, and later Napoleon Bonaparte. They proved that the Asian political volcano was not yet extinct. Nadir Shah of Iran was an international celebrity, potentially a world-historical individual in the Hegelian sense, a Peter the Great in the making. European observers followed his career with almost journalistic interest. What went wrong? The degeneration of Nadir Shah's rule into one of the worst tyrannies in recent Asian history provided a well-documented lesson in moral corruption and the destructive automatism of unbridled military ambition.

Sultan Haidar Ali of Mysore was a far less monstrous figure; he was also not a national leader but one of the more important Indian princes. Haidar was regarded with such fascination in Europe—not just in Great Britain, where imperial interests were at stake—because he seemed to embody a historical principle that had no precedent in Asia: the purposefully modernizing state-builder, the polar opposite of the old-fashioned and decadent "oriental despot." Haidar was the first Asian political leader who seemed to understand that the European invaders had to be beaten at their own game. This made him and his less forward-thinking son, Tipu Sultan, particularly dangerous enemies for Great Britain. The Mysore experiment came to an abrupt end, yet Haidar Ali never completely lost the respect of his former adversaries. In him, the explosive political force of the "elemental-historical" was refined into the ability to create a new state from the rubble of shattered empires. Almost imperceptibly at first, the storms of war unleashed by Timur or Nadir Shah made way for the quieter resistance of Asiatic reform.

IX

Savages and Barbarians

These writers might as well say that all Negroes and all sheep are alike; but this would only prove the carelessness of their scrutiny, that they have not the eye of the shepherd or the slave dealer.
—Constantin-François de Volney (1757–1820), "Observations générales sur les Indiens ou sauvages" (1803)[1]

Volney, who traveled through Egypt and Syria from 1783 to 1787 and narrowly survived the Terror of 1793, moved on to the United States in 1795 and made the New World the subject of wide-ranging studies. At first glance, the quotation from one of his papers on America seems disturbing. Volney appears to bracket Africans and animals in a dehumanizing way. Yet the sentence has a second meaning, quite representative of the time when it was written: the days of the traveling amateur and the impressionistic travel writer are over—a group in which Volney probably also included his younger self as an oriental traveler. The observer now has to be an expert. He has to subject what he sees to the closest possible scrutiny. His main duty is to make scientific distinctions and classify both the natural and the human world. These two worlds meet in the figure of the "savage," now slowly morphing into the less flamboyant "primitive." Wherever the European travels he encounters savages, a mass of nonwhite strangeness that presents a surmountable challenge to the scientific mind.

But let us pick up the thread from the preceding chapter. In the eyes of eighteenth-century Europeans, the "elemental-historical" was a barbaric force that erupted into the civilized world from outside and destroyed it.

Sometimes it also worked to revitalize a civilization that had been debilitated by luxury and lethargy, infusing it with previously untapped primal energies. The barbarian was both the destroyer of refinement and the enemy of *over*refinement. In the best case scenario, where the barbarian invaders proved willing and able to adapt to the vanquished culture, new syntheses could emerge. That helps explain the fascination of China, where it was precisely the "barbarian" Manchus under the Kangxi emperor who ushered in a renaissance of Chinese civilization. Partly for this reason—there were others—Kangxi was in European eyes the most illustrious monarch in all Asia: the barbarian king turned peace-bringing Augustus.[2] Similar to the Gothic ruler Theodoric for Edward Gibbon,[3] Kangxi was for his admirers the paragon of the ideal prince, the self-transcending barbarian.

Not all "barbarians" acted as elemental forces of historical change, however. Most had long since ceased to march at the vanguard of world-historical progress. Having been neutralized as a political and military threat, it was now easy to treat them as objects of ethnographic inquiry. The Others—savages as well as barbarians—were assigned to ethnography and ethnology once they no longer inspired terror. For Asia, this shift commenced in the eighteenth century.

LOST SAVAGES

By the mid-seventeenth century, nobody could seriously expect to find monstrous human-animal hybrids, such as those described by the ancients, prowling the forests of Asia. While the European discourse on Asia in the Enlightenment era was still shot through with illusions and wishful thinking, it no longer resorted to pure fantasy. To the enlightened mind, the same natural laws obtained everywhere in the world. In Asia, much was possible that strained belief when reported in Europe; the ascetic exercises of Indian holy men ("fakirs"), for example, appeared all but incomprehensible. Yet no European scholar believed in the existence of exotic alternative universes in which the laws of physics and physiology were suspended. The fabled East of djinns and flying carpets, but also of violence and debauchery, found its literary monument at the dawn of the eighteenth century in Antoine Galland's translation of the *Tales from the Thousand and One Nights*, before being rediscovered and enriched with gothic elements by William Beckford in his novella *Vathek: An Arabian Tale* (1786); it later became a common setting and source of materials for romantic literature. Writers such as Byron, Coleridge, Pushkin, Wilhelm Hauff, Théophil Gautier, Thomas Moore, and Thomas de Quincey pored over travel reports to stimulate their imaginations.[4] The worlds of Asia as imagined in fiction and Asia as perceived in reality intersected in a variety of ways, yet few contemporaries—least of all creative writers, who often ornamented their works with footnoted references to travel reports—ever confused the two.

If the East had now been unfabled, were there at least still "savages": not human-animal hybrids but human beings who had not yet been ennobled or spoiled (depending on the observer's philosophical taste) by modern civilization? The "noble savage" had been discovered in America and was subsequently rediscovered in the 1760s in the South Seas. The myth of man in the state of nature was staged in the rugged Canadian wilderness and on the sun-drenched islands of the Pacific.[5] In Europe, wildness had been domesticated away to such an extent that even the discovery of wild *horses* set mouths agape.[6] In Asia "primitive" social conditions persisted at the outer edges of the great empires.

Each of the Asiatic high cultures had its own ideas about primitive savagery and barbarism. These often coincided with the views of European observers. When the Jesuits in Peking reported on the imperial campaigns to repress ethnic minorities in the mountains of southern China, they did so entirely from the perspective of the imperial court, which believed itself the center of all civilization.[7] The non-Han aborigines of Formosa and the mountain tribes in the tributary state of Tonking were likewise represented as savages.[8] In June 1822 the British consul Dr. John Crawfurd examined a member of the Ka people introduced to him by his Siamese host:

> I had brought to me to-day an individual of the wild race called Ka. This people inhabit the mountainous country lying between Lao and Kamboja and still preserve their rude independence. The Siamese make no scruple in kidnapping them whenever they can find an opportunity. In consequence of this practice, a good number of them are to be found in a state of slavery at the capital. My present visitor had been taken about three years before. His features differed strikingly from those of the Siamese. . . . In intelligence, I found him greatly superior to what might reasonably have been expected.[9]

In Vietnam the same traveler learned that the neighboring Cambodians were regarded as barbarians, and in Burma the ethnic Karen people were described to him as savages.[10] Chardin had earlier reported that the Persians viewed the Muscovites and Tatars in much the same way.[11] Almost everyone whom Europeans categorized as barbarians looked down on their own barbarians in turn.

By common consent, there were still people on Europe's periphery who remained similarly untouched by civilization: Lapps, Albanians, Irish, Highland Scots, and many more. When the Russian army marched into Paris in 1813 with its Tatar and Caucasian regiments, the sight struck both awe and fear into the hearts of many. The mountain warriors from the Caucasus, in particular, brought home the ambivalence of wildness, since only a minority of them were subjects and auxiliary troops of the tsar. Most peoples of the Caucasus had staunchly defended their freedom against Russian encroachment and now had to put up with being told that they were "ignorant in matters of religion and law, uncouth in manners, more bandits than petty thieves, false, deceptive and disloyal to themselves and others."[12] In the "art of robbery," wrote one of the few Westerners to visit them, the Chechens in particular had attained a "great barbarian mastery."[13] In the Caucasus, as almost nowhere else, the law of the jungle seemed to prevail in an anarchic countersociety: a state of nature under civilization's eyes. Attentive observers noticed, however, that customs such as hospitality or blood vengeance were by no means archaic leftovers from a purported "childhood of humanity"; they served as functional equivalents for stable social institutions.[14]

In the eighteenth century, the most primitive savages of all were deemed to be the native inhabitants of Tierra del Fuego, the New Zealand Maori, and also, towards the end of the century, the Australian Aborigines and South African Bushmen. It was very rare to find conditions in Asia that were equally far removed from what Europeans understood by civilization. The surest sign of this is a paucity of reports on cannibalism, the most drastic indication of barbarism. William Dampier, by no means averse to sensationalist reporting, assured his readers that he had not encountered a single cannibal during his thirteen-year circumnavigation of the world.[15] According to the experts, in the reams of literature devoted to Asia in the seventeenth century there are only two authors who claim to have witnessed cannibalism, in both cases on the Indonesian island of Amboina.[16]

The story was much the same in the eighteenth century. There are occasional reports of people driven by hunger to eat human flesh, such as in the Indian city of Patna in the 1760s.[17] Gibbon claims—half in provocation, half in jest—that the Christians who set out on the First Crusade, and not some woebegone Asiatic starvelings, provided the greatest and almost sole example of medieval cannibalism.[18] William Marsden contends in his *History of Sumatra* that the Batta (Batak) people, otherwise civilized enough to dress in colorful fabrics, play orchestral music, and adroitly handle muskets, engaged in ritual cannibalism. Never having witnessed this with his own eyes, however, he relied mainly on literary tradition and voiced his own doubts at the end of his discussion.[19] After thoroughly looking into the matter, Sir Stamford Raffles concluded that the Battas' former custom of consuming their unproductive elders had been sacrificed to progress. He nonetheless did not completely place his trust in such an alleged improvement in morals, writing as a precaution to his friend Charlotte, Duchess of Somerset:

> Notwithstanding the practices I have related, it is my determination to take Lady Raffles into the interior and to spend a month or two in the midst of these Battas. Should any accident occur to us, or should we never be heard of more, you may conclude we have been eaten.[20]

Sir Stamford and Lady Sophia came back sound in life and limb, but with grisly tales to tell about the alleged juridical cannibalism of the Battas, who were said to sacrifice fifty to sixty convicted criminals each year in peacetime. In principle, Raffles found such behavior, if it had actually occurred, no worse than the public corporal punishment inflicted on malefactors in the recent European past. In both cases he placed his trust in the gradual progress of civilization.[21]

One of the rare descriptions of an Asiatic people languishing in a state of extreme barbarism is found in Captain Michael Symes, the author of two detailed reports on Burma. In early 1795, while traveling from Calcutta on his first mission to Burma on behalf of the EIC, Symes and his entourage visited the Andaman Islands in the Bay of Bengal. Here they encountered a coast-dwelling tribe numbering more than two thousand, "a degenerate race of Negroes with woolly hair, flat noses and thick lips."[22] These people went around stark naked, lived in the simplest wooden huts, subsisted almost entirely on a diet of speared fish, and coated themselves in a layer of hardened mud to protect themselves against insects. Symes recoiled in horror from such brutishness, but he also found words of praise for the virtues of the Andamanese: they never developed a taste for the liquor introduced to them by foreigners, they always longed to regain their liberty when placed in captivity, and they practiced a sun and moon cult that struck him as "the purest devotion of an unenlightened mind."[23] A cautious observer, Symes felt that it would be reckless to declare these people to be cannibals without hard evidence. It was equally impossible to clarify whether or not they believed in an afterlife. He expressed his irritation with reserve, shunning any outright display of abhorrence, but he also showed no sign of wanting to idealize this species of *homme naturel*. Symes instead approached his subjects with clear-eyed realism, as when he diagnosed them with chronic malnutrition resulting from nutrient-poor flora and fauna as well as a lack of cooking utensils. In short, the learned British officer proved an early exponent of what ethnologists today call "cultural materialism" or "cultural ecology."

Travel writers returning from Asia had no other candidates apart from the wretched Andamanese to offer the eighteenth century's yearning for unspoiled wildness. Only the natives of Kamchatka, harder to reach than the South Sea Islanders, had what it took to become something like the Tahitians of the North. In the course of the Great Northern Expedition they were visited and described by two of the most intrepid travelers of the age: the young Russian Stepan Petrovich Krasheninnikov, who spent the period from September 1737 to June 1741 on a research trip to Kamchatka, the easternmost tip of the tsarist empire, and Georg Wilhelm Steller, who arrived on the peninsula in September 1740 and remained there until March 1745.

The question of which qualities defined a people as "primitive" had been a topic of lively debate since the mid-sixteenth century. The usual answer, in brief, was that savages lacked three things: laws, religion, and morals.[24] That more or less remained the state of discussion until, beginning in 1748, Montesquieu, Rousseau, and Ferguson developed a more sociological concept of primitiveness that foregrounded technology and the division of labor. Krasheninnikov, still untouched by these new ideas, applied a tangible criterion to ascertain whether or not he was dealing with savages: they were people who had never come into close contact with Europeans, as could be inferred from their ignorance of alcohol and tobacco.[25] This held true for most Kamchadals.

> The natives of Kamchatka are as wild as their country itself. Some, in the same fashion as the Lapps, have no permanent dwelling place, but move from one location to another, driving their reindeer

herds along with them. . . . The nomadic peoples live in iurts or huts made of reindeer hides, the others in underground dugout iurts. In general, all these natives are idolaters, and are totally ignorant and illiterate.[26]

This was a report from a first-contact situation. A few decades later, under the tsarina Catherine II, official attitudes towards the indigenous population of Siberia softened for a time, and the discourse on the "natives" became calmer and less dismissive. Written in the early 1750s, Krasheninnikov's detailed ethnography draws out the contrasts with Europe. The antipode to Western civilization could be found at the opposite end of Eurasia. All that Europeans and Kamchadals (more precisely: Itelmens) had in common was that both believed themselves to be the happiest people on Earth. The Itelmens had a completely different sense of time from Europeans. Private ownership of property was unknown to them, there being more than enough land for everyone. Their trade with each other and with their neighbors was more a ceremonial exchange of gifts, carried out not for personal gain but to secure the basic necessities of life. Their notions of sin and virtue were utterly utilitarian and amoral: "They regard as acceptable anything that can gratify their desires and passions, and they consider sinful only those actions which make them feel real harm."[27] Divorce was a straightforward matter, while no undue fuss was made about sex before marriage. Their dead were thrown to the dogs—hardly surprising for a society in which dogs were the most valued commodity: "whoever is eaten by the dogs will have good dogs in the other world."[28] Their greatest pleasure was to laze about doing nothing. They only hunted, fished, and worked when they had no other option. They lived entirely in the present; past and future held no interest for them. "They have no knowledge either of riches, of honor, nor of glory; consequently they know neither greed, ambition, nor pride."[29]

Steller, an even shrewder observer, draws a similar picture of the pleasure-loving Itelmens of Kamchatka. Not only did they go through life blessedly unplagued by material concerns, their musical artistry was such as to enthuse even the contemporary of Johann Sebastian Bach and George Frideric Handel:

> Besides eating they take great delight in singing. Just as it may truthfully be said that this jovial nation is predisposed to music above all else, so one can only marvel at their songs, which have nothing wild about them, but are performed *cantabile* and composed in perfect accordance with the rules of music, rhythm and cadence, such that it appears almost inconceivable that this people should be capable of the like. The cantatas of the great Orlandus Lassus . . . are far less pleasing to the ear than the arias of the Itelmens, which are not only sung in unison but also ably supported by middle voices.[30]

In addition, the natives were sexually uninhibited and left their civilized visitors little choice, given the underdeveloped state of the monetary economy, but to partake of the local freedoms:

> Any man who comes to Kamchatka and does not take a woman or live with one in secret companionship will find himself forced to do so by necessity. Nobody will wash for him, sew for him, or perform him the least service without payment in the form of copulation.[31]

Almost two decades before the circumnavigator Bougainville acquainted Europe with the joys awaiting visitors to the earthly paradise of Tahiti, Steller and Krasheninnikov described the naïve happiness of a prelapsarian community in similar terms. But first impressions could be deceptive. In the South Seas, and previously among the "primitive" inhabitants of Tierra del Fuego, Bougainville had been struck by the unhierarchical, quasi-organic democracy that others had already perceived at work in several North American tribes.[32] Krasheninnikov draws on the same register:

> they [the people of Kamchatka] had always lived in complete independence without rulers or laws. The elders, or those who were distinguished for their valor, were preeminent over the others in each

> ostrog [village]. The preeminence, however, consisted only in that preference was given their advice over that of others. Aside from that there existed complete equality among them; no one might command another, nor would anyone presume of his own accord to punish another.[33]

Yet those halcyon days were long gone. By the time the scientific expeditionaries visited the peninsula, the traces of the brutal Cossack conquest launched in 1697 could no longer be overlooked. Large parts of Kamchatka that interested the tsar only as a source of sable furs had become little more than a target for Russian colonial exploitation.[34] Steller and his Russian friend were aware that it was already practically impossible to make statements about the Itelmens' authentic culture. Around 1740 they observed the natives to be conspicuously belligerent; their clans and villages were pushing each other to the brink of extermination. Had it ever been thus, the young European scholars asked themselves? Was their constant infighting an expression of their innate character or a result of the brutalizing effects of the Russian invasion on all aspects of society?[35] The visitors had no way of knowing the answer. They were reluctantly forced to concede that no foreigner had ever seen the Itelmens in their pristine, uncontaminated condition. Steller laments in general "how strongly the loss of natural freedom can change our inclinations and manners" before relating this to the situation in Kamchatka:

> For this reason one can say that Kamchatka has changed beyond recognition within a short time, and finds itself in a far worse state than before. The more the Itelmens fraternize with the Cossacks, the closer they live to the ostrogs,[36] the more they befriend Cossack and Russian customs, the more dishonest, mendacious, deceitful and duplicitious they become: the less they do all these things, the more honesty and virtue they still display in their conduct.[37]

The dream of *homo naturalis* was at an end in Asia before it had even begun in the South Pacific. When the sobering reports from Kamchatka first became known in Western Europe—Krasheninnikov was published in English translation in 1764, Steller in German in 1774—they could suggest at least two things to careful readers. On the one hand, "noble" and "ignoble" savages could not be clearly distinguished from each other in ethnographic reality; on the other, the authentic truth about the primitive Other had already been disturbed by contact. Only a minority of European intellectuals followed Rousseau in his critique of civilization, projecting utopian wishes onto an idealized *homme naturel*. The more common question was how a savage became a barbarian.[38]

FOUR TYPES OF BARBARISM

Until well into the eighteenth century, European ideas about societies organized differently to their own remained dominated by concepts inherited from ancient ethnography. Many early modern ways of coming to grips with the alien had been pioneered by the Greeks: positing a binary contrast between civilization and its opposite, describing civilizations in comparative terms, deriving biological and cultural differences from climatic and other environmental factors, theorizing the origin and evolution of culture.[39] Other civilizations, such as the Chinese and the Arab-Islamic, independently arrived at quite similar ways of classifying, explaining, and dealing with foreignness. In numerous non-European languages there were evaluative words and phrases that roughly matched the semantic field of the "barbarian" in Europe. Of all the terms for designating otherness available to eighteenth-century Europe, "barbarian" and "barbarism" were still the ones bandied about most often. Since the word's meaning became terribly diffuse over time, tracing its etymology back to Greek usage is as futile as trying to arrive at a half-way accurate definition. The Enlightenment had no universally accepted concept of barbarism.

First of all, "Barbary" (*Barbarei, Barbarie*) was the common name for the "Berber lands" of North Africa.[40] Because the buccaneering corsairs who lived there were some of the most notorious troublemakers in the

Mediterranean, they soon became identified with the barbarousness of their conduct. Secondly, inhumane cruelties of all kinds were termed "barbaric," regardless of whether they were committed by Europeans or non-Europeans. Calling Europeans barbaric meant unmasking their claim to superiority as hypocrisy. The implicit assumption—and the ultimate criterion for judgment—was that "real" barbarians could be expected to behave barbarically all the time. Alexander von Humboldt repeats a topos found in early Spanish critics of colonialism (such as Bartolomé de Las Casas) in a diary entry from September 1802, where he contends that Europeans "behave more barbarically when abroad than the Turks—and worse, because they are even more fanatical."[41] In 1762 Justi invites his readers to consider whether there is anything more barbaric than warfare as routinely practiced in Europe today, and he encourages them to find such misconduct more deplorable than the crimes allegedly committed by cannibals half a world away.[42] Faced with the atrocities that accompanied the Ottoman conquest of Cyprus in 1571, Hammer-Purgstall recalls the barbarism "of the whole age," citing Ivan the Terrible, the Huguenot Wars, the Bartholomew's Day Massacre, and the horrors unleashed upon the taking of the Estonian-Finnish fortress of Winterstein by the Russians in 1573 as the most shocking examples: "If this could happen in France and Finland, how could anything different be expected in Turkey?"[43] Gibbon relativizes and neutralizes the accusation of barbarism by showing how Crusaders and Muslims (with whom he sympathizes more than with the Christian knights) "despised each other as slaves and barbarians."[44]

"Barbarian" is used in a third way when an entire community's way of life is characterized as uncivilized. This does not necessarily mean that they are guilty of any barbaric acts (in the second sense); barbarians can also possess vital natural instincts or be harmless dolts. Barbarism is here simply the antonym of civilization; more precisely, it is a negatively charged marker of deficiency. Barbarians are people who do not share the cultural practices that are taken for granted in the imperial center: language, religion, notions of justice, social norms, and so on. But periods of regression within the historical cycle of an empire or high culture can also be barbarian (in the sense of uncivilized): the European Middle Ages, for example, were barbarian from the viewpoint of the Enlightenment, especially the seventh, eleventh, and fourteenth centuries.[45] Voltaire and Gibbon, in particular, never missed an opportunity to point out the lapses into barbarism that punctuated the history of civilization.[46]

Characterizing foreign nations as "barbarian" could give rise to endless disputes. A barbarian, it was said in jest, was someone whose mouth starts watering at the sight of a Jesuit missionary.[47] Arbitrary criteria for exclusion, old stereotypes, and new experiences were all mixed up in these debates. Nobody in Europe ever dreamed of calling the Japanese "barbarians." Japan was the only country in Asia that was always recognized as a civilization in its own right. Differing opinions could be expressed about China, even if the voices proclaiming it to be barbarian remained at all times in a minority. The opposite held true of the Turks, who were respected by Europeans for their military prowess far more than they were admired for their cultural achievements. Even their most vocal champion, Joseph von Hammer-Purgstall, ultimately saw the conflict between Austria and the Ottoman Empire as one "between civilization and barbarism."[48] Such, at any rate, was his verdict on seventeenth-century Turkey; from around 1700 he noted a certain softening of Turkish customs.[49] The Persians, conversely, had been regarded since the days of Herodotus as a highly civilized nation, an appraisal that their political renaissance in the sixteenth and early seventeenth century seemed only to confirm. The chaos that descended on the land in the eighteenth century cast doubt on this judgment. Persia now became the only Asiatic country in which a Hobbesian state of nature—the war of all against all—appeared to have been realized in the present. Many who affirmed the barbarism of Asiatic peoples recognized that the concept was far too sweeping to capture nuances and changes over time. With regard to the Mongols, Hammer-Purgstall suggested, should not a distinction be made between their *savage* barbarism before Genghis Khan and their *organized* barbarism in the aftermath of his institutional reforms and imperial conquests?[50]

Fourth, over the course of the eighteenth century, the idea of barbarism as a state of deficiency gradually came to be supplanted by the notion that barbarism referred to a stage in social development. There had already been stage theories in antiquity, and they would go on to reach a high point of sophistication and complexity in nineteenth-century "evolutionism." In the seventeenth and eighteenth centuries they were bound up with some of the most intellectually contentious questions of the era. In particular:

- What was the relationship between biblical *historia sacra* and its chronology to the potentially far older—even pre-Adamite—history of heathen nations such as the Chinese, Egyptians, and Chaldeans?
- How do religious ideas develop? In particular, how did monotheism first arise?
- What is the origin of language?
- How did social ties, social inequality, and the authority to rule emerge from a primordial state of humankind?

A phase of "barbarism" played a part in almost all the theories that ventured answers to such questions. This could mean different things to different authors.

In the eighteenth century, the idea that the dawn of human history had witnessed a golden age that was succeeded by a decline into barbarism found ever fewer adherents. It endured only in a tradition of primitivism reformulated by Jean-Jacques Rousseau and in the idea that early societies were particularly powerful incubators of artistic talent, as expressed in anonymous folk poetry and in figures like Homer or the Celtic bard Ossian (who turned out to be an invention of the Scottish poet James Macpherson). This template of an early cultural flowering that all too quickly wilted into degeneration was now no longer seen to pertain to the entire human race, however much such ideas continued to be applied to individual civilizations. It was replaced by theories of man's rise from primitive beginnings to the pinnacle of civilization.[51]

Such theories came in two versions.[52] On the one hand, the transition from barbarism to civilization, from the state of nature to the state of culture, could be envisaged as a foundational act: either by a wise lawgiver (*législateur*) or through consensus between parties to a social contract. On the other hand, a gradual *progression* through a series of stages was also conceivable. Whereas sixteenth-century thinkers, confronted with the sacred and profane meaning of the discovery of American Indians, had construed "barbarians" to be human beings left behind by the march of progress,[53] in the late eighteenth century they were generally credited with the potential to advance along the path to civilization. In the best case scenario, barbarians could liberate themselves from their constraints; failing that, they could always be educated to freedom. Why a given people found itself at a given developmental stage at any given time was a question that could only be answered through empirical research.

In the second half of the eighteenth century, "barbarism" was widely regarded as a secondary development following on from a stage in which humans eked out an existence close to nature: barbarians were incompletely denatured savages.

Montesquieu, who tended to apply the concept far more liberally to the European early medieval period than to non-European cultures, distinguished savages from barbarians by arguing that, while savages live in small scattered bands or hordes, barbarians come together to form larger political associations. The former were largely gatherers, the latter herders. He cited the Siberian tribes as examples of the former; in the latter category he placed the Mongols, who proved themselves capable of creating a vast (albeit short-lived) empire.[54] Adam Ferguson saw private property as the key differentiating criterion: while savages have no inkling of it, barbarians recognize it de facto even if there are no legal guarantees put in place to protect it, as there are in more advanced societies. Among barbarians, the relative equality of the first phase gives way to clear power hierarchies, which are ordered and reordered through constant struggles for dominance.[55]

This understanding of barbarism as a transitional phase between savagery and civilization was intended to be descriptive and value-neutral. It was more substantial than the simple concept of barbarism as the opposite of civilization. Yet Montesquieu and Ferguson made little use of it, and Adam Smith, another great social scientist of the time, completely avoided it, preferring instead to distinguish between dominant "modes of subsistence": hunting, pasturage, farming, trade, and manufacturing. The sociological concept of barbarism proved too blunt an instrument to be useful, given that it encompassed all premodern high cultures, wherever they happened to be. By the nineteenth century it could be found only in latter-day stage theorists[56] as well as in some versions of ethnological evolutionism. Its demise in the 1830s as a category pertaining to a universal theory of societal development was sealed by a very narrow definition: "barbarians" are nomadic peoples in the process of forming institutions and establishing permanent settlements, as well as illiterate farmers who lack the higher arts and have nothing but the "rudiments of civil society and a state." This definition was said to include most black Africans, several Malay ethnic groups, and a number of mountain tribes in Asia.[57] By that stage the concept had already migrated to where it would be principally domiciled for the rest of the nineteenth century: the myth of the inner demons that were tormenting Europe.

THE ROOF OF THE WORLD

No contemporary inhabitants of Asia fitted the eighteenth century's image of the "barbarian" better than the Tatars (or Tartars). Unlike the desert Arabs, the competing candidates for the role, the Tatars not only fulfilled the criterion that they were a nomadic people who had moved beyond the stage of primitive savagery; they also embodied the raw forces of history that had been pacified not long before. All the most devastating scourges of history, from the Scythians and Huns via the Turks and Mongols up to the conquering Manchus at the time of the Thirty Years' War, seemed to originate in that "terrible vast land in deepest Asia."[58] As late as 1788, Sir William Jones was still speaking of "the great hive of the northern swarms, the nursery of irresistible legions."[59] In the words of another author, Tartary was "the great *officina gentium* whence such myriads of barbarians have at different periods poured into the more cultivated regions of the earth."[60]

By the late Middle Ages, "the Tatar" was already the best known of all barbarians.[61] In contrast to the Arabs, who besides living in desert tents as Bedouins had developed a sophisticated urban culture, the Tatars appeared never to have risen above a subsistence level.[62] Those living furthest to the west, the Crimean Tatars and the Nogai Horde, were considered "the wildest people in Europe," as one writer was still declaring with a slight shudder in 1820.[63] Calling someone a Tatar was a choice insult. Voltaire hurled it at the English in India, Chateaubriand at the Turks on a number of occasions.[64]

Where was Tartary? Medieval travelers to Asia could still make for an obvious destination: in the first half of the thirteenth century, the court of the Mongol great khan in Karakorum was not just the political heart of Inner Asia but also one of the great power centers of the medieval world. Following the breakup of the Mongol world empire, the revival of Chinese strength under the Ming dynasty (1368–1644), and the beginning of Russian eastward expansion in the late sixteenth century, Inner Asia came to be seen in the West as a kind of no-man's-land between the empires: a world of boundless grass steppes ranged by hordes of nomadic herder-warriors unbeholden to anything resembling a unitary state.

In the seventeenth century, it became common to split Tartary into western (= Mongol) and eastern (= Manchu) halves. Tartary itself, however, seemed to extend far beyond the area controlled by these two peoples or ethnic groupings. At a time when borders between territorial states were becoming increasingly fixed, the very indeterminacy of this space allowed exotic fantasy to take flight. Thus the English geographer Richard

Blome, who takes Tartary to mean the country between the Volga and China, between the Caspian Sea to the south and the Arctic Ocean in the north, remarks in 1670 of the people who inhabit these far-flung regions: "they are very rude, barbarous and revengeful, not sparing their enemies, who in revenge they eate, first letting out their Blood, which they keep, using it as Wine at their Feasts."[65] This was lurid fantasy even by the standards of the time, fed less by distorted travel reports than by the very *lack* of post-medieval reporting. New information was not long in coming. Working independently of each other, Nicolaas Witsen and Pierre Avril compiled the seventeenth century's scattered knowledge of North and Inner Asia.[66] Reports of recent Russian overland voyages to China were publicized, augmented in the 1730s by the accounts given by Swedish prisoners-of-war of their experiences in Siberia.[67] In 1735 Jean-Baptiste Du Halde, drawing on the travels and research of Pater Gerbillon, devoted almost the entire fourth volume of his Chinese encyclopedia to Mongolia, now little more than a Sino-Manchu protectorate.[68] Russian research into Tartary got underway with Daniel Gottlieb Messerschmidt's journey of 1720–27 and was continued in the Great Northern Expedition.[69]

Firsthand observation of the Tatars did much to normalize their image. "We found them to be good company," wrote Johann Georg Gmelin in 1733, "and the once-dreaded name of Tatar held no more terror for us."[70] But achieving greater ethnographic clarity was a slow process. That Tartary was inhabited by "an extraordinary number of peoples"[71] had been a literary commonplace since Pliny. Yet who these peoples were and how they could be told apart from non-Tatars remained uncertain. Those who adopted a maximalist definition treated even China under Mongol (Yuan dynasty, 1279–1368) and Manchu rule (Qing dynasty from 1644) as part of Tatar history.[72] Sometimes Tibet was included, sometimes not. Witsen's map of Tartary (1690) was the first to chart the region with any degree of accuracy; in 1706 it was supplanted by Delisle's map, which in turn was superseded by d'Anville's map in 1735. None of these representations set down sharply defined external borders. The idea that "Greater

Tartary" was the area between the 57th and 160th meridians east and the 37th and 55th parallels north could expect to find some support.[73]

As early as 1730, the Swedish captain and Russian prisoner-of-war Philip Johan Tabbert, subsequently ennobled under the name of Philipp Johann von Strahlenberg, had criticized Europeans' unwillingness to distinguish between the peoples of "High Asia" (as he was one of the first to call it). He saw a symmetry in the way both sides employed sweeping generalizations:

> And likewise to this day the people of High Asia, when they give us Europeans a name, make no distinctions among our nations, but call them all Frang or Frank, whether they be from Germany, France, Spain, Sweden, England or Holland.[74]

In 1768 Johann Eberhard Fischer, the expert on Siberia, justly complained "that when Europeans speak of Tatars, I have not the faintest idea who they are talking about."[75] Such criticism made little impact. Admittedly, towards the end of the eighteenth century it became less attractive to label everyone living in the central part of the continent by that name, and more common to adopt a narrower meaning that excluded Mongols and Manchus.[76] The term was nonetheless fuzzy enough, and in 1824 the researcher on Central Asia, Isaac Jacob Schmidt, still felt compelled to polemicize against that "vacuous, antiquated . . . common name."[77]

"TARTARY" IN GEOGRAPHY, THE PHILOSOPHY OF HISTORY, AND ETHNOGRAPHY

During the second half of the eighteenth century, the astonishing situation came about that three almost unrelated discourses on "Tartary" flowed alongside each other.

Firstly there was a series of *geographical* reflections that gradually dispensed with the notion of Tartary. Philippe Buache, the Cartesian geometrist among eighteenth-century geographers, developed a technique of topographical description that attached cardinal importance to the mapping of mountain ranges and river systems. Such an analysis revealed a high-altitude arid plateau at the center of Asia. All the great Asian mountain chains radiated from this plateau like spokes from a hub, and all the continent's major rivers arose at its edges.[78] Central Asia thus did not consist of endless steppes on which mounted archers rode impetuously from one skirmish to the next, but of deserts, salt lakes and chilly highlands.[79] Paradoxically, these barren landscapes were the natural origin of the great riverine civilizations. This reorientation in spatial perception led to the continent being recategorized into North, Central, and South Asia, as recommended by Gatterer, among others.[80] What was crucial was that, on the one hand, previously unified Tartary was now divided into Central and North Asia; Siberia thus became a distinct geographical entity. On the other hand, the image of Tartary's "endless expanses" underwent revision as the extraordinary height of the central plateau became visible in relief. The geographer August Zeune spoke in 1808 of "High Asia" as an "elevated bowl valley," while Carl Ritter, the era's best-informed expert on Asia, referred in 1817 to the continent's "exalted middle."[81] As a consequence, both North and South Asia, and perhaps China as well, appeared as lowlands extending from High Asia down towards the sea. The gigantic mountain massifs of the Himalaya and the Hindu Kush, still barely known in Europe, became the rooftop of the world. Peter Simon Pallas, who unlike the armchair theorists had at least traveled the Atlas Mountains and had written the most correct orographic description of Central Asia to that point, spoke of the "roof of Asia" (*le toit de l'Asie*) being located amidst "awe-inspiring mountain ranges in the North of India, from which Tibet and the Kingdom of Kashmir radiate outwards."[82]

This new spatial awareness affected the *historico-philosophical* discourse on Tartary. Ever since the biblical teaching that an earthly paradise had once existed had begun to be taken less literally, theorists of the genesis and worldwide dispersal of the human race had been searching for the place where civilization might have originated. Since the seventeenth century, Egypt had been zealously promoted as the fount of all knowledge and wisdom.[83] Pierre Daniel Huet, a bishop of Avranches, even proposed that China had been an Egyptian colony. Half a century later, Joseph de Guignes exerted all his scholarly authority in a vain attempt to demonstrate this thesis.[84] Early nineteenth-century romantics were more drawn to India. In the last third of the eighteenth century, Jean-Sylvain Bailly's hypothesis of a "primal people" met with considerable interest.[85] Bailly eloquently conjured up a vision of the Central Asian high plateau as the birthplace of natural fertility and cultural achievement. In 1778, for example, he wrote in an open letter to Voltaire:

> This great space, where so many rivers have their source, is strewn with towering peaks. They enclose vast valleys where men, sheltered from wind and conquest, were able to settle down undisturbed and found empires.[86]

Directly contradicting the information provided by geographers, Bailly talks up the Edenic bounty of Central Asia, which the nomads had supposedly failed to use to their advantage. Why had they never settled down? Because they wanted to keep themselves in readiness for future conquests abroad. That had not always been the case. In the lush and protected mountain valleys of Tibet, "Brahmans" had meditated on profound truths in ages past. These genial climes had once been well-tended and densely populated. They had only reverted to wilderness when humans had been forced to abandon them following a deterioration in climate.[87]

Bailly's mythic construction of space was nothing if not ingenious. It was based largely on the sparse reports compiled by the abbé Prévost on the topic of Central Asia. Johann Gottfried Herder's exposition of similar ideas in his *Ideen zur Philosophie der Geschichte der Menschheit* (*Outlines of a Philosophy of the History of Man*) rested on only slightly sounder empirical foundations. According to Herder, it was at the heart of Asia, "in the center of the most active organic powers," that "creation had progressed farthest, and had developed most extensively and with the greatest refinement." Envisaged as "an extensive amphitheater, a constellation of mountains, the arms of which extend into various climates," Central Asia was the first abode of all higher life-forms.[88] Herder distinguishes the Mongol conquests of historic times from the "ancient migrations from this highest spine of the earth."[89] The portrait Herder paints of the Mongols is the darkest produced in the eighteenth century. On the basis of writings by Peter Simon Pallas, he depicts their external appearance as being diametrically opposed to the "finely formed peoples" he imagines dwelling in the earthly paradise of Kashmir and the countries to its west. In Herder's racial typology, Mongols and Kalmyks are the most Asiatic Asians of them all: they resemble "human beasts of prey" in their ugly, animalistic facial features.[90] They are also weak and "womanly," developing their strength and power not as individuals but in hordes and masses. It is therefore unsurprising that Herder fails to emulate the fine ambivalence of a Gibbon in evaluating the historical role of the Mongols. He also completely overlooks Genghis Khan's legislative legacy, not least a religion that acted as a long-term civilizing force on his people—Lamaism—as well as a written language. The Mongols were "light birds of prey" (*leichte Raubgeier*), "rapine wolves come down from the Asiatic heights," "despoilers of the world."[91] Hegel's "elemental-historical" has rarely been so chillingly invoked as in these sentences by Herder.

It is remarkable that Herder refrains from equating Tatars and Mongols, thus avoiding the path trodden by so many of his contemporaries—including at times even the great Joseph der Guignes, the doyen of Inner Asian history. Bailly employed just such an all-embracing, blanket concept of "Tartary" and "Tatars," much as Montesquieu had thrown Mongols and Manchus into the same basket in 1748. The abbé Raynal, who did more than anyone else to shape the broader public's views on the non-European world, accurately described the current political situation when he pointed out in 1770 that most "Tatars" were now subjects of the Chinese and Russian Empires.[92] But Raynal all too often mined his sources uncritically and did not always escape self-contradiction. He even went so far as to contend that the Indian Mughal dynasty was Tatar, a claim he could support only through spurious genealogical reasoning. Because he saw the Manchu conquest of China in 1644 as nothing but a repeat performance of the Mongol conquest in the thirteenth century, he missed the point that it was precisely the Manchus who had tamed the "elemental-historical" force of the Mongols. In confronting the unavoidable question of what constituted their shared "Tatarism," Raynal referred neither to a myth of origin nor to common ethnographic or racial characteristics. He instead pointed to the unifying bond of Lamaism, the "doctrine of the Grand Lama, who resides in Potala." So little was known about Tibetan religion at the time that Raynal cannot be blamed for ascribing it the fantastic age of three thousand years.[93] His argument was not inept or flawed per se, but it would necessarily have undermined the historico-philosophical stereotype of the "Tatar." This is because, on the one hand, a significant number of the peoples widely known as Tatars were actually followers of Islam or shamanist cults; on the other, a central place in the imaginary construct "Tartary" was now assigned to the Tibetans, a wholly unexpansive and irenic people without the slightest "elemental-historical" tendencies, at least since the downfall of the Tibetan Empire in the ninth century. Nowhere else do the inner tensions of the notion of Tartary come through so clearly as in Raynal's chapter entitled *Notions générales sur la Tartarie.*

Herder, to return to him, was one of the few historico-philosophical commentators to assimilate some of the subtleties of ethnographic discourse, which he knew inside out as a tireless reader and collector of materials.[94] His Tatars include Uzbeks, Bukharans, and Circassians, among others. He classifies all these ethnic groups among the "finely formed peoples" (*schöngebildeten Völkern*), even if some of them "have run wild on the steppes."[95] Herder draws a curious racial borderline between Tatars, who in his view stand much closer to Russians, and Mongols: "When Russians or Tatars intermix with Mongols, it is reported, handsome children are produced."[96]

The historico-philosophical discourse on Tartary essentially ends with Hegel. We are confronted here with the problem of an unreliable textual transmission. Hegel held lectures on the philosophy of world history between 1822/23 and 1830/31 at the University of Berlin. These lectures are known only from student notes, and the only ones established as critically secure are those from winter semester 1822/23, which survive in three separate transcripts.[97] In these lectures Hegel held forth at length about China, but it was not until 1824/25 that he delivered an appendix on "the Mongolian principle." We know it only from Georg Lasson's edition from 1919, likewise based on auditor notes.

Hegel was so intimately familiar with the literature on Asia[98] that the blunders he makes in his Berlin lectures are hard to explain. It is uncertain which criteria he uses to differentiate between Tatars and Mongols, and he confusingly declares at one point, with the eighteenth century in mind when an Inner Asian dynasty presided over a multiethnic empire: "The Mongols rule over China, which controls the other Mongolia. . . . By Mongols we also mean the Manchus who rule over China. They are unrelated to the Mongols proper and belong instead to the Tungus."[99] Hegel recycles an error already repeatedly corrected by the Jesuits, asserting that the Manchus, a hunting people from the Manchurian forests, were nomadic. Only through such simplifications could the topos of the thundering steppeland warriors be saved. Thanks to the report on Tibet by Samuel Turner (1800), Hegel is better informed about Lamaism, which he analyzes in some detail, than Raynal; unlike Raynal, he recognizes it as a variant of Buddhism. Yet he regards it as a complement to a nomadic way of life,[100] even though the Tibetans' lifestyle was anything but.

Hegel brings together the motifs of the eighteenth century when he additionally emphasizes Central Asia's topographic features. Pastoralism and patriarchy—in other words, the disintegration of society into individual family units in the absence of any central state authority—are both typical of highland dwellers. Highlanders are also unconcerned for the future and lack an understanding of "legal relationships," which is why they oscillate between the polar extremes of hospitality and lawless banditry. For unknown reasons or, as Hegel puts it, impelled "into external motion by some impulse," they periodically descend upon civilized lands "like a devastating storm."[101] High plains, high mountain valleys, and above all the interior of the Asiatic continent were for Hegel the birthplaces of a militarized patriarchalism that from time to time erupted into paroxysms of elemental violence before subsiding once again into inactivity.

It is a characteristic of the historico-philosophical discourse on Central Asia that it largely immunized itself against the results of recent ethnological research. References to pastoral life hardly went beyond the clichés of the ancient world. The peoples of Central Asia and Siberia had been important objects of ethnographic study in the eighteenth century. A history of the *ethnographic* "Tatar" discourse could no more neglect Chinese investigations than it could pass over the report by al-Biruni (973–1048). Ethnographic studies could do little with the coverall term "Tatar." They were locally specific, always having to do with particular ethnic groups, often presented in a comparative framework. They had little interest in macrotheories, such as the hypothesis of a "primal people," or in statements on the role played by apocalyptic horsemen in world history.

In the Chinese Empire and its dependent periphery, Europeans found it difficult to carry out such ethnographic observations. The most thorough, Ippolito Desideri's investigations in Tibet between 1712 and 1733, were disseminated in Europe only in summary form.[102] Fathers Verbiest, Gerbillon, and Régis, whose descriptions became known through Du Halde, gave far more precise and detailed information on the landscape and climate of Mongolia than on the customs of its inhabitants, whose various ethnic and tribal affiliations were known to the Jesuit scholars as a matter of course. To some extent, they saw through the glasses of a victorious China when they presented the Mongols as harmless primitives. In 1735, for example, Du Halde writes about them:

> They are naturally of a good disposition, always gay and chearful, and perpetually inclin'd to laugh, but never pensive or melancholy, and indeed why they should they? since they have commonly

> neither neighbours to manage, enemies to fear, nor superiors to flatter; no difficult affair, no painful occupation, but spend their lives in a continual round of diversions, as fishing, hunting, and other exercises of the body, in which they are very expert.[103]

What this description makes clear is that the Mongols have lost the historical initiative. They have come under the emperor's protection or fallen under his dominion. Imperial rule has had a stultifying, infantilizing effect. In 1822/23 Hegel elevates the tranquility of Mongol life into an idyll that is unparalleled in his writings on Asia:

> Now as for the Mongols and Tibetans, they are described as extremely good-natured, open, trusting, observant, obliging, and far from the deception, cowardice, and baseness of the Hindus. Trusting and friendly, these peoples carry on a peaceful life. The priests are pious on behalf of the entire land. Every one of the laity performs his job in peace and quiet. They are not, on the whole, warlike. Moreover, Tibet has mostly been spared from war.[104]

There are reasons why Hegel can depict the descendants of Genghis Khan's terrifying mounted armies as peace-loving and hence assimilate them to the Tibetans (who in reality were not always quite so pacific). Yet Hegel only hints at what these reasons were and appears to underestimate their historicity. He barely goes beyond the laconic assertion that the peoples of Inner Asia stood "under Russian dominion, with some under Chinese rule."[105] He never discusses how the Mongols could have been defeated and tamed by the Sino-Manchu Qing dynasty, how their fall from hyperactive world conquerors to rural simpletons could have been possible. Perhaps he sensed at least *one* important factor: the pacifying effect of the Lamaist religion, which was deliberately propagated by the Qing emperors as an instrument of rule.[106]

The Mongols, meanwhile, were by no means transformed in European eyes into the noble savages of Asia. The civilizational deficits they were increasingly seen to embody spoke too much against them. Mongols, Du

Halde was already claiming, are dirty, foul-smelling and crude: their social structure, distinguishing only between nobles and commoners, is primitive. Through living in such close proximity to their animals, they appeared to have lost all contact with civilized values and become dumb brutes themselves.[107] Jesuitical primitivism rolled European and Chinese primitivism into one. It expressed the general arrogance of empire. That remained the status quo until 1830/31, when Johann Heinrich Plath published his masterpiece on the history of Inner Asia, especially Manchuria. Influenced by Heeren's perspective on universal history, Plath was the first since Joseph de Guignes to paint a panorama of demographic movements and state formations in Central and North Asia. In doing so, he began a new chapter in the study of the non-Han Chinese peoples who had been pushed to the margins of the Middle Kingdom.[108]

KNIGHTS AND STRANGERS IN THE CRIMEA

When Western European readers in the second half of the eighteenth century were provided with ethnographic information about "Tatars," they were generally not learning about the descendants of Genghis Khan but about tribal societies inside the tsarist empire. In Russia, Voltaire justly observed, "there is a greater number of different species, more singularities, and a greater diversity of manners and customs, than in any country in the known world."[109] While the Tatars were still described in 1737 as "the masters of the third part of Asia,"[110] this assessment soon become obsolete from the vantage point of both Peking and Saint Petersburg. Here is how Johann Gottlieb Georgi summarized his impressions as a participant (from 1771 to 1774) in Peter Simon Pallas's great academy expedition:

> The Tatar hordes are so far from inspiring terror that several of them are forced to seek shelter with each other or with their neighbors: sometimes here and sometimes there, depending on circumstances. The remaining hordes are subjects of Russia, the Otto-

man sultan, the Grand Mughal, China and also Persia, especially before the unrests there; or they are dependent on these powers for their protection.[111]

Taken together, the Tatar hordes formed the largest single "nation" in the tsarist empire after the Russians. The ethnographic findings that gradually became available in Western European languages following the publication of Johann Georg Gmelin's Siberian travels (1751–52) gave rise to a far more nuanced understanding of the Tatars. This new research steered a middle path between demonizing and racially defaming the peoples of Central Asia (Herder) and idealizing them as loyal good savages (Du Halde). The basic attitude—differently accented in the coolly impersonal Peter Simon Pallas than in the chatty, vivacious Johann Georg Gmelin or the detail-infatuated, demonstratively pro-Tatar Johann Gottlieb Georgi—is one of sympathetic objectivity. Samuel Turner likewise contrasts his own fresh experience in Tibet with the shopworn clichés still being peddled about the Tatars: "The Tibetans are very humane, kind people, . . . so different from the ferocity commonly annexed to our ideas of a Tatar."[112]

The reports make clear that by no means all the eastern expanses of the tsarist empire were occupied by typically Mongol nomadic horsemen. The spectrum ranged from the permanently settled Kazan Tatars, whom Georgi believed to be better farmers than many Russian peasants,[113] to the largest ethnic group in Central Siberia, the unusually mobile Tungus, who combined livestock farming with hunting over vast areas.[114] The travelers were keenly interested in shamanism, describing it with precision even as they condemned it as erroneous pagan belief. Reprising a motif that enjoyed widespread appeal in the Enlightenment critique of religion, much that appeared illogical and preposterous could be explained as priestly fraud, in this case "deception worked by shamans and magicians."[115] J. G. Gmelin and G. F. Müller, the scientific leaders of the Great Northern Expedition, had a liking for ethnological experiments and demanded that the shamans conjure something up for them. They were surprised when the discovery that the magicians' tricks were often nothing but hocus-pocus failed to discredit them in the eyes of the native population.[116] Georgi, at least, discovered even in shamanism "the universal ideas of natural religion" and traced the persistence of such beliefs to a hostile nature and a lack of instruction for the young.[117] Rational explanations were pursued as far as possible by most of these authors. A clear correlation between shamanism and primitiveness, such as would become almost obligatory in the nineteenth century, is still nowhere to be found in these early anthropologists of religion.

Ethnographic studies were by no means confined to non-European specimens. Samuel Gottlieb Gmelin, whose description of the Tatars of Astrakhan represented perhaps the most cogent ethnographic study in eighteenth-century travel literature from the tsarist empire, applied similar investigative and literary methods to the Don Cossacks as well, a community that had constituted itself from Russian and Ukrainian peasant stock.[118] The Cossacks were Russia's "savages within," a militia frequently deployed to "civilize" the purportedly even more savage peoples of Asia.[119] Borders were further blurred by the fact that "Asiatic" Tatars could be found in Europe as well. A trip to the Crimea sufficed to be made aware of this.

Adam Olearius, secretary to an embassy sent by the small German state of Holstein, observed in 1634 how emissaries of the Crimea Tatars, "cruel and hostile," defiantly approached the tsar as representatives of an equal power and demanded gifts from him: "His Tsarist Majesty, desirous to buy peace, usually spares no expense on them."[120] At the time those words were written, the Crimean Khanate still controlled significant territories north of the Black Sea as well as the Crimean Peninsula itself; a century later, little remained of its former status as "a great power in its own right."[121] Targeted by increasing Russian aggression, this Ottoman vassal state was nonetheless able to maintain a political and social order unique in all Eurasia until it was finally annexed and the last khan deposed in 1783.

As Nicolaas Witsen emphasized in his brief description from 1692, the Crimean Tatars were notorious slave hunters and traders.[122] As kidnappers, Muslims, and ethnic aliens on European soil, they appeared to be ideally cast for the role of archnemesis to the Christian West. Few Western Europeans cared or dared to enter the Tatar state of their own accord. Interest levels increased in the years when it was being taken over by the tsarist empire, however. The Crimea, a landscape blessed by its favorable climate (and famous to this day for its sparkling wine), attracted visitors who wanted to form a picture of the last Asiatic barbarians on European soil.

In 1771 Nikolas Ernst Kleemann, a merchant trading in chandeliers and mirrors (among other things), described the impressions he picked up on several business trips to the Crimea. Kleemann disliked the "braggart" Turks and contrasted them with the kind-hearted and modest Crimean Tatars, who were said to be better than their reputation would suggest. He was particularly taken with the power of the aristocracy, whose "Consilium or Parliament" imposed strong constraints on the dynastic ruler.[123] Lady Elizabeth Craven, who visited the Crimea in early 1786 following her divorce for adultery by the Earl of Craven, was more intent on collecting "sentimental" impressions. She found herself thrust unawares into the role of guinea pig when the new absolute ruler of the freshly annexed peninsula, Prince Grigory Aleksandrovich Potemkin, used her to trial the elaborate deceptions ("Potemkin villages") he had arranged to conceal the devastation wreaked by war from the pleasure-loving Catherine II on her upcoming tour of the Crimea.[124] Under these circumstances, it is hardly surprising that Lady Elizabeth's travel report should contain little information of any value.

The learned French consul Claude Charles de Peyssonnel (*fils*), by contrast, studied the country with great thoroughness. He evoked the vanquished khanate shortly before its demise, coating it with a patina of historical nostalgia. In the Crimea, squeezed between the oriental despotism of the Ottomans and the despotic absolutism of the Romanovs, he discovered almost early medieval, feudal conditions: a weak monarchy, a strong aristocracy imbued with the values of warrior culture and a free peasantry (unlike their enserfed Russian counterparts), with an underclass consisting mainly of ethnically exogenous slaves. The native aristocratic elite cultivated the same code of honor as the European high nobility. In war and in peace, nothing was more important to the *gentilhommes tartares* than the *point d'honneur*—with the exception that they never dueled.[125] The feudal laws in eighteenth-century Crimea were "by and large the same as those . . . in France at the beginning of the monarchy."[126]

Written on the eve of the French Revolution, Peyssonnel's fantasy of Tatar chivalry Europeanized the Crimean Tatars in extreme fashion. It made them appear to stand far closer to the Western European historical tradition than to their oriental neighbors and Russian conquerors. The French consul showed no interest in their Islamic religion or their "Asiatic" facial features. It is a moot question whether this image of the Crimean Tatars as paragons of feudal nobility was any further removed from reality than the stereotypes of Russian (and later Soviet) propaganda, which depicted them as degraded, criminal savages.[127] At any rate, the Crimean Tatars lacked many of the characteristics typically ascribed to the uncivilized Tatar: they were no shamanists and "heathen idol-worshippers" but devotees of a monotheistic high religion. Their state, led from the 1440s by khans from the Genghisid House of Giray, was among the most important in Eastern Europe in the sixteenth and seventeenth century. Until its final years, it possessed—in the words of one modern historian—"all the requisites of early modern statehood":[128] a functioning central government, a legal system (combining Ottoman and Central Asian elements), a hierarchically structured social system with a high urban population, flourishing foreign trade, and an education system that was equal to anything the Ottoman and Muscovite-Russian Empires had to offer. The khans were patrons of the arts and keen builders; Tatar chroniclers made important contributions to Islamic historiography. Baron de Tott even claimed to have discussed Molière with Khan Sahin Giray.[129] Peyssonnel's message was therefore not wrong: the Crimean Tatars were far from savages. They were only "barbarians" if the most stringent criteria were used for defining civilization, in which case it is difficult to see how their more powerful neighbors, the Russians and Ottomans, would have come off any better.

Only a few years after Peyssonnel, the Crimea presented an altogether different scenario. The English mineralogist Edward Daniel Clarke, who visited the peninsula in 1800–1801, was appalled by the scenes of destruction he witnessed in Kefe (Caffa, now Feodosia), the once-thriving center of the Tatar slave trade. The town had recently been occupied by Russian forces:

> Fifty families are at present the whole population of the once magnificent town of Caffa. . . . During the time we remained, soldiers were allowed to overthrow the beautiful mosques, or to convert them into magazines, to pull down the minarets, tear up the public fountains, and to destroy all the public aqueducts, for the sake of a small quantity of lead they were thereby able to obtain. . . . Some of those fountains were of great antiquity; and they were beautifully decorated with marble reservoirs, exhibiting bas-reliefs and inscriptions. . . . The remains of antient sculpture left by the Grecians in Caffa, had not shared a better fate. All that even Mohammedans had spared of bas-reliefs, of inscriptions, or of architectural pillars, were fractured by the Russians, and sold as materials to construct their miserable barracks. . . . In a short time, nothing will remain in Caffa but the traces of desolation left by its Russian conquerors.[130]

Clarke heard Greek merchants cursing the Russians as "Scythians."[131] With that, the European discourse on Tartary had come full circle. The inheritors of classical civilization were now characterizing their fair-skinned rulers, not the Tatars they had overthrown, with the original byword for Asiatic savagery.

When the geographer Moritz von Engelhardt and the botanist Friedrich Parrott visited the Crimea in the service of the imperial government in 1811, the conditions they saw there—like those encountered seventy years before in Kamchatka—could only be described as colonial. Both Baltic scholars took issue with how the Tatars had been depicted by one of the leading intellectual lights of the tsarist empire: Peter Simon Pallas, councilor of state to Her Imperial Majesty of all the Russias, who had traveled the Crimea between March and July 1794. From 1795 to 1810 Pallas had then returned to the peninsula to live on an estate bestowed on him as a retirement residence by the grateful tsarina. His report on the Crimean trip appeared in German translation in 1799–1801.[132] During the academy expedition, Pallas was the coolest and most distanced observer of the non-Russian nationalities of the tsarist empire. Even in the Crimea, which he toured in the aftermath of the Russian annexation, he lacked all sympathy for the romanticism of the noble savage and the tragedy of his downfall. Pallas saw everything from the viewpoint of how nature could be mastered to maximum economic and material benefit.

Like Pallas before them, Parrott and Engelhardt criticized the poor use the Tatars made of the land, yet they contradicted their illustrious predecessor's claim that the fault lay with the innate "idleness of the working class, which exerts itself only for the most necessary nourishment and is almost entirely lacking in industry."[133] Pallas recommended that the Tatars, "who demonstrate in their economic behavior that same addiction to destruction and improvidence which has always been typical of their nation," be driven out or resettled in Russia.[134] Parrott and Engelhardt denounce this proposal as "unjust and inhumane";[135] fortunately for them, they did not live to see it implemented in the twentieth century. The Tatars, they argued, were not lazy but they had modest needs. Pallas failed to grasp this because, as an official, economist, and administrative expert, he cared only for the good of the state. For him, human worth was determined solely by the product of human labor. But did this mean, they asked, that the Tatars were morally inferior to "people from civilized nations"?[136]

Engelhardt and Parrott proceed to indict Russian land policy in the Crimea. Because a considerable amount of Tatar land had been confiscated and transferred to alien landlords (including Professor Pallas), Tatar peasants had no incentive to make the best use of the soil. The popular complaint about the Tatars' Asiatic torpor, requiring that they labor under strict supervision, was therefore a colonialist pseudo-anthropology—in essence, nothing but a self-fulfilling prophecy on the part of their new overlords.[137] Furthermore, the authors stoutly defend the Tatar moral character against the stereotypical slurs. Tatar hospitality was by no means a sham, as claimed; it was a seriously observed injunction of the Koran. Both travelers find their hosts to be nothing but honest and welcoming. Tatars could be model citizens if treated with decency. Their intelligence and eagerness to learn make them better qualified than anyone else to further the economic development of the Crimea. They should certainly be tapped for their expertise in horticulture and beekeeping. Many of the new colonial landowners, on the other hand, showed no interest in agricultural improvements and had adopted a parasitic relationship to their newly acquired landholdings.[138]

This heartfelt and courageous plea for a free Tatar economy with only limited colonial interference tailored the image of the Crimean Tatars to the dictates of modernity. Whereas Peyssonnel had defended the Tatars by archaizing them, the two Estonian scholars, motivated by similar considerations, aimed to demonstrate that, given the right policy settings, the Tatars could fully satisfy the requirements of Muscovite-Russian late mercantilism. Exoticizing the Tatars and mentally distancing themselves from them was the strategy of their colonial oppressors. Their sympathizers, by contrast, sought to demonstrate that the Tatars' non-European exterior did not entail an anthropological otherness that made them unfit to be integrated as equals into a modernizing society. To be sure, following the mass exodus of Crimean Tatars into the Ottoman Empire and an influx of Russian settlers, the Tatars had by 1800 already become a minority in their own country. Parrott and Engelhardt's humane proposals came too late to prevail over Pallas's rigorous solutions.[139]

THE ETHNOLOGY AND POLITICS OF ARABIC LIBERTY

The Crimean Khanate fitted into none of the theories of the age. Above all, it refuted the simple equation, "Savages = Tatars = Nomads." The nomadic way of life exerted a powerful hold on eighteenth-century intellectuals. The nomad, no less than the carefree *homme naturel* frolicking on a palm-shaded beach in Tahiti, was an emblem of the era.

In accordance with modern anthropologists, the eighteenth century favored a narrow concept of nomadism that, rather than covering every form of mobile existence, was restricted to "pastoral mobility."[140] The nomad was thus generally a herder, recognizable as such from the Old Testament, from ancient ethnographic texts, and from the tradition of bucolic literature. Present-day herder-nomads were found among ethnic groups that had once been major historical actors before being pushed to the margins by the great territorial empires. Besides the Mongols, these were in the first instance the Arabs: once an "effervescent nation" (*brausende Nation*),[141] now overwhelmingly subjected to Ottoman suzerainty. Exact descriptions of the nomadic way of life were rare. People dwelling in houses and cities seem to have found nothing more difficult than to put themselves in the well-worn shoes of those who moved incessantly from place to place. From 1776, the leading and almost only authority on the Mongols was Peter Simon Pallas, who had seen little of them himself and therefore relied on the findings of other travelers (Gerhard Friedrich Müller, Samuel Gottlieb Gmelin, and others).[142] Benjamin Bergmann's marvelously detailed and extraordinarily sympathetic account of his time with the Oirat Mongols or Kalmyks was little known outside the German-speaking realm.[143] Bergmann saw the Kalmyk lifestyle as the polar opposite of the European. Thanks to his Rousseauian affinity for pastoral simplicity, he resisted getting carried away in flights of fancy or "constructing" the Other as a "world turned upside-down." He sought instead to demonstrate with the utmost precision how the Kalmyks tended to their horses and camels, for example.[144]

For a long time, almost as little was known about the nomadic inhabitants of North Africa, Syria, and the Arabian Peninsula. In 1715 Jean de la Roque—or rather the long-serving consul in Aleppo Laurent D'Arvieux, the true author of the report published under de la Roque's name—had popularized the image of the serious, contemplative, silent desert-dweller. Two decades later Dr. Thomas Shaw, still smarting from a number of unpleasant experiences with the Arabs, represented them as barbarian cutpurses. In 1771, nearing the end of a voyage around the world, a well-to-do "philosophical" traveler, the Vicomte de Pagès, had accompanied the caravan from Basra to Aleppo. The insightful account he wrote up after the event betrays a measure of sympathy for the Arabs' way of life. By far the most detailed description of Arab nomadism to that point, however, was that furnished in 1772 by Carsten Niebuhr.[145] Volney, who had studied nomads in Syria, visibly strove to attain Niebuhr's level—apparently with success, judging by the public acclaim that greeted his work.[146] The Swiss Orientalist Johann Ludwig Burckhardt subsequently became the leading authority of the early nineteenth century.[147]

It almost goes without saying that theoretical reflections on nomadism by eighteenth-century authors were influenced by ethnographers like Pallas and Niebuhr, just as the latter in turn were affected by the general intellectual climate. Yet the discourse on nomadism did not necessarily flow from direct observation of the sources. Perhaps its most important characteristic was that it largely avoided a discussion of the *historical* role of peoples such as Mongols and Arabs. It must therefore be kept separate from debates on the "elemental-historical." These peoples were regarded as *un*historical in the sense that they were at once *post*historical and *pre*historic: posthistorical, because they had exited the stage of history following their star appearance; prehistoric, because they appeared to have sunk into an atemporal stasis that made them witnesses and relics of an age-old past. As late as 1820, one traveler found himself reminded of "the happy age of patriarchal life" upon first glimpsing Mongol nomads.[148] Such associations were almost unavoidable when encountering Bedouins, the present-day occupants of the biblical lands. In the case of the Arabs, such archaism was especially conspicuous, given that here—unlike for the entirely nonurban Mongols—a contrast could be drawn between primordial desert Arabs and modern city-dwellers. Europeans' sympathies lay squarely with the sons of the desert, for the urban Arabs, according to one characteristic asseveration, "have all the vices of civilized society, without having quitted those of a savage state."[149]

While Carsten Niebuhr begins his analysis of the Bedouins with the same contrast between town and desert, he is too discerning a writer to equate it simplistically with the dichotomy of civilization and barbarism:

> The inhabitants of Arab cities, and especially those lying by the sea and on the border, have intermingled with foreigners to such an extent that they have lost many of their old customs and manners. The true Arabs however, who have always esteemed their liberty a treasure far greater than riches and comfort, live in tribes under tents and still steadfastly observe the age-old government, rites and customs of their ancestors.[150]

For Niebuhr, life in the desert was not an expression of civilizational backwardness, nor the decree of "Providence,"[151] but the consequence of a free decision for a life lived in simplicity, liberty, and closeness to nature. The Bedouins made the choice that was right and appropriate for them. There were two sides to their love of liberty. On the one hand, they refused to submit to a fixed power structure. They lived in a mosaic-like multiplicity of small communities—clans and tribes—which regularly came together to form higher and larger units. The respective rulers, the sheikhs, exercised patriarchal authority over their families and servants. Following the death or removal of a sheikh, the eldest son did not automatically inherit his place; rather, the ablest male relative was elected to the vacant position. Outside the family, everyone who wielded political authority could be held to account. The "lesser sheikhs" were not the obedient vassals of the greater:

> The great sheikh must regard them rather as his confederates than as his subjects. If they are dissatisfied with their government yet incapable of deposing it, they can always drive their herds to another tribe, which is usually happy to be able to strengthen its party. But each lesser sheikh must also strive to govern his family well, lest they likewise depose or abandon him.[152]

The other side of Bedouin freedom is its contrast with Turkish despotism in the cities. The realistic Niebuhr does not absolutize this contrast in the manner that would later become fashionable. Only a few tribes lived in total isolation; the price they paid for their complete freedom from external influences and ties was a particularly austere way of life.[153] Far more characteristic were contact and conflict between Turkish power and Arab counterpower. Niebuhr feels compelled to defend the Arabs against the charge of lawless brigandage leveled against them by the Turks. The Arabs may have felt no compunction about plundering caravans and individual travelers, but they rarely murdered them or left them to die in the desert. Resistance to Ottoman aggression could be (mis)classified as robbery only for blatantly propagandistic purposes.

> If therefore the Turks appear each year with an army in Arabia, then the Arabs can only assert their rights by countering with an army of their own, particularly in a situation of open war. This army cannot justly be compared with a band of thieves, being commanded by six sheikhs who are indisputably lords of the desert, and hence have every right to oppose all those who would forcibly pass through their domains.[154]

Niebuhr's descriptions, which went on to influence those of Volney and Burckhardt, outline the vision of an unmistakable *genre de vie* (as Volney likes to call it) while at the same time sketching a theory of Bedouin nomadism. If the harder-edged realistic accents are disregarded, such as references to chronic hunger among Syrian Bedouins or the provision of the Baloch people through the international arms trade,[155] such material could be used to construct the partly neo-pastoral, partly heroic idealization of the desert dwellers that would culminate artistically in romantic Orientalist painting before reaching a literary climax in T. E. Lawrence's *Seven Pillars of Wisdom* (1922).[156] Similarly, the discipline of Islamic studies later implicitly or explicitly adopted many of the ideas of these pioneer Arabists.

THEORIES OF NOMADISM

The eighteenth century saw several attempts to arrive at a *general* theory of pastoral nomadism. A particularly wide-ranging one, based mainly on ancient sources, was elaborated by the English physician William Falconer.[157] Falconer saw the pastoral way of life as a stage in cultural development interposed between the invention of money and the universal spread of agriculture. Unlike Adam Smith, Adam Ferguson, and other thinkers of the Scottish Enlightenment, Falconer, one of the earliest ecologists, paid attention to the specific environmental conditions that could cause quite distinct versions of pastoral life to develop in lands as different from each other as Egypt, Sicily, Arabia, and Mongolia.[158] In general terms, according to Falconer, it may be said that in the pastoral stage, human beings are roused to purposeful activity; the previously loose bands of society are drawn tighter; the female sex is treated for the first time with respect. On the other hand, it would be a mistake "to consider the pastoral character as a model of virtue and simplicity."[159] The introduction of property laws leads to greed, miserliness, and new forms of crime. The invention of money draws bribery and indebtedness in its wake, fostering relations of dependency. Warfare is a key element in the life of herders, who sharpen their wits by learning how to fight. Since they have no understanding of urban life, however, they do not know how to lay siege to a city; they lack the patience for it.[160] Because nomads are not tied to any fixed place, temples as well as immobile images of the divine are foreign to them. As a consequence of their way of life, they therefore possess fairly abstract ideas about god, making them receptive to monotheistic religion, particularly Islam, the most aniconic among them.[161]

Defying the era's tendency to binary opposites, Falconer's examples of pastoral life are drawn from both Europe and Asia. Huns and Teutons, Scythes and Celts all share significant affinities in their manner of living and thinking. Edward Gibbon, likewise no friend of East-West antagonism, was interested more specifically in herder societies that had intervened in late antiquity and the early Middle Ages to change the course of history. This led him to a comprehensive interpretation of nomadism that, uniquely for the eighteenth century, combined Hegel's "elemental-historical" with the ethnographic perspective. J.G.A. Pocock, one of the foremost historians of ideas of our time, has dedicated several important studies to it.[162] Because Gibbon identified the various waves of barbarian invasions as an important causative factor for the fall of both the Western and Eastern Roman Empires, it was only natural that he should seek to arrive at an understanding of the motives driving these barbarians.

Gibbon concludes chapter 25 of his *Decline and Fall of the Roman Empire* with the death of Emperor Valentinian I in 375. He begins the next chapter with a depiction of the devastating earthquake and tsunami that struck the greater part of the Roman world on July 21, 376. This natural disaster coincided with a convulsion that was to prove even more fateful: the beginning of Hunnic aggression. Gibbon now pauses before picking up his grand narrative to address some fundamental questions under the heading, *Manners of the Pastoral Nations*.[163]

According to Gibbon, the reality of herder societies had nothing to do with the bucolic idylls painted so lovingly in the pastoral literature of the early modern period.[164] All such peoples closely resemble each other on account of their way of life. Since they follow their herds from place to place rather than settling down to till the soil, they are incapable of forging lasting cultural identities. Killing animals is part of the everyday life of "barbarians" and fosters brutality towards humans, too. There is no taboo on eating horse meat; on the contrary, it is one of the secrets to the nomads' success in mounted warfare. Their perpetual readiness for war issues from their pastoral way of life, not from some immutable Tatar or Scythian “character.” Young men live in mobile camps and test their strength in military contests. No sense of homeland or territorial belonging impedes them in their search for fresh pastures. Living under the harshest conditions provides ideal preparation for the ordeals of far-flung campaigns. Nomads do not live from their herds alone, however. They are also skilled hunters, trained from an early age in marksmanship and quick reactions. The hunt is the training ground for the battlefield. All that was needed to trigger the great “elemental-historical” tidal waves of nomadic horsemen was thus a combination of external stimuli and internal political leadership. Their political structures were flexible enough to allow proven warrior-princes to advance quickly to the fore.

So much for the foundations. Gibbon borrows the notion of a “mode of subsistence” from the Scottish social theorists, who had introduced it shortly before, and refines it into an instrument of historical analysis. In later chapters, individual examples of nomadic military outbreaks are thoroughly investigated in their specific causative contexts: the Huns under Attila, the Arabs in the decades following Muhammad, the Mongols under Genghis Khan. A highpoint is chapter 50, where Gibbon discusses the origins of Islam. He speaks here of the paramount importance of the camel for the life of the desert Arabs, expatiating on its advantages over the less resilient and less versatile horse. He depicts how they gradually departed from their original primitive state, a process that in his account was nothing like a simple leap from one stage of development to the next. In contrast to the Huns and Mongols, the Arabs had already made the transition to urban culture in pre-Islamic times, although this implied no antagonism towards the Bedouin way of life. In the city as in the desert, the social putty was provided less by institutions compelling obedience from above than by voluntary reciprocity on a relatively egalitarian basis. In Gibbon’s eyes, Arab democracy could withstand comparison with both the Greek and Roman versions. It was less dependent than these on prescribed participation rights and institutions—“artificial machinery," in Gibbon's critical phrasing[165]—than on a love of individual liberty that made for a less tractable, more fiercely independent citizenry. This form of government was not so unstable as to lead to outright anarchy, while at the same time it thwarted tendencies to despotic individual rule such as first gradually emerged from the eighth century onwards under Byzantine and Persian influence. Social evolutionary processes were accompanied by a bardic poetry that worked to moralize social relations and inculcate decorum. Gibbon sets out how he saw Islam developing under such conditions and in the interplay of faith and politics in one of the finest examples of universal-historical analysis ever written. Perhaps no other historical figure is so carefully examined in *Decline and Fall* as Muhammad, the founder of the world religion that offered Gibbon his second great case study (after Christianity) for the history-making power of individual charisma combined with exceptional organizational skills.

Gibbon's theory of nomadism lays the foundations for his pan-Eurasian interpretation of the Middle Ages. That interpretation is materialistic insofar as it takes a people's environmental conditions and "mode of subsistence" as its starting point, without thereby lapsing into climatic or geographical determinism. It also never denies the agency of ideas and especially religious convictions, wavering ever precariously between superstition and fanaticism. Gibbon is not content with merely telling a historical narrative. His ambition is to explain the movements that shaped history most profoundly, such as the rise of Islam. In doing so, he steers a middle path between Falconer-style generalizations and close scrutiny of local conditions. Such a historiographical program went far beyond Gibbon's sources and informants; small wonder, then, that he could only implement it in half-speculative fashion. Apart perhaps from Montesquieu in his short book on the greatness and decline of the Romans (1734), nobody had attempted anything of the kind before. Precisely nomads, who for many seemed to stand outside history, became in Gibbon's hands the occasion for the most subtle historical analysis of the Enlightenment era.

TRIUMPH OF THE SETTLERS

The last decades of the eighteenth century and the first decades of the nineteenth witnessed an unparalleled offensive on the part of the settled "civilizations" against mobile "savages" or "barbarians."[166] "The great fear of the primitive world" (Michèle Duchet) had finally been laid to rest.[167] Social theorists reflected this by interpreting pastoral nomadism as a stepping stone on the path of social evolution.[168] Needless to say, the "civilized" were themselves highly mobile. Through military conquest and agricultural colonization, they expanded their living space at the expense of nonagrarian peoples. Mobility was here only a temporary means to an end, not a way of life, despite borderline cases such as Argentinean gauchos, Australian drovers, or (from the 1830s) the South African Trekboer. North American Indians, Kurds, Mongols, and Siberian tribespeople were not the only ones to be driven from their ancestral lands and pushed back into ever smaller reserves. In the same period, the Royal Navy set out to eradicate piracy in the course of their operations against the slave trade—not always with lasting success, at least in the Persian Gulf and the seas around Malaya. Pirates are a nuisance for any great sea power. The British Empire, it was admitted in 1816, might have overthrown or subdued the Indian warrior states but it had so far made little headway against piracy in the Persian Gulf.[169] The fair-skinned buccaneers of the Caribbean, who in the seventeenth century had practically formed their own sovereign terrorist power, had been quashed by the early nineteenth century. Meanwhile, the French navy patrolled the Mediterranean with increasing success; in 1830 the "pirate state" in Algeria, which had posed no serious threat to mercantile shipping for some time, was toppled following a French intervention.

Robbery and vagabondage were closely associated in the imperial mind. Early modern territorial states campaigned against organized robbery and street crime, begging and vagrancy. They attempted to immobilize their subjects in order better to control and tax them.[170] Nomadism was not seen as a legitimate form of self-organization, "but merely as a refusal to organize that posed a challenge to the established order."[171] This attitude was exported to the colonial world. Missionaries complained that nomads were almost impossible to civilize and proselytize and pressed that they be forcibly settled on stations. Colonial reformers saw them as poor material for "improvement."[172] In India, migrant communities—the so-called "criminal tribes"—were violently suppressed, particularly following the "Indian Mutiny," the great anti-British uprising of 1857.[173] The exclusion and persecution of "gypsies," variously interpreted as Indian or Egyptian immigrants or as Turkish spies, increased during the Age of Enlightenment. Even Johann Gottfried Herder's celebrated tolerance went out the window when he turned to the subject of gypsies:

> A rejected Indian caste, separated by birth from everything that calls itself godly, respectable and civil, and remaining faithful for centuries to this debased destiny: for what are they suited in Europe except for military training, which can discipline everything as quickly as possible?[174]

Just as the gypsy could only be romanticized—mysterious foundlings, fiery women, freedom in the rolling wagon, and the like—once effective police measures had been taken against the "Gypsy problem," and just as the North American Indians could only be sentimentalized once they had been destroyed as a viable fighting force, so Europeans only discovered noble barbarians in Asia when they were no longer forced to make their direct acquaintance. The last refuge of liberty, Montesquieu had taught, was to be found among the indomitable mountain tribes.[175] From the late eighteenth century onwards, Afghans, Kurds, Rif Kabyles, Gurkhas, Chechens, along with Tyrolians, Swiss, and Highland Scots, were transfigured into primordial custodians of premodern customs and liberties.[176] With that, mountain peoples underwent an astounding revaluation. They were now no longer perceived as threatening savages, pouring down from their impregnable redoubts with no apparent provocation to bring the sword and the flame to peaceful lowland settlements. Forgotten, too, were the tales of the "Old Man of the Mountain" brought back with them to Europe by the Crusaders and Marco Polo: the head of the Muslim Ismaili sect who held his followers in thrall through his personal charisma and sent young, drug-benumbed "assassins" into the cities of the plain to do his murderous bidding. Such stories still preoccupied Orientalists such as Sylvestre de Sacy and Joseph von Hammer-Purgstall, but they now barely ruffled the popular imagination.[177]

The *new* savages—unsettling precisely because they were unsettled—gradually became more visible in the European metropolises. Friedrich Engels saw the Irish as modern nomads and described them with all the repugnance that eighteenth-century travelers reserved for the most primitive and rootless natives.[178] In 1851 Henry Mayhew began his great social panorama, *London Labour and the London Poor*, with an observation about "Wandering Tribes in General," dividing the global population into "two distinct and broadly marked races, viz., the wanderers and the settlers—the vagabond and the citizen."[179] According to Mayhew, these differed from each other even in their physical appearance, such as their skull shape. Nomads, in Mayhew's opinion, had in all civilizations been the parasites of domesticated society. The noble barbarian and *homme naturel*, pushed to the inhospitable fringes of the great empires, had now been succeeded by the restless tribes peopling the new industrial landscapes at their center. The vendors and lumpenproletariat who thronged the streets of London, as seen by the early social researcher Mayhew, had more in common with the Kalahari Bushmen than with their middle-class neighbors. Mayhew describes them using the very same categories that the eighteenth century had applied to ignoble savages:

> The nomad then is distinguished from the civilized man by his repugnance to regular and continuous labour—by his want of providence in laying up a store for the future—by his inability to perceive consequences ever so slightly removed from immediate apprehension—by his passion for stupefying herbs and roots, and, when possible, for intoxicating fermented liquors—by his extraor-

> dinary powers of enduring privation—by his comparative insensibility to pain—by an immoderate love of gaming, frequently risking his own personal liberty upon a single cast—by his love of libidinous dances—by the pleasure he experiences in witnessing the suffering of sentient creatures—by his delight in warfare and perilous sports—by his desire for vengeance—by the looseness of his notions as to property—by the absence of chastity among his women, and his disregard of female honour—and lastly, by his vague sense of religion—his rude idea of a Creator, and utter absence of all appreciation of the mercy of the Divine Spirit.[180]

By the mid-nineteenth century, pastoral romanticism had become passé. The nomad now served as a negative foil to bring the Victorian bourgeois gentleman into sharper relief. He had become a problem for the police.

X

Real and Unreal Despots

This day, being the Emperor's birthday, we set out for the Court at three o'clock a.m. . . . We immediately descended into the garden, where we found all the great men and Mandarins in their robes of state, drawn up before the Imperial pavilion. The emperor did not show himself, but remained concealed behind a screen, from whence, I presume, he could see and enjoy the ceremonies without inconvenience or interruption. . . .

At length the great band, both vocal and instrumental, struck up with all their powers of harmony; and instantly the whole Court fell flat upon their faces before this invisible Nebuchadnezzar. . . . Indeed, in no religion, either ancient or modern, has the Divinity ever been addressed, I believe, with stronger exterior marks of worship and adoration, than were this morning paid to the phantom of his Chinese Majesty.

—George Macartney, 1st Earl Macartney (1737–1806), Journal (unpublished) of his mission to China, entry for September 17, 1793[1]

A dignified and affable gentleman celebrates his eighty-second birthday. His British visitors have met him three days before, amazed at how sprightly he is for his age. He happens to be the most powerful person in Asia: Qianlong, emperor on the Dragon Throne for the past fifty-eight years. He is not really adored as a deity—the concept of sacred kingship is absent from Confucian political theory—but protocol expects him on this particular day to act the mute role of the numinous center of the universe: an absent presence and a present absence. No European king would be honored by his courtiers prostrating themselves in the dust. One of Qianlong's colleagues among the crowned heads of Europe, long reviled by his enemies as a "despot," mounted the scaffold at the Place de la Révolution in Paris a few months earlier. How different is Qianlong? Is he a despot, perhaps the quintessential oriental despot? Lord Macartney, a sensible and seasoned diplomat who has seen a lot of the world, is not so sure. Qianlong does not seem to be a raving tyrant but rather a hugely experienced politician trapped in the gilded cage of state ceremony. Words from the Bible flit through the ambassador's mind: he has seen "Solomon in all his glory."[2]

THE HEIRS OF NERO AND SOLOMON

In the transcultural typology of leadership styles developed in the early modern period, Cambyses, Attila, Genghis Khan, Timur, and Nadir Shah, the early Islamic caliphs and Sultan Mehmed II (the conqueror of Byzantium), along with Alexander the Great, Caesar, Charles XII of Sweden, and sometimes also Louis XIV of France, were all placed in the category of "conquerors." As warrior princes they were obviously figures of extreme authority. Yet their military charisma tended to overshadow the harshness of their domestic regime. The "tyrants," a second category, included monarchs who even in times of peace were thought to have ruled arbitrarily, cruelly, and unjustly. These too could appear in both East and West. Henry VIII of England belonged in this rogues' gallery, as did Philipp II of Spain (from the Protestant point of view) and Ivan IV, "the Terrible." Peter the Great was also frequently regarded as such a tyrant, at least by those who emphasized his brutality over his constructive achievements. In India the sultan of Delhi, Muhammad bin Tughluq (reigned 1325–51), who allegedly slaughtered his subjects on organized hunts, was long the subject of obloquy.[3] The period's most sadistic ruler, however, was no oriental despot but a marginal Christian petty tyrant who ordered every Turk he had captured to be impaled without further ado: the voivode of Wallachia, Vlad III ("Dracula," "Tepeš"). Hammer-Purgstall calls him the "madman of the stake" (*Pfahlwüterich*) and reports that the voivode's great adversary, Sultan Mehmed II—himself not one to shrink from harsh measures—admired him for his ruthlessness.[4] The reign of terror established in the southwest Chinese province of Sichuan by the rebel Zhang Xianzhong between 1644 and 1647 falls into the category of extraordinary "elemental-historical" violence. The number of fatalities cited by Pater Martin Martini may have been exaggerated—six hundred thousand in the city of Chengdu alone—but Zhang was still undoubtedly one of the worst mass murderers in Chinese history.[5]

Not coincidentally, Zhang Xianzhong was an atypical parvenu and rebel whose atrocities aroused little interest both in later Chinese literature and European writings on China. On the whole, it is striking just how few Asiatic monarchs of the early modern period were represented by European observers as monstrous tyrants: not a single emperor of the late Ming and early Qing dynasty; among the Mughal emperors perhaps only the fratricidal Aurangzeb (r. 1658–1707);[6] elsewhere in South Asia, there is Rajasinha II of Kandy (r. 1635–87), whose cruelties are related by Robert Knox.[7] Among the Ottoman sultans, Mehmed II (r. 1451–81) and Selim I ("the Grim," r. 1512–25) are singled out as particularly unscrupulous power politicians, but only Murad IV (r. 1623–40), whom Cantemir claims to have been personally responsible for fourteen thousand murders,[8] and on a less extreme scale his weaker successors, the psychopathic Ibrahim (r. 1640–48) and his son Mehmed IV (r. 1648–87), seemed to rival a Nero or Domitian in their unquenchable thirst for blood. This "most bloody, vicious and gruesome period of Ottoman history," as the judicious Hammer-Purgstall put it, came to an end in 1656 with the appointment of Köprülü Mehmed Pasha as grand vizier. Granted sweeping powers, he himself ordered the execution of thousands of officials compromised by their complicity with the previous regime.[9] The Safavid shahs seemed in European eyes to come closest to the model of the oriental despot. But tales of capricious misrule and uninhibited bloodlust were only told of two shahs (not without reason, it must be said): Shah Safi I (r. 1629–42), a contemporary of the cruel sultan Mehmed IV, and Shah Safi II, also known as Suleiman (r. 1666–94).[10] No single eighteenth-century Asian ruler was painted in similar colors. Genuine Asiatic despots were thus thin on the ground in the Enlightenment era.

In European texts, thirdly, Asian monarchs were more frequently seen to belong in the positive category of state-founders, empire-builders, and sage legislators than they were pilloried as tyrants. King Solomon was the Asiatic prototype for such figures, who in modern European history included Henri IV of France, Queen Elizabeth, Emperor Charles V, the ambivalent tsar Peter the Great, the tsarina Catherine II, Empress Maria Theresia, and the Prussian kings of the eighteenth century, among others. Their crackdowns on enemies and insubordinate subjects were viewed as evidence of prudent statesmanship, not wanton tyranny. The more philosophical European colonizers of Asia aspired to be *législateurs* themselves: Sir Stamford Raffles fancied himself the Solon of Java, while the judge Sir William Jones had ambitions to be remembered as an Indian Justinian. Voluntary abdication following a successful reign was considered a rare sign of regal wisdom: Diocletian, Charles V, the Qianlong emperor (in 1796, three years after the visit of the Macartney Mission), and Sultan Murad I all distinguished themselves in this way.

Even in the eyes of those who held the Jesuit encomiums to China to be grossly exaggerated, the Kangxi emperor stood beyond reproach, and even the personality of his less easily idealized grandson Qianlong was almost never cast into disrepute.[11] Sir William Jones called him "a man of the brightest genius and the most amiable affections,"[12] and the reports of the near-simultaneous Macartney Mission did nothing to call this judgment into question: not only Lord Macartney himself, but even the more Sinophobic members of the delegation, above all Sir John Barrow, were impressed by the elderly emperor. Joseph de Guignes admired the wisdom and political skills of Genghis Khan's grandson Kublai, whose rule over China (1280–94) he did not even hint at dismissing as primitive Mongol tyranny.[13] Gibbon's assessment of the Ayyubid sultan Saladin, the great adversary of the Crusaders, was ambivalent but generally positive, and he went so far as to call the Seljuq ruler Malek Shah (r. 1072–92) "the greatest prince of his age."[14] Sultan Suleiman "the Magnificent," also known as "the Lawgiver" (*Kânûnî*, r. 1520–66), appeared an ideal ruler even to European observers of the eighteenth century.[15] The Mughal emperor Akbar (r. 1556–1605) had many admirers and few critics in Europe. His celebrated religious pluralism contrasted sharply with the cruel persecution of heretics under his exact contemporary Philipp II of Spain. Even James Mill, the pitiless judge of everything Indian, found little to chide in Akbar.[16] Akbar's great-grandson Aurangzeb (r. 1658–1707), more brutal and closed-minded than almost all his predecessors, found an influential contemporary apologist in François Bernier, who knew him well. Bernier represented him as a kind of enlightened despot, although this evaluation would have better suited his father, Shah Jahan (r. 1628–58). Robert Orme, the official historian of the EIC, considered Aurangzeb worthy of being "ranked with the ablest princes who have reigned in any age or country."[17]

King Narai of Siam (r. 1656–88) was generally represented in Europe as an active and energetic autocrat, who to an unusual degree (recalling his contemporary, the Kangxi emperor) was curious about the world outside his own country.[18] The less well-known King Alaungpaya, who founded the dynasty that went on to rule until 1885, was respected as the restorer of Burma and "a man of great genius and courage."[19] Much the same was said of Emperor Gia-Long, who united a divided Vietnam in 1802. Particularly interesting, finally, is the case of Shah Abbas I, bynamed "the Great" (r. 1588–1629). Given his immense political achievements, European observers like Pietro della Valle and Adam Olearius were willing to forgive this creator of the modern Iranian state for governing his land with the utmost autocratic severity and for having his next-of-kin assassinated (as did Suleiman the Magnificent and Peter the Great) and several of his sons and grandsons blinded. Roubaud, otherwise vehemently opposed to despotism in all its forms, held up Shah Abbas in 1770 as an exemplary ruler. Sir John Malcolm, believing that under conditions of an all-pervasive despotism that penetrated every corner of state and society, rule by oppression and violence was the best option for a prudent statesman, excused him in 1815 through a kind of casuistic justification for murder.[20]

Throughout the seventeenth and eighteenth centuries, Asiatic rulers were thus by no means universally depicted and condemned as heartless oppressors of their own people. On the contrary, it was possible to find only a few verifiable examples of such tyrants. It was much more common to praise Asian monarchs as latter-day Solomons and princes of peace (Akbar, Kangxi), canny statesmen from whom even European sovereigns might learn a thing or two. Lord Macartney had good reason to be dissatisfied with Kangxi's grandson, the Qianlong emperor, as a negotiating partner. Yet he concluded his private notes about their memorable encounter on September 14, 1793, with the following reminiscence:

> Thus, then, have I seen "King Solomon in all his glory." I use this expression, as the scene recalled perfectly to my memory a puppet show of that name which I recollect to have seen in my childhood, and which made so strong an impression on my mind that I then thought it a true representation of the highest pitch of human greatness and felicity.[21]

In no way unusual was Qianlong's categorization as an autocrat who governed strictly but with the best interests of his realm and his subjects at heart. In an age when European territorial states were still in the process of formation, European observers showed respect for similar achievements in Asia. Indeed, in Eurasia as a whole the early modern period was one of incipient state formation, centralization, and bureaucratization. European "grand viziers," such as Thomas Cromwell in England or cardinals Richelieu and Mazarin in France, could easily bear comparison with the Köprülü prime ministers, just as the Tudor monarchs, Louis XIII of France, and the Great Elector of Brandenburg resembled their Asiatic colleagues Shah Abbas I, Tokugawa Ieyasu (the founder of the early modern Japanese state), and Nurhaci, who through his concerted modernization program set the Manchus on track to seize power in China in the next generation. These parallels were widely recognized in Europe at the time, preventing all-too-stark East-West dichotomies from arising. The monarchical state created by Louis XI in France, William Robertson wrote in 1769 without a hint of criticism, was "scarce less absolute, or less terrible, than eastern despotism."[22] When the Jesuits compared Kangxi with Louis XIV in 1700, they thought they were paying *both* of their patrons a compliment.

MONTESQUIEU READS SIR JOHN CHARDIN

> The immemorial despotism of the East is a fact so familiar to every reader, that it seems to be received, as we receive the knowledge of a law of nature, without any troublesome investigation of the causes which produce an effect so wonderful and invariable.[23]

When despotism was presented as a fact of nature, as here by the historian and colonial administrator Mark Wilks in 1810, it happened in a discourse that bore no direct relation to observations of how governments actually operated on the ground. While few Asiatic rulers were personally represented as despots, despotism appeared to be ubiquitous in the East. As a kind of unquestioned axiom, this assumption was largely immune to empirical correction. Anything that contradicted it could be interpreted as the exception that proved the rule. The ambassador Dr. John Crawfurd thus had considerable difficulty admitting "that the country [Siam] prospered under his [King Rama's] administration and that he was rarely guilty of acts of atrocity."[24] Such a sober observation flew in the face of fashionable theory.

"Despotism" was understood as a systemic concept: it referred less to the behavior of specific rulers than to a particular form of political order. How much was ascribed to the system and how much to "performance" varied from case to case. A few options were possible. Firstly, the repressive praxis of individual autocrats could be taken as evidence for the repressive features of the system itself;[25] secondly, the two could be kept separate, opening up the possibility that a virtuous prince could still glean some good from a bad system;[26] thirdly, the system could be presented on its own terms and the praxis then measured against this yardstick. That was the approach taken by the knowledgeable Armenian dragoman of the Ottoman Empire, Ignatius Mouradgea d'Ohsson, when he downplayed some unmistakably tyrannical aspects of Turkish rule with the argument that the Ottomans had been untrue to themselves and their originally good and just state institutions.[27]

Two further aspects of the concept of despotism, besides the systematic nature of the phenomenon, can already be discerned in ancient Greek political theory: despotism as an illegitimate, degenerate form of monocratic rule that rides roughshod over the law, and its specific association with "barbarians." Aristotle fatefully developed a relativizing argument that led to a split in the realm of political norms: even though despotism was the worst of all constitutions for the Hellenes, it could still be appropriate for the "barbarians" since they lacked all awareness of liberty. According to this anthropologically informed argument, "because the barbarians are more servile in their nature than the Greeks, and the Asiatics than the Europeans, they endure despotic rule without resentment."[28] The same form of government could thus be evaluated differently depending on sociocultural context.[29]

The eighteenth century's ideas about "oriental despotism" were in part trivial, serving no other purpose than the polemical one of associating forms of European absolutism with negative stereotypes pertaining to the "Oriental," particularly the Turk. English writers waxed indignant that the tyranny of Louis XIV, for example, surpassed that of the "Grand Turk."[30] David Hume expected his readers to have a basic prior understanding of Ottoman politics when he cast the government of Elizabeth I in a dim light by spotting a resemblance with "that of Turkey at present": "The sovereign possessed every power except that of imposing taxes."[31] The "discourse" in the Elizabethan parliaments, he pointed out, was so tame and docile that it was "more worthy of a Turkish divan than of an

English house of commons."[32] When such associations and analogies laid claim to theoretical substance, they stood in a tension between two genealogies. On one side, early modern political philosophers from Machiavelli through Jean Bodin to John Locke took up the Aristotelian theory of constitutions and sought to make it relevant to the present.[33] On the other side, European observers looked for ways to describe political conditions in Asia. In the sixteenth century, returning Venetian ambassadors produced realistic analyses of how the Ottoman political system functioned in actual practice. These reports ("relazioni"), some of which were read out in public and subsequently printed, remained largely free of anti-Islamic polemics. They offered instead a coolly objective take on the strengths and weaknesses of a neighboring world power that was vitally important to Venice's existential interests. From around 1575, the empire of the sultans was increasingly viewed as illegitimate and subject to arbitrary rule; at the same time, Venetian reports lost something of their factual, sharply observed lucidity and became ever more taken up with denunciations of an order that was increasingly perceived to be alien.[34] The Ottoman Empire continued to be an important factor in European diplomacy, and no foreign office in Christian lands could afford not to gather the best possible information on an empire that remained formidable even in its slow "decline" from superpower status. However, from the seventeenth century European interest was additionally directed towards Iran and Mughal India. Sir Thomas Roe, Bernier, Tavernier, Chardin, Thévenot, Kaempfer, and other travelers did not rest satisfied with relating anecdotes about oriental court life; they tried to explain the particular forms of autocracy they came across in early modern Muslim empires.[35]

Montesquieu's significance for the theory of oriental despotism lies in his having brought together both genealogies—that of normative political philosophy and that of descriptive "political science"—in his magnum opus, *De l'esprit des lois* (*Spirit of the Laws*, 1748). In doing so, he arrived at "the definitive formulation of despotism."[36] Montesquieu combines earlier motifs in a kind of "ideal type" or conceptual construct. He identifies three forms of government—republican (in democratic and aristocratic variants), monarchical, and despotic—and distinguishes them according to the different "principles" that animate their respective political cultures. These are virtue (*vertu*) in a republic, honor in a monarchy, and fear in a despotism. Before he sketched his concept of despotism, Montesquieu had already followed Tacitus in drawing an impressive psychogram of tyranny and fear in the person of Tiberius.[37] The ideal type of despotism, which has to be put together from numerous scattered remarks in *De l'esprit des lois*, also encompasses the *structures* of despotic rule. It reveals the following characteristics, which as a rule distinguish despotism from the princely rule of the monarch:

(1) The despot stands above the law. His will and his whims *are* the law.
(2) There are no largely independent countervailing forces (estates, church) to limit the despot's power.
(3) The despot exercises his power through an administrative elite that, unlike a hereditary aristocracy, is completely under his thumb. Even the highest dignitaries can never be sure of their social standing or even their lives.
(4) Under a despotism subjects are akin to the "slaves" of an overlord. At any rate they see themselves as slaves.
(5) Under a despotism no land is held in private ownership. All land belongs to the despot, who asserts his rights to it to varying degrees. The despot usually also designates himself the heir to all private property.
(6) The predominant affect in a despotic system, fear, determines not only relations with the ruler but also those between his subjects, who see each other as potential informants and close themselves off in mutual suspicion. This prevents the emergence of nonstate solidarities or a bourgeois public sphere.
(7) Despotic conditions reproduce themselves in small-scale units such as the household or family.

(8) Life under a despotism is not geared towards construction, planning for the future, and economic growth. Instead, people live in the present and exploit nature for short-term gain:

> In these states, nothing is repaired, nothing improved. Houses are only built for a lifetime; one digs no ditches, plants no trees; one draws all from the land, and returns nothing to it; all is fallow, all is deserted.[38]

Montesquieu's conception of despotism could be understood independently of context as a universally applicable category. That is what gave it critical force. Precisely because monarchy could slide into despotism in Europe as well, Europeans had no cause to congratulate themselves on their insusceptibility to this form of government. Yet Montesquieu, along with most of his contemporaries, was in no doubt that despotism was peculiarly characteristic of Asia. It had been "naturalized" there.[39] Montesquieu did more than merely assert this; he asked why this should be the case. He found two independent natural variables. On the one hand, the vast spaces that typified Asia, with its boundless, sweeping plains, necessitated a degree of administrative centralization that was possible only under a despotic form of government.[40] On the other hand, its hot climate bred a passivity and servility that made Asians more apt than inhabitants of cooler climes to submit to an authoritarian and arbitrary regime.[41] There was an analogy between immoderate climate and immoderate rule. In historical reality if not in theory, despotism was thus a characteristically *oriental* form of government.

Montesquieu's concept of despotism steered attention away from tyranny's outward appearance towards its structures and causes. The typological approach lived off the constant contrast between monarchy and despotism, and it inevitably made Asia appear—if only for reasons of methodology—as the political antitype to Europe. The ideal type had to be presented as distinctly as possible for it to be set in sharp relief.[42] Montesquieu's hatred of despotism is unmistakable: just thinking about "those monstrous governments" makes him shudder in revulsion.[43] To that extent, Montesquieu played a role in lending intellectual support and respectability to anti-Asiatic sentiments. Asia was a zone of chronic instability lacking in certain "orders of the state" and fundamental laws,[44] home to a primitive form of government founded on the stupefied ignorance of both the leaders and their enslaved subjects. Liberty *here* stood opposed to servitude *there*, the art of politics to an absence of politics, the skillful balance of powers to the forces of despotic command.

Montesquieu built his comparative political sociology on the basis of something like an early form of empirical political science. He himself had no personal knowledge of any political system in Asia, nor did he depict any such system in detail. When his followers traveled to the Orient, they often found the master's analyses confirmed by what they saw.[45] His ideal type is a combination of several traits that he had found mainly in the literature on Muslim empires. The analyses of the Iranian political system carried out by Chardin or Kaempfer had given a much clearer account of how this system functioned and came to a less negative overall verdict than Montesquieu a few decades later. Sir John Chardin, read by Montesquieu in the edition of 1735 and one of his most important sources, may serve as an example. What did Montesquieu borrow from him, what did he neglect or overlook?[46]

For Chardin, Persian rule since Abbas I had been despotic and arbitrary; the Persian people were "the most harshly oppressed in the world."[47] Yet Abbas I, the creator of this system, was content merely to disempower the grandees of his empire. It was his successor Safi I who began to liquidate them at will, a purge that served no practical political purpose. Under his rule, the court became a place of terror. Chardin introduces an important distinction between court and country that is nowhere to be found in Montesquieu:

> In Persia, as in any other country on earth, the great lords are more vulnerable than others. Their fate is most uncertain and often a highly lamentable one. The people, by contrast, enjoy more security and comfort than in certain Christian countries.[48]

Chardin here adopts a socially differentiated perspective that is missing in his famous reader: despotism has little impact on how most people live. If it touches them at all, then it is not necessarily to their detriment.[49] Those who have cause to find this system "lamentable" are the representatives of a threatened aristocracy and an intimidated civil service, not the populace at large.

Whereas despotism appears in Montesquieu as a faceless and highly determined system that leaves little room for statecraft, Chardin emphasizes precisely the extraordinary importance attached to the prince's personal qualities under conditions of extreme autocracy. For someone who knows Iranian history as well as Chardin does, Montesquieu's god-king languishing in his harem, "lazy, ignorant and voluptuous,"[50] is more a phenomenon of weakness and dynastic decrepitude. Successful rulers like Abbas I and to a lesser extent Abbas II were very active despots indeed. They no more conformed to the harem cliché than did the Qing emperors, the sixteenth-century sultans, and the "grand mughals" from Akbar to Aurangzeb. None of these rulers could be said to have been the blind victims of their passions.[51] The organizational problems faced by despotic systems had more to do with a lack of formalized channels for advice, such as a European-style state council or college of nobles, with the influence of a kitchen cabinet consisting of the queen mother, eunuchs, and concubines, and with endless succession disputes brought about by a lack of primogeniture rules (also discussed by Montesquieu).[52] But as Johann Heinrich Gottlieb von Justi drily riposted in 1762, was it really the case that in Europe, the royal favorites and mistresses were less influential, the crown princes better educated, and the dynastic succession principles more rational, given the number of inept or feeble-minded kings on the throne, than in the much-despised "barbaric" states of Asia and Africa?[53] China at least, regarded by many as despotic, seemed to prove the opposite. The fact that emperors there were able to choose the most capable of their (usually) numerous male offspring to succeed them had resulted in the Middle Kingdom being led between 1661 and 1799 by three of the most outstanding rulers to be found anywhere in the world at the time.

Chardin had pointed to a further remarkable context disregarded by his reader Montesquieu: a regime that acts tyrannically in its domestic affairs often adopts an irenic or even defensive foreign policy. Tyranny and a thirst for conquest are structurally distinct. Why? Bloodlust at court stems not from military virtues, such as those cultivated by Abbas I, but from luxury, decadence, and ill discipline. Princes brought up in the harem behave monstrously towards those around them once they ascend to the throne, while at the same time they lack the virile, martial spirit needed to defend the empire, let alone extend it. The most dangerous madmen are therefore also weaklings who squander the national and dynastic interest and leave their kingdom vulnerable to attack from foreign enemies.[54] Moreover, a despot fears his people and so takes the precaution of disarming them, thereby weakening the military power of the state.[55] When Chardin left Persia in 1677, the terrible shah Safi II was in power. The military, however, had fallen into a state of abject decay.[56] This aspect was very rarely considered by theorists of oriental despotism.

Chardin again demonstrates his sociological perspicacity when broaching the question of landed property. In 1669 François Bernier had written and subsequently published a widely read letter to Minister Colbert in which he drew on his authority as a respected traveler to explain how all the land in the Mughal Empire, with the exception of individual houses and gardens, belonged to the emperor.[57] Montesquieu, like many other authors on Asia, had taken up this idea, generalized it, and expressed it a little more cautiously: in many—although not all—despotic states, the ruler declared himself the sole proprietor of all land and heir to all his subjects.[58] In doing so, Montesquieu ignored what he had read on this topic in Chardin. In an extended discussion, Chardin shows that there were four categories of ownership of agricultural land: state land, royal domains, land belonging to religious institutions, and land owned by private citizens. The king could draw direct income from his crown holdings alone, at the customary Iranian rate of a third of the total harvest. State land was managed quite differently; it was administered by provincial governors and was mainly used to supply the military. Lands held by religious institutions (predominantly foundations) were amassed through donations and corporately owned; they were considered sacrosanct and could not be touched by the king. Private land may nominally have been under royal control, but it was rented out at cheap rates in ninety-nine-year leases that were renewed automatically. As such, it was de facto kept permanently in private hands.[59]

Chardin's exact description thus in no way supported the claim that the despot enjoyed monopoly rights on land, a thesis which in Montesquieu, at the latest, lost contact with historical reality and took on an almost mythical life of its own. Indeed, Chardin's account directly contradicted this thesis. There could also be no talk of the peasants being particularly hard pressed. Chardin stresses instead their relatively modest burden of taxation, tolls, interest payments, and seigneurial duties, and comes away impressed by their average living standards: "They live at their ease, and I can affirm that there are incomparably poorer peasants in the most fertile countries of Europe."[60] Chardin was no convinced Iranophile, but at the end of his investigation into the mid-seventeenth-century Persian state and economy, he arrives at an overall assessment that offers only limited support for Montesquieu's later theory of despotism.[61] Compared with many European states, the system shows a number of distinct advantages: there is no head tax and the tax burden is generally light; the populace remains relatively unmolested by the military; peasants are well treated by their landlords, coexisting in what today would be called a functioning "moral economy" of mutual rights and obligations: "It is possible to say that the lord and his subject are connected by a kind of unwritten contract: losses and gains are shared on an equal basis, and the poorest suffer the least."[62] The Persian people are well-off, and were it not for the shah's reign of terror at his court in Isfahan and the occasional malfeasance of corrupt ministers and governors, there would be no reason to characterize the political system of Safavid

Iran as in any way "barbaric." It is ridiculous to claim that the shah's subjects are his "slaves." On the contrary, the Huguenot émigré Chardin adds, the Persians are blessedly free of the pressure that weighs down on Christian societies from the church. There are neither parasitical monasteries and priests nor an intolerant monitoring of people's thoughts.[63]

Europe's best-informed expert on Persia (along with Raphaël Du Mans) was not out to downplay the real evils of despotism, which he depicted impressively enough. But he took them to be a potentially treatable symptom of ruling-class degeneracy rather than the death rattle of the entire system. They affected the majority of Persians only insofar as it was not in their interests to have the central state weakened by an incapable ruler. The best yardstick for measuring the quality of a political order was not provided by court intrigues but by the living conditions of ordinary subjects, particularly the poorest among them. According to this criterion, the system created by the great Abbas I had proved eminently successful.[64] It was wrong, in Chardin's view, to use the word "despotism" as an exhaustive characterization of Iran, or for that matter the entire East. Unlike Montesquieu, he studiously avoided amplifying shades of difference into rigid binary contrasts with Europe. From the viewpoint of its achievements, Safavid Iran by no means came off worse than the other two countries Chardin knew best: France under Louis XIV and Restoration England. At one point he casually mentions a further aspect of the cliché of oriental cruelty: torture in legal cases was far less often applied than in Europe, and although the law foresaw capital punishment for the worst offenses, he had not witnessed a single public execution during his fifteen years in Persia.[65]

The Iran that interested Montesquieu as a case study for his theory of despotism was not the chaotic Iran of the early eighteenth century—ruled in name if not in deed by the hapless last Safavid shahs, overrun by Afghan invaders, and then dominated by the warlord Nadir Shah—but the country at the height of its power, stability, and prosperity under the early dynasty. Montesquieu was concerned less with accounting for the "elemental-historical" forces that periodically laid waste to civilization than with elaborating the ideal type of a particular species of political system. Travel reports provided the great thinker with more than mere data. An author like Chardin had developed a deeply considered description, explanation, and evaluation of conditions in Iran. In doing so, he had kept one eye firmly on Europe: not as an idealized norm, nor as an object to be critiqued from an exotic new standpoint, but as a measure for empirically comparing life in Persia with life as it was lived in other countries around the same time. Montesquieu radicalized and simplified this method into an asymmetrical typology. From Chardin's in-depth analysis of Iran, he extracted only what could be used to illustrate the constructed type of *le despotisme*.

Chardin emerges as the better sociologist and political scientist, Montesquieu as the bolder political philosopher. As chunks of empirical analysis were incorporated into a uniquely varied system for a universal sociology, they took on new meaning, becoming both dogmatized and trivialized in the process. The complications and contradictions of despotism as it actually existed were ironed out into the seamless unity of an idealized negative stereotype that seemed, in an almost visionary way, to anticipate features of twentieth-century totalitarianism, to which it was perhaps better suited than to the Orient of the Enlightenment era. To be sure, Montesquieu himself was clear that his ideal type of oriental despotism was a construct of quasi-geometrical abstraction. In 1734 he had already remarked in his text on the grandeur and decadence of the Romans:

> It is an error to suppose that there is any human authority in the world which is, in all respects, despotic. There never was and there never will be such. The most enormous power is always limited on some side.[66]

Yet this caveat was not repeated in his magnum opus. Although Montesquieu was circumspect enough to allow for exceptions to his general pronouncements, the final impression left with the reader is nonetheless that of a divided world. This division is not derived from any racial or national characteristics. There is no anthropological transfiguration of the Western individual in Montesquieu, no denigration of Asiatic cultures as such, no teleological philosophy of history culminating in the supposedly unique achievements of the West. For all that, there is still something inevitable about Asiatic bondage, given Montesquieu's premise that political and social conditions are determined by environmental factors, that is, by climate and topography. Montesquieu's answer to the question of how this perverse form of (mis)rule can be overcome—a question that stands at the heart of the discourse on despotism—is at bottom pessimistic. While individual despots may come and go in often bewildering succession, the numerous "revolutions" in Asiatic countries lead to nothing more than the eternal return of the ecologically determined same.

DESPOTISM AND THE PHILOSOPHY OF HISTORY

Montesquieu condensed, concentrated, simplified, and generalized the older discourse of despotism to come up with an ideal type that could be used for purposes of comparison.[67] Detached from the framework of *De l'esprit des lois*, this ideal type launched a career of its own that freed it for a variety of uses. It could be polemically exaggerated, empirically tested, or used as material for a philosophy of history. Each involved demolishing the context in which the type had originally appeared in Montesquieu. His great comparative tableau was dismantled and harvested for parts.

By and large, polemical exaggeration served the purpose of denouncing one's neighboring country, or even the rest of the world, as despotic while simultaneously basking in one's own happy exceptionalism. Montesquieu had already praised Europe's unique good fortune in this respect. Such rhetoric was open to the objection voiced by Jean-Charles de Lavie: "Since all nations in the universe, save the Europeans, are subjected to the same type of domination—is it then possible to say that this type is illegitimate?"[68]

A more serious advance on Montesquieu was the historico-philosophical interpretation. It saw despotism as a separate stage in the course of historical evolution. There were a number of different and quite diverse ways of conceiving this. Nicolas-Antoine Boulanger, a civil engineer and admirer of Montesquieu whose main interest lay in human prehistory, conducted research into the "spirit" of myths and rites.[69] In a work published in 1761, two years after the author's premature death, he interpreted despotism as the intensified form of an early theocracy. Its chief characteristics were that the divine now assumed regal features while the political ruler, conversely, came to be viewed as divine. Both characteristics were combined in a quasi-religious cult of the state. The ruler was ascribed magical powers. Religious and political intolerance went hand in hand. Abuse of power led under certain conditions—as in ancient Greece and Rome—to the breakdown of despotic rule and its replacement by a republican form of government. According to Boulanger, what emerged from the original theocracy in the West was not despotism, as in the East, but anarchy. The West, however, has always been exposed to despotic infection through its Asiatic colonies.[70] Yet the ancient republics were themselves inherently unstable, incapable of breaking free from their despotic inheritance; the transition to imperial rule in Rome clearly showed this. Boulanger does not discuss how despotism came to an end once more, but the implications of his ideas for the state and church under Louis XIV were clear.[71] Decades later, incidentally, without referring to Boulanger and most likely in ignorance of his work, the historian of India Mark Wilks would define the essence of despotism in a very similar way, as the fusion of divine and human law.[72]

Boulanger had thoroughly investigated a particular transition in the early development of religious and political institutions without extrapolating from it a general model of progress. Such models only advanced to the center of Enlightenment thought in the years following Boulanger's death. The first example was furnished in impressive fashion by Turgot's various sketches for a fully secular universal history, written around the same time as Montesquieu's masterpiece.

The philosopher, economist, and statesman Turgot analyzed despotism more cogently and searchingly than Montesquieu ever did.[73] He saw it as a phenomenon that inevitably accompanies the formation of large territorial states in highly populated agrarian societies. He dismissed climate as a determining factor; the political sphere is subject to the same laws everywhere on Earth. The cardinal difference between Asia and Europe is that in Asia, a series of conquests meant that despotism arose too early for there to be any established "mores" to offer it concerted resistance. In Europe, it emerged at a later point in time (around the period of the Roman Empire), when it could no longer fully permeate society. In Turgot's eyes, a despotic system is organizationally unstable since it rests on a simple hierarchy of terror and exploitation. There are no crossbeams in place to support the tottering political edifice; a fickle military, frequently in the form of a politically ambitious praetorian guard, plays a decisive role. The position of the supreme executive, the chief minister, or "grand vizier," is often so precarious as to render effective government all but impossible.[74] A despotic system can nonetheless prove long-lasting. It oppresses the entire intellectual life of the country, using education to break the initiative and sap the willpower of its citizens; committed freedom fighters are therefore in short supply. Despotism ultimately becomes a matter of habit: people put up with it because they know nothing else. Turgot describes the political effects of this kind of social despotism even more forcefully than Montesquieu:

> It may be added that in these vast despotic states there is also introduced a despotism which extends over social manners, which dulls men's minds even more; which deprives society of the greater part of its resources, its delights, and the cooperation of women in the running of the family; which by forbidding the social intercourse of the two sexes reduces everything to uniformity, and induces in members of the state a tired lethargy which is opposed to all change and therefore to all progress.[75]

On the whole, Turgot takes despotism to be a more or less permanent fixture of Asian societies that is largely immune to change from within. Its structural weakness is more than made up for by its capacity to lodge itself immovably in the minds of its people.[76] The East appears to have maneuvered itself into a cul de sac of world history.

Condorcet too, greatly influenced by Turgot, lamented in 1793 "a shameful stagnation" of Asia's despotic systems.[77] Several lesser-known authors modified this image. Charles-Athanase Walckenaer, who in 1798 cut back Condorcet's ten-stage model of human history to six, bade farewell to the black legend of despotism and drew his own conclusions from the obvious fact that the descriptions of seventeenth-century travelers no longer captured the reality of late eighteenth-century Asia. The East had not been left untouched by the progress of trade, industry, and the arts. Such progress could strengthen the hand of an individual despot if he could skillfully exploit new opportunities to his advantage. By the same token, however, the inexorable march of progress weakened despotism as a system: a ruler could only profit from growing world trade, for example, by allowing merchants greater freedom of movement. Such liberalizing measures, dictated by the monarch's own interests, would not necessarily spell the end of despotism, but they could at least deprive it of its sting (*ferocité*).[78] In contrast to Turgot, Walckenaer thus does not assume that Asia has gone its own unique way in history; rather, he expects a convergence of systems in the not-too-distant future.

A different argumentative strategy arrived at the opposite results. It tied in with the contradiction—already hinted at by Lavie—between the empirical observation of despotism and its normative evaluation. If despotism could be explained by objective factors such as climate, what possible grounds were there for critique? Julien Joseph Virey, for example, recalled Solon, who when asked whether he had enacted the best laws for the Athenians replied that he had given them the best they would receive. Did not every nation necessarily have the constitution that best matched its character, and was it not conceivable "that despotism is perfectly suitable for Asia, whereas a republican government would only cause a great deal of unrest"?[79] Human society could not, as Condorcet believed, be perfected according to a one-size-fits-all model; there were only culturally specific solutions to problems. With that, the discourse on despotism had been linked up to the great debate on universalism and relativism. The East-West dichotomy that had been so central to Montesquieu's discussion no longer played a central role.

Were "ideal types" claiming global validity and abstract "stage models" covering all of world history of any use at all for understanding reality? In 1774 Linguet answered this question in the negative and argued against "geometric precision." Political systems differ from each other in how they regulate the relationship between commands and their execution; here there are "an infinite number of degrees."[80] Despotism is a pathological degenerative condition that can befall *any* constitution, whether republican or monarchical, a generally fatal "political fever" symptomized by a loss of rationality, morality, reliability, and moderation.[81] Such "putrefaction of a state" does not concentrate power in a single hand but disperses it among many. It is not a form of government because it resembles a government without form.[82] Linguet goes back historically behind Montesquieu, speaking the language of classical republicanism and the theory of political virtue. It is the paradoxical twist of his argument that Asian political systems have been less prone to this kind of decadence than the countries of Europe ever since the sordid drama of late imperial Rome. Why? Their "laws" are older and simpler and thus more resistant to erosion,[83] although this is an idea that Linguet fails to substantiate sufficiently from the evidence he adduces. His "Asia" is, even more than in the cases of Montesquieu or Voltaire, a projection screen for arguments about Europe. His outspoken critique of despotism did not save Linguet from the charge that he wanted to introduce a centralized state to France. In June 1794, this proto-Bonapartist thinker fell to the guillotine.

Other authors, too, tried to escape the orthodoxy of the Montesquieu school. One alternative was "middle range" theories of despotism. Dr. John Crawfurd, the diplomat and Southeast Asia expert who has still yet to be appreciated as a theorist in his own right, was thinking only of the Indonesian archipelago when he attempted in 1820 to detect recurring historical patterns. He took his cue from two observations. Firstly, in that part of the world conquest now played a far less important role as a basis for despotic rule than philosophers of history had been wont to ascribe it. Despotism thus had to be explained from the *internal* affairs of a country. Secondly, political unfreedom tended to increase as societies became more civilized. Crawfurd joins Walckenaer in making a link between political development and civilizational evolution, but the link he identifies is a very different one. Advancing "modernization" does not check despotism; on the contrary, it is what makes despotism possible in the first place. Crawfurd, the philosophical diplomat, develops an evolutionary model consisting of "five distinct forms of social union": (1) the unconstrained egalitarianism of savages; (2) elective kingship; (3) a hereditary monarchy subject to aristocratic oversight and control; (4) federation with an elected head; (5) unrestrained despotism.[84] The last form is characteristic of Java, the island with the most highly developed economy in the region. Crawfurd goes on to depict the extreme subservience of Javans towards their monarch while also noting that the establishment of effective despotic rule is associated with internal peace, greater legal security, better administration, and the abolition of the slave trade. With the loss of *political* freedom, the Javans had gained "a larger share of personal freedom."[85] Crawfurd avoids taking the usual rhetorical potshots at despotism, but neither does he lapse into the cynical relativism that proclaims the "Asiatic" to be both ignorant and unappreciative of liberty and hence deserving of nothing better than oppression.

As if writing in the spirit of an empirically validated Thomas Hobbes, Crawfurd here takes up a countertheme that pervades much of the discourse on despotism: the fear of anarchy, of the Hobbesian state of nature, of the war of all against all. This may have been only a historical memory in a Europe that had left civil and religious wars behind it, but in Asia, which in the eighteenth century had witnessed the collapse of political order in Persia, India, Siam, Vietnam, and several other countries, it was hard to think of a more pressing political problem. Nothing was worse for human beings than a breakdown in public order, and a strong despot was always preferable to a mob of uncontrolled and uncontrollable "petty tyrants"—that, at any rate, was the general tenor of European commentary.[86] This was an all-but-irrefutable objection to the standard denunciations of despotism. There were indeed worse things than an all-powerful autocrat, at least until the advent of totalitarianism in modern times. Yet the argument was not completely disinterested. After all, once the local strongman had left the scene, a new guarantor of peace and stability could move in to take his place: the colonial powers.[87]

Volney, the most experienced philosophizing traveler and the most ambitious traveling *philosophe*, came to similar conclusions. His remarks on oriental despotism reunited what had been torn asunder since Chardin: personal experience and theoretical reflection.[88] Volney's historico-philosophical treatise, *Les Ruines, ou Méditations sur les révolutions des empires* (1791), follows Turgot in deriving despotism from the empire-building activities of great conquerors and in offering psychological and cultural explanations for the longevity of despotic systems.[89] In doing so, Volney draws general conclusions from his first book, the *Voyage en Égypte et en Syrie* from 1787. Here he had literally taken under the microscope despotism's modus operandi and its consequences, above all the economic irrationality of a political order that prevented people from producing wealth and laid waste to nature.[90] Volney was particularly interested in the *causes* of despotism. He advised against all-too-audacious speculations and generalizations à la Montesquieu, arguing instead—like Crawfurd after him—for empirically grounded theories that were regional in scope.[91] He disputed Montesquieu's claim that climate had a determining influence on social and political conditions, and he likewise rejected the anthropological argument for the aversion to labor purportedly shown by Orientals.[92] Evidently, the ancestors of today's Near Easterners had once exerted themselves to titanic feats under near-identical climatic conditions.

For Volney, the military despotism of the Ottomans and the Egyptian Mamluks was not an objectively necessary phenomenon, but one that demanded a political explanation. The Ottoman Empire was a ruthlessly exploitative colonial power, founded on conquest and devoid of legitimacy.[93] The Orient's civilizational backwardness with regard to Europe, the deplorable state of the sciences and stagnation of the arts was not—as Volney's rival Savary had contended—anchored in practically inalterable givens like language and writing; rather, it was due to the fact that political circumstances, working hand in glove with religion, kept people bound in the chains of ignorance: "The true cause is the difficulty of procuring the means for self-education, above all the rarity of books."[94] The West's superiority lay in its scientific and scholarly accomplishments, in its triumph over religious hypocrisy, and in social institutions that promoted the increase of knowledge. Volney accordingly opposed all varieties of physical or anthropological determinism. Because the current state of affairs in the East did not have to be fatalistically accepted, it was amenable to political change. Although Volney did not explicitly call for a European intervention in the Near East, the right and perhaps the duty of progressive Europe to set free the victims of despotism lay on the horizon of his reflections.

"ORIENTAL DESPOTISM" UNDER SUSPICION

By historicizing and politicizing despotism, Volney contributed decisively to the concept's demystification. Despotism was not the Orient's inescapable destiny; it was the outcome of a historical misstep and as such could be corrected. Volney nonetheless continued to demonize the phenomenon of despotism, if anything to a greater extent than his predecessors. Enlightenment stalwarts, by contrast, had cautioned against hysteria. Thus Adam Ferguson, anything but a lackey of princes, had remarked laconically in 1767: "Despotism itself has certain advantages, or at least, in time of civility and moderation, may proceed with so little offence, as to give no public alarm."[95] Christoph Meiners pointed out that it was the great achievement of Roman-Byzantine despotism to have kept the barbarians at bay.[96] And August Hennings, an early German liberal writing around the same time that Volney was condemning Turkish military despotism, voiced his suspicion (apropos the literature on India) that vilifying oriental despotism might be a way of diverting attention from conditions closer to home:

> The exaggerated depictions of Asiatic despotism that may be found even in Raynal and others, the tales of bloodthirsty regents and oppressive Omrahs and Rajahs,[97] are nothing new for the student of European history, and when Bernier castigates the shameful flattery of the Asiatic nobles, in crying out "O Wonder! Wonder!" at every word uttered by the Grand Mughal, this is surely no different from the tone that prevails among us at court today.[98]

The same criticism could have been made of Montesquieu as well. Fed on a diet of such lurid "tales," travelers sometimes expressed their surprise at not encountering the expected horrors. Visiting Vietnam in 1792, Barrow saw nothing of the tyranny he had read about at home. Touring the same country three decades later, Crawfurd found the common people to be lively and happy, "as if they had nothing to complain of."[99]

Many other authors subjected the theories of Montesquieu, Turgot, and their adherents to empirical scrutiny, although their detailed descriptions, unlike Volney's, were divorced from any historico-philosophical interpretive framework. The complete opposite of philosophy of history was provided by Thomas Brooke Clarke in his *Publicistical Survey of the Different Forms of Government of All States and Communities in the World* (1791). This extraordinarily fine-grained attempt to taxonomize all the political systems found on Earth, dedicated to the Margrave of Baden, could not avoid tackling Montesquieu's famous problem of how to distinguish (absolute) monarchy from despotism. Clarke did not define these forms by their internal driving forces but by their observable appearance. He distinguished between limited and unlimited monarchies. In "sovereign or unlimited monarchies," the monarch is beholden to nobody but himself, ruling by laws that either preexist his reign or that he decrees in his own name. Despotism is defined in Aristotelian terms as a degenerative form of sovereign monarchy. It appears "when the monarch has unlimited power over the life and property of his subjects, and without ruling according to law, can treat his subjects arbitrarily as slaves."[100] Tyranny, for its part, is an extreme form of despotism in practice, where citizens are subjected to "wanton and inhuman bondage and torment."[101] Clarke applies this legalistic definition in a culturally neutral fashion when he undertakes a statistical survey of the globe. He must have been an avid reader of travel literature to have been able to gain an overview of even the smallest principalities. The only tyrannies he can discover are in Africa: the kingdom of Morocco as well as fourteen realms in Central Africa, among which he considers "Caffange" and "Monoemugi" to be the worst in the world. There are also a great many despotisms in the same continent. Almost all of Asia is ruled despotically, with some exceptions: China is classified as the sole unlimited monarchy in Asia and thereby placed on an equal footing with Russia, Prussia, France, the Habsburg hereditary lands, and the Papal States. Among the limited monarchies, Clarke lists Korea as well as tributary states or protectorates whose sovereignty is constrained by an external overlord: Tibet, Cochinchina, Golkonda (as a vassal of the Mughal Empire), or various sultanates in the Indonesian archipelago that are subordinate to the Dutch. Democratic states are to found only in Europe; these include the free imperial cities and the cantons and municipalities of Switzerland. Anarchies, on the other hand, are an Asian speciality, found in the Caucasus, the Kalmyk Steppe, and Arabia.

In his quaintly pedantic though insightful tables, Clarke employs a very broad and formal concept of despotism that in its empirical coverage roughly accords with Montesquieu's way of viewing the world. Early on, and long before Montesquieu's radical simplifications, consideration had been given to possible gradations in despotic praxis. Thus the not at all badly informed author of a genealogical handbook observes in 1711 that the Turkish sultan rules absolutely while being at constant risk of palace revolts. The king of Morocco rules even more absolutely, since he is the only greater monarch who treats his subjects as if they were his actual slaves. The grand mughal is richer and more glorious than the sultan and has less reason to fear resistance at his own court. The emperor of China is attended by less pomp and ceremony but is more parsimonious and therefore wealthier than all other despots; he rules less through violence than through his perfect information system, which brings him news from everywhere and carries his commands to the farthest reaches of the empire.[102] Such comparisons within Asia never ceased to fascinate. Montesquieu's subsumption of diverse historical phenomena under the overarching category of "despotism" left many unconvinced. Perhaps there was no such thing as "despotism" per se, only different kinds of despots?[103]

Montesquieu himself had an inkling that his concept of despotism did not quite fit China, in particular. Japan only played a marginal role in his investigation, as a country with particularly draconian laws. While the abbé Raynal depicted it as a paragon of despotism,[104] others insisted that it was the only sizeable country in Asia *not* to have fallen into the clutches of a despot. Far from succumbing to the enervating allurements of the harem, Japan's rulers were the most conscientious in the continent.[105] In this case, the dichotomy of monarchy and despotism seemed completely inapt: was Japan perhaps a composite form of despotism and feudalism?[106] And how was it possible that in immediate vicinity to the Mughal dynasty, and thus under almost exactly the same climatic conditions, the Sikh state could arise, which was republican and perhaps even democratic in constitution?[107]

Against Montesquieu's ideal typology, Voltaire had already objected that there had never been a "pure" despotism. He had also caught the author of *De l'esprit des lois* making reckless use of some very problematic sources.[108] In 1753, while Montesquieu was still alive but without mentioning his name, Voltaire came to some critical insights about negative stereotyping. Political theory, he observed, had always recognized the potential for a monarchical government to degenerate into tyranny. Now such occasional aberrations had suddenly been turned into a distinct political system. The excesses reported by travelers had summarily been declared to be the very essence of this system, and certain peculiarities of the sultan's palace in Constantinople had been used to license sweeping conclusions about the nature of the Ottoman state and even the Orient as a whole. In this way, "a frightful phantom" (*un fantôme hideux*) had been deliberately conjured up in order that that the virtues of European absolute monarchs might shine all the more brightly against this dark background. "Oriental despotism" was thus nothing more than a gigantic attention-deflecting strategy on behalf of the crowned heads of Europe.

The idea of oriental despotism as a lawless reign of terror, Voltaire continues, has no basis whatsoever in historical experience. It is neither credible that ancient civilizations such as those in Persia and China could have flourished without binding legal statutes, nor can it be conceived how anyone could have been induced to transfer absolute rights over their property and their body to a ruler. It is hardly plausible that the son of a craftsman in Constantinople should not be allowed to inherit his father's workshop.[109] And was it even the case, the wise John Richardson asked in the spirit of Voltaire, that premodern state apparatuses were already compact enough to allow for a centralized power of command?[110]

Voltaire did not engage in theoretical debate. For him there was no such thing as a theory of despotism, since the whole notion stood on far too shaky a foundation. His appeal to healthy common sense encouraged others to subject the theory's undisputed assumptions to rigorous scrutiny. The key question was not whether the theory could satisfactorily account for this or that borderline case (China or Japan, for example), but whether it held water even where it claimed the greatest validity: when applied to the Islamic empires of the Ottomans, Safavids, and Mughals. Montesquieu had outlined his worst-case scenario under the impression of some pages that Sir Paul Rycaut had written at the end of the worst period of tyrannical misrule in Ottoman history. They were ideally suited to his purpose. Yet as we have seen, when it came to Chardin's sober and nuanced report on Iran, the political philosopher took liberties that turned what the traveler wrote on its head.

ANQUETIL-DUPERRON: THE DESPOT'S NEW CLOTHES

The most radical reckoning with Montesquieu's theory was undertaken by his compatriot Abraham-Hyacinthe Anquetil-Duperron.[111] Much like Volney a generation later, Anquetil had the advantage of knowing Asia—in his case India, where he had lived for almost six years—and understanding Asian languages.[112] In his comprehensive *Législation orientale* from 1778, he set out to demonstrate that, firstly, a tradition of written law binding both rulers and ruled existed in Turkey, Iran, and Mughal India; and that, secondly, private citizens in all three states enjoyed property rights to mobile and immobile goods, which they were free to do with as they pleased. With that, the idea that there was a *special* form of ("oriental") despotism had become untenable, and the political systems of Muslim Asia could be reintegrated into the *general* theory of monarchical government.[113]

Anquetil-Duperron was a supremely learned man. In 1771 he had published his epochal translation of the ancient Iranian *Zend Avesta*. This was the first scholarly work on an Asiatic text standing completely outside the biblical and classical Mediterranean traditions and, as such, it deserves to be seen as a founding document of a truly polyphonous global history.[114] He had been driven to take an interest in the problem of Asiatic despotism by his experiences around 1760 with British colonial rule in India, then just getting underway before his eyes. The motives for Anquetil-Duperron's anticolonialism were not entirely pure, however, since his increasingly apparent hatred of England made him willing to grant the French certain colonial privileges. He believed postrevolutionary France, unlike Great Britain, to be capable of forging mutually beneficial relations with the Indian states on the basis of equal rights.[115] Within a French domestic context, Anquetil-Duperron belonged—along with Voltaire, the radical writer Simon-Nicolas-Henri Linguet, and the former ambassador to the Sublime Porte and later Foreign Minister (1774–87), the Comte de Vergennes—to a royalist party that attempted to bolster the monarchy by blunting the edge of "despotism" as a polemical weapon against Bourbon "misrule."[116] All this does nothing to alter the fact that *Législation orientale* is animated by the impulse to defend the Muslim peoples and states of Asia against their European detractors, to work against their stigmatization as the countertype and archenemy of the West, and to contest the argument that oriental and occidental history had developed along qualitatively different paths. With an energy unmatched by any of his contemporaries, Anquetil sought to correct the exotic physiognomy and demonic grimace that had long distorted the European portrait of the "Asiatic."[117]

Anquetil begins his work with a dedication *Aux peuples de l'Indoustan*, in which he prophetically draws out the difference between the old conquerors of India, the Mughals, and the new ones, the Europeans. Whereas the fierce Mughal warriors from the north, mollified by the warm climate and gentle customs of India, had assimilated successfully to their new country, the same could not be prophesied of their fanatically rapacious successors from overseas. The English were far more likely to transform India beyond recognition.[118] Anquetil's introduction is a rhetorically dazzling critique of the caricature of the Orient that had taken root in the West. There was method to the absurd exaggerations of the *publicistes*, since they were only pandering to Europe's sense of its own uniqueness: "Europe revels in the wisdom of its laws, while the rest of the world, the Orient in particular, is alleged to be the plaything of a single individual!"[119] Anquetil does not blame the much-maligned travelers for this situation, but rather the great theorists who had systematically misread their reports from the comfort of their leather-backed armchairs. In principle, an unprejudiced and judicious assessment of serious travel reports could have resulted in a correspondingly realistic, reasonable, and plausible view of Asia. This is precisely what Anquetil claimed for his own investigation, which thus became a triumphant vindication of those voyagers whom Anquetil—we have already encountered him as a theorist of "high" travel—credits with an unclouded perspective (*désintéressement*).[120]

His method consists in falsifying arguments claiming general validity by citing refutations from the relevant literature. Where Montesquieu maintains that honor, the hallmark of a monarchy enjoying support from the nobility, is unknown in the fearful climate of despotism, Anquetil-Duperron produces page after page of counterevidence. Where Montesquieu says that despots are ill educated, lazy, and loath to appear in public, Anquetil has no difficulty proving the opposite. Even on the rare occasions when theorists of despotism—occasionally Boulanger comes under attack as well—describe a phenomenon correctly, they still misunderstand its effects. For example, it may well have been the goal of some despots to control their subjects as intensively as possible. But the absence of fixed laws constantly being invoked by the theorists would have thwarted this very intention. In the absence of a built-up bureaucracy, solely the execution of a rule-bound, universally recognized sovereign will could promise success.[121] It would further lie in no despot's interests to be universally feared by his people. He would seek instead to cultivate the good will of those groups in the population, such as city-dwellers, who could ally with him against the ambitions of elite groups. Put anachronistically, Anquetil saw that all regimes rely on the loyalty of the masses to ensure their long-term survival. More generally, he shows that a political system that functions in the way Montesquieu claims despotism to function would be doomed to failure.[122] The ideal type is thus neither the conceptual duplicate of a reality nor the vision of a plausible possibility. And so it goes on for more than three hundred pages. Anquetil-Duperron chases his opponents' arguments up hill and down dale, firing a barrage of quotations and learned commentary in their direction until they have been all but shot to pieces. By the end, the strict opposition of East and West has been transformed into a multitude of finely graded political and social possibilities. Having been dramatized and exoticized by Montesquieu and his ilk, oriental politics is now hauled back into the sphere of experience and common sense.

Anquetil also asks why the discourse on despotism should be so sharply polarized. Things are not always as clear-cut as in the case of a traveler who was said to have been commissioned by the Pope in the 1680s to write an attack on the Turks.[123] Anquetil comes to the conclusion that the theory of despotism is ultimately the ideology of conquerors and plunderers. One's own brutal misconduct is easier to excuse once one has convinced oneself that politics in the Orient is a rougher business than at home, and always will be owing to the unchanging climate. Under the assumption that Indians are strangers to property law, they can be plundered and their lands confiscated with an untroubled conscience.[124] In the eyes of Anquetil-Duperron, who was living in India during the period of early British smash-and-grab imperialism that enriched the "nabobs," the whole theory of imperialism is nothing but a license for Europeans to commit crimes in India and later, as he prophetically foresees, in other parts of the non-European world as well. Finally, Anquetil detects a hypocritical double standard applied by those who come back home and then loudly complain about the arbitrariness of Asiatic governments. Europeans in Asia expect—simply by virtue of being European—to get away with anything, yet if required to pay a toll or surrender contraband in Europe, it would never occur to them to kick up a fuss. In Asia, however, such legitimate assertions of state sovereignty are decried without fail as acts of "despotism."[125]

Anquetil-Duperron's great polemic, carried out in the spirit of Voltairean enlightenment, remained untranslated and was evidently rarely cited; its arguments met overwhelmingly with rejection.[126] The Montesquieuean ideal type, rapidly become the stuff of cliché, was not so readily abandoned by those who found it congenial to their purposes. In 1793, for example, Christoph Meiners was still presenting a completely antithetical viewpoint, buttressed by all the usual evidence on oriental despotism.[127] In 1842 the retired statesman Lord Brougham devoted a lengthy discussion to the "absolute monarchies of the East" in his *Political Philosophy*, one of the last nineteenth-century works of political science to take conditions outside Europe into account. Although he attempted to paint a nuanced picture and excluded China from his list of despotic states, in the end the old clichés survived unscathed, as if Anquetil-

Duperron's objections had never been voiced. Here despots continued to tax and bully their subjects into cowed submission, restrained at best by a few brave priests and the fear of popular revolt; here they continued to strangle, behead, drown, crucify, dismember, and impale their subjects as their fancy pleased them; here the ever-present threat of expropriation continued to block the emergence of any future-oriented commerce.[128]

INDIA: *TRANSLATIO DESPOTICA*

Anquetil-Duperron failed to make headway against the prevailing climate of opinion. He lived long enough, however, to see his findings confirmed by a number of scholars. One of these was Charles William Boughton Rouse, an EIC high official in Bengal and later in London, sometime parliamentarian and translator from the Persian, who sent him a copy of his *Dissertation Concerning the Landed Property of Bengal* (1791). Rouse's contribution can only be understood in the context of the very complicated Anglo-Indian debate on the nature of landed property in India that had been underway since 1769. This debate had direct practical consequences in the so-called Permanent Settlement of Bengal, a revolutionary new system of property law and taxation, introduced by Lord Cornwallis in 1793, that nominally remained in force until the end of British rule in 1947.[129] What interests us here is Rouse's opinion on one of the central questions of the theory of oriental despotism. On the basis of his own on-the-ground investigations, Rouse took the side of those who posited the existence of heritable landed property in India and demanded that the British colonial power recognize the native ownership structure. Because written titles could not be produced in the vast majority of cases, this line of argument had to be based on traditions ("immemorial usage"), customary law ("constant practice"), and tacit recognition ("universal sense of the people").[130] Rouse emphasizes that under Mughal rule the great landowners and patrons, the zamindars, had been arbitrarily deprived of their rights only in exceptional cases. De facto if not de jure, their possession of the land had been inviolable and heritable.[131] He goes on to trace the history of the opposing view back to Bernier and Alexander Dow, giving honorable mention to Voltaire and Anquetil-Duperron for having refused to join the chorus of abuse directed at oriental despotism.[132] Rouse's most important insight was that, in representing Asiatic society as wholly other, European observers were not showing an open-minded acceptance of diversity; on the contrary, they were merely absolutizing their own limited standards of judgment.[133] The construction of difference did not create space for tolerance but confirmed the superiority of the cultural arbiter. Unsurprisingly, Rouse's view had no discernible effect on British policy in India.

Rouse's declared empiricism was not a disinterested scientific stance. It served political ends. The same can be said for almost the entire discourse on despotism towards the end of the eighteenth century. The political battlefield increasingly shifted from the critique and defense of European absolutisms to the question of the legitimacy of European imperial maneuvers abroad. When oriental despotism was discussed around 1760, the real topic of conversation was Europe. Those who spoke of despotism around 1800 and in the years that followed—especially in Great Britain and Germany—were also still talking about Europe; but they now had in mind a new kind of autocracy in the form of Napoleon's postrevolutionary dictatorship, which provoked hugely diverse reactions ranging from ardent enthusiasm to bitter enmity. In this context, Asia became more important than ever: an Asia that for the first time gave Europeans the opportunity to slip into the role of oriental despots themselves.[134]

This was nowhere more obvious than in India. The "oriental despotism" of the Mughal emperors, as popularized by Sir Thomas Roe, François Bernier, and Jean-Baptiste Tavernier, had basically ceased to exist with the death of Aurangzeb in 1707, or at the latest with Nadir Shah's invasion of 1737. There was no longer a "grand mughal"—that mythical figure of wealth and power that had initially been formed in Akbar's image and which Johann Melchior Dinglinger had worked for August the Strong of Saxony into an opulent fantasy of gold and precious gems; it can still be admired today in the Green Vault in Dresden.[135] The British in the guise of the EIC, an armed and quasi-sovereign trading company, were its heirs. This newfangled colonial rule was the target of a critique that availed itself of the catchword "despotism." It first came from the side of imperial rivals. British, French, and German authors denounced the Dutch on Java and Ceylon—not unjustly—as brutal despots. Holland's freedom and wealth, Johann Traugott Plant argued in 1793 in his great work on Asian archipelagos, were built on the tears and sweat of enslaved Indonesians.[136] French observers interpreted British rule in Bengal in particular, where the EIC had its earliest and most secure power base, as a *modernized* form of despotism. The Bengalis, the abbé Raynal contended as early as 1770, only a few years after the British had established their rule on the Ganges Delta, had good reason to mourn the despotism of their former overlords:

> A methodical tyranny has taken the place of an arbitrary one. The raising of revenues has become general and regular, suppression of the people is made permanent and absolute. The destructive power of monopolies has been perfected, and new monopolies have been created. In a word, every source of trust and public happiness has been altered and corrupted.[137]

Other French critics also railed against a new English despotism in South Asia.[138] Whereas Raynal had still depicted Mughal rule as a dark and violent regime that had now been surpassed by the "methodical tyranny" of the EIC,[139] Edmund Burke reserved the concept of despotism for British misdeeds in his parliamentary impeachment of Governor-General Warren Hastings. According to Burke, the British had trampled on a system that could not be denied a certain legitimacy and lawfulness.[140] In an analysis of the Indian political tradition that at times recalled Anquetil-Duperron (whose work Burke appears not to have known, however), Burke demolished point for point Montesquieu's theory of despotism as applied to India; needless to say, Hastings had cited Montesquieu in defense of his own contested administrative methods.[141]

In 1783 Burke's patron and comrade-in-arms, the leading opposition politician Charles James Fox, went so far as to call EIC policy under Hastings "a despotism unmatched in all the histories of the world."[142] British assertions on the structure of the Mughal Empire were henceforth guided by the question of how the newcomers viewed the last power to have unified the greater part of the subcontinent under its scepter. The further back into the past the rule of the great Mughal emperors reached, the more calmly it could be contemplated. Here two tendencies stood opposed to each other. On the one hand, the terrors of the old despotism were kept alive for pedagogical reasons, to inculcate an attitude of gratitude in the Indians for the joyful present.[143] On the other hand, negative judgments were concentrated on the petty tyrants of recent memory—including the sultan of Mysore and the Maratha Peshwas—who had been the target of military operations during the hot phase of British colonization. The more negatively such enemies were portrayed, the more justified measures to unseat them from their thrones could be made to appear. The glory years of the Mughal dynasty were swallowed up in a fog of nostalgia. The fact that Lord Wellesley, the aggressive conqueror, had grandiose and extremely expensive government buildings erected in Calcutta during his governor-generalship was partly motivated by the desire to assert British power on an imperial scale.[144]

It took several more decades, however, before Britannia came into the symbolic as well as territorial inheritance of the Mughals. This first occurred when Queen Victoria was proclaimed empress of India in 1877. Three related visions of how India should be governed were mooted in the period from 1790 to 1830, roughly:

(1) the late Enlightenment idea, represented by the governor-general Lord Cornwallis (in office from 1786–93), the creator of the Permanent Settlement and the colonial bureaucracy, that

personal despotic rule should be replaced by the impersonal rule of law;[145]

(2) opposed to this, the romantic idea, arising in the circle around Lord Wellesley among men like Sir John Malcolm, Sir Thomas Munro, and Mountstuart Elphinstone, that charismatic white leaders and "uncrowned kings" should place themselves at the head of loyal native followings, seeking through a kind of dynamic despotism to catch up with the processes of state formation that had already occurred in early modern Europe;[146]

(3) the idea, promoted by the historian and EIC official James Mill and fellow proponents of utilitarianism or "philosophical radicalism," that the residues of native despotism should be eliminated as quickly as possible; through "a revolution masterminded by skilfull administrators," a temporary British dictatorship would introduce Indians to the benefits of the most valuable (i.e., not all) Western civilizational achievements.[147]

Each of these three models of rulership was trialed at different times in various regions of India.

DESPOTISM WITH CHINESE CHARACTERISTICS

China played an altogether different role in the late eighteenth-century European discourse on despotism. In China, unlike in India, the ancien régime was still intact. Compared with the Ottoman Empire, it had been much less affected by influences from the West. At this point, nobody seriously entertained the idea of military intervention in China, let alone colonial subjugation. The political dimension of discussions on China lay in the fact that here, even in the early nineteenth century, an "eastern" political system appeared neither to be destabilized from within nor to face military threats from without. Two uniquely Chinese characteristics were obvious: on the one hand, imperial rule there was not a foreign import but a two-thousand-year-old product of indigenous culture;

after 1644, the Manchus had introduced reforms to stabilize the system, eliminating structural defects such as the inordinate power wielded by court eunuchs.[148] On the other hand, this long history led to a series of real rulers (as portrayed in the gallery of Confucian historiography) merging into a composite image of the archetypal emperor: the mythical ideal emperors of the early period, decadent monsters,[149] violent dynasty founders, and tyrants such as the first emperors of the Qin (Qin Shi Huangdi, r. 221–210 BCE) and the Ming (Hongwu, r. 1368–98), as well as the wise Tang emperor Taizong (r. 626–49), who struck Johann Heinrich Gottlob von Justi as a paragon of monarchical "moderation"—and of course the active autocrats of the Qing Dynasty: Kangxi, Yongzheng, and Qianlong.[150]

The path from "Sinophilia" at the start of the eighteenth century to "Sinophobia" at its end has been charted on numerous occasions in recent Western literature on China.[151] Even if the texts do not permit us to reconstruct this trajectory in all its particulars, there may be something to it. Only the Jesuits (and their fierce critic, the Dominican Domingo Fernández Navarette) had produced in-depth accounts of the Chinese political system. Du Halde's 1735 encyclopedia of China remained the authoritative source for the remainder of the century. Every assessment of the country, whether positive or negative, was overwhelmingly based on the material assembled there. With the exception of Gemelli Careri, no private travelers reported back from the Middle Kingdom, while most participants in diplomatic missions glimpsed only the externals of court life, relying for all other information on what the Jesuits told them. In the late Ming period, Jesuits had drawn a rather anonymous picture of a static system. During the turbulent and bloody midcentury dynastic overthrow, the raw forces of history—Hegel's "elemental-historical"—had intruded to force a revision of this hieratic perspective. Once the turmoil had subsided, the three great Manchu emperors Kangxi, Yongzheng, and Qianlong ushered in a new era when a perfected bureaucracy was combined in the ruler's person with the charisma of office.

This combination is reflected in Du Halde. In his account, the political system of the Qing period is neither an unbridled despotism nor an authoritarian bureaucracy where the emperor acts as a kind of king in council.[152] Du Halde, partly following his fellow Jesuit Louis Le Comte,[153] develops the following theses on Chinese political order and political culture under the Kangxi and Yongzheng emperors:

(1) The emperor's power is "absolute and almost unlimited"; he exercises it personally as an active autocrat. There are no regional potentates who could potentially stand in his way; the imperial princes have little opportunity to assert their independence from the throne (in obvious contrast to the Mughal Empire).[154]
(2) The emperor's power is nonetheless restrained in its execution by:
   - written laws;
   - the emperor's concern for his public image and for how posterity will judge him;
   - the ideology of paternalism, which expects the emperor to treat his subjects with the stern benevolence of a paterfamilias;[155]
   - the independent Censorate, a bureaucratic agency whose officials could criticize their colleagues and even the emperor and his court in the name of the public good;[156]
   - the tradition of successful popular uprisings against unworthy emperors.
(3) The generally meritocratic examinations for entry into the civil service guarantee the high quality of the bureaucracy.[157]
(4) Mandarins have almost absolute power over the population in matters of civil law. There is nonetheless a measure of protection against malfeasance and incompetence in that unrests are initially blamed on the official in whose administrative district they break out.[158] He is therefore well advised to make sure they do not arise in the first place.

In Du Halde, as indeed in all the literature on China, one searches in vain for vivid evocations of Caesarean madness. (In Southeast Asia too, incidentally, there was only one true homicidal maniac on a throne after the mid-eighteenth century: King Bodawpaya of Burma, who reigned from 1782 to 1819).[159] Chinese despotism thus never exercised the European imagination in the same way as its Iranian or Ottoman counterparts. Readers had to be satisfied with stories that were more amusing than horrifying, like the following tale told by Pater Amiot in 1752: the Qianlong emperor wanted to celebrate his mother's sixtieth birthday with a festive boat ride on a canal. When the day dawned unexpectedly cold, thousands of Chinese were ordered to keep stirring the water to prevent it from freezing over.[160]

Du Halde's solid compendium inspired several European authors, above all French physiocrats from the circle around François Quesnay, to extravagant idealizations of the system they found described there. Their enthusiasm was so palpably implausible that it could not fail to provoke a Sinophobic reaction—from Cornelius de Pauw, for example, who argued the exact opposite. Yet when Christoph Meiners claimed in 1796 that Chinese despotism was the worst in the world,[161] this was no less absurd than earlier declarations that, in modern China, the utopia of wise philosopher-kings had finally been realized.[162] The debate on China conducted during the second half of the eighteenth century, principally in France, was less grounded in reality and less specific than contemporary European discussions of India or the Ottoman Empire. A question of the utmost political significance that could also be subjected to empirical examination, such as the problem of landed property in India, was missing in the Chinese context.[163] Whereas the topic in India was how knowledge of the country could be applied to the benefit of its *own* colonial administration, discussion of China remained stuck on the old question of whether *Europe* had anything to learn from the Middle Kingdom. Even in the nineteenth century, this question was not (yet) answered with a simple "no"; the model of China played a certain role in the introduction of civil service examinations in Great Britain, for example.[164] But after the tempering of European monarchies in the phase of enlightened absolutism, and with the waning in importance of patriarchal ideas in European political theory, the Chinese model seemed to be of continuing relevance only in relatively minor areas such as the agricultural arts and the moral-philosophical foundations of politics.

By the end of the great eighteenth-century debate on China, there was widespread agreement that China should not be considered a clear case of despotism; Montesquieu himself had already expressed reservations on this score.[165] What else was at issue? The Jesuits' last word (almost) came in the form of the abbé Grosier's precise description of the country's public administration. Grosier went far beyond the old schemata for categorizing despotism and completely ignored the big typological concepts of political theory.[166] Neither of the two diplomatic missions from the 1790s yielded fundamentally new information on China's political system.

Sir John Barrow was usually not one to pass up an opportunity to berate the Chinese for their civilizational backwardness. Yet apart from pointing out the usual malpractices (especially corruption), even he found little to criticize in their political order, which he labeled by the conventional name of despotism. He even paid China some surprising compliments: the press was as free there as in England, and there was no censorship. Despotism may have broken the bonds of solidarity between men, but at least it had gifted the country a long period of peace. Although the emperor was nominally regarded as the proprietor of all lands, Chinese farmers and tenants were de facto in secure possession of their fields and landholdings. Markets were free; there were hardly any monopolies. No feudal hunting and fishing privileges or other seigneurial rights barred access to lakes, rivers, and the sea. Taxes were low and were sensibly regulated.[167] In fact, Barrow found very little that was objectionable in the Chinese constitution; he considered it to be essentially rational in design. While it never occurred to him that it might have lessons to teach Europe, he also did not find it particularly alien and "oriental." For the majority of the population, it was even quite bearable. Lord Macartney arrived at a similarly even-tempered judgment. But he perceived the very real fissures in the system more clearly than his subordinate on the mission to China, and he saw that the concentration of power in a single person would turn from a blessing into a curse once the empire passed into the hands of a less capable monarch.[168]

The last great analysis of China to stand under the impression of the magnificent High Qing comes from an author who, like Barrow, adopted a fundamentally critical attitude towards China and who, far excelling Barrow in his knowledge of the land and its language, was taken by the (ex-)Jesuits to be the most dangerous besmircher of China's good name: Chrétien Louis Joseph de Guignes.[169] The son of the famous Orientalist had first visited Peking in 1784 with the Lazarists, the Jesuits' successors in the China mission, and he went on to spend many years representing France in Canton. He accompanied the Dutch Titsingh/Van Braam embassy of 1794/95 as an interpreter before returning to France in 1800. As a Sinologist—he was commissioned by Napoleon to publish a Chinese dictionary (1813)—and long-serving diplomat, he was something like the French counterpart to Sir George Thomas Staunton, then junior member of the Macartney Mission and founding father of British Sinology.

De Guignes eschews the concept of despotism. In his chapter on China's government, he is concerned in the first instance with analyzing its most conspicuous feature: bureaucratic management. At the center of his analysis stands not the emperor but the roughly two-thousand-strong corps of high "mandarins" who administered the empire and held it together. The paternalistic rhetoric that the Jesuits had always taken at face value interests this nonnormative author only in its functionality: the veneration of the *chef de l'empire* by his subjects must be kept alive through constant indoctrination and propaganda.[170] The achievements of the Chinese political system—the preservation of peace, public welfare, and territorial integrity—depended entirely on the quality of the officials, and the principal task of the imperial centers was to ensure that this quality was maintained. De Guignes expressed more clearly than anyone before him that good laws and the Chinese version of an "ancient constitution" posited by a number of authors were not enough, that governing China was a gigantic management task requiring constant vigilance. For all the lip service paid to Confucian ethics, officials were structurally corrupt and tended to tyrannize those under their jurisdiction. A strong central authority was therefore needed to keep the machinery of state in good working order. Just as Barrow and Macartney had already warned of a "revolution" in China, so de Guignes recommended that China not press for Western-style reforms. These would only prove unsuitable, for "it is impossible to govern Asians in the same way as Europeans."[171] To say this about noncolonial China was to argue for the continuation of native despotism; to say it about colonial India was to urge the new, enlightened masters to occupy the positions left vacant by the despots of old.

THE OTTOMAN EMPIRE: PRAETORIAN GUARDS AND PAPER TIGERS

So far as the political system of the Ottoman Empire was concerned, neither an attitude of retrospective nostalgia (as in the case of Mughal India) nor one of wonderment at the survival of a unique form of premodern governance (as in the Chinese case) was possible around 1800. The legitimacy and stability of Ottoman rule palpably affected the foreign policy of the European great powers in the area between North Africa and the Persian Gulf. The Russo-Turkish War of 1768–74 had ended with a crushing defeat for the Sublime Porte. The territories surrendered and concessions granted to Russia in the peace treaty of Küçük Kaynarca (1774) were so considerable that historians conventionally take it to mark the beginning of the Ottoman Empire's decline from great power status to a rump state capable only of acting in its own defense. In the process of mental distancing by which everything Turkish was excluded from a European community of values, the question of whether despotism prevailed in the Ottoman Empire no longer played a primary role. The most important differentiating criterion was not any lack of freedom in the sultan's realm but rather its "civilizational," technological, and economic backwardness with regard to the likes of France and England. Volney was one of many who held this view.

All the same, Volney believed that despotism was an essential *cause* of these retrograde conditions. In his pamphlet *Considérations sur la guerre actuelle des Turcs* (*Reflections on the Current War of the Turks*, 1788), a kind of addendum to his travel report from the previous year, he juxtaposed the old, decadent, and enfeebled Ottoman Empire with the young and dynamic great power Russia, advising the French Foreign Ministry to relinquish its traditional pro-Ottoman stance in favor of a free trade policy and diplomatic (but not military) support of the tsarist regime. The tsarina acknowledged his efforts with a medal, which he felt obliged to return in 1791 following his conversion to revolutionary activism.[172]

Volney was far less interested in the formal organization of power than in a regime's tangible effects on the people over which it ruled. In his travel report from 1787, he had defined despotism as a situation in which "the mass of inhabitants is subjected to the will of a faction of armed men, who treat them according to their own interest and pleasure," citing Ottoman rule in Syria as his prime example.[173] In the *Considérations* as well, he spoke of Turkish despotism as a matter of common knowledge. While conceding that the tsarist empire likewise displayed despotic features, he contended that their consequences were far less devastating. He thereby ignored the judicial line of argument that had played a growing role in the discourse on despotism since Anquetil-Duperron, at the latest. A response to the *Considérations* was promptly fired off by a proponent of this tendency, the consul Charles de Peyssonnel (*fils*), whom we have already met as the chivalrous defender of the Crimean Tatars. Peyssonnel insisted that there was a full-fledged despotism in Russia because the sovereign there stood above the law, whereas in the Ottoman Empire the sultan was subjected to a "code of theocratic laws." On the theme of unfreedom, he remarked in passing that the Turkish soldier was in principle a free man, while his Russian opponent remained a serf and chattel.[174] The consul also took the opportunity to parry Volney's frontal attack on Turkish "barbarism." Thus where Volney, like many before him, blames the Turks for destroying the monuments of classical antiquity, Peyssonnel counters that the Crusaders, the Venetians, the Genoese, and the modern Greeks had also played their part. Had the Turks destroyed Hagia Sophia? And should today's French be held accountable for the ruinous state of the Arena of Nîmes?[175]

Peyssonnel's attempt to salvage the honor of Ottoman culture and the Turkish national character was anachronistic even at the time. It never stood a chance of a fair hearing; his voice was soon drowned out in the chorus of philhellenes baying for revenge against the devilish Turk. On the other hand, however, the revisionist view of the sultan's supposedly lawless and uninhibited autocracy largely carried the day. Montesquieu had presented the Ottoman Empire as an extreme example of the unification of all state powers in a single person, a leviathan that denied its citizens even basic legal protections or the right of redress.[176] The Ottoman Empire seemed further to confirm the "monolith thesis" put forward by the classical theory of despotism, according to which despotic government was marked by an absence of balancing forces. Yet doubt was cast on this thesis through a comparison of specific systems of rule. Cracks were opening up in the smooth façade of Montesquieu's ideal type.

As Hegel recognized more clearly than most,[177] nowhere were the forces working against the sovereign's supreme power weaker than in eighteenth-century China, where there was neither a church nor semiautonomous regional magnates, and where the famous Censorate was always overruled in cases of doubt. For all that, most observers agreed that China was an unusually well-governed, internally peaceful country. The Mughal emperor may not have had a strong Islamic priesthood to contend with, yet he still had to negotiate with the grandees of his empire, as Voltaire rightly maintained against Montesquieu, making the occasional compromise inevitable. Princely revolts were also a structural element of the system. By comparison, the sultan in Istanbul was even more hemmed in.

Voltaire was not the first to point out that hardly any sultans were able to assert effective control over their own infantry units, the Janissaries (Yeniçeri); indeed, many were deposed or even assassinated by this elite guard. Frequently, Voltaire observes, the sultan may terrorize his household and his court with impunity, but he has little power outside the palace walls; he is the "oppressed" rather than the "oppresser."[178] The position of sultan was thus far more precarious than that of a European monarch. "To preserve the fidelity and attachment of the Janizaries," William Robertson remarked in 1769 in his astute dissection of the Ottoman system, "was the great art of government, and the principal object of attention in the policy of the Ottoman court."[179] For long periods, revolt functioned as an ersatz form of government.[180] Along with the military, religion set limits to the sultan's power. Islam had long been regarded as a mainstay of despotism until Sir James Porter demonstrated that the sultan's ability to take unilateral action was constrained by religion and the law.[181] On the one hand, the Islamic hierarchy of the *ulema*, the religious legal scholars, had considerable potential to thwart the sultan's will; on the other, religious and secular law, which guaranteed (among other things) private ownership of landed property, was supported by people's widespread awareness of their rights and could not be violated with impunity, even by the sultan. Commoners in the Ottoman Empire should also not be imagined as a herd of slaves suffering in silent oppression. They were instead a political force to be reckoned with:

> Notwithstanding the transcendant expressions the Turks use when speaking of their Sovereign, they will frequently murmur, talk freely, abuse him and his ministers, throw anonymous scurrilous papers into the mosques, and seem ever ripe for rebellion, if outraged by frequent and unusual oppression and tyranny.[182]

The greatest European authorities of the next two generations joined Porter in emphasizing the importance of the law as a factor in preserving order. Neither Ignatius Mouradgea d'Ohsson (whom Peyssonnel had already cited in 1788 in support of his criticisms of Volney) nor Joseph von Hammer-Purgstall claimed that the Ottoman Empire had anything like a Western-style constitution enshrining habeas corpus and protecting citizens from arbitrary interference by the state. But by familiarizing European readers with the Ottoman legal system, their detailed accounts destroyed the cliché of the oriental despot as an almighty, overbearing tyrant.[183] The knowledgeable Istanbul merchant Thomas Thornton, who argued in a similar vein, called Montesquieu's "pure" despotism "a metaphysical abstraction," a theoretical construct corresponding to nothing in the real world.[184]

Montesquieu's specter of Ottoman despotism was finally put to rest during the reign of Sultan Selim III (1789–1807), a cultivated and cautious reformer.[185] Now there was little talk of despotism as a *system*. Those who still spoke of despotism *alla turca* did so more in Volney's sense, as a terroristic and retrograde *praxis* that arose from time to time. Turkey's problem, according to some of the leading experts on the country, was not so much an excess of autocracy as the lack of a truly enlightened despot. Mouradgea d'Ohsson, the great authority on conditions in Turkey, yearned in 1788 for what the Ottomans' enemies had long feared: "a superior mind, a wise Sultan, enlightened and vigorous," who could jump-start the country into modernity.[186] In 1798 Bonaparte believed that this could be his own role, at least in Egypt, where the French, as Marshall G. S. Hodgson put it, "set up as much as they could of the apparatus of the Enlightenment": a modern state, hospitals, scientific laboratories, and so on.[187]

EX OCCIDENTE LUX

The theory of despotism as a degenerate form of government has a pedigree that can be traced back to ancient Greece. The idea that a violently autocratic form of government was better suited to Asia than to Europe had already arisen among Hellenic authors. In the early modern period—in Jean Bodin, for example—the concept of despotism fitted into a universal taxonomy of constitutions that was no longer (or not yet) aligned with the binary opposition between East and West. Such a dichotomy first became prevalent through Montesquieu's ideal-typical contrast between monarchy and despotism. This could also be interpreted, in a more strongly normative reading than that proposed by Montesquieu himself, as an opposition between legitimate and illegitimate rule. Such an interpretation met with protest from figures such as Voltaire, Burke, and Gibbon, who warned in the name of historical experience and practical reason against a one-sided ideological appropriation of the concept.[188] Their arguments found support among experts who, at a time when it was almost impossible to find any actual rulers in the Orient who lived up to their generic reputation for monstrous tyranny, offered detailed refutations of the theory of despotism: Sir James Porter, Abraham-Hyacinthe Anquetil-Duperron, Claude Charles de Peyssonnel, Ignatius Mouradgea d'Ohsson, C. W. Boughton Rouse, the abbé Grosier, and others. While this counterattack could not be faulted on its own terms, from around the 1780s it flew in the face of the most pressing political issues and the intellectual climate of the day. The topics of chief concern were now the organization of colonial India, the expected breakup of the Ottoman Empire, and the gradual erosion of the social and political system in China. Legal and constitutional questions faded into the background. More important was the alleged *civilizational* split between East and West.

The polemically slimmed-down concept of despotism that Volney introduced into the debate proved ideally suited to this new situation. Arbitrary rule, ignorance, and administrative-economic mismanagement were compressed into a modernized cliché of barbarianism that made up for in propaganda value what it lacked in theoretical sophistication. It became the basis for the rhetoric of liberation that, following the final war against Tipu Sultan and the French invasion of Egypt in 1798, would accompany every subsequent intervention by a European great power in Asia and Africa. This presupposed that the old Montesquieuean environmental and climatic determinism had been abandoned and a new anthropological-racist reductionism had not yet been embraced. The Orient was by no means condemned to eternal bondage through heat and the weakness of the "oriental character." Despotism, Sir William Jones declared in 1792, was the decisive difference between Asia and Europe, and its elimination would usher in a new dawn for the Asiatic nations.[189] The peoples of the Orient were capable of being free, just not of freeing themselves. Freedom had to come from outside. Europeans even took the provisional measure of installing themselves as modernizing despots and *législateurs*: at first in India, then elsewhere. By the Napoleonic era, the Enlightenment discourse on despotism was thus being used to justify an emancipatory imperialism that believed itself to be a temporary expedient, and was still some way removed from the later doctrine that the European master race had a God-given mandate to rule in perpetuity over its racial inferiors.

XI

Societies

At the very commencement of the present dynasty [of the Tokugawa shoguns, 1603–1868] the government made regulations as salutary as the welfare of the state, the happiness of the people and the maintenance of order in the interior of the empire required. The active spirit of the Japanese could not fail to seek new objects, and by degrees their attention was turned to the establishment of fixed bases of all the observances due to each individual, according to his station in the different circumstances of life. So that everyone might have precise rules for the government of his conduct towards others of every class, from the highest to the lowest.

—Isaac Titsingh (1745–1812), *Illustrations of Japan*[1]

This observation made by Isaac Titsingh, a high-ranking official of the VOC who spent forty-four months in Tokugawa Japan during the years 1779 to 1784 and went on to become one of the earliest European japanologists, stands at the end of a long tradition of seeing Western and Eastern countries within a single and common framework, a framework shared by the elites of many Asian societies themselves. One might call it "the primacy of political power." Once the rulers—whether despots or feudal monarchs—had established peace and set down basic laws, a space opened up where their subjects could follow their interests and indulge their passions. When they had nothing else to do, they ordered the relations among themselves in hierarchical systems of rank and protocol. In others words: they invented society.

SOLIDARITY AMONG THE CIVILIZED

In the 1740s Montesquieu hit upon the idea of not just describing political conditions by their system of organization—their "form," as he called it—but also of positing a uniform "principle" that provides the entire community with a point of mental orientation. With that, the step from the constitutional theory of the Aristotelian tradition to political sociology had been taken. In a monarchy it is honor—in a despotism fear—that defines the moral climate of a society and shapes interpersonal relations outside the political sphere. Montesquieu and others further assumed that under a despotism, absolute relations of command and submission were reproduced at every level of social life. The organizing "principle" was diffused throughout a society, which is why the harem, for example, could be taken as a microcosm of the political system. In his *Lettres persanes*, Montesquieu had already presented the world of the harem, with its hierarchically scaffolded arrangement of possessive overlord, watchful eunuchs, and dependent women, as a model of power relations in general. The structure of the state was replicated in that of the seraglio.

These were important insights, but they were still a very blunt instrument for describing actual social relations. In other parts of *De l'esprit des lois*, Montesquieu himself developed concepts and hypotheses that came closer to an adequate descriptive account of forms of socialization. His most comprehensive umbrella term for this is the "esprit général" of any particular nation. This general spirit consists of a nation's "climate, religion, laws, the maxims of the government, examples of past things, mores, and manners."[2] The relative influence of these factors varies from case to case. *Mœurs* (mores) and *manières* (manners and customs) are "universal" institutions that have sprung up organically, so to speak. No recognizable foundational intent lies behind them, whereas *lois* (laws) spring from the active will of a legislator:

> The difference between laws and mores is that, while laws regulate the actions of the citizen, mores regulate the actions of the man. The

> difference between mores and manners is that the first are more concerned with internal, and the latter external, conduct.[3]

Montesquieu then offers a series of reflections on the relationship between laws, mores, and manners. Chinese civilization strikes him as unique because all three aspects coincide there, with religion fitting harmoniously into the picture as a fourth factor. This multilayered, tightly integrated system of values was practically unassailable, as all previous invaders had discovered; conquered China took captive her savage conquerors. At the same time, this made it almost impossible for the country to be converted to Christianity, as Montesquieu clearly recognized.[4] There were very few cracks in the civilizational edifice where a cultural aggressor could secure a grappling hook.

For something like a "sociological" prespective, no category is more important than that of *mœurs*. They are the social code regulating *private* life; they pertain to the lives of individuals as *hommes*, not as politically active *citoyens*. They differ from conventionally mandated forms of social conduct, *manières*, in that they steer the inner motivations of human beings. Although only a few authors from the second half of the eighteenth century adhered to Montesquieu's narrow and precise concept of *mœurs*, his terminological proposals had opened up the possibility of apprehending society in its totality.[5] The point is not to claim Montesquieu as an ancestor of modern Western sociology. He was more than that: the creator of a general framework of a general social science. Few writers of the second half of the eighteenth century were entirely free from his influence, however indirect and refracted it may have been.

It is important to note that Montesquieu considered his categories to be universally valid. The division between Europe and the Orient, which played so important a role in his theory of despotism, was irrelevant to his social theory. He never refers in broadbrush terms to "Asiatic society," as would become commonplace in the nineteenth century. He also never plays off a specific concept of anthropology as the science of "them," the exotic others, against something like "sociology" as the science of "us."

Montesquieuean social theory is transcultural and universal, comparative and counter-teleological, empirical and nonnormative. Societies in all civilizations are studied as they are or as they appear to be; they are not assigned to one of the stages preordained for them by a philosophy of progress.

Montesquieu is as much the cofounder as the symptom of an eighteenth-century intellectual movement that went beyond the mere collection and classification of ethnographic data to inquire into the always-specific rules governing human communal life. Collating curiosities and *variétes d'hommes* from all the world's cultures, as the Nuremberg encyclopedist Erasmus Francisci had done with great flair in the seventeenth century and as the Scottish polymath Lord Kames was still doing in 1778, was no longer enough.[6] On the other hand, the constitutive idea of modern anthropology still lay in the future: the idea that human communities, particularly those of a "primitive" nature, can be characterized by their kinship networks. Montesquieu does not yet employ the concept of society that would be introduced by nineteenth-century sociology and is still familiar to us today. In the few passages where he speaks of *société*, he has in mind—in keeping with contemporary usage—"the fact of human interconnectedness as such,"[7] that is, the opposite of the *vita solitaria*, asocial solitude. All this does nothing to alter the fact that in Montesquieu, as in those who followed in his footsteps, there begins to emerge a synthesizing approach to material culture and rule-governed coexistence in entities like "peoples" or "nations."

Such an approach to non-Western societies was attempted on numerous occasions in the eighteenth century. It would be unfair to label them all categorically as "savage anthropology."[8] While this term may accurately describe Steller's account of the Itelmen on Kamchatka, for example, European commentaries on the social hierarchy in China, say, or the Indian caste system have nothing specifically anthropological about them. Within the realm of literate, agrarian high civilizations, something like solidarity among the civilized was the order of the day. Non-European societies were drawn into the interpretive horizon of what was, in principle, already familiar. They might be alien, but they were still comparable to what was known. It was not until the mid-nineteenth century that theories of a uniquely "oriental society" or "Asiatic mode of production" began to arise.[9]

CITIES

For most Europeans, cities were their first experience of Asia: above all, harbor towns such as Istanbul/Constantinople, Alexandria, Goa, Surat, Calcutta, Batavia, Macao, Canton, or Nagasaki. If these places had anything in common, then it was not some quintessentially Asiatic trait but an ethnic and cultural heterogeneity that was nowhere to be found in Europe at the time. Apart from Canton and especially Nagasaki, where they were prevented from mingling with the local population, Europeans formed just one element in a medley of skin colors, customs, and religions. Many of these trading hubs were migrant cities. Commerce lay less in the hands of a long-established local merchant class than in those of diaspora groups. Even in Canton, where the local Chinese were known for their business acumen and controlled the trade routes with Southeast Asia, Captain Krusenstern could observe in 1805:

> Canton is particularly interesting to strangers as a great commercial mart, on account of the people assembled here from all parts of the globe. Besides Europeans of all nations, there are people of all the trading countries of Asia: Americans, Mahomedans, Hindostanees, Bengales, Parsees, &c. Most of these come by sea from India to Canton, and return in the same manner. Many have their agents at Canton, and remain constantly there, and do not, as the Europeans, pass the summer at Macao.[10]

As a Baltic German in Russian service, and thus not directly involved in the Canton trade, Krusenstern does not overlook the Asian communities in the south Chinese port city, as Western European travelers tended to do. These were even more firmly entrenched as they were there all year round.

Much the same could be said of most of the other great trading centers of Asia, including those in the interior of the continent such as Peshawar, whose colorful street life was memorably described by Mountstuart Elphinstone following his visit there in 1809.[11] In Asiatic cities, religious tolerance was more the rule than the exception. It exceeded what was considered acceptable by European standards. In Turkish Smyrna in the 1670s, well before John Locke wrote his *Essay on Toleration* (1689), there were seven synagogues, three Catholic, three Greek Orthodox, and two Armenian churches as well as a chapel in the English, Dutch, and Genoese consulates.[12] A spirit of commercial enterprise and religious openness fostered the virtue of urbanity, which European observers were far from claiming as a monopoly. Alexander Hamilton, for example, took it to be particularly characteristic of the Arabs in Muscat, while Samuel Turner found it even in Bhutan, a land completely cut off from Western influence.[13]

Other than multiculturalism, oriental cities had few things in common that distinguished them from cities in Europe. In the eighteenth century, the great metropolises of Asia—Istanbul, Cairo, Peking, and Edo (Tokyo)—were unmistakably larger and more populous than their European rivals, London excepted. More remarkable still, there were a great many second-tier cities, especially in China, Japan, and parts of India. In China alone, according to Pater Le Comte, there were more than eighty towns the size of Lyon or Bordeaux. In 1696 he described a phenomenon that had yet to exist anywhere in Europe: urban sprawl on the lower reaches of the Yangzi River.[14] Transportation in Asiatic cities relied to a lesser extent on noisy horse-drawn carriages. Partly for this reason, there were fewer paved roads. Whereas European cities before the era of civic planning seemed to grow in higgledy-piggledy fashion, many Asiatic cities gave the impression of having been carefully set out. This was particularly true of Peking, which provided the model for most other Chinese cities with its quadratic layout. If you had seen one Chinese city, Du Halde maintained, you had seen them all.[15]

Ayudhya, the capital of Siam, was notable for its checkerboard grid of streets and canals.[16] In theory if not always in practice, cities in the Ottoman Empire were set out in concentric circles around the main market and Great Mosque. In the Islamic East, the harmony of architecture, pleasure gardens, and fountains occasionally caught the traveler's eye. This helped gain places like Damascus, Agra, or Isfahan (before its devastation by the Afghans in 1722) their reputation as earthly paradises. In the Orient, more of life was lived outdoors than in Europe, at any rate north of the Alps. The lively social atmosphere in streets and squares was often seen, described, and occasionally admired by travelers, as was the rare appearance of women in such public spaces. Finally, there were numerous comments about the excellent "policing" of oriental cities.[17]

Most descriptions of cities were impressionistic. Occasionally a solid topographical and architectural description was furnished, such as the account of Isfahan given by Chardin or that of Peking provided by the geographers Delisle and Pingré on the basis of Jesuit reports.[18] Travelers like Thévenot or Niebuhr, who were unusually interested in the everday life of ordinary people, made richly detailed observations in laneways and markets. But only a few Europeans, mostly long-term residents of a particular city, were granted a glimpse behind the façade. Sociological analyses of a specific urban society were therefore rare. Even rarer were investigations that heeded the advice once proffered by Bernier: to observe cities not in isolation but in connection with their environment.[19] Samuel Gottlieb Gmelin carried off this feat superbly with his description of Astrakhan.[20]

BATAVIA'S COLONIAL SOCIOLOGY

A sociology of urban life could most easily be venutured where a large expatriate community allowed for greater ease of access. This was above all the case in Batavia. The capital of the VOC's Asian empire was particularly interesting owing to its Janus face. On the one hand, it represented the attempt to replicate a Dutch townscape in the tropics. This gave rise, as the abbé Raynal inferred from several travel reports, to "one of the most beautiful cities in the world."[21] Magnificent coaches were as common here as in the cities of Europe.[22] On the other hand, the Dutch colonialists had succumbed in their everyday life to what many saw as the corrupting influence of the equatorial climate and the Javanese environment. Of the ten thousand Europeans in Batavia, the abbé remarks again, around four thousand had "degenerated to a point that beggars belief."[23] Morally upright visitors from the motherland such as the physician Nicolaas de Graaff, who came out to Batavia several times between 1640 and 1687 and described Batavian society at length and in great detail, were appalled by the worldly splendor and dissipation they encountered there among the Dutch: at the mistresses they kept and the bevy of Eurasian children they sired, at the way they embraced native customs such as the chewing of betel by Dutch ladies, at the idleness and ignorance of the womenfolk, and at their excessive cruelty towards slaves, who were expected to perform all manual labor.[24] Moreover, says de Graaf, Batavia is a popular refuge for good-for-nothings, loafers, bankrupts, failed students, and other dissolute elements who may expect to obtain a comfortable job in the colonial army where they are unlikely ever to see serious military action.[25]

De Graaff's pioneering work of colonial sociology condenses the impressions of earlier travelers into a synoptic image. Visitors in the eighteenth century, such as Pierre Poivre in the 1740s, essentially confirm the good doctor's account of a mestizo society far removed from European models and standards of propriety. Through their foreignness, social relations in Batavia seemed especially suited to awaken a sociographical need. Those who came directly from Europe were greeted, not by the authentic strangeness they might have expected upon first landing in Asia, but by the often shockingly unexpected estrangement of an ethnically diverse class society operating against a Dutch late baroque backdrop. By the late eighteenth century, malaria and the decline of VOC trade in Asia had so sapped the vitality of the European population that the whites in Batavia, a town that struck Captain Cook in 1770 as a filthy, stinking hotbed of disease,[26] gave the impression of having been given the kiss of death.[27]

The members of the Macartney Mission, who stopped off at Batavia in March 1793 on their way to China, were alarmed to see Madeira, port wine, Bordeaux, and Dutch beer flowing in unhealthy quantities even over the breakfast table. They doubted the will to survive of a colonial community that recalled the later Roman Empire in its corruption and sybaritic excess.[28] Sir George L. Staunton described this culturally hybrid class with the disdainful condescension shown by an aggressively expansionist imperial power, convinced of its God-given civilizing mission, towards the betrayal of their civilization and race by those whose continuing rule rested exclusively on habit, bluff, and the ethnic and therefore political fragmentation of their colonial underlings: "The features and outlines of their faces are European; but the complexion, character, and mode of life, approach more to those of the native inhabitants of Java."[29] There was no sign here of solidarity among "whites." The sympathies of the British observers lay mainly with the local Chinese, who, although almost entirely without rights and constantly threatened with a recurrence of the great massacre of 1740, had energetically taken in hand the colony's economic life and much of its foreign trade. The Chinese were hardworking, frugal, and family-minded; they displayed a proto-capitalist mentality and morality that, notwithstanding their weakness for opium and gambling, was more appealing to the British middle and upper classes than the decadent slovenliness of the Dutch colonial burghers. During the Napoleonic wars in 1811, when Sir Stamford Raffles assumed temporary command of Java as lieutenant-governor, it was not the Javans or Chinese who were the object of a British civilizing mission but the Dutch expatriates, whose poor example had long tarnished Europe's reputation in Asian eyes.

CLOSE-UP: URBAN LIFE IN SYRIAN ALEPPO

No Asiatic colonial metropolis, not even Calcutta, Bombay, or Madras, attracted greater sociological interest in the eighteenth century than Batavia. Outside the colonies, few Europeans could gain sufficient insight into the everyday life of the various groups of a given urban population to paint a social portrait of a city.[30] In any event, the statistical data and sociological concepts drawn on by researchers today were unavailable at the time.[31] All the more remarkable is the comprehensive *Natural History of Aleppo* by the Scottish physician Alexander Russell, published in 1756. A considerably enlarged edition appeared in 1794, edited and expanded by Patrick Russell, who in 1753 had succeeded his half-brother as physician in the British factory in the Syrian city while Alexander was off in India making a name for himself as an expert on snakes.[32] The project met with considerable interest and support. Samuel Johnson praised the first edition, while Johann Friedrich Gmelin, a scion of the famous Swabian dynasty of scholars, translated the second into German.[33] Carsten Niebuhr, Sir Joseph Banks, and Daniel Solander assisted Patrick Russell, a friend of Sir William Jones, William Robertson, and Adam Smith, in his revision of Alexander's text. The concept of a "natural" history encompassed not only descriptions of climate, minerals, plants, and animals but also of urban society in all its aspects and ramifications. What it left out were monuments and antiquities—the subject matter of most Western accounts of oriental cities.

The Russell brothers were among the most methodologically careful writers on Asia of their time. Alexander had lived in Aleppo from 1740 to 1753, Patrick from 1750 to 1772. Their wealth of experience by no means predisposed them to offer generalizations about the Ottoman Empire, let alone the Orient as such. Alexander instead emphasized in his foreword to the first edition that the author's knowledge was "confined to one city and its environs only."[34] For all that they recognized the achievements of their predecessors, the two siblings identified the weakness of much of the earlier literature in the fact that observations of one place—

Istanbul, for example—had too quickly been ascribed a more general validity. Furthermore, neither the distinctions between "the different orders of society" nor the changes in "national manners" over time had been given due consideration. The widespread view that nothing ever changed in the Orient stood in the way of an unprejudiced perception of reality.[35] Such an awareness of the spatial, temporal, and social specificity of all observations stood opposed to fashionable, all-encompassing theories about a supposedly immobile and immutable East.

The Russells had a keen eye for the limited perspectives and prejudices of traveling Europeans. They were particularly mistrustful of the numerous Christian monks and pilgrims who hastened through Syria on their way to the Holy Land. They were well aware that only their own medical profession gave them access to a wider variety of milieux than was glimpsed by the ordinary traveler. This in turn allowed them to transform a monograph on the plague-ridden town's flora, fauna, and epidemiological circumstances—Alexander's original intention[36]—into a far more ambitious social panorama of Aleppo. Of the 235,000 residents in 1753 (in Russell's estimation—more recent research has cut the figure in half)[37] there were only fifteen colleagues in the English factory along with eight British private households, reduced to four by 1772. The factory doctor thus had plenty of time left over to pay calls on local patients.[38] Above all, the physicians were granted access to a number of the city's harems, a sphere that otherwise remained totally off-limits to foreigners.

The work begins with an exceptionally careful description of the city: its streets and its squares, its buildings and its gardens, its climate and its supply of food from the surrounding countryside. Readers are guided methodically through the town and its agricultural hinterland, enabling them to paint a mental picture of Aleppo. The following sociographical chapters initially deal with "the inhabitants in general" (their demographic distribution, languages, appearance, clothing, social life) before examining individual ethnoreligious groups in greater detail: Muslims, "Franks," native Christians, and Jews. The Russells do not restrict themselves to describing local customs, although this is what interests them most.

They also inform readers about the city's economic context as well as dedicating a long chapter to Turkish civic governance. In the "thickness" of their description, the sections on Europeans in Aleppo recall the best attempts at a colonial sociology of Batavia from de Graaff to Thunberg. The chapters on native milieux, meanwhile, are unique in eighteenth-century literature on Asia. Only the incomparable Chardin comes close, and Kaempfer could perhaps have achieved something similar on Japan had he been allowed to see more of the country. The same level of descriptive detail would not be reached until Sir Stamford Raffles's description of Java from 1817 and the abbé Dubois's book on India from the same year.

Even if the Russells cannot conceal their distaste for a range of Aleppan peculiarities, from the style of beard worn by the men to the obscenity of the puppet theater and the oppression of the peasantry,[39] they still strive for a stance of objectivity and scholarly neutrality. There is hardly any negative stereotyping of the Arab Muslim population as "barbarians." Time and again, the Orient is defended against its European critics and simplifiers: the official disdain for non-Muslims does nothing to prevent freedom of religion and conscience and a respectful treatment of Christian Europeans.[40] While it may be true in theory that women are held captive in the harem, this is not the case in practice.[41] Men in Aleppo speak of their wives with greater decency and discretion than is customary in Europe.[42] Opium smoking is by no means as widespread as believed. The authors continue in a manner typical of their acute sense of discernment:

> It [opium smoking] prevails indeed more at Constantinopel than at Aleppo, where happily it is hitherto held almost equally scandalous as drinking wine, and practised by few openly, except by persons regardless of their reputation. The natives of Aleppo the least scrupulous in the use of opium are people of the Law; owing probably to the influence of example; for a new Cady coming annually from Constantinopel, it seldom happens that either he himself, or some

> of his officers, do not by their own practice, give a fresh sanction to a custom they have learnt at the capital, where the offence is regarded as venial and stands little in the way of preferment in that line.[43]

Those who consume alcohol in Aleppo never openly admit to doing so, but always plead medicinal grounds.

The authors continually emphasize the purposeful adaptation of *mœurs* to the specific circumstances in Syria. Their admiring description of public baths underscores this point, while at the same time allowing them to return to one of their favorite topics: the separation between private and public space.[44] The theory of oriental despotism had expressly denied such a separation, maintaining that the despot's power extended over all realms of life, just as, conversely, there could be no possibilities for a meaningful social life between the household and the court. In Aleppo however, as is now shown, the public baths where women from all social levels and milieux intermingle form a kind of female public sphere. What Lady Mary Wortley Montagu had already observed in 1717[45] is now expressed more clearly:

> But the Bagnio is almost the only public female assembly; it affords an opportunity of displaying their jewels and fine clothes, of meeting their acquaintance and of learning domestic history of various kinds; for particular Bagnios being more in vogue than others, the ladies are assembled from remote districts, and if accidentally placed near each other on the same Divan, it is reckoned sufficient for joining in confidential conversation, though they were not acquainted before.[46]

Baths are a social microcosm. They have their own rites, symbols, hierarchies, division of labor, and taboos. The male equivalents are the coffee houses for the lower classes and, for the social elite, the reception halls of their residences, where they pay each other visits and discuss political as well as business matters. The private sphere of the harem is reserved not just for the ladies but also for the lord of the house. In its principal function, it is less a site of voluptuous sexuality (as envisaged by European male fantasy) than "a sanctuary into which only the most urgent business dares intrude."[47] The public sphere thus does not end at the doorstep, as it does for the European middle class, but at the threshold to the inner chambers.

The Natural History of Aleppo is also significant for the sketch it offers of a natural and social history of the passions. In contrast to the assumption of static national character types that were a dime a dozen in the literature on foreign countries, Alexander and Patrick Russell insist on a civilizing process that affects and involves the sexes and individual social groups *within* a nation in different ways. Thus Ottoman dignitaries ("the Osmanli") are normally "courteous and polite," not at all the imperious and vengeful patriarchs so often described in print and displayed on the European stage. They are generally friendly towards their social inferiors; only when contradicted do they give way to anger. With those of a higher station, however, they show themselves devoted and eager to please. If vulgar psychology explained despotism through fear of the ruler, the Russells know that emotional self-control plays a more important role:

> they feel, but conceal their emotion. It is an habitual power of controlling the passions, to be acquired only by practice, and consequently is possessed in different degrees, proportionate to the occasions which individuals, in the progress of life, may have for exercising it. The Osmanli of middle age, who have risen slowly from obscurity, to eminent stations, possess this talent in a high degree.[48]

The courtier must be an expert in affect management, regardless of whether he appears before the sultan in Istanbul or at the court of his representative, the pasha of Aleppo. Merchants or rural Arabs behave quite differently. The customary habitus of city-dwelling commoners is "an affected gravity," ever liable to erupt into fits of rage or public disorder. Is there anything specifically Aleppan, Ottoman, or oriental about this? Here too we receive a sociological rather than an ethnological answer: very little, since the courtly character type is in principle much the same across different societies and civilizations; so too is the commercial habitus.[49] If for example the Muslim and "Frankish" merchants in Aleppo could only overcome their mutual suspicion and bridge the social gap that had arisen on *both* sides, they would soon come "to think of one another in a more liberal manner." But the Russells are aware that this will never happen, largely because the Jews and indigenous Christians are constantly stirring up the Europeans against the Muslims, their inveterate enemies.[50] Cultural misunderstandings work to undermine the intrinsically feasible solidarity of social function and class position.

While the Russells thus dispute the all-too-simple clichés of oriental despotism, they do not in principle refuse to broaden their depiction of local ways into a *political* sociology. In their reading, the chief characteristic of the politicial situation in the Ottoman Empire is the exercise of tyranny throughout the social hierarchy, not just at its apex. The pashas or governors under the sultan's command act like absolute sovereigns, as do the agas below them, and so on. The repressive-servile type of the courtier is reproduced at every level, just as Montesquieu's "principles" permeate all spheres of society. Whereas the "courtly vices" are concentrated in the capital city in the European monarchies, in the Ottoman Empire they proliferate in even the most farflung administrative outpost. And because the demand for luxury among the Ottoman upper class had increased over the course of the eighteenth century, illegal confiscations of property—more precisely, the extortion of wealthy subjects through protection rackets—had grown apace.[51]

So much for the doctors' general diagnosis. In a later chapter on the government of Aleppo, this image is then refined and relativized: it turns out that the pashas are not omnipotent after all; they are not permitted to pass the death sentence or confiscate private property; and their edicts can be appealed in Istanbul with a fair chance of success.[52] The Russells do not allow their freedom of judgment to be impaired by European ideological fashions, while their strict empiricism spares them the problems that can arise when firsthand observation is used as the basis of "philosophical" reasoning—a trap into which the great Volney had maneuvered himself. Categories like tyranny and despotism, overburdened with a long history of occidental semantics and Orientalist fantasy, are incapable of capturing the realities of *social* power, such as the role of notables, patrons, and other leaders who operate outside the structure of the state. Such civic worthies are at once the exploiters and the spokespeople of their local communities. They occupy precarious positions as intermediaries that they can turn as much to their own advantage as to the public good.[53] An analysis in categories such as "interests" and "coalitions"—categories that modern political science has yet to supersede—allows the Russells to banish the chimera of oriental despotism even more successfully than had Anquetil-Duperron or Mouradgea d'Ohsson with their legalistic argumentation. Even though the lofty principles of Islamic-Ottoman law were frequently violated, the real antagonism of the contending power factions leads to a situation where, "notwithstanding the frequent violations of the people's rights, the ordinary course of affairs proceeds more equitably than might be expected in a government where the people are commonly supposed to be the mere slaves of despotic power."[54] In the end, popular unrest very often acted as a corrective. Hunger strikes or protests against excessive taxation invariably caused whichever pasha was in charge of the affected province to lose favor with the sultan.

Alexander and Patrick Russell regarded conditions in Syria—and, although they wisely avoided generalizations, in the Ottoman Empire as a whole—with an unexampled cool-headedness that never crossed over into cynicism and indifference. Nobody else so successfully teased apart the interwoven strands of state, society, religion, ethnicity, and national character. The subtlety that Montesquieu developed in his theory, but then largely revoked through the coarseness of his concept of despotism, is preserved in *The Natural History of Aleppo*. The text, far removed from the alienating simplifications of a "savage anthropology," is one of the forgotten founding documents of European sociology. Whether its individual findings have been confirmed by today's Orientalists is as irrelevant a question as whether, say, Tocqueville's analyses of America were "correct." More than two centuries on, the voice of the Russell brothers is still worth listening to—not least because the authors, like Carsten Niebuhr or Lady Mary Wortley Montagu in her many impressionistic letters from Constantinople,[55] communicate a spirit of warm human generosity. Concluding a string of critical remarks about the dark side of socialization in the Ottoman upper class, the Russells assure their readers that nothing lies further from their intention than to purvey a collective stereotype of Turks and Arabs. During their three decades in Aleppo, they had met with "persons of the utmost honor and integrity" at *all* levels of society.[56]

SLAVES

In 1729 Mehmet Efendi traveled to France as ambassador of the Sublime Porte. One of his tasks was to secure the release of Ottoman slaves being held in French galleys in direct contravention of international law.[57] These people, eighty of whom were eventually freed, had been slaves in Istanbul before being captured by French warships. Several decades later, Turkish prisoners-of-war were still reportedly being held in slavery in Italy and other European countries.[58] In 1763 Adam Smith had to admit that in Scotland, many of those employed in mines and saltworks were living in slave-like conditions.[59] In the Age of Enlightenment, not *all* of Europe between the Elbe and the Pyrenees was thus spared the institution of slavery. In 1771, John Millar discussed slavery as something of a universal stage in societal evolution and pointed out three individual paths to absolute dependency: captivity, voluntary submission, and judicial sentencing.[60] He makes clear that slavery is not restricted to earlier barbaric ages. The sentence of a judge presupposes the civilizing achievement of a judical system, and modern slavery almost invariably is justified and regulated by some kind of legal framework.

Yet it is still remarkable that by the mid-eighteenth century, almost the only part of the world where slavery was not the fate of a considerable proportion of the population was Western Europe. By stark contrast, during the same period the transatlantic slave trade and the slave economy in Europe's American colonies were in full swing. On the sugar islands of the Caribbean, especially the French and British colonies, there were slaveholding regimes of a brutality unmatched since the days of the late Roman Republic. Enlightenment philosophers from Montesquieu to Condorcet had forcefully condemned these arrangements yet been powerless to change them. Public attitudes only started to shift—and the momentum for emancipation to build—with the Quaker-founded abolitionist movement. Its most important milestones were the ban on the African slave trade by Parliament in London in 1807 and the release of 780,000 slaves in the British Empire in 1834.

Against this background there is little more to note than that slavery, which was present to some degree almost everywhere in Asia, was *not* viewed as an especially foreign or abhorrent aspect of Asiatic societies. The most critical commentaries were occasioned by two phenomena: on the one hand, the extraordinarily harsh form of slavery (by Asian standards) inflicted on people from the "Outer Islands" of Indonesia—but never Javans—in Dutch Batavia;[61] on the other, the so-called "oriental slave trade," whereby Arab dealers supplied the harems of the entire Islamic world with "black eunuchs," principally from Ethiopia. Countries such as China or Vietnam were barely touched by this international eunuch market, however. They could more than cover their domestic needs—here largely concentrated on the imperial or royal court—by castrating their own subjects.[62] Moreover, eunuchs were no Afro-Asian speciality. They had played a significant role in Byzantium until at least the eleventh century, while church music and opera in seventeenth- and eighteenth-century Italy relied on a steady stream of castrati from the lower classes.

From the Kirghiz Steppe to Burma, from Turkey to Japan, travelers constantly registered slave-like conditions of dependency. Yet with the possible exception of a few small regions in Central Asia, these were nowhere seen as socioeconomically predominant. Even the Orient's harshest critic could not deny that wherever one looked in the world, only

Europeans were in charge of slaveowning societies. There was no such thing as plantation slavery in Asia. Most slaves, it was reported, were employed in the home, often held for limited terms in bondage for debt. By and large, commentators found slaves in Asia to be better treated than those subject to European colonial regimes. They were assigned domestic duties and were frequently valued, even treasured, as sources of prestige. However, as the successes of abolitionism gradually blotted out the greatest stain on Europe's moral reputation, the tone of pronouncements on the remaining forms of slavery in Asia became correspondingly darker.[63]

While the increasingly vulgarized theory of despotism insisted that subjects in most Asiatic countries were the very opposite of free citizens, the application of a more narrow juridical or sociological concept of slavery brought to light the relative unimportance of slavery in Asia. Christoph Meiners sought to explain this apparent contradiction by arguing that the worst despots tended to treat their slaves the best, since they made ideal tools for oppressing the populace.[64] Grand theories of slavery, such as those put forward by Turgot and Linguet, Adam Smith, and John Millar, had few Asiatic examples to draw on. Indirectly, though, they could shed light on conditions in Asia. Thus, Turgot claimed in 1766 that farming with an enslaved workforce became economically unviable once large territorial states were formed.[65] In 1763 Adam Smith demonstrated that tenant farming was always economically superior to slavery. Citing the Mughal Empire, Iran, and Turkey as examples, he pointed out that absolute monarchs would need to move against the institution of agrarian slavery if they wanted to weaken the elites who profited by it; the "arbitrary" character of rule was shown here precisely in the measures taken against private property. Slaves were worst off, he contended, in a slaveholding democracy.[66] John Crawfurd, a later student of the Scottish Enlightenment, argued that a full-blown despotism best guaranteed its security and taxation revenue by preserving the personal freedoms of smallholding farmers.[67] The most conspicuous example he adduced for this was Java, well known to him as a diplomat.

Whatever attempts at explanation were offered, Asia, the homeland of *political* unfreedom in the eyes of many, was clearly not a continent of *personal* unfreedom. This distinction pertained even in Siam, where the king exploited his subjects as a conscript labor force—something that would have been unthinkable in early modern China. The inhabitants of Siam, Simon de La Loubère explained in 1691, were either free or enslaved:

> The difference of the King of Siam's Slaves from his Subjects of free condition is, that he continually employs his Slaves in personal labours, and maintains them; whereas his free Subjects only owe him six months service every year, but at their own expense.[68]

Despite having to perform onerous duties in countries like Siam and Burma, nowhere in Asia were slaves so disenfranchised or so dependent on the goodwill of their masters as on the Caribbean Islands or in the tsarist empire. Likewise, there were no Asian countries where slaves formed a majority of the population. Theorists of despotism thus had no factual basis for claiming that Asians typically languished under the yoke of slavery.

The most perceptive "philosophical" observers of history were interested in a very different phenomenon: the rise of slaves to political power. The most striking example of this was offered by the Mamluks in Egypt.[69] From the ninth century onwards, enslaved members of Turkish nomadic tribes from the steppes of Central Asia had served the Abbasid caliphs as a Praetorian guard. Building up their power over time, by 1250 they had established their own state in Egypt. It collapsed in 1516–17 under an Ottoman invasion. In the early eighteenth century, a Mamluk political revival got underway. By midcentury, something like a neo-Mamluk military caste had come to dominate society and rule Egypt under largely nominal Ottoman suzerainty. European observers were fascinated by a social group that for centuries had reproduced itself, not by the usual means of procreation and aristocratic lineage, but through a constant supply of young Christian slaves from Georgia, the Caucasus, and the Balkans.[70] Uprooted and foreign-born young slaves ruled the country in a situation of permanent usurpation: they had usurped both the legitimate power of the sultan and the social status of a homegrown nobility. Volney, who studied them closely on his travels, called them "a slave militia turned despots" and saw their constant infighting as the realization of something like a Hobbesian state of total anarchy.[71] Destroyed in 1805 by Muhammad Ali, the new autocrat on the Nile, the Mamluk regime appeared as a curious throwback to the dark Middle Ages, but also as an example of the paradoxical coexistence of the most tyrannical order with the most rampant disorder.

SCHOLARS AND AESTHETES IN POWER

In European eyes, Mamluk rule looked typically "oriental" because it was not based on the principle of hereditary aristocracy. The son of a Mamluk did not stand to inherit the political and social status of his father, although as a scion of the ruling class his material needs were provided for. Young men imported into Egypt as slaves, accepted into the Islamic community, and given military training were constantly rising to high positions of power. Did this not prove, once again, that the stabilizing, civilizing element of aristocracy was lacking in oriental societies, or at best was restricted to the descendants of religious founders like Confucius and Muhammad? Had not Francis Bacon and Niccolò Machiavelli already taken the absence of a nobility to be a chief characteristic of despotic states?

If Europeans ever experienced a cognitive shock in their encounters with Asia that prompted a comparative sociological relativization of their own social normality, then it was the seventeenth-century insight that highly sophisticated civilizations could survive and even flourish without an aristocracy. The most obvious example was China under the Ming and Qing dynasties. Here matters could be described very simply: leaving aside a politically powerless Manchu "banner aristocracy" that was utterly dependent on imperial largesse and grew ever more irrelevant as the eighteenth century progressed, there was no such thing as aristocracy in China. There were no dynastic magnates, no vassals, no patrimonial privileges, no feudal dues, no great landholdings, no courtly society outside the imperial power center, no code of chivalry, and no estates-general or parliaments. When an English children's book from 1817 nonetheless attested to "nine orders of nobility in China,"[72] this was not a complete fabrication, for the bureaucratic hierarchy (which was indeed made up of nine ranks) fulfilled many of the functions performed by the aristocracy in European society—or at any rate by the *noblesse de robe* of the French ancien régime.

This was a view shared by some of the Jesuit fathers. The Jesuits had been the first to introduce European readers to China's unique social order. Their reports convey far less a sense of perplexed astonishment than was presumably experienced by other travelers upon encountering a high culture with no aristocracy. The Jesuits themselves were a post-feudal meritocratic elite who derived their sense of self and their claims to status from their intellectual ability. The same could be said of the Chinese "literati," who must therefore have appeared to the padres as congenial colleagues, if not mirror images of themselves. The "mandarins" they encountered at court had spent years mastering the classical texts in preparation for the gruelling and highly competitive state examinations. These were conducted at three levels: regional, provincial, and central. Success at the first level entitled the candidate to the lowest rank, termed the "Baccalaureus" by several European commentators. The scholar could now take his place in the legally privileged elite group of the *shenshi* or "gentry." Only if he went on to achieve success in the central examination, gaining his "doctoral degree" in the presence of the emperor himself, was he now qualified—although by no means guaranteed—to secure one of the few bureaucratic offices in the territorial administration of this enormous country and at the imperial court. These coveted offices, like the title of gentry, were nonhereditary. Each generation had to prove its worth by passing through the gigantic apparatus of the state examination system.[73]

These conditions were without parallel in Europe; at most, they recalled career prospects within the church.[74] They had already been attentively described in the wonderfully detailed reports on China by Matteo Ricci (1615), the founder of the mission there, and the Portuguese missionary Alvarez Semedo (1642), who had traveled through much of the empire between 1613 and 1637.[75] Semedo insisted on calling the meritocratic elite of "mandarins" a "nobility": a nobility of intellectual and aesthetic virtue.[76] An anonymous German author put the matter in a nutshell in 1679: "They [the Chinese] associate nobility with the person and not with his blood."[77] And Mendoza, in the first great modern book on China, had already recognized in 1585 that no Western analogy quite captured what made China so peculiar: the mandarins were something like aristocrats *for the Chinese*, although *we* would consider them to be scholars.[78] Two social roles that were kept apart in Europe were thus conflated in Ming dynasty China.

Those who spoke of the mandarins as China's nobility did so either for didactic purposes, to make a bewilderingly foreign institution more comprehensible to their readers, or because they viewed Chinese society as a variant of a universally valid norm and simply could not imagine a social order without an aristocracy. Such misgivings subsided over the course of the eighteenth century. Ever more authors acknowledged the unique make-up of the social system in China. Those searching for an ideal community particularly approved of the union of a social upper class with a bureaucratic elite in the Middle Kingdom. Here there was no split between an old landed aristocracy and a new urban functionary elite such as that which had accompanied the development of the early modern state in Europe. Put differently, in China inherited wealth played no role as a source of status and power outside the state. Extraordinarily elegant and almost geometrically pleasing in its design, the system was completely defined by the polarity of a competitive machinery that selected qualified candidates from below and an imperial will that deployed them from above, particularly following the elimination of irrational impediments to its smooth functioning such as the eunuch tyranny of the late Ming.

Above all, seventeenth-century men of letters were entranced by the idea that in China erudition and lifelong learning were rewarded by social success. Only naïve enthusiasts could believe, however, that a disinterested pursuit of knowledge for its own sake was what lay behind such studiousness. The social order was set up in such a way that the only chance of improving one's lot lay in education. "Since the fate of the Chinese depends entirely on their merits," Le Comte wrote in 1696, "they devote all their lives to study."[79] In the eighteenth century, the idea of a competent, corruption-free state administration that genuinely worked for the public good fascinated European observers. It attracted authors of the caliber of Justi and Quesnay, who like most of their contemporaries drew their information mainly from Du Halde.[80] The objection that China was idealized in these "Sinophile" texts may be correct, but it misses the point. On the one hand, Chinese bureaucracy in the first half of the eighteenth century was indeed perhaps the best functioning in the world; its idealization was therefore not a flight of fancy, merely an extrapolation from reality. On the other hand, reports from the Middle Kingdom—summarized by Du Halde in 1735 and further popularized in 1749 in the eighth volume of Prévost's travel compendium—gave European theorists their first opportunity to come to grips in a detailed way with the problems of administration and governance (in the sense given the term by political science today). More interested in a political system's capacity to deliver results than in its legitimacy, theorists such as the French physiocrats and the German *Polizeywissenschaftler* regularly cited China as a model polity. It seemed to demonstrate just how much a well-ordered paternalistic state could achieve. Confucian political ethics, whose key works became available in translation from the 1680s, offered surprising and independent support for the old European idea of the monarch as the good shepherd of his flock.

Once it could no longer be denied that China lacked an aristocracy, it depended on the individual commentator's view of the *European* nobility whether this absence was found to be regrettable or not. Those following in the footsteps of Edmund Burke saw the ownership of great estates as a sign of advanced civilization and a necessary guarantor of stability and social harmony.[81] Those who joined James Mill and other exponents of Benthamite utilitarianism in seeing the nobility as a class of parasites, by contrast, welcomed its absence as a crucial step forward on the path to modernity. In the background stood the more general question of whether it was justified to separate power and prestige from inherited wealth and attach it to learning and scholarship instead.[82] Increasingly, that question received a positive answer.

At the same time, reports began to accumulate of growing corruption among Chinese authorities. By the mid-eighteenth century, corruption seemed to have reached endemic proportions under the Qianlong emperor.[83] So long as the trial of the Indian governor-general Warren Hastings—followed with the keenest interest throughout Europe—kept the question of *British* corruption on the table, it was difficult to decry Chinese impropriety without appearing hypocritical.[84] Following the clean-up and restructuring of British administration in India under Lord Cornwallis in the 1790s, however, a new and superior form of rational state organization seemed to have emerged in Asia to rival the long-tainted Chinese bureaucracy. Its driving forces were noninheriting younger sons of the Scottish, English, and Irish landed aristocracy. As a rationally organized and scrupulously fair administration under aristocratic leadership, it stood opposed to the irrational government of China by sedentary pen-pushers mired in corruption and incompetence. What was viewed as inferior was not so much the *idea* of Chinese bureaucracy, which was hardly ever criticized in principle, as its degradation in actual administrative practice.

The lettered aristocracy or scholarly elite was the most striking idiosyncrasy of Chinese societal organization. What could be said about the remainder of society? The *Universal History* identified three classes in China: the mandarins, the literati, and the plebeians.[85] The difference between the officials (the "mandarins") and the far-larger talent pool from which they were recruited (the "literati") was here clearly seen and perhaps even overstated. But what were the distinctive characteristics of the "plebeians"? That they were not segmented into hermetically sealed castes, as many observers had assumed based on their knowledge of

India, was made crystal clear by Pater Parennin in a long letter sent from Peking in September 1735.[86] Unfortunately, the letter came too late to add sociological weight to Du Halde's China encyclopedia, which appeared in the same year. Parennin warned his European readers against unwittingly transferring categories like "caste" or "tribe" from one Asian country to another, but he also emphasized the value of comparison. Precisely the comparison with Europe revealed that—leaving the mandarinate to one side—Chinese society, just like European societies, was made up of merchants, innkeepers, and handworkers as well as an underclass of vagabonds, outsiders, and outlaws.[87] Hardly any livelihoods were inherited. No Chinaman was forced by law or custom to take up his father's trade, and few did so of their own free will. A laborer or artisan who had saved enough money strove to become a merchant and later to invest whatever wealth he may have acquired through trade in preparing his sons for the state examinations.[88] That the Chinese were industrious businesspeople was evident to all who saw them in Southeast Asia, Macao, or Canton. In China trade was allowed to develop freely. The economy as a whole was unencumbered by a leisured and unproductive aristocracy.[89]

The botanist and agronomist Pierre Poivre, one of the few eighteenth-century travelers to show an interest in Chinese agriculture, expressed his admiration for its productivity and what one might call its modernity in lectures held in Lyon in 1763 and 1764. In his view China, and to a lesser extent Cochinchina as well, were successful agrarian societies that had proved themselves capable of feeding a growing population; they were so successful, in fact, that they might serve Europe as a model in many respects. The state vigorously promoted farming. In China there was neither slavery (as in Siam, Malaya, and the European colonies) nor despotic primary ownership of the land, only free labor on the basis of secure private property. Idleness was disdained even in the most elevated circles; women made a productive contribution and were not hidden away in harems; the tax burden was tolerable and easy to predict; upward social mobility was barely hindered by accidents of birth allotting penury to some and privilege to others; valuable land was not wasted, as in Europe, on aristocratic hunting grounds or on raising more horses than were needed.[90]

Poivre obviously shared Quesnay's idealization of China; indeed, he was one of his physiocratic followers. Nonetheless, his analysis is not mistaken in its general tendency. He only exaggerates the profile of a society characterized by nonfeudal agrarian relations, a high degree of social mobility and a widepread work ethic: China as the utopia of bourgeois free enterprise in Asia. Goethe perceived something similar when, having read a Chinese novel recently translated by Jean-Pierre Abel-Rémusat, he remarked to his amanuensis, Johann Peter Eckermann, on January 31, 1827, that he found the characters entirely understandable and familiar: "With them, everything is sensible, bourgeois, without great passion and poetic verve, and their behavior therefore has much in common with my *Hermann and Dorothea* and the English novels of Richardson."[91]

CASTES: RELIGIOUS STRAITJACKET OR SOCIAL UTOPIA?

Whether or not there was an aristocracy and what should be made of it was the subject of lively debate for other Asian countries as well. The results were never clear-cut, as a few samples may suffice to indicate. The social system of Tonkin seemed the most similar to the Chinese, although its hereditary class of military mandarins formed something like a nobility. Society there was strictly divided into mandarins and subjects, it was stated in 1807.[92] In Burma space for "aristocratic commonwealths" was found within a despotic system.[93] Together with Iran, Siam was generally considered to be the most despotic state in all Asia. Here, as in China, there was no hereditary aristocracy, yet the machinery for social advancement provided in China by the examination system and mandarinate was also lacking. As a result, social standing was determined by such fickle forces as commercial success and royal whim. As one of the leading experts on the country put it: "It is the richest man who is respected as the most noble, and true merit is estimated according to the superiority of fortune and the extent of favor shown by the ruler."[94] Chardin's finding that there was no aristocracy in Iran was widely repeated on the strength of his incontestable authority. Those who climbed the social ladder in Iran, Fryer maintained, owed their success to a miracle, not to their own efforts.[95] In Indonesia, nobility was not to be expected according to the theory of despotism, though the indefatigable Dr. Crawfurd still managed to describe it.[96]

The question of aristocracy in the Ottoman Empire was extensively debated. It was agreed that there was no hereditary aristocracy there. Hammer-Purgstall was prepared to acknowledge a kind of aristocracy of merit, nothing more.[97] An investigation of the proto-sociological literature on the Ottoman Empire brings to light an insight that has been hidden by our focus on the problem of despotism: even those who conjured up the despot's heavy hand could not help but recognize the comparatively high incidence of upward mobility. In the mid-sixteenth century the imperial ambassador Ogier Ghiselin de Busbecq, the most influential European authority on the golden age of the Ottomans under Suleiman the Magnificent, had already painted the portrait of a meritocratic society in which the path to high office stood open to the worthy. In a much-quoted passage, first published in 1581, he assured his readers that "those who hold the highest posts under the Sultan are very often the sons of shepherds and herdsmen" and proud of their modest background. "They do not consider that good qualities can be conferred by birth or handed down by inheritance, but regard them partly as the gift of heaven and partly as the product of good training and constant toil and zeal."[98] Like everyone else who expressed their admiration for this kind of meritocratic "open elite," Busbecq was pursuing an antiaristocratic agenda. He did not overlook the main drawback of such an arrangement: everything depended on the autocrat's sound judgment, his ability to pick the right people for the top positions in state and society.

This analysis was confirmed time and again. The Ottoman Empire boasted a mobile, competitive society in which the "virtuous burgher" (*le bourgeois vertueux*) stood in high repute.[99] Merchants, including numerous members of minorities such as Greeks, Jews, and Armenians, had a fair chance of making their own fortunes. Gibbon and others praised the Janissaries, at least at their apogee, as a post-feudal corps of crack troops.[100] Although organized quite differently from China, the Ottoman Empire showed similar meritocratic features that distinguished both systems from the stricter and less permeable social hierarchies prevailing in large parts of Europe.

Yet the opposite extreme to social fluidity could also be found in Asia: a strictly regimented, hierarchical society where people were bound for life to the position assigned to them at birth. The vertical social mobility that impressed many European observers of China and the Ottoman Empire was here conspicuous in its absence. This, at any rate, was how commentators viewed the society of Hindu India, which in many parts of the country coexisted with that of the Muslim conquerors without the two spheres ever coming into alignment, let alone amalgamating.

In the seventeenth century, the more mobile and open conditions in China and the Ottoman Empire were startlingly unfamiliar from the viewpoint of a Europe that was still largely stratified into sharply defined estates. In the course of the eighteenth century, by contrast, when social structure in the more socioeconomically advanced countries of Europe became less rigid, the ossified Indian caste system increasingly came to be seen as both alien and objectionable. The European tendency to engage with the outside world by means of conceptual opposites contributed to this perception of incommensurable strangeness even in a world beyond magic and miracles. India, above all, was transformed from the stuff of oriental fairytale into a paradigm of sociological alterity. This was mainly a matter of evolving terminology.

Until Montesquieu and the Scottish and Göttingen Enlightenment, early European attempts to describe and apprehend the social reality of non-European civilizations had used the same concepts that were applied to Europe as well: estate, order, nobility, peasant, *état*, rank, and so on. The example of China showed that such concepts risked assimilating a foreign reality to what was already known and familiar, thereby obliterating the foreignness that had drawn interest to it in the first place. Yet at least since the first Jesuit reports, attentive observers had been quite capable of capturing the *differentia specifica* of a non-European society through the modified application of European concepts. Alongside this there emerged concepts of European origin that nonetheless referred exclusively to Asiatic conditions and had no referent in European reality: "mandarin," for example. Many originated with the earliest European observers of Asia, the Portuguese.

One such concept was that of "caste." This word had at first been widely and flexibly used to denote many possible human collectives in Asia. It was not until the eighteenth century that the semantic elements of segregation, internal homogeneity, or even biological purity were pushed into the foreground, causing the term's meaning to become narrower and more precise. This too did not yet mean that castes were seen as something typically and exclusively Indian. Up to Max Weber and beyond, "caste" could be defined as a culturally neutral sociological category, for instance as a special case of the concept "class." Thus Conrad Malte-Brun spoke of caste in 1812 as "a hereditary class that is exclusively engaged in a particular occupation."[101] Although he found this phenomenon confined to Asia, he identified it not just in India but in Iran, Arabia, and Egypt as well. In 1835 Frédéric de Rougemont, a historical geographer who took extraordinary care with his terminology, ventured the following definition: "A class is a caste if birth irrevocably determines the way of life (*genre de vie*) and social rank of the individual."[102] In principle, such castes could feature in very different types of societies.

By the time Rougemont was writing, however, two interrelated ideas had prevailed: firstly, that "caste" was something typically Indian and secondly, that the phenomenon was intimately linked with the native religion, now dubbed "Hinduism"—a coverall term that had no indigenous equivalent.[103] This exoticization or perhaps anthropologization of Indian sociology proceeded gradually during the eighteenth century. It was no mere figment of the Western imagination, nor an arbitrary imposition of alien categories onto a social world whose patterns and logic remained inscrutable to European observers. What happened was more complicated and occurred within an epistemic triangle. Firstly, there was that complex mosaic of social formations that, to this day, makes up "Indian society," in other words: the incontrovertible reality of power and hierarchy, of social inclusion and exclusion, of unevenly distributed life chances. Secondly, Indian groups and individuals had their own highly diversified and contradictory interpretations of social reality, interpretations that seeped into the perceptions formed by foreign observers. And thirdly, these observers brought with them their own conceptual equipment that, through comparison and analogy, helped to make sense of a social world that was strange though hardly less complex than conditions in Europe at the same time. European observers were particularly intrigued by the contrast between high upward mobility in China and the freezing of vertical mobility in India where—not just among the Hindu population—hereditary caste status could not be changed by individual effort or preferment. The only hope for advancement lay in a slow, long-term elevation of the collective status of one's caste in the overall social hierarchy. European countries during the incipient transition to bourgeois society occupied a place between these extremes, moving in a "Chinese" direction from the last quarter of the eighteenth century, the very time when meritocratic mechanisms in the Chinese Empire began to lose their efficacy. In the same process, an India under European rule became, in European eyes, stranger than it had ever been before, at least as far as its society was concerned.

The first account of an Indian society to be based on firsthand observation over many years was written by Bartholomäus Ziegenbalg. From 1706 until his death in 1719 at the age of thirty-six, he was active as a Pietist missionary in the small Danish colony of Tranquebar (south of Madras).[104] Ziegenbalg learned to speak and read the local language, Tamil, with great fluency. In close contact with natives, he undertook extensive social and cultural research as a participant observer. Only a few of the reports he sent to Europe were published at the time. The editors at mission central in Halle made sure that Ziegenbalg's all-too-understanding attitude towards the Indians and their social and religious life did not reach the public uncensored. Ziegenbalg's masterpiece, the great monograph *Malabarisches Heidentum* (*Malabar Heathendom*), had been sent to Halle in manuscript form in 1711; it was kept there under lock and key until it was finally published in 1926. Ziegenbalg was less interested in the social organization of the Tamils than in their religion and other aspects of their life and ideas. All the same, something akin to a sociology of southwest India can still be distilled from his brief remarks.[105]

Ziegenbalg found that the social cosmos he was studying was primarily structured around a multitude of occupational groups. He was fascinated by the equal opportunities for participating in public affairs that all these groups were afforded. This led him to place greater emphasis on the openness and flexibility of Tamil society than on its character as a strictly segmented, coercive order. [106] He rarely speaks of "castes," never of a "caste system." The (South) India of 1700, as presented by Ziegenbalg, was thus a kind of "open" society, no different fundamentally from the Chinese and Ottoman social orders described by his contemporaries. Corporatively structured Europe with its guilds and estates was hardly more modern in comparison.[107]

The simplistic image of India as a world of self-contained castes that from the mid-eighteenth century came to dominate European perceptions arose on the basis of reports whose authors could seldom benefit from Ziegenbalg's rich experience and linguistic expertise. Montesquieu gave this image forceful expression in a laconic remark: in India, unlike in Europe, the social order was defined by religion. This led to a situation where the individual castes regarded each other with a kind of horror born of a sense of religious propriety (Montesquieu plays with the words *honneur* and *horreur*): "A certain honor established by religious prejudices in the Indies makes the various castes hold one another in horror."[108] With that, the natural hierarchy regulating other societies was suspended: there were Indians who for reasons of caste affiliation felt dishonored if they had to eat with their king. *Noblesse oblige*, the sense of paternalistic obligation felt by European higher-ups towards those less fortunate than themselves, is absent here too.

As so often, Voltaire is more cautious. He emphasizes how difficult it is to make valid generalizations about non-Muslim India. The subcontinent is "inhabited by twenty different nations whose manners and religions show few similarities."[109] Over the following decades, commentators shuttled to and fro between these two broad approaches: Voltaire stood for a more discriminating view of regional cultures that refused to see India as Europe's Other, Montesquieu for a more sweeping, vigorously generalizing approach that posited the existence of a homogeneous Indian civilization with the caste system, the subcontinent's most characteristic institution, at its center.[110]

Information about the lifeworld of the non-Muslim majority was drawn from a wide range of scattered European sources. During the eighteenth century no large-scale summative work on South Asia appeared that was comparable in stature to Chardin on Iran, Du Halde on China, or La Loubère on Siam. Not only did the great Indian manuscript by the Protestant Ziegenbalg remain inaccessible, so too did the original version of the *Mœurs et coutumes des Indiens* (1777) by the Jesuit father Gaston-Laurent Cœurdoux, subsequently quarried in 1817 by the unscrupulous abbé Dubois. The *Lettres édifiantes et curieuses*, which the Jesuits dispatched from India, therefore had to be studied separately and augmented by Dutch, English, and French sources for want of handy summaries.[111] This was the only way that even a minimally adequate impression of Indian society could be gained by European scholars. In Jesuit letters and travel reports, many of the Indian castes that would go on to be explored in twentieth-century anthopology and sociology were described or at least mentioned for the first time.[112]

Those wanting to present a rough outline of Indian society often made do with the classification into four major caste groupings or *varna* (in European texts sometimes called "estates"): spiritually exalted Brahmins, warriors and rulers, traders, and manual laborers, often in a servile position.[113] The abbé Raynal memorably depicted such a four-caste society in his portrait of India. Castes, he informed his sizeable readership, had existed unchanged since time immemorial. While they demonstrated the incomparable precociousness of Indian high culture, they also presented the greatest possible barrier to the "natural progress of society."[114] Raynal, who often calls castes "classes" (which in relation to the *varna* is not entirely false), emphasizes the religiously sanctioned impermeability of the social hierarchy while also pointing out ways in which it could be bypassed: either temporarily on journeys of pilgrimage, where rules prohibiting intercaste contact could not be rigorously enforced, or permanently by taking on the "monastic" status of a fakir.[115]

Raynal, a radical and sometimes maverick proponent of Enlightenment values, was in 1770 still remarkably measured in his critique of the caste system, which he presented as a kind of exacerbated class society. A few years later, the economist Adam Smith and the natural scientist and traveler Pierre Sonnerat pronounced more damning judgments. Smith took the castes to be an important (although by no means the decisive) factor retarding India's economic development, a deplorable systemic flaw that falsified the natural yield on capital and the market price of labor.[116] Sonnerat, who appears to have seen little of the country itself on his journey to India, denounced castes as an expression of collective irrationality and a violation of man's "natural equality."[117]

A remarkable link between the two objections, the economic and the philosophical, was made by August Hennings, an acolyte of Raynal's and friend of Moses Mendelssohn's. As a Danish public servant, Hennings had access to unpublished or untranslated reports of the Danish-Pietist mission in Tranquebar. Hennings was full of praise for the Indians' and especially the Tamils' natural aptitude for science, the arts, and handicrafts. Such talents were still in evidence here or there but were coming—in his view at least—to be ever more imperfectly realized. No anthropological reasons lay behind this; human agency was solely to blame. Society had been split up into self-perpetuating castes, which Hennings interprets not as timeless religious institutions but as historical instruments of class domination; despotism, exacerbated in large parts of India by Muslim and especially European conquest, further intensified the process of social atomization. As a consequence, the Indian mind and soul had atrophied and social productivity had stymied. Hennings places the responsibility for this squarely and solely on the "barbarism of the government,"

> which instead of encouraging sociability, utterly severs the bonds of society, and instead of stimulating people to common reflection, keeps them isolated or cut off, as it were. That is why thirty Indians are incapable of accomplishing the work of ten Europeans, they have almost nothing in the way of tools, machines and the like, and taste and inventiveness have dried up entirely.[118]

Unlike Raynal, whom he otherwise admired for his anticolonial stance, the Enlightenment radical Hennings thus did not see the caste system as a time-honored, quintessential, and ineradicable element of Indian civilization that condemned the latter to perpetual stagnation, but rather as a sociopathological aberration to be eliminated through reform or even revolution. Starting from a principle of equality that owed less to natural law than to Christian conviction, the high EIC official Charles Grant came to a similar finding in 1792: the caste system was an instrument of extreme slavery.[119]

Despite such harsh judgments, it is astonishing how many defenders the Indian caste system nonetheless found in the Age of Enlightenment. Edmund Burke admired what today might be called the identity-forming power of caste affiliation.[120] The abbé Perrin, an eminent authority on the country, denied that castes, *pace* August Hennings, debilitated the soul. On the contrary, every caste, even the least respected, infused whoever belonged to it with a sense of pride in their group, its traditions, and its venerable age. Granted, a member's loyalty extended only to the border of the caste and no further. Each caste formed its own self-contained "moral republic"; that is why patriotism and a striving for social advancement were so foreign to Indians.[121] Pater Cœurdoux praised the castes for the successful social control they exerted over their members through their caste-specific laws, customs, and institutions. The Indians were accordingly prevented from relapsing into barbarism through a kind of internal self-discipline. The castes also thereby mitigated the effects of despotism, since the state would have no cause for meddling with a society that could already regulate itself.[122] Finally, the high Brahmin castes were the Indian version of an aristocracy, which, unlike its French counterpart, protected itself from mésalliances and social decline by strictly prohibiting exogamy.[123]

In Cœurdoux's socially conservative interpretation, blood ties united only family members and did not suffice "to foster the mutual aid and support required in civil society."[124] People therefore had to be brought together into larger groups (*corps*) in which they could develop and defend their common interests. The bonds (*liens*) between individuals needed to be made unbreakably strong. In this respect, the "ancient Indian legislators" had been astonishingly successful. In 1777 Cœurdoux and his editor Desvaulx did not see the longevity of the caste system as a symptom of Indian backwardness. Quite the contrary: in their eyes it was proof of a wise dispensation, one that forged the sense of solidarity that was indispensable to "civil" life. Johann Gottfried Herder agreed: "Undoubtedly, the system of the bramins, when it was first established, was good: otherwise it could not have spread so wide, penetrated so deep, and endured so long."[125] This interpretation was the polar opposite of that put forward by Hennings: castes here provided the strongest bulwark *against* social atomization and fragmentation. Herder (who does not overlook the dark side of the caste system) and the abbé Dubois contributed the additional idea that a spirit of tolerance governed relations between castes. In lifestyle, customs, and religion, members of every caste could be happy in their own way, "as long as the general and universally respected laws of good behaviour are not infringed."[126]

The hymns in praise of the caste system would be less interesting if they had been sung exclusively by conservative French priests. Yet William Robertson, one of the most respected Enlightenment historians, arrived at similar results in his late work on India (1791). To be sure, Robertson admitted in anticipation of the predicted Enlightenment counterargument, the caste system erects "artificial barriers" between people and so sets limits on the natural "operations of the human mind."[127] Men of genius would struggle under such a system. The promotion of genius was not the main goal of societies, however. The caste structure presented average human beings with a meaningful division of labor, channeling their abilities into particular occupations that gave them a chance to shine. This explained the extraordinary perfection of Indian craftsmanship as well as the abundant supply of commodities for domestic consumption and export.[128] There was a key difference, however, between Robertson's words in praise of castes and those of an author like Cœurdoux: whereas the French Jesuit ascribes a kind of universal exemplarity to the caste system, for the Scottish historian it was suited only to preindustrial India, while Europeans in his own day, living in a completely different social order, understandably regarded it with the greatest distaste.

In the early nineteenth century, such relativism could barely be tolerated. On the basis of new studies on India carried out since 1784 by learned members of the Asiatick Society in Calcutta gathered around Sir William Jones,[129] two very different philosophical critics published influential condemnations of the caste system. In James Mill's *History of British India* (1817), the first volume of which was largely taken up with a systematic investigation of Indian civilization, castes appear as intrinsically abhorrent: "that institution, which stands as a more effectual barrier against the welfare of human nature than any other institution which the workings of caprice and selfishness have ever produced."[130] While most defenders of the caste order saw India's Muslim conquerors as barbarian outsiders whose best efforts to break the resistance of "Hindu" society had proved unavailing, James Mill, otherwise no friend of Islam, credited the Muslims with the superior civilization. In his eyes, the absence of caste barriers and even of a European-style hereditary aristocracy recommended Islamic nations, notwithstanding their tendency to despotism, as places where effort could be rewarded with social advancement. It was therefore only fitting that he took umbrage at British attempts—above all in the Permanent Settlement of 1793—to create in India, alongside the existing caste system, something like a class structure dominated by a new landowning aristocracy.[131]

By somewhat willfully interpreting Brahmins as "priests," Mill was able to marshall the entire "priestly fraud" rhetoric of the Enlightenment. At no other time and place in history had priests attained such power over the thoughts and deeds of a majority of the population as in India; and they had continued to wield this ever more anachronistic power to the present day.[132] For Mill, the caste system was only one of many indications that an antiquated social order was standing in the way of progress. The romantic idea that the wise Brahmin "legislators" of India had created a perfect system in the infancy of mankind, only for it to fall into decay in later ages, was of no interest to Mill, the progress-minded reformer and avowed enemy of all that was obsolete.

Soon after the appearance of Mill's book, Hegel engaged much more extensively with the caste phenomenon. Before critiquing the phenomenon, he set out to describe it objectively on the basis of the widest possible range of sources available to him at the time; he was familiar not only with Mill's *History of British India* but also with the most recent work by the abbé Dubois and the Indologist Henry Thomas Colebrooke, among others.[133] Approaching the phenomenon from a completely different angle, Hegel ultimately arrived at similar findings to the utilitarian James Mill. Whereas in China everyone was equally subject to the sovereign's unchecked will, the Indian world was founded on an elemental inequality that had become second nature. Given the immovable rigidity of caste divisions, "people relate themselves to the divine and to other people as they do to natural things."[134] Society remained opaque and hence insusceptible to reform.

Hegel's argument against the caste system owes nothing to ideas of equality grounded in natural law or Christianity. The system's obstruction of economic development is also of little concern to him. What displeases him is, firstly, the fact that individuals are "naturally" socialized into a group that they joined by accident of birth (rather than by "ethical" decision) and which they cannot leave of their own volition.[135] Every aspect of life is dictated by requirements that nobody dares measure against the yardstick of reason: "The most inane things are imposed on Hindus. The Hindu institutions rule out all that rests upon one's own free will."[136] Subjective freedom and an individual conscience could not arise under such conditions. Secondly, Hegel misses in India (before the British colonial period) a legal order that encompasses and transcends particular communities.[137] If China is in Hegel's view a civilization of boundless and unstructured universality, its substance exhausted in the imperial will and a limited number of very general ethical maxims, India strikes him as an *overly* structured civilization where differences and particularities are rendered absolute. This is nowhere more obvious than in the caste system.

To sum up, castes had already made an impression on the first modern visitors to India. They remained a stock theme of travel literature and were made the subject of sociological or ethnographic inquiry by several authors, especially Ziegenbalg and Cœurdoux. If they had at first been one element among many in the Indian social landscape, by the second half of the eighteenth century they had moved to the center of Western views of India. The decline of the Mughal Empire and the social groups it drew on for support made India appear all the more "Hindu." The sociological quintessence of this Hinduized India appeared to be the globally unique phenomenon of the caste, which came to be schematized in early nineteenth-century European perceptions into a caste *system*.

How this system was judged went through several phases. To missionaries like Ziegenbalg, it aroused suspicion only when it stood in the way of their efforts to convert the heathen. With Montesquieu's brief remark from 1748 there began a line of criticism that saw castes as standing in the sharpest possible antithesis to the free organization of social life, owing to the massive constraints they imposed on individuals by virtue of birth, tradition, and spiritual particularism, as well as their underlying postulate of natural human inequality. Until the turn of the century, such criticism was opposed by those who lauded the caste system as a bedrock of social order. Similar views lingered on in romantic idealizations of small-scale, hierarchical relations, although they proved unable to overturn the verdicts of Hegel and the philosophically coarser yet still (in the English colonial and scientific context) highly influential James Mill. The caste system became emblematic of the perverse, deviant path taken by India in modern world history.[138]

The abbé Dubois should be given the final word. He will not easily be forgiven for copying his chapters on the Brahmins from Pater Cœurdoux. But it should not be forgotten that the 1825 edition of his *Mœurs, institutions et cérémonies des peuples de l'Inde*—far superior to the English edition of 1816—contains a great deal of additional material that appears to derive from the abbé's personal observations. This includes a chapter "On the Wretched Condition of the Indians."[139] Dubois here fully frees himself from the perspective on caste that otherwise defines his work, describing the poverty and misery he saw in India with an unpolemical precision unmatched in the Western literature on Asia of the time. Many Europeans admired, he remarks, the fine materials and handicrafts exported from India. Yet they had no idea that most were manufactured in mud huts under conditions of abject poverty. From such observations, Dubois goes on to develop a hierarchical model of eight *income* classes, each with its own vividly described economic and social way of life. He begins with the poorest class, which in his estimate encompasses the half of the Indian population owning less than 120 francs' worth of property. They perform the most unpleasant or arduous forms of agricultural labor. This class includes pariahs living outside the caste order, members of almost all the castes, and nomadic tribespeople. At the tip of this social pyramid, which lies athwart the caste order, stand the wealthiest urban merchants as well as men who have been able to accumulate riches over years of government service. Remarkably, Dubois's completely modern-sounding sociology of contemporary India, which refrains from all exoticizing distortion, is embedded in a work that, through its extensive depictions of caste practices, did more than any other to cultivate the impression of India as an alien world.

FEUDALISM

The judgments made by European observers on social conditions in Asia were not just determined by the circumstances under which they were observing and the extent of their prior knowledge; they were also influenced by normative ideas. A conservative Catholic priest like Cœurdoux, who could only conceive of a good society as one ordered along lines of hierarchy and class privilege, naturally took a more favorable view of the caste system than a philosophical radical and egalitarian liberal like James Mill, who condemned the inheritability of social status and political rights as fundamentally illegitimate and therefore also attacked the privileges of the English aristocratic elite. Similarly divided reactions were provoked by what was termed "Asiatic feudalism." At one end of the spectrum stood a social romantic like Edmund Burke, who admired the Indian princes as guarantors of stability akin to the English nobles. At the other end, an early bourgeois economic theorist like Pierre Poivre blamed the incessant warmongering of an archaic and parasitic aristocracy in Malaya for the country's economic backwardness, contrasting it with the exemplary order in utterly unfeudal China.[140]

In the early modern period, the term "feudal" had been restricted to feudal law. Montesquieu expanded it in 1748 to the seigneurial system, understood as rule by local lords over subjects who enjoyed only limited freedoms. Voltaire saw a reform-minded monarchy in a more positive light than Montesquieu and therefore held the nobility's political wisdom in lower esteem. He spoke critically of a *système féodale*, which he characterized as a splintering of state power among innumerable petty tyrants. After Charlemagne, this kind of "anarchy" had at first proliferated throughout Europe; in some countries, including France and England, it had eventually been replaced by a strong monarchy or a mixed constitution, but in Germany it had persisted down to the present day.[141] Whereas Montesquieu regarded feudalism as a primarily European development, just as he understood its opposite, despotism, to be an Asiatic speciality, Voltaire found evidence of the phemomenon in Asia as well. With that he took the "first step towards a universal-historical typology."[142] Anquetil-Duperron, thoroughly familiar with conditions in India, suggested that South Asia had produced a combination of feudalism and despotism that had no parallel in early modern Europe.[143]

Travelers recognized feudal conditions in a strong aristocracy, which either was barely held in check by a comparatively powerless central authority or dispensed with a ruler altogether in a *république féodale*,[144] as well as in a warlike "spirit of chivalry" that pervaded all of society, or at least its uppermost stratum. Besides the Malays, such conditions were detected among the Afghans, Ceylonese, Sikhs, Marathas, Kurds, Circassians, Crimean Tatars, and even on Tahiti.[145] If early seventeenth-century European observers had marveled at how countries like China and Vietnam could be ruled in despotic-bureaucratic rather than feudal-chivalric fashion, by around 1800 the tables had been turned: oriental feudalism now appeared as a curious relic of the Middle Ages or as a reminder of the archaic conditions that still persisted on Europe's periphery. James Baillie Fraser felt reminded of his Scottish homeland when visiting Nepal, a country he had studied in depth. He recalled

> that condition of things which existed in the highlands of Scotland during the height of the feodal system, where each possessor of a landed estate exercised the function of a sovereign and made wars and incursions on his neighbours, as a restless spirit of ambition or avarice impelled him.[146]

Like the Scots before them, so too the Indian Marathas with their decentralized command structure ultimately succumbed to the more strictly organized English forces. Contemporary observers described the Marathas as "a military republic, composed of chiefs independent of each other,"[147] and drew parallels to the European Middle Ages or the recently dissolved Holy Roman Empire. Hegel summarized this image in 1822/23 when describing the anarchic and unstable "feudal condition" in India before the Pax Britannica was imposed: an internally riven warrior caste that was little more than a "pack of thieves" (*Raubgesindel*), endlessly locked in blood feuds with the princes above them and the subject population below.[148]

In such assertions, feudalism figured as a form of society that was spread all over the world. John Richardson, never one to shrink from bold claims, even expressed the view that feudalism first arose in Asia before later being introduced into Europe.[149] Many specific instances of classification were contested. Were the Indian princes, particularly following the downfall of "despotic" Mughal supremacy, a "feudal" elite, as contended by Voltaire (India was ruled by "thirty tyrants") and disputed by James Mill?[150] Were there regional pockets left within the vast and fragmented social landscape of South Asia where a fragile kind of chivalric feudalism survived under Hindu auspices? The former colonial official James Tod believed this happened among the Rajputs and in 1830 devoted a bulky work of romantic historiography, both fanciful and erudite, to the subject.[151] Later in the nineteenth century, when the question of an autonomous Indian feudalism had become academic, the British colonial masters entertained the romantic illusion that the Indian princes remaining under their sovereignty constituted an authentic feudal nobility.[152]

In *one* country, nonetheless, a viable feudal system seemed to have survived to the present day: Japan. In the 1660s François Caron, whose knowledge of the country was second to none, had already described an order in which there was an effective center of power, the shogun in Edo, with a layer of ruling princes under him, the daimyo, who in turn were surrounded by vassals of their own.[153] The shogun was far from omnipotent: he himself was bound by the laws of the realm, was forbidden from confiscating the property of princes, and had only a limited right to interfere in their domains. Unlike the emperor of China, he was not supported by a centralized bureaucracy. For Montesquieu and the theorists of despotism who leaned on his authority (such as the abbé Raynal), Japan subsequently figured as another example of despotic conditions. Engelbert Kaempfer, long the most influential and indeed practically the only expert on Japan, had described the Japanese political system in far less detail than the Iranian. That is why the "despotic misunderstanding" was possible; the sparse material presented by Kaempfer could be interpreted in this way.

In 1769 the independent-minded Louis Castilhon pointed to the role played by territorial princes and nobles in Japan, which was uncommonly large for a supposedly despotic state. He made some extraordinary statements that stand diametrically opposed to the dominant tendency of his age: while almost all of Asia from the Mediterranean to the Sea of China languished under the yoke of despotism, only the Japanese—for all that they lacked European science and customs—enjoyed "our rights and our freedom."[154] In Japan, according to Castilhon, there was a hereditary aristocracy and a military mentality. Ambition and honor—utterly foreign to the essence of despotism, in Montesquieu's view[155]—were primary motivating factors. In short, the Japanese were the "English of Asia."[156] Of all the countries in Asia, only Japan bore a resemblance to European nations in its institutions and national character. The figure of the Japanese knight came to fascinate Europe only in its decline; the nineteenth century's interest in the sword-bearing samurai far surpassed that of earlier periods. Yet Japan's exceptional role as a country that in many respects was closer to Europe than any other Asian civilization was already apparent in the eighteenth century.

MASKS AND EMOTIONS

Sociological analysis need not just be the study of groups, strata, and classes—something like "macrosociology." In the eighteenth century there was also a "microsociology" that took an interest in everyday culture. There was a receptiveness to sociability, to human contact, to the movements of the soul in situations of cooperation and conflict.[157]

"Civil society," discussed mainly by French and Scottish thinkers since the midcentury, was not just understood as a space where the interests of private subjects could compete against each other free of state interference;[158] it was also a sphere of controlled affects and refined emotions beyond schematic roles. Around 1800 the view was frequently expressed that one of Europe's advantages over the rest of the world—and over its own classical past as well—lay in the gentleness and courtesy of its human interactions. Europeans congratulated themselves on being more empathetic social creatures and on having attained a higher degree of individualization: European society was held together more through a finely calibrated balance of personalities than through the dictates of convention. With that, an anthropological distinction was made that continues to shape our view of Asians. It was summed up with pithy irony by social anthropologist Jack Goody: "They have customs, we have sentiments."[159]

This view coincided with an important shift in the focus of attention. The former preoccupation with *mœurs* or, as Démeunier 's book title puts it, with *usages et coutumes*, assumed that every society was governed by its own set of rules. Customs are the recurring patterns of everyday life, above all in the preparation and consumption of food and in ceremonies for festive occasons: weddings, funerals, religious rites, and so on. Travel accounts from the sixteenth and seventeeth centuries linger—often with great care and attention to detail—on this rule-bound and ritualized side of foreign societies.[160] The notion of *sociabilité* that arose in the late eighteenth century reflected this schematic behavior at a higher level and shone a light on it from outside. What was at issue now was no longer just the rules themselves but also the extent to which different societies were rule-governed in the first place. That such differences even existed was in itself a new insight.

Changing assessments of Chinese politeness may serve to illustrate this shift. Ever since the first early modern reports on China had appeared, it had been clear that assiduous politeness, a serene composure, or however else one might choose to designate a high degree of affect control was a distinguishing feature of the Chinese people—or at any rate the literati. European visitors should therefore take pains to preserve an unruffled demeanor at all times, Pater Du Halde advised in 1735, lest they seriously damage their standing with the Chinese through temperamental outbursts and fits of rage.[161] In China there were rules of conduct for every situation, the Dominican Navarette had already remarked in 1670; no room was left for spontaneity, and the precision of the unwritten rules of propriety left little room for interpretation and conflict.[162] Du Halde stressed that the formality and solemnity of the Chinese was by no means the expression of a fixed national character but rather the result of a long socialization process, "for they are not lacking in temperament and liveliness but learn early on to become masters of themselves."[163] Once a closer acquaintance with the Chinese had been formed and trust established, however, social relations proceeded "with the same familiarity and ease as would be the case in Europe."[164] The imperturbable *politesse* displayed by upperclass Chinese was thus something of a public mask. Du Halde had nothing against it, simply observing that this was the Chinese idea of civilized behavior.

John Barrow visited China with the Macartney Mission in 1793/94, later writing a book that, for all its pomposity and prejudice, contained some remarkable notes towards a sociology of the Chinese people. Far more strongly than the Jesuits, whose reports Du Halde had worked up in his China encyclopedia, Barrow was struck by the split between the social masks worn by the Chinese and their innermost being. This entailed an extreme disparity between public and private conduct. Almost all the Qing dignitaries

> with whom we had any concern, whether Tartars or Chinese, when in our private society, were easy, affable and familiar, extremely good-humoured, loquacious, communicative. It was in public only, and towards each other, that they assumed their ceremonious gravity, and practiced all the tricks of demeanour which custom requires of them.[165]

These observations are similar to those cited by Du Halde, yet the assessment has shifted considerably during the intervening seventy years. The ritualization of social life (or at least that part of it that plays out in public view) is no longer depicted neutrally as a Chinese peculiarity, still less presented as a laudable cultural achievement. It now serves instead to indicate social petrification. "Unsociable distance" defines not just relations between the sexes and generations but the entire life of society.[166] In Barrow's analysis, China was lacking what Alexis de Tocqueville would later call *les liens*, social bonds. In public life, too, there were hardly any unions, civic associations, or religious communities that made it easier for people to come together and articulate their common interests. The younger generation, in particular, suffered a great deal as a result:

> The young people have no occasional assemblies for the purpose of dancing and of exercising themselves in feats of activity, which, in Europe, are attended with the happy effects of shaking off the gloom and melancholy that a life of constant labour and seclusion from society is apt to promote. They have not even a fixed day of rest set apart for religious worship. Their acts of devotion partake of the same solitary cast that prevails in their domestic life.[167]

For Barrow, the isolation of individuals in China—an instance of social atomization on a grand scale—mainly results from society being dominated by a despotic state apparatus. With this interpretation, he places himself in the Montesquieuean line of thought that saw the "principle" of despotism in fear. Writing half a century after Montesquieu, however, he had a clearer notion of civil society, understood to be more than the mere absence of control from above. China was for him a society of isolated and mistrustful mask-wearers, damned to stagnation and intellectual sterility.[168]

The incomparable civility of the West, so often discussed in the late eighteenth century, continued to be seen in its mastery of social niceties. These included the art of conversation, as cultivated in English coffeehouses and country manors and in the salons of Paris. Its first great theorist was David Hume. The great classical orators who had been studied and emulated to date appeared to him as alien and unrefined. Greco-Roman antiquity was for him a purely rhetorical civilization, a culture of declamation and stilted figures of speech. Modern Europe, by constrast, was a civilization of witty conversation in intimate settings. One was defined by monologue, the other by dialogue.[169] As other commentators registered, formal speech was characteristic of non-European cultures as well, albeit not of China, where eloquence was neglected in favor of written communication.[170] The art of speaking was highly developed among the Arabs and stood, as Sir William Jones explained, in close connection with an oral tradition of folk poetry.[171] The missionary Pierre Lemonnier de La Bissachère made the astonishing discovery that in Tonkin, almost the only way to be exempted from onerous labor duties for the state was to win over the mandarins through well-composed addresses. That is why the Tonkinese were trained from an early age in the art of public speaking.[172] In his ethnographic description of southeast India, completed in 1711, Bartholomäus Ziegenbalg was full of praise for the "natural eloquence" of the Tamils. Unfettered by the rigid rules of formal rhetoric, they were possessed "of a glib tongue" and able "to discourse at length" on any suitable subject. Their fluency and spontaneousness might serve as an example to Europeans.[173]

In the later eighteenth century, European observers expressed ambivalence about the value of such achievements. On the one hand, displays of oratorical virtuosity (in a Malay court, for example) were impressive and bespoke the speaker's civilizational merits.[174] On the other hand, the art of public speaking belonged to a stage of social development that Western Europe had put behind it: communications in Europe were now mostly conducted in the medium of writing; besides on the stage, the spoken word had all but disappeared from literature; eloquence in court had become the preserve of specially trained lawyers. The intimacy of speech, its ennoblement from an instrument of rhetoric to a vehicle of free conversation, further demonstrated the superiority of European modernity.

Not all travelers and commentators on Asia were convinced, however, that life in the West was clearly preferable to an average existence in the East. William George Browne, an important researcher on Africa and the Near East who from 1792 to 1798 had traveled widely between thc Sudan and Asia Minor, concluded his travel report by offering a "comparative view of life and happiness in the East and in Europe."[175] Browne begins by contrasting general characteristics: the European is impatient, active, and sanguine, whereas the Oriental is indolent, grave, and unimaginative. These qualities are not anthropological invariants; they result from differences in education. Each system has its advantages. The same holds true of the way women are treated. Confining them to a harem means that "social intercourse is . . . rendered less vivacious and amusing" than in Europe, "but numberless inquietudes are avoided." Adultery, which in the West exposes the husband to ridicule, his wife to scandal, and her lover to penury, is unknown in the East.[176]

The "easy compliance" that distinguishes social relations in the Orient likewise has much to recommend it over European restlessness. Quarrels are fewer, formalities less burdensome, and there is less pressure to keep up conversation than in the salon culture of the North, where "the abortions of fancy and caprice" are taken for outpourings of wit. The abstinence in food and drink habitually shown at the table by Easterners contrasts with the gluttony of European dinner guests. Browne is no Rousseauian enthusiast, no ideologist of a simple life close to the fountainhead of nature. He is an open-minded observer of two very different life forms whose respective advantages he evaluates with pragmatic shrewdness.

THE BIRTH OF SOCIOLOGY FROM THE SPIRIT OF CULTURAL DIFFERENCE

The eighteenth-century literature on Asia produced numerous texts of great sociological distinction. Being confronted with strange climes and customs led their authors to eschew the simplistic dichotomies offered by many an armchair traveler. They endeavored instead to describe, in as painstaking and realistic a manner as possible, the foreign ways they had often experienced themselves as participant observers. Who were the best of these pioneer sociologists? The great travelers of the seventeenth century may be considered their precursors: Bernier on the Mughal Empire, Chardin on Iran, Semedo on China. In the eighteenth and early nineteenth century, no text from the quill of a European eyewitness surpasses the volume on Aleppo by the brothers Alexander and Patrick Russell in the "thickness" of its sociological description. But several approach this high standard: Desideri on Tibet, Marsden on Sumatra, Elphinstone on Afghanistan, Kirkpatrick on Nepal, Cœurdoux, Dubois, and Buchanan on India, Koffler on Cochinchina, Malcolm on Iran, Niebuhr, Jaubert and Volney on the Arab Near East.

Volney, a member of the late Enlightenment group of intellectuals, the *Idéologues*, is the foremost theorist of them all. His theoretical contribution lies in the concept of *genre de vie*, designating a society's way of life. This concept took on enormous significance in France, becoming extraordinarily important for the human geography of the early twentieth century, above all for Paul Vidal de la Blache and his followers. Although Volney frequently uses it in a considered manner, he never offers an abstract definition.[177] *Genre de vie* is a theoretical construct that mediates between the macrolevel of society as a whole and the microperspective of observed social activity. The concept draws the consequences from an insight that could only fully be grasped through the study of non-Western societies: that societies differ from each other not just hierarchically—according to estates, ranks, or classes—but also spatially, ethnically, and in their lifestyles. Talking about *genres de vie* made it possible to describe what later came to be known as *milieux*. For Volney, the concept lies at the intersection of his two intimately connected points of view: the *état physique*, that is, the natural environment, and the *état politique*, the political and social conditions of a country. Within a country there can be a multitude of very different *genres de vie*: those of Syria's urban notables and rural Bedouins, Egypt's Mamluk elite and dirt-poor fellahin.

When he wanted to make a trenchant point, Volney did not shrink back from advancing the most general historico-philosophical speculations or from sharply opposing East and West. Yet the concept of *genres de vie* allowed him as an empiricist (which is what he was above all else) to concentrate on observable social contexts. The "Orient" cannot be seen, only constructed. A way of life, by contrast, can be studied through the evidence it presents to the senses. Overseas travelers of the late eighteenth and early nineteenth centuries were the pioneers of just such an experiential science of lifestyles and their material presuppositions. Alexander von Humboldt and Alexis de Tocqueville were its greatest practitioners.[178] Through their writings, the New World became the best described and analyzed part of the world, at least until the mid-nineteenth century. For all the justified attention they have received, however, the best studies on Asia should not be allowed to fall into oblivion. They too contributed to the birth of sociology from the spirit of cultural difference.

ON HOSPITALITY[179]

Finally, a few remarks on how societies behave at the very concrete and tangible interface with the Other. Societies differ tangibly in the ways they respond to foreigners approaching them from outside. Reactions vary on a scale from killing the trespasser or shipwreck survivor to hailing strangers as long-awaited deities. In the famous murder of Captain Cook on February 14, 1779, in Kealakekua Bay (Hawai'i), the extremes of welcome and violence merged into a single contradictory event of emblematic stature. Hardly any other question is of greater political relevance today than the issue of how foreigners should be received.

The strict policing and surveillance experienced by Europeans in closed countries with strong law enforcement institutions such as China and, even more so, Japan, was an exception that affected relatively few travelers to Asia. In most other Asian countries, travelers' freedom of movement was unimpeded by systematic state interference.[180] Travel in the Islamic world, India, and Southeast Asia may have been arduous and not infrequently dangerous, but at least it was possible; indeed, it was arguably easier than traveling through Christian countries would have been for Muslims (very few tried before about 1830). Western travelers who had experienced religious intolerance at home—the French Protestant refugee Sir John Chardin was a case in point—cherished the greater religious freedom in Islamic countries.[181]

At the end of the eighteenth century only a few regions, notably the area around Bombay with its famous Elephanta Caves, boasted anything like an embryonic tourist infrastructure. Everywhere else, the traveler had to rely either on the logistics of public transport—the caravanserais in Persia and North India were a celebrated example—or the help of the local population. Remarks on the treatment shown foreign guests were therefore a standard feature of travel narratives.

On the basis of such depictions, there developed a more general discourse on hospitality and its various modifications (although these were rarely clearly distinguished): hospitability—that is, hospitality extended in a spirit of friendship—and the right to hospitality of strangers in a strange land. A second source of this discourse was the ancient historians and geographers. Time and again, for example, the passage in the *Germania* (written probably in 98 CE) was cited where Tacitus credits the Germans with unequalled hospitality (*hospitium*). Nobody, whether familiar or unknown, has the door shut in his face: "they do not distinguish those they know from strangers." The visitor was escorted from house to house; guest and host plied each other with gifts without giving a thought to their value or feeling under any obligation to the giver.[182]

Hospitality and hospitability could mean different things to different people. At the very least, it meant placing the foreign guest under the protective authority of the head of the household, but it often also entailed more than the mere guarantee that the traveler would come to no harm: extending a warm welcome, sharing hearth and home ungrudgingly and without expectation of return, assisting travelers in their onward journey. European travelers were rarely exposed to the full repertoire of hospitality for the simple reason that they were almost never refugees seeking asylum. The cash, gold, and other valuables they brought with them mostly sufficed to defray any costs to the host. A friendly reception of traveling guests is reported of almost all peoples outside East Asia: the inhabitants of the Indonesian isles,[183] the Hindus in Bengal,[184] the Iranians,[185] the Turks,[186] the Kurds,[187] the "Tatars" on the Crimea and in the Central Asian provinces of the Russian Empire,[188] the Balochs in present-day Pakistan, whose propensity to cruelty—thankfully suspended when hosting guests from abroad—is highlighted in the reports,[189] and the Burmese, who are singled out for praise for being hospitable on principle, not out of naivety and weakness.[190] On the Aleutian Islands, a stranger goes from hut to hut, "and they all share their food with him."[191]

Even Europeans who took pride in their critical view of the Orient acknowledged the widespread hospitality they encountered there as a particularly attractive feature of the East. "No part of oriental manners," wrote the traveler to Syria and antiquarian Robert Wood in 1757, "shows those people in so amicable a light as their discharge of the duties of hospitality." And he added: "Indeed the severities of Eastern despotism have ever been softened by this virtue, which so happily flourishes most where it is most wanted."[192] Many statements of this kind reflect the clichés of the travelogue genre and an ethnic stereotyping that expects hospitality from wild mountain warriors and peaceful camel herders. But particularly accurate travelers sometimes allow reality to shine through with its mixed offer of experiences.

In 1738, for example, Dr. Thomas Shaw, esteemed by both contemporary readers and posterity as a reporter of impeccable integrity, gave exact information about his travel experiences in the Maghreb and the Levant.[193] Understandably, the most helpful source of hospitality had been his compatriots: the numerous British merchants in the Near East who ran trading posts on the coast. In the cities and villages of the interior, the traveler could take heart whenever he came across a special guest house in which strangers were put up for the night at the expense of the local community. But it might already be occupied, or the custodian with the key could prove impossible to track down. Where such public facilities were unavailable, and where private inns or hostels were also not to be had, Shaw sometimes discovered that the much-vaunted hospitality of the East was nothing more than a pious legend. On these occasions, the wandering preacher found himself forcibly reminded of words from the Old Testament: ". . . and when he went in, he sat him down in a street of the city: for there was no man that took them into his house to lodging."[194] Shaw was never taken in for the night by Arab families, at any rate. When traveling in open countryside, he and his few companions slept under the stars; a tent would have marked them as well-to-do and made them easy prey for robbers.

Only those who had lived in a country for a long time were capable of looking beyond their own limited travel experiences. Alexander Russell pointed out that not *every* foreigner was accorded a friendly reception in Aleppo. The oft-described kindnesses of the oriental host were reserved for those who had been accepted as guests. Among private Turks, this required a recommendation. Hospitality thus functioned only within a preexisting network of relations.[195] Those who entered the tent of a Bedouin, Volney wrote later, could feel assured of their safety, but getting into the tent in the first place was no straightforward matter.[196] Carsten Niebuhr, the most renowned eighteenth-century traveler to Arabia, agreed with Russell that the famous Arab and Turkish hospitality had already disappeared in the cities: "A stranger can no more expect there than in Europe that people who do not know him will invite him into their homes."[197] In villages where the arrival of a European was perhaps still a novelty, however, the Arabs were "hospitable to this day."[198] "To this day"—with that, Niebuhr answered one of the questions set him by the Paris Académie des Inscriptions et des Belles Lettres: whether the Arab hospitality attested to in the Bible still existed.[199]

The literature of romanticism was again densely populated by hospitable Arabs. Tales of Arab tribesmen who allegedly placed their own wives and daughters at their guests' disposal were indispensable for painting a romantic picture of the Orient.[200] The Swiss traveler to the Orient Johann Ludwig Burckhardt, a sober and precise witness, also mentions this "barbaric system of hospitality," adding a nice story about a particular branch of the Asyr tribe living south of Mecca:

> If the stranger rendered himself agreeable to his fair partner, he was treated next morning with the utmost attention by his host, and furnished, on parting, with provisions sufficient for the remainder of his journey; but if, unfortunately, he did not please the lady, his cloak was found the next day to want a piece, cut off by her as a signal of contempt. This circumstance being known, the unlucky traveler was driven away with disgrace by all the women and children of the village or encampment.[201]

The Grand Theory of hospitality that was popular in Enlightenment-era Europe mostly operated at a remove from such ethnographic details.[202] From around 1760, hospitality was widely associated with "barbaric" phases of social evolution. William Robertson, a good empiricist who regarded with skepticism the more audacious attempts by his friends and contemporaries to sketch a "conjectural history," saw late antiquity and the Middle Ages as something like a golden age of hospitality. There was much need of it at the time: the dissolution of the political, economic, and cultural ties that had held together the ancient world had led to such a fragmentation of life in Europe that a bare minimum in traffic and trade between nations could only be maintained by guaranteeing the security of strangers. Robertson points out that hospitality in the Middle Ages was more than a mere custom or moral imperative; it was a legally enforcable duty.[203] This leads him to formulate a law of inverse proportion: "hospitality abounded while the intercourse among men was inconsiderable."[204] According to Robertson, hospitality moves to the fore in times of crisis as a functional equivalent to a well-regulated society. It comes to assume vital importance in the dark and anarchic periods of transition between the renaissances of world history.

Adam Smith, who approached history with greater speculative brio than his fastidious friend Robertson, developed his own version of a functionalist explanation several years later. In societies where a lack of overseas trade and investment opportunities means that there are few possibilities for employing surplus production, “rustick hospitality at home” presents an obvious avenue for conspicuous consumption.[205] Smith had in mind not just hospitality towards strangers but also the munificence of feudal lords, who would often expend fortunes on their retainers and clients. In Smith’s account, this simple economic mechanism is found in *all* commercially and industrially less developed societies, in Scotland as much as in Arabia. It thus does not stand in any particularly close connection with the Orient. The only thing that prevents hospitality—generally a costly undertaking for the host—from becoming economically ruinous is the fact that travel is dangerous and therefore rare in times of barbarism.[206] In primitive ages, hospitality is thus an economic necessity; later, in more complex societies, it becomes economically irrational. Around the same time, another Scottish social theorist, Adam Ferguson, situated hospitality more precisely in the stage of pastoral nomadism. Rather than offering an economic explanation, he understood it as part of a moral economy of honor that largely disappears with the transition to the next stage of social development.[207]

Even the earliest theorists of post-feudal modernization had seen the fate of hospitality as an index of social development. Montesquieu was one of the first to note that hospitality was made defunct by trade. Commercialization brought with it peace, but only between nations, not between individuals, since now everything in life could be bought or sold at a fixed price: “the smallest things, those required by humanity, are done or given for money.”[208] Conversely, the combination of robbing the neighboring *collective* and demonstrating hospitality towards *individuals* remains in place where commerce is not yet in the ascendant. Condorcet, the apostle of progress, refused to acknowledge the conflict between hospitality and commercialization identified by Montesquieu. He saw *both* as civilizing, pacifying factors that promote intertribal contacts in the agrarian stage that follows on from nomadism.[209]

Unjustly forgotten today, Dr. William Falconer was an encyclopedist and universalist social thinker in the Age of Enlightenment as well as a physician of some repute. Like Montesquieu before him—and in contrast to Rousseau and his disciples—Falconer warned in 1781 against idealizing the pastoral life in the manner of the old bucolic tradition. When studying the customs of "pastoral nations" in their "barbarous state," he was amazed "that although addicted to pillaging strangers, they practice hospitality to a great degree."[210] The *individual* stranger enjoys the freedom to journey unmolested, since he poses no threat to the host society and robbing him would bring neither practical advantages nor glory. Yet Falconer then makes an interesting observation that takes him a step beyond both his master Montesquieu and stage theorists such as Smith, Ferguson, and Condorcet: "As to internal corruption, or that which arises from the influence of money, I am inclined to think that this also is diminished by the change of the way of life. The nations who live in a pastoral state, are the most venal and corrupt in the world. The Arabs and the Tartars will do any thing for money."[211] In short, monetarization is no reliable indicator of modernity. At an early stage of societal evolution, money can already dictate relations within a community and wreak havoc by attenuating social bonds and eroding solidarity. Already in ancient times, warlike nomadic tribes had repeatedly sold their military services or their neutrality for cash, while the Romans' famed political virtues would have been inconceivable without their society's foundation in agriculture. According to Falconer, the decline of hospitality is thus not primarily caused by commercialization and the spread of a monetary economy. He sees it rather as having fallen victim to social hierarchization. The condition of nomadism, being overwhelmingly egalitarian in structure, demands a certain degree of ceremony to allow status and prestige to be allotted when people come together. This encompasses the various forms of hospitality:

> But an agricultural state is nearly, in every respect, the reverse of that just described. There is a necessity for different ranks, as well as functions and occupations, in such a society; the nature of their

> employment being local, precludes them from variety of acquaintance; and their sense of honor is seldom so nice as to render transgressions in point of behaviour, unless accompanied with some substantial injury, great objects of concern. In short, the politeness of agricultural nations, like what Mr. Montesquieu has observed of the English, is rather in their morals than in their behavior.[212]

They have a moral sympathy for helpless strangers but are little inclined to do anything for them.

Falconer observed the development of hospitality with the cool gaze of an early sociologist. Others judged more resolutely. David Hume regarded the demise of "antient hospitality [which] was the source of vice, disorder, sedition and idleness" as a welcome sign of progress.[213] In his ethnographic material, Jean-Nicolas Démeunier found confirmation of the thesis advanced by the Scottish philosopher Henry Home (Lord Kames) that there was no more universal human inclination than an aversion to strangers.[214] Wise legislators and trade had temporarily been able to take the edge off such instincts and inculcate a more hospitable attitude, yet in a further step, "administrators" in many nations had promoted a spirit of patriotism ("un goût exclusif pour la patrie") that had reversed the civilizational gains.[215] The treatment of strangers had gone from being a matter for individual families and local communities to a political concern; governments had taken control of alien affairs. This was the only satisfactory explanation for why, in the modern age, there were once again states that had completely closed themselves off from the outside world. Démeunier thus detects a more complicated pattern in the history of hospitality than the linear narrative of progressive modernization offered by many a stage theorist. He cites as an example an unusual case: the Paulistas in Brazil, a criminal frontier squad, ten to twelve thousand men strong, who maintained their own quasi-state, treated strangers with the utmost brutality, and admitted new recruits into their ranks only after subjecting them to severe trials. But he could also have been thinking of Japan, given that, of all the theorists discussed here, he was the one best equipped to grasp the nub of the Japanese case: the manipulation of xenophobic impulses by the state.

Démeunier 's pessimistic scenario runs counter to the Enlightenment sensibilities of his time. These are presented in distilled form in a particularly extensive, richly documented discussion of hospitality published in Leipzig in 1777, one year after Démeunier . The author of this extraordinary book, entitled *On Hospitality. An Apology for the Human Race* (*Von der Gastfreundschaft. Eine Apologie für die Menschheit*), was Christian Cayus Lorenz Hirschfeld, still known today for his five-volume *Art of Gardening*. Here we find a thorough compilation of the ethnographic material and a discussion of many motives that also play a major role in the contributions of other authors. Hirschfeld views hospitality as a collective, national affair rather than as a merely personal one. It is a "natural" human "drive," but it can only come to fruition when certain obstacles are overcome, such as the "absurdity" shown by men "still in their primitive state" in taking flight from approaching strangers.[216] That hospitality is a natural drive is experimentally confirmed by the fact that islanders in rarely traveled seas extend a warm welcome to strangers.[217] The most recent Tahitian reports of Bougainville and Cook, which Hirschfeld was able to read in time to incorporate their findings, appeared to support this view. Hirschfeld further contours his basic idea when he speaks of an "indirect natural drive, rooted in the drives of sociability and sympathy."[218] That is why this drive can be historicized. Hirschfeld operates within the parameters of Franco-Scottish stage theory, which he was one of the first German authors to draw on, going into great detail to discuss hospitality at the various developmental stages of hunting, fishing, herding, and so on. As a strident critic of colonialism, he generally sees defensive xenophobic reactions as provoked.[219] After all, only those under attack feel the need to defend themselves.

Hirschfeld shows particular interest in the emergence of a culture of hospitality in its classical homeland, the Orient. He places more emphasis on a conducive natural environment than on the functional-sociological factors to which Adam Smith was drawing attention around the same time:

> The mildness and brightness of the sky, the enjoyment of so much natural beauty lying all around, roused people's spirits and and enlivened their sensations. In lands such as these, the stage of initial savagery could be neither intense nor long-lasting.[220]

Such anthropological factors explained why Arabs, Iranians, and Turks, in particular, received strangers with such openness. Hirschfeld then distinguishes between the naïve hospitality of the Arabs, which "is rather a natural kindheartedness born of simplicity," and the more elegant and civilized, largely postnomadic Iranians, who treat their guests with "refined courtesy."[221] Hospitality also serves in all Islamic countries—and especially in Turkey—to moderate the despotic form of government. The severity of the political system is partly balanced out by the social virtues of ordinary citizens.[222]

For Hirschfeld, unlike for Hume, the decline of hospitality, culminating in its disappearance from present-day European society, is less a sign of successful modernization than a deeply ambivalent phenomenon. "What goes by the name of hospitality in civilized nations" is no longer a "time-honored virtue" but a mere social convention.[223] Europe has become the homeland of commercial travel:

> The spirit of trade, which connects all nations, has broken the bonds of charity among private persons. It has furthered and strengthened the love of profit, and so, as this has extended its dominion, it has disrupted the tender motions of nature which linked man to his fellow men. The only party that has benefited is the rich.[224]

Hospitality has become a saleable commodity in the progressive societies of the West. We have entered the era of the hotel trade and tourism. Hirschfeld takes up and extends Montesquieu's analysis. The unstoppable commercialization of life transforms the guest from a hospitably received stranger into a paying customer. The host makes way for the hotelier.

The last beacon of the European Enlightenment, Alexander von Humboldt, also recognized the dialectic of social modernization and the dissolution of the interpersonal ties that had formerly been stabilized by tradition:

> It has been remarked that, with the exception of a few very populous towns, hospitality has not yet perceptibly diminished since the first establishment of the Spanish colonists in the New World. It is distressing to think, that this change will take place, when population and the colonial economy shall have made more rapid progress; and that this state of society, which we are agreed to call an advanced state of civilization, will by degrees have banished "the old Castilian generosity."[225]

Humboldt noted this in July 1799 in Cumaná, a town on the coast of today's Venezuela. Carsten Niebuhr had experienced something similar thirty years before in Yemen. The end of hospitality as a right, custom, and duty, its transformation into private virtue or commercial enterprise, was a harbinger of more fundamental change in societies that had long been deemed all but unchangeable. In far-off corners of the non-European world, watchful travelers heeded the dawning of a new age.

The Grand Theory of hospitality, as formulated by authors such as Montesquieu, Falconer, Ferguson, and Hirschfeld, was a curious episode in the early history of sociology. It revealed that the forces of social development, never more virulently on display than at the time these authors were writing, had turned the age-old tradition of hospitality into a dysfunctional luxury. As a private and common-law institution, the right to "hospitality"—which Immanuel Kant, in his *Perpetual Peace* from 1795, was still seeking to ground in international law—had fallen victim to a process of modernization that had begun even *before* the onset of industralization. From now on, hospitality could no longer be claimed; it was left to the individual's whims, feelings, and interests. Europe had been alienated from traditional ways of dealing with the alien. Now, whenever such customs were still encountered abroad, they were regarded as a curiosity, an archaic remnant of stages in human evolution that the West had long since outgrown. The more self-consciously European universalism celebrated its triumph, the greater the distance that opened up between itself and everyone else. In the end, Europe was left on its own.

XII

Women

It was not enough that fields and meadows had been partitioned and assigned masters. The least that they achieved was to station around their cabins slaves who were bound to them in service. The regulations thus introduced concerned needs only; soon others were required to maintain order, even in the realm of the pleasures. Some of these pleasures had brought about an unwitting debasement of humankind: others would have led to its utter ruin. The most intense of them all was undoubtedly union between the sexes; it was also necessarily the first to be affected by the strange revolution the world had undergone.

—Simon-Nicolas-Henri Linguet (1736–94), *Théorie des lois civiles ou principes fondamentaux de la société* (1767)[1]

Not all male commentators on questions of gender emulated Linguet, that colorful ancien régime radical and underrated political and social theorist, in rising to the heights of a general theory. In the footsteps, or the shadow, of Montesquieu, a frequent target of his critical pen, Linguet sketched a theory of the subjugation of women by men in the course of societal evolution. The scope of this idea was vast and not specific to any one civilization, and the basic thesis was simple: everywhere, the progress of society was built upon the subjugation and misery of women and the toiling lower classes.

Christoph Meiners at Göttingen, ostracized today from the history of ideas for his crassly racist attitudes towards Africans and what he called "Mongols," told a different story. In that story, the oppression and exploitation of women was not a consequence of an early fall from grace in a mythical past but persisted into the present day, showing no sign of diminishing with the march of civilization. Meiners later loses himself in the lurid anecdotes he loved to cull from travel accounts. But the beginning of the four-volume world history of women that he published in German between 1788 and 1800 is a powerful and passionate indictment in the best Enlightenment tradition:

> The history of no people, of no other class of society, presents a spectacle so revolting, a spectacle that so powerfully excites the sentiments of horror and compassion, as the history of the condition of the female sex among most of the nations of the globe. . . . Among more than one half of the human race, the life of women was an uninterrupted series of hardships and humiliations, the patient endurance of which could scarcely be expected of human nature; and the condition of the maid, the wife, and the widow, was a state of progressively aggravated subjection and misery on which all the mortifications and evils of life were accumulated and from which, on the other hand, almost all its pleasures and enjoyments were excluded.[2]

These conditions prevailed "among more than one half of the human race," says the Göttingen professor. Which half? Meiners's answer throughout his lengthy work is a mixture of predictable praise of modern Europe and unexpected censure spanning the "us and them" divide. The question that most intrigued Meiners and many of his contemporaries was that of nonbinary difference or, to use the plural that alone is appropriate here, of differences in the social situation of women. Even if the enslavement of the female half of humanity were to be found nearly everywhere, a closer ethnographic look tried to detect characteristic forms and special paths. This is the particular focus of the present chapter, which follows up directly on what the previous chapter had to say about the representation of society. Eighteenth-century travel writers and their European readers were at least as interested in questions of gender and sexuality as were the later "founding fathers" of the social sciences in the nineteenth century.

THE CARDINAL DIFFERENCE

More than anything else, visitors from the East were amazed at the position of women in Europe. Yirmisekiz Mehmed Çelebi Efendi, also known as Mehmed Efendi, who stayed in France for eleven months in 1720–21 as an Ottoman special envoy, described his experiences in a report (*sefâretnâme*) that, for the first time, documented the attempts made by a Turkish dignitary to understand the West. Mehmed Efendi was surprised at how great a portion of personal life played out in public view and at the relative insignificance accorded the private sphere. Men and women ate in each other's company, not just in their homes, but even at public dinners. Women went to the theater and the opera, took part in public balls, and received male guests in their private chambers. Actresses displayed unrestrained emotion on stage. On all public occasions, women were treated with respect and honor; even the king received them with the greatest courtesy. Efendi found Paris to be a much livelier city than Istanbul, mainly because women of all classes could be seen out on the streets.[3] In no other area were cultural differences so strikingly conspicuous.

European observers of Asia took a similar view. "The cardinal difference between us and the Orientals," Voltaire asserted in the concluding remarks to his *Essai sur les mœurs*, "lies in how we treat our womenfolk."[4] Travel writers could be assured of public interest when they included the all-but-obligatory chapter on women in their reports.

The observers were almost exclusively male. The period before 1830 saw the publication of only a handful of texts by female travelers to Asia. None of the great scientific reports was written by a woman. East and Central Asia, Siberia, and Persia were purely masculine domains. Reports were sent from India by Jemima Kindersley, whose letters communicate a narrowly colonial mentality,[5] and her polar opposite, the highly unorthodox Eliza Fay. The daughter of an English shipwright, Fay married a lawyer who in 1780 was admitted to the Supreme Court of Calcutta, only to become tied up in debts, intrigues, and love affairs. She left him, returned to London in 1782, and was back in Calcutta two years later to set up shop as a milliner, although with little success. A few years later she embarked—quite literally—on a new career in transoceanic trade between Britain, India, and the United States. One of her ships caught fire, another barely escaped shipwreck. Fay finally opened a boarding school for girls in Surrey, returned to India once more, and died in Calcutta in 1816 at the age of sixty. Towards the end of her life, she seems to have decided that travel literature might be a good money-spinner. Her travel letters were sold posthumously to the *Calcutta Gazette* to pay off her debts.[6] Eliza Fay's letters break with the generic conventions of travel literature and make no claim to scholarly accuracy or philosophical profundity. They convey the impression of an uncommonly vivacious woman. "Her age produced many greater letters," the novelist E. M. Forster wrote in tribute, "but few that so faithfully reflect the character of their author."[7]

In the Near East, the resolute and unbiased Lady Mary Wortley Montagu, who in 1717–18 had come to know Istanbul as the wife of the British ambassador, remained a unique phenomenon; there will be more to say about her shortly. Lady Elizabeth Craven, the gullible tourist in the Crimea,[8] cut a much less impressive figure. Women are almost completely silent in Enlightenment-era travel literature on Asia. In the texts as well, their voices are heard only on rare occasions. One of them occurs in an amusing anecdote related by Carsten Niebuhr, who had a fine eye for the telling detail. In September 1762 he had the following experience near Suez:

> It is well-known that Arabs are permitted to have up to four wives at once. However, most of them content themselves with only one in their lifetime, provided she generally does her husband's bidding. Our sheikh Beni Said had two wives, one of whom, living near where we had put up our tent, was charged with supervising the servants who tended to the livestock. The other lived in a different area and was responsible for a garden of date palms. His domestic affairs

> were thus managed by his two wives when he was visiting friends, or was away in Suez earning money fetching water, or when he brought his wares to market in Suez or Káhira [Cairo]. Our neighbor, the foremost lady in the camp, honored us one afternoon with a visit in the company of several other Arab women. She brought with her a chicken and some eggs as a gift. Now, I had been in the Orient for some time already, but this was the first time I had spoken with a Mohammedan lady, leaving aside the dancing girls of Káhira. Since the Arab women were unwilling to enter our tent they all sat outside, but close enough for them to sit in the shade and for us to be able to converse at ease. Of all we told them about Europe, nothing pleased them so much as that a Christian was forbidden to take more than one wife. The wife of our sheikh lamented that she had a rival; her chief complaint was that her husband loved this rival more than her, even though she had wed him first and behaved at all times as a good wife should.[9]

In this brief passage, Niebuhr touches on several motifs that define how oriental women were perceived: polygamy, love, servitude, but also independence in their working life. As always, he eschews pretentious "philosophical" commentary and thus also turns down the opportunity—eagerly seized by many other travelers—to push the message of Christian monogamy.

IN THE REALM OF THE SENSES

Among travelers, there was extended discussion about the extent to which women in Asiatic countries were in fact "shut away" or were a visible part of the urban streetscape. There was no lack of dramatic examples. In 1766 Mrs. Kindersley reported from Patna that women and children had recently perished when a fire had broken out in their harem: they did not dare flee the burning building for fear of bringing shame on themselves and incurring their master's wrath.[10] The story was repeatedly told—first of the shah of Persia, then transposed to other settings—that during an outing of the princely harem, all local males over the age of six had been ordered to evacuate the streets. Almost everyone fled as if a lion were on the loose, Chardin says, and the curious few who stayed behind to watch the procession were given a taste of the whip or even run through with the executioner's sword.[11] Backed up by the threat of punishment, this taboo on looking (*qoruq* in Persian) proved the same thing from the other side: either women were hidden away or the relationship between private and public was reversed and the ruler's subjects were forced to conceal themselves.

To be sure, European witnesses were permitted to see neither the women shut away behind closed doors nor those borne in sedan chairs through the streets. At most, the controversy therefore concerned the extent to which Asiatic women were kept out of sight in their homes: how many of them were seen in public and under what circumstances? It was widely assumed, although almost never demonstrated, that they were held "captive" against their will. Alexander Russell suggested that the invisibility of females in the Muslim world had nothing to do with coercion, but was instead the result of the border between public and private space being drawn differently than in Europe; but this sensible solution was heeded by few.[12]

The fact that so little was known about what went on behind harem and seraglio walls,[13] with at best an occasional glimpse afforded to female visitors like Lady Mary Wortley Montagu or Baron de Tott's mother-in-law, left vast scope for the imagination. A European master builder succeeded in smuggling Engelbert Kaempfer into the less dangerous outer wings of the royal seraglio in Isfahan for a short time to carry out some work there.[14] The most systematic and scientific observer of early modern Iran took the opportunity to register the architectural form of the buildings—but little else. Even the inquisitive Chardin found out very little about the seraglio, leading him to indulge in uncharacteristically bold speculations.[15] Small private harems were more promising targets for investigation. Montesquieu's *Lettres persanes* had already shifted attention away from the huge seraglios at court—*political* institutions with clear hierarchies where princes were educated, eunuchs schemed, and dowager sultanas held sway—to the normal harems of average oriental lords.[16]

These boasted nowhere near the two thousand women that Sultan Selim I and the grand mughal Aurangzeb were said to have possessed, still less the three thousand attributed to the last Ming emperors; they could not even match the four hundred companions of Shah Safi II, nor the roughly three hundred held in their seraglios by eighteenth-century sultans.[17] Moreover, each of the monarch's women had her own maidservants, so that courts could enclose vast female worlds. The number of eunuchs may serve to indicate the distance between the royal harem and polygamous private households: whereas the shah employed three thousand eunuchs in Chardin's day, private houses made do with six to eight, while simpler folk rarely had more than two.[18]

Yet precisely the more modest ménages with half a dozen or so wives guarded by a couple of eunuchs seemed to offer ideal conditions for vice to flourish. From serious travel accounts all the way to exotically veiled pornography, the literature abounds in fantasies of lust and longing bred in the hothouse atmosphere of harem intrigue. Lesbian trysts, fornicating eunuchs, and the cruelties that could ensue when the sexuality of young women was left unsatisfied were among the standard themes.[19] Behind them lay the view that climate, strong libido, and weakness of character condemned Easterners to a life of sexual excess. Even the almighty despot was a slave to his drives and passions. The Iranians in particular were viewed as insatiable libertines. As John Fryer wrote in a passage that could just as easily have been written by many other authors, they "put no bounds to their lascivious Desires" and "outdo the Sensuality of the hottest Beasts."[20] William Marsden later sarcastically objected that, while high temperatures may indeed arouse desire, they weaken the constitution at the same time. As a result, the unfortunate men of Iran were caught in a trap between their burning lust and their physical inability to satisfy it.[21]

Openly practiced pederasty—"sodomy," in the parlance of the day—was considered no less abominable. It was believed to be particularly widespread under the Ottoman ruling class (such as under the Janissaries), among the Egyptian Mamluks and Algerian Corsairs, in Bukhara,[22] in Japan, and wherever Buddhist priests were to be found. Marsden, meanwhile, thought that the unspeakable sin was unknown in Sumatra, so much so that there was no word for it in the local tongue.[23] Joost Schouten, a successful agent for the VOC, was said to have acquired a taste for "sodomy" during his posting in Siam, where it was quite normal. In 1644 he was put to death for it in Batavia.[24] Sonnini reported that bestiality was openly practiced in Egypt.[25]

The view of the Orient as a sexually uninhibited and perverse counterworld to Europe could also, needless to say, serve as a projection screen for the writer's own repressed sexual urges. Robert Knox, the shipwreck survivor on Ceylon, contended that there were no prostitutes there because *all* women were whores.[26] William Marsden, who took the women of Sumatra to be the chastest in all the world, complained that travelers formed their image of oriental women from those they encountered in the brothels of port cities.[27] There may have been an element of truth to this, although surely not in Knox's case.

In the eighteenth century, however, this image did not yet have the all-surpassing significance it would assume in nineteenth-century exoticism. Coolly functional explanations existed alongside lustful voyeurism. Hammer-Purgstall's political sociology of pederasty is a fine example of the former. According to Hammer, the role of Ottoman court pages as pleasure boys had little to do with sexuality. Rather, since the late fourteenth century it had been a route to lucrative feudal fiefs and high state office, the "most effective means of gaining honor and riches."[28] Wars against Christians had at times been unleashed solely in order to replenish the supply of page boys. "From these nurseries," the Austrian diplomat and scholar concludes with barely a trace of irony or moral indignation, "emerged some of the greatest men of the Ottoman Empire."[29]

The confinement of women in harems provoked varied responses from commentators. There were three basic templates. Firstly, many European travelers showed a male understanding for polygamy, the trade in concubines, and the custom of keeping women indoors during daylight hours. After all, did not the bloom of oriental beauty fade all too soon? Montesquieu thought that girls in the East were sexually mature at eight and old by twenty[30]—and needed to be replaced with fresh blood if their master's sexual needs were to be satisfied.[31]

Secondly, a more sophisticated, even theoretical-sounding idea was frequently aired. Popularized above all by Montesquieu, it claimed that in hot climates, females tended to moral dissolution and had to be protected from their own unbridled lust by being kept under lock and key. This brought with it the additional advantage that men would be safe from their ravenous clutches. "In these countries," Montesquieu says, "there must be bolted doors instead of precepts."[32] In medieval Europe, W. G. Browne speculated, sublimation through romantic chivalry had served a similar purpose. This noninstitutionalized solution had broken down over time, however, and recently there had been signs that women were straining against the bounds of Christian wedlock.[33] In Asia, Montesquieu believed, female morals were at their purest where the sexes were most successfully separated.[34] Montesquieu was generally mistrustful of women and wanted to prevent them exerting an influence on politics and culture; in principle, he had no objection to female segregation and servitude. He interpreted this as a sensible regulatory measure and a logical supplement to Asia's unavoidable despotism. Unsupervised women, as Montesquieu had already depicted them in semifictional form in his *Lettres persanes*, undermined (their) man's sexual as well as political authority.

Other European commentators saw, thirdly, the harem's function in sheltering women from male assault. For women who had never learned to be independent, the harem at least offered food and board as well as a comfortable and secure living space.[35] Yet the social costs were high, as even the Ottomans' staunchest defenders pointed out. They consisted in the segregation of the sexes within a single household as well as in the distance separating individual households or families, making it extremely difficult for them to meet in private. The exchange of visits between harems was also unusual. All this stood in the way of the emergence of civil society in the Orient. The public sphere was almost completely male, lacking the private basis in regular contact between families that existed in Europe.

The most unconventional interpretation of the harem was proposed by Lady Mary Wortley Montagu.[36] Her letters from Turkey, written between 1717 and 1718 but first published posthumously in 1763, tell of her visits to various harems and ladies' baths. This uniquely privileged position gave her depictions a special weight, while her racy style ensured they were widely read. How reliable the English aristocrat was in her reporting remains a moot question. The authenticity that appears to speak through her letters, supported by multiple verification strategies, should not be divorced from the context of her deliberate self-representation as an emancipated woman. What she reported from Adrianople (now Edirne) and Istanbul was entirely in keeping with this self-portrait.

Lady Mary, who plunged into foreign climes with great élan and loved to poke fun at the caution and reserve shown by European ladies in the East, was an energetic critic of all constructions of the Ottoman-Turkish culture as the Other. She dealt particularly briskly with ambivalent (male) fantasies—at once appalled and titillated—of oriental women as slaves to their men. Lady Mary was convinced that Turkish ladies need not fear comparison with their European counterparts: "The Turkish Ladys have at least as much wit and Civility, nay, Liberty, as Ladys Amongst us."[37] The women who moved in the highest Ottoman circles, to which Lady Mary had access as the ambassador's wife, were the equals of European ladies in "civility," in manners, education, and taste. Their dependence and helplessness had been widely exaggerated in previous European reports. The harem was governed by rules that not even the lord could flout; under some circumstances, even he was forbidden from entering at will. The harem was essentially the domain of the powerful primary wife and her mother-in-law, who between them ruled absolutely over their own slaves and servants. Through legally guaranteed property, upper-class women were also materially independent.[38] For these women, "liberty" meant being able to arrange extramarital liaisons with relative ease, notwithstanding the strict surveillance to which they were nominally subjected.

Joseph Pitton de Tournefort, one of the most knowledgeable commentators on Turkey in the early eighteenth century, had already pointed out that the death penalty for adultery did little to deter Turkish wives from pursuing their affairs.[39] Lady Mary went still further, arguing that Turkish women enjoyed greater erotic freedom than those in England or Europe. The chief reason for this was that, whenever they left their inner chambers, they went about covered from head to toe, guaranteeing them a unique anonymity. Slipping away to have sex with their lovers was the simplest matter in the world:

> The Great Ladys seldom let their Gallants know who they are, and 'tis so difficult to find it out that they can very seldom guess at her name they have corresponded with above halfe a year together. You may easily imagine the number of faithful Wives very small in a country where they have nothing to fear from their Lovers' Indiscretion.[40]

Lady Mary came to the finding that Turkish women were, "upon the Whole, . . . the only free people in the [Ottoman] Empire."[41] To be sure, these words were written before Montesquieu famously made the connection between female bondage and political despotism. Lady Mary Wortley Montagu's concept of freedom is in this sense pre-political.

DOMESTICITY

Lady Mary's portrayal of the life of Turkish women was limited to only a few passages in her letters. The effect of this portrayal on readers was ambivalent. On the one hand, it acted as a counterweight to the widespread sensationalist exoticization of what went on behind harem walls;

on the other, with its captivating descriptions of beautiful women, exquisite clothing, and sumptuous interiors,[42] it created a visual reservoir from which the Orientalizing painters of the nineteenth century were still drawing. The odalisques of an Ingres or Delacroix, often condemned today as offensive examples of the male gaze colonizing the female body, paradoxically *also* owed much to the curiosity—not to mention the feminine voyeurism—of a twenty-eight-year-old politician's daughter.[43]

To be sure, by far the most in-depth analysis of the harem in eighteenth-century European literature was the product of just such a male gaze. It was written by Alexander Russell and his brother Patrick, the consular physicians in Aleppo. In the first volume of their *Natural History of Aleppo* (1794), they expanded their remarks on the harem as a sphere of privacy into two comprehensive chapters.[44] This text contradicts every "postcolonial" theory of the late twentieth century, avoiding the stereotypical view of the East that European observers supposedly could not help but purvey.

We have already gotten to know the Russells as empathetic and perceptive sociologists. They interpret the harem as a social rather than as an erotic space. They do so with the authority of physicians who had the rare privilege of inspecting and vividly describing the ladies' chambers in Aleppo. The European doctor, a trusted companion after years of regular visits, is led to his fully veiled patient but also approached by other women who wish to consult him about their minor ailments. He enters into conversation with the ladies, who sometimes invite him to stay for coffee and quiz him about the Land of the Franks, especially the conditions of women there. Far from sharing the customary view of the harem dwellers' dull and empty-headed voluptuousness, the Russells are full of praise for their intelligence and attentiveness: "Their questions are generally pertinent, and the remarks they occasionally make on manners differing so widely from their own, are often sprightly and judicious."[45]

Without ever polemicizing against earlier describers of harem life, the Russells set about correcting their more outlandish claims. Cruelties and murders in the harem, as expected by the European public ever since

Montesquieu's *Lettres Persanes*, occurred very rarely. The clandestine and anonymous love affairs gushingly recounted by Lady Mary Wortley Montagu were equally uncharacteristic. In twenty years hardly a single adulterous affair had come to the public eye in Aleppo, one of the great Near Eastern metropolises at the time; the generally very effective supervision of women, combined with their close monitoring of each other's movements, made erotic assignations almost impossible. Higher-placed women would also have exposed themselves to the risk of blackmail.[46]

It is typical of the Russells' determination to get to the bottom of things that they do not rest content with such outer appearances. Instead, they question the tacit assumption shared by almost all European authors, up to and including Lady Mary Wortley Montagu, that the oversexed and overheated race of Orientals had no control over their lustful impulses, which could therefore only be held in check by external constraints. When it came to the women, "innate modesty, cherished from its first dawnings with maternal care, and, in riper years, sheltered from the contagion of insidious gallantry, ought in candor to be allowed some share in the protection of the sex from irregularities."[47] Turkish men, too, were less hot-blooded, and less versed in the arts of seduction, than Western fantasy made them out to be.

Alexander and Patrick Russell depict the harems in the urban upper class milieu of Aleppo—the sultan's seraglio in Istanbul is not their theme—as a cozy, sometimes even idyllic domestic space. Alone among European observers, they allow that the harem might serve a number of other, very natural human purposes. For example, a husband might sometimes visit the harem to play with his children.[48] Chatting with the often Jewish or Christian women who regularly came in and out of the harem to sell fabrics, as well as with the wet nurses, often recruited from desert tribes, was a further nonsexual attraction of life in the ladies' chambers. Exempted from strict hijab requirements, these women were a welcome source of political and social gossip for the secluded harem dwellers—and sometimes for their lord as well. The wet nurses, in particular, enjoyed "a licensed privilege of speaking freely to the men."[49]

There were certainly tyrants who inspired fear in those around them, and sons would notice and adopt the condescending tone towards women taken by their fathers. Yet the Russells observe with fine psychology how bullying and bluster were intended only to assert male authority in a setting where it by no means went unchallenged:

> The men perhaps judge it politic to assume this demeanor in a situation when dominion may be supposed to be maintained with more difficulty than among male dependents; and therefore venture only in hours of retirement to avow that gentleness, which, as if derogatory from their dignity, they think prudent, in their general conduct, to conceal, from persons whose obedience they believe can alone be secured by an air of stern authority.[50]

The sociological observer pushes up against a limit here. Since even a doctor is denied access to intimate hours of private retirement, even he can only ever perceive people from a different culture as social actors, never in the domestic seclusion where their true nature stands revealed. That is why the Russells are extremely reluctant to add to the ever-growing stockpile of statements about the Arabic or Turkish "character." How could such a character be recognized? Crosscultural stereotyping is undermined here through epistemological reflection.

How do the Russells judge the "confinement" of women? Firstly, it was not nearly as strict as commonly supposed, since the ladies of the harem were given ample opportunity to go on outings. Secondly, knowing nothing else, they did not suffer unduly from their restrictions.[51] Thirdly, life in the harem was regulated by unwritten rules that were far from turning women into the hapless victims and supine playthings of an all-powerful overlord. Fourthly, women considered to be past their prime were not left to fend for themselves. They continued to be looked after in old age and, in the best case scenario, could rise to become respected matrons.[52] Finally, the vast majority of men in Aleppo lived monogamously and lacked the means to maintain a harem. In short, so far as marriage and family life were concerned, the constantly invoked cultural differences between the Ottoman Empire and the European powers proved not to be so great after all: "The conjugal state may perhaps in general be deemed not less happy in Turkey than in other countries."[53]

Alexander and Patrick Russell were hardly representative of the mainstream European discourse on the harem. More characteristic by far were the voices cited at the beginning of this chapter. Additional variants included an argument in support of the harem on almost eugenic grounds: particularly in Turkey, wives were procured "from every nation." From the viewpoint of optimal breeding, this was a much better arrangement than limiting procreation to members of a single group. According to John Carne, it explained why Turks today were so much more beautiful than the ethnically pure Greeks.[54] The extensive discussion of the harems as a social site that makes *The Natural History of Aleppo* so unique for its time, however, shows that the sensationalist exoticization of dusky oriental women was neither inevitable nor predetermined by the discursive conditions of the epoch. Turkish women—this was the Russells' great insight—were quite familiar with what, in the eyes of many Europeans, constituted the superior worth of polite Western society: domesticity.[55]

POLYGAMY

If a discourse on sexuality and power, openness and secrecy, grew up around the harem, its anthropological basis, polygamy, was treated primarily as a demographic question. Polygamy had long been regarded as a stain on Islam and the "heathen" religions, its absence from Christian Europe as a sign of moral superiority. It appeared to be a universal characteristic of the Orient; for even Solomon, the wisest of all monarchs, had, as the Bible reports, seven hundred primary wives and three hundred concubines.[56] Polygamy was found everywhere in Asia. Of particular interest to travelers were discrepancies between theory and practice. In China, for example, the laws as well as the ethical maxims of Confucianism promoted monogamy, yet in upper-class households it was commonplace for the legitimate lady of the house to live with several wives of a lesser rank, called "concubines" in Europe. Conversely, Europeans knew that the Koran—in stipulations that George Sale, its most important European exegete in the Enlightenment era, considered both severe and rational[57]—permitted four wives. There were many more than that in the great harems, whose existence therefore had to be justified through non-Koranic legal traditions. On the other hand, it was far from clear that the opportunities that the prophet had provided in theory would be realized in every Muslim country. Among the Crimea Tatars, for example, polygamy was extremely rare even in the nobility.[58] When Johann Gottlieb Georgi visited the Kazan Tatars, he learned that they shunned the practice to conserve their peace of mind as well as their expenses. "Wives," the scholar from Tübingen reports, "are costly to purchase and maintain, and keeping several usually disturbs the domestic peace, therefore most men take only one."[59]

Outrage over polygamy was nowhere greater than among missionaries. Their concerns were more than just theological. Although polygamy was not sanctioned by religion in China, the isolation of women it entailed represented one of the greatest obstacles to Christian evangelization. Women could not be addressed directly; any attempt on the part of missionaries to approach them risked degenerating into scandal.[60] The oddities of family life in China in general, above all the ease of divorce and child marriage, did more than anything else to tarnish the country's image as an ideal society. The Jesuits made no attempt to conceal this, but they sought to offset it with the image, propagated by state Confucianism, of the demure and virtuous Chinese wife. It would not be relativized until the nineteenth century, when China's erotic literature gradually became known in the West. Until then, fantasies of harem debauchery had been associated almost exclusively with the Muslim world. Chinese polygamy appeared more innocuous and more domestic by comparison.

It should not be forgotten that Europeans' own relationship to sexuality and the flesh could give offense to non-Europeans. The Chinese were perplexed by the vow of celibacy taken by the Jesuit missionaries. Displaying the human body in the nude was taboo. When Portuguese emissaries presented the Kangxi emperor with a mirror decorated around the edges with naked sirens, the gift provoked an imperial outburst and a diplomatic crisis. Tensions only eased when Pater Ferdinand Verbiest, the most skilled diplomat among the missionaries, managed to convince the emperor that the sirens were a kind of fish.[61] The episode illustrates what Démeunier argued in 1776 in a lengthy chapter of his ethnographic encyclopedia: ideas of nakedness and shame were culturally specific constructs, not anthropological universals. This author, skeptically disposed towards all supposed advances in the civilizing process, further contested any link between cultural maturity and a sense of shame: the prudery shown by New Zealanders recalled the most exquisite European moral sensibilities, yet they thought nothing of eating their enemies. The Tahitians, by contrast, stood on a similar level of civilization but were both peaceful and completely uninhibited in their sexuality.[62]

The philosophers of the Enlightenment could more or less agree to consider polygamy as one among several basically legitimate forms of conjugal and sexual life, albeit one that ran counter to the amorous sensations of the human heart and therefore did not allow human nature to develop to the full. That is how David Hume saw the matter in a much-cited essay on "Polygamy and Divorces."[63] Montesquieu did not join later authors in denying Orientals the capacity to sublimate their animal drives in a loving marriage. But he did point out that in polygamous relationships, children were shown greater care and affection by their mother than by their father, for no man could distribute his emotions equally among twenty or more children.[64]

Neither Hume nor Montesquieu went so far as to see polygamy as a barrier to civilization.[65] Montesquieu was on his guard against moralizing critics, though, expressly emphasizing his intention merely to explain polygamy, not to excuse it.[66] He saw it as the consequence of a hot climate, which also provided, he believed, an elegant explanation for the undeniable fact that Islam had met with far greater success in Asia than Christianity.[67] This was flanked by the demographic argument that more girls than boys were born in a hot climate. Polygamy thus absorbed a natural surplus of women. Montesquieu quoted a statistic from Engelbert Kaempfer in support of this dubious claim, along with a Dutch report contending that women outnumbered men ten to one in the Banten Sultanate.[68] The same statistics were recycled by everyone who believed polygamy to be a natural practice in Asia, yet they strained readers' credulity. For all his respect for the great philosopher, William Marsden, the strict empiricist, considered the figures quoted by Montesquieu to be "not only manifestly absurd, but positively false."[69]

In the second half of the eighteenth century, the demographic aspect of polygamy overshadowed the earlier religious and moral interest in the phenomenon. In 1762 Johann David Michaelis commissioned the Danish expedition to Arabia to investigate "the influence of polygamy on the increase or decrease of the human population."[70] Carsten Niebuhr, the sole surviving member of the expedition, tendered a response based on his usual mixture of experience and sound common sense. On the one hand, polygamy was far less widespread in the East than was commonly supposed in Europe. On the other, a lack of statistics and "political arithmetic" made it impossible to get hold of accurate demographic data.[71] This second point rendered futile all speculation on whether polygamy helped or hindered population growth. More important than the answers was the displacement of the question itself. Early eighteenth-century authors up to Montesquieu and the Scottish minister and philosopher Robert Wallace, who summarized reflections of this kind in 1753, had fretted about the world's dwindling population.[72] The explanation appeared simplest in the Islamic world, which was generally believed to be sparsely inhabited. Following Montesquieu's lead, Turgot and Volney attributed this to political oppression and polygamy, which in turn was a consequence of despotism undergirded by Islam.[73] Yet in another Islamic country, Java, Sir Stamford Raffles came to the conclusion that polygamy was *not* a significant impediment to population growth; native and Dutch misrule was a far more important inhibiting factor.[74]

By the end of the century, overpopulation had become a far greater concern than underpopulation. During the entire early modern period,

China's teeming masses had filled onlookers with admiration and awe. Anyone who wished to speak ill of the Middle Kingdom had done so (rather unconvincingly) by disputing the high figures taken by the Jesuits from Chinese sources. There was much speculation about the reasons for the unusually rapid rate of population growth in China; to this day, the question has yet to receive a definitive answer. In 1785 the abbé Grosier put together a résumé of earlier deliberations, enumerating sixteen natural and cultural factors that, notwithstanding recurring famine, helped promote Chinese fecundity.[75] These included long-lasting inner peace, a light and reliable taxation regime, the widespread practice of adoption, and the fact that soldiers were permitted to marry. Although Grosier does not mention polygamy directly, he does speak of "the wives' isolation," which led them to devote much of their time to child-rearing.[76]

From around 1800, the Middle Kingdom's populousness was increasingly seen as a weakness and liability. In India, too, overcrowding was now considered to exacerbate rather than alleviate the misery of the masses.[77] Behind this reevaluation lay fundamental shifts in the way people understood their relationship with the environment. Against the optimism of philosophers like Condorcet and William Godwin, who believed in human perfectibility and the Earth's capacity to nourish an infinite number of living things, Robert Wallace had been the first to draw attention to the ecological limits to demographic growth.[78] From such considerations the Anglican cleric Thomas Robert Malthus, one of the most influential thinkers of the modern age, derived the natural law of disparity between the potential rate of increase of a population and the potential growth in its means of subsistence. If all Malthus had set out to do was to present a universally valid law, then his *Essay on the Principle of Population* (1798) would have been a far shorter text. But because he was interested in *how* this law expressed itself in different ways in different civilizations, and in the mechanisms societies developed in response, he became one of the most attentive readers of travel literature from all around the world.[79] That is what makes his *Essay*—particularly in the sixth edition from 1826, the last to be authorized by Malthus himself—a treasure trove of materials and judgments on reproductive behavior, population policy, family life, and the status of women in every continent.

Malthus was the first to grapple with the phenomenon that societies do not always establish an equilibrium with their natural environment; rather, they continue to grow even when the food supply remains constant. He observed this happening almost everywhere in Asia, claiming that it explained the untold amount of human suffering that could be read between the lines of many travel reports. His prime example was the desert Arabs, whom he saw primarily through Volney's eyes. The injunction to go forth and multiply urged on them by their religion was strengthened by the political interests of the sheikhs. Because a chief's power and prestige depended largely on the number of heads in his tribe, it was imperative for him "to encourage population, without reflecting how it may be supported."[80] Malthus did not ascribe any paramount importance to polygamy. Its effects were varied: it accelerated population growth among the desert Arabs while slowing it among the Turks and the city-dwelling Arabs.[81]

Malthus's explanations are far less grounded in naturalistic or anthropological speculation than Montesquieu's. He almost entirely dispenses with the cliché that Orientals, particularly oriental women, were in thrall to an overheated sensuality. Not sexual impulses but religion, politics, and war governed reproductive behavior in *all* civilizations. The rational insight that people should only bring children into the world if they could feed them played a role in very few cases. The unchecked proliferation of the Arabs was an example of extreme irrationality that could only be countered through a different kind of irrationality: mutual decimation via tribal warfare.[82] When the number of men drastically declined as a result of such feuding, polygamy became functionally unavoidable. In China, by contrast, wars were too infrequent to dent the increases in population demanded by cultural norms and promoted by the state. Agricultural production failed to keep pace with the extra mouths to feed, notwithstanding the best efforts of the hardworking Chinese to extract higher yields from their land.[83] In the Ottoman Empire, meanwhile, there was no such lack of resources, but conditions were unconducive to agriculture owing to a weak and arbitrary despotic regime. The consequence here was a long-term decline in population, exacerbated by outbreaks of plague and other diseases.[84] Tibet was an exception in Asia for Malthus, since here—and nowhere else—the population had been deliberately kept low in recognition of the harsh environmental conditions. In his view, the Tibetans had put in place the same rational measures otherwise found only in the middle and upper classes of Europe.[85]

With Malthus, the topic of polygamy disappears from the philosophy of history and from discussions about the cultural differences between East and West. It becomes one factor among many in a demographic system that is susceptible to causal analysis. The contrast between a monogamous Christian West and a polygamous heathen East is toned down considerably. The true cause of Asia's demographic deficit is now seen to lie in the growing prosperity of the core nations of Europe, on the one hand, and economic decline (Turkey, India) or stagnation (China, Japan), on the other. With this switch to an economic perspective on cultural differences, polygamy loses much of its explanatory power. We are in the realm of the Great Divergence.

In the question of polygamy, as in many others, Arnold Hermann Ludwig Heeren is the last but by no means least original thinker to speak the language of Enlightenment sociology. His *Ideen über die Politik, den Verkehr und den Handel der vornehmsten Völker der alten Welt* (*Ideas on the Politics, Traffic and Trade of the Foremost Nations of the Ancient World*) appeared in the same decade as Malthus's *Essay*. Heeren takes up a theme that from Montesquieu to Volney had been touched on repeatedly but never properly followed through: the connection between despotism and polygamy. Montesquieu had expressed himself cautiously on this point, suggesting analogies without positing any causal relationships:

> the servitude of women is very much in conformity with the genius of despotic government, which likes to abuse everything. Thus in

> Asia domestic servitude and despotic government have been seen to go hand in hand in every age.[86]

The French theorists of despotism tended to attribute this particular form of unchecked autocracy to climate or conquest. Once it had been established as the form of government, the despotic principle penetrated all of society from above. Every head of family behaved like the caricature of a sultan. For Heeren, by contrast, despotism was built up from below. Its most solid support lay in polygamy, which Heeren treats as an independent variable. The most fundamental and intractable problem of civilizations was not the defectiveness of their "civil institutions" but the peculiarity (for which Heeren has no "philosophical" explanation to offer) of their "domestic society" (*häusliche Gesellschaft*).[87] Under a system of polygamy, "domestic virtues" were nipped in the bud along with their desirable consequences: patriotism and a freedom-loving civic consciousness:[88]

> Polygamy at once produces domestic tyranny, by making woman a slave and man a tyrant; and society at large thus becomes a combination not of fathers of families, but of household tyrants, who by the practice of tyranny have been fitted to endure it. He who is tyrannical in authority will be abject in submission.[89]

The bourgeois paterfamilias differs from the despot in that, rather than selfishly indulging his passions, he "takes an interest . . . in the preservation and continuance of the whole." This virtue animates him as a husband and father but also as a citizen and protector of his fatherland. Anyone who sacrifices himself for his family does so as much for the political community as a whole. Asiatic societies make too strict a separation between state and family.[90] The polygamist can never be a *citoyen*. To be sure, the despot's autocracy only extends so far. The higher up in Asiatic society one looks, the larger, more powerful, and more autonomous the harems become. In the end, many a godlike emperor had found himself reduced to a puppet in the hands of his wives and eunuchs. The ultimate specter of rule by women thus arises before Heeren's eyes.[91]

"When a system of despotism was based on the general practice of polygamy, it is evident that the nations of the East could never hope to shake off the former, so long as their domestic relations continued unaltered."[92] Yet why should they, especially since the existing practice was sanctioned by religion? Heeren accordingly ends up adopting a fatalistic position. For him, despotism is more surely determined by "domestic relations" than it was for Montesquieu by climatic conditions. It will never be swept away in Asia, as Volney expected; but it will also never cross into Europe, as Montesquieu feared at times. Heeren's consoling message is "that Europe is secured by a more perfect state of morals from a despotism like those of the East."[93] Europe's greatest world-historical advantage lies in the institution of monogamy. Was this a specifically Christian achievement? Heeren does not venture an answer to this question, but Lord Kames, the Scottish eccentric, had already offered his response: in Coptic Ethiopia and among the Christians of the Congo, polygamy was very much the norm.[94]

LABOR, LIBERTY, AND SACRIFICE

Not all women in Asia were passive "slaves" and hence, from the European point of view, objects of both pity and voyeuristic fantasy. Not all were the tradable goods and property of their masters. Lady Mary Wortley Montagu had waxed lyrical about the erotic self-determination enjoyed by the more fortunate ladies in the Turkish harem, while Arnold Heeren had feared rule by women, "the silken web of the harem" (Gibbon) from which no tyrant was safe.[95] Since François Bernier, it had been known that women occasionally exerted an extraordinary influence on politics—not just in the Ottoman Empire but in the Mughal Empire as well.[96] Yet nothing similar had been reported from China, Japan, and Southeast Asia. Gibbon, who may have been unaware of the Chinese empress Wu (r. 683–705), was of the opinion that, apart from the half-mythical Semiramis, only one woman in the entire history of Asia had ever asserted herself "with superior genius" against "the servile indolence imposed on her sex by the climate and manners of Asia": the Syrian queen Zenobia, who had rebelled against the Roman emperor Aurelian in 272 CE and thereby condemned her own state of Palmyra to destruction.[97] Otherwise, there was very little to say about women's involvement in the politics of Asiatic countries in the age of Catherine the Great. Almost nobody believed in the existence of Amazons any more.

Attention was drawn to situations where a woman failed to act in "typically Asiatic" (i.e., servile) fashion, yet got off more lightly than the harem stereotype required. In Tibet there was polyandry, a practice whereby a woman was simultaneously married to several men, usually brothers, and was recognized as head of the family. Ippolito Desideri's early description of polyandry was mixed with repugnance, Montesquieu had read about the practice in Pater Du Halde, the abbé Grosier had reported on it from Chinese sources in 1785, and Captain Samuel Turner got to know it very well when visiting Tibet in 1783.[98] Turner chose neither to demonize what he saw nor to retreat into the detached distance of the professional ethnographer. His judgment was unambiguously positive: polyandry was ideally suited to the specific conditions of Tibet. It helped prevent overpopulation, the greatest calamity that could befall an arid country. Above all, it played a part in refining the manners and reining in the passions of the unfailingly polite Tibetans. Hardly anywhere else in Asia were women in so advantageous a position. A comparison with India made this clear:

> Comparatively with their southern neighbors, the women of Tibet enjoy an elevated station in society. To the privileges of unbounded liberty, the wife here adds the character of mistress of the family, and companion to her husbands. The company of all, indeed, she is not at all times entitled to expect. Different pursuits, either agricultural employments or mercantile speculations, may occasionally cause the temporary absence of each; yet whatever be the result, the profit

of the laborer flows into the common store; and when he returns, whatever may have been his fortune, he is secure of a grateful welcome to a social home.[99]

There could be no talk of women's idleness. As Ippolito Desideri had already observed at the beginning of the century, women in Tibet shouldered the bulk of agricultural labor, toiling constantly and to the brink of exhaustion.[100] Everywhere in Asia women worked in agriculture, manufacture, and trade, often unnoticed by European travelers. This was reported from Southeast Asia with particular frequency. In Siam, a mid-seventeenth-century description states, women did all the work while their menfolk lazed around.[101] Both there and in Vietnam they were mostly in charge of trade.[102] Few seem to have noticed that this contradicted the theory of a close connection between political and domestic despotism. In his extensive analysis of agriculture on Java, Raffles repeatedly placed emphasis on the contribution of women. Their work in the field was rated almost as highly as that of men, while clothing was made exclusively by women working from home. Families lived off "the fruits of their joint industry."[103] According to Sir John Barrow, women in Vietnam performed most of the work on the land; likewise in several provinces of China, where they were sometimes hitched to a light plow.[104] Among nomads, women were involved in tending animals and making animal products. In India they were even employed in construction, and there was in general, at least in Elphinstone's considered opinion, "scarcely any difference between the work done by the two sexes."[105] Up and down the coast of Japan, specially trained "fisherwomen" (as Kaempfer calls them) went diving for seaweed, an expensive delicacy.[106]

Women's social and legal position was not as low everywhere as the cliché of the submissive harem dweller would suggest. Just how deeply this cliché was rooted is shown when conditions that appeared to be favorable to women were consistently regarded as exceptions to the rule. While some may have claimed that Turkish men held their wives in low esteem and "hardly do them the Honor of looking upon them as rational

Creatures,"[107] elsewhere the opposite was true. Captain Robert Percival confirmed Robert Knox's old report of the extremely loose morals of Ceylonese (here: Singhalese) women, yet he interpreted this as an expression of female freedom: "A Ceylonese woman scarcely ever experiences the treatment of a slave, but is looked upon by her husband, more after the European manner, as a wife and companion."[108] Female labor was often—in Vietnam, for example—rewarded with considerable personal freedom.[109] In 1812 one missionary even drew a favorable comparison with Europe:

> Women [in Tonkin] are by no means, as in many parts of the world, kept as slaves and prisoners in their own homes. Nor are they, as in some European states, bound by ties of legal dependence. In the laboring classes, they work alongside their husbands as equal partners. In the higher classes, they occupy themselves with anything that provides them with the means to give pleasure. . . . They enjoy great liberty, and, although they seldom venture abroad, they are free to visit their friends at will.[110]

In Burma wives were treated with disdain by their husbands: "They consider women as little superior to the brute stock of their farms." Yet even here, women were indispensable for production and mostly controlled the purse strings.[111]

Throughout Asia, attentive travelers thus registered women's working life and conditions, their legal standing, and their scope for freedom. Yet such observations tend to be scattered haphazardly throughout the reports. They do not cohere into a general impression that might have challenged woman's preassigned role as victim and/or seductress. There was no portrait of a peasant wife or female trader to match the covert allure of harem scenes and the overt horror of widow burning ceremonies.

Widow burning (*sati*) had been a standard topic in the literature on India since the first European reports in the days of Alexander the Great.[112] This ritual for "following the departed into the grave" (Jörg Fisch) was particularly attention-grabbing because, unlike the institution of slavery, which many Europeans found equally repulsive, there had never been anything like it in Christendom or in the neighboring sphere of Islam.[113] Widow burning appeared to be unique to Hindu India. As a rule, the reports give no indication that it was a rare occurrence, suggesting instead that most or even all widows met their end on the funeral pyre.[114] It is especially difficult in this case to decide which of the numerous descriptions left behind by travelers were based on eyewitness testimony, which of them drew from the storehouse of literary motifs, and which embroidered observed fact with fantasy. While the causes of this phenomenon may have been subject to dispute, the basic elements of the scene were always the same: the widow (often young), the relatives, the presiding Brahmins, the public; the corpse on its bier, the funeral pyre, the oil for feeding the flames. Beauty and death, violence and consent, individual suffering and the weight of tradition, religious ritual and crime: these tensions lent the rite of widow burning its incomparable fascination.[115]

Sati found few defenders in Europe. The view that the practice was necessary to discipline the wives of India, who might otherwise be tempted to murder their husbands and take on lovers, was rarely expressed so crassly.[116] Once heretics and witches were no longer burned at the stake in Europe—the last judicial killing of a woman under the charge of witchcraft took place in Switzerland in 1782—*sati* became fully identified as a macabre Indian peculiarity. Given that many reports stressed the widow's calm acquiescence to her cruel fate, or even her eagerness to die, the question of consent received an inordinate amount of attention. Enlightenment authors saw the widow in large part as the victim of her circumstances. The case was clear-cut if physical force was applied. Bernier had already depicted the Brahmin ceremony organizers as diabolical monsters who did not think twice about pushing unwilling wives back into the flames.[117] But even the widows who expressed a wish to be sacrificed were mistrusted, since such a wish seemed not so much a free decision as the result of what the Enlightenment critique of religion pathologized as fanaticism and superstition. From this viewpoint, the widow was less the victim of physical violence than that of a misogynist cultural system, which here stood revealed in all its archaism and moral inferiority.[118]

The ban on widow burning imposed in 1829 by the British colonial powers in Bengal, and then in 1830 in the presidencies of Bombay and Madras, was preceded by a series of debates in which Indians were active participants on both sides. These debates were not conducted solely in terms of legality, morality, and Christian values.[119] From a cultural relativist viewpoint, tolerance for *sati* could be recommended out of respect for "age-old" indigenous customs; it could also be justified on pragmatic grounds with reference to the unrest that might break out if colonial authorities were to outlaw the practice.[120] In the early years of Indology, the additional question arose of whether widow burning could be derived from the texts of Indian orthodoxy and tradition. For a time, this perspective assumed extraordinary significance for the arguments of both defenders and critics of *sati*. Human rights, especially the rights of women, threatened to disappear behind the battles of textual scholars and the ploys of political strategists. Women were just passive pawns, both for those "conservatives" who held them up as emblems of a tradition to be defended and for their "liberal" opponents who claimed to rescue them from the clutches of this very tradition.[121]

PROGRESS AND CIVILIZATION

Voltaire's idea, quoted near the beginning of this chapter, that the cardinal difference between East and West consisted in their treatment of women, points to a further context in which the topic of femininity was embedded: the civilizing process.

From around the mid-eighteenth century, the tripartite division of the world into Christians, other monotheists (Jews and Muslims), and "heathens" made way for its secular categorization into primitives, barbarians, and the civilized. To be sure, these categories were less sharply defined than membership of religious communities. There were subtle gradations and smooth transitions on the scale of human "refinement," ranging from the wretched savage of Tierra del Fuego all the way to the Paris salon queen, English lord, and German professor. In particular, how was the step from barbarism to civilization to be defined, or the level of civilization attained at any given time? And what role did the contrast between East and West have to play? There was one line of thought that followed Voltaire's lead in seeing the position of women as an important criterion—if not the most important—for gauging the quality of social life.

This criterion gradually took shape over the second half of the eighteenth century. In the older ethnographic literature, as summarized in 1776 by Jean-Nicolas Démeunier , there had been much talk of marriage rites and sexuality, conjugal relations and divorce.[122] Montesquieu was no exception in this regard. But these facets of human community were not read as signs of societal evolutionary success. They were not singled out from the general mass of customs and mores. This first occurred in 1742 in some brief remarks made by David Hume, the instigator of the High Enlightenment in Europe, in his essay *Of the Rise and Progress of the Arts and Sciences*. Here Hume asks what makes the moderns superior with regard to the politeness and refinement shown in their interpersonal relations. Somewhat hesitantly, he contemplates whether "modern notions of gallantry" might not best account for this progress in civilization.[123] Hume takes "gallantry" to mean a particular form of considerate conduct between the sexes involving the correction of natural differences through self-imposed male "generosity":

> As nature has given man the superiority above woman, by endowing him with greater strength both of mind and body; it is his part to alleviate that superiority, as much as possible, by the generosity of his behavior, and by a studied deference and complaisance for all her inclinations and opinions. Barbarous nations display this superiority, by reducing their females to the most abject slavery; by confining them, by beating them, by selling them, by killing them. But the male sex, among a polite people, discover their authority in a

> more generous, though not a less evident manner; by civility, by respect, by complaisance, and, in a word, by gallantry.[124]

In 1761 Hume sketched the origins of such gallantry in his *History of England*, a work that offered not just a national narrative history but also a theoretical history of the rise of civilization in Europe. Gallantry was interpreted as the most important and long-lasting legacy of the feudal Middle Ages. The independence granted the military elites under the feudal system awakened in knights and barons a new sense of honor and a dawning awareness of their duty to protect those weaker than themselves, especially women. This was a watershed in the history of culture. The oath of loyalty sworn to the feudal lord was now transferred to the relationship between the sexes. Chivalry emerged from political independence and the individualism expressed in the ideal of single combat, the tournament.[125] In Hume's view, it shone out from the surrounding medieval darkness as the most important outcome of a major civilizational advance. It was then further refined and purified of feudal dross in the courtly societies of early modern monarchies.

Other Scottish thinkers took up and extended Hume's analysis. In 1767 Adam Ferguson characterized the monopolization and rationalization of violence by the state, the decreased brutality of behavior in society, and hence also the improved lot of women, as a hallmark of "polished nations." Like Hume, he attributed this development to the salutary effects of medieval "chivalry."[126] John Millar—the third great social theorist of the Scottish Enlightenment alongside Adam Smith and Adam Ferguson—was the first to treat the position of women as symptomatic of the overall condition of social life. In his *Origins of the Distinction of Ranks in Society* from 1771, he reconstructed the universal history of society, from its uncouth beginnings all the way to the achievements of present-day Europe, as a history of relations between the sexes.[127]

Millar cites the usual travel literature but uses it for convergent purposes. In other words, he is less interested in cultural differences than in the commonalities that could contribute to a universal cultural history of the human race. The East-West binary is as irrelevant for him as it was for Hume and Ferguson. For Millar, the barbaric state that modern Europe had left behind it was a universal condition. Just as it had once prevailed in the ancient Mediterranean, so too it continued to hold sway across the length and breadth of Asia. Hardly any of the Scottish authors posit a stark antagonism between East and West. In their eyes, Europe had reached a level of civilization that could eventually be attained by other cultures as well. In all these writers, Christianity is ascribed only secondary importance as a civilizing force.

The Scottish jurist and cultural theorist Henry Home, appointed to high judicial office as Lord Kames in 1752, likewise operated on the basis of such pan-Scottish ideas.[128] In the long chapter on "Progress of the Female Sex" from his magnum opus, *Sketches of the History of Man* (1774), he gathered together material from all the world's epochs and regions to substantiate his claim that "women, formerly considered as objects of animal love merely, are now valued as faithful friends and agreeable companions."[129] Kames, however, placed far greater emphasis than his Scottish contemporaries on the power of polygamy to impede the progress of civilization. Indeed, for him—as later for Heeren—the Great Map of Mankind sometimes appears to be divided into only two hemispheres, dominated by polygamy and monogamy, respectively. He adds the important point that under conditions of barbarism, women are treated as objects for sale and exchange. Even in the stage of "savagery," only "the northern nations of Europe" had escaped the worldwide curse of bride-buying, thereby qualifying for later advances in civilization.[130] Kames further differs from his compatriots in reaching back to Montesquieu's climate theory, embraced by neither Adam Smith nor Adam Ferguson. That "modern" chivalry (as Hume puts it) could have arisen in Europe is, in Lord Kames's view, itself the consequence of a pre-Christian repudiation of the threat of polygamy.[131] This in turn presupposed a climate that curbed the animalistic drives of both men and women. Kames is thus far less hopeful than the other Scottish philosophers that Asians and Africans might one day break free from the shackles of nature. The criterion of gallantry is here conceived deterministically.

John Richardson—likewise a jurist, albeit an English one—responded with an objection worthy of Gibbon's acute sense of comparative justice: was there not, as the Crusades had shown, an Oriental-Muslim version of chivalry closely related to the more familiar European-Christian variety? Was it not even older than that found to the north of the Mediterranean? Had it not led to women enjoying a similarly high standing among the Arabs and "Tatars"? Did not the special circumstances of mobile life ("roving habits") among the Arabs increase "sentimental" passion—Richardson in the 1770s still lacks a notion of "romantic love"—and even tragedy? The English Orientalist suggests a kind of materialist explanation:

> Many tribes are often encamped together; and the young men of one fall naturally in love with the damsels of another. In the midst of their courtship, the heads of the tribe suddenly order the tents to be struck: one goes to the right hand, the other takes the left. The lovers are separated, perhaps never more to meet; and if we can draw any conclusions from their elegies in their language, those separations have often been fatal.[132]

Had not the significance of polygamy in the Orient—which, incidentally, had little to do with climate, being found even in frosty Kamchatka—been vastly overstated by European travelers? And had they not ignored the fact that, at least from the days of the Prophet, "Arabian women of rank seem indeed to have taken a very active concern both in civil and military concerns?"[133]

Under Scottish influence, from around 1800 the aspect of male-female relations became established as a standard of judgment that could be applied to specific societies. Sir John Barrow, philosophically the most ambitious of the English travelers to Asia around the turn of the century, formulated the following universal truth:

> It may, perhaps, be laid down as an invariable maxim, that the condition of the female part of society in any nation will furnish a tolerable just criterion of the degree of civilization to which that nation has arrived.[134]

And James Mill, the philosophical hanging judge of all Indian follies, set out as a general law: “Among rude people, the women are generally degraded; among civilized people they are exalted.”[135] A sentence of this kind could be twisted and turned in such a way that tautologous self-congratulation always came out at the end: to be civilized meant to treat women with respect, and to treat women with respect meant to be civilized. From there it was but a small step to the simple equations: “rude” = Asiatic and “civilized” = European. But could this kind of specious reasoning be considered at all meaningful?

Several years before the appearance of Mill’s *History of British India*, the perceptive Constantinople-based merchant Thomas Thornton set down his own thoughts on the matter. European views on the lives led by Turkish women were completely false, warped by anti-Islamic prejudice and grotesquely distorted by “the glow of a heated imagination.”[136] That every European was pure and civilized was nothing more than a myth. Had not Europe been strongly influenced by Asia in ancient times and again during the period of the Crusades? And did not the customs and mores of Eastern and Southeastern Europeans, from Greece to Poland and Russia, betray unmistakably Asiatic features? The segregation of women in the Ottoman Empire, which should on no account be understood as their “enslavement,” barely differed from the exclusion of Spanish women from mixed society; Moorish influence was surreptitiously at work here.[137] Thornton acknowledges woman’s high standing among the Germanic tribes, which later gave rise to “the almost idolatrous gallantry of the chevaliers,” which in turn produced “the modern European character.”[138] But such customs and character types could make no claim to universal validity. They had value and permanence only when they emerged organically from natural refinement. That is why Thornton thinks it absurd to want to liberate oriental women from their alleged captivity. Conversely, he finds no spectacle more disgusting than the immoral Russian imperial court, which was nothing but the result of an unnaturally forced Westernization of a semi-Asiatic society.[139]

In the judgment of observers like Richardson and Thornton, respect for women was possible under a wide array of cultural preconditions. Its contents were culturally specific: whereas a wife received public recognition in the West as the beloved partner of her husband, Turkish civilization held her in incomparably greater "reverence" as the loving mother of her children.[140] The criterion of gallantry did not apply to the progress of civilization as a whole, only to that of a *particular* civilization.

XIII

Into a New Age

The Rise of Eurocentrism

The love of lengthened tones and modulated sounds, different from those of speech, and regulated by a stated measure, seems a passion implanted in human nature throughout the globe; for we hear of no people, however wild and savage in other particulars, who have not music of some kind or other, with which we may suppose them to be greatly delighted, by their constant use of it upon occasions the most opposite.

—Charles Burney (1726–1814), *A General History of Music: From the Earliest Ages to the Present Period* (1776)[1]

It [musical criticism] must acknowledge as beautiful what any human being, what any nation would deem to be beautiful by the lights of its knowledge and by the degree to which it has developed its capabilities. . . . The modern Greeks, the Turks, the Persians, the Chinese, the American savages, form melodies from scales which differ so greatly from our own that we are unable to find the least order and beauty therein. Their music is nonetheless beautiful, because it pleases them and because they would discern in our own music the very disorder that we criticize in theirs.

—Johann Nikolaus Forkel (1749–1818), *Allgemeine Geschichte der Musik* (*General History of Music*, 1788)[2]

Throughout antiquity, and among oriental nations in the present era, the sole ingredients of music have been melody and rhythm, whereas among modern Europeans, and in their colonies in the new world, a simultaneous harmony of sounds has been added to the other elements to form a complete art. . . . In all times and at all places there have been popular songs and religious chants; only among modern Europeans has there been an art of music.

—François-Joseph Fétis (1784–1871), *Histoire générale de la musique depuis les temps les plus anciens jusqu'à nos jours* (*General History of Music from the Most Ancient Times to Our Days*, 1869)[3]

We now draw an arc from the years of a mature Enlightenment to the mid-nineteenth century. Consider a seemingly marginal issue: is a world history of music possible, and if so, how should it be written? This question intrigued some of the foremost musicologists of their respective ages. And because they were fully aware of the advanced philosophical and historiographical tendencies of their times, their judgments carry considerable weight and are symptomatic of fundamental intellectual shifts. Each of the three quotations in the epigraph is embedded in complex aesthetic arguments and theories of cultural evolution.

It is easy to do an injustice to the great Belgian scholar François-Joseph Fétis, who knew as much about music among the Arabs, Iranians, Turks, and South Asians as it was possible to know before the advent of empirical ethnomusicology in the late nineteenth century.[4] He was certainly no bigoted "Eurocentrist." Yet the fact remains that the great Enlightenment scholars Charles Burney in London and Johann Nikolaus Forkel at Göttingen, who almost simultaneously published the first world histories of music that transcended the Occident, were of one mind in their generous acknowledgment and appreciation of non-Western music—music that was almost entirely unknown to them given the lack of recording techniques and the uncertainty of notation at the time. Their arguments were more of a "conjectural" than of an empirical nature: "music" is to be found everywhere, and even if it has reached the highest pitch of perfection in Europe, there is no reason to condemn the sonic expressions and social music-making of other civilizations by the universal and absolute standards embodied in the art of Joseph Haydn (Burney's good friend) and Johann Sebastian Bach (on whom Forkel was the leading expert). With Fétis, we enter a different world: a dichotomous world of music versus nonmusic, art versus folklore, refinement versus primitivism. Non-Europeans are left behind in the race for perfection, they lose the right to their own taste, and Europeans no longer even show them the courtesy of finding their music interesting.[5]

BALANCE AND EXCLUSION

The eighteenth century was an age of balance between little Europe and big Asia. Having long been on the defensive, "Europe" now launched a counterattack on the Turkish great power, although it was unable to establish anything more than colonial outposts in the empires of the East prior to the conquest of Bengal in the 1760s. Only the opening up of North Asia—the trans-Ural expanses of the tsarist empire—continued apace, barely noticed outside the region. When early modern Asian states did collapse, this was hardly ever the result of European intervention; the Crimean Khanate was a notable exception. The British, for example, played no part in the breakup of Aurangzeb's Mughal Empire; they merely understood how to use it to their advantage. During the century and a half following the Manchu conquest of China in 1644, breakouts of continental tribal societies were at least as important a factor in Asian history as the seaborne incursions of European maritime powers. In the seventeenth and eighteenth century, Europeans, now armed with the highly efficient institution of the militarized chartered company, set about integrating Asia's coastal regions into worldwide trading networks. Overseas shipping routes extended from Yemen and the Persian Gulf all the way to the port of Nagasaki on the East China Sea. Asiatic trade was linked with the Atlantic via the Cape of Good Hope and with the Americas via the Spanish Acapulco-Manila link. Nonetheless, at this stage the

European powers did not yet one-sidedly dominate the Asian market and force it to operate by their laws. Native shipping remained respected as a competitor and indispensable as a partner; Europeans only gradually came to play a role in this so-called "country trade" between Asian ports. In order for European products to penetrate their vast hinterlands, native merchants were always essential.

Above all, Europeans succeeded in taking over the production of coveted export commodities only in exceptional cases, as in some areas of the spice trade. Taking advantage of booming European demand, Asian producers dramatically expanded their volume of trade in goods such as tea and cotton ware. Towards the end of the eighteenth century, the economies of entire regions of China and India were geared towards the European export market. The later colonial-mercantilist relationship between an Asia that produced raw materials and a Europe that sold them back in the form of manufactured industrial and commercial goods was not yet in sight. The advantages accruing to Asia from its intensified commerce with Europe, particularly in view of its positive balance of trade, more than outweighed the damage done by marauding EIC "nabobs." Around 1820, when industrialization had already gotten underway in parts of Western Europe, per capita income in Asia and Oceania was still probably around half the level of Western Europe.[6] The great disparity in wealth between Europe and Asia first opened up over the following decades.

The balance of power and two-way commerce between Asia and Europe were not reflected in symmetrical mutual perceptions. Modern Europe emerged as the culture of learning and knowledge par excellence. A steady stream of Europeans traveled to Asia, conquering the continent with the pen before subjugating it with the sword and the gunboat. Asia, represented in a voluminous travel literature, in translations of oriental texts, in images and *objets d'art*, aroused keen interest as a field of inquiry for a universal science of humankind: an Anglo-Scottish "science of man," whose groundwork was laid by the era's great philosophers; a French *science de l'homme*, more strongly oriented towards the natural sciences; and a *Kulturgeschichte* or "cultural history" of the human race, Germany's characteristic contribution to the late Enlightenment study of the world.[7]

By contrast, Asian interest in Europe was desultory. Phases of mental opening to the West, such as the high water mark of Chinese curiosity about Europe reached in the second half of the Kangxi emperor's reign (circa 1690–1720)[8] and the Ottoman "Tulip Period" shortly thereafter (1718–30), proved short-lived. Only in Japan, the most inaccessible of all Asian countries after Korea, was Europe studied in anything like a systematic way on the basis of imported books, mainly in Dutch.[9] This willingness to learn from the outside world was the legacy of a centuries-long absorption of Chinese civilization.[10]

In the realm of ideas, the equilibrium of the eighteenth century was thus not expressed in the back and forth of cross-cultural perception but rather in ambivalences and a broad spectrum of judgments within the European mind itself. Europe fantasized the Orient as a fairytale alternative universe while simultaneously investigating it with the instruments provided by the new experiential sciences. It created both colonialism and the critique of colonialism, most forcefully in such rhetorically skilled authors as Edmund Burke, Denis Diderot, and the abbé Raynal. Such tensions and contradictions in how Europeans perceived the world came especially to the fore under conditions of a temporarily reduced dogmatism. On the one hand, the seventeenth century's astonishment at the splendor and wealth of Asiatic courts and cities had given way to a more skeptical view. The spell cast by the old mother culture had been broken.[11] On the other hand, the nineteenth century's smug assumption of superiority still lay some way off. Asiatic civilizations—at first mainly China, later India—posed intellectual challenges that seemed worthy of discussion and debate. Experimenting with different perspectives, playfully adopting the viewpoint of the non-European Other, and relativizing one's own criteria of evaluation were more than just literary tricks. Theories of perception and travel, combined with sophisticated procedures for critically interrogating the most important medium of intercultural information, the travel report, worked against naïve credulity and unfounded speculation. Few were convinced by simple dichotomies. Before 1790 hardly anyone saw a stark opposition between the cultural macrospheres "East" and "West," fewer still believed them to be incompatible, and no one posited a "clash of civilizations." Those who nonetheless heightened the contrasts, as Montesquieu did with clear methodical intent in his theory of despotism, had to reckon with forceful criticism.

For eighteenth-century Europeans, the history of Asia was a subject of burning interest. It had not yet—as the nineteenth century would have it—come to itself in European global supremacy. A new understanding of history, informed by a sense that the West's recent great leap forward was both unique and unprecedented, was developing not only in contrast to Europe's past but also against the backdrop of Asia's present. Europe's self-extrication from the old uniformity of Eurasia was becoming a central theme in the philosophy of history.

A second motif resonated alongside it: the final pacification of the "barbarian hordes" who had once ridden forth from their Central Asian homelands to unleash wave upon wave of destruction on the settled civilizations of the West. The taming of the primal forces of history was so recent a phenomenon that it still impressed Edward Gibbon as one of the signal achievements of the modern age. He ends the first half of his great work with a deep sigh of relief that the progress of civilization, and specifically agriculture, had finally defused the peril of militant nomadism. In a passage dating from 1780–81,[12] written with Catherine the Great's "powerful and civilized empire" in mind, he proclaims the successful subjugation of the steppe—and he adds a rider in the next sentence:

> The reign of independent Barbarism is now concentrated to a narrow span; and the remnants of Calmucks or Uzbeks, whose forces may be almost numbered, cannot seriously excite the apprehensions of the great republic of Europe. Yet this apparent security should not tempt us to forget, that new enemies, and unknown dangers, may

> *possibly* arise from some obscure people, scarcely visible in the map of the world.[13]

Gibbon, like most of his European contemporaries, was unaware of what was then brewing among a less-than-obscure people right on his Swiss doorstep. He contemplated the various declines and falls offered to a student of the past and seems not to have completely discounted the prospect of future empire-building. But he certainly did not perceive the looming general crisis, and he failed to predict the French Revolution and Napoleon.

The Hunnic, Arab, Mongol, and Turkish threats that had struck fear in the hearts of earlier generations now faded from view, leaving only Nadir Shah, the "comet of war," to overawe eighteenth-century European spectators. The anticolonial self-strengthening reforms undertaken by Haidar Ali in India, later pursued with similar intent by Pasha Muhammad Ali in Egypt, belong to a new era: they are already reactions to Europe's burgeoning power. In them, for the first time, Asiatic dynamism appears not as a storm from the steppes but in the more sober guise of institutional modernization. However imperfect in execution, herein lie the beginnings of a strategy that the Japanese would come to master in the nineteenth century: the appropriation of Western means to acquire immunity to Western domination.

The wide range of societies in Asia was carefully examined in Europe. They could not be dismissed wholesale as "barbarian," nor were they banished to a separate ethnological discourse that interested experts and no one else. A universally oriented, comparative approach to society had not yet been split into sociology, the science of "us," and anthropology, the science of "them." Travelers such as Engelbert Kaempfer, the brothers Alexander and Patrick Russell, Carsten Niebuhr, and the Comte de Volney made the social orders and ways of life they encountered in civilized Asia the objects of a detailed sociography, while for theorists such as Montesquieu and Adam Ferguson these were incentives for establishing a social science from the spirit of cultural difference. By investigating other worlds—worlds that did not necessarily strike them as incommensurably alien—such writers arrived at a more clear-sighted understanding of their own. European societal forms emerged in sharper profile the more clearly they could be distinguished in their particulars from their Asiatic counterparts. Asia was comparable to Europe so long as Europe did not yet take itself to be incomparable.

Curiosity, openness, and respect for the people of Asia are found for the last time in the generation that includes the historians Arnold Hermann Ludwig Heeren and Joseph von Hammer-Purgstall and the geographers Carl Ritter and Alexander von Humboldt. We have heard frequently from Heeren and Hammer-Purgstall in earlier chapters. A few brief remarks about Humboldt and Ritter may suffice. Alexander von Humboldt knew Asia only from his late Russian journey; he had written little about the continent, most of what he did write being limited to questions of physical geography. It is enticing to imagine what might have come about had the same empirical and critical approach that makes his account of Mexico from 1808 one of the founding documents of modern social analysis been applied to an Asian country.[14]

Carl Ritter never set foot on Asian soil, yet his importance as the last great synthesizer of what Europeans knew about Asia in the early modern period cannot be overestimated. His gigantic *Erdkunde* (*World Geography*), which appeared in its definitive second edition from 1832 onwards and never went beyond Asia, is a historically oriented cultural geography of Asia's macroregions or, put differently, a history of Asiatic civilization in a spatio-ecological context. The breadth of Ritter's vision would not be equaled until the mid-twentieth century, when the French historian Fernand Braudel published his epochal work on the Mediterranean world in the sixteenth century. In a herculean feat of empirically grounded imagination, Ritter went beyond the obsessive collection of data pursued by the older German sciences of "statistics" and *Staatenkunde* to compile descriptions of Asian cultural landscapes as historical "individualities." Ritter was convinced that divine creation had been purposefully tailored to human needs. He was particularly interested in the (mostly) successful attempts made by human communities to adapt to given physical and climatic conditions.

Because he favors functionalist explanations, drawing out how cultural practices and societal institutions relate to their always-specific natural environments, Ritter steers clear of thinking in terms of national or racial characteristics. It is obvious which side he stands on in the debate between biological and geographical determinism. He nonetheless avoids ascribing a causative influence to environmental factors. Instead, he regards nature and landscape as the stage on which humans secure their survival and develop their culture. Like Johann Gottfried Herder before him, whose imprint on his thinking is unmistakable, Ritter disputes the possibility of an absolute standpoint from which civilizations could be judged. In his eyes, civilizations differ not through any substantive value (such as the degree to which they are "civilized") but in the measure to which they successfully husband the limited resources at their disposal—in their environmental management, so to speak.[15]

From the 1770s onwards, however, the Herderian position increasingly came under attack from Asia's "philosophical" critics. Distancing themselves from the crassly Asiaphobic attitudes of some older travel reports,[16] they claimed to have penetrated the veil of appearances through exact study and careful reasoning. After the eccentric Cornelius de Pauw, the naturalist Pierre Sonnerat was the first serious proponent of such an evaluative approach, which was common to later authors whose philosophical convictions could otherwise not have been more different: travelers such as the *idéologue* Volney and the utilitarian Barrow, or sedentary commentators on Asia such as the Scottish stage theorist James Mill, the Christian philosopher of history Friedrich Schlegel, and in many respects also Hegel, whose highly nuanced judgments appear to have been purged of all subjective opinion. Asiatic civilizations were now summoned before a tribunal that judged them by the supposedly universal criteria of rationality, efficiency, and justice—and generally found them wanting. Others applied the alternative criterion of these civilizations' receptiveness to Christianity.

In the second quarter of the nineteenth century, research into ancient and medieval Asia was organized into new academic disciplines, but only a few outsiders, such as the historian and long-serving governor of Bombay, Mountstuart Elphinstone, defended the dignity of *modern* Asia.[17] At the same time, the hitherto self-evident interest in Asia disappeared from discourses such as history, political economy, and sociology. They narrowed their focus to Europe and lost their comparative dimension in the process.[18]

It would be too simplistic to describe the development that led to this end point solely as a shift from a "positive" to a "negative" image of Asia. It is better characterized as a slow movement from an *inclusive* Eurocentrism, which regarded European superiority as a working hypothesis subject to correction in individual cases, to an *exclusive* Eurocentrism that took such superiority as axiomatic. From around the 1780s, this fundamental shift in "self-description" at the level of semantics was bound up with *real* cases of exclusion: for example, the Orientalization of the Ottoman Empire in European Great-Power diplomacy, the exoticization and ethnic cleansing of the Crimean Tatars and other peoples on the fringes of the Islamic world, the exclusion of Indians from judicial and higher administrative appointments in the EIC, and the refusal of European ambassadors to submit any longer to Asiatic court ceremony. No single action better illustrates this new distance than Lord Macartney's bow to the Qianlong emperor on September 14, 1793. Prior to Macartney, who was far from a rabid imperialist and arrogant Eurocentric, every European ambassador had consented to perform the kowtow, prostrating himself three times before the Dragon Throne.[19]

At the same time as it distanced itself from Asia, Europe tightened its grip on the continent. The British took to heart the cautionary examples of the Portuguese and Dutch, whose excessive familiarity with their colored subjects had supposedly diminished their authority and white man's mystique. They wanted to rule like the Romans, not the Greeks, who had succumbed to the temptations of the East in their Hellenistic late period.

The rise and triumph of European exceptionalism put an end to the solidarity among Eurasian civilizations that had still been taken for granted in the Enlightenment era. But it also concealed a more far-reaching tectonic shift in mentality. The decades around 1800, the European "saddle period," witnessed a change in the mental map of the *world* as well. It was around this time that there first formed a sense of Europeanness as we know it today, which was just as much an awareness of Europe's position among the world's continents and civilizations as it was one of what the postmedieval nations of the West had in common. Exclusion and self-definition went hand in hand. Europe projected itself on the screen of the non-European. It did so, above all, as the only culture that had instituted systems claiming universal validity. The closer the contact with foreign cultures—whether in India, Egypt, or the Caucasus—the greater the challenge to the European sense of order. It was no accident that scientific colonization followed on the heels of military invasion. The conscientious and methodical note-taking of individual travelers such as Volney made way, particularly in India and Egypt, for systematic data collection by the colonial state or occupying power.[20] The disenchantment of Asiatic civilizations began with the wish that they be forced to give up their secrets.

The unfabling of the East deprived these civilizations of their enigmatic self-evidence. They became objects of scientific curiosity, tasks for the acumen of learned specialists and the organizational talent of energetic administrators. Ambiguities dissolved in the acid bath of professionalized rationality. A line was now drawn between the two worlds, making it more difficult to cross borders and switch roles. It would not have been easy to affix a single identity to a Jesuit in China in 1720; the church had often sought to do so in vain. Were the court Jesuits in Peking Europeans, representatives of particular nations, or members of a supranational elite? Were they Christian clerics, experts in natural science, or Confucian scholars? Nineteenth-century missionaries were barely affected by this problem: in their minds, they were bringing light from the West to the benighted heathen. Or to take another example: when Carsten Niebuhr or even Johann Ludwig Burckhardt traveled in Arab dress, they did so because they found it both practical and courteous towards their hosts. Their nineteenth-century successors like Richard Burton turned this into costume and masquerade, dramatized in tales of bloodthirsty fanatics plotting against the life of the heroic traveler. The superior white master mixed incognito with the natives.

The unfabling of the East also led to a narrowing of intellectual horizons. The humor of a Niebuhr, the irony of a Gibbon (who when in doubt reserved a dash more caustic wit for the civilized than for the barbarians) gave way to sarcasm and condescending caricature. The assumption of European superiority poisoned intercultural good taste. At best, the default position of permanent condescension tolerated its polar opposite: exalted infatuation with the East. Yet the starry-eyed Orientalists all too often remained Eurocentrically or narcissistically trapped in their quest for a deeper authenticity that had somehow been betrayed in present-day Asia.

The sweeping changes that occurred in the decades around 1800 have called forth a number of ambitious interpretations. Reinhart Koselleck, who introduced the concept of a "saddle period," emphasizes the temporalization and acceleration of perception, Michel Foucault the replacement of tableau-like classificatory thinking by the discovery of an active depth dimension, Niklas Luhmann the end of old-European semantics, Martin Thom the build-up and breakthrough of a new kind of ethnic nationalism.[21] While each of these interpretations contains important impulses that bear directly on our topic, they do not add up to anything like a coherent overview. The following concluding pages make no claim to offer a general theory of the European mind around 1800. They attempt solely to shed more light on the discursive transition that occurred between (roughly) 1780 and 1830.

FROM ALADDIN'S CAVE TO DEVELOPING NATION

This transition can be clearly traced in economic assessments. Throughout the seventeenth century, travelers had rubbed their eyes in astonishment before the unimaginable splendor of the courts of Istanbul, Isfahan, and Agra. The sultan's wealth was "incredible," Tavernier states in 1675.[22] Once the glory of these courts had faded and fear of the morally corrupting influence of oriental luxury had grown, the emperor of China, who maintained a more frugal court and seemed to preside over a better managed economy, was widely considered to be the richest monarch in the world. Travelers such as Bernier or Gemelli Careri as well as some missionaries were dismayed by the poverty they encountered in many parts of India.[23] Yet until the mid-eighteenth century, visitors to countries like China, Japan, Siam, and Cochinchina were still struck by the prosperity of the common people.[24] The ancient topos of Asia's superior fertility seemed to have been confirmed anew. These reports and judgments were surely not unfounded. Visitors who did not hail from such wealthy regions of Europe as the Netherlands, the Île de France, or southern England must have been favorably impressed by living standards in many parts of Asia. The superficial impression that tropical or subtropical nature rained its blessings on the spoiled children of the East with them barely having to lift a finger, condemning them to lives of indolence and torpor, was gradually overlaid by admiration for the agricultural, horticultural, and hydrological achievements of Asiatic countries.[25] As late as 1818, a German geographical handbook was still proclaiming the Japanese to be the best farmers in the world.[26]

Very few of these positive judgments withstood the new barrage of criticism. In 1817 James Mill described Indian farming techniques—more precisely, those of the Hindus—as primitive.[27] The abbé Dubois concluded a careful analysis by finding that India was an underdeveloped country—but at least it was a civilized one: "Among all the civilized countries in the world, this one was the poorest and most miserable."[28] This could of course reflect an *actual* decline that would have to be corroborated from native sources, yet the criteria of judgment had shifted in the meantime. To the same extent that economically and structurally determined food shortages became less common in Europe, their existence in Asia became all the more conspicuous. While the terrible famines that ravaged India between 1770 and 1800 could still be discussed partly as a problem of the native economy, partly as a consequence of EIC economic policy,[29] the great hunger that afflicted China around the same time was clearly a domestic Chinese phenomenon for which no foreign intervention could be blamed. China's defenders found themselves placed in a difficult position, one that their opponents were only too happy to exploit. There gradually arose a new image of China as a land of mass starvation.[30]

The new science of economics played its part in causing the once-gleaming jewels of the East to lose some of their luster. Broadly speaking, European notions of rationality were deployed against Asiatic irrationality, as when Chardin reproached the Iranians for their poor saving habits,[31] or when it was correctly pointed out that the value of gifts exchanged in China was determined by the rank of the donor, not by equivalence—a completely irrational and premodern form of behavior, in European eyes.[32] Economic analysis became more sophisticated once the observer avoided taking nature's bounty and the ruler's visible riches as a direct measure of the overall wealth and economic potential of a society, seeking instead to move beyond surface appearances. The first to do so, writing in the 1760s, was the traveler, botanist and physiocrat Pierre Poivre.

Poivre, who had visited India, China, and several Southeast Asian countries, was unresponsive to court spectacle and refused to see it as an indicator of a nation's wealth. He drew on many examples to show that a favorable climate and fertile soil were not enough to ensure a thriving agriculture. Only an agrarian constitution guaranteeing farmers legal freedom and the maximum enjoyment of the fruits of their labor, combined where possible with a policy that stimulated economic activity, was conducive to human happiness.[33] Poivre consequently opposed despotism and royal proprietary rights; slavery, forced labor, and serfdom; parasitic aristocrats and indolent monks; monopolies and excessive taxation. He saw his ideal of an affluent society of legally protected farmer-proprietors under a benign and patriarchal ruler realized in China and partly also in Vietnam, but nowhere else in Asia.[34] He reserved withering scorn for what he saw as the dire economic conditions in the maladministered Mughal Empire, despotic Siam, anarchic Cambodia, feudal Malaya, and colonial Java.

As a good physiocrat, Pierre Poivre regarded agriculture as the fountainhead of public welfare. Wherever he went, he gave his opinion on local conditions with the trained eyed of the botanist and agronomist. As one of the first travelers to pay almost no attention to urban Asia, including the dazzling artisanal achievements that had so fascinated earlier visitors, he was instrumental in creating the image of Asia as a continent of peasant societies. Village life, not glittering cities, stood at the center of Poivre's physiocratic reports and observations.

Later travelers, schooled in the ideas of Adam Smith and political economy, applied different criteria of rationality. They paid attention to the efficiency of means—and chided the Indian princely states for their extravagance; they subjected economic policy to cost-benefit analysis—and found the system of conscript labor (*corvée*) in Siam and Cochinchina to be senseless; they trusted in the invisible hand of the market—and saw public granaries in China and Cochinchina, not as a sign of paternal concern and a form of natural disaster insurance, but as a market-distorting instance of hoarding. To be sure, the new doctrine also discovered redeeming features in some Asiatic countries: the free trade system in the Ottoman Empire, for example, or the exemplary absence of poor laws in China.[35]

Several leading theorists—Adam Smith, Thomas Robert Malthus, Jean-Baptiste Say, James Mill, and his son John Stuart—already recognized the problems caused by unequal rates of economic development around the world. The great problem of the "static" character of Asiatic countries, which had long preoccupied philosophers of history, received its most intellectually ambitious treatment to date in Adam Smith's theory of the stationary or steady-state economy, itself part of a larger theory of the conditions of wealth creation. Jean-Baptiste Say and others continued this line of investigation. The wonderment provoked at the beginning of our epoch, around 1680, by the grand mughal's fabulous splendor had been replaced at its end, around 1830, by a sophisticated theory of underdevelopment.[36] From now on, the key phenomenon calling for explanation was Asia's relative backwardness, not its wealth.

DECLINE, DEGENERATION, STAGNATION

Nineteenth-century theories of global economic development, with their differentiation between dynamic and static or backward countries, were but the latest manifestation of an older discourse of stagnation and decline. This discourse cannot be retraced here in all its multiple ramifications, only sketched in a few aspects.

In the eighteenth century, the idea that "savages" had no history was a commonplace boasting an ancient pedigree. Very few thought to question it. The ahistorical nature of primitive society was confirmed by a negative finding: they left no traces—no ruins, no inscriptions, no books. Such an absence of material remains was less common in Asia than in other parts of the non-European world. The continent was strewn with the relics and rubble of earlier civilizations. These needed explaining. Many of these ruins were obviously modern in origin and hence bore witness to military turbulences and those "revolutions" that, prior to the French Revolution, tended to be associated more with Asia than with Europe. Others pointed to a prehistoric past.

What amazed and sometimes shocked people about Asia were its extremes. On the one hand, European visitors to China, Japan, and Korea were constantly struck by what they did *not* see: ruins. The wooden construction techniques traditionally used there meant that temples and palaces quickly succumbed to fire, termites, or organic decay. Little was more than four or five centuries old. Given the absence of ancient monuments, Europeans accustomed to ruins found it hard to orient themselves in unmarked landscapes that, unlike the trackless forests and boundless plains of North America, were nonetheless clearly home to age-old cultures.[37]

On the other hand, there still existed monuments of colossal dimensions that had withstood the combined assault of climate, natural disasters, and history: antiruins created by a race of titans, so unlikely did it seem that they were the work of human hands. In 1585 Mendoza had already interpreted the Great Wall of China as part human project, part geological process.[38] Johann Michael Wansleb's awestruck reaction upon catching sight of the Egyptian Pyramids on October 3, 1664, was typical: "One is almost appalled at the sight and cannot comprehend how such enormous stones could have been raised so high."[39] Later travelers were not so naïve. Volney noted the contradictory feelings that overcame him when he first beheld the Pyramids: astonishment, terror, admiration, respect, a sense of human insignificance in the grand scheme of things. Yet these soon gave way to mounting anger at the self-indulgence and brutality of the despots who had forced "these barbarous works" on their people.[40] There was widespread agreement, meanwhile, that both the Pyramids and the Great Wall were *not* ruins.[41] Only a few Europeans saw the Central Asian sections of the Wall that had already collapsed by the eighteenth century, and hardly anyone shared Edward Gibbon's realistic insight that the great border defenses would rarely have been of much use against barbarians, anyway.

The Pyramids and the Great Wall of China had a unique standing in the knowledge of the eighteenth century as timeless, apparently everlasting monuments. More characteristic was the ruin as an emblem of transience. In Europe, north of the Mediterranean, there was nothing to match in scale the ruined cities and landscapes that could be seen in Asia even before the archeologists arrived on the scene. These included Ephesus in Asia Minor, Baalbek and Palmyra in Syria, and above all Persepolis in Iran, the subject of frequent description and commentary from the 1670s, at the latest.[42] Before Europeans began studying the figures and inscriptions of Persepolis and interpreting them as prototypical oriental antiquities, other questions stood in the foreground, such as whether Alexander the Great had the right to burn down the Achaemenid summer residence in 330 BCE. While some deplored the deed as an act of vandalism, the influential art historian Dubos claimed that Alexander had destroyed the palace with good reason, on account of its unsightly design flaws.[43] At any rate, there was no doubt as to who was responsible for the ruinous state of the ancient Persian palace complex: the ruins of Persepolis were the work of a Hellenic conqueror.

There was nothing puzzling or picturesque about the ruins of Alexandria, by contrast, nothing that stimulated deeper reflection: a gigantic, desolate rubblefield that had been known north of the Mediterranean ever since Jean de Thévenot's visit in 1657.[44] An English traveler noted upon inspecting it in 1817:

> The outer gate leads to an enclosure that presents a scene of wretchedness unequaled even in this land of desolation. A considerable part is occupied by ruined cottages and prostrate temples: the mouldering remains of ancient splendour lie mingled in confused masses with the havoc of modern rapine.[45]

The process that transformed a ruin into a heap of rubble was difficult to arrest, and at some point such a degree of formlessness was reached that nothing was left for the imagination to work upon. Once "the plan of the whole" could no longer be discerned, the ruin lost its aesthetic appeal and historical expressiveness.[46] In Asia, that was very often the case even for relics of relatively recent origin. European travelers saw the evidence of the latest havoc wreaked by war or earthquake in the Near East, in China after the Manchu conquest, in Iran following the Afghan invasion of 1722, and in and around Delhi, where traces of the destruction unleashed by Timur in 1399 had still not entirely been eradicated by the time Nadir Shah sacked the city in 1739.[47]

Modern Europeans had themselves already left behind ruins in Asia, such as abandoned Portuguese and Dutch forts. In the case of Georgia and Armenia, whole countries were described as having gone to rack and ruin.[48] In 1799 the Saxon writer Johann Adam Bergk characterized the entire Old World as a single rubblefield, advising his readers to migrate to America, the only place where new construction efforts stood a chance of success; there alone was it possible to resume the project of "educating the human race for the better."[49] The ruin metaphor here takes on the broader meaning that made it possible for Raynal to describe the customs of the "currently living" Indians as a field of ruins, or for Herder to state that China, "like a prehistoric ruin, has stayed stuck in its semi-Mongolian condition."[50]

Because European visitors lacked the awareness of historical continuity that made monuments of the classical past and the Middle Ages seem essentially familiar to them, Asiatic ruins rarely occasioned aesthetic contemplation, romantic rumination, or melancholic brooding on the transience of earthly things. All the more important were the historical and historico-philosophical reflections linked to observations of Asia. Three broad thematic trends may be distinguished here: the discourse of decline, the discourse of decadence, and the discourse of stagnation.

The *discourse of decline* derives from ancient ideas about the ineluctable rise and fall of empires. Charting this movement had always been considered one of the historian's primary tasks; the revival of cyclical notions of history in the Renaissance gave it fresh impetus and it was subsequently adopted by Enlightenment historiography. Joseph von Hammer-Purgstall, writing at the end of this line of tradition, still speaks the old language of classical fatality when he declares decline to be the "lot of all empires" and inscribes his own history of the Ottoman Empire into the cyclical model.[51]

Projected onto Asia at the start of the early modern period, this pattern of thought had a significance that was more topical than historico-philosophical. From the late sixteenth century, confrontation with the Ottomans made it imperative to look for weaknesses and first cracks in the imposing façade of Turkish power. This lent a strong empirical accent to the discussion of decline in relation to the Ottoman Empire. The fall of the Iranian Safavid state and the Indian Mughal Empire proceeded far more rapidly and more surprisingly than the creeping debilitation of the Ottoman Empire, restricting European observers to the role of posthumous chroniclers.

In particular, the Mughal collapse following the death of the emperor Aurangzeb in 1707 aroused considerable interest, since each of its possible interpretations held implications for the self-legitimation of the new European overlords as well as lessons for the future.[52] For example, those who assigned principal responsibility for the Mughal debacle to military overextension and the rise of religious intolerance under the "fanatical" Muslim Aurangzeb warned the British against repeating these mistakes and urged them to refrain from proselytizing their Indian subjects.[53] The eighteenth-century discourse of decline dealt with Asiatic cases individually while also encompassing the erosion of the Portuguese and Dutch empires.[54] Only towards the end of the century were the individual examples drawn together into a scenario of pan-Asiatic decline: triumphantly by those who heralded the dawning of European global supremacy, elegiacally by anticolonial critics who lamented the despoliation of South and Southeast Asia through foolish self-destruction and foreign conquest.[55]

Although the discourse of imperial decline had its basic template in classical antiquity, it was transposed to modernity when applied to Asia. Gibbon built a bridge between the two with his great interpretation of the downfall of the Byzantine Empire. The Scottish engineer, economist, and statistician William Playfair even developed a remarkable general theory of imperial decline that still has much to contribute to today's discussion.[56] Yet such universality was uncharacteristic. All that interested those who deployed this discourse about India, for example, was the fate of the early modern Mughal Empire, not that of the illustrious ancient Hindu culture.

The *discourse of degeneration*, by contrast, was concerned with precisely such phenomena. It stood on the border between older myths of a golden age and more recent theories of cultural evolution. The fundamental theme, subject to multiple variations, can be easily summarized: nations that present themselves to us today as savage, barbarian, or effetely pseudo-civilized are in truth descended from age-old high cultures, although they have long been estranged from their origins. Philosophers elaborated on this theme with great ingenuity; Jemima Kindersley expressed it in her usual no-nonsense manner:

> However pure the system of religion might originally be, it is certain the *Hindoos* have no reason, at present, to boast; for the whole of it, at this time, consists in absurd unaccountable ceremonies, which the people do not understand the meaning of; nor, I may venture to say, do many of the *Brahmins* themselves.[57]

The discourse of degeneration can already be found in English authors of the Renaissance. They regarded the kind of "savagery" encountered by sailors in America, not as a primitive state of nature from which the human race had gradually emerged, but as the product of an early cultural flowering that had long since gone to seed. Savages were thus, unbeknownst to them, something like the living ruins of their own past.[58] Such reflections were transferred primarily to India in the eighteenth century. India seemed to offer an example for how the originally pure light of religion had been all but snuffed out by superstition and ritual. This was conceived more as a slow process of inner decay than as a catastrophic barbarian incursion from outside.

Around the mid-eighteenth century, when Europeans were still unable to read Sanskrit and knew next to nothing about ancient India (far less than about ancient China), Voltaire had enthused about the wisdom of the ancient Indians and found support from no less an expert on India than John Zephaniah Holwell.[59] Once philologically informed research into ancient India had gotten underway under Sir William Jones's leadership in the 1780s, this interpretation was given a new lease on life, even if the negative judgment on the later Hindus expressed by those affiliated with the Asiatick Society of Bengal was not so damning as that reached by less scholarly proponents of a similar viewpoint.

The degeneration discourse implied a linear, discontinuous concept of time, not a cyclical one. The figure of discontinuity could, if it was deemed necessary, easily be used to justify a lack of interest in the present state of Asia, since this to all appearances was only a pale imitation of its former glory. At the same time, Europeans could see it as their mission—either on their own or in concert with native collaborators—to revive and restore the cultural authenticity they believed had gone lost in the present age. Such a program sounds "Orientalist" but was in fact subversive in the early nineteenth-century context because the high culture that was to be reconstructed was a non-Christian one.[60] Interpretations of India in the decades around 1800 overwhelmingly spoke the language of degeneration.[61] They linked up with speculation on the origin of language, poetry, art, and wisdom, with the Aryan myth, and with the hypothesis of a single *Urvolk*,[62] stimulating new theories of human prehistory and ethnogenesis.

The "conjectural," only partly demonstrable idea of a decline from a pure Brahmin archaic past did not remain uncontested. Goethe and Hegel, for example, looked askance at their romantic contemporaries' predilection for primal myths and primordial Vedic wisdom. Edmund Burke was of the opinion that the obvious decadence of modern India had not been brought about by some legendary early diminution of cultural vitality, nor by Muslim foreign rule, but by the far more recent crimes of European colonizers.[63] Evangelical politicians disliked the misty-eyed veneration of India's heathen legacy. And James Mill, who as an Enlightenment radical and modernizer was unsparing in his critique of the Indian tradition, saw in the degeneration thesis nothing more than a weak fallback position taken up by Asia's muddle-headed defenders.[64] The mental slavery he claimed to observe in present-day India had always been a defining feature of Indian civilization. Mill remained firmly wedded to the idea of Asiatic stagnation.

This *discourse of stagnation* differed fundamentally from that of degeneration in presupposing a progress in human evolution that had reached its climax in modern Western Europe. Stasis could only be recognized in its distinction from dynamism. "Stagnation" figured here as a concept pertaining to the history of civilizations. It did not contend that a stagnating nation lacked history in the conventional narrative sense. On the contrary, a constant parade of new leaders or a series of "revolutions" was eminently compatible with stagnation. Stagnation could be diagnosed when mores and customs, knowledge and mentalities, forms of government and modes of material subsistence remained unchanged over long periods of time, when the material life and intellectual capacities of a nation or an entire civilization were stuck in neutral, so to speak. This idea was obviously nuanced and developed in various ways, and it formed a stock part of the European interpretation of the world from the mid-eighteenth century, at the latest.

To be sure, Europeans rarely had the opportunity to observe other nations and civilizations long enough to be able to adduce any real evidence for their immobility. The standard argument resulted from comparing modern travel experiences with ancient texts: present-day Arabs lived just like the biblical patriarchs; travelers to the Near East thought they saw "the very people spoken of by Moses and the Prophets."[65] In India the works of Arrian and Megasthenes could still be taken as valid descriptions of social conditions.[66] And James Mill—in an uncharacteristically florid passage—even pictured the Indians of his own day as the living representatives of the entire ancient Orient: "By conversing with the Hindus of the present day, we, in some measure, converse with the Chaldeans and Babylonians of the time of Cyrus; with the Persians and Egyptians of the time of Alexander."[67]

Edward Gibbon, who was not only the era's most philosophically subtle historian but also an exacting empiricist, shied away from such flights of fancy. He chose as his own example of societal petrification and cultural ossification the only tolerably well-documented case: the Byzantine Empire. Others were less cautious, claiming for example that the customs of the nomadic Arabs had not changed in the last three to four thousand years,[68] or that the Chinese today made the same unmelodious and unharmonious music as "in their first infancy."[69] Of course, nobody could know this with any certainty. Writers were mostly trading in clichés that then took on a life of their own. Yet when an unimpeachable authority such as Sir John Malcolm maintained that the inhabitants of Persia "have remained unchanged in their appearance and character for more than twenty centuries," who would have dared contradict him?[70]

When it came to the idea that the age-old, historiographically long-documented Chinese civilization had persisted in a state of immutable identity with itself, the Jesuits who broadcasted this view to the West were faithfully following the Chinese self-interpretation, or more precisely the influential neo-Confucianism of the thirteenth century. Here at least the stagnation thesis was not merely a European "invention" but at least as much the application of an image that the Others had made of themselves. Scholars such as Joseph de Guignes, who knew the East and Central Asian historical sources better than any other European, or Jean-Baptiste d'Anville, who as a mapmaker was keenly aware of the Celestial Empire's constantly shifting borders, permitted themselves to correct some of the more dubious claims advanced in support of the stagnation thesis.[71] Others adopted a more theoretical approach: expressed in modern terms, it was simply not credible that *all* subsystems of a civilization could exist in a state of suspended animation. Was it not conceivable that—to recall Montesquieu's distinction—*les mœurs* could have evolved while *les loix* lagged behind, making China's ancient laws unsuitable for the modern Chinese?[72]

The diagnosis of static conditions could be evaluated in different ways. It was possible, for example, to see the supposedly unvarying dress sense in the East in a positive light. Vast sums of money otherwise spent on keeping up with the latest fashions were thereby saved, and sartorial solutions perfectly adapted to the local environment were not put at risk by capricious changes in taste.[73] According to William Marsden, the people of Sumatra were perplexed to see Europeans changing their clothes so often, assuming that they must find all their garments equally unsatisfactory.[74] Asians' conservatism in this regard could be favorably interpreted as signaling their affectionate attachment to the old ways, while the absence of political change could be welcomed as a sign of stability and sound governance.[75] Such judgments became increasingly rare from the 1760s onwards. In his *Geschichte der Kunst des Altertums* (*History of the Art of Antiquity*, 1764), Johann Joachim Winckelmann opposed the progressive development of Greek art to the stagnation and uniformity shown by the Egyptians and Persians, particularly in their representations of the human form.[76] Changes in style became a further index of Western superiority. Style was the ennobled version of fashion.

As time went by, dichotomies such as those between vitality and moribundity, creativity and spiritual sterility, "improvement" and the preservation of bad traditions became ever more sharply polarized. In the light of the new evolutionary thinking, stasis could no longer be justified and stability was a moral defect. This showed up particularly clearly in a newly emerging semantic divergence. While the history of Europe was described in a language suggestive of active, strong-willed subjecthood, mechanical or biological metaphors were increasingly applied to Asian societies that appeared to European observers as backward or inert. In 1782 Pierre Sonnerat characterized China as a culture of repetition, lacking the spark of true imagination and genius: "everything is done mechanically or by rote."[77] A little later Herder invoked a similar image of a society that for all its incessant bustle seemed to be incapable of propelling itself forward. He spoke of a "mechanical engine of [Confucian] morals" that was "forever checking the progress of the mind,"[78] and claimed of the Chinese nation that its "internal circulation" was "that of a dormouse in its winter sleep."[79]

Burke's Great Map of Mankind, where individual nations differed from each other only by degree, was replaced by the bipolarity of East and West. This in turn was interpreted in the light of the opposition between nature and history. The history of the East was passive, organic, and plantlike; or, in an equally unflattering metaphor, it was nothing but a clattering mechanism reproducing the same stale uniformity. In short, it was unconscious and without purpose. In this view, only the history of the West rose to the higher sphere of ethical volition.

At the summit of evolutionary thinking, in Condorcet and above all in Hegel, this opposition is drawn out with considerable sophistication. In Hegel an unprecedented historico-philosophical apotheosis of contemporary European superiority is combined with an attempt to do justice to the philosophically devalued cultures of Asia in their particularity and individuality. These are portrayed in a manner that surpasses even Herder in its careful empiricism.[80] Hegel's coupling of historico-*philosophical* exclusion and historico-*scientific* inclusion had no lasting impact. Over the course of the nineteenth century, the stagnation thesis was absolutized to the point where the peoples of Asia could be described as "ahistorical," an outcome already anticipated in Herder. Asia, it was now suggested, had never boarded the train of world history.[81] The fact that, in some quarters, even Slavs were denied a history of their own shows how tightly the circle of world-historical subjects was drawn. The best rational presentation of what might have been meant by this, Adam Smith's and Jean-Baptiste Say's theory of the stationary economy, was largely ignored outside a small coterie of economists. It influenced history writing and the philosophy of history only in Karl Marx's late reflections on an "Asiatic mode of production" and in a few scattered remarks of John Stuart Mill.

Of the three discourses that Europeans used to make sense of Asian history, the stagnation discourse was to prove by far the most influential in the nineteenth century. Imperial cyclical models seemed to have become obsolete once almost all the Asiatic empires had capitulated to the Western powers and Victorian colonial strategists had convinced themselves that they could escape the sad fate of their Portuguese, Spanish, and Dutch predecessors. The sun would never set on the British Empire, at the very least, which seemed to have broken definitively with the pattern of rise and fall that had foredoomed the empires of old. The discourse of cultural degeneration fell out of intellectual favor as the new Orientalist disciplines and Middle East archaeology, beginning in 1810 with the first investigations of Claudius Rich, the young British resident in Baghdad, caused notions of an early golden age to appear in a more realistic light.[82] The degeneration discourse was driven into the underground of a scientifically undisciplined, mythopoetic romanticism, only to be revived midcentury by doctrines of racial decadence as a result of "miscegenation." Solely the stagnation discourse appeared to accord with both the imperialist zeitgeist and the most up-to-date scientific knowledge. In the eyes of its proponents, modern Europe had left Asia trailing in the dust as it stormed from one success to the next.

FROM THE THEORY OF CIVILIZATION TO THE CIVILIZING MISSION

A simplistic view of the world that divided humankind into an active, history-making "West" and the passive, ahistorical "rest" was not the only legacy of the far more subtle reflections made by thinkers of the stature of Voltaire, Gibbon, Schlözer, Ferguson, or even the Janus-headed Herder, who placed unprecedented emphasis on the intrinsic value and meaning of all cultures while at the same time preparing the ground for many a later simplification. Another line in the history of ideas leading from the eighteenth to the nineteenth century can be traced by following ideas of "civilization."

The Enlightenment's underlying conception of history and social evolution was universal and unitary. It was based on the idea that people of all nations and races, for all that they differed in appearance, were endowed with the same basic faculties. It was therefore inconceivable that particular nations should be excluded from global processes. "Savages" and "barbarians" partook of them just as much as the so-called "polished" nations found predominantly in Europe, although not just in Europe. Obviously discriminatory terms such as "primitives" were not yet a part of the general discourse. The uncouth behavior of savages may have been repellent, but hardly anyone saw fit to deny them the potential for future development. Were not today's Europeans descended from the rude heathen tribes described by Caesar and Tacitus? In 1789 poet and dramatist Friedrich Schiller vividly articulated this view of history in his inaugural address as professor of history at Jena:

> The discoveries which our European seafarers have made in distant oceans and on remote shores afford us a spectacle which is as

> instructive as it is entertaining. They show us peoples arrayed around us at various levels of development, as an adult might be surrounded by children of different ages, reminded by their example of what he himself once was and whence he started.[83]

For Schiller history is that of "education" (*Bildung*); for others, such as Turgot and the Scottish Enlightenment, it concerns modes of material subsistence and the law. There were many rival conceptions. What they almost all had in common was the idea of human perfectibility and the conviction that individual peoples and nations would move at their own pace through the human civilizing process, often envisaged as a sequence of progressive stages. There would thus always be leaders and stragglers. The ultimate explanation for such variations was to be found in environmental conditions, not in anthropological or cultural deficits. The stragglers, provided they had enough wisdom, could see in the leaders a shimmer of their own possible future, while the leaders saw in the people dallying behind them a reminder of their own youthful past: a contrast confirming what they had already achieved but also a warning not to let it slide.

If civilization was a process rather than the sudden result of divine or prophetic intervention, the problem arose of how these graduated stages were to be described and named. The old triad of "savages—barbarians—polished nations" proved too coarse to be of much use. The sequence proposed by the Scots, "hunters—shepherds—farmers—traders," was easier to "operationalize" but it presupposed a material theory of civilization that not everyone agreed with. There was broad consensus from the 1760s that universal history should be written as *Kulturgeschichte* or "history of civilization" rather than as a mere summation of national histories. Even some of the most important early accounts of a particular national history—above all David Hume's *History of England* (1754–62) and William Robertson's *History of Scotland* (1759)—were essentially histories of civilizing processes exemplified in national case studies. As early as the 1780s, however, the learned Anglo-Irish cleric George

Gregory was pondering whether a history of human civilization ought not to be confined to the early phases up to the consolidation of agriculture and a centralized state, given that national characteristics became ever more pronounced thereafter as a consequence of more or less coincidental "casual interventions."[84] For the time being, however, this methodical doubt did nothing to dampen the enthusiasm for histories of the entire human race. A high point was reached in 1793, when Condorcet described ten eras in the progress of the human mind since the first tribes were formed.

Individual histories of civilization differed, above all, in how they responded to a single key question: were their authors more interested in the *origins* of civilization, in "the great taming of the human race," as the Scottish geographer Hugh Murray memorably put it?[85] Or did they instead—like Hume, Robertson, and Gibbon—have in mind the later *evolution* of civilization in Europe since late antiquity?[86] There were as many different opinions on what specifically constituted civilization and which forces were driving it as there were participants in the debate.

The possibility, first mooted by Fréret and Voltaire, that there could be distinct non-European paths to civilization was ever present in the minds of universal historians such as Gibbon and Schlözer. In a highly significant undertaking, the Jena Orientalist Johann Gottfried Ludwig Kosegarten, an adviser to Goethe in his studies on world literature, wrote a history of Eastern civilization that was based on extensive knowledge of the sources while still being cast in the theoretical-"philosophical" Enlightenment mold: a worthy counterpart to William Robertson's celebrated analysis of European history since the fall of the Western Roman Empire.[87]

Kosegarten, whose Orient extends geographically from the Hebrews and Phoenicians to India, tracks the evolution of Asiatic societies from the first emergence of tribal cultures, via the innovations of early legislators and the appearance of religion, ritual, and priesthood, all the way to the threshold of civilizational development he calls the "social and ethical state."[88] Avoiding overly bold deductions, he draws above all on the ancient "law books" of the various nations to describe what the great civilizations of the Orient have in common: a productive agricultural sector, a highly differentiated division of labor, elaborate social hierarchies, the institution of slavery (omnipresent, albeit of relatively minor importance), obligations of hospitality and mutual aid, veneration of the elderly and respect for women, and so on. He then distinguishes variants within this pan-Asiatic evolutionary path: for example, societies where priests enjoy the highest honors and those where these are accorded to warriors instead. The modern history of the East had preserved many such early idiosyncrasies without justifying talk of "stagnation." Change was a constant, and not just in the sense of an inexorable march of progress: women in Arabia had formerly enjoyed greater freedoms than they did today.[89]

Kosegarten offers little more than a broad outline. His social history of the East, which recalls Heeren in many respects, was never fully worked out. What makes his book so significant is that—perhaps in conscious opposition to what Hegel had declared from the lectern shortly before—it recognizes the history of Asiatic civilization as an integral part of the common history of humankind without judging it by Western standards. Although not published until 1831, the year of Hegel's death, the book reads like a document of the mature Enlightenment.

Over time, the concealed normativity of the concept of civilization grew ever more apparent. The relativism of Sir William Jones, who in 1787 proclaimed that everyone took civilization to mean only "the habits and prejudices of his own country,"[90] had already gone out of fashion by 1800. It was not a question of drawing a line between the civilized and the uncivilized. That only began to happen at the end of our period, as when Friedrich Schlegel declared in 1828 that Islam had failed to produce a civilization.[91] For the time being, the widespread assumption of a uniform civilizing process in which individual nations had reached varying degrees of maturity, yet were still capable of making further evolutionary progress, ruled out such strict dichotomies. The problem was rather that of determining how much further a particular community had to advance before it arrived at a fully civilized state, generally identified with present-day Western Europe. This index could be a temporal one, as when Volney precisely located the spirit of the Egyptian Mamluks in the twelfth century, while the rest of the country was still stuck in the tenth.[92] Alternatively, each nation was assigned its place on a scale of civilization, much like the United Nations's Human Development Index today. Needless to say, this called for the creation of relevant criteria (or "indicators," as we would say now). Rather than being diametrically opposed to barbarism, civilization was thus regarded as a finely graded cultural achievement.

This way of thinking endeared itself especially to British authors. The English had already attempted in the sixteenth and seventeenth centuries to distance themselves from their neighbors and would-be colonial underlings, the "wild Irish." From around 1800 they felt impelled to gain an overview of conditions within their newly acquired territories in Asia and beyond. Now the task was to demonstrate "to every society the place which they occupy in the great chain of human things."[93] The old cosmological idea of a "great chain of beings" still resonates in this programmatic statement by Hugh Murray from 1808, yet it has been detached from its biological context and transformed into an instrument of social and cultural analysis. It is easy to see how a scale of civilization could be interpreted as a racial hierarchy. This momentous development was portended from the late eighteenth century onwards but did not fully ensue until after 1830.[94]

William Marsden, alongside his contemporaries Volney and Georg Forster perhaps the most impressive specimen of the late Enlightenment scientific and "philosophical" traveler, was one of the originators of this new, finely graded hierarchical conception of civilization. The crucial passage in his *History of Sumatra*, published in 1783 and last reissued in 1811, deserves to be quoted at length:

> Considered as a people occupying a certain rank in the scale of civil society, it is not easy to determine the proper situation of the inhabitants of this island. Though far distant from that point to which the polished states of Europe have aspired, they yet look down, with an

> interval almost as great, on the savage tribes of Africa and America. Perhaps if we distinguish mankind summarily into five classes; but of which each would admit of numberless subdivisions; we might assign a third place to the more civilized Sumatrans, and a fourth to the remainder.
>
> In the first class, I should of course include some of the republics of ancient Greece, in the days of their splendor; the Romans, for some time before and after the Augustan age; France, England and other refined nations of Europe in the latter centuries; and perhaps China. The second might comprehend the great Asiatic empires at the period of their prosperity; Persia, the Mogul, the Turkish, with some European kingdoms. In the third class, along with the Sumatrans, and a few other states of the eastern archipelago, I should rank the nations of the northern coast of Africa, and the more polished Arabs. The fourth class with the less civilized Sumatrans, will take in the people of the new discovered islands in the South Sea; perhaps the celebrated Mexican and Peruvian empires; the Tartar hordes, and all those societies of people in various parts of the globe, who, possessing personal property, and acknowledging some species of established subordination, rise one step above the Caribs, the New Hollanders, the Laplanders, and the Hottentots, who exhibit a picture of mankind in its rudest and most humiliating aspect.[95]

Although Marsden later expands on his criteria for civilization, his categorization is impressionistic, albeit based on extensive historical and ethnographical research. It is remarkable not least because it manages to avoid the kind of rigid East-West dichotomies that would proliferate soon after. Marsden clearly places Europe at the apex of the hierarchy, yet it has to share the top two classes with Asiatic societies. China "perhaps" even belongs in the highest category. "Some European kingdoms"—Marsden may be thinking of Spain, Scandinavia, and the states of Eastern Europe—are by no means superior to the Muslim empires of the early modern period. The categorization cuts across religion, skin color, and national characteristics. Marsden is far removed from constructing a racial hierarchy along the lines proposed by Christoph Meiners, who had earlier distinguished between light, fair, and dominant nations, on the one hand, and dark, ugly, and subservient nations, on the other.[96] Marsden also distinguishes between a civilization's golden ages and its periods of decline: Augustan Rome merits top ranking, not Rome per se. The comparison is between historically precise cultural situations, not entire civilizations.

Once the "scale of civilization" came into vogue around the turn of the century, hardly anyone persisted with the judicious multidimensionality of Marsden's classification. Clear-cut rankings were now the order of the day. In 1804 John Barrow did not rest content with telling his readers what he had witnessed and experienced when visiting China a decade earlier as part of Lord Macartney's entourage. His goal was to equip them to determine "the point of rank which China may be considered to hold in the scale of civilized nations."[97] It is worth noting that China was still included among the "civilized nations" here. Everything depended on *how* civilized or uncivilized it was. The scale also made it possible to trace movements and make comparisons. A century earlier, Barrow points out, Russia had begun under Peter the Great to work itself out of a state of barbarism. Another hundred years hence "she will make a conspicuous figure among European nations, both in arts and arms."[98] China, by contrast, had already been highly civilized two millennia ago but was now chronically enfeebled and arrested in its development: "under its present state of existence" it was "not likely to advance in any kind of improvement."[99] "*Under its present state . . .*": it is telling that, in Barrow's view, China's fate was far from sealed. It could still be saved by reforms, perhaps taken in hand by a Chinese Peter the Great. Barrow's guidelines recur in the writings of many others on Asia. When John Malcolm wrote on Iran, James Mill on India, Mountstuart Elphinstone on Afghanistan, Stamford Raffles on Java, John Crawfurd on Siam, Burma, and Cochinchina, Constantin François de Volney on Syria and Egypt, or Alexis de

Tocqueville on Algeria, they were inquiring into the degree of civilization attained by the respective population or specific ethnic and social groups. There were practical reasons for doing so in some cases. The prudent imperial legislator needed to give careful consideration to the conditions to which he tailored his regulations.

Blithely oblivious to Marsden's scruples, pedants set about ranking nations in regular league tables. The Burmese, Crawfurd remarked in 1834, are far less civilized than the Hindu Indians and even more so the Chinese, but they are on the same level as the Siamese and the Javans. They are superior to the inhabitants of the eastern Indonesian islands, although Crawfurd had his doubts about whether these even permit comparison.[100] In 1800 the unpedantic traveler Michael Symes had already recognized how problematic such point-scoring could be: "The Birmans in some points of their disposition, display the ferocity of barbarians, and in others, all the humanity and tenderness of polished life."[101] Symes here rekindled a spark of High Enlightenment irony, recalling a time when it was still possible to praise the kindheartedness of cannibals and to see Asiatic nations as one's equals or even (in some respects) one's betters.[102]

In this way, the universalist theory and history of civilization of the Enlightenment became, in the nineteenth century, a tool for slotting every society on Earth into a hierarchy based on how far they had progressed—or failed to progress—on the path to modernity. What was beyond dispute was that Victorian England or France, where an important historian of civilization, François Guizot, played a leading political role, stood at the top of the civilizational leaderboard.[103] A consciousness of European superiority, bolstered by the theory of civilization, now gave rise to new justifications for imperial expansion. Exclusive Eurocentrism fed into the ideology that Europe was called on to remake the world in its own image. The theory of civilization spawned the conviction of a *mission civilisatrice*: the right or even duty of enlightened Europe to assert the universal values of progress against Asiatic darkness.[104] The expansive sense of mission awakened by the French Revolution had prepared the ground for such an awareness. Ever since, what international law had once excluded on principle seemed a distinct possibility: support for a popular rebellion against intolerable tyranny, or even intervention from outside when despotism or the dead weight of an inhumane tradition nipped protest in the bud.

Until the end of the eighteenth century, the appropriation of land for colonies had been justified, depending on circumstances, with economic goals, princely glory, the need to secure a strategic advantage in the contest between great powers, self-defense in a just war, the right to acquire "unowned" territory (*terra nullius*), or a Pauline mandate to convert the heathen, but not with humanitarian motives. It was instead the *critique* of colonialism, reaching a high point in Raynal/Diderot and Burke, that adopted humanitarian arguments. It was in this sense that Condorcet wrote in 1793 in a book that appeared the following year:

> Run through the history of our projects and establishments in Africa or Asia, and you will see our monopolies, our treacheries, our sanguinary contempt for men of a different complexion or different creed, and the proselyting fury or the intrigues of our priests, destroying that sentiment of respect and benevolence which the superiority of our information and the advantages of our commerce had at first obtained.
>
> But the period is doubtless approaching when, no longer exhibiting to the view of these people corruptors only or tyrants, we shall become to them instruments of benefit, and the generous champions of their redemption from bondage.[105]

Condorcet, a tireless campaigner against slavery, was serious about these accusations and expectations. He hoped for a future partnership between East and West, North and South. Yet under what conditions and with what intentions should the "generous champions" spring into action? This was the crux of the matter.

A standpoint that assumes—whether on universalist or relativist grounds—that all civilizations and religions are equal in value, and that all political systems enjoy more or less equal legitimacy (provided they do not degenerate into tyranny), cannot condone the exercise of imperial power. This was the view of Engelbert Kaempfer, Edmund Burke (at least on the India question), Herder, and Kant. In a weaker form, it was shared by most authors of the Enlightenment. Even Montesquieu never called for a crusade against oriental despotism, which he partly attributed to inalterable climatic conditions, anyway. By contrast, the doctrine of the white race's natural superiority fueled Social Darwinist justifications for aggression and annexation, derived from the right of conquest and the privilege enjoyed by the strong over the weak. This doctrine underpinned the high imperialism of the late nineteenth century. Between these two extremes lay a third position, which had its greatest practical impact between around 1790 and 1830. It flowed from a normative concept of civilization.

The civilization theory of the late Enlightenment operated, as we have seen, with a "scale of civilization." It was dynamic: the hierarchical ranking of the world's societies was not set in stone. Geographical-climatic and anthropological-racial conditions, which were largely unamenable to change, could not be assigned primary responsibility for lags in development. The main reasons why a country's often-enormous natural potential failed to be tapped were of human origin and could therefore be addressed. Despotism and religious "superstition" kept Asia bound in iron chains. They prevented the arts and sciences from flowering, the spirit of invention from prospering, and industry from booming. "Generous champions" (Condorcet) from the free countries of the West could help unleash all that pent-up potential.

This was a secular and pragmatic chain of ideas that had no need of religious and moral backing. Yet once there was added a sense of Christian mission and—as in the case of the influential evangelical politician Charles Grant—a program of moral reform, the interventionist impetus could be further strengthened.[106] Intervention from the more civilized West was necessary because the forces of social evolution could not be trusted to ripen of their own accord. After hundreds or even thousands of years of political and spiritual slavery, the people of Asia were incapable of liberating themselves from despotism and superstition. Like Bonaparte in Egypt in 1798, Condorcet's "generous champions" therefore had to act on their own initiative rather than in response to cries for help from a desperate citizenry. They took it upon themselves to topple despots and rogue states such as the slave-robbing pirate regime of Algiers, to curb religious "excesses" such as the *sati*, and to introduce legal institutions that would be conducive to modernization. They set about reforming existing colonial systems in the same way, seeking to "uplift" the morals and improve the economic welfare of their subject populations; the British saw this as their task on the Cape of Good Hope, on Ceylon, and for several years (1811–16) also on Java when they took over from what they saw as the selfish and depraved colonial administration of the Dutch VOC. In other cases pressure needed to be applied to recalcitrant native governments: in 1779 the German Enlightenment thinker Christian Wilhelm Dohm, a valiant champion of the rights of women and Jews, had already called for the "unnaturally closed kingdom" of the Tokugawa shoguns to be pried open—if necessary by force of arms—so that the Japanese would come into contact with "culture and enlightenment" and the whole world could profit from trading with them.[107] On this view, military intervention was a permissible last resort against such despicable tyrants as Tipu Sultan of Mysore or the Ottoman oppressors of the freedom-loving Hellenes. It was reprehensible for Europeans to keep their new-found happiness to themselves. Civilization, the great Indologist Henry Thomas Colebrooke announced in 1823 when founding the Royal Asiatick Society, came from India; now modern Europe had the opportunity and indeed the duty to repay its debt by taking in hand the project of civilizing Asia.[108]

It would be short-sighted to burden Enlightenment theories of civilization with sole responsibility for the belligerence that Great Britain, France, and Russia started to display in Asia and North Africa in the 1790s. They were one factor among many that a satisfactory explanation of this development would need to consider. But the real-world consequences of shifts in ideas, values, and attitudes ought not to be overlooked. A newly strengthened sense of European exceptionalism in the Napoleonic era, combined with an upsurge in intra-European nationalism, brought about a paradoxical result. On the one hand, it promoted a Eurocentric self-preoccupation that pushed Asia to the margins of public consciousness and elevated the collective narcissism of the world's number one civilization to previously unknown heights. On the other, it opened up a space for a secular civilizing mission whose ideologists clamored for the chance to impose their will on a crisis-ridden, vulnerable continent.[109]

The Enlightenment is not to blame for imperialism. No one criticized European world dominance more pointedly and attacked it more vociferously than Burke, Raynal, Diderot, Kant, Forster, or Alexander von Humboldt. But there are connections. The civilization that took itself to be the best performing and most humane in the world did not wait for Asia to show an interest in it. It gave its laws to Asia. In the age of the educational mission—from Lord William Bentinck's campaign to save the widows of India from the flames to the introduction of good diplomatic manners in East Asia[110]—the tone became earnest and severe, didactic and unfrivolous. The playful irony of a Johann Georg Gmelin, George Bogle, Edward Gibbon, William Jones, or Carsten Niebuhr disappeared from view. From now on Asia needed to be ruled and schooled, lectured and hectored, exploited and reconnoitered. Asia was hard work. The unencumbered Europe of the Enlightenment made the fateful decision to take up the white man's burden.

Notes

CHAPTER I. INTRODUCTION: LOOKING TO THE EAST

1. "Nos peuples occidentaux ont fait éclater dans toutes ces découvertes une grande supériorité d'esprit et de courage sur les nations orientales. Nous nous sommes établis chez elles, et très souvent malgré leur résistance. Nous avons appris leurs langues, nous leur avons enseigné quelques-uns de nos arts. Mais la nature leur avait donné sur nous un avantage qui balance tous les nôtres; c'est qu'elles n'avaient nul besoin de nous, et que nous avions besoin d'elles." Voltaire, "Essai sur les mœurs," in *Œuvres complètes de Voltaire*, vol. 26A (2013), 181; Voltaire, *The Works of M. de Voltaire*, 1761–65, vol. 4 (1761), 179.
2. Hammer-Purgstall, *Chane der Krim*, 1856, 141–49.
3. "Et que si ces Tartares n'avoient pas des guerres continuelles entre eux, ils seroient capables d'inonder und grande partie du monde, comme Chingis-chan a fait autres fois." Leibniz, *Briefwechsel mit den Jesuiten in China*, 2006, 204 (Leibniz to Antoine Verjus, S. J., April 20, 1699).
4. "Die materialistische Geschichtsauffassung" (1909), in Wieser, *Recht und Macht*, 1910, 114–15.
5. Huntington, *The Clash of Civilizations*, 1996, esp. chs. 5, 10, 11.
6. The present book does not have the ambition to propose yet another overall interpretation of the Enlightenment. For the major issues concerning the historical Enlightenment, its influence, and its continuing relevance see Ferrone, *The Enlightenment*, 2015; Pagden, *The Enlightenment*, 2013; an outstanding historical introduction is Tortarolo, *L'illuminismo*, 2007.
7. Cheneval, *Philosophie in weltbürgerlicher Bedeutung*, 2002; Albrecht, *Kosmopolitismus*, 2005.
8. See Schlereth, *The Cosmopolitan Ideal*, 1977. On patriotic countertendencies see Fink, "Patriotisme et cosmopolitisme," 1992.
9. On correspondence networks in the "republic of letters" see Goodman, *Republic of Letters*, 1994; Withers, *Placing the Enlightenment*, 2007, 42–61.
10. Withers, *Placing the Enlightenment*, 2007, 35–41; Kraus and Renner, *Orte eigener Vernunft*, 2008; Butterwick, Davies, and Sanchez Espinosa, *Peripheries of the Enlightenment*, 2008; Hardtwig, *Die Aufklärung und ihre Weltwirkung*, 2010; Conrad, "Enlightenment in Global History," 2012.
11. See as a case study of an Asian hub of global knowledge: Raj, "The Historical Anatomy of a Contact Zone," 2011.
12. P. Burke, *A Social History of Knowledge*, 2000 (table of contents); similarly Withers, *Placing the Enlightenment*, 2007, 87–135.
13. Collet, *Die Welt in der Stube*, 2007.
14. Schneider, *Kulturen des Wissens im 18. Jahrhundert*, 2008.
15. See Blanke, *Politische Herrschaft*, 1997, vol. 2, 1–20.
16. Golvers, *Libraries of Western Learning for China*, 2012–15.
17. See Plewe, *Die Carl Ritter Bibliothek*, 1978.

18. Plant, *Türkisches Staats-Lexicon*, 1789, "Vorbericht" (unpaginated).
19. E. Burke, *Correspondence*, 1958–78, vol. 3 (1961), 351. This famous quotation opens as an epigraph the pioneering work by Marshall and Williams, *Great Map of Mankind*, 1982.
20. Démeunier , *L'esprit des usages et des coutumes des différens peuples*, vol. 1, v. On similar judgments among authors related to the *Encyclopédie* see Vyverberg, *Human Nature*, 1989, 89.
21. Ferguson, *Essay on the History of Civil Society*, 1966, 21. Similarly Denis Diderot in 1770, quoted in Landucci, *I filosofi*, 1972, 20–21.
22. On this tangible presence of the East see Dermigny, *La Chine et l'Occident*, 1964, vol. 1; McCabe, *History of Global Consumption*, 2015; Berg, *Goods from the East*, 2015.
23. Derks, *History of the Opium Problem*, 2012; Milligan, *Pleasures*, 1995; Hayter, *Opium*, 1968; Berridge and Edwards, *Opium*, 1981.
24. Bruzen de la Martinière, *Introduction à l'histoire de l'Asie*, 1735, vol. 1, xii.
25. For Germany, the emergence of special sciences of the "Orient" has been dated to around 1810. See Mangold, *Eine "weltbürgerliche Wissenschaft,"* 2004, 42–46; for a more nuanced picture that avoids sharp periodization see Marchand, *German Orientalism in the Age of Empire*, 2009.
26. For more detail see Osterhammel, "'Peoples without History,'" 2000.
27. See Schulin, *Die weltgeschichtliche Erfassung des Orients bei Hegel und Ranke*, 1958, 235–69; Muhlack, "Das Problem der Weltgeschichte bei Leopold Ranke," 2010.
28. Compare my discussion, retained from the orginal of 1998, with Sanjay Subrahmanyam's recent mapping of the debate: Subrahmanyam, *Europe's India: Words, People, Empires, 1500–1800*, 2017, 212–15.
29. See Said, *Orientalism*, 1978, 86–87. More modestly, it could be said that Bonaparte's invasion of 1798 "pushed relations between Europe and the Muslim world into a new phase." Fowden, "Gibbon on Islam," 2016, 292.
30. For example, Inden, *Imagining India*, 1990, esp. 36ff.
31. Measured formulations of this argument that avoid the excesses of "deconstructionism" may be found in Dalmia and Stietencron, "Introduction," 1995, 20–21; Quigley, *Interpretation of Caste*, 1993, 12ff.
32. Kupperman, "Introduction," 1995, 5.
33. See also Ryan, "Assimilating New Worlds in the Sixteenth and Seventeenth Centuries," 1981. Peter Burke detects a deeper awareness and appreciation of the epistemological challenges posed by America emerging only in the eighteenth century: Burke, "America and the Rewriting of World History," 1995, 47. Other important advocates of the idea that America had only a minor impact on the European mind are John H. Elliott and Giovanni Gliozzi.
34. This is a central insight in Gadamer, *Truth and Method*, 1988, 245–74.
35. See Haase and Reinhold, *The Classical Tradition*, 1994; Grafton, *New Worlds and Ancient Texts*, 1993.
36. Boulainvilliers, *Histoire des Arabes*, 1731, 6.
37. Adelung, *Geschichte der Schiffahrten*, 1768, 2–3.
38. See Said, *Culture and Imperialism*, 1993.
39. Such a "Whig interpretation" of European insightfulness still informs Donald F. Lach's gigantic, unsurpassably copious encyclopedia of seventeenth-century European views of Asia: Lach, *Asia in the Making of Europe*, vol. 2, 1970–77; Lach and Van Kley, *Asia in the Making of Europe*, vol. 3, 1993.
40. B. Lewis, "Eurozentrismus," 1995, 650.

41. The point of departure today for any discussion of European perceptions of Asiatic religions must be the work of Urs App, esp. his *Birth of Orientalism*, 2010.
42. From many related publications by this author see esp. Pocock, "The Concept of a Language," 1987, 21–22.
43. See also Rousseau and Porter, "Introduction," 1990, 1. The studies by Gilman on coping with difference are of particular importance; see for example *Difference and Pathology*, 1985.
44. See Blanke, *Politische Herrschaft*, 1997, vol. 2, 28–33.
45. Kaempfer, *Heutiges Japan*, 2001. Again, in a neat parallel to the editorial history of the text in the eighteenth century, this definitive edition was preceded by a new translation, replacing Scheuchzer's version of 1727, of the manuscript in the British Library: Kaempfer, *Kaempfer's Japan*, 1999.
46. See Haberland, *Von Lemgo nach Japan*, 1990, 17–28. On many different aspects of Kaempfer's life and work see Haberland, *Engelbert Kaempfer*, 2004.
47. Kaempfer's Europe-wide reception has been ably reconstructed by Kapitza, "Engelbert Kaempfer und die europäische Aufklärung," 1980.
48. Burckhardt was born in Lausanne; his family belonged to the patriciate of Basel. He was educated at Göttingen and Leipzig. For biographical details, see Henze, *Enzyklopädie der Entdecker und Erforscher der Erde*, 1978–2004, vol. 1, 399–407; Wollmann, *Scheich Ibrahim*, 1984.
49. See Subrahmanyam, "One Asia, or Many?" 2016.
50. C. Niebuhr, *Beschreibung von Arabien*, 1772, 32.
51. See for example Vicziany, "Imperialism, Botany and Statistics," 1986.
52. In their encyclopedic work on European perceptions of Asia (see note 39 above), Donald F. Lach and Edwin J. Van Kley confine themselves for good logistical reasons to South, Southeast, and East Asia, excluding Central Asia, Siberia, and the entire Islamic world.
53. See for example Murphey and Stapleton, *A History of Asia*, 2016.
54. Chaudhuri, *Asia before Europe*, 1990.
55. Gibbon, *Decline and Fall of the Roman Empire*, 1994, vol. 1, 53.
56. Such as J. de Guignes, *Mémoire*, 1759.
57. A magisterial synthesis is Gascoigne, *Encountering the Pacific in the Age of the Enlightenment*, 2014.
58. At least for England, such a periodization even makes sense in the national historical context: see O'Gorman, *The Long Eighteenth Century*, 1997.
59. Thus, for example, the discussion of the "end" of Enlightenment in Outram, *The Enlightenment*, 2013, ch. 10.
60. See Baridon, "Lumières et enlightenment," 1978, 46, 56; Schneiders, "Einleitung," 1995, 167–68.
61. On France, for example, see Harth, *Ideology and Culture*, 1983, 289ff.
62. See Martino, *L'Orient*, 1906, 173–76; Makdisi and Nussbaum, *"The Arabian Nights" in Historical Context*, 2008.
63. Impey, *Chinoiserie*, 1977, 12, places the transition from oriental ornament to full-blown China fantasy in the 1730s.
64. Lach and Van Kley, *Asia in the Making of Europe*, vol. 3, 1993, 498, see 1676 as the turning point in the Dutch literature on Asia. See also ibid., 506–8, 591.
65. See also Wills, *The World from 1450 to 1700*, 2009, 140–54; Wills, *1688: A Global History*, 2001.
66. See Osterhammel, *China und die Weltgesellschaft*, 1989, chs. 6 and 7.

67. G. K. Goodman, *Japan and the Dutch*, 2000, 14–15.
68. G. K. Goodman, *Japan and the Dutch*, 2000, 18–24. A vivid description is provided in Thunberg, *Reise durch einen Theil von Europa, Afrika und Asien*, 1794, vol. 2, pt. 1, 1027.
69. According to Totman, *Early Modern Japan*, 1993, 233–347.
70. On the decline of Southeast Asia in the second half of the seventeenth century: Reid, *Southeast Asia in the Age of Commerce*, vol. 2 (1993), 267ff.
71. Ricklefs, *A History of Modern Indonesia*, 2008, 98.
72. Wyatt, *Thailand*, 1982, 107–17; of fundamental importance: Van der Cruysse, *Louis XIV et le Siam*, 1991, 441–78. On the repercussions in Europe, see Lach and Van Kley, *Asia in the Making of Europe*, vol. 3, 1993, 1185–96; Trakulhun, *Asiatische Revolutionen*, 2017, ch. 6.
73. Richards, *The Mughal Empire*, 1993, 252, 282.
74. Savory, *Iran under the Safavids*, 1980, 226–54.
75. On this concept see Hodgson, *The Venture of Islam*, 1974, vol. 3; McNeill, "Gunpowder Empires," 1993.
76. Rousseau and Porter, "Introduction," 1990, 14.
77. Ricklefs, *A History of Modern Indonesia*, 2008, ch. 12.
78. Yakovaki, "'Ancient and Modern Greeks' in the Late 18th Century," 2007, 200–201.
79. Kappeler, *Russian Empire*, 2001, 171.
80. See Osterhammel, "Alexander von Humboldt," 1998; Ette, *Alexander von Humboldt und die Globalisierung*, 2009.
81. Grosier, *De la Chine*, 1818–20.
82. Société Asiatique, *Livre du centinaire* (1922), containing the history of the Society by L. Finot (pp. 1–65); Pargiter, *Centenary Volume of the Royal Asiatic Society*, 1923; Kumar, "The Evolution of Colonial Science in India," 1990, 59ff.
83. See M. Koch, *Weimaraner Weltbewohner*, 2002; Goßens, *Weltliteratur*, 2011; and, above all, the many valuable studies by Karl S. Guthke.
84. Rückert quoted in Jacob Grimm and Wilhelm Grimm, *Deutsches Wörterbuch*, vol. 7, Leipzig, 1889, col. 1396–97 ("Ost").
85. See Buzard, *The Beaten Track*, 1993, chs. 12.
86. *Allgemeine deutsche Real-Encyclopädie für die gebildeten Stände: Conversationslexicon*, 10th ed., Leipzig 1855, vol. 15, 153.
87. P. Dumont, "Le voyage en Turquie," 1982, 339.
88. Pückler-Muskau, *Aus Mehemed Alis Reich*, 1985, 354.
89. Cited in Erker-Sonnabend, *Orientalische Fremde*, 1987, 3.
90. Kaukiainen, "Shrinking the World," 2001.
91. A. v. Humboldt, *Zentral-Asien*, 2009, clxxxii.
92. M. Weber, *Die Wirtschaftsethik der Weltreligionen*, 1989, 512.
93. See Delanty, *Europe and Asia beyond East and West*, 2006.

CHAPTER II. ASIA AND EUROPE: BORDERS, HIERARCHIES, EQUILIBRIA

1. Hammer-Purgstall, *Erinnerungen aus meinem Leben*, 1940, 44.
2. Gollwitzer, *Europabild und Europagedanke*, 1964, 59.
3. Pocock, "Deconstructing Europe," 1994, 336, and passim.
4. Lewis and Wigen, *Myth of Continents*, 1997, esp. 21–72.
5. Ellis, *Journal*, 1818, vol. 1, 37.
6. Barchewitz, *Ost-Indianische Reisebeschreibung*, 1730, 87.

7. R. K. Porter, *Travels in Georgia*, 1821–22, vol. 1, 192.
8. Morier, *Second Journey through Persia*, 1818, 246–47.
9. On this fundamental opposition in world history see Bulliet, *The Camel and the Wheel*, 1975, 7.
10. See Kappeler, *Russian Empire*, 2001, 114–53.
11. A. v. Humboldt, *Reise durchs Baltikum*, 1983, 121; A. v. Humboldt, *Zentral-Asien*, 2009, cxvi–cxx. See his day-to-day itinerary in A. v. Humboldt, *Briefe aus Russland 1829*, 2009, 45–52.
12. Alexander to Wilhelm v. Humboldt, Aug. 29, 1829, in A. v. Humboldt, *Briefe aus Russland 1829*, 2009, 182 (original letter in French).
13. On Humboldt's visit: A. v. Humboldt, *Briefe aus Russland 1829*, 2009, 104–8, 116. A. v. Humboldt, *Zentral-Asien*, 2009, cvi–cxi. A comprehensive description of this border, based on a visit in 1806, is offered in Klaproth, *Reise in den Kaukasus*, 1812–14, vol. 2, 450–78.
14. Unverzagt, *Gesandtschaft Ihrer Kayserlichen Majestät von Groß-Rußland an den Sinesischen Kayser*, 1727, 47.
15. Klaproth, *Reise in den Kaukasus*, 1812–14, vol. 2, 467. See also Foust, *Muscovite and Mandarin*, 1969, 77–82.
16. Bell, *Journey from St. Petersburg to Pekin 1719–22*, 1965, 116.
17. Bell, *Journey from St. Petersburg to Pekin 1719–22*, 1965, 120.
18. R. K. Porter, *Travels in Georgia*, 1821–22, vol. 1, 179. On the war's impact on the region, see Atkin, *Russia and Iran*, 1980, 145ff.
19. See Buisseret, *Monarchs, Ministers and Maps*, 1992.
20. Klug, "Das 'asiatische' Rußland," 1987, 271. For example: Zedler, *Grosses vollständiges Universal-Lexicon*, 1732–50, vol. 8 (1734), col. 2194.
21. Wolff, *Inventing Eastern Europe*, 1994, 153.
22. Bassin, "Russia between Europe and Asia," 1991, 6–7.
23. "Si après avoir parcouru de l'œil toutes ces vastes provinces, vous jetez la vue sur l'orient, c'est là que les limites de l'Europe de l'Asie se confondent encore." Voltaire, "Histoire de l'Empire de Russie sous Pierre le Grand" [1759], in *Œuvres complètes de Voltaire*, vol. 46, 1999, 459.
24. Pallas, *Reise durch die verschiedenen Provinzen des Rußischen Reiches*, 1771–76, vol. 1, 365; a fundamental account remains Wisotzki, *Zeitströmungen*, 1897, 418ff.
25. W. H. Parker, "Europe: How Far?," 1960, 286.
26. The following remarks according to Bassin, "Inventing Siberia," 1991, 767–71.
27. Ludwig Wekhrlin 1780, quoted in Gollwitzer, *Europabild*, 1964, 68.
28. "*Ésclaves attachés aux terres*": Montesquieu, "De l'esprit des lois," 22/14, in *Œuvres complètes*, 1949–51, vol. 2, 671; Montesquieu, *Spirit of the Laws*, 1989, 417 (revised).
29. See Lemberg, "Zur Entstehung des Osteuropabegriffs im 19. Jahrhundert," 1985, 74–77. On the debate in Russia see Bassin, "Russia," 1991, 8–17; Bassin, *Imperial Visions*, 1999, 49–57.
30. Gibbon, *Decline and Fall of the Roman Empire*, 1994, vol. 1, 817–18. Gibbon here discusses the recruitment of the Janissaries from among non-Turkish peoples of the empire.
31. See P. Ritter, *Leibniz' Ägyptischer Plan*, 1930; Antognazza, *Leibniz*, 2009, 117–18. The relevant documents are in Leibniz, *Sämtliche Schriften und Briefe. Politische Schriften*, vol. 1, 1983, 217–410. A joint offensive of the European princes against the Ottomans was also suggested by the cleric and former French consul Jean Coppin: *Le Bouclier de L'Europe*, 1686, 23ff.
32. Housley, *Later Crusades*, 1992, 455; Yapp, "Europe in the Turkish Mirror," 1992, 143.

33. H. M. Scott, *Birth of a Great Power System*, 2006, 137–49.
34. Businello, who was highly regarded as an expert on the Ottoman Empire, also saw Ottoman foreign policy as essentially rational: Businello, *Historische Nachrichten*, 1778, 168–73.
35. Quoted in Schumann, *Edmund Burkes Anschauungen*, 1964, 107.
36. See Gatterer, *Ideal einer allgemeinen Weltstatistik*, 1773.
37. Spittler, *Entwurf der Geschichte der europäischen Staaten*, 1793–94, vol. 2, 197–241.
38. Deleyre, *Tableau de l'Europe*, 1774, 10–11.
39. Schumann, *Edmund Burkes Anschauungen*, 1964, 105–7; Chabod, *Storia dell'idea d'Europa*, 1995, 19.
40. Herder, *Ideen*, 1989, 699; *Outlines*, 1800, 484.
41. Herder, *Ideen*, 1989, 701–2; *Outlines*, 1800, 485–86.
42. Herder, *Ideen*, 1989, 705; *Outlines*, 1800, 360.
43. Herder, *Ideen*, 1989, 705; *Outlines*, 1800, 360.
44. Gibbon, *Decline and Fall of the Roman Empire*, 1994, vol. 1, 49, draws a contrast between good Roman administration in Asia Minor and bad Ottoman rule over the same region.
45. Thornton, *Present State of Turkey*, 1809, vol. 1, ccxxvii–ccxxviii.
46. "Les Turcs sont campés en Europe." Quoted in Chateaubriand, *Itinéraire de Paris à Jérusalem*, 1968, 63.
47. Meiners, *Betrachtungen*, 1795–96, vol. 1, 79.
48. Eton, *Survey of the Turkish Empire*, 1801, 13.
49. Schroeder, *Transformation of European Politics*, 1994, 739–40.
50. See J. Wallace, *Shelley and Greece*, 1997, 119ff.
51. Hammer-Purgstall, *Constantinopolis und der Bosporos*, 1822, vol. 2, 387.
52. See Bernal, *Black Athena*, 1987, 161ff. The controversy surrounding this three-volume work has not diminished the worth of the author's remarks in volume 1 on the history of ideas.
53. A notion of Eurasia as a geological entity seems to date back to the Austrian geologist Eduard Suess in 1885: W. H. Parker, "Europe: How Far?," 1960, 288.
54. Valéry, *Œuvres*, 1957–60, vol. 1, 995. A similar formula can be found as early as 1829 in writings of the French geographer Pierre Lapie: W. H. Parker, "Europe: How Far?," 1960, 288.
55. For example, Bruzen de la Martinière, *Grand Dictionnaire Géographique*, 1768, vol. 1, 457; Prichard, *Researches into the Physical History of Mankind*, 1836–47, vol. 3, 1–3 ; vol. 5, 602.
56. A. v. Humboldt, *Ansichten der Natur*, 1987, 81; *Views of Nature*, 2014, 84.
57. See chapter 8 in this book.
58. For example Subrahmanyam, "Connected Histories," 1997.
59. For example, Blome, *Geographical Description*, 1670, 1–2; Zedler, *Grosses vollständiges Universal-Lexicon*, 1732–50, vol. 2 (1732), col. 1844.
60. Diez, *Denkwürdigkeiten*, 1811–15, vol. 1, v; similarly: Adelung, *Mithridates*, 1806–17, vol. 1, 3.
61. Paulus, *Sammlung*, 1792–1803, vol. 1 ("Plan," unpaginated).
62. Büsching, *Große Erdbeschreibung*, 1787, 12.
63. Heeren, "Ideen," in *Historische Werke*, 1821–26, vol. 10 (1824), 47; Heeren, *Historical Researches*, 1846, vol. 1, 1.
64. Heeren, "Ideen," in *Historische Werke*, 1821–26, vol. 10 (1824), 48; Heeren, *Historical Researches*, 1846, vol. 1, 1.

65. Said, *Orientalism*, 1978, 79.
66. Ogilby, *Asia*, 1673, "The General Description of Asia" (unpaginated).
67. Beawes, *Lex Mercatoria Rediviva*, 1754, esp. vol. 1, 627ff.
68. Guthrie, *A New Geographical, Historical, and Commercial Grammar*, 1771, vol. 1, vii; see also vol. 2, 188ff.
69. "L'Asie a joué longtemps un grand rôle dans l'Univers; il ne lui en reste plus que le souvenir." Grasset de Saint-Sauveur, *Encyclopédie des voyages*, 1796, vol. 3, 4.
70. Volney, "Les ruines, ou méditation sur les révolutions des empires," in Volney, *Œuvres*, 1989–98, vol. 1, 248; Volney, *The Ruins*, 1849, 65.
71. Volney, "Les ruines, ou méditation sur les révolutions des empires," in Volney, *Œuvres*, 1989–98, vol. 1, 248; Volney, *The Ruins*, 1849, 66.
72. Leibniz, *Der Briefwechsel mit den Jesuiten in China*, 2006.
73. Jaubert, *Voyage en Arménie et en Perse*, 1821, 314.
74. Robertson, *Progress of Society in Europe*, 1972, 25.
75. Mailly, *L'esprit des Croisades*, 1780, vol. 1, 3.
76. Heeren, "Ideen," in *Historische Werke* (1821–26), vol. 10 (1824), 1–2, 43.
77. Malte-Brun, *Précis de la géographie universelle*, 1812–29, vol. 3 (1812), 18–19. On Malte-Brun's attititude towards non-Europeans see Godlewska, "Napoleon's Geographers," 1994, 44–45. Immobility wherever it might be found was seen by geographers of the Napoleonic generation as an ideal precondition for grand schemes of domination and reform. See Godlewska, *Geography Unbound*, 1999, 214.
78. "Airs, Waters, Places," 16, in *Hippocrates*, 1923, 114–17.
79. *Asiatisches Magazin*, vol. 1, pt. ("Stück") 1, 1806, iii.
80. Salaberry, *Histoire de l'Empire Ottoman*, 1813, vol. 4, 150.
81. Ellis, *Journal*, 1818, vol. 1, 55.
82. Morier, *The Adventures of Hajji Baba of Ispahan*, 1824.
83. Dabashi, *Persophilia*, 2015, 163–64.
84. A profound study of d'Herbelot is now Bevilacqua, "How to Organize the Orient," 2016.
85. In exhaustive detail: Omont, *Missions archéologiques*, 1902, vol. 1 (853ff: lists of the manuscripts collected).
86. D'Herbelot, *Bibliothèque Orientale* (1777–79), vol. 1, vi (Introduction by Antoine Galland). This edition, which made the work well known in late eighteenth-century Europe, was the result of a thorough revision of the original by a team of Dutch oriental scholars. See Laurens, *Aux sources de l'orientalisme*, 1978, 21.
87. The supplemenary volume of the Dutch edition (vol. 4, 1779) also contains more recent materials on China and Central Asia, among them a history of the "tartars" (i.e., mainly the Mongols) by the learned Jesuit and missionary to China, Claude Visdelou (pp. 46–294).
88. He uses it extensively, for example, in chapter 57 of *Decline and Fall of the Roman Empire*, 1994, vol. 3, 523–54.
89. See the careful analysis in Laurens, *Aux sources de l'orientalisme*, 1978, 37ff.
90. The conclusion that the alphabetically ordered encyclopedia is nothing but a "pale shadow of polyhistorism" (Schmidt-Biggemann, *Topica Universalis*, 1983, 291) does not apply in this case.
91. Fisch, "Der märchenhafte Orient," 1984, 250.
92. Hager, *Ausführliche Geographie*, 1773, vol. 1, 107.
93. J. R. Forster, *Bemerkungen über Gegenstände der physischen Erdbeschreibung*, 1783, 256; Godwin, *Enquiry Concerning Political Justice*, 1971, 21.

94. Büsching, *Auszug aus seiner Erdbeschreibung*, 1785, 20. On Büsching's significance for the history of geography see M. Bowen, *Empiricism and Geographical Thought*, 1981, 154–59; on Büsching as a scholar with international connections see Hoffmann and Osipov, *Geographie, Geschichte und Bildungswesen*, 1995, esp. 18–29.
95. Riello, *Cotton*, 2013, chs. 5 and 10.
96. Meiners, *Grundriß der Geschichte der Menschheit*, 1793, 29–30.
97. "En vérité, je crois toujours de plus en plus qu'il y a un certain Génie qui n'a point encore été hors de notre Europe, ou qui du moins ne s'en est pas beaucoup éloigné." Fontenelle, "Entretiens sur la pluralité des mondes habités," 1991, 129–30.
98. Dubos, *Reflexions*, 1719, vol. 2, 146. Very similar: Hager, *Ausführliche Geographie*, 1773, vol. 1, 111.
99. Gibbon, *Decline and Fall of the Roman Empire*, 1994, vol. 1, 228. In a similar way, Heeren points out that Europe surpassed all other parts of the world in the maximization and efficient use of its military and political power resources: Heeren, *Historische Werke*, 1821–26, vol. 15 (1826), 4.
100. See chapter 10 in this volume.
101. Brougham, *An Inquiry into the Colonial Policy of the European Powers*, 1803, vol. 2, 198.
102. Brougham, *An Inquiry into the Colonial Policy of the European Powers*, 1803, vol. 2. 235.
103. "Seuls nous sousmittons à nos volontés les forces même les plus rédoutables de la nature." Malte-Brun, *Précis de la géographie universelle*, 1812–29, vol. 6 (1826), 2. See also Adas, *Machines*, 1989, 79.
104. Gibbon, *Decline and Fall of the Roman Empire*, 1994, vol. 3, 803, note 28.
105. Jean-Jacques Rousseau, "Discours sur l'origine et les fondements de l'inégalité parmi les hommes" (1755), in Rousseau, *Œuvres complètes*, 1959–95, vol. 3 (1975), 208.
106. Sprengel, *Vom Ursprung des Negerhandels*, 1779, who chronicles, in a highly critical spirit, the emergence of the slave trade up to the mid-seventeenth century. Chronologically speaking, Sprengel, in his provincial German backwater, was among the earliest European critics of the slave trade. On the Anglo-American mainstream of early abolitionism see D. B. Davis, *Problem of Slavery*, 1975.
107. Robertson, *Historical Disquisition*, 1812, 181.
108. Beawes, *Lex Mercatoria*, 1754, 18.
109. Pradt, *Les trois âges des colonies*, 1801–2, vol. 1, 21.
110. Thanks to the efforts of European scholars such as Sir William Jones und Charles-Marie de La Condamine.
111. Zimmermann, *Die Erde und ihre Bewohner*, 1810–14, vol. 1 (1810), 8–15.
112. J. R. Forster, *Geschichte der Entdeckungen und Schiffahrten im Norden*, 1784, 8. On the civilizing effects of shipping already in ancient times see Dunbar, *Essays on the History of Mankind*, 1781, vol. 2, 299ff.
113. Immanuel Kant, "Perpetual Peace: A Philosophical Sketch," in Kant, *Political Writings*, 1970, 106; Immanuel Kant, "Zum ewigen Frieden. Ein philosophischer Entwurf," in Kant, *Werke*, 1968, vol. 9, 214 ("entfernte Weltteile mit einander friedlich in Verhältnisse kommen").
114. Kant, "Perpetual Peace," 1970, 106–7 (emphases in original); Kant, "Zum ewigen Frieden," in Kant, *Werke*, 1968, vol. 9, 214–16: "Vergleicht man hiermit das *inhospitable* Betragen der gesitteten, vornehmlich handeltreibenden Staaten unseres Weltteils, so geht die Ungerechtigkeit, die sie in dem *Besuche* fremder Länder und Völker (welches ihnen mit dem *Erobern* derselben für einerlei gilt) beweisen, bis zum Erschrecken weit. Amerika, die Negerländer, die Gewürzinseln, das Kap etc. waren,

bei ihrer Entdeckung, für sie Länder, die keinem angehörten; denn die Einwohner rechneten sie für nichts. In Ostindien (Hindustan) brachten sie, unter dem Vorwande bloß beabsichtigter Handeldsniederlagen, fremde Kriegsvölker hinein, mit ihnen aber Unterdrückung der Eingebornen, Aufwiegelung der verschiedenen Staaten desselben zu weit ausgebreiteten Kriegen, Hungersnot, Aufruhr, Treulosigkeit, und wie die Litanei aller Übel, die das menschliche Geschlecht drücken, weiter lauten mag. China und Japan (Nippon), die den Versuch mit solchen Gästen gemacht hatten, haben daher weislich, jenes zwar den Zugang, aber nicht den Eingang, dieses auch den ersteren nur einem einzigen europäischen Volk, den Holländern, erlaubt, die sie aber doch dabei, wie Gefangene, von der Gemeinschaft mit den Eingebornen ausschließen." On the eighteenth-century debate about closed countries and the desirability of their being "opened up" see Osterhammel, "Gastfreiheit und Fremdenabwehr," 1997, 404–12.

115. Schlözer, *WeltGeschichte*, 1785–89, vol. 1, 116–17.
116. Schlözer, *WeltGeschichte*, 1785–89, vol. 1, 75.
117. Schlözer, *WeltGeschichte*, 1785–89, vol. 1, 86.
118. "Compaß, Pulver, Papir und Druckerei, Brillen, Uhren und Posten." Schlözer, *WeltGeschichte*, 1785–89, vol. 1, 104.
119. Schlözer, *WeltGeschichte*, 1785–89, vol. 1, 105. See also his charming world history for children: Schlözer, *Vorbereitung zur Weltgeschichte für Kinder*, 2001.
120. On the iconography of European primacy in the eighteenth century see the magnificent study: Wintle, *The Image of Europe*, 2009, 282–348.
121. "Der uns nicht nur über alle unsre ZeitGenossen der übrigen WeltTheile, sondern auch über die aufgeklärtesten Völker der älteren Zeiten hoch erhebt." Schlözer, *WeltGeschichte*, 1785–89, vol. 1, 104–5. Schlözer's concept of world history, though never developed at length, is more interesting today than that of any of his contemporaries. A good summary is Muhlack, *Geschichtswissenschaft im Humanismus und in der Aufklärung*, 1991, 133–37.
122. On the history of this enormous project see Abbattista, "The Business of Paternoster Row," 1985. An almost complete, and in many places augmented, German translation was Baumgarten and Semler, *Uebersetzung der Algemeinen Welthistorie*, 1744–67.
123. See Pigulla, *China in der deutschen Weltgeschichtsschreibung*, 1996, 150, 222.
124. See the great biography: Franklin, *Orientalist Jones*, 2011.
125. W. Jones, *Works*, 1807, vol. 1, 10.

CHAPTER III. CHANGING PERSPECTIVES

1. Georg Christoph Lichtenberg. "Sudelbücher," Heft G [1779–83], Aphorismus 183, in Lichtenberg, *Schriften und Briefe* (1968–74), vol. 2 (1971), 166.
2. Richardson, *Dissertation on the Languages, Literature and Manners of Eastern Nations*, 1778, pt. 2, 154.
3. For example (a testimonial from the mid-1740s) Poivre, *Un manuscrit inédit de Pierre Poivre*, 1968, 40.
4. An example for this is coastal Sri Lanka under the VOC (from c. 1670 onwards). Silva, *History of Sri Lanka*, 1981, 197–98.
5. Two excellent, and complementary, surveys are C. H. Parker, *Global Interactions in the Early Modern Age*, 2010; Gunn, *First Globalization: The Eurasian Exchange*, 2003; Braudel, *Civilization and Capitalism*, 1981–84, is inexhaustible.
6. Riello, *Cotton*, 2013.
7. Hanway, *Historical Account of the British Trade over the Caspian Sea*, 1753, vol. 2, 27.

8. Symes, *Account of an Embassy to the Kingdom of Ava*, 1800, 312, 319, 321ff.
9. S. Turner, *Account of an Embassy to the Court of the Teshoo Lama,* 1800, 263.
10. S. Turner, *Account of an Embassy to the Court of the Teshoo Lama,* 1800, 81. At a later stage, Turner and the raja exchanged medicines (153–54).
11. See in general Thomas, *Entangled Objects*, 1991.
12. Castilhon, *Considérations*, 1769, 24.
13. Démeunier , *L'esprit des usages et des coutumes*, 1776, vol. 1, v.
14. As general surveys see Walvin, *Fruits of Empire*, 1997; McCabe, *History of Global Consumption,* 2015; Berg, *Goods From the East*, 1600–1800, 2015.
15. See also Chaudhuri, *Trading World of Asia*, 1978, 15.
16. See Winch, *Classical Political Economy*, 1965, 9–14; Pitts, *A Turn to Empire,* 2005, 52–58.
17. Very important on Burke's critique of empire and colonialism is Whelan, *Edmund Burke and India*, 1996, esp. chs. 1 and 4; see also Bourke, *Empire and Revolution*, 2015, esp. chs. 7 and 10.
18. E. Burke, "Opening of Impeachment, 16 February 1788," in Burke, *India: The Launching of the Hastings Impeachment,* 1991, 346.
19. See Pagden, *Encounters*, 1993, 141–88.
20. Robertson, *Historical Disquisition*, 1812.
21. Schlegel, "Über die Sprache und Weisheit der Indier," 1975. The most common English translation is "On the Indian Language, Literature, and Philosophy," 1849.
22. On Herder and India see Halbfass, *India and Europe*, 1988, 69–72; Ghosh, *Johann Gottfried Herder's Image of India*, 1990.
23. See also the excellent chapter on Robertson in O'Brien, *Narratives of Enlightenment*, 1997, 129–66; on Robertson's view on India's unique position in world history see Kontler, *Translations, Histories, Enlightenments*, 2014, 141–45.
24. Shackleton, *Montesquieu*, 1961, 32–33; Dodds, *Les récits des voyages*, 1929, 41–56.
25. The earliest text featuring an "exotic observer" of Europe seems to have been *L'espion du Grand-Seigneur* (1684) by Jean-Paul Marana (1642?–1693). See Weißhaupt, *Europa sieht sich mit fremdem Blick*, 1979, vol. 2, pt. 1, 3–15.
26. Montesquieu, "Lettres persanes," in *Œuvres complètes de Montesquieu*, vol. 1 (2004), 403; Montesquieu, *Persian Letters*, 1973, 185. The numbering of the letters in the critical edition differs from the conventional numbering as used in this English translation.
27. Montesquieu, "Lettres persanes," in *Œuvres complètes de Montesquieu*, vol. 1 (2004), 243–44; Montesquieu, *Persian Letters*, 1973, 98–99.
28. A motif in numerous travel accounts. As late as the 1820s, the Scottish diplomat John Crawfurd was annoyed by the Siamese penchant to put themselves above anyone else: *Journal of an Embassy to the Courts of Siam and Cochin China*, 1967, 345–46.
29. D. Campbell, *Journey over Land to India,* 1796, pt. 2, 21.
30. Adelung, *Geschichte der Schiffahrten*, 1768, 439.
31. Court de Gebelin, *Monde Primitif,* 1777–81, vol. 8, lix.
32. Ferguson, *Essay on the History of Civil Society*, 1966, 22–23.
33. This is how Pocock characterizes Ferguson's work: Pocock, *Barbarism and Religion*, vol. 2, 1999, 330.
34. Ferguson, *Essay on the History of Civil Society*, 1966, 75.
35. Dunbar, *Essays on the History of Mankind*, 1781, vol. 2, 161.
36. Dunbar, *Essays on the History of Mankind*, 1781, vol. 2, 162.
37. Sir William Temple, "Of Heroic Virtue," in Temple, *Works*, 1814, vol. 3, 322.

38. See Dreitzel, "Justis Beitrag zur Politisierung der deutschen Aufklärung," 1987, 167–68.
39. J. Campbell, *Present State of Europe*, 1750, 12–13.
40. Justi, *Vergleichungen*, 1762, Preface ("Vorrede"), 3.
41. Justi, *Vergleichungen*, 1762, 165–87.
42. Justi, *Vergleichungen*, 1762, 170.
43. Justi, *Vergleichungen*, 1762, 168.
44. See M. Harbsmeier, *Wilde Völkerkunde*, 1994, 209–24.
45. His source is a report, often cited in the eighteenth century, by the Franconian naturalist, Michael Peter Kolb, who spent the years 1704 to 1707 at the cape: *Caput Bonae Spei Hodiernum* (1719).
46. Justi, *Vergleichungen*, 1762, 178.
47. Justi mistakenly writes "Sineser" (Chinese).
48. Justi, *Vergleichungen*, 1762, 182.
49. Justi, *Vergleichungen*, 1762, 246.
50. Justi, *Vergleichungen*, 1762, 187.
51. Varenius, *Descriptio*, 1974, 142. For the Chinese see similar remarks in Le Gobien, *Histoire de l'édit de l'Empereur de la Chine*, 1698, 218–19.
52. David Hume. "Of the Standard of Taste," in Hume, *Essays*, 1987, 227.
53. Quoted in Vyverberg, *Human Nature*, 1989, 60.
54. Démeunier , *L'esprit des usages et des coutumes*, 1776, vol. 1, viii.
55. Walckenaer, *Essai sur l'histoire de l'espèce humaine*, 1798, 249–50.
56. For example, Hammer-Purgstall, *Geschichte des Osmanischen Reiches*, 1827–35, vol. 1 (1827), 414–15.
57. Hammer-Purgstall, *Geschichte des Osmanischen Reiches*, 1827–35, vol. 2 (1828), 508–10.
58. Hammer-Purgstall, *Geschichte des Osmanischen Reiches*, 1827–35, vol. 9 (1833), vii.
59. A. Hamilton, *New Account of the East Indies*, 1930, vol. 1, 144.
60. The medical doctor, botanist, and North African traveler, Johann Ernst Hebenstreit (1731), quoted in Thomson, *Barbary and Enlightenment*, 1987, 38. Similarly (on the Knights of Malta): C. Niebuhr, *Reisebeschreibung nach Arabien*, 1774–1837, vol. 1, 18.
61. Justi, *Vergleichungen*, 1762, 252.
62. See Gibbon, *Decline and Fall of the Roman Empire*, 1994, vol. 3, 151–232.
63. Hammer-Purgstall, *Geschichte der Goldenen Horde*, 1840, 79, also 81. See also the strong condemnation of the "barbarity" of the crusaders in Hammer-Purgstall, *Constantinopolis*, 1822, vol. 1, 93–95, 131 -32.
64. Montesquieu, "Lettres persanes," in *Œuvres complètes de Montesquieu*, vol. 1 (2004), 328; Montesquieu, *Persian Letters*, 1973, 148–49.
65. Societas Jesu, *Lettres édifiantes et curieuses*, 1780–83, vol. 24, 330–76. On Benoist see Pfister, *Notices biographiques et bibliographiques sur les Jésuites*, 1934, vol. 2, 813–26; on his work as a hydraulic engineer see Zheng Yangwen, *China on the Sea*, 2012, 190–98.
66. Societas Jesu, *Lettres édifiantes et curieuses*, 1780–83, vol. 24, 334.
67. Societas Jesu, *Lettres édifiantes et curieuses*, 1780–83, vol. 24, 375. See also Kästner, "Das Gespräch des Orientreisenden mit dem heidnischen Herrscher," 1997.
68. An English translation, with a detailed introduction by the editiors, is Jeyaraj and Young, *Hindu-Christian Epistolary Self-Disclosures*, 2013.
69. "Introduction," in Jeyaraj and Young, *Hindu-Christian Epistolary Self-Disclosures*, 2013, 3–4; Nørgaard, *Mission und Obrigkeit*, 1988 (still a good account; 308 on the number of missionaries).
70. Liebau, *Die indischen Mitarbeiter der Tranquebarmission*, 2008, 212.

71. "Was anlanget, was unter den Christen zu verwerffen ist, so sind viel böse Gebräuche bey ihnen eingeführet. Sie reinigen die Zähne nicht. Sie waschen sich nicht, wenn sie auf dem Abtritt gewesen. Sie reinigen sich nicht in heiligen Teichen. Die Weiber halten nach ihrer Zeit keine Reinigung. Sie halten sich mit dem Speichel nicht reinlich. Wenn sie Leute von verachtetem Geschlecht anrühren, reinigen sie sich nicht wieder. Sie schweren und fluchen zu allen Dingen. Wenn sie das Sacrament geben, so sagen sie, dass das Brodt der heilige Leib sey, und trincken Christi heiliges Blut, welches ich nicht recht begreifen kan. Und weil unter ihnen in vielen Dingen ein Mangel der Reinlichkeit ist, dabey auch Kuh-Fleisch essen, so wäre zu wünschen, dass diese Dinge nicht unter ihnen wären, es würden alle Malabaren zu ihrer Religion treten." Ziegenbalg and Gründler, *Malabarische Correspondenz*, pt. 2 (1717), 902–3; Jeyaraj and Young, *Hindu-Christian Epistolary Self-Disclosures*, 2013, 254.
72. "Nun ist es zwar wahr, dass viele Sachen unter uns zu tadeln seyn; auch gehen allerley Sünden und Ungerechtigkeiten bey uns im Schwange, welches nicht seyn solte, aber gleichwol kan man nicht alles verwerffen. Wären wir Heiden und hätten einen gantz falschen GOttes-Dienst, so würden gantz keine Tugenden und gute Wercke unter uns zu finden seyn. Nun aber sind ja so viel Tugenden unter uns, und werden allenthalben von diesen und ienen gute Wercke ausgeübet: Ja man findet Leute unter uns, die so heilig leben, dass man sie keiner Sünden überzeugen kan. Soll denn nun ein solch Gesetz, das alle Sünden verwirfft und zum Guten führet, ein falsches Gesetz seyn, dadurch man nicht selig werden könne? Eine jedwede Nation hat ihre besondere Tracht, Sitten und Rechte, die der andern Nation ungereimt vorkommen. Also ists auch mit der Religion. Gott ist mannigfältig in seinen Creaturen und mannigfältig in seinen Wercken. Daher will er auch mannigfältig verehret werden. . . . Hiernebst finden wir gleichfals an den Christen, die aus Europa in unser Land kommen, vieles zu tadeln und sollen wir anders die Religion aus den Wercken urtheilen, so können wir gar wenig Gutes von der christlichen Religion gedencken. Denn wir sehen, dass wenig Gerechtigkeit und Keuschheit unter ihnen sey. Sie üben wenig gute Wercke aus, geben wenig Almosen, haben keine Buße unter sich, nehmen gern Geschencke, trincken sich voll in starckem Geträncke, martern die lebendige Creaturen und gebrauchen sie zu ihrer Speise, halten gar wenig auf die leibliche Reinigkeit, verachten alle andere neben sich, sind sehr geitzig, hoffärtig und zornig." Ziegenbalg and Gründler, *Malabarische Correspondenz*, pt. 1 (1714), 456–57; Jeyaraj and Young, *Hindu-Christian Epistolary Self-Disclosures*, 2013, 186 (translation amended).
73. Poivre, "Voyage de Pierre Poivre en Cochinchine," 1885, 382.
74. Hüttner, *Nachricht von der britischen Gesandtschaftsreise durch China und einen Teil der Tartarei*, 1996, 117.
75. C. Niebuhr, *Reisebeschreibung nach Arabien*, 1774–1837, vol. 1, 299.
76. See the superb biography: Baack, *Undying Curiosity*, 2014.
77. C. Niebuhr, *Reisebeschreibung nach Arabien*, 1774–1837, vol. 1, 189.
78. *Mémoires concernant l'histoire . . . des Chinois*, 1776–1814, vol. 2 (1777), 372–73. These *mémoires* were written and edited by ex-Jesuits after the suppression of their order.
79. H. Burney, *Burney Papers*, 1910–14, vol. 1 (1910), 59.
80. Moltke, *Briefe über Zustände und Begebenheiten in der Türkei*, 1987, 349.
81. C. Niebuhr, *Reisebeschreibung nach Arabien*, 1774–1837, vol. 1, 426
82. Thunberg, *Reise durch einen Theil von Europa, Afrika und Asien*, 1794, vol. 2, pt. 1, 21.
83. Thunberg, *Reise durch einen Theil von Europa, Afrika und Asien*, 1794, vol. 2, pt. 1, 12.

84. Thunberg, *Reise durch einen Theil von Europa, Afrika und Asien*, 1794, vol. 2, pt. 1, 20.
85. C. Niebuhr, *Reisebeschreibung nach Arabien*, 1774–1837, vol. 1, 442–43.
86. Crawfurd, *Journal of an Embassy from the Governor General of India to the Court of Ava*, 1834, vol. 2, 114.
87. C. Niebuhr, *Reisebeschreibung nach Arabien*, 1774–1837, vol. 1, 337. Indigenous amazement at the Europeans' strange penchant for traveling is a frequent motive in travel accounts. Chardin (*Voyages . . . en Perse et autres lieux de l'Orient*, 1735, vol. 2, 53) encountered it in Persia, Alexander von Humboldt (*Reise auf dem Río Magdalena*, 1986, 93) in South America.
88. S. Turner, *Account of an Embassy to the Court of the Teshoo Lama*, 1800, 269–78.
89. Barrow, *Travels in China*, 1806, 74, similar remarks: 59, 65. On Barrow see Walter, *John Barrow*, 1994; Angster, *Erdbeeren und Piraten*, 2012.

CHAPTER IV. TRAVELING

1. Elphinstone, *Account of the Kingdom of Caubul*, 1839, vol. 1, 34.
2. C. A. Bayly, "Elphinstone, Mountstuart (1779–1859)," *Oxford Dictionary of National Biography*, Oxford University Press, 2004; online ed., Jan. 2008 [http://www.oxforddnb.com/view/article/8752, accessed Dec. 10, 2016].
3. The scene is described in Malcolm's diary, partly published in Kaye, *Life and Correspondence of Major-General Sir John Malcolm*, 1856, vol. 2, 444–46.
4. On Malcolm as an imperial commander and administrator see Pasley, *"Send Malcolm!,"* 1982; on his scholarly work and his role as an "ideologue of the British Empire" see Harrington, *Sir John Malcolm*, 2010.
5. Harrington, *Sir John Malcolm*, 2010, 77–78.
6. One of his many pamphlets (around 1811) carries the frightening title "Leichenstein auf dem Grabe der chinesischen Gelehrsamkeit des Herrn Joseph Hager" ("Tombstone on the grave of Mr. Joseph Hager's Chinese scholarship").
7. Mommsen, "Goethe und China in ihren Wechselbeziehungen," 1985, 32.
8. For example: A. v. Humboldt and Ritter, *Briefwechsel*, 2010. Further study of this cosmopolitan academic operator has to be based on the documents collected in Klaproth, *Briefe und Dokumente*, 1999; Walravens, *Julius Klaproth*, 1999.
9. Schwab, *Oriental Renaissance*, 1984, 184.
10. Cordier, *Mélanges d'histoire et de géographie orientale*, 1814–23, vol. 4, 53, 56–57. Potocki was the author of *The Manuscript Found in Saragossa*.
11. G. T. Staunton, *Memoirs*, 1856.
12. See G. T. Staunton, *Ta Tsing Leu Lee*, 1810.
13. H. Beck, *Alexander von Humboldt*, 1959–61, vol. 2, 91–92.
14. *Edinburgh Review*, October 1815, 417–18.
15. A massive compendium on all aspects of early modern travel, mainly in Europe, is Roche, *Humeurs vagabondes*, 2003, supplemented by Roche, *Les circulations dans l'Europe moderne*, 2011. For an introduction to travel writing see Hulme and Youngs, *Cambridge Companion to Travel Writing*, 2002.
16. ". . . des travaux pénibles et dangereux." Volney, *Voyage en Égypte et en Syrie*, 1959, 29. On connections between "travel" and "travail" (French for "work") see Buzard, *Beaten Track*, 1993, 33.
17. A question already asked in the sixteenth century by Jean Bodin. See Grafton, *New Worlds and Ancient Texts*, 1993, 124, 126.

18. Joseph Dehergne, "Chronologie du P. Antoine Gaubil." Appendix in Gaubil, *Correspondance de Pékin*, 1970, 867ff.; see also Pfister, *Notices biographiques et bibliographiques*, 1934, 667–93.
19. Sacy, *Henri Bertin*, 1970, vi.
20. Lemny, *Les Cantemir*, 2009.
21. Penzer, *The Harêm*, 1936, 44–49.
22. See Thomaz de Bossière, *Jean-François Gerbillon, S. J.*, 1994, 169–71.
23. See the translation of his report: Hasan, *Westward Bound: Travels of Mirza Abu Taleb*, 2005. On him and other eighteenth-century Indian observers see Khan, *Indian Muslim Perceptions of the West during the Eighteenth Century*, 1998; Alam and Subrahmanyam, *Indo-Persian Travels in the Age of Discoveries*, 2007, 243–95; Green, *The Love of Strangers*, 2016 (mainly based on the diary of the Persian student Mirza Salih).
24. Alam and Subrahmanyam, *Indo-Persian Travels in the Age of Discoveries*, 2007, 244–45.
25. Tahtāwi, *An Imam in Paris*, 2004.
26. I mention only texts of which Western translations are available: Peyrefitte, *Un choc de cultures*, vol. 1: *La vision des Chinois*, 1992; M. H. Fisher, *The Travels of Dean Mahomet*, 1997; Philipp and Perlman, *Abd-al-Rahman al-Jabarti's History of Egypt*, 1994; Khodja, *Le Miroir*, 2003.
27. Since the history of "discoveries" has somewhat fallen out of favor in recent years, the best surveys can be found in the older literature: Devèze, *L'Europe et le monde à la fin du XVIIIe siècle*, 1970; Duchet, *Anthropologie et histoire au siècle des lumières*, 1971, 25ff.; Parry, *Trade and Dominion*, 1971, 273ff.; Villiers and Duteil, *L'Europe la mer et les colonies*, 1997. A recent magisterial summary of enormous size is Reinhard, *Unterwerfung der Welt*, 2016. A unique biographical tool is Henze, *Enzyklopädie der Entdecker und Erforscher der Erde*, 1978–2004.
28. Spate, *Paradise Found and Lost*, 1988, remains an excellent survey. For present-day approaches to the region see Armitage and Bashford, *Pacific Histories*, 2014.
29. Shelvocke, *A Voyage round the World*, 1726, 460.
30. "Die vormahls unbekannte Länder sind von den curieusen Europæern so offt besuchet und nach allen Umstände beschrieben, daß sie uns nach gerade eben so bekandt als unser eignes Vaterland werden." Unverzagt, *Gesandtschaft*, 1727, preface ("Vorrede," unpaginated). Similarly already Magalhães, *New History of China*, 1688, preface (unpaginated).
31. Barchewitz, *Reisebeschreibung*, 1730, unpaginated.
32. Perry, *View of the Levant*, 1743, ii. The glut of literature on Turkey was already lamented by Grelot, *Relation nouvelle d'un voyage de Constantinopel*, 1680, "Avis au lecteur" (unpaginated).
33. E. Scott Waring, *A Tour to Sheeraz*, 1807, v.
34. Moor, *Hindu Pantheon*, 1810, 354. Nonetheless, the author then proceeds to offer his impressions at great length.
35. J. Johnson, *Oriental Voyager*, 1807, vi. See also C.L.J. de Guignes, *Voyages à Peking*, 1808, vol. 2, 147.
36. Ellis, *Journal*, 1818, vol. 1, 61–62. A comment on this in *Asiatic Review* 1818, 480. See also Krusenstern, *Voyage round the World*, 1813, vol. 2, 302.
37. Sprengel, *Geschichte der Maratten*, 1791, 13.
38. A. Hamilton, *New Account of the East Indies*, 1930, vol. 1, 5–6. A prominent culprit was Fryer, *A New Account of East India and Persia* (1909–15).

39. Societas Jesu, *Lettres édifiantes et curieuses*, 1780–83, vol. 18, 416ff.
40. Du Halde, *Description géographique*, 1735, vol. 4, 423ff.; Grosier, *Description générale de la Chine*, 1785, 177–87; *Universal History*, 1779–84, vol. 7 (1781), 323ff.
41. See Lee Ki-baik, *New History of Korea*, 1984, 239–40.
42. Lee Ki-baik, *New History of Korea*, 1984, 241; P. H. Lee, *Sourcebook of Korean Civilization*, 1996, vol. 2, 109–59.
43. Translations 1670 into French, 1672 into German, 1704 into English, published in Churchill and Churchill, *A Collection of Voyages and Travels* (3rd ed., 1744–46: vol. 4, 607–32), reprinted in Ledyard, *The Dutch Come to Korea*, 1971, 169–226, with a good introduction. A more recent translation is Hamel, *Hamel's Journal*, 1994. See also Lach and Van Kley, *Asia in the Making of Europe*, 1993, 486–88, 1785–97. The first European to reach Korea was a Dutch castaway in 1628.
44. B. Hall, *Account of a Voyage of Discovery*, 1818; M'Leod, *Voyage of His Majesty's Ship Alceste*, 1819.
45. B. Hall, *Account of a Voyage of Discovery*, 1818, 6.
46. B. Hall, *Account of a Voyage of Discovery*, 1818, 7.
47. B. Hall, *Account of a Voyage of Discovery*, 1818, 10.
48. B. Hall, *Account of a Voyage of Discovery*, 1818, 17.
49. B. Hall, *Account of a Voyage of Discovery*, 1818, 32–33.
50. B. Hall, *Account of a Voyage of Discovery*, 1818, 33–34.
51. B. Hall, *Account of a Voyage of Discovery*, 1818, 37.
52. British travelers were always delighted to encounter non-European "gentlemen." In a similar vein, aristocratic visitors from the European continent to the United States were enthralled by nobility among the Native Americans. See Cannadine, *Ornamentalism*, 2001; Liebersohn, *Aristocratic Encounters*, 1998.
53. B. Hall, *Account of a Voyage of Discovery*, 1818, 41.
54. M'Leod, *Voyage of His Majesty's Ship Alceste*, 1819, 104ff.
55. Societas Jesu, *Lettres édifiantes et curieuses*, 1780–83, vol. 23, 182ff. Apparently Father Gaubil in Peking had also met with tribute bearers from the Ryûkyû Islands: Gaubil, *Correspondance de Pékin*, 1970, 708.
56. Jartoux's letter from Peking (dated April 12, 1711) was first published in issue 10 of the *Lettres édifiantes et curieuses*. It gained widespread circulation through a reprint in a popular collection of travel accounts: Bernard, *Recueil de voyages du Nord*, 1732–34, vol. 4, 348–65. Jartoux's fellow Jesuit Joseph François Lafitau read it in Quebec in 1715 and came to the conclusion that the same plant was used in Iroquois pharmacology, which he held in high esteem: Lafitau, *Mémoire concernant la precieuse plante du Gin seng de Tartarie*, 1718, 6–12, 49–50.
57. See Sobel, *Longitude*, 1996.
58. Spate, *Pacific since Magellan*, 1979–88, vol. 3, 191.
59. Kotzebue, *Entdeckungs-Reise in die Süd-See*, 1821, vol. 2, 176. See more generally Lawrence, "Disciplining Disease," 1996.
60. On the rise of scientific travel and navigation see Macdonald and Withers, *Geography, Technology and Instruments of Exploration*, 2015.
61. Vogel, *Zehn-Jährige, Jetzo auffs neue revidirt und vermehrte Ost-Indianische Reise-Beschreibung*, 1716, preface ("Vorrede," unpaginated). About the author see Gelder, *Het Oost-Indisch avontuur*, 1997, 267–68. In this excellent book see also a detailed account of life onboard VOC East Indiamen (149–72).
62. Vogel, *Zehn-Jährige, Jetzo auffs neue revidirt und vermehrte Ost-Indianische Reise-Beschreibung*, 1716, 149.

63. Vogel, *Zehn-Jährige, Jetzo auffs neue revidirt und vermehrte Ost-Indianische Reise-Beschreibung*, 1716, 153–54.
64. Poivre, *Un manuscrit inédit de Pierre Poivre*, 1968, 17–25.
65. Schlözer, *Vorlesungen über Land- und Seereisen*, 1962, 18.
66. J. Forbes, *Oriental Memoirs*, 1813, vol 1, 12.
67. See as a case study Edwards, *Story of the Voyage*, 1994, 53ff.
68. Hoskins, *British Routes to India*, 1928, 82. On the route to China see Dermigny, *La Chine*, 1964, vol. 1, 265–73. A hugely detailed contemporary source is Elmore, *Directory*, 1802.
69. Morier, *Journey through Persia*, 1812, 181, 269–70; E. Scott Waring, *Tour to Sheeraz*, 1807, 84.
70. Beckmann, *Litteratur der älteren Reisebeschreibungen*, 1807–10, vol. 1, 492.
71. Wessels, *Early Jesuit Travelers*, 1924, 1–41 (a masterpiece of travel history).
72. Wessels, *Early Jesuit Travelers*, 1924, 164–202.
73. Wessels, *Early Jesuit Travelers*, 1924, 205–82; Luciano Petech, "Introduzione," in Petech, *I missionari italiani nel Tibet e nel Nepal*, 1954–56, vol. 5, xiii–xviii; Pomplun, *Jesuit on the Roof of the World*, 2010, 45–71.
74. Henze, *Enzyklopädie der Entdecker und Erforscher der Erde*, 1978–2004, vol. 1, 373–77.
75. Bruce, *Travels to Discover the Source of the Nile*, 1790, vol. 1, dedication.
76. His papers were edited by the Swiss polymath Johann Bernoulli: Bernoulli, *Description historique et géographique de l'Inde*, 1786–89. See also Windisch, *Geschichte der Sanskrit-Philologie*, 1917–20, vol. 1, 14–15.
77. Leibniz, *Briefwechsel mit den Jesuiten in China*, 2006, 627–28 (fn. 1); Duteil, *Le mandat du ciel*, 1994, 76.
78. The Izmailov-Bell embassy of 1719/20 needed sixteen months. The Ides Mission of 1692/93 required twenty months to make its way from Moscow to Peking but marched speedily back in less than a year. Much detail in Joyeux, *Der Transitweg von Moskau nach Daurien*, 1981.
79. Jenour, *Route to India*, 1791, 5–6.
80. See Douglas Carruthers, "Introduction," in Carruthers, *Desert Route to India*, 1928, xv, xxii, xxvi–xxx.
81. E.g., Chatfield, *Historical Review of the Commercial, Political and Moral State of Hindostan*, 1808, xxvi et seq., including speculations about Napoleon's possible route to India.
82. See G. K. Goodman, *Japan and the Dutch*, 2000.
83. See Elison, *Deus Destroyed*, 1973, 238. A contemporary report is in Kapitza, *Japan in Europa*, 1990, vol. 2, 153–59.
84. Raffles, *Report on Japan*, 1929; Wurtzburg, *Raffles*, 1954, 282–84.
85. See Golovnin, *Memoirs of a Captivity in Japan*, 1824; Rikord, *Narrative of My Captivity in Japan*, 1818; Kapitza, *Japan in Europa*, 1990, vol. 2, 954–1007; Keene, *Japanese Discovery of Europe*, 1969, 144–47; Barratt, *Russia in Pacific Waters*, 1981, 164–72.
86. See Krusenstern, *Voyage round the World*, 1813, vol. 1, 251; Kapitza, *Japan in Europa*, 1990, vol. 2, 848–90; Barratt, *Russia and the South Pacific*, 1988–92, vol. 2, 9–19, 91–97.
87. Kaempfer, *History of Japan*, 1727, vol. 2, 393–568; Kaempfer, *Geschichte und Beschreibung Japans*, 1777–79, vol. 2, 143–382; critical edition: Kaempfer, *Heutiges Japan*, 2001, vol. 1, 308–500; modern English translation: Kaempfer, *Kaempfer's Japan*, 1999, 239–397; Thunberg, *Reise durch einen Theil von Europa, Afrika und Asien*, 1794, vol. 2,

pt. 1, 61–136. On the circumstances of travel in Japan at the time see G. K. Goodman, *Japan*, 1986, 27–29. Rietbergen, "Ten hove gegaan," 2004, 284–96, deals with the Dutch diplomatic missions to Edo on the basis of VOC sources.

88. A typical description of Canton in this manner is Wathen, *Journal of a Voyage in 1811 and 1812 to Madras and China*, 1814, 185ff. With amazingly little prejudice: Lisiansky, *A Voyage round the World in the Years 1803, 4, 5, & 6*, 1814, 278–93.
89. This was the opinion, for example, of Sir William Chambers, the architect and promotor of the Chinese landscape garden. His Chinese experience was limited to Canton. See John Harris, *Sir William Chambers*, 1970, 146.
90. This is not the place to provide bibliographical details of the huge literature on China produced by the Jesuits. For the seventeenth century see Lach and Van Kley, *Asia in the Making of Europe* (1993), books 1 and 4; a similar survey for the eighteenth century is still lacking. On the Jesuit presence in general see Standaert, "Jesuits in China," 2008; in more detail: Standaert, *Handbook of Christianity in China*, 2001.
91. An excellent list of the most influential European sources on China from Marco Polo to the Opium Wars is in Lehner, *China in European Encyclopaedias*, 2011, 83–90.
92. Le Comte, *Nouveaux mémoires sur l'état present de la Chine* (1697). On this see Mungello, *Curious Land*, 1985, 329–42.
93. A good survey of this innovative and long-running serial is F. C. Hsia, *Sojourners in a Strange Land*, 2009, 132–36.
94. Du Halde, *Description géographique*, 1735.
95. F. C. Hsia, *Sojourners in a Strange Land*, 2009, 140. A superbly detailed study of the making and impact of the work is Landry-Deron, *La preuve par la Chine*, 2002.
96. Lenglet-Dufresnoy, *Méthode pour étudier la géographie*, 1741, vol. 1, 397.
97. Grosier, *Description générale de la Chine*, 1785; Grosier, *De la Chine*, 1818–20.
98. On the decline and termination of the Jesuit mission in China see the classic work Rochemonteix, *Joseph Amiot*, 1915, esp. 251ff.; also Krahl, *China Missions*, 1964, 223ff.; and at a more general level Hsia, "The End of the Jesuit Mission in China," 2015.
99. See the list in Demel, *Als Fremde in China*, 1992, 388.
100. See Hevia, *Cherishing Men from Afar*, 1995.
101. See Foust, *Muscovite and Mandarin*, 1969, 323–28; Fu Lo-shu, *Documentary Chronicle*, 1966, vol. 1, 361–62, 367.
102. Conder, *Modern Traveller*, 1830, vol. 13, 267.
103. Historical surveys of the European knowledge about Southeast Asia in the early nineteenth century are W. Hamilton, *East-India Gazetteer*, 1828, and, in staggering detail, C. Ritter, *Erdkunde*, 1832–47, vol. 3 (1835); vol. 4, pt. ("Abteilung") 1 (1835).
104. See Lach and Van Kley, *Asia in the Making of Europe*, 1993, 380–81, and 1248–99 as a survey of European knowledge about Vietnam.
105. For example Grosier, *Description générale de la Chine*, 1785, 187–229.
106. On travel and exploration in the Himalayas up to 1829 see C. Ritter, *Erdkunde*, 1832–47, vol. 2 (1833), 482–585.
107. Kirkpatrick, *An Account of the Kingdom of Nepaul*, 1811; F. Hamilton, *An Account of the Kingdom of Nepal*, 1819.
108. Hüllmann, *Historisch-kritischer Versuch über die Lamaische Religion*, 1796, 45.
109. Grosier, *Description générale de la Chine*, 1785, 229–41.
110. Barthold, *Die geographische und historische Erforschung des Orients*, 1913, 187–88.

111. On both, see Bishop, *Myth of Shangri-La*, 1989, 25–64.
112. See Lach and Van Kley, *Asia in the Making of Europe*, 1993, 1895–96; Richards, *Mughal Empire*, 1993, 287.
113. See Schwab, *Oriental Renaissance*, 1984.
114. Schwab, *Vie d'Anquetil-Duperron*, 1934, 105.
115. J. Forbes, *Oriental Memoirs*, 1813, vol. 1, 428.
116. Rennell, *Memoir of a Map of Hindoostan*, 1793; Duff, *History of the Mahrattas*, 1826; Buchanan, *Journey from Madras*, 1807. On Buchanan and other writers who saw Indian landscapes and local life in terms of "improvement" see Nayar, *English Writing and India*, 2008, 75–93.
117. Bastian, *Geschichte der Indochinesen*, 1866, 4.
118. Zimmermann, *Versuch einer Anwendung der zoologischen Geographie auf die Geschichte der Erde*, 1783, 99–100. On the history of European travel to and in Iran see Gabriel, *Erforschung Persiens*, 1952, 60ff.; Firby, *European Travellers*, 1988; Chaybany, *Les voyages en Perse*, 1971.
119. E. Bowen, *The Gentleman, Tradesman and Traveller's Pocket Library*, 1753, 285.
120. A survey of the most important accounts of Iran between 1722 and 1800 is Gabriel, *Erforschung Persiens*, 1952, 120–31.
121. On the complex diplomacy involving Iran around 1800 see Greaves, "Iranian Relations with Great Britain and British India," 1991.
122. See Thomson, *Barbary and Enlightenment*, 1987; Brahimi, *Voyageurs français du XVIIIe siècle in Barbarie*, 1976.
123. Thompson, *Wonderful Things*, 2015, 71–72. This is now the standard history of Egyptology.
124. Blount, *Voyage into the Levant*, 1671, 3.
125. Thompson, *Wonderful Things*, 2015, 79–82. On Pocock see also a good chapter in Damiani, *Enlightened Observers*, 1979, 70–104.
126. See Höllmann, *Ägyptisches Alltagsleben*, 1990.
127. The antiquarian knowledge prior to Volney's travels is summarized in Carré, *Voyageurs et écrivains français*, 1990, vol. 1, 65–78.
128. See the impressive documentation for the golden age of Ottoman power: Yerasimos, *Les voyageurs dans l'Empire Ottoman*, 1991.
129. Pitton de Tournefort, *Relation d'un voyage du Levant*, 1717, vol. 1, 464, 469. An anthology of French descriptions of Instanbul around 1800 is Berchet, *Le voyage en Orient*, 1985, 429ff.; see also Constantine, *Early Greek Travellers*, 1984.
130. Hammer-Purgstall, *Constantinopolis*, 1822, vol. 1, xiii, here on pp. xi–xxvii a commentary on the earlier literature. Hammer, in his time the leading authority, considers the best accounts of the city to be those by Busbecq (1581), Du Cange (1682), Pitton de Tournefort (1717), Pococke (1743–45), Lady Mary Wortley Montagu (1763), and Andreossy (1818). See also Hammer's own vision of medieval Byzantium: *Geschichte des Osmanischen Reiches*, 1827–35, vol. 1, 513ff.
131. For instance the Marquis de Villeneuve, ambassador to the Sublime Porte from 1728 to 1740. See Omont, *Missions archéologiques*, 1902, vol. 2, 663ff.
132. See J. Porter, *Observations on the Religion, Law, Government, and Manners of the Turks*, 1768.
133. Rycaut, *History of the Turkish Empire*, 1680; even more popular (and translated into six languages) was Rycaut, *Present State of the Ottoman Empire*, 1667.
134. Babinger, "Die türkischen Studien in Europa," 1919, 128. On this fascinating figure see Theolin et al., *The Torch of the Empire*, 2002; E. A. Fraser, "Dressing Turks," 2010; Findley, *Enlightening Europe on Islam*, forthcoming.

135. Angelomatis-Tsougarakis, *Greek Revival*, 1990, 1.
136. R. Morrison, *Memoir of Principal Occurrences*, 1819, 186–87.
137. Gehrke, "Die wissenschaftliche Entdeckung des Landes *Hellás*," 1992–93, pt. 1, 29–30.
138. "J'ai toujours dérobé quelque chose aux monuments sur lesquels j'ai passé." Chateaubriand, *Itinéraire de Paris à Jérusalem*, 1968, 147.
139. This perspective on Near Eastern travel literature is also dominant in Harmer, *Observations on Divers Passages of Scripture*, 1786–87.
140. E.g., Chateaubriand, *Itinéraire de Paris à Jérusalem*, 1968, 200.
141. Chateaubriand, *Itinéraire de Paris à Jérusalem*, 1968, 261.
142. Hennings, *Gegenwärtiger Zustand der Besitzungen der Europäer in Ostindien*, 1784–86, vol. 3, 415, laments the comparatively low intellectual level of travel literature on East and Southeast Asia and sees the reason for this in the prevalence of soldiers of fortune in that part of the world. On the characteristic "nabobs" see Marshall, *East India Fortunes*, 1976.
143. Lach and Van Kley, *Asia in the Making of Europe*, 1993, 529–33. Many of those texts are collected in L'Honoré Naber, *Reisebeschreibungen von deutschen Beamten und Kriegsleuten*, 1930–31. J. S. Semler included long excerpts from these accounts in volume 26 (1764) of the enlarged German edition of the *Universal History*: Baumgarten and Semler, *Uebersetzung der Algemeinen Welthistorie.*
144. Knox, *Historical Relation of the Island Ceylon*, 1681.
145. An early representative is Lord Valentia, *Voyages and Travels to India*, 1809.
146. Abbé Prévost, *Histoire générale des voyages*, 1746–61, vol. 7 (1749), 261.
147. Lach and Van Kley, *Asia in the Making of Europe,* 1993, 386–87; Henze, *Enzyklopädie der Entdecker und Erforscher der Erde*, 1978–2004, vol. 2, 332–33; Zoli, "Le polemiche sulla Cina," 1972, 409–16.
148. The caravan traffic was organized in a highly complex way and constituted a "great highway system of Asia": Chaudhuri, *Trade and Civilisation in the Indian Ocean*, 1985, 167–75 (quotation 169). An excellent analysis of the caravan trade was already offered in Heeren, *Historische Werke*, 1821–26, vol. 10 (1824), 23–29.
149. A. Hamilton, *New Acccount of the East Indies*, 1930.
150. Benyowski, *Memoirs and Travels*, 1893; Adams, *Travelers and Travel Liars,* 1962, 81–83.
151. Hoare, *Tactless Philosopher*, 1975, 293–94, 363.
152. Ghirardini, *Relation*, 1700. He was a bit weak on geography, telling his readers that Java was an island within the Kingdom of Siam (30).
153. Tombe, *Voyage aux Indes Orientales*, 1810, vol. 1, 186ff. on Batavia.
154. Cochrane, *Narrative of a Pedestrian Journey*, 1824.
155. Drummond, *Travels*, 1754.
156. Bennassar and Bennassar, *Les Chrétiens d'Allah*, 1989.
157. S. Anderson, *An English Consul in Turkey*, 1989, 203–204.
158. Laurens, *L'Expédition d'Égypte*, 1989, sec. 199.
159. E.g., the Saint-Simonist Lambert as well as "Osman Effendi": see Thompson, "Osman Effendi," 1994.
160. C. Niebuhr, *Reisebeschreibung nach Arabien*, 1774–1837, vol. 1, 456.
161. Kroell, "Douze Lettres de Jean Chardin," 1982, 307; Hammer-Purgstall, *Erinnerungen*, 1940, 26.
162. *Vanity Fair*, 2001, ch. 51, 596.
163. See Pearson, *Before Colonialism*, 1988, S61.
164. Bernier, *Travels in the Mogul Empire*, 1934, 73, 82, 93–94, 217.
165. Zaidi, "European Mercenaries in the Indian Armies," 2011, 56–57.

166. See S. J. Shaw, *Between Old and New*, 1971, 10–11, 121; Tott, *Memoirs of Baron de Tott*, 1786. The first military adviser in the Ottoman Empire was Count Alexandre de Bonneval (Ahmed Pascha), who arrived in 1729. Rather late in our period, the British officer William Wittman, who was a member of the British military mission in support of the sultan against Bonaparte, observed Constantinople, the Levant, and Egypt with "cool" cultural detachment: Wittman, *Travels in Turkey*, 1803.
167. Rochemonteix, *Joseph Amiot*, 1915, 108, 251ff.
168. Broc, *La géographie des philosophes*, 1975, 285; H. Woolf, *Transits of Venus*, 1959.
169. The following section is indebted to Henning, "Die Reiseberichte über Sibirien von Herberstein bis Ides," 1905; Wendland, "Das Russische Reich am Vorabend der Großen Nordischen Expedition," 1990; Wendland, *Peter Simon Pallas*, 1992, 80–268; Robel, "Der Wandel des deutschen Sibirienbildes im 18. Jahrhundert," 1980; Robel, "Bemerkungen zu deutschen Reisebeschreibungen," 1992; Kollmann, *The Russian Empire*, 2017, 84–102; Black, *G.- F. Müller and the Imperial Russian Academy*, 1985, 47–77; Lincoln, *Conquest of a Continent*, 1994, 100–121; Hintzsche and Nickol, *Die Große Nordische Expedition*, 1996; Dahlmann, "Einleitung," 1999; Dahlmann, "Die Weite Sibiriens und des Ozeans," 2014; Cecere, "Russia and Its 'Orient,'" 2007.
170. Strahlenberg, *Das Nord- und Ostliche Theil von Europa und Asia*, 1730.
171. This journey can be reconstructed in detail from the sources: Steller, Kraŝeninnikov, and Fischer, *Reisetagebücher 1735 bis 1743*, 2000; Steller, *Briefe und Dokumente 1740*, 2000.
172. Wendland, "Das Russische Reich am Vorabend der Großen Nordischen Expedition," 1990, 367.
173. See Stagl, "Die Methodisierung des Reisens im 16. Jahrhundert," 1989.
174. Broc, *La géographie des philosophes*, 1975, 38–39, 116–21.
175. On Niebuhr as a scientific traveler see Baack, *Undying Curiosity*, 2014.
176. Hoare, *Tactless Philosopher*, 1976, 12.
177. Laurens, *L'Expédition d'Égypte*, 1989, esp. chs. 9–11; Cole, *Napoleon's Egypt*, 2007; on the scientific aspects of the expedition see Laissus, *L'Égypte*, 1998.
178. See Broc, "Les grandes missions scientifiques françaises au XIXe siècle," 1981.
179. On the special role of British military officers in gathering intelligence and authoring accounts of Asian countries see Peers, "Colonial Knowledge and the Military in India," 2005.
180. Markham, *Rennell*, 1895, 42; Edney, *Mapping an Empire*, 1997, 9–18, 134–35; Raj, *Relocating Modern Science*, 2006, 60–94.
181. Edney, *Mapping an Empire*, 1997, 17, emphasizes the discrepancy between ideal and real accuracy.
182. On Mackenzie see Dirks, "Colonial Histories and Native Informants," 1993; Edney, *Mapping an Empire*, 1997, 152–55, 206–9; Barrow, *Making History, Drawing Territory*, 2003, 76–79. Of general importance is Jasanoff, *Edge of Empire*, 2005.

CHAPTER V. ENCOUNTERS

1. Morier, *Second Journey through Persia*, 1818, 144.
2. This embassy is of particular interest because the ambassador's report later appeared in French translation: Galland, *Relation de l'ambassade de Mehmet Effendi*, 1757. New edition: Mehmed efendi, *Le paradis des infidèles*, 1981. For an earlier (1707–8) semiprivate visit to France by a young Maronite Christian from Aleppo see Diyāb, *D'Alep à Paris*, 2015.

3. Van der Cruysse, *Louis XIV et le Siam*, 1991, 263–92, 373–410; Göçek, *East Encounters West*, 1987, 7ff.; Aksan, *An Ottoman Statesman in War and Peace*, 1995, 34ff.
4. Rietbergen, "Witsen's World," 1985, 126–27.
5. Spence, *The Question of Hu*, 1988.
6. Sacy, *Henri Bertin*, 1970, 158–67.
7. Blumenbach, *Abbildungen naturhistorischer Gegenstände*, 1810, unpaginated.
8. Barrett, *Singular Listlessness*, 1989, 56, fn. 1.
9. M. H. Fisher, *Counterflows to Colonialism*, 2004, 1–3.
10. Gaastra, *De geschiedenis van de VOC*, 1991, 82 (table 8).
11. Sörlin, *Scientific Travel*, 1989, 103, 121 (fn. 23).
12. Henze, *Enzyklopädie der Entdecker und Erforscher der Erde* (1978–2004), vol. 1, 372.
13. Lunt, *Bokhara Burnes*, 1969, 206. On Burnes's achievement as an imperial geographer see Withers, "On Enlightenment's Margins," 13–17. See also Dalrymple, *Return of a King*, 2013, 267–73, which draws on Afghan as well as English sources to narrate Burnes's death.
14. His extant manuscripts were later published by his co-traveler, the botanist Johann Gottlieb Georgi: Falck, *Beyträge zur Topographischen Kenntnis des russischen Reiches*, 1785–86.
15. Alder, *Beyond Bokhara*, 1985, 357.
16. Van der Brug, *Malaria en malaise*, 1994, 55, 59–60.
17. Marshall, *East India Fortunes*, 1976, 217–19.
18. Kaempfer, *Reisetagebücher*, 144. On the climatic terrors of that region see also Arbuthnot, *An Essay Concerning the Effects of Air on Human Bodies*, 1733, 79.
19. J. G. Gmelin, *Reise durch Sibirien*, 1751–52, vol. 1, preface ("Vorrede," unpaginated).
20. S. Turner, *Account of an Embassy to the Court of the Teshoo Lama*, 1800, 93.
21. J. G. Gmelin, *Reise durch Sibirien*, 1751–52, vol. 2, 445ff.; vol. 4, 6–7; Wurtzburg, *Raffles*, 1954, 678–82.
22. Seetzen, *Reisen durch Syrien*, 1854–59, vol. 1, 278.
23. A. v. Humboldt, *Briefe aus Russland*, 2009, 52. Journeys to the Inner Asian border zones of the Tsarist Empire always required a military escort. See also Pallas, *Bemerkungen auf einer Reise in die südlichen Statthalterschaften des Russischen Reichs*, 1799–1801, vol. 1, 323.
24. Posselt, *Große Nordische Expedition*, 1990, 192.
25. Posselt, *Große Nordische Expedition*, 1990, 177–78.
26. Unverzagt, *Gesandtschaft*, 1727, 45.
27. Elphinstone, *Account of the Kingdom of Caubul*, 1839, vol, 1, 376, mentions the reasons for this.
28. Schlözer, *Vorlesungen über Land- und Seereisen*, 1962, 40. Caravanserais existed even in Bengal. See Hodges, *Travels in India*, 1793, 32. There is a wealth of material on Persia in Kaempfer's travel diaries: Kaempfer, *Reisetagebücher*, 1968, 45, 80–81, 86–87, 92, 111–12, 119. See also Still, *Enlightenment Hospitality*, 2011, 155–58.
29. J. Johnson, *Journey from India to England*, 1818, 87, 100–101.
30. One of the last travelers to praise the Chinese roads was C.L.J. de Guignes, *Voyages à Peking*, 1808, vol. 2, 214ff. (also vol. 1, 361). Around 1800 it took an official message from Peking fifteen days to reach the governor-general at Canton (Morse, *Chronicles of the East India Company*, 1926–29, vol. 3, 256). Compare at the same time the numerous complaints about the sorry state of roads in Asia Minor and Persia, for example Macdonald Kinneir, *Geographical Memoir of the Persian Empire*, 1813, 43.

31. E.g., Magalhães, *New History of China*, 1688, 114ff.; Klaproth, *Mémoires relatifs à l'Asie*, 1826–28, vol. 3, 312–31.
32. Steller, *Beschreibung von dem Lande Kamtschatka*, 1774, 133–39.
33. Gemelli Careri, "Voyage round the World," 1745, 220; Singh, *Surat*, 1977, 27, see also Qaisar, *Indian Response*, 1982, 37–43.
34. Perrin, *Voyage dans l'Indostan*, 1807, vol. 1, 101.
35. T. Shaw, *Travels or Observations Relating to Several Parts of Barbary*, 1808, vol. 1, xvii.
36. With marvelous detail: C. Niebuhr, *Reisebeschreibung nach Arabien*, 1774–1837, vol. 1, 214–16. On the caravans to Mekka in a slightly earlier period see Faroqhi, *Pilgrims and Sultans*, 1994.
37. Sestini, *Voyage de Constantinopel à Bassora en 1781*, 1797, v.
38. See Sonnini, *Voyage Voyage dans la haute et basse Égypte*, 1799, vol. 1, 5.
39. Lequin, *Isaac Titsingh in China*, 2005, 96: Titsingh's diary entry of December 10, 1794. This happened in Nanchang, the provincial capital of Jiangxi. The entire diary is a register of travel horrors.
40. Lequin, *Isaac Titsingh in China*, 2005, 119.
41. Thus the malicious comment in Barrow, *Autobiographical Memoir*, 1847, 98. See also Duyvendak, "The Last Dutch Embassy to the Chinese Court (1794–95)," 1938, 40ff.; Boxer, "Isaac Titsingh's Embassy," 1939, 16.
42. Blussé, *Visible Cities*, 2008, 87, 89.
43. Societas Jesu, *Lettres édifiantes et curieuses*, 1780–83, vol. 23, 160–61.
44. See Klaproth's reminiscences: Klaproth, *Briefe und Dokumente*, 1999, 205.
45. Caillié, *Travels through Central Africa to Timbuctoo*, 1830, vol. 2, 49.
46. Æ. Anderson, *Narrative of the British Embassy to China*, 1795, 133.
47. Schrödter, *See- und Landreise nach Ostindien und Aegypten*, 1800, vi–vii.
48. Schrödter, *See- und Landreise nach Ostindien und Aegypten*, 1800, 11.
49. See J. R. Forster, *Bemerkungen*, 1783, 350–51; J. R. Forster, *Observations*, 1996, 251–52.
50. S. Turner, *Account of an Embassy to the Court of the Teshoo Lama*, 1800, sec. 174; Bogle and Manning, *Narratives*, 1879, 103ff.
51. D. Campbell, *Journey over Land to India*, 1796, pt. 3, 10.
52. Eversmann, *Reise von Orenburg nach Buchara*, 1823, viii. Similarly J. G. Gmelin in Posselt, *Große Nordische Expedition*, 1990, 75; Timkovski, *Voyage à Pekin*, 1827, vol. 1, 438.
53. This passage is based on Markham, "Introduction," 1879, clix–clxv; Stifler, "The Language Students of the East India Company's Canton Factory," 56–57; Bishop, *Myth of Shangri-La*, 1989, 76–80.
54. Bogle and Manning, *Narratives*, 1879, 256.
55. Bogle and Manning, *Narratives*, 1879, 256.
56. Bogle and Manning, *Narratives*, 1879, 258.
57. Bogle and Manning, *Narratives*, 1879, 224.
58. Bogle and Manning, *Narratives*, 1879, 216. The entry is free of Manning's habitual self-irony.
59. Bogle and Manning, *Narratives*, 1879, 266.
60. Pomplun, *Jesuit on the Roof of the World*, 2010, 156–59; Petech, "Introduzione," in Petech, *I missionari italiani nel Tibet e nel Nepal* (1954–56), vol. 5, xxii–xxiv, see also Desideri's own account in the same volume: 193ff. George Bogle and Samuel Turner did not have time to pick up more than a smattering of Tibetan.
61. C. Harbsmeier, "La connaissance du Chinois," 1992, 307–8.
62. Lemny, *Les Cantemir*, 2009, 29–160.

63. Collani, *P. Joachim Bouvet, S. J.*, 1985, 13; Cantemir, *Historisch-geographische und politische Beschreibung der Moldau*, 1771, 22; Leezenberg, "The Oriental Origins of Orientalism," 2012, 247; Reith, *Life of Dr. John Leyden*, 1923, 379; Hoare, "Introduction," 1982, 2.
64. Hammer-Purgstall, *Erinnerungen*, 1840, 57.
65. Franklin, *Orientalist Jones*, 2011.
66. Rabault-Feuerhahn, *Archives of Origins*, 2013, 45–46.
67. Fück, *Die arabischen Studien in Europa*, 1955, 127–29.
68. Hammer-Purgstall, *Des osmanischen Reiches Staatsverfassung und Staatsverwaltung*, 1815, vol. 2, 117–18.
69. Philliou, *Biography of an Empire*, 2011, 112.
70. W. Turner, *Journal of a Tour in the Levant*, 1820, vol. 1, 62–63 (fn.).
71. E.g., Björnstahl, *Briefe auf seinen ausländischen Reisen*, 1777–83, vol. 4, 64–65.
72. Russell, *Natural History of Aleppo*, 1794, vol. 2, 4.
73. The only senior representative of the VOC in Nagasaki who made his mark as a Japanologist was Isaac Titsingh, with several interruptions from 1779 to 1784 head of the Dutch factory on the artificial island of Dejima. See Titsingh, *Private Correspondence of Isaac Titsingh*, 1990–92, vol. 1, xv–xxi.
74. Keene, *Japanese Discovery of Europe*, 1969, 78–79.
75. Adami, *Eine schwierige Nachbarschaft*, 1990, 89.
76. Demel, *Als Fremde in China*, 1992, 97–98.
77. Nieuhof, *An Embassy from the East-India Company of the United Provinces, to the Grand Tartar Cham*, 1669, 117.
78. Schefer, "Introduction," 1890, cviii–cix.
79. Cranmer-Byng, *An Embassy to China*, 1962, 319–20. The designated secretary of the embassy, Sir George L. Staunton, had personally traveled to France and Italy to recruit translators. See G. L. Staunton, *An Authentic Account of an Embassy from the King of Great Britain to the Emperor of China*. 1797, vol. 1, 38–41.
80. Dabringhaus, "Einleitung," 1996, 51.
81. Dabringhaus, "Einleitung," 1996, 69–70.
82. Russell, *Natural History of Aleppo*, 1794, vol. 2, 1–2.
83. Cohn, *Colonialism and Its Form of Knowledge*, 1996, 19, 33–36.
84. Cohn, *Colonialism and Its Form of Knowledge*, 1996, 16–56.
85. Osbeck, *Voyage to China and the East Indies*, 1771, vol. 1, 274–75.
86. Finlayson, *Mission to Siam and Hué*, 1826, 146.
87. Symes, *Account of an Embassy to the Kingdom of Ava*, 1800, 295.
88. C. A. Bayly, *Empire and Information*, 1996, 63.
89. C. A. Bayly, *Empire and Information*, 1996, 71.
90. Yule and Burnell, *Hobson-Jobson*, 1886, 581.
91. C. A. Bayly, *Empire and Information*, 1996, 74. There are parallels to the rise of literate administrators in Iran in the early seventeenth century.
92. C. A. Bayly, *Empire and Information*, 1996, 75.
93. C. A. Bayly, *Empire and Information*, 1996, 77–78.
94. See above, chapter 4, section 2: "A Weeping Mandarin."
95. Barrow, *Voyage to Cochin China*, 1806, 288.
96. Barrow, *Voyage to Cochin China*, 1806, 327.
97. Crawfurd, *Journal of an Embassy to the Courts of Siam and Cochin China*, 1828, 73–74, 81. At almost the same time the British diplomat James Justinian Morier witnessed in Iran the dinner *à l'anglais* alluded to in the epigraph to the present chapter (*Second Journey through Persia*, 1818, 144).

98. W. Jones, Preface to "A Grammar of the Persian Language" [1771], in Jones, *Works*, 1807, vol. 5, 179.
99. W. Jones, "Fifth Anniversary Discourse" [1788], in Jones, *Works*, 1807, vol. 3, 71. In a similar vein another great authority: Anquetil-Duperron, "Recherches historiques et géographiques sur l'Inde," 1787, vol. 2, xiii–xiv.
100. D'Ohsson, *Tableau générale de l'Empire Othoman*, 1788–1824, vol. 1, ii–v.
101. Tott, *Mémoires*, 1786, vol. 1, xvii–xviii (meant as criticism of Lady Mary Wortley Montagu).
102. Hachicho, "English Travel Books about the Arab Near East," 1964, 104.
103. C. Niebuhr, *Reisebeschreibung nach Arabien,* 1774–1837, vol. 1, 274–75.
104. C. Niebuhr, *Reisebeschreibung nach Arabien,* 1774–1837, vol. 1, 362.
105. C. Niebuhr, *Reisebeschreibung nach Arabien,* 1774–1837, vol. 1, x–xi; on von Haven's academic credentials and his studies in Rome see Baack, *Undying Curiosity*, 2014, 45–46.
106. C. Niebuhr, *Reisebeschreibung nach Arabien,* 1774–1837, vol. 1, 414–15; see also C. Niebuhr, *Beschreibung von Arabien*, 1772, xv.
107. C. Niebuhr, *Reisebeschreibung nach Arabien,* 1774–1837, vol. 1, 232.
108. Burnes, *Travels into Bokhara*, 1834, vol. 1, 281.
109. Greenblatt, *Marvellous Possessions*, 1991, 99.
110. Charles-Roux, *Les échelles de Syrie et de Palestine,* 1928, 16; Russell, *Natural History of Aleppo*, 1794, vol. 2, 2.
111. R. K. Porter, *Travels in Georgia*, 1821–22, vol. 1, 240.
112. C. Niebuhr, *Reisebeschreibung nach Arabien,* 1774–1837, vol. 1, 322, 378, 410.
113. C. Niebuhr, *Reisebeschreibung nach Arabien,* 1774–1837, vol. 2, 168.
114. J. White, *Voyage to Cochin China*, 1824, 227.
115. E. Morrison, *Memoirs of the Life and Labours of Robert Morrison*, 1839, vol. 1, 188.
116. Cohn, *Colonialism and Its Form of Knowledge*, 1996, 111.
117. Cohn, *Colonialism and Its Form of Knowledge*, 1996, 112; Dalrymple, *White Mughals,* 2002, 50.
118. "Entdeckerfreundschaften": See M. Harbsmeier, "Kadu und Maheine," 1991.
119. Bogle and Manning, *Narratives*, 1879, 83–89, 95, 110, 135–45; Lamb, *Bhutan and Tibet*, 2002, 149–55.
120. Bogle and Manning, *Narratives*, 1879, 92, 104; S. Turner, *Account of an Embassy to the Court of the Teshoo Lama,* 1800, 235. See also a universal history of the game of chess: Wahl, *Geist und die Geschichte des Schach-Spiels*, 1798.
121. Colley, *Britons*, 1992, 127ff.
122. Volney, *Voyage en Égypte et en Syrie*, 1959, 119.
123. Bruce, *Travels to Discover the Source of the Nile*, 1790, vol.1, lxxi–lxxii.
124. Percy, *Hau Kiou Choaan, or the Pleasing History*, 1761, vol. 1, xviii–xix.
125. Based on the author's personal experience as a medical doctor on Lord Amherst's mission to China in 1816: Abel, *Narrative of a Journey into the Interior of China*, 1819, 232–33; see also Grosier, *De la Chine*, 1818–20, vol. 1, v–vi.
126. Nieuhof, *An Embassy from the East-India Company of the United Provinces to the Grand Tartar Cham*, 1669, 25.
127. This is what happened in 1716 to a Swedish diplomat in Russian employment who served in China: Lange, "Journal von Lorenz Langens Reise nach China," in F. C. Weber, *Das veränderte Rußland*, 1738–39, pt. 1 [first ed. 1721], 83.
128. This must have occurred regularly; see, for example, the Ottoman embassy to France in 1720/21: Göçek, *East Encounters West*, 1987, 41ff.

129. Elphinstone, *Account of the Kingdom of Caubul*, 1839, vol. 1, 37. Niebuhr regarded traveling as an opportunity for mutual learning: *Reisebeschreibung nach Arabien*, 1774–1837, vol. 1, 272–73.
130. Bogle and Manning, *Narratives*, 1879, 77.
131. Bernier, *Travels in the Mogul Empire*, 1934, 91–92.
132. For example Otter, *Voyage en Turquie et en Perse*, 1748, vol. 1, 100; Kaempfer, *Reisetagebücher*, 1968, 62–63.
133. Posselt, *Große Nordische Expedition*, 1990, 47–49.
134. Bogle and Manning, *Narratives*, 1879, 267–68, 280–81, 286–87.
135. Alder, *Beyond Bokara*, 1985, passim (see entry "medicine" in the index).
136. C. Niebuhr, *Reisebeschreibung nach Arabien*, 1774–1837, vol. 1, 262, 300–301, 407; vol. 2, 308–9.
137. Chamisso, "Reise um die Welt," 1883, vol. 3, 250.
138. See Schäbler, "Ulrich Jasper Seetzen," 1995, 124.

CHAPTER VI. EYEWITNESSES–EARWITNESSES: EXPERIENCING ASIA

1. J. R. Forster, *Observations*, 1996, 211; German original: J. R. Forster, *Bemerkungen*, 1783, 290.
2. Dédéyan, *Montesquieu ou l'alibi persan*, 1988, 14–15.
3. The standard edition is now Goethe, "West-östlicher Divan 1819: Besserem Verständnis," 2010. This prose part of the "Divan" has traditionally been known as *Noten und Abhandlungen zum besseren Verständnis des West-östlichen Diwan*. On Goethe's extensive use of travel literature in the preparation of this work see Guthke, *Goethes Weimar*, 2001, 89–106.
4. Layton, *Russian Literature and Empire*, 1994, 29–30, 34.
5. *Denckwürdige Beschreibung des Königreichs China*, 1679, 6.
6. See Robinet, *Vue philosophique de la gradation naturelle des formes de l'être*, 1768, 160–61.
7. Adams, *Travelers and Travel Liars*, 1980, 19–43. The problem is discussed with utter seriousness in 1749 by Buffon, "Histoire naturelle de l'homme," 2009, 554–57, and three decades later by the German geographer and zoologist E.A.W. von Zimmermann: *Geographische Geschichte des Menschen*, 1778–83, vol. 2, 60ff.
8. Zimmermann, *Geographische Geschichte des Menschen*, 1778–83, vol. 2, 138–64; a similar consideration in Barrow, *Account of Travels into the Interior of Southern Africa*, 1801, 313–19.
9. S. Turner, *Account of an Embassy to the Court of the Teshoo Lama*, 1800, 157.
10. Hammer-Purgstall, *Constantinopolis*, 1822, vol. 1, xxiii.
11. From a letter of Sir James Porter, read at a meeting of the Royal Society in London on April 10, 1755. Quoted in Boogert, *Aleppo Observed*, 2010, 11.
12. For example, in Poivre, *Un manuscrit inédit de Pierre Poivre*, 1968, 19–20.
13. ". . . des vues plus relevées, des considerations plus puissantes." Sonnini, *Voyage dans la haute et basse Égypte*, 1799, vol. 1, 3. The author was a naturalist and former collaborator of Buffon. He traveled in Egypt from 1777 to 1780.
14. Diez, *Denkwürdigkeiten*, 1811–15, vol. 1, xvii.
15. Köhler, *Sammlung neuer Reisebeschreibungen*, 1767–69, vol. 1, pt. 2, 571; Hausleutner, *Geschichte der Araber in Sicilien*, 1791–92, vol. 1, xv.
16. Parennin, in Societas Jesu, *Lettres édifiantes et curieuses*, 1780–83, vol. 19, 277–78.
17. Savary, *Lettres sur l'Égypte*, 1785–86, vol. 1, i–iii.

18. "Le vrai Voyageur, c'est-à-dire celui qui, aimant tous les hommes comme ces frères, inaccessible aux plaisirs & aux besoins, au-dessus de la grandeur & de la bassesse, de l'estime & de blame, de la richesse et de la pauvreté, parcourt le monde, sans attache qui le fixe à aucun lieu, spectateur du bien & du mal, sans égard à celui qui le fait, aux motifs propre à telle Nation: ce voyageur, s'il est instruit, s'il a un jugement sain, saisit sur-le-champ le ridicule, le faux d'un procédé, d'un usage, d'une opinion." Anquetil-Duperron, *Dignité du commerce*, 1789, 4.
19. Robert Hooke, "Preface," in Knox, *Historical Relation of the Island of Ceylon*, 1681, unpaginated.
20. Anonymous review in *The British Critic* (December 1817, 591) of Ellis, *Journal*, 1818. A similar remark in Diez, *Denkwürdigkeiten*, 1811–15, vol. 1, xiii: "How many times has an entire nation been condemned because children mocked the traveler or adults did not appreciate his supposedly elevated rank?"
21. For example, see Businello, *Historische Nachrichten*, 1778, 2.
22. Thornton, *Present State of Turkey*, 1809, vol. 1, xii–xiii.
23. Thornton, *Present State of Turkey*, 1809, vol. 1, 3.
24. S. Turner, *Account of an Embassy to the Court of the Teshoo Lama*, 1800, 65, 302, 343.
25. C. Niebuhr, *Reisebeschreibung nach Arabien*, 1774–1837, vol. 1, 31.
26. For example, Semedo, *History of that Great and Renowned Monarchy of China*, 1655, 25; and as a summary Du Halde, *Description géographique*, 1735, vol. 1, ii. There is an echo in such remarks of the Confucian literatis' contempt for commerce.
27. See the preface to *Travels of the Jesuits*, 1743, viii–ix.
28. Pauw, *Recherches philosophiques sur les Egyptiens et les Chinois*, 1773, vol. 1, v. On this influential author see Duchet, *Le partage des savoirs*, 1985, 82–104, and on his controversial views concerning the alleged inferiority of America: Gerbi, *Dispute of the New World*, 1973, 52–79.
29. A powerful refutation was published by Father Amiot in *Mémoires concernant l'histoire . . . des Chinois*, 1776–1814, vol. 2 (1777), 365–574, with additions in vol. 6 (1780), 275ff.; part of the same response was Grosier, "Discours préliminaire," 1777, xxxvi et seq.
30. Pauw, *Recherches philosophiques sur les Egyptiens et les Chinois*, 1773, vol. 1, 84; Amiot in *Mémoires concernant l'histoire . . . des Chinois*, 1776–1814, vol. 6 (1780), 277–307; G. L. Staunton, *Authentic Account of an Embassy from the King of Great Britain to the Emperor of China*, 1797, vol. 2, 615ff.; Barrow, *Travels in China*, 1806, 575; Cranmer-Byng, *Embassy to China*, 1962, 246; Pinkerton, *Modern Geography*, 1807, vol. 2, 99 (in a sense the final word on de Pauw).
31. Sonnerat, *Voyages aux Indes Orientales et à la Chine*, 1782, vol. 2, 2–4.
32. Barrow, *Travels in China*, 1806, 30–31, quotation: 3.
33. Leguat, *Voyages et aventures*, 1708, vol. 1, xviii; on this see Adams, *Travelers and Travel Liars*, 1962, 100ff.
34. Dubois, *Description of the Character, Manners and Customs of the People of India*, 1817, xv.
35. Dubois, *Description of the Character, Manners and Customs of the People of India*, 1817, v.
36. Max Müller, "Prefatory Note," in Dubois, *Hindu Manners, Customs and Ceremonies*, 1906, vii.
37. Cœurdoux and Desvaulx, *Mœurs and coutumes des Indiens*, 1987. This extremely complex story has been painstakingly unraveled by Sylvia Murr in *L'indologie du Père Cœurdoux*, 1987.

38. Quoted in Schäbler, "Ulrich Jasper Seetzen," 1995, 122–23.
39. Schäbler, "Ulrich Jasper Seetzen," 1995, 122.
40. This was reported by one of their number, the Polish Count Jan Potocki: *Voyages*, 1980, vol. 2, 45.
41. Braam Houckgeest, *Authentic Account of the Embassy of the Dutch East India Company*, 1798, vol. 1, xix.
42. Bruce, *Travels to Discover the Source of the Nile*, 1790, vol. 1, lxvi.
43. Early travelers with a "realist" outlook were Herberstein (1549), Busbecq (1589), Sandys (1615), Blount (1636), and Olearius (1647). They may be contrasted with the ever-gullible diplomat Sir Thomas Herbert (1634), who was always on the alert for the sensational and spectacular.
44. Hammer-Purgstall, *Constantinopolis*, 1822, vol.1, xi–xii.
45. See Roger, *Les sciences de la vie*, 1963, 163–64.
46. Milburn, *Oriental Commerce*, 1813—a work of incredible detail.
47. "J'allais chercher des images, voilà tout." Chateaubriand, *Itinéraire de Paris à Jérusalem*, 1968, 41.
48. C. Niebuhr, *Beschreibung von Arabien*, 1772, xx–xxi; Volney, *Voyage en Égypte et en Syrie*, 1959, 25; J. B. Fraser, *Journal of a Tour through Part of the Snowy Range of the Himala Mountains*, 1820, preface.
49. Gemelli Careri, "Voyage round the World," 1745, 205.
50. Adams, *Travelers and Travel Liars*, 1980, 210–22.
51. Shelvocke, *Voyage round the World*, 1726, 459–60.
52. Ellis, *Journal*, 1818, vol. 1, 334.
53. Thévenot, *Travels*, 1687, vol. 1, 59; Gervaise, *Natural and Political History of Siam*, 1928, 38; Merklein, *Reise nach Java*, 1930, 14.
54. Hodges, *Travels in India*, 1793, iv.
55. Castilhon, *Considérations*, 1769, 218–19.
56. Societas Jesu, *Lettres édifiantes et curieuses*, 1780–83, vol. 23, 321ff. (quotation from a report by Father Joseph Amiot). A similar experience of chaos is mentioned in Heissig, *Mongoleireise zur späten Goethezeit*, 1971, 101.
57. J. G. Gmelin, *Reise durch Sibirien*, 1751–52, vol. 1, 196.
58. See Abbattista, *James Mill e il problema indiano*, 1979, 93–94; Majeed, *Ungoverned Imaginings*, 1992), 140ff.
59. Mill, *History of British India*, 1817, vol. 1, 7.
60. Mill, *History of British India*, 1817, vol. 1, 9.
61. Elphinstone, *Account of the Kingdom of Caubul*, 1839.
62. See also the discussion in Despoix, *Le monde mesuré*, 2005, ch. 2.
63. Bruce, *Travels to Discover the Source of the Nile*, 1790, vol. 1, lxv–lxvi; Hammer-Purgstall, *Constantinopolis*, 1822, vol. 1, xxiv; Osbeck, *Voyage to China and the East Indies*, 1771, xviii; C. Niebuhr, *Beschreibung von Arabien*, 1772, xvii.
64. A. Smith, *Journal of His Expedition into the Interior of South Africa*, 1975, ix.
65. Of fundamental importance: Stagl, *History of Curiosity*, 1995.
66. See Dharampal-Frick, *Indien im Spiegel deutscher Quellen der Frühen Neuzeit*, 1994, 72–75.
67. Fried, "Auf der Suche nach der Wirklichkeit," 1986, 316, also 302–4. On the empirical element in medieval reports on Inner Asia and China see Reichert, *Begegnungen mit China*, 1992, 88–111.
68. Caron and Schouten, *True Description of the Mighty Kingdom of Japan*, 1935. Lucas's questionnaire is in Kapitza, *Japan in Europa*, 1990, vol. 1, 537–38. For Caron's response see Kapitza, 538–50.

69. For example, S. Anderson, *An English Consul in Turkey*, 1989, 210–11; Shapin, *Social History of Truth*, 1994, 245ff.
70. Leibniz, *Briefwechsel mit den Jesuiten in China*, 2006, 11–15.
71. Turgot, "Questions sur la Chine adressées à deux Chinois" (1766), in Turgot, *Œuvres*, 1913–23, vol. 2 (1914), 523–33. On a different Chinese informant, Arcadius Hoang, see Elisseeff-Poisle, *Nicolas Fréret*, 1978, 39ff., 166ff.
72. Michaelis, *Fragen an eine Gesellschaft gelehrter Männer*, 1762, 386.
73. C. Niebuhr, *Beschreibung von Arabien*, 1772, xvii.
74. Michaelis, *Fragen an eine Gesellschaft gelehrter Männer*, 1762, "Instruction," unpaginated.
75. Wendland, *Peter Simon Pallas*, 1992, vol. 1, 89–93.
76. Buchanan, *Journey from Madras*, 1807, vol. 1, viii–xiii.
77. "Classe essentiellement questionneuse": Volney, "Questions de statistique à l'usage des voyageurs," in Volney, *Œuvres*, 1989–98, vol. 1, 663.
78. A. v. Humboldt, *Relation historique*, 1814–25, vol. 2, 158.
79. Volney, *Voyage en Égypte et en Syrie*, 1959, 147.
80. "Pour une telle étude, il faut communiquer avec les hommes que l'on veut approfondir, il faut épouser leurs situations afin de sentir quels agens influent sur eux, quelles affections en résultent; il fait vivre dans leur pays, apprendre leur langue, pratiquer leurs coutumes." Volney, *Voyage en Égypte et en Syrie*, 1959, 399.
81. "Le cœur est partial, l'habitude puissante, les faits insidieux, et l'illusion facile. L'observateur doit donc être circonspect sans devenir pusillanime; et le lecteur obligé de voir par des yeux intermédiaires, doit surveiller à la fois la raison de son guide et sa propre raison." Volney, *Voyage en Égypte et en Syrie*, 1959, 399.
82. Broc, "Les grandes missions," 1981.
83. Stagl, *History of Curiosity*, 1995, 279.
84. Volney, *Œuvres*, 1989, vol. 1, 667.
85. Volney, *Œuvres*, 1989, vol. 1, 669–79.
86. Volney, *Œuvres*, 1989, vol. 1, 664–65. A different instruction for scientific observation and reporting by travelers was developed in 1800 by a fellow-*idéologue*, Joseph-Marie Degérando. His emphasis is on ethnological and anthropological aspects whereas Volney is more interested in politics and economics. See Degérando's document in Copans and Jamin, *Aux origines de l'anthropologie française*, 1978, 129–69; see also Chappey, *La Société des observateurs de l'homme*, 2002, 247–57.
87. On his biography: Marsden, *Brief Memoir*, 1838; for an interpretation, see Gascoigne, *Joseph Banks and the English Enlightenment*, 1994, 164–71.
88. Marsden, *History of Sumatra*, 1811, vi (preface of 1783).
89. Marsden, *History of Sumatra*, 1811, 399–400.
90. On trust and the acceptance of scientific propositions see Shapin, *Social History of Truth*, 1994, 22–36.
91. Burnes, *Travels into Bokhara*, 1834, vol. 1, 277; Barrow, *Voyage to Cochin China*, 1806, 296; J. White, *Voyage to Cochin China*, 1824, 226; Barrow, *Travels in China*, 1806, 79; Morier, *Second Journey through Persia*, 1818, 229–30.
92. A. Hamilton, *New Account of the East Indies*, 1930, vol. 1, 141.
93. Bernier, *Travels in the Mogul Empire*, 1934, 121–22; Morier, *Journey through Persia*, 1812, 116.
94. Percival, *Account of the Island of Ceylon*, 1805, 266.
95. Hammer-Purgstall, *Geschichte des Osmanischen Reiches*, 1827–35, vol. 5, 287.
96. Cantemir, *History of the Growth and Decay of the Ottoman Empire*, 1734–35, vol. 2, 379. See also Businello, *Historische Nachrichten*, 1778, 65.

97. Hammer-Purgstall, *Des Osmanischen Reiches Staatsverfassung*, 1815, vol. 2, 57.
98. Cantemir, *History of the Growth and Decay of the Ottoman Empire*, 1734–35, vol. 2, 379.
99. Hammer-Purgstall, *Des Osmanischen Reiches Staatsverfassung*, 1815, vol. 1, 218–19. On mute servants in the harem see Grosrichard, *The Sultan's Court*, 1998, 139–41.
100. Vogel, *Zehn-Jährige, Jetzo auffs neue revidirt und vermehrte Ost-Indianische Reise-Beschreibung*, 1716.
101. A. Hamilton, *New Account of the East Indies*, 1930, vol. 1, 9.
102. Ellis, *Journal*, 1818, vol. 1, 90 (fn.); Mason, *Costume of China*, 1800.
103. T. Shaw, *Travels or Observations Relating to Several Parts of Barbary*, 1808, xxv–xxvi.
104. See Du Mans, *Estat de la Perse*, 1890; Schefer, "Introduction," 1890, cviii–cvix.
105. Angelomathis-Tsougarakis, *Greek Revival*, 1990, 14ff.
106. Tavernier, *Nouvelle relation de l'interieur du Serraill du Grand Seigneur*, 1675, 541; Bernier, *Travels in the Mogul Empire*, 1934, 267; Peirce, *Imperial Harem*, 1993, 115–16.
107. Peirce, *Imperial Harem*, 1993, 114.
108. Georgi, *Bemerkungen einer Reise im Rußischen Reich*, 1775; Kapitza, *Japan in Europa*, 1990, vol. 2, 628–32; Thunberg, *Voyages de C. P. Thunberg au Japon*, 1796, vol. 2, 405ff.
109. Stavorinus, *Reise nach dem Vorgebirge der Guten Hoffnung*, 1796, 83. In Bombay, Niebuhr experienced the same problem but, characteristically, faulted himself for being unable to speak the local language: *Reisebeschreibung nach Arabien*, 1774–1837, vol. 2, 22.
110. Dallaway, *Constantinopel Ancient and Modern*, 1797, 12.
111. S. Turner, *Account of an Embassy to the Court of the Teshoo Lama*, 1800, 45.
112. C. Niebuhr, *Reisebeschreibung nach Arabien*, 1774–1837, vol. 1, 226, also 61; also C. Niebuhr, *Beschreibung von Arabien*, 1772, 404–5.
113. C. Niebuhr, *Reisebeschreibung nach Arabien*, 1774–1837, vol. 2, 219.
114. C. Niebuhr, *Beschreibung von Arabien*, 1772, 209.
115. C. Niebuhr, *Beschreibung von Arabien*, 1772, xi.
116. C. Niebuhr, *Beschreibung von Arabien*, 1772, xviii.
117. J. G. Gmelin, *Reise durch Sibirien*, 1751–52, vol. 2, preface ("Vorrede," unpaginated).
118. Crawfurd, *Journal of an Embassy to the Courts of Siam and Cochin China*, 1967, 263.
119. Poivre, "Voyage de Pierre Poivre en Cochinchine," 1885, 462.
120. Gibbon, *Decline and Fall of the Roman Empire*, 1994, vol. 3, 937, fn. 11.
121. Percival, *Account of the Island of Ceylon*, 1805, 3.
122. Bernier, *Travels in the Mogul Empire*, 1934, 311.
123. J. G. Gmelin, *Reise durch Sibirien*, 1751–52, vol. 2, preface ("Vorrede," unpaginated).
124. W. Jones, "Tenth Anniversary Discourse" [1792], in Jones, *Works*, 1807, vol. 3, 217. See also G. T. Staunton, *Ta Tsing Leu Lee*, 1810, xii.
125. Foss, "A Western Interpretation of China," 1988, 230–31; Hostetler, *Qing Colonial Enterprise*, 2001, 71.
126. See Fuchs, *Jesuiten-Atlas der Kanghsi-Zeit*, 1943, vol. 2 (Atlas, including the edition of 1721), 222–23.
127. D'Anville, *Nouvel Atlas de la Chine*, 1737.
128. Harley and Woodward, *History of Cartography*, 1994, 185.
129. Rennell, *Memoir of a Map of Hindoostan*, 1793, ii, viii.
130. Edney, *Mapping an Empire*, 1997, 308–9, 328, 311; for an account covering the entire nineteenth century see Waller, *The Pundits*, 2004.

131. Fischer, *Sibirische Geschichte*, 1768, vol. 1, 46.
132. Gaubil, *Traité de la chronologie chinoise*, 1814, 282. A general assessment of Chinese historiography by a learned ex-Jesuit: Grosier, "Discours préliminaire," 1777, xxix et seq.
133. J. de Guignes, *Histoire générale des huns*, 1756–58, vol. 1, pt. 1, preface; see also Fourmont, *Reflexions critiques sur les histoires des anciens peuples*, 1735, vol. 2, 406.
134. Ockley, *History of the Saracens*, 1757, vol. 1, xvii; similarly: Margat de Tilly, *Histoire de Tamerlan*, 1739, xv–xvi.
135. Ockley, *History of the Saracens*, 1757, vol. 2, vii.
136. Sale, "Preliminary Discourse," 1764. See also Bevilacqua, "The Qur'an Translations of Maracci and Sale," 2013.
137. Titsingh, *Private Correspondence*, 1990–92, vol. 1, xviii.
138. W. Jones, "On the Philosophy of the Asiaticks" [1794], in Jones, *Works*, 1807, vol. 3, 235.
139. Gladwin, *Ayeen Akbery*, 1800, vol. 1, x. On Gladwin see Grewal, *Muslim Rule in India*, 1970, 25–27.
140. Goethe, "West-östlicher Divan 1819: Besserem Verständnis," 2010, 270.
141. Kleuker, *Anhang zum Zend-Avesta*, 1781–83, vol. 1, pt. 1, 168.
142. Mailla, *Histoire générale de la Chine*, 1777–80. The most competent and penetrating critic was Father Antoine Gaubil. See his *Correspondance*, 1970, 262, 511, 674. Father Dominique Parennin, apprently a better Sinologist than de Mailla, made his own translations of parts of the *Tongjian gangmu*. It remained unpublished.
143. See Pinot, *La Chine et la formation de l'esprit philosophique en France*, 1932, 250–52; Guy, *French Image of China*, 1963, 393–94; Mackerras, *Western Images of China*, 1989, 95–96.
144. *Encyclopedia of Islam*. New ed., vol. 2, 1983, 923. On Dow see Grewal, *Muslim Rule in India*, 1970, 6–22; Van Aalst, *British View of India*, 1970, 312–13. Dow had neglected any critical examination of the Ferishta manuscript at his disposal. His carelessness became apparent in 1829 when John Briggs published a new translation based on the philological standards of the day: *History of the Rise of Mahomedan Power in India*.
145. Gibbon, *Decline and Fall of the Roman Empire*, 1994, vol. 3, 529, fn. 13.
146. Dow, *History of Hindostan*, 1812, vol. 1, viii.
147. Bernier, *Travels in the Mogul Empire*, 1934, 320, 343–44.
148. Lach and Van Kley, *Asia in the Making of Europe*, 1993, 1030.
149. The following passage follows Windisch, *Geschichte der Sanskrit-Philologie*, 1917–20, vol. 1, 22ff., Schwab, *Oriental Renaissance*, 1984, 51–80; Kejariwal, *Asiatic Society*, 1988; Rocher, *Orientalism, Poetry, and the Millenium*, 1993, 234–40; Teltscher, *India Inscribed*, 1995, 92–228; Franklin, *Orientalist Jones*, 2011.
150. Rocher and Rocher, *The Making of Western Indology*, 2012, 67–82.
151. See Grotsch, "Das Sanskrit und die Ursprache," 1989, 88ff.
152. Windisch, *Geschichte der Sanskrit-Philologie*, 1917–20, vol. 1, 55.
153. ". . . de tirer de cete nation tout ce qui peut servir à la perfection de nos Sciences et de nos Arts. . . ." Leibniz, *Briefwechsel mit den Jesuiten in China*, 2006, 228 (letter no. 32 of September 19, 1699).
154. Bouvet, *Eine wissenschaftliche Akademie für China*, 1989, 27–31.
155. Leibniz, *Briefwechsel mit den Jesuiten in China*, 2006, 396 (letter no. 49 of May 18, 1703). Leibniz was right: the reign of the Kangxi emperor was the high point of intercultural openness and exchange. See Jami, *The Emperor's New Mathematics*, 2012.

156. See also Leibniz, *Preface to Leibniz' Novissima Sinica*, 1957, 68–71; the best edition of the Latin original is Leibniz, *Briefe über China*, 2017, 4–9.
157. Gascoigne, *Joseph Banks and the English Enlightenment*, 1994, 179–80, 182.
158. Muntschik, "Die floristische Erforschung Japans um 1700," 1983, 13.
159. Muntschik, "Die floristische Erforschung Japans um 1700," 1983, 20, 22.
160. Fournier, "Enterprise in Botany," 1987, 128–29; Heniger, *Hendrik Adriaan van Reede tot Drakenstein*, 1986, esp. 41–45, 59–64; Grove, *Green Imperialism*, 1995, 85–90; Grove, "Indigenous Knowledge," 1996.

CHAPTER VII. REPORTING, EDITING, READING: FROM LIVED EXPERIENCE TO PRINTED TEXT

1. S. Johnson, *Selected Poetry and Prose*, 1977, 270.
2. Drijvers, de Hond, and Sancisi-Weerdenburg, *"Ik hadde de nieusgierigheid,"* 1997; Schmidt, *Inventing Exoticism*, 2015, 43–45. On earlier visual representations of Turks and the Ottoman Empire see Harper, *The Turk and Islam*, 2011.
3. Peyrefitte, *Images de l'Empire immobile*, 1990; Tillotson, *Artificial Empire*, 2000; Bernard Smith, *European Vision and the South Pacific*, 1985, 56–82; Bernard Smith, *Imagining the Pacific*, 1992, 111–35. A classic on the illustrated travel account is Stafford, *Voyage into Substance*, 1984; see also Jacobs, *Painted Voyage*, 1995, 18–79 on Asia.
4. See Archer, *Early Views of India*, 1980; Shellim, *Oil Paintings of India and the East*, 1979.
5. See Bernard Smith, *European Vision and the South Pacific*, 1985; Bernard Smith, *Imagining the Pacific*, 1992.
6. On the emergence of the "philosophical traveler" in humanism and Renaissance see the excellent article by Rubiés, "Travel Writing and Humanistic Culture: A Blunted Impact?," 2007. Rubiés's analysis confirms for an earlier age my own interpretation of the eighteenth century as developed in 1998 in the German original of the present book. This is not the place to discuss the extensive literature on travel writing that has appeared since 1998. Starting points are Hulme and Youngs, *Cambridge Companion to Travel Writing*, 2000; Rubiés, *Travelers and Cosmographers*, 2007; Elsner and Rubiés, *Voyages and Visions*, 1999. The comparison of travel writing in European and Chinese contexts has been pioneered in Rubiés and Ollé, "The Comparative History of a Genre," 2016 (with a good introduction to travel writing in early modern Europe: 5–20).
7. A brief vignette of such a voracious reader (the Göttingen polymath Christoph Meiners) is provided in Carhart, *Science of Culture in Enlightenment Germany*, 2007, 228–29.
8. Beaglehole, *Life of Captain James Cook*, 1974, 290, 459–71; Robel, "Bemerkungen zu deutschen Reisebeschreibungen," 1992, 25 (on the Great Nordic Expedition); Potocki, *Voyages*, vol. 2, 52 (on the Russian mission to China in 1805).
9. Elphinstone, *Account of the Kingdom of Caubul*, 1839, vol. 1, xxiv–xxxv.
10. See Abbott, *John Hawkesworth*, 1982, 137ff.
11. Gelder, *Het Oost-Indisch avontuur*, 1997, 260.
12. Duchet, *Anthropologie et histoire*, 1971, 56.
13. Castoldi, *Il fascino del colibrí*, 1972, 77, 79. A good example is Capper, *Observations on the Passage to India*, 1783.
14. Duchet, *Le partage du savoir*, 1985, 19.

15. Kaempfer, *Phoenix Persicus*, 1987, 42.
16. T. Shaw, *Travels or Observations Relating to Several Parts of Barbary*, 1808, ix–x.
17. Quoted in Osbeck, *Voyage to China and the East Indies*, 1771, vol, 2, 127–28.
18. Batten, *Pleasurable Instruction*, 1978, 79; Hentschel, "Die Reiseliteratur am Ausgang des 18. Jahrhunderts," 1991, 54–63.
19. Sonnerat, *Voyages aux Indes Orientales et à la Chine*, 1782, vol. 2, xv.
20. T. Shaw, *Travels or Observations Relating to Several Parts of Barbary*, 1808, xi.
21. Chardin, *Le couronnement de Soleimaan*, 1671; Kroell, "Douze Lettres de Jean Chardin," 1982, 299.
22. Preface to Baumgarten, *Uebersetzung der Algemeinen Welthistorie*, 1744–67, vol. 26 (1764), 4; also vol. 29 (1765), 2; Matthias Christian Sprengel's introduction to Barrow, *Reisen durch die inneren Gegenden des südlichen Africa*, 1801, xvii.
23. General reflections on the value of detail in travel accounts: C. Niebuhr, *Reisebeschreibung nach Arabien*, 1774–1837, vol. 1, 312–13.
24. Elphinstone, *Account of the Kingdom of Caubul*, 1839, vol. 1, ix.
25. Typical examples are Forrest, *Voyage from Calcutta to the Mergui Archipelago*, 1792, or Lucas, *Voyage du Sieur Paul Lucas au Levant*, 1720.
26. S. G. Gmelin, *Reise durch Rußland zur Untersuchung der drey Natur-Reiche*, 1770–84, vol. 1, 48. His uncle J. G. Gmelin has kept his own diary in a less methodical way, regarding it as a "hodgepodge of countless particulars": *Reise durch Sibirien von dem Jahr 1733 bis 1743*, 1751–52, prefaces (unpaginated) to vols. 1 and 2.
27. ". . . der uns das Fremdeste, Seltsamste, mit seiner Lokalität, mit aller Nachbarschaft, jedesmal in dem eigensten Elemente zu schildern und darzustellen weiß." J. W. v. Goethe, "Die Wahlverwandtschaften," in Goethe, *Sämtliche Werke. Münchner Ausgabe*. Ed. Karl Richter, vol. 9, Munich, 1987, 457; *Goethe's Collected Works*. Ed. Victor Lange, Eric A. Blackall, and Cyrus Hamlin, vol. 11, New York, 1988, 212.
28. T. Shaw, *Travels or Observations Relating to Several Parts of Barbary*, 1808, xi.
29. Grundy, *Lady Mary Wortley Montagu*, 1999, 134–66.
30. Kindersley, *Letters from the Island of Teneriffe*, 1777.
31. Abel-Rémusat, *Nouvelles mélanges asiatiques*, 1829, vol. 1, 284. For a fitting example of a perpetuated error see Chateaubriand, *Itinéraire de Paris à Jerusalem*, 1968, 93ff.
32. *Edinburgh Review*, July 1804, 314 (anonymous).
33. On Lahontan see Pagden, *European Encounters with the New World*, 1993, 120–25; see also the general reflections in Gearhart, *Open Boundary of History and Fiction*, 1984; Constantine, "The Question of Authenticity," 1988.
34. Liebersohn, *The Travelers's World*, 2006, 8.
35. Desideri, *Account of Tibet*, 1932, 302–6.
36. Volney, *Voyage en Égypte et en Syrie*, 1959, 34.
37. Chateaubriand, *Itinéraire de Paris à Jerusalem*, 1968, 27, 45, 105, 111, 131, 271–72.
38. See Rehbinder, *Nachrichten und Bemerkungen über den algierischen Staat*, 1798–1800, vol. 1, 3–5, on his failed attempts to disprove and refute Shaw's observations. James Bruce, too, and even travelers from the nineteenth century confirmed Shaw's accuracy and reliability during his travels through the Near East from 1720 to 1733.
39. Walckenaer, *Vies de plusieurs personnages célèbres*, 1830, vol. 2, 74, makes the point that Bernier's reputation kept growing continuously after his death.
40. Wilson's detailed introduction to Mill, *History of British India*, 1858, vol. 1, vii–xxxvi.
41. Grosier, *De la Chine*, 1818–20, vol. 1, xiv.
42. Thompson, *Wonderful Things*, 2015, 78.
43. Markham, "Introduction," in Bogle and Manning, *Narratives*, 1879, clxii.

44. Grewal, *Muslim Rule in India*, 1970, 114.
45. Those who debriefed him included famous scholars like Athanasius Kircher and Lorenzo Magalotti: see Zoli, *La Cina e la cultura italiana*, 1973, 105–11.
46. Moorcroft and Trebeck, *Travels in the Himalayan Provinces of Hindustan*, 1841; Alder, *Beyond Bokhara*, 1985.
47. Examples are Roque, *Voyage de l'Arabie Heureuse*, 1715 (the standard account of Yemen before Niebuhr's work); Turpin, *Histoire civile et naturelle du royaume de Siam*, 1771; Richard, *Histoire naturelle, civile et politique du Tonquin*, 1778; Renouard de Sainte-Croix, *Voyage commercial et politique aux Indes Orientales*, 1810, who used unpublished papers written by missionaries.
48. *Travels of the Jesuits*, 1743, vi. However, the anonymous editor then proceeds to praise the acuity of the Jesuits' observations.
49. See Richards, *Mughal Empire*, 1993, 306.
50. Catrou, *History of the Mogul Dynasty*, 1826.
51. Manucci, *Storia do Mogor* (1906–8); Manuzzi's life and the fate of his work have been carefully reconstructed in Subrahmanyam, *Three Ways to Be Alien*, 2011, 136–72.
52. On the dissemination and celebrity of this work see Lemny, *Les Cantemir*, 2009, 305–19.
53. On the early collections see Broc, *La géographie de la Renaissance*, 1980, 37–42, on the eighteenth century Boerner, "Die großen Reisesammlungen des 18. Jahrhunderts," 1982.
54. Rietbergen, "Witsen's World," 1985, esp. 124–15. A kind of continuation of Witsen's work was a French collection of reports on Northern Asia: Bernard, *Recueil de voyages du Nord*, 1732–34.
55. Valentyn, *Oud en nieuw Oost-Indien*, 1724–26.
56. Fisch, *Hollands Ruhm in Asien*, 1986, 17–19.
57. Fisch, *Hollands Ruhm in Asien*, 1986, 22. On Valentyn see also Beekman, *Troubled Pleasures*, 1996, 119–44.
58. Crone and Skelton, "English Collections of Voyages and Travels," 1946, 84–85.
59. Harris and Campbell, *Navigantium atque Itinerantium Bibliotheca*, 1744–48; *Modern Part of an Universal History*, 1759–66. See Abbattista, *Commercio, colonie e impero*, 1990, 69, 267ff.
60. Astley and Green, *A New General Collection of Voyages and Travels*, 1745–47. John Green was the editor, Thomas Astley the publisher and at the same time owner of the library from which the texts were drawn.
61. Astley and Green, *A New General Collection of Voyages and Travels*, 1745–47, vol. 1, vii (preface).
62. Astley and Green, *A New General Collection of Voyages and Travels*, 1745–47, vol. 1, vii (preface).
63. Crone and Skelton, "English Collections of Voyages and Travels," 1946, 101.
64. See Astley and Green, *A New General Collection of Voyages and Travels*, 1745–47, vol. 4, 3.
65. See Prévost, *Histoire générale des voyages*, 1746–59. A detailed table of contents is in Prévost, *Œuvres*, vol. 8, 1986, 400–401. An excellent discussion is Duchet, *Anthropologie et histoire*, 1971, 81–95.
66. Prévost, "Avertissement" of vol. 11, in *Œuvres*, vol. 8, 1986, 436.
67. Duchet, *Anthropologie et histoire*, 1971, 91.
68. "Un système complet d' histoire et de géographie moderne, qui représentera l'état actuel de toutes les nations." Quoted in Duchet, *Anthropologie et histoire*, 1971, 84.

69. Examples are Newberry, *World Displayed*, 1759–61; Derrick, *Collection of Travels thro' Various Parts of the World*, 1762.
70. Schwabe, *Allgemeine Historie aller merckwürdigen Reisen*, 1747–74, vol. 1, preface ("Vorrede," unpaginated).
71. "Das Werck an sich selbsten ist so beschaffen, daß je weiter man darinnen lieset, je lieblicher und angenehmer es wird: Und obschon gleich Anfangs manche Umstände, wegen der angeführten unbekannten Länder und Oerter, sehr dunckel vorkommen, so werden sie in den nachfolgenden Relationen dergestalt erläutert, daß gar kein Zweiffel mehr übrig bleibet. So gehet einem das Licht immer mehr auf, und so vermehret sich alle Augenblicke die Lust, diese Historie weiter einzusehen." Schwabe, *Allgemeine Historie aller merckwürdigen Reisen*, 1747–74, vol. 1, preface ("Vorrede," unpaginated).
72. Laharpe, *Abrégé de l'Histoire Générale des Voyages*, 1813–15, vol. 1, 7.
73. Boucher de la Richarderie, *Bibliothèque universelle des voyages*, 1808, vol. 1, 93.
74. Beckmann, *Litteratur der älteren Reisebeschreibungen*, 1807–10, vol. 1, 200.
75. Hakluyt, *Hakluyt's Edition of the Early Voyages, Travels, and Discoveries of the English Nation*, 1809–12.
76. Pinkerton, *General Collection*, 1808–14.
77. At the same time, a precious novelty was presented by Paulus in volume 3 (1794) of his *Sammlung der merkwürdigsten Reisen in den Orient* (1792–1803), where he had unearthed reports on Egypt by the seventeenth-century traveler Johann Michael Wansleb.
78. Pinkerton, *General Collection*, 1808–14, vol. 1, v.
79. Pinkerton, *Modern Geography*, 1807. The first edition came out in two volumes in 1802.
80. Walckenaer, *Histoire générale des voyages*, 1826–31. See especially Walckenaer's magisterial survey of the history of geographical knowledge from antiquity to the early Portuguese voyages. The author deals extensively with the Arab contribution: vol. 1, 1–55.
81. Marsden, *Travels of Marco Polo*, 1818, xviii.
82. For example E.A.W. Zimmermann's *Annalen der Geographie und Statistik*, Braunschweig 1790–92, in three volumes.
83. Pinkerton, *General Collection*, 1808–14, vol. 7 (1811), 652ff.
84. *Annales de Voyages*, vol. 24 (1814), 214–26.
85. Sprengel, *Auswahl der besten ausländischen geographischen und statistischen Nachrichten*, vol. 10 (1798), 1–328; vol. 11 (1798), 1–349.
86. Sprengel, *Auswahl der besten ausländischen geographischen und statistischen Nachrichten*, vol. 10 (1798), vi–vii.
87. Fabian, "English Books and Their Eighteenth-Century German Readers," 1976, 165–74; Fabian, "Englisch als neue Fremdsprache des 18. Jahrhunderts," 1985, 178.
88. See a study on Scheuchzer's English translation (1727) of Kaempfer's German manuscript about his stay in Japan: Bodart-Bailey, "Kaempfer Restor'd," 1988, esp. 14ff., and the same author's introduction to her own new translation of the source: Kaempfer, *Kaempfer's Japan*, 1999, 7–10.
89. Bruce, *Reisen in das Innere von Africa*, 1791, vol. 1, i.
90. Bruce, *Reisen zur Entdeckung der Quellen des Nils*, 1791. No lesser scholar than the famous anthropologist Johann Friedrich Blumenbach of Göttingen University provided the annotations to this edition.

91. Percy, *Hau Kiou Choaan*, 1761. See also D. Porter, *Chinese Taste in Eighteenth-Century*, 2010, 156.
92. Tzoref-Ashkenazi, "Romantic Attitudes toward Oriental Despotism," 2013, 291.
93. Translator's preface, in Valentia, *Reisen nach Indien*, 1811, vol. 1, v.
94. Barrow, *Reise durch China*, 1804, vol. 2, preface ("Vorbericht," unpaginated).
95. Barrow, *Reise durch China*, 1804, vol. 1, 85.
96. New edition: Hüttner, *Nachricht von der britischen Gesandtschaftsreise durch China*, 1996.
97. Guthke, *Die Reise ans Ende der Welt*, 2011, 161–89.
98. Hoare, *Tactless Philosopher*, 1976, 236–37.
99. See the impressive bibliography of Johann Reinhold Forster's activities as an editor and translator of travel literature in Hoare, *Tactless Philosopher*, 1976, 353–72.
100. Hoare, *Tactless Philosopher*, 1976, 202.
101. The following is based on Friese, "Einleitung," 1991, xxiii–xxx, as well as Thunberg, *Voyages de C. P. Thunberg au Japon*, 1796, vol. 1, vi–vii.
102. See Brot, "L'abbé Raynal, lecteur de l'Histoire générale des voyages," 1995.
103. See the English translation Valentyn, *Description of Ceylon*, 1978. Only in 1803 was Knox's old account superseded by a description based on a recent visit to the country: Percival, *Account of the Island of Ceylon*, 1805. Somewhat derivative in relation to Percival is Cordiner, *Description of Ceylon*, 1807.
104. Wolf, *Reise nach Zeilan*, 1781–84.
105. Rietbergen, *Japan verwoord*, 2003, 285–300.
106. Prichard, *Researches into the Physical History of Mankind*, vol. 4 (1844), 521.
107. Morison, *"Old Bruin,"* 1967, 276.
108. See Willson, *Mythical Image*, 1964, 53, 87, 212; Goerres, *Mythengeschichte der asiatischen Welt*, 1810, vol. 1, 40, 45. Johann Christoph Adelung was another prominent supporter of the idea that the "Urvolk" was located in Kashmir: *Mithridates*, 1806–17, vol. 1, 8–9. See also Petri, *Urvolkhypothese*, 1990.
109. Busbecq, *Travels into Turkey*, 1744; for a modern edition see Busbecq, *Turkish Letters*, 1927.
110. See Hammer-Purgstall, *Constantinopolis*, 1822, vol. 1, xiii–xiv; Hammer-Purgstall, *Geschichte des Osmanischen Reiches* (1827–35), vol. 3 (1828), 333–35.
111. Kühn, *Neugestaltung der deutschen Geographie im 18. Jahrhundert*, 1939, 9.
112. Abel-Remusat, *Nouveaux mélanges asiatiques*, 1829, vol. 1, 291–92.
113. For example Thornton, *Present State of Turkey*, 1809, vol. 1; D. Stewart, *Collected Works*, 1854–60, vol. 9, 391.
114. Hammer-Purgstall, *Des osmanischen Reiches Staatsverfassung und Staatsverwaltung*, 1815, vol. 1, x.
115. Woodhead, "'The Present Terrour of the World,'" 1987, 23.
116. For example, Martini, *De bello tartarico historia*, 1654, 4; Kircher, *China*, 1667, 87–90; Du Halde, *Description géographique*, 1735, vol. 1, i. The typical assessment of the mid-eighteenth century is summarized in Harris and Campbell, *Navigantium atque Itinerantium Bibliotheca*, 1744–48, vol. 1, 593.
117. C. Ritter, *Erdkunde*, vol. 3 (1835), 514. Also Hegel, *Die orientalische Welt*, 1923, 277.
118. Bruzen de la Martinière, *Grand dictionnaire géographique*, 1768, vol. 1, vii.
119. Meiners, *Grundriß der Geschichte der Menschheit*, 1793, 324; he thinks that only Simon de La Loubère's acount of Siam is of comparable quality (351). For a modern assessment of Chardin see Emerson, "Sir John Chardin," 1992: "Whenever an

important Persian text on a particular topic is available, it confirms not only the general accuracy of Chardin's reports but also its usefulness in clarifying and supplementing that text" (373–74).

120. Review of Morier, *Journey through Persia, Armenia, and Asia Minor* (1812), in *Eclectic Review* vol. 8, pt. 1 (1812), 116.
121. Büsching to Müller, August 19, 1780, in Hoffmann and Osipov, *Geographie, Geschichte und Bildungswesen*, 1995, 467.
122. B. G. Niebuhr, *Lebensnachrichten über Barthold Georg Niebuhr*, 1838–39, vol. 1, 227, also 168.
123. Cited in Grafton, *The Footnote*, 1997, 49.
124. See Gaulmier, *L'idéologue Volney*, 1951, 114–21, on the sensational success of Volney's book.
125. Oliver, *American Travelers on the Nile: Early U.S. Visitors to Egypt, 1774–1839*, 2014, 24.
126. Volney, "Tableau du climat et du sol des États-Unis," in *Œuvres* (1989–98), vol. 2, 21–285, quote 30. However, this book is replete with descriptions of landscapes that might be compared to Humboldt's contemporaneous work on Latin America.
127. Harrison and Laslett, *Library of John Locke*, 1971, 27.
128. Schultz, "Goethe and the Literature of Travel," 1949, 446ff.; see also numerous contributions by Karl S. Guthke, e.g., his *Goethes Weimar*, 2001, and also Guthke, *Die Erfindung der Welt*, 2005; Guthke, *Die Reise ans Ende der Welt*, 2011.
129. *Magazin von . . . Reisebeschreibungen*, vol. 1 (1790), preface ("Vorwort"); Plewe, *Carl Ritter Bibliothek*, 1978.
130. Bernoulli, *Unterrichtendes Verzeichniß einer Berlinischen Privatbibliothek*, 1783, preface ("Vorbericht"). On library holdings of travel literature see also Duchet, *Anthropologie et histoire*, 1971, 66–75; Blanke, *Politische Herrschaft und soziale Ungleichheit*, 1997, vol. 2, 1–20.
131. Montesquieu, *Œuvres complètes de Montesquieu*, vol. 16: *Geographica*, 2007; Minuti, *Una geografia politica della diversità*, 2015, 163–90, esp. 165; Dodds, *Les récits de voyages*, 1929.
132. Grundmann, *Die geographischen und völkerkundlichen Quellen*, 1900, on Asia: 42–64; Jäger, "Herder als Leser von Reiseliteratur," 1986.
133. Curley, *Samuel Johnson and the Age of Travel*, 1976, quote 238–39.
134. Platteau, *Les économistes classiques et le sous-développement*, 1978, vol. 1, 14, 53ff.
135. The sixth, extensively revised edition (1826) of his *Essay on the Principle of Population* (first edition 1798) shows Malthus as a particularly well-informed reader of the most up-to-date literature on societies outside Europe. See Malthus, *Works*, 1986, vols. 2 and 3 (with a bibliography of the books cited: vol. 3, 701ff.).
136. Marshall, "Introduction," in Burke, *India: The Launching of the Hastings Impeachment*, 1991, 20ff.
137. Falconer, *Remarks*, 1781; Hirschfeld, *Von der Gastfreundschaft*, 2015.
138. See Keighren, Withers, and Bell, *Travels into Print*, 68–99.
139. Castoldi, *Il fascino del colibrí*, 1972, 187.
140. 1813 in *Jenaische Allgemeine Literatur-Zeitung*, see Blanke, "Verfassungen," 1983, 154–55.
141. A. v. Humboldt, *Zentral-Asien*, 2009, 27.
142. See, for example, the translator's "avertissement" (unpaginated) in Pétis de la Croix, *Histoire de Timur-Bec*, 1723.

143. On the significance and impact of the work see Gierl, *Geschichte als präzisierte Wissenschaft,* 2012, 361–65.
144. Baumgarten and Semler, *Uebersetzung der Algemeinen Welthistorie,* 1744–67, vol. 1 (1744), 27, also 18; Pigulla, *China in der deutschen Weltgeschichtsschreibung,* 1996, 125–27.
145. Baumgarten and Semler, *Uebersetzung der Algemeinen Welthistorie,* 1744–67, vol. 21 (1760), 515–16.
146. Du Halde, *Description géographique,* 1735, vol. 2, xii–xiii.
147. Gibbon, *Decline and Fall of the Roman Empire,* 1994, vol. 3, 844–47.
148. A charge leveled at Prince Cantemir, the historian of the Ottoman Empire, by the anonymous authors of the volume on the Ottomans as part of the German *Uebersetzung der Algemeine Welthistorie*: vol. 27, 1764, 330–32. A modern assessment comes, basically, to a similar conclusion: Leezenberg, "The Oriental Origins of Orientalism," 2012, 254–55.
149. "Daß man die bisherigen Beschreibungen bald als die einzige mögliche Quelle nöthig haben wird, um das ächtorientalische, welches so lange fast ungeändert fortgepflanzt war, von dem modernisierten und europäisierten zu unterscheiden," Paulus, *Sammlung,* 1792–1803, vol. 5 (1799), preface ("Vorrede," unpaginated).
150. Jean-Jacques Rousseau, "Discours sur l'inégalité," 1755, in Rousseau, *Œuvres,* 1959–95, vol. 3 (1975), 212–13. Rousseau, *Basic Political Writings,* 1987, 100.
151. Quoted in Duchet, *Anthropologie et histoire,* 1971, 99.
152. Johann Salomo Semler, in Baumgarten and Semler, *Uebersetzung der Algemeinen Welthistorie,* 1744–67, vol. 26 (1764), 5.
153. The clear-cut distinction between scholars and gentlemen that Shapin (*Social History of Truth,* 1994) wishes to draw is difficult to find in eighteenth-century sources.
154. Langsdorff, *Bemerkungen auf einer Reise um die Welt,* 1813, vol. 1, ix.
155. Barrow, *Travels in China,* 1806, 579.
156. S. Johnson, "Essay on the 'Description of China,'" 1742, 320.
157. S. Johnson, "Essay on the 'Description of China,'" 1742, 320.
158. Anonymous review of Edward Scott Waring, *Tour to Sheeraz* (1807), in *Edinburgh Review,* April 1807, 63. The other worked mentioned in the review is Francklin, *Observations Made on a Tour from Bengal to Persia,* 1790.
159. Swiderski, *The False Formosan,* 1991; Keevak, *The Pretended Asian,* 2004, 1–6; Breen, "No Man Is an Island," 2013.
160. Psalmanazar, *Historical and Geographical Description of Formosa,* 1704.
161. Millar, *Origins of the Distinction of Ranks,* 2006, 90.
162. Pauw, *Recherches philosophiques sur les Egyptiens et les Chinois,* 1773, vol. 1, v, 9, 70.
163. G. L. Staunton, *Authentic Account of an Embassy from the King of Great Britain to the Emperor of China,* 1797, vol. 2, 159; Barrow, *Travels in China,* 1806, 170.
164. C.L.J. de Guignes, *Voyages à Peking,* 1808, vol. 2, 288; Abel, *Narrative of a Journey into the Interior of China,* 1819, 234.
165. Sonnerat, *Voyages aux Indes Orientales et à la Chine,* 1782, vol. 2, 22.
166. Voltaire, "Essai sur les mœurs," in *Œuvres complètes de Voltaire,* vol. 26A (2013), 322.
167. In private letters that seem to have been unrelated to the public relations initiatives of the Jesuit order, Père Gaubil reports amazing numbers of those dying children. In 1752 he claims that, during the past couple of years, more than six thousand had been baptized per annum. Gaubil, *Correspondance de Pékin,* 1970, 722, also 387, 445, 535.

168. Père Joseph Amiot, in *Mémoires concernant l'histoire . . . des Chinois*, 1776–1814, vol. 6 (1780), 327–31.
169. Malthus, *Works*, 1986, vol. 2, 130–36.
170. Chambers, *A Dissertation on Oriental Gardening*, 1772.
171. Hirschfeld, *Theorie der Gartenkunst*, 1779–85, vol. 1, 99.
172. Bruce, *Travels to Discover the Source of the Nile*, 1790, vol. 1, xxv–xxvi.
173. Shapin, *Social History of Truth*, 1994.

CHAPTER VIII. THE RAW FORCES OF HISTORY: APOCALYPTIC HORSEMEN, CONQUERORS, USURPERS

1. Heeren, "Ideen," in *Historische Werke*, 1821–26, vol. 10 (1824), 60; the English translation quoted here was published half a century after the original: Heeren, *Historical Researches*, 1846, vol. 1, 9; translation modified.
2. This is the basic narrative line in the best English-language history of Central Asia: Beckwith, *Empires of the Silk Road*, 2009.
3. Frankopan, *The Silk Roads*, 2015, 508–21.
4. Hegel, *Die orientalische Welt*, 1923, 342.
5. Avril, *Voyage en divers états d'Europe et d'Asie*, 1692, 195.
6. For example, Pufendorf et al., *Introduction à l'Histoire moderne*, 1753–69, vol. 7, 299.
7. The Manchu conquest of China was not a one-time event but a lengthy process. See Rowe, *The Great Qing*, 2009, 11–30.
8. See C. A. Bayly, *Imperial Meridian*, 1989, 35–40; Gommans, *Rise of the Indo-Afghan Empire*, 1995, esp. 33ff. Among contemporary historians, Alexander Dow was particularly obsessed with what he termed the "Afghan Empire."
9. A contemporary account for the British public was C. Hamilton, *An Historical Relation of the Origin, Progress, and Final Dissolution of the Government of Rohilla Afgans*, 1787, 21ff., where the author shows considerable sympathy for the Rohillas' point of view. See also Francklin, *History of the Reign of Shah-Aulum*, 1798. 60ff. Warren Hastings' brutal treatment of the Rohillas in this war later, in 1786, was one of the main charges in Edmund Burke's impeachment of Hastings. See Burke, *India: The Launching of the Hastings Impeachment*, 1991, 79–119; Whelan, *Edmund Burke and India*, 1996, 142–45. A German author accused Hastings of what would today be called genocide: Breitenbauch, *Ergänzungen der Geschichte von Asien und Afrika*, 1783–87, vol. 2, 122. For the historical background see Husain, *Ruhela Chieftaincies*, 1994.
10. For the full range of European responses, culminating in Johann Ludwig Burckhardt, see Bonacina, *The Wahhabis Seen through European Eyes*, 2015.
11. Perdue, *China Marches West*, 2005, 270–87.
12. Condorcet, *Esquisse d'un tableau historique des progrès de l'esprit humain*, 1988, 270; Condorcet, *Outlines of an Historical View of the Progress of the Human Mind*, 1796, 257. See also Leibniz's worries of 1699: ch. 1 above, fn. 3.
13. Kappeler, *Russian Empire*, 2001, 123.
14. "Verpesteter Windhauch": A. v. Humboldt, *Ansichten der Natur*, 1987, 7.
15. Volney, "Les ruines, ou méditation sur les révolutions des empires," in Volney, *Œuvres*, 1989–98, vol. 1, 225. On this remarkable work as a "cosmic" theory of decadence see Moravia, *Il tramonto dell'illuminismo*, 1986, 163–67.
16. Gibbon, *Decline and Fall of the Roman Empire*, 1994, vol. 3, 691–98, 727 (quote).
17. Gibbon, *Decline and Fall of the Roman Empire*, 1994, vol. 3, 588.

18. Voltaire, "Histoire de Charles XII," in *Œuvres complètes de Voltaire*, vol. 4, 1996, 542.
19. Lueder, *Geschichte der vornehmsten Völker der alten Welt*, 1800, 77.
20. Strahlenberg, *Das Nord- und Ostliche Theil von Europa und Asia*, 1730, 16.
21. Temple, "Of Heroic Virtue," in *Works*, 1814, vol. 3, 357–59.
22. Temple, "Of Heroic Virtue," in *Works*, 1814, vol. 3, 397–98; a later discussion is Virey, *Histoire naturelle du genre humain*, 1824, vol. 1, 469ff.
23. Ranke, *Weltgeschichte* (1881–88), pt. 8, 420, 417.
24. Ranke, *Weltgeschichte* (1881–88), pt. 9, sec. 1, 271.
25. Ranke, *Weltgeschichte* (1881–88), pt. 1, sec., ix; pt. 8, 417.
26. Ranke, *Weltgeschichte* (1881–88), pt. 9, sec. 1, 274.
27. Ranke, *Weltgeschichte* (1881–88), pt. 4, sec. 1, 300.
28. See Müller, *Geschichte der antiken Ethnographie*, 1972–80, vol. 2, 192–94.
29. Fessler, *Attila*, 1794, 96.
30. Robertson, *Progress of Society in Europe*, 1972, 15.
31. Gibbon, *Decline and Fall of the Roman Empire*, 1994, vol. 2, 297–98, 306–7. For Gibbon's view on the impact of the Huns on the fate of the Western empire see Pocock, *Barbarism and Religion*, vol. 6, 2015, 391–414.
32. Richardson, *Dissertation on the Languages, Literature and Manners of Eastern Nations*, 1778, pt. 2, 149.
33. Montesquieu, "Considérations sur les causes de la grandeur des Romains et de leur decadence," ch. 19, in *Œuvres complètes de Montesquieu*, vol. 2, 2000, 242.
34. See the editorial comments in *Œuvres complètes de Montesquieu*, vol. 2, 2000, 242, fn. 12; Minuti, *Una geografia politica della diversità*, 2015, 91.
35. Schmidt, *Forschungen im Gebiete der älteren religiösen, politischen und literärischen Bildungsgeschichte der Völker Mittel-Asiens*, 1824, 1–2.
36. For example, Sir William Jones, "On Asiatic History, Civil and Natural" [1792], in Jones, *Works*, 1807, vol. 3, 208–11. This would become a favorite motif in romantic conceptions of history. See the idea of "Völkerströme" (ethnic flooding) in Goerres, *Mythengeschichte der asiatischen Welt*, 1810. The history of migrations later assumes a central position in Prichard, *Researches into the Physical History of Mankind*, 1836–47.
37. Volney, "Les ruines, ou méditation sur les révolutions des empires," in Volney, *Œuvres*, 1989–98, vol. 1, 221.
38. Peyssonnell, *Observations historiques & géographiques*, 1765, 19 and passim.
39. See, in general, Mohnhaupt, "Spielarten 'revolutionärer' Entwicklung," 1988. A parallel development was that of the concept of "revolution" in geology. Peter Simon Pallas and Georges Cuvier were particularly important in this regard.
40. Achenwall, *Staatsverfassung der heutigen vornehmsten Europäischen Reiche und Völker*, 1768, 6.
41. Gatterer, *Versuch einer allgemeinen Weltgeschichte bis zur Entdeckung Amerikens*, 1792, 1.
42. Anquetil-Duperron, *Dignité du commerce*, 1789, 41.
43. Gibbon, *Decline and Fall of the Roman Empire*, 1994, vol. 1, 1 (preface).
44. "Great Revolution": Baumgarten and Semler, *Uebersetzung der Algemeinen Welthistorie*, 1744–67, vol. 25 (1763), 152–248 (the most detailed and comprehensive description of the events in China in eighteenth-century European literature); the classic source is Martini, *De bello tatarico historia*, 1654; see also Van Kley, "News from China," 1973; Mungello, *Curious Land*, 1985, 110–16.
45. See Goldstone, *Revolution and Rebellion in the Early Modern World*, 1991; G. Parker, *Global Crisis*, 2013.

46. Dunbar, *Essays on the History of Mankind*, 1781, vol. 2, 275–76; Castilhon, *Considérations*, 1769, 252; Roubaud, *Histoire générale de l'Asie*, 1770–72, vol. 2, 283.
47. A number of contemporaries applied the term "revolution" to the British expansion in India, e.g., Francklin, *History of the Reign of Shah-Aulum*, 1798, 185; Herrmann, *Gemählde von Ostindien*, 1799, 54; Dubois, *Description of the Character, Manners and Customs of the People of India*, 1817, xiv.
48. E. Burke, "Speech on Fox's India Bill" (December 1, 1783), in Burke, *India: Madras and Bengal 1774–1785*, 1981, 402.
49. Maurice, *Modern History of Hindostan*, 1802–10, vol. 1, 181. On the author see Grewal, *Muslim Rule in India*, 1970, 58–62.
50. Tott, *Memoirs of Baron de Tott*, 1786, vol. 1, x. Similar: Fischer, *Sibirische Geschichte*, 1768, 50.
51. Baumgarten and Semler, *Uebersetzung der Algemeinen Welthistorie*, 1744–67, vol. 21 (1760), 512.
52. Baumgarten and Semler, *Uebersetzung der Algemeinen Welthistorie*, 1744–67, vol. 21 (1760), 636–37.
53. Gibbon, *Decline and Fall of the Roman Empire*, 1994, vol. 3, 793, fn. 6. Similarly, Malcolm, *History of Persia*, 1829, vol. 1, 254–56.
54. Two centuries later, the Elizabethan writer Richard Knolles, still reprinted in the eighteenth century, takes the side of Timur in the struggle between the two "tyrants" Timur and Sultan Bajazit I: *Turkish History*, 1687–1700, vol. 1, 153–54, 157–58.
55. Voegelin, *Anamnesis*, 1966, 154, 156–59, 169–70; Nagel, *Timur der Eroberer*, 1993, 9–10. On the image of Timur in the eighteenth century see also Minuti, *Oriente barbarico*, 1994, 17ff., 22ff.; on the historical Timur see Manz, *Rise and Rule of Tamerlane*, 1989; Roemer, *Persien auf dem Weg in die Neuzeit*, 1989, 57–120; Nagel, *Timur der Eroberer*, 1993. George Frideric Handel's opera ("dramma per musica") *Tamerlano* was first staged in 1724. My analysis focuses on the *political* Timur leaving aside a different line of reception that emerged in the 1670s and placed Timur's amorous entanglements at the center of attention. Handel is part of that tradition.
56. This made it possible for British authors of the nineteenth century to claim the ambivalent tradition of Timur for the British raj.
57. D'Herbelot, *Bibliothèque Orientale*, 1777–79, vol. 3, 500–521.
58. Visdelou, "Histoire abregée de la Tartarie," 1779, 277–78.
59. D'Anville, *L'Empire Turc*, 1772, 28. See also Rennell, *Memoir of a Map of Hindoostan*, 1793, liv: Timur was "an inhuman monster."
60. Margat de Tilly, *Histoire de Tamerlan*, 1739, vol. 2, 385; also Catrou, *History of the Mogul Dynasty*, 1826, 8; Manucci, *Storia do Mogor*, 1906–8, vol. 1, 97–103. The peak of enthusiasm for Timur was reached with Pétis de la Croix, *Histoire de Timur-Bec*, 1723, vol. 4, 296–300; also Holberg, *Vergleichung der Historien und Thaten*, 1748–54, vol. 1, 29ff.
61. Margat de Tilly, *Histoire de Tamerlan*, 1739, vol. 2, 386–87.
62. Baumgarten and Semler, *Uebersetzung der Algemeinen Welthistorie*, 1744–67, vol. 22 (1761), 439.
63. White, *Institutes Political and Military . . . of Timour*, 1783; Remer, *Darstellung der Gestalt der historischen Welt in jedem Zeitraume*, 1794, 172.
64. Justi, *Vergleichungen*, 1762, 130ff.
65. White, *Institutes Political and Military . . . of Timour*, 1783, vii.

66. For example, Thornton, *Present State of Turkey*, 1809, lxii et seq.; Mills, *History of Muhammedanism*, 1817, 214–15.
67. Maurice, *Modern History of Hindostan*, 1802–10, vol. 2, vii, 3ff., 12–13.
68. Voltaire, "Essai sur les mœurs," in *Œuvres complètes de Voltaire*, vol. 24, 2011, 359–78, quote 375. See also a long editorial comment on Voltaire's perception of Timur: 359–63, unnumbered footnote. See Briant, *Alexandre des Lumières*, 2012, 104–9, 273–77, on Voltaire's image of Alexander.
69. On Joseph de Guignes, one of the greatest of eighteenth-century historians, see Minuti, *Oriente barbarico*, 1994, 141–69; Pocock, *Barbarism and Religion*, vol. 4, 2005, 133–53.
70. Gibbon, *Decline and Fall of the Roman Empire*, 1994, vol. 3, 828.
71. J. de Guignes, *Histoire générale des huns*, 1756–58, vol. 4, 13.
72. J. de Guignes, *Histoire générale des huns*, 1756–58, vol. 4, 27, 31.
73. Gibbon, *Decline and Fall of the Roman Empire*, 1994, vol. 3, 850, and he adds a characteristic footnote (850, fn. 67): "The Mogul emperor was rather pleased than hurt with the victory of a subject: a chess-player will feel the value of this encomium!"
74. Gibbon, *Decline and Fall of the Roman Empire*, 1994, vol. 3, 849.
75. Gibbon, *Decline and Fall of the Roman Empire*, 1994, vol. 3, 852.
76. Malcolm, *History of Persia*, 1829, vol. 1, 312; a similar view in Hammer-Purgstall, *Geschichte des Osmanischen Reiches*, 1827–35, vol. 1 (1827), 253–337.
77. Hammer-Purgstall, *Geschichte des Osmanischen Reiches*, 1827–35, vol. 1 (1827), 315–16.
78. Curzon, *Problems of the Far East*, 1894, 2.
79. Herrmann, *Gemählde von Ostindien*, 1799, 177.
80. Tucker, *Nadir Shah's Quest for Legitimacy*, 2006, 71–72.
81. Lockhart, *Nadir Shah*, 1938, 20. On the historical Nadir Shah see Avery, "Nâdir Shâh and the Afsharid Legacy," 1991; Axworthy, *Sword of Persia*, 2006; Tucker, *Nadir Shah's Quest for Legitimacy*, 2006 (with a useful chronology: xi–xiv); see also Subrahmanyam, *Explorations in Connected History*, 2005, 185–209.
82. Lockhart, *Nadir Shah*, 1938, 148–54. A highly dramatized narrative of the events is Claustre, *Histoire du Thamas Kouli-Kan*, 1743, 426ff., a mostly derivative work.
83. For example, Pufendorf et al., *Introduction à l'Histoire moderne*, 1753–69, vol. 7, 539.
84. Dalrymple, *Koh-i-Noor*, 2017.
85. Hanway, *Historical Account of the British Trade over the Caspian Sea*, 1753, vol. 1, 331.
86. Baumgarten, "Vorrede," 1744, 12.
87. A digest of those report for an eighteenth-century reading public was Marigny, *Histoire des révolutions de l'empire des Arabes*, 1750–52, vol. 4, 260–525. Nadir Shah is also included.
88. Voltaire, "Histoire de l'Empire de Russie sous Pierre le Grand," in *Œuvres complètes de Voltaire*, vol. 47 (1999), 913–14.
89. Excerpts in Laurens, *Les origines intellectuels de l'expédition d'Égypte*, 1987, 133–35.
90. On his biography see Lockhart, *Fall of the Safavi Dynasty*, 1958, 516–25.
91. The result was Clodius, *Chronicon Peregrinantis*, 1731. Krusinski's report—"very reliable" even by the standards of critical scholarship (Lockhart, "European Contacts with Persia 1350–1736," 1986, 409)—is extensively used, alongside many other sources, in the most respectable of several mid-seventeenth histories of modern Persia: Clairac, *Histoire de Perse depuis le commencement de ce siècle*, 1750.
92. Krusinski, *History of the Revolution in Persia*, 1728, vol. 1, 149.

93. Krusinski, *History of the Revolution in Persia*, 1728, vol. 2, 9.
94. Krusinski, *History of the Revolution in Persia*, 1728, vol. 2, 99.
95. Hammer-Purgstall, *Geschichte des Osmanischen Reiches*, 1827–35, vol. 8, 30; Orme, *History of the Military Transactions of the British Nation in Indostan*, 1763–78, vol. 1, 2.
96. See Laurens, *Les origines intellectuels de l'expédition d'Égypte*, 1987, 139–40.
97. On Fassmann as a major representative of early eighteenth-century orientalism see Dreyfürst, *Stimmen aus dem Jenseits*, 2014, 415–563.
98. Quelle, *Herkunft, Leben und Thaten des Persianischen Monarchens Schach Nadyr*, 1738, 573, 665.
99. Lockhart, *Nadir Shah*, 1938, 312; also C. Niebuhr, *Reisebeschreibung nach Arabien*, 1774–1837, vol. 2, 275.
100. Lockhart, *Nadir Shah*, 1938, 304–5.
101. J. Fraser, *History of Nadir Shah*, 1742, 130.
102. J. Fraser, *History of Nadir Shah*, 1742, 185, 220–23.
103. J. Fraser, *History of Nadir Shah*, 1742, 227–34.
104. Claustre, *Histoire du Thamas Kouli-Kan*, 1743, 437.
105. For example, see J.- P. Bougainville, *Parallèle de l'expédition d'Alexandre dans les Indes avec la conquête des mêmes par Thamas Kouli Khan*, 1752, 140–41, who mainly relies on Otter's travel account of 1748; Hanway, *Historical Account of the British Trade over the Caspian Sea*, 1753, vol. 4, 143–46.
106. Hanway, *Historical Account of the British Trade over the Caspian Sea*, 1753, vol. 4, 263.
107. Hanway, *Historical Account of the British Trade over the Caspian Sea*, 1753, vol. 4, 271–83. On Hanway see Pugh, *Jonas Hanway*, 1787.
108. *Ta'rikh-i-Nadiri*. William Jones's translation: Jones, *Histoire de Shah Nader*, 1770; also in Jones, *Works*, 1807, vols. 11 and 12 (on Nadir in the later stage of his career—Nadir's nadir, so to speak—see esp. book 6). See Franklin, *Orientalist Jones*, 2011, 64–66.
109. W. Jones, *Works*, 1807, vol. 11, iii.
110. Meiners, *Betrachtungen über die Fruchtbarkeit, oder Unfruchtbarkeit, über den vormahligen und gegenwärtigen Zustand der vornehmsten Länder in Asie*, 1795–96, vol. 1, 179. A similar assessment, though with less hyperbole, from the same year by the historian Thomas Maurice is quoted in Grewal, *Muslim Rule in India*, 1970, 60.
111. "Je suis celui que Dieu envoie contre les Nations sur lesquelles il veut faire tomber sa colère." Nadir quoted by Otter, *Voyage en Turquie et en Perse*, 1748, vol. 1, 414.
112. Bernoulli, *Des Pater Joseph Tieffenthaler's . . . Beschreibung von Hindustan*, 1785–88, vol. 2, pt. 2, 39.
113. Grewal, *Muslim Rule in India*, 1970, 67.
114. Malcolm paints the brutality of the conquest and occupation of Persia by the Afghans in the darkest colors. He estimates the demographic losses at nearly one million lives. Malcolm, *History of Persia*, 1829, vol. 1, 472.
115. From Indian sources he took the figure of (only) eight thousand deaths among the population of the city: Malcolm, *History of Persia*, 1829, vol. 2, 33.
116. More contemporary evidence of atrocities in Persia: Bonnerot, *La Perse dans la littérature et la pensée françaises au XVIIIe siècle*, 1988, 43–67.
117. Bonnerot, *La Perse dans la littérature et la pensée françaises au XVIIIe siècle*, 1988, 52.
118. Bonnerot, *La Perse dans la littérature et la pensée françaises au XVIIIe siècle*, 1988, 47.
119. E.g., Brougham, *Political Philosophy*, 1842–43, vol. 1, 125.

120. Wilson, *India Conquered*, 2016, 82.
121. W. Jones, *Works*, 1807, vol. 11, vii.
122. See as a general survey C. A. Bayly, *Indian Society and the Making of the British Empire*, 1988, 18–32, and a more dramatic political account: Wilson, *India Conquered*, 2016, ch. 3.
123. This had not escaped the notice of contemporary European observers, see Lach and Van Kley, *Asia in the Making of Europe*, 1993, 765–68.
124. E.g., J. Scott, *Historical and Political View of the Deccan*, 1791, 22. See also S. Gordon, *Marathas*, 1993, 178ff.
125. There has been considerable historiographical interest in late-eighteenth-century Mysore. For an introduction see Habib, *Confronting Colonialism*, 1999; Prakash, et al. *Haidar Ali and Tipu Sultan*, 2001; more specifically on Mysore politics and politico-religious culture see Brittlebank, *Tipu Sultan's Search for Legitimacy*, 1997.
126. Marshall, "Cornwallis Triumphant," 1992, 61ff.; Teltscher, *India Inscribed*, 1995, 229–58.
127. Teltscher, *India Inscribed*, 1995, 230.
128. Tennant, *Indian Recreations*, 1803, 184.
129. Maistre de la Tour, *History of Ayder Ali Khan*, 1784, vol. 1, v.
130. Maistre de la Tour, *History of Ayder Ali Khan*, 1784, vol. 1, 159.
131. See S. Gordon, *Marathas*, 1993, 158.
132. Robson, *Life of Hyder Ally*, 1786, 103.
133. Robson, *Life of Hyder Ally*, 1786, 105.
134. Fullarton, *A View of the English Interests in India*, 1788, 62.
135. Fullarton, *A View of the English Interests in India*, 1788, 63–65. Also Michaud, *Histoire des progrès et de la chûte de l'empire de Mysore*, 1801, vol. 1, 33ff.
136. Sprengel, *Geschichte der Maratten*, 1791, 13, 19. The sophistication of Sprengel's analysis becomes apparent when compared with other contemporary treatments of the same or related topics: naive narratives (J. Kerr, *Mahrattah State*, 1782) or simple chronicles of rulers (a prime example in Asian history is Hüllmann, *Geschichte der Mongolen*, 1796).
137. Sprengel, *Hyder Aly und Tippo Saheb*, 1801, 3. See also Perrin, *Voyage dans l'Indostan*, 1807, vol. 1, 193.
138. Sprengel. *Hyder Aly und Tippo Saheb*, 1801, 13–14.
139. Sprengel. *Hyder Aly und Tippo Saheb*, 1801, 34–36. There is a similar portrait of Tipu Sultan in Buchanan, *Journey from Madras*, 1807, vol. 1, 70ff., who emphasizes the decline of Mysore's economy after Haidar Ali.
140. Wilks, *Historical Sketches of the South of India*, 1810–17, especially vol. 2.
141. Mill, *History of British India*, 1817, vol. 2, 444.

CHAPTER IX. SAVAGES AND BARBARIANS

1. "Sûrement ces écrivains diraient aussi que tous les Nègres et tous les moutons se ressemblent; mais cela prouve seulement qu'il n'y ont pas regardé de si près que le berger et le marchand d'esclaves." Volney, *Œuvres*, 1989–98, vol. 2 (1989), 342.
2. The peak of Kangxi panegyrics is represented by d'Orléans, *Histoire des deux conquerans tartares*, 1690, 145ff.; Bouvet, *Histoire de l'Empereur de la Chine*, 1699, esp. 12–13, 18ff.; Du Halde, *Description géographique*, 1735, vol. 1, 545 –46; vol. 2, 5ff.; Mailla, *Histoire générale de la Chine*, 1777–80, vol. 11, 354ff.; Abel-Rémusat, *Nouveaux*

mélanges asiatiques, 1829, vol. 2, 21–44. Very interesting general reflections in Turgot, "Plan du premier discours sur la formation des gouvernement et le mélange des nations" [c. 1751], in Turgot, *Œuvres*, 1913–23, vol. 1 (1913), 289–90.

3. Gibbon, *Decline and Fall of the Roman Empire*, 1994, vol. 2, 534–47.
4. Fundamentally important for the transformation of travel reports into fiction are Lowes, *Road to Xanadu*, 1927 and Barrell, *Infection of Thomas De Quincey*, 1991.
5. This topic has been discussed frequently, see Landucci, *I filosofi e i selvaggi*, 1972; Krauss, *Zur Anthropologie des 18. Jahrhunderts*, 1979; Kohl, *Entzauberter Blick*, 1986; Batra, *Wild Men in the Looking Glass*, 1994; Ellingson, *Myth of the Noble Savage*, 2001 (mainly on American Indians); Muthu, *Enlightenment against Empire*, 2003, ch. 2.
6. S. G. Gmelin, *Reise durch Rußland zur Untersuchung der drey Natur-Reiche*, 1770–84, vol. 1, 44–47.
7. E.g., Societas Jesu, *Lettres édifiantes et curieuses*, 1780–83, vol. 22, 328–29; *Mémoires concernant l'histoire . . . des Chinois*, 1776–1814, vol. 3 (1788), 387–412 (an account of the Qing dynasty's war against the Miao people in 1775). See also J. de Guignes, *Histoire générale des huns*, 1756–58, vol. 2, 92.
8. Societas Jesu, *Lettres édifiantes et curieuses*, 1780–83, vol. 18, 413ff., esp. 430; Grosier, *Description générale de la Chine*, 1785, 212–13.
9. Crawfurd, *Journal of an Embassy to the Courts of Siam and Cochin China*, 1967, 177.
10. Crawfurd, *Journal of an Embassy to the Courts of Siam and Cochin China*, 1967, 488; Crawfurd, *Journal of an Embassy from the Governor General of India to the Court of Ava*, 1834, vol. 2, 170ff., 262ff.
11. Chardin, *Voyages du Chevalier Chardin en Perse*, 1735, vol. 1, 121.
12. Güldenstädt, *Reise durch Rußland und ins Caucasische Gebürge*, 1787–91, vol. 1, 471 (on the Ossetes); see also Pallas on the Chechens: *Bemerkungen auf einer Reise in die südlichen Statthalterschaften des Russischen Reichs*, 1799–1801, vol. 1, 418, and in general Pallas's magnificent enthnography of the peoples of the Caucasus: 364ff.
13. Reineggs, *Allgemeine historisch-topographische Beschreibung des Kaukasus*, 1796–97, vol. 1, 40.
14. Sommer, *Neuestes Gemälde von Asien*, 1834, vol. 1, 83–84.
15. Dampier, *A New Voyage round the World*, 1697, 485.
16. Lach and Van Kley, *Asia in the Making of Europe*, 1993, 1913. In the eighteenth century, the motif of cannibalism was mainly linked to the Pacific islands, as in Daniel Defoe's *Robinson Crusoe* (1719/20). More generally, Rennie, *Far-Fetched Facts*, 1996, 181–97. On the motif of cannibalism in America see Still, *Enlightenment Hospitality*, 2011, 87–135.
17. Stavorinus, *Reise nach dem Vorgebirge der Guten Hoffnung*, 1796, 59, an author who admits that he, like so many others, knows of cannibalism only by hearsay.
18. Gibbon, *Decline and Fall of the Roman Empire*, 1994, vol. 3, 589; 796 on cannibalism during the siege of Peking by Genghis Khan.
19. Marsden, *History of Sumatra*, 1811, 390. The true scandal, in European eyes, was *ritual* cannibalism without any urgent physical need. But need, too, could turn into some kind of routine, as pointed out in Steeb, *Versuch einer allgemeinen Beschreibung von dem Zustand der ungesitteten und gesitteten Voelker*, 1766, 51.
20. Quoted in Wurtzburg, *Raffles*, 1954, 559.
21. Wurtzburg, *Raffles*, 1954, 562.
22. Symes, *Account of an Embassy to the Kingdom of Ava*, 1800, 130–31
23. Symes, *Account of an Embassy to the Kingdom of Ava*, 1800, 133.
24. Landucci, *I filosofi e i selvaggi*, 1972, 389 and, in great detail, 394ff.

25. Krashenninikov, *Explorations of Kamchatka*, 1972, 70 (referring to "the Americans").
26. Krashenninikov, *Explorations of Kamchatka*, 1972, 193.
27. Krashenninikov, *Explorations of Kamchatka*, 1972, 242.
28. Krashenninikov, *Explorations of Kamchatka*, 1972, 275.
29. Krashenninikov, *Explorations of Kamchatka*, 1972, 205.
30. Steller, *Beschreibung von dem Lande Kamtschatka* 1774, 332. Orlando di Lasso (1532–1594): composer and master of vocal polyphony, employed at the Bavarian court.
31. Steller, *Beschreibung von dem Lande Kamtschatka* 1774, 288, fn a. On sexual practices in Kamchatka, especially pedophilia and transvestism, see 350–51. Herder explained the "impertinent lecherousness" of the people of Kamchatka with reference to the many volcanos and hot springs on the island: *Ideen zur Philosophie der Geschichte der Menschheit*, 1989, 301.
32. L.-A. Bougainville, *Voyage autour du monde*, 1982, 166. The classic passage on North America is Lafitau, *Mœurs des sauvages ameriquains,* 1724, vol. 1, 464.
33. Krashenninikov, *Explorations of Kamchatka*, 1972, 203. This was no utopian fantasy of European zealots: "Like the other tribes of north-east Siberia, the Itelmens had no hereditary chiefs, and their social equality was modified only insofar as the opinion of a particularly brave or intelligent man would be listened to at clan gatherings." Forsyth, *History of the Peoples of Siberia*, 1992, 132. Or is this judgment based on Krashenninikov?
34. Forsyth, *History of the Peoples of Siberia*, 1992, 131–36; for a wider context see Slezkine, *Arctic Mirrors*, 1994, 60–71.
35. Krashenninikov, *Explorations of Kamchatka*, 1972, 233.
36. Russian settlements surrounded by wooden palisades.
37. Steller, *Beschreibung von dem Lande Kamtschatka* 1774, 285.
38. See Meek, *Social Science and the Ignoble Savage*, 1976, passim and 129.
39. See Nippel, *Griechen, Barbaren und "Wilde,"* 1990; Dihle, *Die Griechen und die Fremden*, 1994; Müller, *Geschichte der antiken Ethnographie*, 1972–80.
40. See the major dictionaries: *Oxford English Dictionary*, 2nd ed., vol. 1, Oxford 1989, 945–47; *Trésor de la langue française*, vol. 4, Paris 1975, 162–64; Grimm, *Deutsches Wörterbuch*, vol. 1, 854, col. 1124.
41. "Les conquérants espagnols ne firent pas seulement pas entretenir ces canaux, mais les détruisirent de même que les chemins. Tel serait le sort de la Chine si les Européens s'en rendaient maître. Les Européens hors de leur pays sont aussi barbares que les Turcs et plus encore, car ils sont plus fanatiques." A. v. Humboldt, *Reise auf dem Río Magdalena durch die Anden und Mexico*, 1986, 272.
42. Justi, *Vergleichungen*, 1762, 239, 241.
43. Hammer-Purgstall, *Geschichte des Osmanischen Reiches*, 1827–35, vol. 3 (1828), 588; Knolles already expressed a similar viewpoint, *Turkish History*, 1687–1700, vol. 1, 765.
44. Gibbon, *Decline and Fall of the Roman Empire*, 1994, vol. 3, 583. Gibbon never applies the even more pejorative term "savages" to Muslims, but he uses it for the Christian mob during the First Crusade: "The promiscuous multitudes of Peter the Hermit were savage beasts, alike destitute of humanity and reason" (583).
45. To dramatic effect in Gibbon's portrait of Europe in the sixth century: Gibbon, *Decline and Fall of the Roman Empire*, 1994, vol. 2, ch. 42.
46. See Michel, *Un mythe romantique*, 1981, 37–38.
47. Muratori, quoted in Michel, *Un mythe romantique*, 1981, 39.
48. Hammer-Purgstall, *Geschichte des Osmanischen Reiches*, 1827–35, vol. 3 (1828), 221.

49. Hammer-Purgstall, *Geschichte des Osmanischen Reiches*, 1827–35, vol. 7 (1831), 1–4.
50. Hammer-Purgstall, *Geschichte der Goldenen Horde*, 1840, 38.
51. An important author in this connection was Giambattista Vico. See Rossi, *Dark Abyss of Time*, 1984, 183ff.
52. A different distinction, disregarded here, would be that between normative and empirical concepts. See the excellent study Medick, *Naturzustand und Naturgeschichte der bürgerlichen Gesellschaft*, 1972.
53. Pagden, *Fall of Natural Man*, 1982, 26.
54. Montesquieu, "De l'esprit des lois," 18/11, in *Œuvres* (1949–51), vol. 2, 537. Almost an echo of this is *Encyclopédie*, 1751–66, vol. 30, 188.
55. Ferguson, *Essay on the History of Civil Society*, 1966, 82, 98–99, 105; Salvucci, *Adam Ferguson*, 1972, 374.
56. For example, in the view of the French socialist Charles Fourier (1772–1837) who interposed a stage of "patriarchy" between savagery and barbarism.
57. Rougemont, *Précis d'ethnographie*, 1835–37, vol. 1, 19.
58. Hübner, *Kurtze Fragen aus der Politischen Historia*, 1727–31, vol. 9, 473.
59. W. Jones, "Fifth Anniversary Discourse" [1788], in *Works*, 1807, vol. 3, 75.
60. Richardson, *Dissertation on the Languages, Literature and Manners of Eastern Nations*, 1778, pt. 2, 141; Chateaubriand, *Itinéraire de Paris à Jerusalem*, 1968, 82.
61. W. R. Jones, "The Image of the Barbarian in Medieval Europe," 1971, 398.
62. Blome, *Geographical Description*, 1670, 88–89.
63. Report by a certain Mr. Whitting in Walpole, *Travels in Various Countries of the East*, 1820, 468.
64. Voltaire to Bailly, November 19, 1776, in Bailly, *Lettres sur l'origine des sciences*, 1776, 5; Chateaubriand, *Itinéraire des Paris à Jérusalem*, 1968, 82.
65. Blome, *Geographical Description*, 1670, 88–89.
66. Witsen, *Noord en Oost Tartayre*, 1705; Avril, *Voyage en divers états d'Europe et d'Asie*, 1692. See also Lach and Van Kley, *Asia in the Making of Europe*, 1993, 1755–59.
67. Ides, *Three Years Travels from Moscow Over-Land to China*, 1706; Brand, *Beschreibung der Chinesischen Reise*, 1698; the standard edition of Ides and Brand is Hundt, *Beschreibung der dreijährigen chinesischen Reise*, 1999; Lorentz Lange's China journal in F. C. Weber, *Das veränderte Rußland*, 1738–39, pt. 1, 73–111; Bernard, *Recueil de voyages du Nord*, 1731–38, vols. 4, 8, and 10; *Relation de la Grande Tartarie*, 1737.
68. Du Halde, *Description géographique*, 1735, vol. 4, esp. 75–422. The eight voyages by Gerbillon are comprehensively summarized in Prévost, *Histoire générale des voyages*, 1746–59, vol. 9 (1749).
69. Messerschmidt, *Forschungsreise durch Sibirien 1720–1727*, 1962–77, also the book by a Swedish officer who accompied Messerschmidt from 1720 to 1922: Strahlenberg, *Das Nord- und Ostliche Theil von Europa und Asia*, 1730. Messerschmidt's travel diary was only known in manuscript to a few experts; only brief excerpts were published during the eighteenth century.
70. J. G. Gmelin, *Reise durch Sibirien von dem Jahr 1733 bis 1743*, 1751–52, vol. 1, 88.
71. Visdelou, "Histoire abregée de la Tartarie," 1779, 47.
72. Visdelou, "Histoire abregée de la Tartarie," 1779, 277–89, on the Yuan Dynasty.
73. Baumgarten and Semler, *Uebersetzung der Algemeinen Welthistorie*, 1744–67, vol. 21 (1760), 243.
74. Strahlenberg, *Das Nord- und Ostliche Theil von Europa und Asia*, 1730, 54.
75. Fischer, *Sibirische Geschichte*, 1768, 142.

76. A brief summary of contemporary knowledge is given in Pinkerton, *Modern Geography*, 1807, vol. 1, 52. The older usage is still found in Aikin, *Geographical Delineations*, 1806, vol. 1, 364.
77. Schmidt, *Forschungen im Gebiete der älteren religiösen, politischen und literärischen Bildungsgeschichte der Völker Mittel-Asiens*, 1824, 5. Similarly, Heeren, "Ideen," in Heeren. *Historische Werke*, 1821–26, vol. 10 (1824), 57; Heeren, *Historical Researches*, 1846, vol. 1, 7, fn. 8. On semantics see Klaproth, *Mémoires relatifs à l'Asie*, 1826–28, vol. 1, 461ff.
78. Wisotzki, *Zeitströmungen*, 1897, 444–45; Broc, *Les montagnes*, 1969, 56–70.
79. Joseph de Guignes arrived at similar results around the same time, basing himself on Chinese geographical works: *Histoire générale des Huns*, 1756–58, esp. vols. 2, pt. 2, and 3.
80. Gatterer, *Kurzer Begriff der Geographie*, 1789, vol. 2. Gatterer's nomenclature is quite unorthodox: "Mittelasien" includes Korea and Japan; South Asia encompasses the entire Southern belt from Anatolia via China through present-day Indonesia.
81. Quoted in Wisotzki, *Zeitströmungen*, 1897, 448, 455.
82. Pallas, *Observations sur la formation des montagnes*, 1779, 27.
83. Gay, *Enlightenment*. 1966–69, vol. 1, 77–78.
84. J. de Guignes, *Mémoire*, 1759. His principal critic was Cornelius de Pauw who, for once, was right. See also Zoli, *La Cina e la cultura italiana*, 1973, 140–49.
85. See Petri, *Urvolkhypothese*, 1990, 120ff.
86. Bailly, *Lettres sur l'Atlantide*, 1779, 220.
87. Bailly, *Lettres sur l'Atlantide*, 1779, 224–25, 228–29, 232. An early German exponent of the thesis of Tartary as the "original home" of mankind was Zimmermann, *Ueber die Verbreitung und Ausartung des Menschengeschlechts*, 1778, 116. In Britain, the final rejection of the thesis came in 1801 with Lord Woodhouselee's *Elements of General History*, 1825, vol. 2, 313–14.
88. Herder, *Ideen*, 1989, 386; Adler and Menze, *Herder on World History*, 1997, 200. As a result of lengthy considerations, Prichard opted for Iran: *Researches zur Philosophie der Geschichte der Menschheit*, 1837–47, vol. 4, 603.
89. Herder, *Ideen*, 1989, 218–19; Adler and Menze, *Herder on World History*, 1997, 170. On Herder's view of nomads see Muthu, *Enlightenment against Empire*, 2003, 238–46.
90. Herder, *Ideen*, 1989, 217; Adler and Menze, *Herder on World History*, 1997, 169.
91. Herder, *Ideen*, 1989, 218, 700–701, also 881. An entirely different story is told by the great geographer Carl Ritter: that of the slow growth of civilization among the Mongols after Genghis Khan. C. Ritter, *Erdkunde*, 1832–47, vol. 2 (1833), 388–95.
92. Raynal, *Histoire philosophique et politique*, 1775, vol. 1, 541.
93. Raynal, *Histoire philosophique et politique*, 1775, vol. 1, 541. The standard source, probably known to Raynal, was Georgius, *Alphabetum Tibetanum*, 1762.
94. On Herder as a supreme empiricist see Zammito, *Kant, Herder, and the Birth of Anthropology*, 2002, 309–45.
95. Herder, *Ideen*, 1989, 224.
96. Herder, *Ideen*, 1989, 218; Adler and Menze, *Herder on World History*, 1997, 169.
97. Hegel, *Vorlesungen über die Philosophie der Weltgeschichte: Berlin 1822/1823*, 1996; an English translation (minus the editorial comment) of this superb edition is Hegel, *Lectures on the Philosophy of World History*, 2011.
98. Hegel, as usual, was very well informed. He read many of the reports sent by the ex-Jesuits from Peking and edited by the abbé Grosier. See the editorial comment in Hegel, *Vorlesungen über die Philosophie der Weltgeschichte: Berlin 1822/1823*, 1996, 538–40.

99. Hegel, *Die orientalische Welt*, 1923, 332: "Die Mongolen herrschen über China, und ihm ist das andere Mongolische unterworfen. . . . Wir verstehen unter Mongolen auch die Mandschu, die über China herrschen. Sie hängen mit den eigentlichen Mongolen nicht zusammen und gehören zu den Tungusen."
100. Hegel, *Die orientalische Welt*, 1923, 336. On Lamaism in Tibet see also Hegel, *Lectures on the Philosophy of World History*, 2011, 293–303.
101. Hegel, "Vorlesungen über die Philosophie der Geschichte. Einleitung. Geographische Grundlagen der Weltgeschichte," in Hegel, *Sämtliche Werke*, 1927–40, vol. 11 (1928), 132; in a different textual tradition also Hegel, *Lectures on the Philosophy of World History: Introduction*, 1975, 157ff.
102. The most pertinent texts are: Petech, *I missionari Italiani nel Tibet e nel Nepal*, 1954–56, vol. 5, 32–40, 44–46. Of special ethnographic interest are chapters 13 to 18 of book 2 in Petech's edition of Desideri's *Relazione*: vol. 6, 75–114.
103. Du Halde, *Description géographique*, 1735, vol. 4, 27; *The General History of China*, 1739, vol. 4, p. 132.
104. Hegel, *Lectures on the Philosophy of World History*, 2011, 302 (translation modified); Hegel, *Vorlesungen über die Philosophie der Weltgeschichte: Berlin 1822/1823*, 1996, 231.
105. Hegel, *Lectures on the Philosophy of World History*, 2011, 302.
106. See Fletcher, "Ch'ing Inner Asia," 1978, 52–56.
107. Du Halde, *Description géographique*, 1735, vol. 4, 38.
108. Plath, *Geschichte des östlichen Asiens*, 1830–31. See H. Franke, *Zur Biographie von Johann Heinrich Plath*, 1960, 11ff.
109. "C'est ainsi que dans l'empire de Russie il y a plus de différentes espèces, plus de singularités, plus de mœurs différentes que dans aucun pays de l'univers." Voltaire, "Histoire de l'empire de Russie sous Pierre le Grand" [1763], in *Œuvres complètes de Voltaire*, vol. 46 (1999), 472–73; Voltaire, *The History of Peter the Great*, 1848, vol. 1, 30.
110. *Relation de la Grande Tartarie*, 1737, 4.
111. Georgi, *Beschreibung aller Nationen des Rußischen Reichs*, 1776–80, vol. 2, 88. The entire second volume of this work is devoted to the "Tatar nations."
112. S. Turner, *Account of an Embassy to the Court of the Teshoo Lama*, 1800, 209, also 305.
113. Georgi, *Beschreibung aller Nationen des Rußischen Reichs*, 1776–80, vol. 2, 96.
114. For a full account of the Tungus, see Georgi, *Beschreibung aller Nationen des Rußischen Reichs*, 306–25; Georgi, *Bemerkungen einer Reise im Rußischen Reich im Jahre 1772*, 1775, 242ff; Pallas, *Reise durch die verschiedenen Provinzen des Rußischen Reiches*, 1771–76, vol. 3, 238–43; Fischer, *Sibirische Geschichte*, 1768, 110ff.
115. Georgi, *Beschreibung aller Nationen des Rußischen Reichs*, 1776–80, vol. 2, 392.
116. For example: J. G. Gmelin, *Reise durch Sibirien von dem Jahr 1733 bis 1743*, 1751-52, vol. 1, 283ff., 397ff.; vol. 2, 44ff., 351ff.
117. Georgi, *Beschreibung aller Nationen des Rußischen Reichs*, 1776–80, vol. 2, 395. On European perceptions of Asian shamanism see Flaherty, *Shamanism and the Eighteenth Century*, 1992, 45ff.
118. S. G. Gmelin, *Reise durch Rußland zur Untersuchung der drey Natur-Reiche*, 1770–84, vol. 2, 120–46, also vol. 1, 173–82; on the Don Cossacks also E. D. Clarke, *Travels in Various Countries of Europe, Asia and Africa* (1816–18), vol. 1, chs. 11 to 13.
119. Fischer, *Sibirische Geschichte*, 1768, 186ff., believes that the Cossacks themselves came to be civilized during this process of expansion.

120. "Ihro Zaare-Mayest. umb den Frieden zuerkauffen, sihet alsdann etwas Unkosten an sie zu wenden nicht an." Olearius, *Vermehrte Newe Beschreibung der Muscowitischen vnd Persischen Reyse*, 1656, 48.
121. Thus Kappeler, *Russian Empire*, 2001, 45. The following passage is based on A. W. Fisher, *Crimean Tartars*, 1978, 49–69; for Crimean history, mainly in the seventeenth century, see Klein, *The Crimean Khanate between East and West*, 2012.
122. Witsen, *Noord en Oost Tartarye*, 1705, vol. 2, 567.
123. Kleemann, *Reisen von Wien über Belgrad bis Kilianova*, 1771, 39, 148–49, 158.
124. S. Franke, *Die Reisen der Lady Craven durch Europa und die Türkei 1785–1786*, 1995, 169–70; the source is: Craven, *A Journey through the Crimea to Constantinopel*, 1789. The tsarina undertook her famous "Taurida Voyage" to the South from January to July 1787.
125. Peyssonnell, *Traité sur le commerce de la Mer Noire*, 1787, vol. 2, 235–36, 267–76.
126. Peyssonnell, *Traité sur le commerce de la Mer Noire*, 1787, vol. 2, 279. The autonomy of the great aristocratic houses is also emphasized in Pallas, *Bemerkungen auf einer Reise in die südlichen Statthalterschaften des Russischen Reichs*, 1799–1801, vol. 2, 357.
127. See A. W. Fisher, *Crimean Tatars*, 1978, 26. In this light, it was easy to give a propagandistic gloss to the deportation of the Crimean Tatars during World War II.
128. A. W. Fisher, *Crimean Tatars*, 1978, 17. See also Lazzerini, "The Crimea under Russian Rule," 1988, 125ff.
129. Tott, *Memoirs of Baron de Tott*, 1786, vol. 1, pt. 2, 135.
130. E. D. Clarke, *Travels in Various Countries of Europe, Asia and Africa*, 1816–18, vol. 2, 144–47. This account is confirmed by Pallas's depiction of devastated Kefe, although Pallas assures his readers that things were not so bad elsewhere in the Crimea: *Bemerkungen auf einer Reise in die südlichen Statthalterschaften des Russischen Reichs*, 1799–1801, vol. 2, 261–63, also 32–33. Many authors were similarly impressed by the fountains and aqueducts they saw in Islamic societies, regarding them as a technological speciality even of more backward peoples such as the Kurds: Kinneir, *Journey through Asia Minor, Armenia, and Koordistan*, 1818, 395.
131. E. D. Clarke, *Travels in Various Countries of Europe, Asia and Africa*, 1816–18, vol. 2, 145.
132. Pallas, *Bemerkungen auf einer Reise in die südlichen Statthalterschaften des Russischen Reichs*, 1799–1801. On this see Wendland, *Peter Simon Pallas*, 1991, 272–73, 474–83.
133. Pallas, *Bemerkungen auf einer Reise in die südlichen Statthalterschaften des Russischen Reichs*, 1799–1801, vol. 2, 360 (also 427, 440); Engelhardt and Parrott, *Reise in die Krym und den Kaukasus*, 1815, vol. 1, 29–30.
134. Pallas, *Bemerkungen auf einer Reise in die südlichen Statthalterschaften des Russischen Reichs*, 1799–1801, vol. 2, 368.
135. Engelhardt and Parrott, *Reise in die Krym und den Kaukasus*, 1815, vol. 1, 30.
136. Engelhardt and Parrott, *Reise in die Krym und den Kaukasus*, 1815, vol. 1, 30.
137. Engelhardt and Parrott, *Reise in die Krym und den Kaukasus*, 1815, vol. 1, 33.
138. Engelhardt and Parrott, *Reise in die Krym und den Kaukasus*, 1815, vol. 1, 48.
139. For a nuanced and not overly critical view of the treatment of Crimea during the first years of Russian rule see Jobst, "Vision und Regime," 2012, 215–21.
140. For a definition see Khazanov, *Nomads and the Outside World*, 1984, 14.
141. Hausleutner, *Geschichte der Araber in Sicilien*, 1791–92, vol. 1, iii (preface).

142. Pallas, *Sammlungen historischer Nachrichten über die Mongolischen Völkerschaften*, 1776–1801, vol.1, see also Pallas, *Reise durch die verschiedenen Provinzen des Rußischen Reiches*, 1771–76, vol. 1, 307ff. (on the Kalmyks).
143. Bergmann, *Nomadische Streifereien unter den Kalmüken in den Jahren*, 1804–5, esp. vol. 2, entitled *Die Kalmüken zwischen der Wolga und dem Don: Ein Sittengemählde*. This charming and profound text would merit extensive discussion.
144. Bergmann, *Nomadische Streifereien unter den Kalmüken in den Jahren*, 1804–5, vol. 2, 66ff.
145. C. Niebuhr, *Beschreibung von Arabien*, 1772, 379–99.
146. Volney, *Voyage en Égypte et en Syrie*, 1959, 195–214.
147. Especially Burckhardt, *Travels in Syria and the Holy Land*, 1822; Burckhardt, *Travels in Arabia*, 1829; Burckhardt, *Notes on the Bedouins and Wahábys*, 1830. Burckhardt wrote his books in English. Other important descriptions of nomadic life in the Middle East are Jaubert, *Voyage en Arménie et en Perse*, 1821, 251ff.; Malcolm, *History of Persia*, 1829, vol. 2, 61–63, 325–34, 431–40; Elphinstone, *Account of the Kingdom of Caubul*, 1839, vol. 1, 302ff.
148. Timkovski, *Voyage à Pekin*, 1827, vol. 1, 13. More evidence on North Africa in Thomson, *Barbary and Enlightenment*, 1987, 103–4.
149. Valentia, *Voyages and Travels to India*, 1809, vol. 2, 354.
150. C. Niebuhr, *Beschreibung von Arabien*, 1772, 379.
151. Thus Heeren, "Ideen," in *Historische Werke*, 1821–26, vol. 10 (1824), 58; Heeren, *Historical Researches*, 1846, vol. 1, 10.
152. C. Niebuhr, *Beschreibung von Arabien*, 1772, 380. As early as 1751 Turgot gave a similar analysis of rule in "small states": "Plan du premier discours sur la formation des gouvernement et le mélange des nations," in Turgot, *Œuvres*, 1913–23, vol. 1 (1913), 286.
153. An example in C. Niebuhr, *Reisebeschreibung nach Arabien*, 1774–1837, vol. 1, 292–93.
154. C. Niebuhr, *Beschreibung von Arabien*, 1772, 382. A similar argument in Volney, *Voyage en Égypte et en Syrie*, 1959, 211: The Arabs did nothing but defend their legitimate position under international law. On nomads according to the European *ius gentium* see Fisch, *Die europäische Expansion und das Völkerrecht*, 1984, 275ff.
155. Volney, *Voyage en Égypte et en Syrie*, 1959, 204; Pottinger, *Travels in Belochistan and Sinde*, 1816, 65–66.
156. On romantic and Victorian images of Arabs and Arabia see Tidrick, *Heart-Beguiling Araby*, 1989.
157. Falconer, *Remarks*, 1781, 321–52; Also of interest is Klaproth, *Tableaux historiques de l'Asie*, 1826, 233ff.
158. On Falconer's place in the history of environmental thought, see Glacken, *Traces on the Rhodian Shore*, 1967, 601–5.
159. Falconer, *Remarks*, 1781, 334.
160. Falconer, *Remarks*, 1781, 336, 339–40.
161. Falconer, *Remarks*, 1781, 352.
162. Pocock, "Gibbon's 'Decline and Fall,'" 1977; Pocock, "Gibbon and the Shepherds," 1981; these crisp articles have not been entirely superseded by Pocock's much more extensive treatment in *Barbarism and Religion*, especially vol. 6, 2015, 255–64. Still useful are a few pages in Burrow, *Gibbon*, 1985, 67–79, and on Gibbon's Eurasian take on the Middle Ages: Giarrizzo, *Gibbon*, 1954, 403ff.; Fowden, "Gibbon on Islam," 2016, is excellent.
163. Gibbon, *Decline and Fall of the Roman Empire*, 1994, vol. 1, 1023–83.

164. Montesquieu already considered the proximity of *les sauvages* to nature as a curse rather than a blessing as it made them victims of climate and vegetation.
165. Gibbon, *Decline and Fall of the Roman Empire*, 1994, vol. 3, 61.
166. For the nineteenth century, this is a major theme in C. A. Bayly, *Birth of the Modern World*, 2004, ch. 12.
167. Duchet, *Anthropologie et histoire*, 1971, 59.
168. For example Pastoret, *Histoire de la législation*, 1817–37, vol. 1, 22.
169. Heude, *Voyage up the Persian Gulf*, 1819, 36.
170. Roche, *La France des Lumières*, 1993, 64, 67.
171. Röttgers, *Kants Kollege und seine ungeschriebene Schrift über die Zigeuner*, 1993, 103.
172. Raffles, *History of Java*, 1817, 58.
173. Metcalf, *Ideologies of the Raj*, 1994, 123–31.
174. Herder, *Ideen*, 1989, 703.
175. Montesquieu, "De l'esprit des lois," 18/2, in *Œuvres complètes*, 1949–51, vol. 2, 532.
176. A summary of this discourse in Rougemont, *Précis d'ethnographie*, 1835–37, vol. 1, 7–8. See also Volney, *Voyage en Égypte et en Syrie*, 1959, 115–16; Elphinstone, *Account of the Kingdom of Caubul*, 1839, vol. 2, 73ff.; Malte-Brun, *Précis de la géographie universelle*, 1812–29, vol. 2 (1812), 611.
177. See Olschki, *Marco Polo's Asia*, 1960, 368–81; Daftary, *Assassin Legends*, 1994. Turgot mentions this case in 1748, pillorying it as an example of despotic superstition: Turgot, "Recherches sur les causes des progrès et de la décadence des sciences et des arts" [1748], in Turgot, *Œuvres*, 1913–23, vol. 1 (1913), 134.
178. Engels, "Die Lage der arbeitenden Klasse in England," 1957, 320–23.
179. Mayhew, *London Labour and the London Poor*, 1861–62, vol. 1, 1.
180. Mayhew, *London Labour and the London Poor*, 1861–62, vol. 1, 2.

CHAPTER X. REAL AND UNREAL DESPOTS

1. Cranmer-Byng, *An Embassy to China*, 1962, 131. The journal was first published in 1908 in a truncated and imperfect edition. The full manuscript, kept in Tokyo, was only made accessible in J. L. Cranmer-Byng's edition from which we quote.
2. Matthew 6:29. Cranmer-Byng, *An Embassy to China*, 1962, 124. But Macartney does not quote directly from the Gospels. As we will soon see, he recalls a "puppet show" by the same name that he had seen in his childhood.
3. Elphinstone, *History of India*, 1841, vol. 2, 61–62; Canetti, *Masse und Macht*, 1960, 488–500. Canetti calls him "the purest case of a paranoid ruler" (499). The assessment of a modern authority is more nuanced: Jackson, *The Delhi Sultanate*, 1999, 255–77. Jackson nicely notes that Muhammad's regime became "the prisoner of its own reputation for harshness" (270).
4. Hammer-Purgstall, *Geschichte des Osmanischen Reiches*, 1827–35, vol. 2 (1828), 65.
5. Martini, *De bello tatarico*, 1654, 134ff.; Parsons, *Peasant Rebellions*, 1970, 176–82.
6. Depending on the loyalties of the European observers: Manuzzi supported Aurangzeb in the succession struggle while Bernier took the side of the eventual loser, Aurangzeb's brother Dara Shukoh.
7. Knox, *Historical Relation*, 1681, 43–47.
8. Cantemir, *History of the Growth and Decay of the Ottoman Empire*, 1734–35, vol. 1, 249–51; an earlier source is Rycaut, *History of the Turkish Empire*, 1680, 89. An eyewitness account by the Venetian ambassador Pietro Foscarini from 1637 is quoted in Valensi, *Venise et la Sublime Porte*, 1987, 7–9. On the atrocities of Sultan Murad

IV see in great detail Hammer-Purgstall, *Geschichte des Osmanischen Reiches*, 1827–35, vol. 5 (1829), 187–88, 257–58, 283–94. Murad's bloody score was surpassed by Sultan Mawlay Isma'il of Maroc (r. 1672–1727) who was credited by European observers with forty thousand murders that he had committed in person. See Allison, *Crescent Obscured*, 1995, 53.

9. Hammer-Purgstall, *Geschichte des Osmanischen Reiches*, 1827–35, vol. 5 (1829), 658. The grand viziers of the Köprülü family—Mehmed (in office 1656–61), and his sons Fâzil Ahmed (1661–76) and Fâzil Mustafa (1689–91)—are usually portrayed in the accounts of contemporary European observers as highly competent, immune to corruption, and devoted to the public good.
10. The tyrannical excesses of Shah Safi I were described by eyewitnesses like the German scholar and diplomat Adam Olearius. See his *Vermehrte Newe Beschreibung*, 1656, 654–62. The best European source is Du Mans, *Estat de la Perse*, 1890, 14ff., 151ff., a report for the minister Colbert that remained unpublished in its day; a new edition is Richard, *Raphaël du Mans*, 1995, vol. 2. The Capuchin Father Du Mans who spent decades at Isfahan was Engelbert Kaempfer's teacher and friend and shared his knowledge with the younger scholar. Kaempfer himself, in his Latin report of 1712 (*Am Hofe des persischen Großkönigs*, 1940, 47–61), strove for a characteristically balanced assessment of Safi II, whom he met in person. Krusinski's popular account (*Revolution in Persia*, 1728, vol. 1, 43–48, 54–58) was not based on first-hand knowledge. It presented both Safi shahs as uninhibited butchers. Modern authorities hardly paint a brighter picture, see Roemer, *Persien*, 1989, 330–31, 359–61.
11. See the enthusiatic praise of both emperors from the pen of an author who otherwise was an avatar of the new "Sinophobia" of the 1790s: Barrow, *Travels in China*, 1806, 412–14.
12. W. Jones, "On the Second Classical Book of the Chinese," in *Works*, 1807, vol. 4, 117.
13. J. de Guignes, *Histoire générale des Huns*, 1756–58, vol. 3, 138–90. See also this authority's finely balanced evaluation of the tyrannical first emperor, Qin Shi Huangdi: vol. 1, pt. 1, 18–19.
14. Gibbon, *Decline and Fall of the Roman Empire*, 1994, vol. 3, 542.
15. For example: Cantemir, *History of the Ottoman Empire*, 1734–35, vol. 1, 96, 172, 217, and Hammer-Purgstall, who devotes almost an entire volume to this great monarch: *Geschichte des Osmanischen Reiches*, 1827–35, vol. 3 (1828), as a summary: 488, 492ff.
16. Mill, *History of British India*, 1817, vol. 1, 594–607.
17. Orme, *History of the Military Transactions*, 1763–78, vol. 1, 18.
18. Ruangsilp, *Dutch East India Company Merchants*, 2007, 143–47.
19. Brougham, *Political Philosophy*, 1842–43, vol. 1, 131; Symes, *Account of an Embassy to the Kingdom of Ava*, 1800, 6ff.
20. Olearius, *Vermehrte Newe Beschreibung*, 1656, 335–42, esp. 339; Bietenholz, *Pietro Della Valle*, 1962, 188ff.; Roubaud, *Histoire générale de l'Asie*, 1770–72, vol. 2, 590ff.; Malcolm, *History of Persia*, 1829, vol. 2, 366–78. On possible good reasons for killing a crown prince see the reflections in Voltaire, "Histoire de l'Empire de Russie sous Pierre le Grand," in *Œuvres complètes de Voltaire*, vol. 47, 1999, 849–50.
21. Cranmer-Byng, *An Embassy to China*, 1962, 124.
22. Robertson, *Progress of Society in Europe*, 1972, 81, also 131.
23. Wilks, *Historical Sketches of the South of India*, 1810–17, vol. 1, 22.
24. Crawfurd, *Journal of an Embassy to the Courts of Siam and Cochin China*, 1967, 136–37, also 327.

25. Turgot, "Recherches sur les causes des progrès et de la décadence des sciences et des arts" [1748], in Turgot, *Œuvres*, 1913–23, vol. 1 (1913), 124, points out that the most tender human being is transmogrified into a criminal once he slips into the role of a despot.
26. Thus Dow, *History of Hindostan*, 1812, vol. 1, xiii.
27. D'Ohsson, *Tableau générale de l'Empire Othoman*, 1787–1824, vol. 1, xxxii–xxiii. See also the strict distinction between system and operative politics in Guer, *Mœurs et usages des Turcs*, 1747, vol. 2, 355ff.
28. Aristotle, *Politics*, 1967, 1285a 18–23, 249. As Hume or Gibbon might have added: What used to be character turned into habit.
29. On the origins of an East-West dichotomy see Springborg, *Western Republicanism*, 1992, 23ff.; on Greek views of Indian politics: Embree, "Oriental Despotism," 1971, 255–64.
30. Examples in D. Forbes, *Hume's Philosophical Politics*, 1975, 142–45, 150, 155ff.
31. Hume, *History of England,* 1983, vol. 4, 360.
32. Hume, *History of England,* 1983, vol. 4, 346. The wider context of these remarks is Hume's analysis of "Tudor despotism." See James Harris, *Hume,* 2015, 368–87.
33. See Mandt, "Tyrannis, Despotie," 1990, 672–76; still unsurpassed: Koebner, "Despot and Despotism," 1951.
34. Valensi, *Venise et la Sublime Porte*, 1987, 97–99; Valensi, "The Making of a Political Paradigm," 1990, 191ff.
35. On the topic of oriental despotism in seventeenth-century travel literature see Grosrichard, *The Sultan's Court,* 1998, chs. 1–2; Krader, *The Asiatic Mode of Production,* 1975, 19–28, as well as (partly based on Krader) O'Leary, *The Asiatic Mode of Production*, 1989, 51–58.
36. Shackleton, *Essays on Montesquieu*, 1988, 483. There is a rich literature on Montesquieu's concept of despotism. A classic is Richter, *The Political Theory of Montesquieu*, 1977, 45–50, 71, 77ff. On *oriental* despotism in Montesquieu see Curtis, *Orientalism and Islam*, 2009, 72–102. See also Young, "Montesquieu's View of Despotism," 1978.
37. Montesquieu, "Considérations sur les causes de la grandeur des Romains et de leur decadence," ch. 14, in *Œuvres complètes de Montesquieu*, vol. 2 (2000), 193–98. Montesquieu cites Paul Rycaut's 1668 description of Turkey as his source for this assertion (in the French edition of 1678).
38. Montesquieu, "De l'esprit des lois," 5/14, in *Œuvres*, 1949–51, vol. 2, 294–95; Montesquieu, *Spirit of the Laws*, 1989, 61.
39. "La partie du monde où le despotisme est, pour ainsi dire, naturalisé, qui est l'Asie." Montesquieu, "De l'esprit des lois," 5/14, in *Œuvres*, 1949–51, vol. 2, 296; Montesquieu, *Spirit of the Laws*, 1989, 63.
40. Montesquieu, "De l'esprit des lois," 18/19, in *Œuvres complètes*, 1949–51, vol. 2, 365; also 17/6, vol. 2, 529.
41. Montesquieu, "De l'esprit des lois," 17/3, in *Œuvres complètes*, 1949–51, vol. 2, 524–26.
42. On Montesquieu as a methodologist of the "ideal type" see Cassirer, *Philosophy of the Enlightenment*, 1951, 210–12.
43. Montesquieu, "De l'esprit des lois," 3/9, in *Œuvres complètes*, 1949–51, vol. 2, 259; Montesquieu, *Spirit of the Laws*, 1989, 28.
44. Montesquieu, "De l'esprit des lois," 5/11, in *Œuvres complètes*, 1949–51, vol. 2, 290–91; Montesquieu, *Spirit of the Laws*, 1989, 57.

45. An example is the Baron de Tott who spent the years 1769 to 1774 as a military advisor in the Ottoman Empire. On Montesquieu's influence on him see Çırakman, *From the "Terror of the World" to the "Sick Man of Europe,"* 2002, 141–45.
46. My 1998 thesis of a highly selective reading of Chardin by Montesquieu has later been supported by a historical sociologist: "In his thousands of pages, Chardin had offered a wealth of other accurate information about Iranian society that Montesquieu found no use for." Arjomand, "Coffeehouses, Guilds and Oriental Despotism," 2004, 30.
47. Chardin, *Voyages du Chevalier Chardin en Perse,* 1735, vol. 3, 289.
48. Chardin, *Voyages du Chevalier Chardin en Perse,* 1735, vol. 3, 295–96.
49. See Dubos, *Reflexions*, 1719, vol. 2, 192: The tyranny of Roman emperors was only aimed at the elite, never at the people.
50. Montesquieu, "De l'esprit des lois," 2/5, in *Œuvres complètes*, 1949–51, vol. 2, 249; Montesquieu, *Spirit of the Laws*, 1989, 20. That this is true for *all* despots was a long-lived claim with evidence ranging from Tavernier, *Nouvelle relation*, 1675, 226, to D. Stewart, "Lectures on Political Economy" [1809–10], in *Collected Works*, 1854–60, vol. 8 (1855), 390.
51. One example among many: Bruin, *Voyages,* 1718, vol. 1, 208.
52. Chardin, *Voyages du Chevalier Chardin en Perse,* 1735, vol. 3, 296–99, 314; Montesquieu, "De l'esprit des lois," 5/14, in *Œuvres complètes*, 1949–51, vol. 2, 295–96.
53. Justi, *Vergleichungen*, 1762, 98–102, 330–36, 390–93. On the much-underrated political theory that Justi developed in many other works see Adam, *The Political Economy of J.H.G. Justi*, 2006, 93–141.
54. Chardin, *Voyages du Chevalier Chardin en Perse,* 1735, vol. 3, 313–14; Bruin, *Voyages,* 1718, 206–7.
55. Robertson, *Progress of Society in Europe*, 1972, 11.
56. Chardin, *Voyages du Chevalier Chardin en Perse,* 1735, vol. 3, 322.
57. Bernier, *Travels in the Mogul Empire,* 1934, 204. A similar thought had been uttered a few decades earlier by Sir Thomas Roe, an English ambassador to the Mughal court.
58. Montesquieu, "De l'esprit des lois," 5/14, in *Œuvres complètes*, 1949–51, vol. 2, 294.
59. Chardin, *Voyages du Chevalier Chardin en Perse,* 1735, vol. 3, 339–40, 344–49. See also Kaempfer, *Am Hofe des persischen Großkönigs*, 1940, 89–95.
60. Chardin, *Voyages du Chevalier Chardin en Perse,* 1735, vol. 3, 343–44.
61. Esp. Chardin, *Voyages du Chevalier Chardin en Perse,* 1735, vol. 3, 368.
62. Chardin, *Voyages du Chevalier Chardin en Perse,* 1735, vol. 3, 368.
63. Chardin, *Voyages du Chevalier Chardin en Perse,* 1735, vol. 3, 369, on religious tolerance in Persia (that did not, however, apply to the Christian mission) see 426ff.
64. Chardin, *Voyages du Chevalier Chardin en Perse,* 1735, vol. 3, 369.
65. Chardin, *Voyages du Chevalier Chardin en Perse,* 1735, vol. 3, 415, 420–21.
66. Montesquieu, "Considérations sur les causes de la grandeur des Romains et de leur decadence," ch. 22, in *Œuvres complètes*, 1949–51, vol. 2, 202; Montesquieu, *Considerations on the Causes of the Grandeur and Decadence of the Romans*, 1882, 460.
67. A magisterial survey of the issue of "oriental despotism" up to Montesquieu is Rubiés, "Oriental Despotism and European Orientalism," 2005.
68. Lavie, *Des corps politiques et de leur gouvernements*, 1764, vol. 1, 228.
69. Venturi, *L'antichità svelata*, 1947, 29.
70. Boulanger, "Recherches sur les origines du despotisme oriental" [1761], in *Œuvres*, 1794, vol. 3, 1–182; summarized in "Essai philosophique sur le gouvernmement," in *Œuvres*, 1794, vol. 3, 215–16, 224–27, 229, 236.

71. See the "Lettre de l'auteur à M. *** [Helvétius]," composed by friends of the deceased philosopher and appended to the first edition of his *Recherches* (*Œuvres*, vol. 3, 1–9). On the letter see Venturi, *L'antichità svelata*, 1947, 66ff.
72. Wilks, *Historical Sketches of the South of India*, 1810–17, vol. 1, 25, 29.
73. Turgot, "Plan du premier discours sur la formation des gouvernements et le mélange des nations," in Turgot, *Œuvres*, 1913–23, vol. 1 (1913), 290–94. Many resonances of Turgot's interpretation of despotism in the context of a theory of the emergence of the state can be found in the 1790s in Heeren, "Ideen," in *Historische Werke*, 1821–26, vol. 10 (1824), 12–14, 66–70, and also in Heeren's description of ancient Iran: 440ff.
74. The figure of the prime minister under a despotic regime was a source of particular fascination to Europeans. See, e.g., Thévenot, *Travels*, 1687, vol. 1, 63–65; Pitton de Tournefort, *Relation*, 1717, vol. 2, 24–27; *Universal History*, 1779–84, vol. 37, 27–28.
75. Turgot, "Plan du premier discours sur la formation des gouvernements et le mélange des nations," in Turgot, *Œuvres*, 1913–23, vol. 1 (1913), 294; English translation in D. Gordon, *The Turgot Collection*, 2011, 368. On propaganda and brainwashing in despotism, see D. Stewart, "Lectures," in *Collected Works*, 1854–58, vol. 8, 395ff.
76. In 1792 despotism is then reduced by the influential British-Indian colonial politician Charles Grant to the predominance of a heathen religion in the minds of the populace: Embree, *Charles Grant*, 1962, 146.
77. Condorcet, *Esquisse d'un tableau historique des progrès de l'esprit humain*, 1988, 120; Condorcet, *Outlines of an Historical View of the Progress of the Human Mind*, 1796, 60.
78. Walckenaer, *Essai sur l'histoire de l'espèce humaine*, 1798, 278–79.
79. Virey, *Histoire naturelle du genre humain*, 1824, vol. 3, 225. Rycaut already makes a very similar argument, *Present State of the Ottoman Empire*, 1668, 3.
80. Linguet, *Du plus heureux gouvernement*, 1774, vol. 1, 10, 12.
81. Linguet, *Du plus heureux gouvernement*, 1774, vol. 1, 18
82. Linguet, *Du plus heureux gouvernement*, 1774, vol. 1, 22–23.
83. Linguet, *Du plus heureux gouvernement*, 1774, vol. 1, 34.
84. Crawfurd, *Indian Archipelago*, 1820, vol. 3, 11.
85. Crawfurd, *Indian Archipelago*, 1820, vol. 3, 26.
86. Malcolm, *History of Persia*, 1829, vol. 1, 379ff., 384–85; vol. 2, 2, 41; also Poivre, "Voyage de Pierre Poivre en Cochinchine," 1885, 473–74; Grose, *A Voyage to the East Indies*, 1772, vol. 1, 85–86; Heeren, "Ideen," in *Historische Werke*, 1821–26, vol. 10 (1824), 79, 81; Ferrières-Sauvebœuf, *Mémoires historiques*, 1790, vol. 1, iii–iv; Ramsay, *An Essay upon Civil Government*, 1732, iv (and passim).
87. For example, Tennant, *Thoughts on the Effects of the British Government*, 1807, 76ff.
88. See Laurens, *Les origines intellectuels*, 1987, 67–78. A slightly different reading of Volney from my own is to be found in Harvey, *The French Enlightenment and Its Others*, 2012, 187–91.
89. Volney, "Les ruines, ou méditation sur les révolutions des empires," in Volney, *Œuvres*, 1989–98, vol. 1, 217–18.
90. A very similar analysis made in a different context is Turpin, *Histoire civile et naturelle du royaume de Siam*, 1771, vol. 1, 79ff., 103ff.
91. Volney, *Voyage en Égypte et en Syrie*, 1959, 114.
92. Volney, *Voyage en Égypte et en Syrie*, 1959, 400–406. Against Montesquieu's coupling of despotism and climate, see the summary account in Murray, *Enquiries Historical and Moral*, 1808, 139–48.

93. Volney, *Voyage en Égypte et en Syrie*, 1959, 361ff.
94. Volney, *Voyage en Égypte et en Syrie*, 1959, 395, 397–98.
95. Ferguson, *Essay on the History of Civil Society*, 1966, 270. Similarly Malte-Brun, *Précis de la géographie universelle*, 1812–29, vol. 2 (1812), 596.
96. Meiners, *Betrachtungen*, 1795–96, vol. 1, 37, 172.
97. Hennings here implies close parallels between enfeoffed feudal lords in Europe and in India.
98. Hennings, *Gegenwärtiger Zustand*, 1784–86, vol. 1, 12–13.
99. Barrow, *A Voyage to Cochin China*, 1806, 333; Crawfurd, *Journal of an Embassy to the Courts of Siam and Cochin China*, 1967, 487.
100. T. B. Clarke, *Publicistical Survey*, 1791, 8.
101. T. B. Clarke, *Publicistical Survey*, 1791, 8.
102. *Durchläuchtige Welt*, 1710–11, vol. 3 (pt. 7), 16, 48, 72–73, 86–87.
103. Symes, *An Account of an Embassy to the Kingdom of Ava*, 1800, 176.
104. Raynal, *Histoire philosophique et politique*, 1775, vol. 1, 141–45.
105. Castilhon, *Considérations*, 1769, 244–45; Thunberg, *Reise durch einen Theil von Europa, Afrika und Asien*, 1794, vol. 2, pt. 2, 18.
106. Pinkerton, *Modern Geography*, 1807, vol. 2, 184.
107. G. Forster, *A Journey from Bengal to England*, 1808, vol. 1, 328ff.; Malcolm, "Sketch of the Sikhs," 1810, 240; Wilks, *Historical Sketches of the South of India*, 1810–17, vol. 1, 28. More on interpretations of Sikh politics in Khurana, *British Historiography on the Sikh Power*, 1985, chs. 1–2. Georgi portrays the political system of the Kyrgyz people as democratic: *Beschreibung aller Nationen des Rußischen Reichs* (1776–80), vol. 2, 216–17.
108. Voltaire, "Commentaire sur L'Esprit des lois" [1777], in *Œuvres complètes de Voltaire*, vol. 80B, 2009, 339.
109. Voltaire, "Supplément au siècle de Louis XIV" [1753], in *Œuvres complètes de Voltaire*, vol. 32C, 2012, 334–35. See also Richter, "Despotism," 1973, 1–11.
110. Richardson, *Dissertation on the Languages, Literature and Manners of Eastern Nations*, 1778, pt. 2, 151–52, also 353, 365. For India see Orme, *Historic Fragments of the Mogul Empire*, 1974, 255: The greater the spatial distance towards the court, the weaker the despot's power.
111. For an extensive discussion see Whelan, "Oriental Despotism," 2001.
112. On his biography see Schwab, *Vie d'Anquetil-Duperron*, 1934. Anquetil's significance for the debate on despotism was powerfully pointed out by Franco Venturi: "Oriental Despotism," 1963, 136–41; important is Stuurman, "Cosmopolitan Egalitarianism," 2007. The place of Anquetil-Duperron within the various polemics of his time—with William Robertson, Cornelius de Pauw, the abbé Raynal, and others—is carefully outlined in Imbruglia, "Tra Anquetil-Duperron et 'L'Histoire des deux Indes,'" 1994.
113. Anquetil-Duperron, *Législation orientale*, 1778, vi.
114. Schwab, *Oriental Renaissance*, 1984, 17.
115. Anquetil-Duperron, *L'Inde en rapport avec l'Europe*, 1798, vol. 1, viii.
116. Kaiser, "The Evil Empire?," 2000, 17. In terms of international politics, this group favored close relations between France and the Ottoman Empire.
117. One could even follow Stuurman and regard Anquetil-Duperron as a global thinker dedicated to "a life-long defense of the equality and dignity of non-European peoples, from India to the Americas and the Arctic zone." Stuurman, "Cosmopolitan Egalitarianism," 2007, 256.

118. Anquetil-Duperron, *Législation orientale*, 1778, "Dédicace."
119. Anquetil-Duperron, *Législation orientale*, 1778, 1.
120. Anquetil-Duperron, *Législation orientale*, 1778, 45. Anquetil's chief authorities are Chardin for Iran and Sir James Porter for the Ottoman Empire; for Mughal India that he knew very well, he relied on sources in Persian, the official language of the Mughal Empire; see, for example, 41–42, 193–209.
121. Anquetil-Duperron, *Législation orientale*, 1778, 16.
122. Anquetil-Duperron, *Législation orientale*, 1778, 179–80.
123. Anquetil-Duperron, *Législation orientale*, 1778, 200.
124. Anquetil-Duperron, *Législation orientale*, 1778, 18, 31–32, 175–77, 212ff.
125. Anquetil-Duperron, *Législation orientale*, 1778, 32.
126. On the French (non-)reception of Anquetil-Duperron see Imbruglia, "Despotisme et féodalité" 1995, 108–11.
127. Meiners, *Grundriß der Geschichte der Menschheit*, 1793, 204–19.
128. Brougham, *Political Philosophy*, 1842–43, vol. 1, 102, 105, 108, 119.
129. Guha, *Rule of Property*, 1963, on Rouse: 50–60; Minuti, "Proprietà della terra," 1978, 103–23.
130. Rouse, *Dissertation*, 1791, 20.
131. Rouse, *Dissertation*, 1791, 77.
132. Rouse, *Dissertation*, 1791, 91–93, 95, 107–9.
133. Rouse, *Dissertation*, 1791, 180.
134. This is a weaker formulation than the one used in the German original of this book. I gratefully accept the critique in Tzoref-Ashkenazi, "Romantic Attitudes toward Oriental Despotism," 2013, 280, 318.
135. See Syndram, *Thron des Großmoguls*, 1996.
136. Plant, *Handbuch einer vollständigen Erdbeschreibung und Geschichte Polynesiens*, 1792–99, vol. 1, 130–31; similar remarks in Raffles, *History of Java*, 1817, vol. 1, 65–66, 76, 151, 266ff.; Tombe, *Voyage aux Indes Orientales*, 1810, vol. 1, 213; Percival, *Account of the Island of Ceylon*, 1805, 192, 199–200, 280, 363.
137. Raynal, *Histoire philosophique et politique*, 1775, vol. 1, 351.
138. Anquetil-Duperron, *L'Inde en rapport avec l'Europe*, 1798, vol. 1, iii; Sonnerat, *Voyages aux Indes Orientales*, 1782, vol. 2, 18; Langlès, *Monuments anciens et modernes de l'Hindoustan*, 1821, vol. 1, 19, also 268.
139. Raynal, *Histoire philosophique et politique*, 1775, vol. 1, 29ff., 430–51.
140. See Marshall, "Introduction," *India: Madras and Bengal*, 1981, 23ff.; Marshall, "Introduction," in Burke, *India: The Launching of the Hastings Impeachment*, 1991, 31ff., and numerous remarks on Burke's views on many different kind of despotism in Whelan, *Edmund Burke and India*, 1996, esp. 230–42.
141. Whelan, *Edmund Burke and India*, 242–60. Whelan points out parallels between Burke and Voltaire (246).
142. Quoted in Marshall, *Impeachment of Warren Hastings*, 1965, 21.
143. Embree, *Imagining India*, 1989, 31.
144. Valentia, *Voyages and Travels to India*, 1809, vol. 1, 235–36.
145. See Jain, *Outlines of Indian Legal History*, 1966, 193ff.
146. McLaren, "From Analysis to Prescription," 1993, 470; for a different view: Stein, *Thomas Munro*, 1989, 218ff.; the military character of this concept is emphasized by Peers, *Between Mars and Mammon*, 1995, 44ff.
147. Zastoupil, *John Stuart Mill and India*, 1994, 26. See also Stokes, *The English Utilitarians and India*, 1959; Majeed, *Ungoverned Imaginings*, 1992, 144–45.

148. This was already understood by early modern commentators. See for example Palafox y Mendoza, *History of the Conquest of China*, 1676, 480–81; d'Orléans, *Histoire des deux conquerans tartares*, 1690; *Universal History*, 1779–84, vol. 7, 141–42.
149. Martini (*Histoire de la Chine*, 1692, vol. 1, 134–43) mentions a semimythical ruler Kieu (probably King Jie, traditionally 1728–1675 BCE, the last king of the Xia dynasty) who is described as a kind of Nero-like monster.
150. Justi, *Vergleichungen*, 1762, 144ff. Justi took much of his material from Du Halde, *Description géographique*, 1735, esp. vol. 1, 436–42. Justi has long been overlooked as a commentator on China, but see now Jacobsen, "Limits to Despotism," 2013, 367–70, and 384–85 on Justi's influence on Catherine the Great, 382 on that of his pupil Joseph von Sonnenfels on the Habsburg emperor Joseph II.
151. Appleton, *A Cycle of Cathay*, 1951, 63; Guy, *French Image of China*, 1963; Étiemble, *L'Europe chinoise*, 1989.
152. This is an interpretation already developed by Matteo Ricci, the founder of the Jesuit mission in China, who watched at close distance the less-than-autocratic political style of the Wan Li emperor (r. 1573–1620). The same view was explained at length in a popular book authored by the French Orientalist and royal historiographer to Louis XIII, Michel Baudier: *Histoire de la cour du roy de la Chine*, 1624, later much anthologized, for instance in Osborne, *Collection of Voyages and Travels*, 1745, vol. 2, 1–24 (esp. 11–13). A similar idea in Temple, "Of Heroic Virtue" (1694), in *Works*, 1814, vol. 3, 337.
153. Le Comte, *Nouveaux Mémoires sur l'état present de la Chine*, 1697, vol. 2, 1–92.
154. Du Halde, *Description géographique*, 1735, vol. 1, 120, also vol. 2, 9–11.
155. Du Halde, *Description géographique*, 1735, vol. 2, 12, 22; vol. 3, 128ff. The most important Jesuit writings on political patriarchalism were collected in *Mémoires concernant l'histoire . . . des Chinois*, 1776–1814, vol. 4 (1779), a kind of themed issue. Hegel later put this argument at the center of his interpretation of China.
156. Du Halde, *Description géographique*, 1735, vol. 1, 120.
157. Du Halde, *Description géographique*, 1735, vol. 2, 255ff. See also Societas Jesu, *Lettres édifiantes et curieuses*, 1780–83, vol. 2, 359ff., vol. 24, 125–35. The examination system in Tonking (Northern Vietnam) was organized along the Chinese model: Tissanier, *Relation du Voyage*, 1663, 122ff.
158. Du Halde, *Description géographique*, 1735, vol. 1, 120; vol. 2, 38; also Clerc, *Yu Le Grand et Confucius*, 1769, 419.
159. See, for example, Sangermano, *Description of the Burmese Empire*, 1885, 74ff.
160. Societas Jesu, *Lettres édifiantes et curieuses*, 1780–83, vol. 23 (1781), 164ff.
161. Pauw, *Recherches philosophiques sur les Egyptiens et les Chinois*, 1773, vol. 2, 330–31; Meiners, *Betrachtungen*, 1795–96, vol. 2, 158, 210ff.
162. All these idealizing motives are somewhat naively summarized in Raynal, *Histoire philosophique et politique*, 1775, vol. 1, 89–98; later in that work, the assessment becomes more realistic and critical: 563–64.
163. An exception in taking this issue seriously and discussing it a length is Patton, *Principles of Asiatic Monarchies*, 1801, 217ff.
164. Teng, "Chinese Influence on the Western Examination System," 1942–43.
165. Montesquieu, "De l'esprit des lois," 19/17–20, in *Œuvres*, 1949–51, vol. 2, 567–71.
166. Grosier, *Description générale de la Chine*, 1785, 509–22; Grosier, *De la Chine*, 1818–20, vol. 5, 209–69; also several artikel by Père Joseph Amiot in *Mémoires concernant l'histoire . . . des Chinois*, 1776–1814, vol. 6 (1780), 331ff.; vol. 8 (1782), 220ff.
167. Barrow, *Travels in China*, 1806, 392, 395, 397–98.

168. Cranmer-Byng, *An Embassy to China*, 1962, 238–39.
169. Grosier attacks him vehemently: *De la Chine*, 1818–20, vol. 1, xiv et seq. Grosier's *opus maximum* is the final word on China in the Jesuit tradition but its basic lines of interpretation had already been developed in the shorter first edition of 1785.
170. C.L.J. de Guignes, *Voyages à Peking*, 1808, vol. 2, 432.
171. C.L.J. de Guignes, *Voyages à Peking*, 1808, vol. 2, 450.
172. Volney, *Considérations*, 1788, summarized in Gaulmier, *L'idéologue Volney*, 1951, 126–32. See also Deneys, "Le récit de l'histoire selon Volney," 1989, 52–53.
173. Volney, *Voyage en Égypte et en Syrie*, 1959, 361.
174. Peyssonnell, *Examen*, 1788, 98–100.
175. Peyssonnell, *Examen*, 1788, 251–52.
176. Montesquieu, "De l'esprit des lois," 11/6, in *Œuvres*, 1949–51, vol. 2, 397, adds: it is exactly like that in Venice.
177. Hegel, *Lectures on the Philosophy of World History*, 2011, 226; Hegel, *Vorlesungen über die Philosophie der Weltgeschichte: Berlin 1822/1823*, 1996, 135.
178. Voltaire, "Essai sur les mœurs," in *Œuvres complètes de Voltaire*, vol. 26C, 2015, 260; in this assessment Voltaire follows the authority of Cantemir's *History of the Ottoman Empire*. A similar assessment is given in Pitton de Tournefort, *Relation*, 1717, vol. 2, 4; see also Gibbon's comment on the modernity of the early Janissaries: Gibbon, *Decline and Fall of the Roman Empire*, 1994, vol. 3, 817–18. During the eighteenth century, however, says Eton (*Survey of the Turkish Empire*, 1801, 28), the sultans had disciplined the Janissaries so harshly as to undermine the empire's military capability.
179. Robertson, *Progress of Society in Europe*, 1972, 147.
180. So too Hammer-Purgstall, *Geschichte des Osmanischen Reiches*, 1827–35, vol. 5 (1829), 552.
181. J. Porter, *Observations*, 1768, vol. 1, 84.
182. J. Porter, *Observations*, 1768, vol. 1, 107.
183. D'Ohsson, *Tableau générale de l'Empire Othoman*, 1788–24, esp. vol. 5; Hammer-Purgstall, *Des osmanischen Reiches Staatsverfassung*, 1815.
184. Thornton, *Present State of Turkey*, 1809, vol. 1, 89.
185. On Selim III and his age see S. J. Shaw, *Between Old and New*, 1971.
186. D'Ohsson, *Tableau générale de l'Empire Othoman*, 1788–1824, vol. 1, xxxiii; Dallaway, *Constantinopel Ancient and Modern*, 1797, 43. On the European fear of an "Ottoman Peter the Great" see Laurens, *Les origines intellectuels*, 1987, 173.
187. Hodgson, *The Venture of Islam*, 1974, vol. 3, 216.
188. Gibbon's views on despotism—Imperial Roman, Byzantine, and oriental—are a huge topic that cannot be dealt with adequately here. The key text is Gibbon, *Decline and Fall of the Roman Empire*, 1994, vol. 1, esp. chs. 3 and 7.
189. "On Asiatick History, Civil and Natural," in W. Jones, *Works*, 1807, vol. 3, 215.

CHAPTER XI. SOCIETIES

1. First published in 1822, ten years after Titsingh's death, as an English translation from his French manuscripts. Quoted from a modern edition: Titsingh, *Secret Memoirs of the Shoguns*, 2006, 174.
2. Montesquieu, "De l'esprit des lois," 19/4, in *Œuvres*, 1949–51, vol. 2, 558; Montesquieu, *Spirit of the Laws*, 1989, 310.
3. Montesquieu, "De l'esprit des lois," 19/16, in *Œuvres*, 1949–51, vol. 2, 566; Montesquieu, *Spirit of the Laws*, 1989, 317.

4. Montesquieu, "De l'esprit des lois," 19/18, in *Œuvres*, 1949–51, vol. 2, 568.
5. A careful explanation of Montesquieu's terminology is found in Binoche, *Introduction*, 1998.
6. For example: Francisci, *Ost- und West-Indischer wie auch Sinesischer Lust- und Stats-Garten*, 1668; Francisci, *Neu-polirter Geschicht- Kunst- und Sitten-Spiegel ausländischer Völcker*, 1670; Dharampal-Frick, *Indien im Spiegel deutscher Quellen*, 1994, 76–85; Kames, *Sketches of the History of Man*, 1778, vols. 1 and 2. Démeunier (*L'esprit des usages et des coutumes*, 1776) basically also belongs to this type of collector and arranger of vast amounts of material and Marvin Harris overstates his case when he calls him "possibly the greatest ethnographer of the eighteenth century" (*Rise of Anthropological Theory*, 1968, 17).
7. Riedel, "Gesellschaft, Gemeinschaft," 1975, 808.
8. M. Harbsmeier, *Wilde Völkerkunde*, 1994.
9. Krader, *The Asiatic Mode of Production*, 1975.
10. Krusenstern, *Voyage round the World*, 1813, vol. 1, 324.
11. Elphinstone, *An Account of the Kingdom of Caubul*, 1839, vol. 1, 74–76. Similarly on Bukhara: Burnes, *Travels into Bokhara*, 1834, vol. 1, 272ff. A rich and colorful text is also Joseph Rehmann's recollection of the fair at Makariev on the river Volga that he visited in 1805: Heissig, *Mongoleireise zur späten Goethezeit*, 1971, 99–121.
12. S. Anderson, *An English Consul in Turkey*, 1989, 7.
13. A. Hamilton, *New Account of the East Indies*, 1930, vol. 1, 48–49; S. Turner, *Account of an Embassy to the Court of the Teshoo Lama*, 1800, 72.
14. Le Comte, *Nouveaux Mémoires sur l'état present de la Chine*, 1697, vol. 1, 130–33.
15. Du Halde, *Description géographique*, 1735, vol. 1, 109. Plenty of material in support of this thesis can be found in Nieuhof, *An Embassy from the East-India Company of the United Provinces, to the Grand Tartar Cham*, 1669.
16. Kaempfer, *Geschichte und Beschreibung Japans*, 1777–79, vol. 1, 37; Kaempfer, *Engelbert Kaempfer in Siam*, 2003, 232; Baker, et al., *Van Vliet's Siam*, 2005, 1–20.
17. Justi, who draws on some of these sources, believed public order in Asian cities to be far superior to that in Europe: *Vergleichungen*, 1762, 255ff.
18. Chardin, *Voyages*, 1735, vol. 2, 1–120; Delisle and Pingré, *Description de la ville de Peking*, 1765, 7ff.
19. Bernier, *Travels in the Mogul Empire*, 1934, 239–40.
20. S. G. Gmelin, *Reise durch Rußland zur Untersuchung der drey Natur-Reiche*, 1770–84, vol. 2, 43ff.
21. Raynal, *Histoire philosophique et politique*, 1775, vol. 1, 186.
22. Poivre, *Un manuscrit inédit de Pierre Poivre*, 1968, 33.
23. Raynal, *Histoire philosophique et politique*, 1775, vol. 1, 186.
24. Graaff, *Oost-Indise spiegel*, 2010, 69–82; on the author and his text see Barend-van Haeften, *Oost-Indïe gespiegeld*, 1992, 131ff.; also Poivre, *Un manuscrit inédit de Pierre Poivre*, 1968, 40–41. A survey of reports on Batavia in the seventeenth century is Lach and Van Kley, *Asia in the Making Europe*, 1993, 1313–22; see also M. Harbsmeier, *Wilde Völkerkunde*, 1994, 199–209. A modern social history of Batavia in the (late) eighteenth century is Taylor, *Social World of Batavia*, 2009, 33–77.
25. Graaff, *Oost-Indise spiegel*, 2010, 106.
26. Beaglehole, *Life of Captain James Cook*, 1974, 257–64. A basic condition of Batavian society was indeed the extreme unhealthiness of the place. See in great detail: Van der Brug, *Malaria en malaise*, 1994, esp. 55–67.

27. Similar: G. L. Staunton, *Authentic Account of an Embassy from the King of Great Britain to the Emperor of China*, 1797, vol. 1, 242.
28. G. L. Staunton, *Authentic Account of an Embassy from the King of Great Britain to the Emperor of China*, 1797, vol. 1, 260–61. Slightly less critical is a traveler who visited Batavia a few years earlier: Thunberg, *Reise durch einen Theil von Europa, Afrika und Asien*, 1794, vol. 1, pt. 2, 203–12.
29. G. L. Staunton, *Authentic Account of an Embassy from the King of Great Britain to the Emperor of China*, 1797, vol. 1, 260. See also Barrow, *Voyage to Cochin China*, 1806, 202–42.
30. The comprehensive description and depiction of Chinese everyday life in Breton de la Martinière, *La Chine en miniature* (1811–12), was not based on first-hand knowledge but drew on material collected by the French statesman and Sinophile Bertin. See Sacy, *Henri Bertin*, 1970.
31. See, for example, Raymond, *Artisans et commerçants au Caire au XVIIIe siècle*, 1973, esp. vol. 2, 373–415, on the social structure of Cairo. See also Boyar and Fleet, *A Social History of Ottoman Istanbul*, 2010.
32. When the German original of this book was published in 1998, there was very little interest in the Russell brothers. Now we have a magnificently illiustrated monograph: Boogert, *Aleppo Observed*, 2010. Readers with less patience should turn to Boogert, "Patrick Russell and the Republic of Letters in Aleppo," 2005, or Starkey, "No Myopic Mirage," 2002. Another Western source on Aleppo that would merit a detailed comparison with the work of the Russell brothers is Seetzen, *Tagebuch des Aufenthalts in Aleppo 1803–1805*, 2011. Seetzen repeatedly refers to the *Natural History of Aleppo*. See also Braune, "Ulrich Jasper Seetzens Leben in der Community der Franken in Aleppo," 2014.
33. However, this remained the only full translation of the work in any language. Boogert, *Aleppo Observed*, 2010, 18.
34. Russell, *Natural History of Aleppo*, 1794, vol. 1, xvii.
35. Russell, *Natural History of Aleppo*, 1794, vol. 1, xii, also 108–9 (on fashions in the Orient).
36. See in vol. 2 the analysis of the various plague epidemics since 1719, the administrative and medicinal measures taken to combat them, and their accompanying social symptoms (Russell, *Natural History of Aleppo*, 1794, vol. 2, 335ff.). As an early sociological analysis of catastrophe, the Russells' account is rivaled only by Alexander von Humboldt's investigation into the earthquake of Caracas (*Relation Historique*, 1814–25, vol. 2, 1–28).
37. Marcus, *The Middle East on the Eve of Modernity*, 1989, 339, gives a figure of around 110,000 for the mid-eighteenth century. It would be intriguing to compare Russell's social portrait with Marcus's similar undertaking over two centuries later. On Aleppo's contacts with the outside world, see Masters, *Origins of Western Economic Dominance*, 1988. Boogert gives an excellent paraphrase of the Russells' work on the town of Aleppo and on Ottoman society: *Aleppo Observed*, 2010, 83–97, 185–230.
38. Russell, *Natural History of Aleppo*, 1794, vol. 2, 3.
39. Russell, *Natural History of Aleppo*, 1794, vol. 1, 99, 147–48.
40. Russell, *Natural History of Aleppo*, 1794, vol. 1, 214, 216–17, 222–23.
41. Russell, *Natural History of Aleppo*, 1794, vol. 1, 141.
42. Russell, *Natural History of Aleppo*, 1794, vol. 1, 181.
43. Russell, *Natural History of Aleppo*, 1794, vol. 1, 126–27.

44. Russell, *Natural History of Aleppo,* 1794, vol. 1, 131ff.
45. Montagu, *Complete Letters,* 1965–67, vol. 1, 312–14.
46. Russell, *Natural History of Aleppo,* 1794, vol. 1, 137.
47. Russell, *Natural History of Aleppo,* 1794, vol. 1, 177.
48. Russell, *Natural History of Aleppo,* 1794, vol. 1, 223–24.
49. Russell, *Natural History of Aleppo,* 1794, vol. 1, 225–26.
50. Russell, *Natural History of Aleppo,* 1794, vol. 1, 226.
51. Russell, *Natural History of Aleppo,* 1794, vol. 1, 229, also 316ff.
52. Russell, *Natural History of Aleppo,* 1794, vol. 1, 325. Compare Marcus, *The Middle East on the Eve of Modernity,* 1989, ch. 3.
53. Russell, *Natural History of Aleppo,* 1794, vol. 1, 327.
54. Russell, *Natural History of Aleppo,* 1794, vol. 1, 327
55. Montagu, *Complete Letters,* 1965–67. Lady Mary lived in the Ottoman Empire from 1717–18.
56. Russell, *Natural History of Aleppo,* 1794, vol. 1, 230.
57. Göçek, *East Encounters West,* 1987, 66–67.
58. Thornton, *Present State of Turkey,* 1809, vol. 1, 291.
59. A. Smith, *Lectures on Jurisprudence,* 1978, 191.
60. Millar, *Origins of the Distinction of Ranks,* 2006, 245.
61. See stories of punishment and torture that recall the horrors of the Caribbean in Vogel, *Zehn-Jährige, Jetzo auffs neue revidirt und vermehrte Ost-Indianische Reise-Beschreibung,* 1716, 105, 117; Barchewitz, *Reisebeschreibung,* 1730, 612; Stavorinus, *Reise nach dem Vorgebirge der Guten Hoffnung,* 1796, 203. Yet Raffles, who estimates that there were nineteen thousand slaves in Batavia in 1814, emphasizes that they were better treated than slaves in the European colonies in the West Indies (*History of Java,* 1817, vol. 1, 76–78). See also Wurtzburg, *Raffles,* 1954, 264–67, with excerpts from other reports by Raffles.
62. On the history of this trade see already Sprengel, *Ursprung des Negerhandels,* 1779, 11ff. More detailed contemporary information on the origin and employment of these black eunuchs can be found in Rycaut, *Present State of the Ottoman Empire,* 1668, 35–37; Tavernier, *Nouvelle relation,* 1675, 17–19, and also (with the physician's clinical gaze) in Fryer, *A New Account of East India and Persia,* 1909–15, vol. 3, 125–26; a summary in Hammer-Purgstall, *Des osmanischen Reiches Staatsverfassung,* 1815, vol. 2, 63ff. European observers were less interested in other forms of slavery in the Ottoman Empire.
63. There is a good summary of early nineteenth-century information and evaluation in the anonymous article, "On Slavery in the East," *Asiatic Journal,* vol. 23 (January–June 1827).
64. Meiners, *Grundriß der Geschichte der Menschheit,* 1793, 230–31.
65. Turgot, "Reflexions sur la formation et la distribution des richesses," in Turgot, *Œuvres,* 1913–23, vol. 2 (1914), 547–48.
66. A. Smith, *Lectures on Jurisprudence,* 1978, 182, 185–87; A. Smith, *Wealth of Nations,* 1976, vol. 1, 387; vol. 2, 587.
67. Crawfurd, *History of the Indian Archipelago,* 1820, vol. 3, 27.
68. La Loubère, *A New Historical Relation of the Kingdom of Siam,* 1693, vol. 1, 77. Most but not all free subjects in Siam did indeed have to perform such labor service for up to six months a year. Owen, *Emergence of Modern Southeast Asia,* 2005, 26.
69. For the eighteenth century see Hathaway, *The Politics of Households in Ottoman Egypt,* 1997. On all aspects see Philipp and Haarmann, *The Mamluks in Egyptian Politics and Society,* 1998, on the eighteenth century esp. 114–16, 118–49, 196–204.

70. Voltaire, "Essai sur les mœurs," in *Œuvres complètes de Voltaire*, vol. 23A (2013), 347–49; Gibbon, *Decline and Fall of the Roman Empire*, 1994, vol. 3, 860–61, above all Volney, *Voyage en Égypte et en Syrie*, 1959, 71–77, 101–9.
71. Volney, *Voyage en Égypte et en Syrie*, 1959, 73. This accords with the findings of modern research, e.g., Crecelius, "Mamluk Beylicate of Egypt," 1998, 128–29. Whereas Volney developed a kind of leadership sociology of the late Mamluk period, Pococke (*Description of the East*, 1743–45, vol. 1, 161–85) had submitted the problem of Egyptian governance to a proto-politological analysis from an Ottoman viewpoint. See also Bergk, *Aegypten*, 1799, 291–317.
72. Wakefield, *The Traveller in Asia*, 1817, 229.
73. Semedo (*The History of that Great and Renowned Monarchy of China*, 1655, 35–45) described the system fairly accurately, while Navarette realistically pointed out its dark side: Navarette "An Account of the Empire of China," 1744, 51–52; Navarette, *Travels and Controversies*, 1962, vol. 1, 153. The standard reference is Elman, *A Cultural History of Civil Examinations*, 2000.
74. This striking parallel between the Chinese and the Roman Catholic hierarchy as career elevators is made by Du Halde, *Description géographique*, 1735, vol. 2, 58.
75. See Duteil, *Le mandat du ciel*, 1994, 232–50.
76. Semedo, *The History of that Great and Renowned Monarchy of China*, 1655, 46, 121–23; somewhat less euphorically Magalhães, *A New History of China*, 1688, 145–48; similar too is Winterbotham, *An Historical, Geographical, and Philosophical View of the Chinese Empire*, 1795, 268.
77. *Denckwürdige Beschreibung*, 1679, 7.
78. Mendoza, *History of the Great and Mighty Kingdom of China*, 1853–54, vol. 1, 125.
79. Le Comte, *Nouveaux mémoires sur l'état present de la Chine*, 1697, vol. 12, 51. A fine sociological analysis in this sense is undertaken by C.L.J. de Guignes, *Voyages à Peking*, 1808, vol. 2, 412ff.
80. Justi, *Vergleichungen*, 1762, 413ff.; Quesnay, "Despotisme de la Chine," 1888, 620–21.
81. Thus Crawfurd, *Journal of an Embassy from the Governor General of India to the Court of Ava*, 1834, vol. 2, 161–62.
82. Barrow, *Travels in China*, 1806, 386.
83. *Universal History*, 1779–84, vol. 7, 135, 137, 145; Sonnerat, *Voyages aux Indes Orientales*, 1782, vol. 2, 20; an interesting analysis is found in C.L.J. de Guignes, *Voyages à Peking*, 1808, vol. 2, 434ff. De Guignes is still yet to receive the attention he deserves.
84. Even Barrow was aware of this: *Some Account of the Public Life . . . of the Earl of Macartney*, 1807, vol. 1, vii–viii, 67ff.; on the theme of corruption in the Hastings trial, see Marshall, *Impeachment of Warren Hastings*, 1965, 130ff.; Whelan, *Edmund Burke and India*, 1996, 64–122.
85. *Universal History*, 1779, vol. 7, 136.
86. Societas Jesu, *Lettres édifiantes et curieuses*, 1780–83, vol. 22, 132ff. See also Mairan, *Lettres de M. de Mairan au R. P. Parennin*, 1759, 78.
87. Georg Hassel ventures a fine analysis of China's "different estates" on the basis of a similar stratified model in Gaspari, *Vollständiges Handbuch*, vol. 15 (1822), 65–69. See also the paraphrase of Louis-François Jauffret's ethnographic analysis of China (c. 1800) in Moravia, *La scienza dell'uomo nel Settecento*, 1978, 79–82.
88. Societas Jesu, *Lettres édifiantes et curieuses*, 1780–83, vol. 22, 158.
89. Silhouette, *Idée générale*, 1731, 18.
90. Poivre, *Voyages d'un philosophe*, 1768, 106–19.

91. Eckermann, *Gespräche mit Goethe,* 1999, 223. The novel in question was "Yü-kiau-li [Yu Jiao Li] ou les deux cousines," published in 1826. Friedrich Schlegel's response to the translation around the same time was very similar: Schlegel, "Philosophie der Geschichte," 1971, 63–64.
92. Tissanier, *Relation du Voyage,* 1663, 121; Maybon, *La relation sur le Tonkin,* 1920, 149ff.
93. A. Hamilton, *New Account of the East Indies,* 1930, vol. 2, 26.
94. Gervaise, *Natural and Political History of Siam,* 1928, 50.
95. Chardin, *Voyages,* 1735, vol. 3, 312; Fryer, *A New Account of East India and Persia,* 1909–15, vol. 3, 133.
96. Crawfurd, *History of the Indian Archipelago,* 1820, vol. 3, 31ff.
97. Hammer-Purgstall, *Geschichte des Osmanischen Reiches,* 1827–35, vol. 9, xli.
98. Busbecq, *Turkish Letters,* 1927, 60.
99. Guer, *Mœurs et usages des Turcs,* 1747, vol. 2, 393, and 389–96; also de Tott, *Memoirs,* 1786, vol. 1, xxv–xxvi; Thornton, *Present State of Turkey,* 1809, vol. 1, 4–5.
100. Gibbon, *Decline and Fall of the Roman Empire,* 1994, vol. 3, 860–62, 946.
101. "Une classe héréditaire qui est chargé exclusivement d'un genre d'occupation." Malte-Brun, *Précis de la géographie universelle,* 1812–29, vol. 2 (1812), 599.
102. Rougemont, *Précis d'ethnographie,* 1835–37, vol. 1, 21.
103. Documents on the early Western perception and construction of "Hinduism" are collected in Marshall, *The British Discovery of Hinduism,* 1970.
104. See Dharampal-Frick, *Indien im Spiegel deutscher Quellen,* 1994, 95–108.
105. The following is based on Dharampal-Frick, *Indien im Spiegel deutscher Quellen,* 1994, 228–42; Dharampal-Frick, "Shifting Categories in the Discourse on Caste," 1995, 92–97. See also chapter 3 in the present book. Susan Bayly's great work on castes gives a detailed account of European and Indian views of caste in the nineteenth and twentieth centuries but has little to say about our period: S. Bayly, *Caste, Society and Politics in India,* 1999, 97–186.
106. Dharampal-Frick, *Indien im Spiegel deutscher Quellen,* 1994, 236.
107. See also Krader, *The Asiatic Mode of Production,* 1975, 75–79, for early ideas about open and closed societies.
108. "Un certain honneur que des préjugés de religion établissent aux Indes, fait que les diverses castes ont horreur les unes des autres." Montesquieu, "De l'esprit des lois," 24/22, in *Œuvres,* 1949–51, vol. 2, 731. Montesquieu, *Spirit of the Laws,* 1989, 474.
109. "peuplée de vingt nations différentes, dont les mœurs et les religions ne se semblent pas."

    Voltaire, "Essai sur les mœurs," in *Œuvres complètes de Voltaire,* vol. 26A (2013), 172. The Comte de Modave, who had seen a great deal of India as an officer between 1757 and 1777, came to a quite different conclusion: India was "une grande nation uniforme dans toutes ses parties et sans mélanges de peuples étrangers" (*Voyage en Inde,* 1971, 407).
110. A similar polarity can still be found in the literature of the twentieth century; see Embree, *Imagining India,* 1989, 9.
111. On eighteenth-century Jesuit reporting, see Murr, "Les Jésuites et l'Inde," 1986, 13ff.
112. Lach and Van Kley, *Asia in the Making of Europe,* 1993, 1102–10.
113. Wahl, *Erdbeschreibung von Ostindien,* 1805, 866. For a nuanced decription by a modern anthropologist, see S. Bayly, *Caste, Society and Politics in India,* 1999, 8–9.
114. Raynal, *Histoire philosophique et politique,* 1775, vol. 1, 33.

115. Raynal, *Histoire philosophique et politique*, 1775, vol. 1, 37.
116. A. Smith, *Wealth of Nations*, 1776, 81; on this see Platteau, *Les économistes classiques*, 1978, vol. 1, 119ff. Smith's arguments were later reprised and developed in Tennant, *Indian Recreations*, 1803, vol. 1, 83–92: the caste system stands in the way of the functional division of labor.
117. Sonnerat, *Voyages aux Indes Orientales*, 1782, vol. 1, 43–63.
118. Hennings, *Gegenwärtiger Zustand*, 1784–86, vol. 3, 478–79, also 499.
119. Embree, *Charles Grant*, 1962, 147.
120. E. Burke, "Opening of the Impeachment" (Feb. 15, 1788), in Burke, *India: The Launching of the Hastings Impeachment*, 1991, 303.
121. Perrin, *Voyage dans l'Indostan*, 1807, vol. 1, 299.
122. Another Catholic conservative later expressed the same idea more forcefully still: the Indian caste system offers optimal protection against despotism. Schlegel, "Philosophie der Geschichte," 1971, 86–87.
123. Cœurdoux and Desvaulx, *Mœurs and coutumes des Indiens*, 1987, 8–9. That the Brahmins universally cultivated an elite lifestyle—as was widely believed in Europe—was disputed by travelers who reported seeing Brahmins behind a plow: Deleury, *Les Indes florissantes*, 1991, 790ff.
124. Cœurdoux and Desvaulx, *Mœurs and coutumes des Indiens*, 1987, 9.
125. Herder, *Outlines*, 1800, 307: "Ohne Zweifel war die Einrichtung der Brahmanen, als sie gestiftet war, gut: sonst hätte sie weder den Umfang noch die Tiefe und Dauer gewonnen, in der sie dasteht." (Herder, *Ideen*, 1989, 454).
126. Dubois, *Description of the Character, Manners and Customs of the People of India*, 1817, 4; similarly Herder, *Ideen*, 1989, 455; Herder, *Outlines*, 1800, 308.
127. Robertson, *Historical Disquisition*, 1812, 200.
128. Robertson, *Historical Disquisition*, 1812, 202. On Robertson's views on castes, see also Carnall, "Robertson and Contemporary Images of India," 1997, 214–15.
129. See in summary Kejariwal, *Asiatic Society*, 1988; Windisch, *Geschichte der Sanskrit-Philologie*, 1917–20, vol. 1, 22ff.; Franklin, *Orientalist Jones*, 2011, 205–50. On Hegel's use of these studies (especially that of H. T. Colebrooke), see Halbfass, *India and Europe*, 1988, 84ff.
130. Mill, *History of British India*, 1817, vol. 1, 701.
131. See Majeed, *Ungoverned Imaginings*, 1992, 159–63.
132. Mill, *History of British India*, 1817, vol. 1, 48, also 50, 73–75, 161, 370, 472, 702–3, 720. Even more dismissive in tone is a Baptist missionary: Ward, *A View of the History, Literature, and Religion of the Hindoos*, 1817–20, vol. 3, xxvi, 64ff., likewise Tennant, *Indian Recreations*, 1803, 115.
133. See the minutely detailed evidence in Hegel, *Vorlesungen über die Philosophie der Weltgeschichte: Berlin 1822/1823*, 1996, 570–96. Not included in the English translation of 2011.
134. Hegel, *Lectures on the Philosophy of World History*, 2011, 260: "wie zu Naturdingen" (Hegel, *Vorlesungen über die Philosophie der Weltgeschichte: Berlin 1822/1823*, 177).
135. Hegel, *Die orientalische Welt*, 1923, 371.
136. Hegel, *Lectures on the Philosophy of World History*, 2011, 271 (corrected); Hegel, *Vorlesungen über die Philosophie der Weltgeschichte: Berlin 1822/1823*, 1996, 191.
137. Hegel, *Die orientalische Welt*, 1923, 377; Hegel, *Lectures on the Philosophy of World History*, 2011, 263; Hegel, *Vorlesungen über die Philosophie der Weltgeschichte: Berlin 1822/1823*, 181. On Hegel's interpretation of the Indian castes, see also Leuze, *Die außerchristlichen Religionen bei Hegel*, 1975, 97–104.

138. On further developments in the nineteenth century see Inden, *Imagining India*, 1990, 49–84; Metcalf, *Ideologies of the Raj*, 1994, 114–25.
139. Dubois, *Mœurs, institutions et cérémonies des peuples de l'Inde*, 1825, vol. 1, 96–123. On Dubois see Dirks, *Castes of Mind*, 2001, 21–26.
140. Poivre, *Voyages d'un philosophe*, 1768, 52–54.
141. Voltaire, "Essai sur les mœurs," in *Œuvres complètes de Voltaire*, vol. 24 (2011), 481–88.
142. Brunner, "Feudalismus, feudal," 1975, 341 (on Voltaire).
143. Imbruglia, "Tra Anquetil-Duperron e 'L'Histoire des deux Indes,'" 1994, 168. As Imbruglia shows, a similar approximation of Montesquieu's pure "ideal types" can be found in Raynal and Diderot's *Histoire des deux Indes* (169–74).
144. Virey, *Histoire naturelle du genre humain*, 1824, vol. 1, 445.
145. Important in-depth analyses of such feudal conditions in Asia are: Marsden, *History of Sumatra*, 1811, 210ff., 350ff.; G. Forster, *A Journey from Bengal to England*, 1808, vol. 1, 135ff., vol. 2, 89, 99–100; J. Forbes, *Oriental Memoirs*, 1813, vol. 2, 39–63 (on the Marathas); Pallas, *Reise in die südlichen Statthalterschaften des Russischen Reichs*, 1799–1801, vol. 2, 355ff., 383–85; Volney, *Voyage en Égypte et en Syrie*, 1959, 197, 207–8 (on the Kurds). J. R. Forster (*Bemerkungen*, 1783, 311) recognized Poivre's description of Malay feudalism in Tahiti: Poivre, *Voyages d'un philosophe*, 1768, 52–54.
146. J. B. Fraser, *Journal of a Tour through Part of the Snowy Range of the Himala Mountains*, 1820, 4. Elphinstone saw parallels between Scotland and Afghanistan: McLaren, "From Analysis to Prescription," 1993, 475.
147. Tone, "Illustrations of Some Institutions of the Mahratta People," 130, on military organization 136ff. This also becomes evident from Duff's narrative history, which never gives a systematic analysis of the Mahratha system: Duff, *History of the Mahrattas*, 1826.
148. See Hegel, *Lectures on the Philosophy of World History*, 2011, 282–83 (quote 283); Hegel, *Vorlesungen über die Philosophie der Weltgeschichte: Berlin 1822/1823*, 1996, 206–7. For him, too, the Marathas are the last and worst of these feudal powers.
149. Richardson, *Dissertation on the Languages, Literature and Manners of Eastern Nations*, 1778, pt. 2, 151; later in this work, the author compares the different styles of "feudal war" in Europe and the "East" (212ff.).
150. Voltaire, "Essai sur les mœurs," in *Œuvres complètes de Voltaire*, vol. 26C (2015), 281–82 (quote 282); Mill, *History of British India*, 1817, vol. 1, 70, 476.
151. Tod, *Annals and Antiquities of Rajasthan*, 1920; the work came out in three volumes with around 1,500 pages in 1829–32. See Peabody, "Tod's 'Rajast'han,'" 1996, esp. 194–200; on Tod's scholarship see Rietbergen, *Europa's India*, 2007, 249–77 (for his views on chivalry among the Rajputs see 265–68).
152. Cohn, *An Anthropologist among the Historians*, 1987, 652–76.
153. Caron and Schouten, *A True Description of the Mighty Kingdom of Japan and Siam*, 1935, 30–36.
154. Castilhon, *Considérations*, 1769, 244–45.
155. That is why there was said to be no duelling in despotic states; see for example Le Comte, *Nouveaux Mémoires sur l'état present de la Chine*, 1697, vol. 1, 367; Bruin, *A Voyage to the Levant*, 1702, 97.
156. Castilhon, *Considérations*, 1769, 248.
157. See Heilbron, *Rise of Social Theory*, 1995, 72ff.; also Woolf, "The Construction of a European World View," 1992, 93.

158. See Keane, "Despotism and Democracy," 1988.
159. Goody, *The East in the West*, 1996, 181; a whole chapter on this motif in a later book: Goody, *The Theft of History*, 2006, 267–85.
160. A paradigmatic example is Nieuhof, *An Embassy from the East-India Company of the United Provinces, to the Grand Tartar Cham*, 1669, 172–215.
161. Du Halde, *Description géographique*, 1735, vol. 2, 75.
162. Navarette, *Travels and Controversies*, 1962, vol. 2, 173–74.
163. Du Halde, *Description géographique*, 1735, vol. 2, 75.
164. Du Halde, *Description géographique*, 1735, vol. 2, 75–76.
165. Barrow, *Travels in China*, 1806, 186–87, also 177–78, 192–93.
166. Barrow, *Travels in China*, 1806, 149, also 142.
167. Barrow, *Travels in China*, 1806, 153.
168. Barrow, *Travels in China*, 1806, 395. See also C.L.J. de Guignes, *Voyages à Peking*, 1808, vol. 2, 163.
169. Hume, "Of the Rise and Progress of the Arts and Sciences" (1741–42), in Hume, *Essays*, 1987, 127.
170. Bayer, *Museum Sinicum*, 1730, vol. 1, 122–25; see also *Mémoires concernant l'histoire . . . des Chinois*, 1776–1814, vol. 8 (1782), 246ff.
171. W. Jones, "Fourth Anniversary Discourse, on the Arabs," in *Works*, 1807, vol. 3, 66–67; also Russell, *Natural History of Aleppo*, 1794, vol. 1, 178ff.; Boulainvilliers, *Histoire des Arabes*, 1731, 36–37.
172. Maybon, *La relation sur le Tonkin*, 1920, 168.
173. Ziegenbalg, *Malabarisches Heidenthum*, 1926, 236–37.
174. For example Marsden, *History of Sumatra*, 1811, 283–84.
175. Browne, *Travels in Africa, Egypt and Syria*, 1799, 425–43.
176. Browne, *Travels in Africa, Egypt and Syria*, 1799, 430.
177. Volney, *Voyage en Égypte et en Syrie*, 1959, 61, 195, 198, 199.
178. For an interpretation of Humboldt in this context, see Osterhammel, "Alexander von Humboldt," 1998.
179. This section is based on Osterhammel, "Gastfreiheit und Fremdenabwehr," 1997. On the realities of hospitality, especially in Europe, see a magnificent chapter in Roche, *Humeurs vagabondes*, 2003, 479–566.
180. See above chapter 4.
181. Still, *Enlightenment Hospitality*, 2011, 167–70.
182. Tacitus, *Germania*, 1999, sec. 21.2, 86.
183. Crawfurd, *History of the Indian Archipelago*, 1820, vol.1, 53.
184. Hodges, *Travels in India*, 1793, 45.
185. Francklin, *Observations Made on a Tour from Bengal to Persia*, 1790, 156.
186. D. Campbell, *Journey over Land to India*, 1796, 31.
187. Jaubert, *Voyage en Arménie et en Perse*, 1821, 75ff.
188. Engelhardt and Parrott, *Reise in die Krym und den Kaukasus*, 1815, 24, 41; Georgi, *Beschreibung aller Nationen des Rußischen Reichs*, 1776–80, vol. 2, 101; Züge, *Der russische Colonist*, 1988, 194–96.
189. Pottinger, *Travels in Belochistan and Sinde*, 1816, 61–63. Balochs also live in parts of Iran and Afghanistan.
190. Hunter, *Concise Account of the Kingdom of Pegu*, 1785, 32–33.
191. Merck, *Das sibirisch-amerikanische Tagebuch aus den Jahren 1788–1791*, 2009, 338.
192. Wood, *Ruins of Balbec*, 1757, 4.
193. T. Shaw, *Travels or Observations Relating to Several Parts of Barbary*, 1808, xii–xxiv.

194. Judges 19:15, King James Bible.
195. Russell, *Natural History of Aleppo,* 1794, vol. 1, 231.
196. Volney, *Voyage en Égypte et en Syrie*, 1959, 211.
197. C. Niebuhr, *Beschreibung von Arabien*, 1772, 46.
198. C. Niebuhr, *Beschreibung von Arabien*, 1772, 47.
199. Michaelis, *Fragen an eine Gesellschaft gelehrter Männer*, 1762, 386.
200. For example, Lane, *Account of Manners and Customs of the Modern Egyptians,* 1895, 297.
201. Burckhardt, *Travels in Arabia*, 1829, vol. 2, 378.
202. If there is such a theory for our own time, it was provided by Jacques Derrida. See his *Of Hospitality*, 2000.
203. Robertson, *Progress of Society in Europe,* 1972, 166, also 63–64.
204. Robertson, *Progress of Society in Europe,* 1972, 167.
205. A. Smith, *Inquiry into the Nature and Causes of the Wealth of Nations*, 1976, vol. 1, 413.
206. A. Smith, *Correspondence*, 1977, 142: Letter to Lord Hailes, March 5, 1769.
207. Ferguson, *Essay on the History of Civil Society*, 1966: 101–2.
208. "Les plus petites choses, celles que l'humanité demande, s'y font ou s'y donnent pour de l'argent." Montesquieu, "De l'esprit des lois," 19/4, in *Œuvres*, 1949–51, vol. 2, 586; Montesquieu, *Spirit of the Laws*, 1989, 339.
209. Condorcet, *Esquisse d'un tableau historique,* 1988, 109.
210. Falconer, *Remarks on the Influence of Climate*, 1781, 334.
211. Falconer, *Remarks on the Influence of Climate*, 1781, 367.
212. Falconer, *Remarks on the Influence of Climate*, 1781, 369.
213. Hume, *History of England*, 1983, vol. 4, 383.
214. Kames, *Sketches of the History of Man*, 1778, vol. 1, 30, also vol. 2, 176–87.
215. Démeunier , *L'esprit des usages et des coutumes*, 1776 vol. 2, 113.
216. Hirschfeld, *Von der Gastfreundschaft*, 1777, 16. A new edition (with a good afterword by Maurizio Pirro) is Hirschfeld, *Von der Gastfreundschaft*, 2015. See also Jancke, *Gastfreundschaft in der frühneuzeitlichen Gesellschaft,* 2013, 440–74.
217. Hirschfeld, *Von der Gastfreundschaft*, 1777, 27.
218. Hirschfeld, *Von der Gastfreundschaft*, 1777, 27.
219. Hirschfeld, *Von der Gastfreundschaft*, 1777, 84.
220. Hirschfeld, *Von der Gastfreundschaft*, 1777, 100–101.
221. Hirschfeld, *Von der Gastfreundschaft*, 1777, 120.
222. Hirschfeld, *Von der Gastfreundschaft*, 1777, 129.
223. Hirschfeld, *Von der Gastfreundschaft*, 1777, 168.
224. Hirschfeld, *Von der Gastfreundschaft*, 1777, 169–70.
225. A. v. Humboldt, *Relation historique,* 1814–25, vol. 1, 293; A. v. Humboldt, *Personal Narrative,* 1815, 360; translation modified.

CHAPTER XII. WOMEN

1. "Il ne suffisoit pas d'avoir divisé les champs et les prairies, et de leur avoir donné des maîtres. C'étoit peu que d'être parvenu à fixer autour de leurs cabanes des esclaves destinés à les servir. Les réglements faits de cette matiere, ne concernoient que des besoins: bientôt il en fallut faire pour mettre de l'ordre, même dans les plaisirs. Les uns avoient donné lieu à la dégradation involontaire du genre humain: les autres auroient amené sa ruine totale. De tous ces plaisirs, le plus vif étoit sans

contredit l'union des deux sexes; il dut aussi se ressentir le premier de l'étrange revolution qui venoit d'arriver sur la terre." Linguet, *Théorie des lois civiles,* 1984, 183.

2. Meiners, *History of the Female Sex*, 1808, vol. 1, 1. A slightly earlier "world history" of women was Alexander, *The History of Women,* 1779. In contrast to Meiners's more or less ethnographic attitude, that work by an English medical doctor was written from a male "us and them" perspective: women as "the other sex."
3. Mehmed Efendi, *Le paradis des infidèles*, 1981, 73–74, 94 (this ambassadorial journal was first published in French in 1757); see also Göçek, *East Encounters West*, 1987, esp. 38–48; and from an Iranian perspective: Ghanoonparvar, *In a Persian Mirror*, 1993, 15ff.
4. "La plus grande différence entre nous et les Orientaux, est la manière dont nous traitons les femmes." Voltaire, "Essai sur les mœurs," in *Œuvres complètes de Voltaire*, vol. 26C (2015), 326.
5. On Kindersley see Dyson, *A Various Universe*, 1978, 122ff.
6. Melman, *Women's Orients*, 1995, 36–37. E. M. Forster's "Introductory Notes" to his edition of the letters begin with a compliment: "Eliza Fay is a work of art." Fay, *Original Letters from India*, 1925, 7. The *Letters* are still in print, the latest reissue dating from 2010. On Eliza Fay's life see http://www.oxforddnb.com/view/article/45846.
7. Fay, *Original Letters from India*, 1925, 16.
8. See above, chapter 9, section 5: "Knights and Strangers in the Crimea."
9. C. Niebuhr, *Reisebeschreibung nach Arabien*, 1774–1837, vol. 1, 241.
10. Kindersley, *Letters from the Island of Teneriffe*, 1777, 102.
11. Chardin, *Voyages*, 1735, vol. 3, 392; descriptions of such scenes are frequent; see for example, Du Mans, *Estat de la Perse*, 1890, 95–96.; Kaempfer, *Am Hofe des persischen Großkönigs*, 1940, 184–85.
12. See above, chapter 11, section 4: "Close-Up: Urban Life in Syrian Aleppo." See several articles in Zilfi, *Women in the Ottoman Empire*, 1997.
13. A "seraglio" was generally taken to refer only to the monarch's harem, especially that of the sultan in Istanbul.
14. Kaempfer, *Am Hofe des persischen Großkönigs* 1940, 180–81. On the precision of Kaempfer's observations and their lack of bias see Gronke, "Am Hofe von Isfahan," 2004, 191, 193–94.
15. Chardin, *Voyages*, 1735, vol. 3, 383–92.
16. See Peirce, *Imperial Harem*, 1993, on the harem in Istanbul as a power center. Its organizational structure is described with the objectivity of an administrative manual in d'Ohsson, *Tableau générale de l'Empire Othoman*, 1788–1824, vol. 7, 62–88. European descriptions of the sultan's seraglio between 1551 and 1845 are discussed in Penzer, *The Harêm,* 1936, 27–50; he considers the best to have been that of the Venetian ambassador Ottaviano Bon, who was active in Istanbul between 1604 and 1607.
17. D'Ohsson, *Tableau générale de l'Empire Othoman*, 1788–1824, vol. 7, 68; Businello, *Historische Nachrichten*, 1778, 22; Manucci, *Storia do Mogor*, 1906–8, vol. 2, 330 (on pp. 330–40 an extensive description on the basis of the author's knowledge as Aurangzeb's personal physician); Semedo, *The History of that Great and Renowned Monarchy of China*, 1655, 113; Kaempfer, *Am Hofe des persischen Großkönigs*, 1940, 182 (Roemer, *Persien*, 1989, 362, ascribes eight hundred harem concubines to Shah Safi II).
18. Chardin, *Voyages*, 1735, vol. 3, 396.
19. For example, Grose, *A Voyage to the East Indies*, 1772, 136; Sonnini, *Voyage dans la haute et basse Égypte*, 1799, vol. 1, 285–86; Habesci, *The Present State of the Ottoman*

Empire, 1784, 170–72; Hill, *A Full and Just Account of the Present State of the Ottoman Empire*, 1709), 163ff. These last two books are sensationalist works of little source value.

20. Fryer, *A New Account of East India and Persia*, 1909–15, vol. 3, 131; see also Olearius, *Vermehrte Newe Beschreibung*, 1656, 311; *Allgemeine Geschichte der neueren Entdeckungen*, 1777–86, vol. 2, 271ff. On the Indians, Roubaud strikes a similar note: *Histoire générale de l'Asie*, 1770–72, vol. 2, 91ff.
21. Marsden, *History of Sumatra*, 1811, 271.
22. One traveler claimed to have discovered that the khan of Bukhara, along with his seraglio of concubines, kept a harem of forty to sixty pleasure boys and also took carnal delight in donkeys: Eversmann, *Reise von Orenburg nach Buchara,* 1823, 84. Reports on pederasty in the travel literature are compiled in Démeunier , *L'esprit des usages et des coutumes,* 1776, vol. 2, 309ff.
23. Marsden, *History of Sumatra*, 1811, 261.
24. Caron and Schouten, *A True Description of the Mighty Kingdom of Japan and Siam*, 1935, 142–43.
25. Sonnini, *Voyage dans la haute et basse Égypte*, 1799, vol. 1, 279.
26. Knox, *Historical Relation*, 1681, 91.
27. Marsden, *History of Sumatra*, 1811, 261. Detailed accounts of prostitutes are rare; for an exception, see Grose, *A Voyage to the East Indies,* 1772, 138–44.
28. Hammer-Purgstall, *Geschichte des Osmanischen Reiches*, 1827–35, vol. 1 (1827), 231.
29. Hammer-Purgstall, *Geschichte des Osmanischen Reiches*, 1827–35, vol. 1 (1827), 232.
30. Montesquieu, "De l'esprit des lois," 16/2, in *Œuvres*, 1949–51, vol. 2, 509.
31. E.g., R. K. Porter, *Travels in Georgia*, 1820–21, 340–41.
32. Montesquieu, "De l'esprit des lois," 16/8, in *Œuvres*, 1949–51, vol. 2, 514; Montesquieu, *Spirit of the Laws*, 1989, 269. Malthus (*Works*, 1986, vol. 2, 119) cites a passage from William Jones's 1794 translation of the *Mânava-Dharmasâstra*, the "Ordinances of Menu," which says much the same.
33. Browne, *Travels in Africa, Egypt and Syria*, 1799, 429–32.
34. Montesquieu, "De l'esprit des lois," 16/10, in *Œuvres*, 1949–51, vol. 2, 516.
35. Verelst, *A View of the Rise, Progress, and Present State of the English Government in Bengal*, 1772, 138–39.
36. See also Garcia, *Islam and the English Enlightenment*, 2012, 68–82.
37. Montagu, *Complete Letters*, 1965–67, vol. 1, 407.
38. Montagu, *Complete Letters*, 1965–67, vol. 1, 329. On the background of these letters see Grundy, *Lady Mary Wortley Montagu*, 1999, 134–66.
39. Pitton de Tournefort, *Relation*, 1717, vol. 2, 95.
40. Montagu, *Complete Letters*, 1965–67, vol. 1, 328.
41. Montagu, *Complete Letters*, 1965–67, vol. 1, 329. An almost word-for-word echo of this sentence can still be found in Salaberry, *Histoire de l'Empire Ottoman*, 1813, vol. 4, 165.
42. Montagu, *Complete Letters*, 1965–67, vol. 1, 312–15, 349–52, 381–82.
43. On forms of voyeurism in the harem literature (Montesquieu, Diderot), see Pucci, "The Discrete Charms of the Exotic," 1990.
44. This important source does not figure in several of the leading contributions: F. Davis, *The Ottoman Lady*, 1986; Peirce, *Imperial Harem*, 1993; Booth, *Harem Histories*, 2010.
45. Russell, *Natural History of Aleppo*, 1794, vol. 1, 247–48.

46. Russell, *Natural History of Aleppo,* 1794, vol. 1, 260, 263. See as a modern corrective to Enlightenment authorities such as the Russells and Lady Mary Wortley Montagu: Ambros, "Frivolity and Flirtation," 2016.
47. Russell, *Natural History of Aleppo,* 1794, vol. 1, 261.
48. Russell, *Natural History of Aleppo,* 1794, vol. 1, 242.
49. Russell, *Natural History of Aleppo,* 1794, vol. 1, 242.
50. Russell, *Natural History of Aleppo,* 1794, vol. 1, 243.
51. Russell, *Natural History of Aleppo,* 1794, vol. 1, 257, 291.
52. Russell, *Natural History of Aleppo,* 1794, vol. 1, 292, see also 282 on the power and reputation of a "Turkish matron."
53. Russell, *Natural History of Aleppo,* 1794, vol. 1, 291.
54. Carne, *Letters from the East,* 1826, 12.
55. Closely related to the Russells in its stance and assertions is the long chapter on women in Thornton, *Present State of Turkey,* 1809, vol. 2, 226–96.
56. 1 Kings 11:3.
57. Sale, "Preliminary Discourse," 1764, 176–77.
58. Pallas, *Reise in die südlichen Statthalterschaften des Rußischen Reiches,* 1799–1801, vol. 2, 359.
59. Georgi, *Beschreibung aller Nationen des Rußischen Reichs,* 1776–80, vol. 2, 102–3. Niebuhr makes similar remarks on Arabia: *Beschreibung von Arabien,* 1772, 73–74.
60. Duteil, *Le mandat du ciel,* 1994, 277.
61. Duteil, *Le mandat du ciel,* 1994, 277–80.
62. Démeunier , *L'esprit des usages et des coutumes,* 1776, vol. 2, sec. 275.
63. See Hume, "Of Polygamy and Divorces," in Hume, *Essays,* 1987, 181–90, esp. 184.
64. Montesquieu, "De l'esprit des lois," 16/9, in *Œuvres,* 1949–51, vol. 2, 514.
65. Unlike Malcolm, *History of Persia,* 1829, vol. 2, 452, who mainly blamed polygamy for the civilizational backwardness of Muslim lands.
66. Montesquieu, "De l'esprit des lois," 16/4, in *Œuvres,* 1949–51, vol. 2, 511. Even so, Montesquieu saw himself later compelled to defend his interpretation of polygamy in his "Défense de l'Esprit des Lois": *Œuvres,* 1949–51, vol. 2, 1141–43.
67. Montesquieu, "De l'esprit des lois," 16/2 in *Œuvres,* 1949–51, vol. 2, 510.
68. Montesquieu, "De l'esprit des lois," 16/4, in *Œuvres,* 1949–51, vol. 2, 511; and 23/12, 690.
69. Marsden, *History of Sumatra,* 1811, 272.
70. Michaelis, *Fragen an eine Gesellschaft gelehrter Männer,* 1762, unpaginated.
71. C. Niebuhr, *Beschreibung von Arabien,* 1772, 70ff. Examples of early serious demographic discussions on Asiatic countries are Raffles, *History of Java,* 1817, vol. 1, 61ff.; H. Burney, *Report on the Mission to Siam,* 1911, 51–52.
72. R. Wallace, *A Dissertation on the Numbers of Mankind,* 1809, on polygamy 86–87. Wallace reacted to the opposite view of his acquaintance David Hume, who devoted one of his longest and most erudite essays to the theme: "Of the Populousness of Ancient Nations," in *Essays,* 1987, 377–464.
73. Montesquieu, "Lettres persanes," in *Œuvres complètes de Montesquieu,* vol. 1 (2004), 439–41; Montesquieu, *Persian Letters,* 1973, 206–7; Laurens, *Les origines intellectuels,* 1987, 108–9.
74. Raffles, *History of Java,* 1817, vol. 1, 73–74.
75. Grosier, *Description générale de la Chine,* 1785, 289–90.
76. Grosier, *Description générale de la Chine,* 1785, 289.

77. Dubois, *Mœurs, institutions et cérémonies des peuples de l'Inde*, 1825, vol. 1, 117ff.
78. See Glacken, *Traces on the Rhodian Shore*, 1967, 632–34.
79. Bashford and Chaplin, *The New Worlds of Thomas Robert Malthus*, 2016, have made this abundantly clear for the Americas. A parallel study could be undertaken on Malthus's views on Asia.
80. Malthus, *Works*, 1986, vol. 2, 82.
81. Malthus, *Works*, 1986, vol. 2, 82–83, 113. See also the general reflections in the chapter on Africa, 94.
82. Malthus, *Works*, 1986, vol. 2, 80–81, also among the Kyrgyz: 84.
83. Malthus, *Works*, 1986, vol. 2, 125ff.
84. Malthus, *Works*, 1986, vol. 2, 113.
85. Malthus, *Works*, 1986, vol. 2, 122. Malthus borrows not just the data but also their interpretation from Samuel Turner (*Account of an Embassy to the Court of the Teshoo Lama Tibet*, 1800, esp. 351).
86. Montesquieu, "De l'esprit des lois," 16/9, in *Œuvres*, 1949–51, vol. 2, 514–15; Montesquieu, *Spirit of the Laws*, 1989, 270.
87. Heeren, "Ideen," in *Historische Werke*, 1821–26, vol. 10 (1824), 72; Heeren, *Historical Researches*, 1846, vol. 1, 16. The English translator speaks of "domestic relations" and thus misses the point that Heeren sees the household as a basic element of "society."
88. Heeren, "Ideen," in *Historische Werke*, 1821–26, vol. 10 (1824), 72; Heeren, *Historical Researches*, 1846, vol. 1, 17.
89. "Vielweiberey gründet nothwendig Familiendespotismus, weil sie das Weib zur Sklavin und eben dadurch den Mann zum Herrscher macht. Die Gesellschaft der Staatsbürger besteht also hier nicht aus einer Zahl von Hausvätern, sondern häuslichen Despoten, die, weil sie selber despotisiren, auch wieder despotisirt seyn wollen. Wer blind befiehlt, ist auch nur geschickt, blind zu gehorchen." Heeren, "Ideen," in *Historische Werke*, 1821–26, vol. 10 (1824), 73; Heeren, *Historical Researches*, 1846, vol. 1, 17. Similarly Hammer-Purgstall, *Umblick auf einer Reise von Constantinopel nach Brussa*, 1818, 45.
90. Heeren, "Ideen," in *Historische Werke*, 1821–26, vol. 10 (1824), 73; Heeren, *Historical Researches*, 1846, vol. 1, 17.
91. Heeren, "Ideen," in *Historische Werke*, 1821–26, vol. 10 (1824), 74; Heeren, *Historical Researches*, 1846, vol. 1, 18.
92. Heeren, "Ideen," in *Historische Werke*, 1821–26, vol. 10 (1824), 74; Heeren, *Historical Researches*, 1846, vol. 1, 18.
93. Heeren, "Ideen," in *Historische Werke*, 1821–26, vol. 10 (1824), 75; Heeren, *Historical Researches*, 1846, vol. 1, 18.
94. Kames, *Sketches of the History of Man*, 1778, vol. 2, 53–54.
95. Gibbon, *Decline and Fall of the Roman Empire*, 1994, vol. 3, 627. See also Hammer-Purgstall, *Geschichte des Osmanischen Reiches*, 1827–35, vol. 5, 298ff., 354ff.
96. Bernier, *Travels in the Mogul Empire*, 1934, 16, 40–41, 374ff.
97. Gibbon, *Decline and Fall of the Roman Empire*, 1994, vol. 1, 313. The most influential discussion of Zenobia was R. Wood, *The Ruins of Palmyra*, 1753, 4ff.
98. Petech, *I missionari italiani nel Tibet e nel Nepal*, 1954–56, vol. 6, 106; Montesquieu, "De l'esprit des lois," 14/4, in *Œuvres*, 1949–51, vol. 2, 511; Grosier, *Description générale de la Chine*, 1785, 235–36; S. Turner, *Account of an Embassy to the Court of the Teshoo Lama Tibet*, 1800, 348–53.
99. S. Turner, *Account of an Embassy to the Court of the Teshoo Lama Tibet*, 1800, 350.

100. Petech, *I missionari italiani nel Tibet e nel Nepal*, 1954–56, vol. 6, 100.
101. Caron and Schouten, *A True Description of the Mighty Kingdom of Japan and Siam*, 1935, 107.
102. A. Hamilton, *New Account of the East Indies*, 1930, vol. 2, 96; Poivre, "Voyage de Pierre Poivre en Cochinchine," 1885, 390.
103. Raffles, *History of Java*, 1817, vol. 1, 109–10.
104. Barrow, *A Voyage to Cochin China*, 1806, 303; Barrow, *Travels in China*, 1806, 141.
105. Elphinstone, *An Account of the Kingdom of Caubul*, 1839, vol. 1, 241.
106. Kaempfer, *Geschichte und Beschreibung Japans*, 1777–79, vol. 1, 138; Kaempfer, *Heutiges Japan*, 2001, vol. 1, 99. "Wives of fishermen" (*Kaempfer's Japan*, 1999, 69) seems to be an incorrect translation. Further evidence of women's work in Kames, *Sketches of the History of Man*, 1778, vol. 1, 35–37.
107. Bruin, *A Voyage to the Levant*, 1702, 102.
108. Percival, *An Account of the Island of Ceylon*, 1805, 194.
109. Barrow, *A Voyage to Cochin China*, 1806, 305; Crawfurd, *Journal of an Embassy to the Courts of Siam and Cochin China*, 1967, 521.
110. La Bissachère, *Etat actuelle du Tunkin*, 1812, vol. 2, 42 (42–62 on the position of women in Vietnam, also vol. 1, 270ff., on their legal position).
111. Symes, *An Account of an Embassy to the Kingdom of Ava*, 1800, 217; Crawfurd, *Journal of an Embassy from the Governor General of India to the Court of Ava*, 1834, vol. 1, 244.
112. A valuable anthology is Major, *Sati*, 2007 (with two British and two Indian accounts from the nineteenth century: 44–61). See also the same author's analysis of these and other sources: Major, *Pious Flames*, 2006.
113. Fisch, "Jenseitsglaube, Ungleichheit und Tod," 1993, 295.
114. By a rough estimate, perhaps one in four hundred widows immolated herself in Bengal at the beginning of the nineteenth century. Fisch, "Jenseitsglaube, Ungleichheit und Tod," 1993, 269. The standard monograph on widow burning and similar phenomena is Fisch, *Burning Women*, 2006.
115. Some examples of descriptions: Bernier, *Travels in the Mogul Empire*, 1934, 305–15; Tavernier, *Travels in India*, 1889, vol. 2, 162–72; Hodges, *Travels in India*, 1793, 79–83; Sonnerat, *Voyages aux Indes Orientales et à la Chine*, 1782, vol. 1, ch. 8; J. Forbes, *Oriental Memoirs*, 1813, vol. 1, 279–83; Dubois, *Mœurs, institutions et cérémonies des peuples de l'Inde*, 1825, vol. 2, 18–34. There were also serious observers who did not give undue prominence to widow burning in their wide-ranging ethnographic accounts, e.g., San Bartolomeo, *Viaggio alle Indie orientale*, 1796.
116. Lenglet-Dufresnoy, *A New Method of Studying History*, 1728, vol. 1, 31.
117. Bernier, *Travels in the Mogul Empire*, 1934, 313–15.
118. This is the summary offered by Ward, *A View of the History, Literature, and Religion of the Hindoos*, 1817–20, vol. 3, xxv–xxvi, xliv et seq.
119. Major, *Sati*, 2007, 75–151.
120. See Narasimhan, *Sati*, 1990, 132–42.
121. Mani, *Contentious Traditions*, 1998, 79.
122. See Démeunier , *L'esprit des usages et des coutumes*, 1776, vol. 1, 68ff. This is also an important topic in Picart's and Bernard's huge encyclopedia of religious customs: Picart, *Cérémonies et coutumes religieuses*, 1723–37. The unacknowledged coauthor of this work, along with the engraver Bernard Picart, was Jean-Fréderic Bernard. See Hunt, Jacob, and Mijnhardt, *The Book that Changed Europe*, 2010.
123. Hume, *Essays*, 1987, 131.

124. Hume, *Essays*, 1987, 133.
125. Hume, *History of England*, 1983, vol. 1, 486–87.
126. Ferguson, *Essay on the History of Civil Society*, 1966, 200–203.
127. Millar, *Origins of the Distinction of Ranks*, 2006, 93–156. Many of Millar's viewpoints were further developed in the first years of the nineteenth century by the early French socialist (and late Enlightenment thinker) Charles Fourier.
128. However, there were also less progressivist voices in Scotland. On the dissident author Gilbert Stuart who took a dim view of the liberty of women in modern commercial society see Sebastiani, *The Scottish Enlightenment*, 2012, 141–43.
129. Kames, *Sketches of the History of Man*, 1778, vol. 1, 41.
130. Kames, *Sketches of the History of Man*, 1778, vol. 1, 69–70.
131. Kames augments the usual theory of knighthood (Kames, *Sketches of the History of Man*, 1778, vol. 1, 82–84) by investigating the decline of the first, medieval form of "chivalry" and its revival in the less naïve, "more substantial" modern form of "gallantry" (85).
132. Richardson, *Dissertation on the Languages, Literature and Manners of Eastern Nations*, 1778, pt. 2, 200.
133. Richardson, *Dissertation on the Languages, Literature and Manners of Eastern Nations*, 1778, pt. 2, 335. Hobhouse, a staunch defender of Turkish womanhood, later pursues a similar line of argument: *A Journey through Albania and Other Provinces of Turkey*, 1813, vol. 1, 345–47.
134. Barrow, *Travels in China*, 1806, 138.
135. Mill, *History of British India*, 1817, vol. 1, 279.
136. Thornton, *Present State of Turkey*, 1809, vol. 2, 257. The passage is polemically directed against the Montesquieu of the *Lettres Persanes*.
137. Thornton, *Present State of Turkey*, 1809, vol. 2, 191.
138. Thornton, *Present State of Turkey*, 1809, vol. 2, 192.
139. Thornton, *Present State of Turkey*, 1809, vol. 2, 194–95.
140. Thornton, *Present State of Turkey*, 1809, vol. 2, 232.

CHAPTER XIII. INTO A NEW AGE: THE RISE OF EUROCENTRISM

1. C. Burney, *A General History of Music*, 1935, vol. 1, 11 (preface).
2. "Sie [die musikalische Kritik] muß für schön erkennen, was jeder Mensch, was jedes Volk nach dem Maaße seiner Kenntniß, nach dem Grade der Entwickelung seiner Fähigkeiten für schön gehalten wissen will. . . . Der Neugrieche, der Türke, der Perser, der Chinese, der amerikanische Wilde, dessen Tonleitern, woraus er seine Melodien bildet, von den unsrigen so sehr abweichen, daß wir nicht im Stande sind, nur die mindeste Ordnung und Schönheit darin zu finden, hat dennoch eine schöne Musik, weil sie ihm gefällt und weil er die nämliche Unordnung, die wir der seinigen vorwerfen, auch an der unsrigen gewahr zu werden glaubt." Forkel, *Allgemeine Geschichte der Musik*, 1788–1801, vol. 1 (1788), xiv.
3. "Dans toute l'antiquité, et chez les nations orientales de l'époque actuelle, la musique n'est constituée que par la mélodie et par le rhythme, tandis que chez les Européens modernes, et dans leurs colonies du nouveau monde, l'harmonie simultanée des sons s'est ajoutée aux autres éléments pour former un art complet. . . . Partout et dans tous les temps il y a eu des chants populaires et religieux: chez les Européens modernes seul il y a eu une art de musique." Fétis, *Histoire générale de la musique*, 1869–76, vol. 1 (1869), 5.

4. This is also true of a few of Fétis's contemporaries. See Bohlman, "The European Discovery of Music in the Islamic World," 1987.
5. This changed to some extent with the rise of musical exoticism from the 1880s onwards. For a comprehensive discussion, see Osterhammel, "Globale Horizonte europäischer Kunstmusik," 2012.
6. According to the estimates of Maddison, *The World Economy*, 2001, 28 (tables 1–2).
7. Schleier, *Geschichte der deutschen Kulturgeschichtsschreibung*, 2003.
8. On this moment of openness see especially Jami, *The Emperor's New Mathematics*, 2012.
9. G. K. Goodman, *Japan and the Dutch*, 2000, chs. 11–14.
10. On Asian interest in Europe in the early modern period see several of the contributions in Schwartz, *Implicit Understandings*, 1994. On Japan see Keene, *Japanese Discovery of Europe*, 1969. The topic is explored under the heading of "Occidentalism" in Carrier, *Occidentalism*, 1995.
11. See also the parallel investigations on Europe's efforts to distance itself from its oriental origins in Bernal, *Black Athena*, 1987.
12. The dating is Pocock's: *Barbarism and Religion*, vol. 6, 2015, 489–90.
13. Gibbon, *History of the Decline and Fall of the Roman Empire*, 1994, vol. 2, 512. Gibbon's emphasis. See also Pocock, *Barbarism and Religion*, vol. 6, 2015, 497–98.
14. A. v. Humboldt, *Essai politique sur le Royaume de la Nouvelle-Espagne*, 1825–27.
15. More critical on Ritter is Schröder, *Das Wissen von der ganzen Welt*, 2011, see, for example, pp. 117–22 on his geography of Africa.
16. Above all in the account of Admiral George Anson's famous circumnavigation of the globe from 1740–44: Walter and Robins, *A Voyage round the World*, 1974. This report, which was widely read and highly regarded throughout Europe, contains one of the earliest anti-Chinese polemics.
17. Especially in his history of India: Elphinstone, *History of India*, 1841.
18. There were exceptions of course. Among thinkers of the first rank, these included Marx and Tocqueville, whose writings on Algeria and India merit greater attention: Tocqueville, *Œuvres complètes*, vol. 3, 1962. But see Pitts, *A Turn to Empire*, 2005, 204–39.
19. See Osterhammel, "Gastfreiheit und Fremdenabwehr," 1997, 397–404. On the Macartney Mission: Peyrefitte, *The Immobile Empire*, 1992; Hevia, *Cherishing Men from Afar*, 1995; Dabringhaus, "Einleitung," 1996.
20. For Egypt on the basis of unpublished correspondence: Laissus, *L'Égypte*, 1998, for India C. A. Bayly, *Empire and Information in India*, 1996.
21. Koselleck, *Futures Past*, 1985; Foucault, *The Order of Things*, 1971; Luhmann, *Theory of Society*, 2012–13, vol. 2, ch.5; Thom, *Republics, Nations and Tribes*, 1995.
22. Tavernier, *Nouvelle relation*, 1675, 130. Others made detailed calculations of such riches, such as Catrou (based on Manuzzi), *History of the Mogul Dynasty*, 1826, 306ff.
23. Bernier, *Travels in the Mogul Empire*, 1934, 223ff.; Gemelli Careri, "A Voyage round the World," 1745, 235; also Tavernier, *Travels in India*, 1889, vol. 1, 391.
24. If even the ever-critical Barrow was impressed by the affluence he observed in the Vietnam of the early 1790s, there must have been something to it: Barrow, *A Voyage to Cochin China*, 1806, 311ff.; similarly also Crawfurd, *Journal of an Embassy to the Courts of Siam and Cochin China*, 1967, 236.
25. See for example the detailed descriptions in Kaempfer, *Phoenix Persicus*, 1987; Poivre, *Voyages d'un philosophe*, 1768; Ekeberg, *Précis historique de l'économie rurale des Chinois*, 1771; Thunberg, *Reise durch einen Theil von Europa, Afrika und Asien*,

1794, vol. 2, pt. 2, 55–73; Colebrooke, *Remarks on the Husbandry and Internal Commerce of Bengal*, 1806; Buchanan, *Journey from Madras*, 1807.

26. Hassel, *Geographisch-statistisches Handwörterbuch*, 1817–18, vol. 2, 374.
27. Mill, *History of British India*, 1815, vol. 1, 331ff.; Tenant had already adopted a similar line, *Indian Recreations*, 1803, vol. 2, 8–20.
28. Dubois, *Mœurs, institutions et cérémonies des peuples de l'Inde*, 1825, vol. 1, 96.
29. Ambirajan, *Classical Political Economy and British Policy in India*, 1978, 59ff.; Picht, *Handel, Politik und Gesellschaft*, 1993, 216–18.
30. The Jesuits did not have much to say about famines. There is, however, an interesting early (1735) analysis of Chinese food supplies in a letter from Pater Parennin to Jean-Jacques d'Ortous de Mairan: Societas Jesu, *Lettres édifiantes et curieuses*, 1780–83, vol. 22, 174–87. The discussion at the end of the century begins with provocations from de Pauw and Grosier's response, *Description générale de la Chine*, 1785, 290–95.
31. Chardin, *Voyages*, 1735, vol. 2, 46ff.; vol. 3, 296ff.
32. C.L.J. de Guignes, *Voyages à Peking*, 1809, vol. 3, 166. European diplomats complained at times about the inferior value of the gifts they received from the Chinese. But from a Chinese viewpoint, a jade scepter that issued directly from the emperor's hand was no less valuable than an English coach.
33. Poivre, *Voyages d'un philosophe*, 1768, 5–8 and passim.
34. Holberg, *Vergleichung der Historien und Thaten*, 1748–51, vol. 1, 237–38, had already noted that China flourished because private ownership of land was allowed there, whereas India stagnated because it was forbidden.
35. Thornton, *Present State of Turkey*, 1809, vol. 1, 65ff.; Barrow, *Travels in China*, 1806, 397–401 (here 401), also 566–71, 578.
36. Platteau, *Les économistes classiques*, 1978, esp. vol. 1, 105ff.; vol. 2, 412ff. The impression of Asian stasis lingered on at a lower level of generalization in mercantile discourses; see for example Blake Smith, "Myths of South Asian Stasis," 2016.
37. On the absence of ruins in Asia, see Barchewitz, *Reisebeschreibung*, 1730, preface; Hodges, *Travels in India*, 1793, 10–11; Meiners, *Betrachtungen*, 1795–96, vol. 1, 267; Barrow, *Travels in China*, 1806, 4–5; Barrow, *A Voyage to Cochin China*, 1806, 312; later Curzon, *Problems of the Far East*, 1894, 83.
38. Mendoza, *The History of the Great and Mighty Kingdom of China*, 1853–54, vol. 2, 282.
39. Wansleb, "Beschreibung von Aegypten im Jahre 1664," 1794, 111.
40. Volney, *Voyage en Égypte et en Syrie*, 1959, 156.
41. For example, Du Halde, *Description géographique*, 1735, vol. 1, 317.
42. See M. Harbsmeier, "Before Decypherment," 1991.
43. Bruin, *Voyages*, 1718, 291, as critic of Alexander; Dubos, *Reflexions*, 1719, vol. 2, 147. The more recent history of Europeans as producers of ruins begins with Cortéz's depredations in Mexico.
44. Thévenot, *Travels*, 1687, vol. 1, 121–23.
45. Joliffe, *Letters from Palestine*, 1822, vol. 2, 108; see also Bruin, *A Voyage to the Levant*, 1702, 172; Volney, *Voyage en Égypte et en Syrie*, 1959, 26; Valentia, *Voyages and Travels to India*, 1809, vol. 3, 455–63.
46. See for example Hammer-Purgstall, *Umblick auf einer Reise von Constantinopel nach Brussa*, 1818, 43.
47. Delhi was still surrounded by vast neighborhoods of ruins in the 1820s: Heber, *Narrative of a Journey through the Upper Provinces of India*, 1828, vol. 2, 290–94, 316–17.
48. Lucas, *Voyage du Sieur Paul Lucas au Levant*, 1731, 246; Güldenstaedt, *Reise durch Rußland*, 1787–91, vol. 1, 326.

49. Bergk, *Aegypten*, 1799, 10.
50. Raynal, *Histoire philosophique et politique*, 1775, vol. 1, 30; Herder, *Ideen*, 1989, 440; see also Volney, "Les ruines, ou méditation sur les révolutions des empires," in Volney, *Œuvres*, 1989–98, vol. 1, 165–439. An interpretation of this fascinating text must be dispensed with here.
51. Hammer-Purgstall, *Geschichte des Osmanischen Reiches*, 1827–35, vol. 1 (1827), xiv. Hammer's view in a nutshell: ibid., 62 (the Peace of Karlowitz of 1699 as the starting point of decline).
52. A contemporary overview of the various interpretations is provided by Chatfield, *Historical Review of the Commercial, Political and Moral State of Hindostan*, 1808, 56ff.
53. See Grewal, *Muslim Rule in India*, 1970, 35, 117.
54. See for example Raynal. *Histoire philosophique et politique*, 1775, vol. 1, 108–20, 203–36; Macpherson, *The History of the European Commerce with India*, 1812, 70ff.; Lueder, *Geschichte des holländischen Handels*, 1788, 243ff.
55. See for example Herrmann, *Gemählde von Ostindien*, 1799, vol. 1, 6–7. Early pan-Asiatic reflections in Holberg, *Vergleichung der Historien und Thaten*, 1748-51, vol. 1, 1ff., 235–36; Harris and Campbell, *Navigantium atque Itinerantium Bibliotheca*, 1744–48, vol. 2, 821ff. Between triumph and elegy: Volney, *Voyage en Égypte et en Syrie*, 1959, 413–14.
56. Playfair, *An Inquiry into the Permanent Causes*, 1805, esp. 70ff. Renaudot, despite calling his book *Révolutions des empires*, 1769, does not offer a general theory of empires.
57. Kindersley, *Letters from the Island of Teneriffe*, 1777, 113.
58. See Hodgen, *Early Anthropology*, 1964, 263–69, 379–80. Similar ideas are found in Enlightenment dress in J. R. Forster, *Bemerkungen*, 1783, 262–63; J. R. Forster, *Observations*, 1996, 196; Marsden, *History of Sumatra*, 1811, 207; Raffles, *History of Java*, 1817, vol. 1, 57.
59. Marshall, "Introduction," in Marshall, *The British Discovery of Hinduism*, 1970, 26–27; Van Aalst, *British View of India*, 1970, 336, 338. On other proponents of this thesis see Mitter, *Much Maligned Monsters*, 1977, 116, 144–45.
60. For more detail see Kopf, *British Orientalism and the Bengal Renaissance*, 1969.
61. See Halbfass, *India and Europe*, 1988, 60–61; Willson, *A Mythical Image*, 1964.
62. See Poliakov, *Aryan Myth*, 1974, 183–214; Jauß, *Studien zum Epochenwandel der ästhetischen Moderne*, 1989, 23–66.
63. See Marshall, "Introduction," *India: Madras and Bengal*, 1981, 15.
64. Mill, *History of British India*, 1817, vol. 1, 460.
65. Diez, *Denkwürdigkeiten*, 1811–15, vol. 1, vi. Travelers obsessed with antiquity, such as Robert Wood, felt themselves transported back into the days of Homer upon seeing peasants in Asia Minor.
66. Tennant, *Indian Recreations*, 1803, vol. 1, 4.
67. Mill, *History of British India*, 1817, vol. 1, 483.
68. Baumgarten, *Algemeine Welthistorie*, 1744–67, vol. 16, 1756, 377.
69. Johann Nikolaus Forkel, quoted in Wang, *Die Rezeption des chinesischen Ton-, Zahl- und Denksystems*, 1985, 194.
70. Malcolm, *History of Persia*, 1829, vol. 1, 82.
71. J. de Guignes, *Histoire générale des Huns*, 1756–58, vol. 1, pt. 1, 76–77 (though a different note is struck in vol. 2, 92–93); d'Anville, *Mémoire . . . sur la Chine*, 1776, 31.
72. Castilhon, *Considérations*, 1769, 234.
73. See for example Hanway, *Historical Account of the British Trade over the Caspian Sea*, 1753, vol. 1, 332–34.

74. Marsden, *History of Sumatra*, 1811, 206.
75. One of the last cautiously sympathetic pronouncements (from 1791): Robertson, *Historical Disquisition*, 1812, 202.
76. Winckelmann, *History of the Art of Antiquity*, 2006, 128–51. On Winckelmann's influence on how oriental art was viewed, see Mitter, *Much Maligned Monsters*, 1977, 192ff.
77. Sonnerat, *Voyages aux Indes Orientales et à la Chine*, 1782, vol. 2, 23.
78. Herder, *Ideen*, 1989, 441; Herder, *Outlines*, 1800, 298.
79. Herder, *Ideen*, 1989, 438; Herder, *Outlines*, 1800, 296.
80. This was shown by Ernst Schulin in an investigation that has yet to be superseded: *Die weltgeschichtliche Erfassung des Orients bei Hegel und Ranke*, 1958, esp. the summary on pp. 137–41; see also Kittsteiner, "Hegels Eurozentrismus in globaler Perspektive," 2010.
81. Pigulla, *China in der deutschen Weltgeschichtsschreibung*, 1996, 155ff.
82. See Lloyd, *Foundations in the Dust*, 1989, 12ff.; Rich, *Narrative of a Journey to the Site of Babylon*, 1839.
83. Schiller, "Was heißt und zu welchem Ende studiert man Universalgeschichte?," in Schiller, *Sämtliche Werke*, 1966, vol. 4, 754; Schiller, "The Nature and Value of Universal History," 1972, 325.
84. Gregory, *Essays Historical and Moral*, 1788, 47.
85. Murray, *Enquiries Historical and Moral*, 1808, 412.
86. See Stocking, *Victorian Anthropology*, 1987, 19. On the diversity of Enlightenment theories of civilization see Slotkin, *Early Anthropology*, 1965, 175–460. Among the prominent Scottish authors of the late eighteenth century, Lord Kames came closest to a general theory of human evolution where stages did not play a leading role. See Sebastiani, "Storia universale e teoria stadiale," 1998, 128.
87. Kosegarten, *Morgenländische Alterthumskunde*, 1831; Robertson, *Progress of Society in Europe*, 1972.
88. Kosegarten, *Morgenländische Altherthumskunde*, 1831, 77.
89. Kosegarten, *Morgenländische Altherthumskunde*, 1831, 95.
90. W. Jones, "Fourth Anniversary Discourse, on the Arabs," in *Works*, 1807, vol. 3, 50.
91. See Hourani, *Europe and the Middle East*, 1980, 32.
92. Volney, *Voyage en Égypte et en Syrie*, 1959, 103, 133.
93. Murray, *Enquiries Historical and Moral*, 1808, 5.
94. Burrow's study remains a classic: *Evolution and Society*, 1966.
95. Marsden, *History of Sumatra*, 1811, 204. Fisch, "Der märchenhafte Orient," 1984, 260–61, had already drawn attention to Marsden as a theorist of civilization.
96. Meiners, *Grundriß der Geschichte der Menschheit*, 1793, 29–31.
97. Barrow, *Travels in China*, 1806, 4, also 32.
98. Barrow, *Travels in China*, 1806, 383.
99. Barrow, *Travels in China*, 1806, 383.
100. Crawfurd, *Journal of an Embassy from the Governor General of India to the Court of Ava*, 1834, vol. 2, 94–95.
101. Symes, *An Account of an Embassy to the Kingdom of Ava*, 1800, 330. Also p. 123 on the high degree of civilization attained by the Burmese.
102. Edmund Burke made a stirring case for the coequality of Europe and India in his speech to Fox's East India Bill of 1783: Burke, *India: Madras and Bengal*, 1981, esp. 389–90. To the best of my knowledge, the last author who acknowledges Asiatic superiority is Thunberg (writing around 1790). He expresses a *general* preference for

the governmental and social institutions of Japan over their European counterparts: Thunberg, *Reise durch einen Theil von Europa, Afrika und Asien*, 1794, vol. 2, pt. 1, 213. Later authors were still prepared to concede *particular* advantages, e.g., the better mental asylums in Turkey: Hammer-Purgstall, *Constantinopolis*, 1822, vol. 1, 509.

103. Guizot, *Histoire de la civilisation en Europe*, 1985. On the idea of "civilization" in the nineteenth century see Mazlish, *Civilization and Its Contents*, 2004; Osterhammel, *Transformation of the World*, 2014, ch. 17.
104. There are few studies to date on the genesis of the new missionary imperialism. Among the most important is Duchet, *Anthropologie et histoire*, 1971, ch. 4. What follows is only a preliminary sketch.
105. Condorcet, *Esquisse d'un tableau historique*, 1988, 268; Condorcet, *Outlines of an Historical View of the Progress of the Human Mind*, 1796, 254.
106. On Grant see Embree, *Charles Grant*, 1962, 118–17, 156.
107. Dohm, "Nacherinnerungen des Herausgebers," in Kaempfer, *Geschichte und Beschreibung Japans*, 1777–79, vol. 2, 422; see also various materials in Kapitza, *Japan in Europa*, vol. 2, 1990.
108. Colebrooke, *Miscellaneous Essays*, 1873, vol. 2, 1.
109. See also Barth and Osterhammel, *Zivilisierungsmissionen*, 2005; Osterhammel, *Europe, the "West" and the Civilizing Mission*, 2006; and, from a rapidly growing literature on the history of humanitarian intervention: Simms and Trim, *Humanitarian Intervention*, 2011.
110. See Gong, *Standard of "Civilization,"* 1984.

Bibliography

Publishers are included only for titles from 1850 onwards. The date of first publication in any language—or, in the case of manuscripts that were only edited much later, the likely year(s) of composition—is provided in square brackets.

Abbattista, Guido. *James Mill e il problema indiano: Gli intellettuali britannici e la conquista dell'India*. Milan: Giuffrè, 1979.

Abbattista, Guido. "The Business of Paternoster Row: Towards a Publishing History of the 'Universal History.'" *Publishing History* 17 (1985): 5–50.

Abbattista, Guido. *Commercio, colonie e impero alla vigilia della rivoluzione americana: John Campbell pubblicista e storico nell'Inghilterra del sec. XVIII*. Florence: Olschki, 1990.

Abbattista, Guido. "At the Roots of the 'Great Divergence': Europe and China in an 18th Century Debate." In Middell, *Cultural Transfers, Encounters and Connections in the Global Eighteenth Century*, 2014, 113–62.

Abbott, John Lawrence. *John Hawkesworth: Eighteenth-Century Man of Letters*. Madison: University of Wisconsin Press, 1982.

Abel, Clarke. *Narrative of a Journey into the Interior of China, and of a Voyage to and from that Country, in the Years 1816 and 1817*. London, 1819.

Abel-Rémusat, Jean-Pierre. *Mélanges asiatiques*. 2 vols. Paris, 1825–26.

Abel-Rémusat, Jean-Pierre. *Nouveaux mélanges asiatiques*. 2 vols. Paris, 1829.

Achenwall, Gottfried. *Staatsverfassung der heutigen vornehmsten Europäischen Reiche und Völker im Grundriße*. 5th ed. Göttingen, 1768.

Adam, Ulrich. *The Political Economy of J.H.G. Justi*. Berne: Lang, 2006.

Adami, Norbert R. *Eine schwierige Nachbarschaft: Die Geschichte der russisch-japanischen Beziehungen*. Vol. 1. Munich: Iudicium, 1990.

Adams, Percy G. *Travelers and Travel Liars, 1660–1800*. Berkeley: University of California Press, 1962.

Adas, Michael. *Machines as the Measure of Men: Science, Technology, and Ideologies of Western Dominance*. Ithaca, NY: Cornell University Press, 1989.

Adas, Michael, ed. *Islamic and European Expansion: The Forging of a Global Order*. Philadelphia, PA: Temple University Press, 1993.

Adelung, Johann Christoph. *Geschichte der Schiffahrten und Versuche, welche zur Entdeckung des Nordöstlichen Weges nach Japan und China von verschiedenen Nationen unternommen worden*. Halle, 1768.

Adelung, Johann Christoph. *Versuch einer Geschichte der Cultur des menschlichen Geschlechtes*. Leipzig, 1782.

Adelung, Johann Christoph. *Mithridates oder allgemeine Sprachenkunde*. 4 pts. in 6 vols. Berlin, 1806–17.

Adler, Hans, and Ernest A. Menze, eds. *Herder on World History: An Anthology*. Armonk, NY: Sharpe, 1997.

Aikin, John. *Geographical Delineations; or a Compendious View of the Natural and Political States of All Parts of the Globe*. 2 vols. London, 1806.

Aksan, Virginia H. *An Ottoman Statesman in War and Peace: Ahmed Resmi Efendi, 1700–1783*. Leiden: Brill, 1995.

Alam, Muzaffar, and Sanjay Subrahmanyam. *Indo-Persian Travels in the Age of Discoveries, 1400–1800*. Cambridge: Cambridge University Press, 2007.

Albrecht, Andrea. *Kosmopolitismus: Weltbürgerdiskurse in Literatur, Philosophie und Publizistik um 1800*. Berlin: de Gruyter, 2005.

Alder, Gerry J. *Beyond Bokhara: The Life of William Moorcroft, Asian Explorer and Pioneer Veterinary Surgeon, 1767–1825*. London: Century, 1985.

Alexander, William. *The History of Women, from the Earliest Antiquity to the Present Time*. 2 vols. Dublin, 1779.

Allgemeine Geschichte der neueren Entdeckungen, welche von den verschiedenen gelehrten Reisenden in vielen Gegenden des rußischen Reichs und Persien . . . sind gemacht worden. 6 pts. in 3 vols. Berne, 1777–86.

Allison, Robert J. *The Crescent Obscured: The United States and the Muslim World, 1776–1815*. Oxford: Oxford University Press, 1995.

Almond, Philip C. *The British Discovery of Buddhism*. Cambridge: Cambridge University Press, 1988.

Ambirajan, S. *Classical Political Economy and British Policy in India*. Cambridge: Cambridge University Press, 1978.

Ambros, Edith Gülçin. "Frivolity and Flirtation." In Ebru Boyar and Kate Fleet, eds., *Ottoman Women in Public Space*. Leiden: Brill, 2016, 150–86.

Amiot, Joseph. *Art militaire des Chinois, ou Receuil d'anciens traités sur la guerre*. Paris, 1772.

Amiot, Joseph. *Mémoire sur la Musique des Chinois, tant anciens que modernes*. Paris, 1779.

Anderson, Æneas. *A Narrative of the British Embassy to China in the Years 1792, 1793, and 1794*. London, 1795.

Anderson, Sonia P. *An English Consul in Turkey: Paul Rycaut at Smyrna, 1667–1678*. Oxford: Oxford University Press, 1989.

Angelomatis-Tsougarakis, Helen. *The Eve of the Greek Revival: British Travellers' Perceptions of Early Nineteenth-Century Greece*. London: Routledge, 1990.

Angster, Julia. *Erdbeeren und Piraten. Die Royal Navy und die Ordnung der Welt 1770–1860*. Göttingen: Vandenhoeck and Ruprecht, 2012.

Annales des voyages, de la géographie et de l'histoire. . . . publiés par M. Malte-Brun. 2e éd. revue et corrigée. 25 vols. Paris, 1809–13.

Anquetil-Duperron, Abraham Hyacinthe. *Législation orientale*. Amsterdam, 1778.

Anquetil-Duperron, Abraham Hyacinthe. "Recherches historiques et géographiques sur l'Inde" (= Bernoulli, *Description historique*, 1786–89. vol. 2, 1787).

Anquetil-Duperron, Abraham Hyacinthe. *Dignité du commerce, et de l'état du commerçant*. n.p. [Paris], 1789.

Anquetil-Duperron, Abraham Hyacinthe. *L'Inde en rapport avec l'Europe*. 2 vols. Paris, 1798.

Antognazza, Maria Rosa. *Leibniz: An Intellectual Biography*. Cambridge: Cambridge University Press, 2009.

App, Urs. *The Birth of Orientalism*. Philadelphia: University of Pennsylvania Press, 2010.

Appleton, William W. *A Cycle of Cathay: The Chinese Vogue in England during the 17th and 18th Centuries*. New York: Columbia University Press, 1951.

Arbuthnot, John. *An Essay Concerning the Effects of Air on Human Bodies*. London, 1733.

Archer, Mildred. *Early Views of India: The Picturesque Journeys of Thomas and William Daniell 1786–1794*. London: Thames and Hudson, 1980.

Aristotle. *Politics* (Loeb Classical Library). Trans. H. Rackham. Cambridge, MA: Harvard University Press, 1967.

Arjomand, Saïd Amir. "Coffeehouses, Guilds and Oriental Despotism: Government and Civil Society in Late 17th to Early 18th-Century Istanbul and Isfahan, and as Seen from Paris and London." *European Journal of Sociology* 45 (2004): 23–42.

Armitage, David, and Alison Bashford, eds. *Pacific Histories: Ocean, Land, People*. Basingstoke: Palgrave Macmillan, 2014.

Asiatic Annual Register. Vols. 1–12 (1800–1812).

Asiatic Journal. Vols. 1–28 (1816–1829).

Asiatick Researches, or Transactions of the Society, Instituted in Bengal. Vols. 1 (1788) to 20 (1836), Calcutta.

Asiatisches Magazin. Ed. Johann Adam Bergk, et al. 3 vols. Leipzig, 1806–11.

Astley, Thomas, [and John Green]. *A New General Collection of Voyages and Travels*. 4 vols. London, 1745–47.

Atkin, Muriel. *Russia and Iran, 1780–1828*. Minneapolis: University of Minnesota Press, 1988.

Auch, Eva-Maria, and Stig Förster, eds. *"Barbaren" und "Weiße Teufel": Kulturkonflikte und Imperialismus in Asien vom 18. bis zum 20. Jahrhundert*. Paderborn: Schöningh, 1997.

Avery, Peter, Gavin Hambly, and Charles Melville, eds. *From Nâdir Shah to the Islamic Republic*. Cambridge: Cambridge University Press, 1991 (= *The Cambridge History of Iran*, 7).

Avery, Peter. "Nâdir Shâh and the Afsharid Legacy." In Avery, Hambly, and Melville, *From Nâdir Shah to the Islamic Republic*, 1991, 3–62.

Avril, Pierre. *Voyage en divers états d'Europe et d'Asie, entrepris pour découvrir un nouveau chemin à la Chine*. Paris, 1692.

Axworthy, Michael. *The Sword of Persia: Nader Shah, from Tribal Warrior to Conquering Tyrant*. London: Tauris, 2006.

Baack, Lawrence J. *Undying Curiosity: Carsten Niebuhr and the Royal Danish Expedition to Arabia (1761–1767)*. Stuttgart: Steiner, 2014.

Babinger, Franz. "Die türkischen Studien in Europa bis zum Auftreten Joseph von Hammer-Purgstalls." *Die Welt des Islams* 7 (1919): 103–29.

Bailly, Jean Sylvain. *Lettres sur l'origine des sciences, et sur celle des peuples de l'Asie*. London, 1777.

Bailly, Jean Sylvain. *Lettres sur l'Atlantide de Platon et sur l'ancienne histoire de l'Asie*. London, 1779.

Baker, Chris, et al. *Van Vliet's Siam*. Chiang Mai: Silkworm Books, 2005 [1636–40].

Barchewitz, Ernst Christian. *Allerneueste und wahrhaffte Ost-Indianische Reisebeschreibung*. Chemnitz, 1730.

Barend-van Haeften, Marijke. *Oost-Indië gespiegld: Nicolaas de Graaff, een schrijvend chirugijn in dienst van de VOC*. Zutphen: Walburg Pers, 1992.

Baridon, Michel. "Lumières et enlightenment: Faux parallèle ou vraie dynamique du mouvement philosophique?" *Dix-huitième siècle* 10 (1978): 45–69.

Barratt, Glynn. *Russia in Pacific Waters 1715–1825: A Survey of the Origins of Russia's Naval Presence in the North and South Pacific*. Vancouver / London: University of British Columbia Press, 1981.

Barratt, Glynn. *Russia and the South Pacific*. 4 vols. Vancouver / London: University of British Columbia Press, 1988–92.
Barrell, John. *The Infection of Thomas De Quincey: A Psychopathology of Imperialism*. New Haven, CT: Yale University Press, 1991.
Barrett, T. H. *Singular Listlessness. A Short History of Chinese Books and British Scholars*. London: Wellsweep, 1989.
Barrow, Ian J. *Making History, Drawing Territory: British Mapping in India, c. 1756–1905*. New Delhi: Oxford University Press, 2003.
Barrow, John. *An Account of Travels into the Interior of Southern Africa in the Years 1797 and 1798*. London, 1801.
Barrow, John. *Reisen durch die inneren Gegenden des südlichen Africa in den Jahren 1797 und 1798*. Trans. Matthias Christian Sprengel. Weimar, 1801.
Barrow, John. *Reise durch China von Peking nach Canton im Gefolge der Großbritannischen Gesandtschaft in den Jahren 1793 und 1794*. Trans. Johann Christian Hüttner. 2 vols. Weimar, 1804.
Barrow, John. *Travels in China*. 2nd ed. London, 1806 [1804].
Barrow, John. *A Voyage to Cochin China, in the Years 1792 and 1793*. London, 1806.
Barrow, John. *Some Account of the Public Life and a Selection from the Unpublished Writings of the Earl of Macartney*. 2 vols. London, 1807.
Barrow, John. *An Autobiographical Memoir of Sir John Barrow, Bart*. London, 1847.
Barth, Boris, and Jürgen Osterhammel, eds. *Zivilisierungsmissionen: Imperiale Weltverbesserung seit dem 18. Jahrhundert*. Konstanz: UVK Verlag, 2005.
Barthold, Vasily V. *Die geographische und historische Erforschung des Orients mit besonderer Berücksichtigung der russischen Arbeiten*. Leipzig: Wigand, 1913.
Bashford, Alison, and Joyce E. Chaplin. *The New Worlds of Thomas Robert Malthus: Rereading the "Principle of Population."* Princeton, NJ: Princeton University Press, 2016.
Bassin, Mark. "Inventing Siberia: Visions of the Russian East in the Early Nineteenth Century." *American Historical Review* 93 (1991): 763–94.
Bassin, Mark. "Russia between Europe and Asia: The Ideological Construction of Geographical Space." *Slavic Review* 50 (1991): 1–17.
Bassin, Mark. *Imperial Visions: Nationalist Imagination and Geographical Expansion in the Russian Far East, 1840–1865*. Cambridge: Cambridge University Press, 1999.
Bastian, Adolf. *Die Geschichte der Indochinesen*. Leipzig: Wigand, 1866.
Batra, Roger. *Wild Men in the Looking Glass: The Mythic Origins of European Otherness*. Ann Arbor: University of Michigan Press, 1994.
Batten, Charles L. *Pleasurable Instruction: Form and Convention in 18th Century Travel Literature*. Berkeley: University of California Press, 1978.
Baudier, Michel. *Histoire de la cour du roy de la Chine*. Paris, 1624.
Baumgarten, Siegmund Jacob. "Vorrede." In Baumgarten and Semler, eds., *Uebersetzung der Algemeinen Welthistorie*, vol. 1 (1744), 3–58.
Baumgarten, Siegmund Jacob, and Johann Salomo Semler, eds. *Uebersetzung der Algemeinen Welthistorie, die in Engeland durch eine Geselschaft von Gelehrten ausgefertiget worden. Nebst den Anmerkungen der holländischen Uebersetzung*. 30 vols. Halle, 1744–67.
Baumgarten, Siegmund Jacob, and Johann Salomo Semler, eds. *Samlung von Erleuterungsschriften und Zusätzen zur Algemeinen Welthistorie*. 6 vols. Halle, 1747–65.
Bayer, Theophil Siegfried. *Museum Sinicum*. 2 vols. Saint Petersburg, 1730.
Bayly, C. A. *Indian Society and the Making of the British Empire*. Cambridge: Cambridge University Press, 1988.

Bayly, C. A. *Imperial Meridian: The British Empire and the World 1780–1830*. London: Longman, 1989.

Bayly, C. A. *Empire and Information: Intelligence Gathering and Social Communication in India, 1780–1870*. Cambridge: Cambridge University Press, 1996.

Bayly, C. A. *The Birth of the Modern World 1780–1914: Global Connections and Comparisons*. Oxford: Blackwell, 2004.

Bayly, Susan. *Caste, Society and Politics in India from the Eighteenth Century to the Modern Age*. Cambridge: Cambridge University Press, 1999.

Beaglehole, J. C. *The Life of Captain James Cook*. Stanford, CA: Stanford University Press, 1974.

Bearce, George D. *British Attitudes toward India, 1784–1858*. London: Oxford University Press, 1961.

Beasley, W. G., and E. G. Pulleyblank, eds. *Historians of China and Japan*. London: Oxford University Press, 1961.

Beawes, Wyndham. *Lex Mercatoria Rediviva, or, the Merchant's Directory*. Dublin, 1754.

Beck, Brandon H. *From the Rising of the Sun: English Images of the Ottoman Empire to 1715*. New York: Lang, 1987.

Beck, Hanno. *Alexander von Humboldt*. 2 vols. Wiesbaden: Steiner, 1959–61.

Beckmann, Johann. *Litteratur der älteren Reisebeschreibungen: Nachrichten von ihren Verfassern, von ihrem Inhalte, von ihren Ausgaben und Uebersetzungen*. 2 vols. Göttingen, 1807–10.

Beckwith, Christopher I. *Empires of the Silk Road: A History of Central Eurasia from the Bronze Age to the Present*. Princeton, NJ: Princeton University Press, 2009.

Beekman, E. M. *Troubled Pleasures: Dutch Colonial Literature from the East Indies, 1600–1950*. Oxford: Clarendon Press, 1996.

Behdad, Ali. *Belated Travelers: Orientalism in the Age of Colonial Dissolution*. Durham, NC: Duke University Press, 1994.

Beiträge zur Völker- und Länderkunde. Ed. Johann Reinhold Forster and Matthias Christian Sprengel. 14 vols. Leipzig, 1781–90.

Bell, John. *A Journey from St. Petersburg to Pekin 1719–22*. Ed. John Lynn Stevenson. Edinburgh: Edinburgh University Press, 1965.

Bennassar, Bartolomé, and Lucile Bennassar. *Les Chrétiens d'Allah: L'histoire extraordinaire des renégats, XVIe–XVIIe siècles*. Paris: Perrin, 1989.

Benyowski, M. A. *The Memoirs and Travels of Mauritius Augustus Count de Benyowsky in Siberia, Kamchatka, Japan, the Liukiu Islands and Formosa*. Ed. P. Oliver. London: T. F. Unwin, 1893 [1790].

Berchet, Jean-Claude, ed. *Le voyage en Orient: Anthologie des voyageurs français dans le Levant au XIXe siècle*. Paris: Laffont, 1985.

Berg, Maxine, ed. *Goods from the East, 1600–1800: Trading Eurasia*. Basingstoke: Palgrave Macmillan, 2015.

Berghaus, Heinrich. *Die ersten Elemente der Erdbeschreibung*. Berlin, 1830.

Bergk, Johann Adam. *Aegypten in historischer, geographischer, physikalischer, wissenschaftlicher, artistischer, naturgeschichtlicher, merkantlischer, religiöser, sittlicher und politischer Hinsicht*. Berlin, 1799.

Bergmann, Benjamin. *Nomadische Streifereien unter den Kalmüken in den Jahren 1802 und 1803*. 2 vols. Riga, 1804–5.

Bernal, Martin. *Black Athena: The Afroasiatic Roots of Classical Civilization*. Vol. 1: *The Fabrication of Ancient Greece 1785–1985*. London: Free Association Books, 1987.

Bernard, Jean Frédéric, ed. *Recueil de voyages du Nord, Contenant divers mémoires très utiles au commerce & à la Navigation*. 10 vols. Amsterdam, 1731–38.
Bernier, François. *Travels in the Mogul Empire A.D. 1656–1668*. Trans. A. Constable. 2nd ed. Revised by V. A. Smith. London: Oxford University Press, 1934 [1670–71].
Bernoulli, Johann. *Unterrichtendes Verzeichniß einer Berlinischen Privatbibliothek*. Berlin, 1783.
Bernoulli, Johann, ed. *Des Pater Joseph Tieffenthaler's d. S. J. und apostol. Mißionarius in Indien historisch-geographische Beschreibung von Hindustan*. 3 vols. in 4 pts. Gotha, 1785–87.
Bernoulli, Johann, ed. *Description historique et géographique de l'Inde*. 3 vols. Berlin, 1786–89.
Berridge, Virginia, and Griffith Edwards. *Opium and the People: Opiate Use in Nineteenth-Century England*. London: Allen Lane, 1981.
Bevilacqua, Alexander. "The Qur'an Translations of Maracci and Sale." *Journal of the Warburg and Courtauld Institutes* 76 (2013): 93–130.
Bevilacqua, Alexander. "How to Organize the Orient: D'Herbelot and the Bibliothèque Orientale." *Journal of the Warburg and Courtauld Institutes* 79 (2016): 213–61.
Bevilacqua, Alexander. *The Republic of Arabic Letters: Islam and the European Enlightenment*. Cambridge, MA: Harvard University Press, 2018.
Bevilacqua, Alexander, and Helen Pfeifer. "Turquerie: Culture in Motion, 1650–1750." *Past and Present* 221 (2013): 75–118.
Bietenholz, Peter G. *Pietro della Valle (1586–1652): Studien zur Geschichte der Orientkenntnis und des Orientbildes im Abendlande*. Basle: Helbing and Lichtenhahn, 1962.
Binoche, Bertrand. *Introduction à "De l'esprit des lois" de Montesquieu*. Paris: Presses Universitaires de France, 1998.
Bishop, Peter. *The Myth of Shangri-La: Tibet, Travel Writing and the Western Creation of Sacred Landscape*. London: Athlone, 1989.
Bitterli, Urs. *Cultures in Conflict: Encounters between European and Non-European Cultures, 1492–1800*. Trans. Ritchie Robertson. Cambridge: Polity Press, 1989.
Björnstahl, Jacob Jonas. *Briefe auf seinen ausländischen Reisen an den königlichen Bibliothekar C.C. Gjörwell in Stockholm*. Trans. J. E. Groskurd and C. H. Groskurd. 6 vols. Leipzig, 1777–83.
Black, J. L. *G.- F. Müller and the Imperial Russian Academy*. Kingston: McGill-Queen's University Press, 1986.
Blanke, Horst Walter. "Verfassungen, die nicht rechtlich, aber wirklich sind: A.H.L. Heeren und das Ende der Aufklärungshistorie." *Berichte zur Wissenschaftsgeschichte* 6 (1983), 143–64.
Blanke, Horst Walter. *Politische Herrschaft und soziale Ungleichheit im Spiegel des Anderen: Untersuchungen zu den deutschsprachigen Reisebeschreibungen vornehmlich im Zeitalter der Aufklärung*. 2 vols. Waltrop: Spener, 1997.
Blome, Richard. *A Geographical Description of the Four Parts of the World*. London, 1670.
Blount, Sir Henry. *A Voyage into the Levant*. 8th ed. London, 1671 [1636].
Blumenbach, Johann Friedrich. "Vorrede." In Bruce, *Reisen in das Innere von Africa*, vol. 1, 1790, iii–xxiii.
Blumenbach, Johann Friedrich. *Abbildungen naturhistorischer Gegenstände*. Göttingen, 1810.
Blussé, Leonard. *Visible Cities: Canton, Nagasaki, and Batavia and the Coming of the Americans*. Cambridge, MA: Harvard University Press, 2008.

Blussé, Leonard, and Femme Gaastra, eds. *On the Eighteenth Century as a Category of Asian History*. Aldershot: Ashgate, 1998.

Bod, Rens, Jaap Maat, and Thijs Weststeijn, eds. *The Making of the Humanities*. Vol. 2: *From Early Modern to Modern Disciplines*. Amsterdam: Amsterdam University Press, 2012.

Bodart-Bailey, Beatrice M. "Kaempfer Restor'd." *Monumenta Nipponica* 43 (1988): 1–33.

Bödeker, Hans Erich, and Ulrich Herrmann, eds. *Aufklärung als Politisierung—Politisierung der Aufklärung*. Hamburg: Meiner, 1987.

Boerner, Peter. "Die großen Reisesammlungen des 18. Jahrhunderts." In Maçzak and Teuteberg, *Reiseberichte als Quellen europäischer Kulturgeschichte*, 1982, 65–72.

Bogle, George, and Thomas Manning. *Narratives of the Mission of George Bogle to Tibet, and of the Journey of Thomas Manning to Lhasa*. Ed. Clements R. Markham. 2nd ed. London: Trübner, 1879.

Bohlman, Philip V. "The European Discovery of Music in the Islamic World and the 'Non-Western' in Nineteenth-Century Music History." *Journal of Musicology* 5 (1987): 147–63.

Bonacina, Giovanni. *The Wahhabis Seen through European Eyes (1772–1830): Deists and Puritans of Islam*. Leiden: Brill, 2015.

Bonnerot, Olivier H. *La Perse dans la littérature et la pensée françaises au XVIIIe siècle: de l'image au mythe*. Paris: Champion-Slatkine, 1988.

Boogert, Maurits H. van den. "Patrick Russell and the Republic of Letters in Aleppo." In Alastair Hamilton, Maurits H. van den Boogert, and Bart Westerweel, eds., *The Republic of Letters and the Levant*. Leiden: Brill, 2005, 223–64.

Boogert, Maurits H. van den. *Aleppo Observed: Ottoman Syria through the Eyes of Two Scottish Doctors, Alexander and Patrick Russell*. Oxford: Arcadian Library, 2010.

Booth, Marilyn, ed. *Harem Histories: Envisioning Places and Living Spaces*. Durham, NC: Duke University Press, 2010.

Boucher de la Richarderie, Gilles, ed. *Bibliothèque universelle des voyages*. 6 vols. Paris 1808.

Bougainville, Jean-Pierre de. *Parallèle de l'expédition d'Alexandre dans les Indes avec la conquête des mêmes par Thamas Kouli Khan*. Paris, 1752.

Bougainville, Louis-Antoine de. *Voyage autour du monde*. Ed. Jacques Proust. Paris: Gallimard, 1982 [1771].

Boulainvilliers, Henry de. *Histoire des Arabes; avec la Vie de Mahomed*. Amsterdam, 1731.

Boulanger, Nicolas Antoine. *Œuvres de Boullanger* [*sic*], 6 vols. Amsterdam, 1794.

Bourguignon-d'Anville, Jean-Baptiste: see d'Anville.

Bourke, Richard. *Empire and Revolution: The Political Life of Edmund Burke*. Princeton, NJ: Princeton University Press, 2015.

Bouvet, Joachim. *Histoire de l'Empereur de la Chine*. The Hague, 1699.

Bouvet, Joachim. *Eine wissenschaftliche Akademie für China: Briefe des Chinamissionars Joachim Bouvet S. J. an Gottfried Wilhelm Leibniz und Jean-Paul Bignon über die Erforschung der chinesischen Kultur, Sprache und Geschichte*. Ed. Claudia von Collani. Stuttgart: Steiner, 1989.

Bowen, Emanuel. *The Gentleman, Tradesman and Traveller's Pocket Library*, London, 1753.

Bowen, Margarita. *Empiricism and Geographical Thought: From Francis Bacon to Alexander von Humboldt*. Cambridge: Cambridge University Press, 1981.

Boxer, Charles R. "Isaac Titsingh's Embassy to the Court of Ch'ien Lung (1794–1795)." *T'ien Hsia Monthly* 8 (1939): 9–33.

Boxer, Charles R. *The Dutch Seaborne Empire 1600–1800*. London: Hutchinson, 1965.

Boyar, Ebru, and Kate Fleet. *A Social History of Ottoman Istanbul*. Cambridge: Cambridge University Press, 2010.

Braam Houckgeest, Andreas Everard van. *An Authentic Account of the Embassy of the Dutch East India Company to the Court of the Emperor of China, in the Years 1794 and 1795*. 2 vols. London, 1798.

Brahimi, Denise. *Voyageurs français du XVIIIe siècle in Barbarie*. Paris: Champion, 1976.

Brahimi, Denise. *Arabes des Lumières et bédouins romantiques: un siècle des "voyages en Orient" 1735–1835*. Paris: Le Sycomore, 1982.

Braithwaite, John. *The History of the Revolutions in the Empire of Morocco, upon the Death of the Late Emperor Muley Ishmael*. London, 1729.

Brand, Adam. *Beschreibung der Chinesischen Reise Welche vermitteltst Einer Zaaris. Gesandtschaft Durch Dero Ambassadeur Herrn Isbrand Ao. 1693, 94 und 95 . . . verrichtet worden*. Hamburg, 1698.

Braudel, Fernand. *Civilization and Capitalism, 15th to 18th Centuries*. Trans. Siân Reynolds. 3 vols. New York: Harper and Row, 1981–84.

Braune, Michael. "Ulrich Jasper Seetzens Leben in der Community der Franken in Aleppo (1803–1805)." In Detlef Haberland, ed. *Ulrich Jasper Seetzen (1767–1811): Jeveraner—aufgeklärter Unternehmer—wissenschaftlicher Orientreisender*. Oldenburg: Isensee, 2014, 167–85.

Breckenridge, Carol A., and Peter van der Veer. eds. *Orientalism and the Postcolonial Predicament: Perspectives on South Asia*. Philadelphia: University of Pennsylvania Press, 1993.

Breen, Benjamin. "No Man Is an Island: Early Modern Globalization, Knowledge Networks, and George Psalmanazar's Formosa." *Journal of Early Modern History* 17 (2013): 391–417.

Breitenbauch, Georg August von. *Ergänzungen der Geschichte von Asien und Afrika in dem mittleren und neueren Zeitalter*. 4 vols. Dessau, 1783–85; Halle, 1787.

Brenner, Peter J., ed. *Der Reisebericht: Die Entwicklung einer Gattung in der deutschen Literatur*. Frankfurt a.M.: Suhrkamp, 1989.

Breton de la Martinière, J.B.J. *La Chine en miniature, ou Choix de costumes, arts et métiers de cet Empire*. 6 vols. Paris, 1811–12.

Briant, Pierre. *Alexandre des Lumières: fragments d'histoire européenne*. Paris: Gallimard, 2012.

Briggs, John. *History of the Rise of Mahomedan Power in India*. London, 1829.

Brittlebank, Kate. *Tipu Sultan's Search for Legitimacy: Islam and Kingship in a Hindu Domain*. Delhi: Oxford University Press, 1997.

Broc, Numa. *Les montagnes vues par les géographes et les naturalistes de la langue française au XVIIIe siècle*. Paris: Bibliothèque Nationale, 1969.

Broc, Numa. *La géographie des philosophes: géographes et voyageurs français au XVIIIe siècle*. Paris: Éd. Ophrys, 1975.

Broc, Numa. *La géographie de la Renaissance (1420–1620)*. Paris: Bibliothèque Nationale, 1980.

Broc, Numa. "Les grandes missions scientifiques françaises au XIXe siècle (Morée, Algérie, Mexique) et leurs travaux géographiques." *Revue d'histoire des sciences* 34 (1981): 319–58.

Brockey, Liam Matthew. *Journey to the East: The Jesuit Mission to China, 1579–1724*. Cambridge, MA: Harvard University Press, 2007.

Brot, Muriel. "L'abbé Raynal, lecteur de l'Histoire générale des voyages: de la description à la démonstration." In Lüsebrink and Strugnell, *L'Histoire des deux Indes*, 1995, 91–104.
Brougham, Henry. *An Inquiry into the Colonial Policy of the European Powers.* 2 vols. Edinburgh, 1803.
Brougham, Henry. *Political Philosophy.* 3 vols. London, 1842–43.
Brown, Stewart J., ed. *William Robertson and the Expansion of Empire.* Cambridge: Cambridge University Press, 1997.
Browne, William George. *Travels in Africa, Egypt and Syria, from the Year 1792 to 1798.* London, 1799.
Bruce, James. *Travels to Discover the Source of the Nile, in the Years 1768, 1769, 1770, 1771, 1772 and 1773.* 5 vols. Edinburgh, 1790.
Bruce, James. *Reisen in das Innere von Africa nach Abyssinien an die Quellen des Nils.* Aus dem Englischen mit nöthiger Abkürzung in das Deutsche übers. v. E. W. Cuhn. Mit zur Naturgeschichte gehörigen Berichtigungen und Zusätzen vers. v. J. F. Gmelin. 2 vols. Rinteln, 1791.
Bruce, James. *Reisen zur Entdeckung der Quelle des Nils in den Jahren 1768, 1769, 1770, 1771, 1772 und 1773.* Ins Deutsche übers. v. J. J. Volkmann u. mit einer Vorrede u. Anm. vers. v. J. F. Blumenbach. 5 vols. Leipzig, 1791.
Bruin, Cornelis de. *A Voyage to the Levant; or, Travels in the Principal Parts of Asia Minor, the Islands of Scio, Rhodes, Cyprus &c.* Trans. into English by W. J. London, 1702 [1698].
Bruin, Cornelis de. *Voyages de Corneille le Brun par la Moscovie en Perse et aux Indes Orientales.* 2 vols. Amsterdam, 1718 [1714].
Brunner, Otto. "Feudalismus, Feudal." In Brunner, Conze, and Koselleck, *Geschichtliche Grundbegriffe*, vol. 2, 1975, 337–50.
Brunner, Otto, Werner Conze, and Reinhart Koselleck, eds. *Geschichtliche Grundbegriffe: Historisches Lexikon zur politisch-sozialen Sprache in Deutschland.* 8 vols. Stuttgart: Klett-Cotta, 1972–97.
Bruzen de la Martinière, Antoine-Augustin. *Introduction à l'histoire de l'Asie, de l'Afrique, et de l'Amérique.* 2 vols. Amsterdam, 1735.
Bruzen de la Martinière, Antoine-Augustin. *Le grand dictionnaire géographique, historique et critique.* Nouv. éd. 6 vols. Paris, 1768.
Buchanan, Francis. *A Journey from Madras through the Countries of Mysore, Canara, and Malabar.* 3 vols. London, 1807.
Buchanan, Francis: see also Hamilton (Francis).
Buffon, Georges-Louis-Leclerc de. "Histoire naturelle de l'homme" [1749]. In Buffon, *Œuvres complètes III: Histoire naturelle, gènérale et particulière.* Vol. 3. Ed. Stéphane Schmitt. Paris: Honoré Champion, 2009, 343–573.
Buisseret, David, ed. *Monarchs, Ministers and Maps: The Emergence of Cartography as a Tool of Government in Early Modern Europe.* Chicago: University of Chicago Press, 1992.
Bulliet, Richard W. *The Camel and the Wheel.* New York: Columbia University Press, 1975.
Burbank, Jane, and Frederick Cooper. *Empires in World History: Power and the Politics of Difference.* Princeton, NJ: Princeton University Press, 2010.
Burckhardt, Johann Ludwig. *Travels in Syria and the Holy Land.* London, 1822.
Burckhardt, Johann Ludwig. *Travels in Arabia.* 2 vols. London, 1829.

Burckhardt, Johann Ludwig. *Notes on the Bedouins and Wahábys, Collected during His Travels in the East*. London, 1830.
Burke, Edmund. *The Correspondence of Edmund Burke*. Ed. Thomas W. Copeland. 10 vols. Cambridge: Cambridge University Press, 1958–78.
Burke, Edmund. *India: Madras and Bengal 1774–1785*. Ed. P. J. Marshall. Oxford: Clarendon Press, 1981 (= *The Writings and Speeches of Edmund Burke*, 5).
Burke, Edmund. *India: The Launching of the Hastings Impeachment 1786–1788*. Ed. P. J. Marshall. Oxford: Clarendon Press, 1991 (= *The Writings and Speeches of Edmund Burke*, 6).
Burke, Edmund. *India: The Hastings Trial, 1789–1794*. Ed. P. J. Marshall. Oxford: Clarendon Press, 2000 (= *The Writings and Speeches of Edmund Burke*, 7).
Burke, Peter. "America and the Rewriting of World History." In Kupperman, *America in European Consciousness*, 1995, 33–51.
Burke, Peter. *A Social History of Knowledge: From Gutenberg to Diderot*. Cambridge: Polity Press, 2000.
Burnes, Alexander. *Travels into Bokhara*. 3 vols. London, 1834.
Burney, Charles. *A General History of Music: From the Earliest Ages to the Present Period*. 4 vols. With critical and historical notes by Frank Mercer. New York: Harcourt, Brace and Co., 1935 [1776–89].
Burney, Henry. "Report on the Mission to Siam [2. Dezember 1826]." In *The Burney Papers*. Vol. 2. Bangkok, 1911, 14–76.
Burrow, J. W. *Evolution and Society: A Study in Victorian Social Theory*. Cambridge: Cambridge University Press, 1966.
Burrow, J. W. *Gibbon*. Oxford: Oxford University Press, 1985.
Busbecq, Ogier Ghiselin de. *Travels into Turkey*. London, 1744 [1589].
Busbecq, Ogier Ghiselin de. *The Turkish Letters*. Trans. Edward Seymour Forster. Oxford: Clarendon Press, 1927.
Büsching, Anton Friedrich. *Auszug aus seiner Erdbeschreibung. Erster Theil, welcher Europa und den nordlichen Theil von Asia enthält*. 6th ed. Hamburg, 1785.
Büsching, Anton Friedrich. *Große Erdbeschreibung*. Vol. 23: *Asien*, pt. 1. Brünn (Brno), 1787.
Businello, Pietro. *Historische Nachrichten von der Regierungsart, den Sitten und Gewohnheiten der osmanischen Monarchie*. Leipzig, 1778.
Butterwick, Richard, Simon Davies, and Gabriel Sanchez Espinosa, eds. *Peripheries of the Enlightenment*. Oxford: Voltaire Foundation, 2008.
Buzard, James. *The Beaten Track: European Tourism, Literature, and the Way of "Culture," 1800–1918*. Oxford: Clarendon Press, 1993.
Caillié, René. *Travels through Central Africa to Timbuctoo; and across the Great Desert to Morocco, Performed in the Years 1824 to 1828*. 2 vols. London, 1830.
Campbell, Donald. *Journey over Land to India, Partly by a Route Never Gone before by Any European*. London, 1796.
Campbell, John. *The Present State of Europe*. London, 1750.
Canetti, Elias. *Masse und Macht*. Hamburg: Claassen, 1960.
Cannadine, David. *Ornamentalism: How the British Saw Their Empire*. London: Allen Lane, 2001.
Cannon, Garland H., and Kevin R. Brine, eds. *Objects of Enquiry: The Life, Contributions and Influence of Sir William Jones (1746–1794)*. New York: New York University Press, 1995.

Cantemir, Demetrius. *The History of the Growth and Decay of the Ottoman Empire.* Written originally in Latin. Trans. into English from the author's own manuscript by N. Tindal. 2 vols. London, 1734–35.
Cantemir, Demetrius. *Historisch-geographische und politische Beschreibung der Moldau.* Frankfurt a.M., 1771.
Capper, James. *Observations on the Passage to India through Egypt and across the Great Desert.* London, 1783.
Carhart, Michael C. *The Science of Culture in Enlightenment Germany.* Cambridge, MA: Harvard University Press, 2007.
Carnall, Geoffrey. "Robertson and Contemporary Images of India." In S. J. Brown, *William Robertson,* 1997, 210–30.
Carne, John. *Letters from the East.* London, 1826.
Caron, François, and Joost Schouten. *A True Description of the Mighty Kingdom of Japan and Siam.* Reprinted from the English ed. of 1663 with introduction, notes, and appendices by C. R. Boxer, London, 1935 [1638].
Carré, Jean-Marie. *Voyageurs et écrivains français en Égypte.* 2nd ed. 2 vols. Cairo: Institut Français d'Archéologie Orientale, 1990.
Carrier, James G., ed. *Occidentalism: Images of the West.* Oxford: Clarendon Press, 1995.
Carruthers, Douglas, ed. *The Desert Route to India, Being the Journals of Four Travellers by the Great Desert Caravan Route between Aleppo and Basra 1745–1751.* London: Hakluyt Society, 1929.
Carter, Harold B. *Sir Joseph Banks 1743–1820.* London: British Museum, 1988.
Cassirer, Ernst. *The Philosophy of the Enlightenment.* Trans. Fritz C. A. Koelln and James P. Pettegrove. Princeton, NJ: Princeton University Press, 1951 [1932].
Castilhon [Jean-Louis]. *Considérations sur les causes physiques et morales de la diversité du génie, des mœurs, et du gouvernement des nations.* N.p., 1769.
Castoldi, Alberto. *Il fascino del colibrì: Aspetti della letterature di viaggio esotica nel settecento francese.* Florence: La nouva Italia, 1972.
Catrou, François. *History of the Mogul Dynasty in India from Its Foundation by Tamerlan, in the Year 1399, to the Accession of Aurangzebe, in the Year 1657.* London, 1826 [1705].
Cecere, Giulia. "Russia and Its 'Orient': Ethnographic Exploration of the Russian Empire in the Age of Enlightenment." In Wolff and Cipolloni, *Anthropology of the Enlightenment,* 2007, 185–208.
Chabod, Federico. *Storia dell'idea d'Europea.* Rome: Laterza, 1995 [1961].
Chambers, William. *A Dissertation on Oriental Gardening.* London, 1772.
Chamisso, Adelbert von. "Reise um die Welt mit der Romanzoffischen Entdeckungs-Expedition in den Jahren 1815–1818 [1836]." In Chamisso, *Gesammelte Werke.* Ed. Max Koch. 4 vols. Stuttgart: Cotta, 1883. Vols. 3 and 4.
Chandler, Richard. *Travels in Asia Minor.* Oxford, 1775.
Chappey, Jean-Luc. *La Société des Observateurs de l'homme (1799–1804): Des anthropologues au temps de Bonaparte.* Paris: Société des Études Robespierristes, 2002.
Chardin, Sir John. *Le couronnement de Soleimaan, troisième Roy de Perse.* Paris, 1671.
Chardin, Sir John. *Voyages du Chevalier Chardin en Perse et autres lieux de l'Orient.* New ed. 4 vols. Amsterdam, 1735.
Chardin, Sir John. *Voyages du Chevalier Chardin en Perse et autres lieux de l'Orient.* Ed. Louis Mathieu Langlès. 10 vols. Paris, 1811.
Charles-Roux, François. *Les échelles de Syrie et de Palestine au XVIIIe siècle.* Paris: Paul Geuthner, 1928.

Chateaubriand, François-René de. *Itinéraire de Paris à Jérusalem*. Paris: Garnier-Flammarion, 1968 [1811].

Chatfield, Robert. *An Historical Review of the Commercial, Political and Moral State of Hindostan*. London, 1808.

Chaudhuri, K. N. *The Trading World of Asia and the English East India Company 1660–1760*. Cambridge: Cambridge University Press, 1978.

Chaudhuri, K. N. *Trade and Civilisation in the Indian Ocean: An Economic History from the Rise of Islam to 1750*. Cambridge: Cambridge University Press, 1985.

Chaudhuri, K. N. *Asia before Europe: Economy and Civilization of the Indian Ocean from the Rise of Islam to 1750*. Cambridge: Cambridge University Press, 1990.

Chaybany, Jeanne. *Les voyages en Perse et la pensée française au XVIIIe siècle*. Teheran: Nastarine, 1971.

Cheneval, Francis. *Philosophie in weltbürgerlicher Bedeutung: Über die Entstehung und die philosophischen Grundlagen des supranationalen und kosmopolitischen Denkens der Moderne*. Basle: Schwabe, 2002.

Çırakman, Asli. *From the "Terror of the World" to the "Sick Man of Europe." European Images of Ottoman Empire and Society from the Sixteenth Century to the Nineteenth*. New York: Lang, 2002.

Churchill, Awnsham, and John Churchill, eds. *A Collection of Voyages and Travels*. 3rd ed. 6 vols. London, 1744–46 [1704].

Clairac, Louis-André de La Mamie de. *Histoire de Perse depuis le commencement de ce siècle*. 3 vols. Paris, 1750.

Clarke, Edward Daniel. *Travels in Various Countries of Europe, Asia and Africa*. Part 1: *Russia, Tartary and Turkey*. 4th ed. 8 vols. London, 1816–18 [1810].

Clarke, J. J. *Oriental Enlightenment: The Encounter between Asian and Western Thought*. London: Routledge, 1997.

Clarke, Thomas Brooke. *Publicistical Survey of the Different Forms of Government of All States and Communities in the World*. London, 1791.

Claustre, André de. *Histoire du Thamas Kouli-Kan, Roi de Perse*. Nouv. éd. Paris, 1743.

Clerc, Nicolas Gabriel. *Yu Le Grand et Confucius, Histoire Chinoise*. Soissons, 1769.

Clodius, Johann Christian. *Chronicon Peregrinantis sei Historia ultimi belli Persarum cum Aghwanis gesti*. Leipzig, 1731.

Cochrane, John Dundas. *Narrative of a Pedestrian Journey through Russia and Siberian Tartary, from the Frontiers of China to the Frozen Sea and Kamtchatka, Performed during the Years 1820, 1821, 1822 and 1823*. London, 1824.

Cœurdoux, Gaston-Laurent, S. J., and Nicolas-Jacques Desvaulx. *Mœurs and coutumes des Indiens*. Texte établi et annoté par Sylvia Murr. Paris: École Française d'Extrême-Orient, 1987 [1777].

Cohn, Bernard S. *An Anthropologist among the Historians and Other Essays*. Delhi: Oxford University Press, 1987.

Cohn, Bernard S. *Colonialism and Its Form of Knowledge: The British in India*. Princeton, NJ: Princeton University Press, 1996.

Cole, Juan R. *Napoleon's Egypt: Invading the Middle East*. Basingstoke: Palgrave Macmillan, 2007.

Colebrooke, Henry Thomas. *Remarks on the Husbandry and Internal Commerce of Bengal*. Calcutta, 1806 [1804].

Colebrooke, Henry Thomas. *Miscellaneous Essays*. 3 vols. London, 1873.

Collani, Claudia von. *P. Joachim Bouvet, S. J: Sein Leben und sein Werk*. Nettetal: Steyler Verlag, 1985.

Collet, Dominik. *Die Welt in der Stube: Begegnungen mit Außereuropa in Kunstkammern der Frühen Neuzeit*. Göttingen: Vandenhoeck and Ruprecht, 2007.

Colley, Linda. *Britons: Forging the Nation 1707–1837*. New Haven, CT: Yale University Press, 1992.

Conder, Josiah. *The Modern Traveller: A Description, Geographical, Historical and Topographical of the Various Countries of the Globe*. 30 vols. London, 1830.

Condorcet, Marie-Jean-Antoine-Nicolas Caritat de. *Outlines of an Historical View of the Progress of the Human Mind*. Trans. from the French. Philadelphia, PA, 1796.

Condorcet, Marie-Jean-Antoine-Nicolas Caritat de. *Esquisse d'un tableau historique des progrès de l'esprit humain*. Introduction par Alain Pons. Paris: Flammarion, 1988 [1794].

Conrad, Sebastian. "Enlightenment in Global History: A Historiographical Critique." *American Historical Review* 117 (2012): 999–1027.

Constantine, David. *Early Greek Travellers and the Hellenic Ideal*. Cambridge: Cambridge University Press, 1984.

Constantine, David. "The Question of Authenticity in Some Early Accounts of Greece." In Graeme W. Clarke, ed., *Rediscovering Hellenism: The Hellenic Inheritance and the English Imagination*. Cambridge: Cambridge University Press, 1988, 1–22.

Cook, Alexander. "'The Great Society of the Human Species': Volney and the Global Politics of Revolutionary France." *Intellectual History Review* 23 (2013): 309–28.

Cook, Alexander, Ned Curthoys, and Shino Konishi, eds. *Representing Humanity in the Age of Enlightenment*. London: Routledge, 2016.

Copans, Jean, and Jean Jamin, eds. *Aux origines de l'anthropologie française: les Mémoires de la Société des Observateurs de l'Homme en l'an VIII*. Paris: Le Sycomore, 1978.

Coppin, Jean. *Le Bouclier de l'Europe, ou la Guerre Sainte . . . avec une relation de voyages faits dans la Turquie*. Lyon, 1686.

Cordier, Henri. *Mélanges d'histoire et de géographie orientale*. 4 vols. Paris: Maisonneuve, 1914–23.

Cordiner, James. *A Description of Ceylon*. 2 vols. London, 1807.

Court de Gebelin, Antoine. *Monde Primitif, analysé et comparé avec le monde moderne*. New ed. 8 vols. Paris, 1777–81.

Courtney, Cecil, and Jenny Mander, eds. *Raynal's 'Histoire des deux Indes': Colonialism, Networks and Global Exchange*. Oxford: Voltaire Foundation, 2015.

Cowan, Robert. *The Indo-German Identification: Reconciling South Asian Origins and European Destinies, 1765–1885*. Rochester, NY: Camden House, 2010.

Cranmer-Byng, J. L., ed. *An Embassy to China: Being the Journal Kept by Lord Macartney during His Embassy to the Emperor Ch'ien-lung 1793–1794*. London: Longman, 1962.

Craven, Elizabeth. *A Journey through the Crimea to Constantinopel, in a Series of Letters from the Right Honourable Elizabeth Lady Craven to His Serene Highness the Margrave of Brandebourg, Anspach and Bareith, Written in the Year 1786*. London, 1789.

Crawfurd, John. *History of the Indian Archipelago: Containing an Account of the Manners, Arts, Languages, Religions, Institutions, and Commerce of Its Inhabitants*. 3 vols. Edinburgh, 1820.

Crawfurd, John. *Journal of an Embassy from the Governor General of India to the Court of Ava*. 2nd ed. 2 vols. London, 1834.

Crawfurd, John. *A Descriptive Dictionary of the Indian Islands & Adjacent Countries*. London, 1856.

Crawfurd, John. *The Crawfurd Papers: A Collection of Official Records Relating to the Mission of Dr. John Crawfurd Sent to Siam by the Government of India in the Year 1821.* Bangkok: Vajirañāṇa National Library, 1915.

Crawfurd, John. *Journal of an Embassy to the Courts of Siam and Cochin China.* Kuala Lumpur: Oxford University Press, 1967 [1828].

Crecelius, Daniel. "The Mamluk Beylicate of Egypt in the Last Decades before Its Destruction by Muhammad ᶜAli Pasha in 1811." In Philipp and Haarmann, *The Mamluks in Egyptian Politics and Society*, 1998, 128–49.

Crone, G. R., and R. A. Skelton. "English Collections of Voyages and Travels 1625–1846." In Lynam, *Richard Hakluyt and His Successors,* 1946, 63–140.

Curley, Thomas M. *Samuel Johnson and the Age of Travel.* Athens: University of Georgia Press, 1976.

Curtis, Michael. *Orientalism and Islam: European Thinkers on Oriental Despotism in the Middle East and India.* Cambridge: Cambridge University Press, 2009.

Curzon, George Nathaniel. *Problems of the Far East.* London: Longmans, Green, and Co., 1894.

Dabashi, Hamid. *Persophilia: Persian Culture on the Global Scene.* Cambridge, MA: Harvard University Press, 2015.

Dabringhaus, Sabine. "Einleitung." In Hüttner, *Nachricht von der britischen Gesandtschaftsreise durch China und einen Teil der Tartarei,* 1996, 7–92.

Daftary, Farhad. *The Assassin Legends: Myths of the Isma'ilis.* London: Tauris, 1994.

Dahlmann, Dittmar. "Einleitung." In J. G. Gmelin, *Expeditionen ins unbekannte Sibirien,* 1999, 7–84.

Dahlmann, Dittmar. "Die Weite Sibiriens und des Ozeans in Berichten und Aufzeichnungen von Forschungsreisenden von der Mitte des 18. bis zur Mitte des 19. Jahrhunderts." *Zeitschrift für Ostmitteleuropa-Forschung* 63 (2014): 55–73.

Dallaway, James. *Constantinopel Ancient and Modern, with Excursions to the Shores and Islands of the Archipelago and to the Troad.* London, 1797.

Dalmia, Vasudha, and Heinrich von Stietencron. "Introduction." In Dalmia and Stietencron, *Representing Hinduism,* 1995, 17–32.

Dalmia, Vasudha, and Heinrich von Stietencron, eds. *Representing Hinduism: The Construction of Religious Traditions and National Identity.* New Delhi: Sage, 1995, 17–32.

Dalrymple, William. *White Mughals: Love and Betrayal in Eighteenth-Century India.* London: HarperCollins, 2002.

Dalrymple, William. *Return of a King: The Battle for Afghanistan, 1839–42.* New York: Knopf, 2013.

Dalrymple, William. *Koh-i-Noor: The History of the World's Most Infamous Diamond.* London: Bloomsbury, 2017.

Damiani, Anita. *Enlightened Observers: British Travellers to the Near East 1715–1850.* Beirut: American University of Beirut, 1979.

Dampier, William. *A New Voyage round the World.* London, 1697.

Daniel, Norman. *Islam, Europe and Empire.* Edinburgh: Edinburgh University Press, 1966.

d'Anville, Jean-Baptiste Bourguignon. *Nouvel Atlas de la Chine, de la Tartarie chinoise et du Thibet.* The Hague, 1737.

d'Anville, Jean-Baptiste Bourguignon. *L'Empire Turc, considéré dans son établissement et dans ses accroisemens successifs.* Paris, 1772.

d'Anville, Jean-Baptiste Bourguignon. *Mémoire . . . sur la Chine.* Paris, 1776.

Darwin, John. *After Tamerlane: The Global History of Empire since 1405.* London: Allen Lane, 2007.

David-Fox, Michael, Peter Holquist, and Alexander Martin, eds. *Orientalism and Empire in Russia*. Bloomington, IN: Slavica Publishers, 2006.

Davis, David Brion. *The Problem of Slavery in the Age of Revolution, 1770–1823*. Ithaca, NY: Cornell University Press, 1975.

Davis, Fanny. *The Ottoman Lady: A Social History from 1718 to 1918*. Westport, CT: Greenwood Press, 1986.

Dawson, Raymond. *The Chinese Chameleon: An Analysis of European Conceptions of Chinese Civilization*. London: Oxford University Press, 1967.

Dédéyan, Charles. *Montesquieu ou l'alibi persan*. Paris: Sedes, 1988.

Dehergne, Joseph. *Répertoire des Jésuites de Chine de 1552 à 1800*. Rome: Gregorian University Press, 1973.

Delanty, Gerard, ed. *Europe and Asia beyond East and West*. London: Routledge, 2006.

Deleury, Guy, ed. *Les Indes florissantes: Anthologie des voyageurs français (1750–1820)*. Paris: Laffont, 1991.

Deleyre, Alexandre. *Tableau de l'Europe: pour servir de supplement à l'Histoire philosophique & politique des établissements & du commerce des Européens dans les deux Indes*. Amsterdam, 1774.

Delisle Jean-Nicolas, and Alexandre Pingré. *Description de la ville de Peking*. Paris, 1765.

Demel, Walter. *Als Fremde in China: Das Reich der Mitte im Spiegel frühneuzeitlicher Reiseberichte*. Munich: Oldenbourg, 1992.

Démeunier , Jean-Nicolas. *L'esprit des usages et des coutumes des différens peuples, ou observations tirées des voyageurs & des historiens*. 3 vols. London, 1776.

Denckwürdige Beschreibung des Königreichs China. . . . Eisenach, 1679.

Deneys, Henry. "Le récit de l'histoire selon Volney." In Henry Deneys and Anne Deneys, eds., *C.- F. Volney (1757–1820)*. Paris: Fayard, 1989, 43–71.

Derks, Hans. *History of the Opium Problem: The Assault on the East, ca. 1600–1950*. Leiden: Brill, 2012.

Dermigny, Louis. *La Chine et l'Occident: le commerce à Canton au XVIIIe siècle*. 3 vols. and album. Paris: S.E.V.P.E.N, 1964.

Derrick, Samuel, ed. *A Collection of Travels thro' Various Parts of the World*. 2 vols. London, 1762.

Derrida, Jacques. *Of Hospitality*. Trans. Rachel Bowlby. Stanford, CA: Stanford University Press, 2000.

Description de l'Égypte, ou Receuil des observations et des recherches qui ont été faites en Égypte pendant l'expedition de l'armée française. 23 vols. Paris, 1809–23.

Desideri, Ippolito. *An Account of Tibet: The Travels of Ippolito Desideri of Pistoia, S. J., 1712–1727*. Ed. Filippo de Filippi. London: Routledge, 1932.

Desideri, Ippolito: see also Petech (1954–56).

Despoix, Philippe. *Le monde mesuré: dispositifs de l'exploration à l'âge des Lumières*. Geneva: Droz, 2005.

Devèze, Michel. *L'Europe et le monde à la fin du XVIIIe siècle*. Paris: Michel, 1970.

Dharampal-Frick, Gita. *Indien im Spiegel deutscher Quellen der Frühen Neuzeit (1500–1750): Studien zu einer interkulturellen Konstellation*. Tübingen: Niemeyer, 1994.

Dharampal-Frick, Gita. "Shifting Categories in the Discourse on Caste: Some Historical Observations." In Dalmia and Stietencron, *Representing Hinduism*, 1995, 82–100.

d'Herbelot, Barthélemi. *Bibliothèque Orientale, ou Dictionnaire Universel contenant Tout ce qui fait connoître les Peuples de l'Orient*. 4 vols. The Hague, 1777–79 [1697].

Diez, Heinrich Friedrich von. *Denkwürdigkeiten von Asien, . . . aus Handschriften und eigenen Erfahrungen gesammelt.* 2 vols. Berlin, 1811–15.

Dihle, Albrecht. *Die Griechen und die Fremden.* Munich: C. H. Beck. 1994.

Dirks, Nicholas B. "Colonial Histories and Native Informants: Biography of an Archive." In Breckenridge and Van der Veer, *Orientalism and the Postcolonial Predicament,* 1993, 279–313.

Dirks, Nicholas B. *Castes of Mind: Colonialism and the Making of Modern India.* Princeton, NJ: Princeton University Press, 2001.

Diyāb, Hannā. *D'Alep à Paris: Les pérégrinations d'un jeune Syrien au temps de Louis XIV.* Trans. Paul Fahmé-Thiéry, Bernard Heyberger, and Jérôme Lentin. Arles: Actes Sud, 2015.

Dodds, Muriel. *Les récits de voyages: sources de l'Esprit des Lois de Montesquieu.* Paris: Champion, 1929.

d'Ohsson, Ignatius Mouradgea. *Tableau générale de l'Empire Othoman.* 7 vols. in octavo. Paris, 1788–1824.

d'Orléans, Pierre Joseph. *Histoire des deux conquerans tartares qui ont subjugé la Chine.* Paris, 1690.

Dow, Alexander. *The History of Hindostan; Translated from the Persian. To Which Are Prefixed Two Dissertations; the first Concerning the Hindoos and the Second the Origin and Nature of Despotism in India.* New ed. 3 vols. London, 1812 [1768–72].

Dreitzel, Horst. "Justis Beitrag zur Politisierung der deutschen Aufklärung." In Bödeker and Herrmann, *Aufklärung als Politisierung,* 1987, 158–77.

Dreyfürst, Stephanie. *Stimmen aus dem Jenseits: David Fassmanns historisch-politisches Journal "Gespräche aus dem Reich der Todten" (1718–1740).* Berlin: de Gruyter, 2014.

Drijvers, Jan Willem, Jan de Hond, and Heleen Sancisi-Weerdenburg, eds. *"Ik hadde de nieusgierigheid": De reizen door het Narbij Oosten van Cornelis de Bruijn (ca. 1652–1727).* Leiden: Brill, 1997.

Drueck, Friedrich Ferdinand. *Gemählde des asiatischen Rußlands.* Stuttgart, 1822.

Drummond, Alexander. *Travels through Different Cities of Germany, Italy, Greece and Several Parts of Asia, as far as the Banks of the Euphrates.* London, 1754.

Du Halde, Jean-Baptiste. *Description géographique, historique, chronologique et politique de l'Empire de la Chine et de la Tartarie chinoise.* 4 vols. Paris, 1735.

Du Mans, Raphaël. *Estat de la Perse en 1660.* Ed. Charles Schefer. Paris: Leroux, 1890.

Dubois, abbé Jean-Antoine. *Description of the Character, Manners and Customs of the People of India, and of Their Institutions, Religious and Civil.* Trans. from the French manuscript. London, 1817.

Dubois, abbé Jean-Antoine. *Mœurs, institutions et cérémonies des peuples de l'Inde.* 2 vols. Paris, 1825.

Dubois, abbé Jean-Antoine. *Hindu Manners, Customs and Ceremonies.* Trans. H. K. Beauchamp. 3rd ed. Oxford: Clarendon Press, 1906.

Dubos, Jean-Baptiste. *Reflexions critiques sur la poésie et sur la peinture.* 2 vols. Paris, 1719.

Duchet, Michèle. *Anthropologie et histoire au siècle des lumières: Buffon, Voltaire, Rousseau, Helvétius, Diderot.* Paris: Flammarion, 1971.

Duchet, Michèle. *Le partage des savoirs: discours historique et discours ethnologique.* Paris: La Découverte, 1985.

Duff, James Grant. *A History of the Mahrattas.* 3 vols. London, 1826.

Dumont, Jean. *Nouveau voyage au Levant.* Paris, 1694.

Dumont, Paul. "Le voyage en Turquie: Du touriste romantique au vacancier d'aujourd'hui." *Journal Asiatique* 270 (1982): 339–61.

Dunbar, James. *Essays on the History of Mankind in Rude and Cultivated Ages*. 2 vols. London, 1781.

Durchläuchtige Welt. Die Durchläuchtige Welt / Oder Kurtzgefaßte Genealogische, Historische und Politische Beschreibung / meist aller jetztlebenden Durchläuchtigen Hohen Personen / sonderlich in Europa. 4 vols. Hamburg, 1710–11.

Duteil, Jean-Pierre. *Le mandat du ciel: le rôle des jésuits en Chine*. Paris: Arguments, 1994.

Duyvendak, J.J.L. "The Last Dutch Embassy to the Chinese Court (1794–95)." *T'oung Pao*. 2e sér. 34 (1938): 1–137.

Dyson, Ketaki Kushari. *A Various Universe: A Study of the Journals and Memoirs of British Men and Women in the Indian Subcontinent, 1765–1856*. Delhi: Oxford University Press, 1978.

Eckermann, Johann Peter. *Gespräche mit Goethe in den letzten Jahren seines Lebens*. Ed. Christoph Michel. Frankfurt a.M.: Deutscher Klassiker-Verlag, 1999 [1836].

Eclectic Review. Vols. 1–10 (1805–1813).

Edinburgh Review. Vols. 1–50 (1803–1830).

Edney, Matthew H. *Mapping an Empire: The Geographical Construction of British India, 1765–1843*. Chicago: University of Chicago Press, 1997.

Edwards, Philip. *The Story of the Voyage: Sea Narratives in Eighteenth-Century England*. Cambridge: Cambridge University Press, 1994.

Ekeberg, Carl Gustav. *Précis historique de l'économie rurale des Chinois*. Publié par M. Linnaeus, & traduit du Suedois par M. Dominique de Blackford. Milan, 1771 [1754].

Elison, George. *Deus Destroyed: The Image of Christianity in Early Modern Japan*. Cambridge, MA: Harvard University Press, 1973.

Elisseeff-Poisle, Danielle. *Nicolas Fréret (1688–1749): réflections d'un humaniste du XVIIIe siècle sur la Chine*. Paris: J. Floch, 1978.

Ellingson, Ter. *The Myth of the Noble Savage*. Berkeley: University of California Press, 2001.

Ellis, Henry. *Journal of the Proceedings of the Late Embassy to China*. 2nd ed. 2 vols. London, 1818.

Elmore, H. M. *British Mariner's Directory and Guide to the Trade and Navigation of the Indian and China Seas*. London, 1802.

Elphinstone, Mountstuart. *An Account of the Kingdom of Caubul*. 3rd ed. 2 vols. London, 1839 [1815].

Elphinstone, Mountstuart. *The History of India*. 2 vols. London, 1841.

Elman, Benjamin A. *A Cultural History of Civil Examinations in Late Imperial China*. Berkeley: University of California Press, 2000.

Elsner, Jas, and Joan-Pau Rubiés, eds. *Voyages and Visions: Towards a Cultural History of Travel*. London: Reaktion Books, 1999.

Embree, Ainslie T. *Charles Grant and British Rule in India*. London: George Allen and Unwin, 1962.

Embree, Ainslie T. "Oriental Despotism: A Note on the History of an Idea." *Societas* 1 (1971): 255–69.

Embree, Ainslie T. *Imagining India: Essays on Indian History*. Delhi: Oxford University Press, 1989.

Emerson, John. "Sir John Chardin." In Ehsan Yarshater, ed. *Encyclopædia Iranica*. Vol. 5. New York: Encyclopaedia Iranica Foundation, 1992, 368–77.

Engelhardt, Moritz von, and Friedrich Parrott. *Reise in die Krym und den Kaukasus.* 2 vols. Berlin, 1815.

Engels, Friedrich. “Die Lage der arbeitenden Klasse in England.” In Karl Marx and Friedrich Engels. *Werke* (MEW). Vol. 2. Berlin: Dietz, 1957, 229–506 [1845].

Erker-Sonnabend, Ulrich. *Orientalische Fremde: Berichte deutscher Türkeireisender des späten 19. Jahrhunderts.* Bochum: Studienverlag Brockmeyer, 1987.

Etiemble, [René]. *L'Europe chinoise.* Vol. 2: *De la sinophilie à la sinophobie.* Paris: J. Floch, 1989.

Eton, William. *Survey of the Turkish Empire.* 3rd ed. London, 1801.

Ette, Ottmar. *Alexander von Humboldt und die Globalisierung: Das Mobile des Wissens.* Frankfurt a.M.: Insel, 2009.

Eversmann, Eduard. *Reise von Orenburg nach Buchara.* Berlin, 1823.

Fabian, Bernhard. “English Books and Their Eighteenth-Century German Readers.” In Korshin, *Widening Circle*, 1976, 117–96.

Fabian, Bernhard. “Englisch als neue Fremdsprache des 18. Jahrhunderts.” In Kimpel, *Mehrsprachigkeit*, 1985, 178–96.

Falck, Johann Peter. *Beyträge zur Topographischen Kenntnis des russischen Reiches.* 3 vols. Ed. Johann Gottlieb Georgi. Saint Petersburg, 1785–86.

Falconer, William. *Remarks on the Influence of Climate, Situation, Nature of Country, Population, Nature of Food, and Way of Life, on the Disposition and Temper, Manners and Behaviour, Intellects, Laws and Customs, Form of Government, and Religion, of Mankind.* London, 1781.

Faroqhi, Suraiya. *Pilgrims and Sultans: The Hajj under the Ottomans, 1513–1683.* London: Tauris, 1994.

Faroqhi, Suraiya, ed. *The Later Ottoman Empire, 1603–1839.* Cambridge: Cambridge University Press, 2006 (= *The Cambridge History of Turkey*, 3).

Faßmann, David: see Quelle, Pithander von der.

Fay, Eliza. *Original Letters from India (1779–1815).* Ed. E. M. Forster. London: Hogarth Press, 1925 [1817].

Ferguson, Adam. *Essay on the History of Civil Society.* Ed. Duncan Forbes. Edinburgh: Edinburgh University Press, 1966 [1767].

Ferrières-Sauvebœuf, Louis François Comte de. *Mémoires historiques, politiques et géographiques . . . , faits en Turquie, en Perse et en Arabie, depuis 1782, jusqu'en 1789.* 2 vols. Paris, 1790.

Ferrone, Vincenzo. *The Enlightenment: History of an Idea.* Trans. Elisabetta Tarantino. Princeton, NJ: Princeton University Press, 2015.

Fessler, Ignaz Aurelius. *Attila: König der Hunnen.* Breslau, 1794.

Fétis, François-Joseph. *Histoire générale de la musique depuis les temps les plus anciens jusqu'à nos jours.* 5 vols. Paris: Didot, 1869–76.

Fillafer, Franz Leander, and Jürgen Osterhammel. “Cosmopolitanism and the German Enlightenment.” In Helmut Walser Smith, ed. *Oxford Handbook of Modern German History.* Oxford: Oxford University Press, 2011, 119–43.

Findley, Carter Vaughn. *Enlightening Europe on Islam and the Ottomans: Mouradgea d'Ohsson and His Masterpiece.* Leiden: Brill, forthcoming [2018].

Fink, Gonthier-Louis. “Patriotisme et cosmopolitisme en France et en Allemagne.” *Recherches germaniques* 22 (1992): 3–51.

Fink-Eitel, Hinrich. *Die Philosophie und die Wilden: Über die Bedeutung des Fremden für die europäische Geistesgeschichte.* Hamburg: Junius, 1994.

Finlayson, George. *The Mission to Siam and Hué, the Capital of Cochin China, in the Years 1821–2.* London, 1826.

Firby, Nora Kathleen. *European Travellers and Their Perceptions of Zoroastrians in the 17th and 18th Centuries*. Berlin: Reimer, 1988.

Fisch, Jörg. "Der märchenhafte Orient: Die Umwertung einer Tradition von Marco Polo bis Macaulay." *Saeculum* 35 (1984): 246–66.

Fisch, Jörg. *Die europäische Expansion und das Völkerrecht: Die Auseinandersetzungen um den Status der überseeischen Gebiete vom 15. Jahrhundert bis zur Gegenwart*. Stuttgart: Steiner, 1984.

Fisch, Jörg. "A Solitary Vindicator of the Hindus: The Life and Writings of General Charles Stuart (1757/58–1828)." *Journal of the Royal Asiatic Society*, 1985, 35–57.

Fisch, Jörg. *Hollands Ruhm in Asien: François Valentyns Vision des niederländischen Imperiums im 18. Jahrhundert*. Stuttgart: Steiner, 1986.

Fisch, Jörg. "Zivilisation, Kultur." In Brunner, Conze, and Koselleck, *Geschichtliche Grundbegriffe*, vol. 7 (1992), 679–774.

Fisch, Jörg. "Jenseitsglaube, Ungleichheit und Tod: Zu einigen Aspekten der Totenfolge." *Saeculum* 44 (1993): 265–99.

Fisch, Jörg. *Burning Women: A Global History of Widow Sacrifice from Ancient Times to the Present*. Trans. Rekha Kamath Rajan. London: Seagull Books, 2006.

Fischer, Johann Eberhard. *Sibirische Geschichte von der entdekkung Sibiriens bis auf die eroberung dieses landes durch die Russische (!) waffen*. 2 vols. Saint Petersburg, 1768.

Fisher, Alan W. *The Crimean Tartars*. Stanford, CA: Stanford University Press, 1978.

Fisher, Michael H., ed. *The Travels of Dean Mahomet: An Eighteenth-Century Journey through India*. Berkeley: University of California Press, 1997.

Fisher, Michael H. *Counterflows to Colonialism: Indian Travellers and Settlers in Britain 1600–1857*. Delhi: Permanent Black, 2004.

Flaherty, Gloria. *Shamanism and the Eighteenth Century*. Princeton, NJ: Princeton University Press, 1992.

Fletcher, Joseph. "Ch'ing Inner Asia c. 1800." In John K. Fairbank, ed. *The Cambridge History of China*. Vol. 10. Cambridge: Cambridge University Press, 1978, 35–106.

Fontenelle, Bernard Le Bovier de. "Entretiens sur la pluralité des mondes habités." In Fontenelle, *Œuvres complètes*. Ed. Alain Niderst. Vol. 2. Paris: Fayard, 1991 [1686], 9–140.

Forbes, Duncan. *Hume's Philosophical Politics*. Cambridge: Cambridge University Press, 1975.

Forbes, James. *Oriental Memoirs*. 4 vols. London, 1813.

Forkel, Johann Nikolaus. *Allgemeine Geschichte der Musik*. 2 vols. Leipzig, 1788–1801.

Forrest, Thomas. *A Voyage from Calcutta to the Mergui Archipelago*. London, 1792.

Forster, Georg. *Sämtliche Schriften, Tagebücher, Briefe*. 18 vols. Ed. Deutsche Akademie der Wissenschaften zu Berlin. Berlin: Akademie-Verlag, 1958–2003.

Forster, George. *Sketches of the Mythology and Customs of the Hindoos*. London, 1785.

Forster, George. *A Journey from Bengal to England through the Northern Part of India, Kashmire, Afghanistan and Persia and into Russia by the Caspian Sea*. 2 vols. London, 1808.

Forster, Johann Reinhold. *Bemerkungen über Gegenstände der physischen Erdbeschreibung, Naturgeschichte und sittlichen Philosophie, auf seiner Reise um die Welt gesammlet*. Berlin, 1783.

Forster, Johann Reinhold. *Geschichte der Entdeckungen und Schiffahrten im Norden*. Frankfurt a.d. Oder, 1784.

Forster, Johann Reinhold. *Indische Zoologie*. 2nd ed. Halle, 1795.

Forster, Johann Reinhold. *The "Resolution" Journal of Johann Reinhold Forster*. Ed. Michael E. Hoare. 4 vols. London: Hakluyt Society, 1982.

Forster, Johann Reinhold. *Observations Made during a Voyage round the World*. Ed. Michael Dettelbach, Harriet Guest, and Nicholas Thomas. Honululu: University of Hawaii Press, 1996 [1783].

Forsyth, James. *A History of the Peoples of Siberia: Russia's North Asian Colony, 1581–1990*. Cambridge: Cambridge University Press, 1992.

Foss, Theodore Nicholas. "A Western Interpretation of China: Jesuit Cartography." In Charles E. Ronan and Bonnie B. C. Oh, eds., *East Meets West: The Jesuits in China*. Chicago: University of Chicago Press, 1988, 209–51.

Foucault, Michel. *The Order of Things: An Archaeology of Human Sciences*. New York: Pantheon, 1971 [1966].

Fourmont, Etienne. *Reflexions critiques sur les histoires des anciens peuples*. 2 vols. Paris 1735.

Fournier, Marian. "Enterprise in Botany: Van Reede and His 'Hortus Malabaricus.'" *Archives of Natural History* 14 (1987): 123–58, 297–338.

Foust, Clifford M. *Muscovite and Mandarin: Russia's Trade with China and Its Setting, 1727–1805*. Chapel Hill: University of North Carolina Press, 1969.

Fowden, Garth. "Gibbon on Islam." *English Historical Review* 131 (2016): 262–92.

Francisci, Erasmus. *Ost- und West-Indischer wie auch Sinesischer Lust- und Stats-Garten*. Nürnberg, 1668.

Francisci, Erasmus. *Neu-polirter Geschicht- Kunst- und Sitten-Spiegel ausländischer Völcker*. Nürnberg, 1670.

Francklin, William. *Observations made on a Tour from Bengal to Persia, in the Years 1786–7*. London, 1790.

Francklin, William. *The History of the Reign of Shah-Aulum, the Present Emperor of Hindostan*. London, 1798.

Francklin, William. *Tracts, Political, Geographical and Commercial; on the Dominions of Ava and the North Western Parts of Hindostaun*. London, 1811.

Frängsmyr, Tore, ed. *Science in Sweden: The Royal Swedish Academy of Sciences 1739–1989*. Canton, MA: Science History Publications, 1989.

Frank, Othmar. *Persien und Chili als Pole der physischen Erdbreite und Leitpunkte zur Kenntnis der Erde*. Nürnberg, 1813.

Franke, Herbert. *Zur Biographie von Johann Heinrich Plath (1802–1874)*. Munich: Bayerische Akademie der Wissenschaften, 1960.

Franke, Susanne. *Die Reisen der Lady Craven durch Europa und die Türkei 1785–1786: Text, Kontext und Ideologien*. Trier: Wissenschaftlicher Verlag Trier, 1995.

Franklin, Michael J. *Orientalist Jones: Sir William Jones, Poet, Lawyer, and Linguist, 1746–1794*. Oxford: Oxford University Press, 2011.

Frankopan, Peter. *The Silk Roads: A New History of the World*. London: Bloomsbury, 2015.

Fraser, Elisabeth A. "'Dressing Turks in the French Manner': Mouradgea d'Ohsson's Panorama of the Ottoman Empire." *Ars Orientalis* 39 (2010): 198–230.

Fraser, James. *The History of Nadir Shah, Formerly Called Thamas Kuli Khan, the Present Emperor of Persia*. London, 1742.

Fraser, James Baillie. *Journal of a Tour through Part of the Snowy Range of the Himala Mountains, and to the Sources of the Rivers Jumma and Ganges*. London, 1820.

Fraser, James Baillie. *Travels and Adventures in the Persian Provinces on the Southern Banks of the Caspian Sea*. London, 1826.

Fraser, James Baillie. *An Historical and Descriptive Account of Persia, from the Earliest Ages to the Present Time*. 2nd ed. Edinburgh, 1834.

Fried, Johannes. "Auf der Suche nach der Wirklichkeit: Die Mongolen und die europäische Erfahrungswissenschaft im 13. Jahrhundert." *Historische Zeitschrift* 243 (1986): 287–332.
Friese, Eberhard. "Einleitung." In reprint of Thunberg, *Reise* (1794). Heidelberg, 1991, vol.1, vii–lv.
Frost, Alan. *The Global Reach of Empire: Britain's Maritime Expansion in the Indian and Pacific Oceans, 1764–1815*. Carlton (Victoria): Miegunyah Press, 2003.
Fryer, John. *A New Account of East India and Persia, Being Nine Years Travels, 1672–1681*. Ed. William Crooke. 3 vols. London: Hakluyt Society, 1909–15 [1698].
Fu Lo-shu. *A Documentary Chronicle of Sino-Western Relations (1644–1820)*. 2 vols. Tucson: University of Arizona Press, 1966.
Fuchs, Walter. *Der Jesuiten-Atlas der Kanghsi-Zeit*. 2 vols. Peking: Fu-jen University, 1943.
Fück, Johann. *Die arabischen Studien in Europa bis in den Anfang des 20. Jahrhunderts*, Leipzig: Harrassowitz, 1955.
Fullarton, William. *A View of the English Interests in India*. London, 1788.
Fundgruben des Orients. Ed. Joseph von Hammer-Purgstall. 6 vols. Vienna, 1809–18.
Gaastra, Femme S. *De geschiedenis van de VOC*. Leiden: Walburg Pers, 1991.
Gabriel, Alfons. *Die Erforschung Persiens: Die Entwicklung der abendländischen Kenntnis der Geographie Persiens*. Vienna: Holzhausen, 1952.
Gadamer, Hans-Georg. *Truth and Method*. Trans. Garrett Barden and John Cumming. New York: Crossroad, 1988.
Galland, Julien-Claude, trans. *Relation de l'ambassade de Mehmet Effendi à la cour de France en 1721, écrite par lui-même et traduite du turc*. Paris, 1757.
Garcia, Humberto. *Islam and the English Enlightenment, 1670–1840*. Baltimore, MD: Johns Hopkins University Press, 2012.
Gascoigne, John. *Joseph Banks and the English Enlightenment: Useful Knowledge and Polite Culture*. Cambridge: Cambridge University Press, 1994.
Gascoigne, John. *Encountering the Pacific in the Age of the Enlightenment*. Cambridge: Cambridge University Press, 2014.
Gaspari, Adam Christian, ed. *Vollständiges Handbuch der neuesten Erdbeschreibung*. Vols. 14–15. Weimar, 1822.
Gatterer, Johann Christoph. *Einleitung in die synchronistische Universalgeschichte zur Erläuterung seiner synchronistischen Tabellen*. 2 vols. Göttingen, 1771.
Gatterer, Johann Christoph. *Ideal einer allgemeinen Weltstatistik*. Göttingen, 1773.
Gatterer, Johann Christoph. *Kurzer Begriff der Geographie*. 2 vols. Göttingen, 1789.
Gatterer, Johann Christoph. *Versuch einer allgemeinen Weltgeschichte bis zur Entdeckung Amerikens*. Göttingen, 1792.
Gaubil, Antoine. *Histoire de Gentchiscan et de toute la dinastie des Mongous ses successeurs, conquérans de la Chine, tirée de l'histoire Chinoise*. Paris, 1739.
Gaubil, Antoine. *Traité de la chronologie chinoise*. Ed. Sylvestre de Sacy. Paris, 1814.
Gaubil, Antoine. *Correspondance de Pékin 1722–1759*. Ed. Renée Simon. Geneva: Droz, 1970.
Gaulmier, Jean. *L'idéologue Volney 1757–1820: Contribution à l'histoire de l'orientalisme en France*. Beirut: Imprimerie catholique, 1951.
Gay, Peter. *The Enlightenment. An Interpretation*. 2 vols. New York: Knopf, 1966–69.
Gearhart, Suzanne. *The Open Boundary of History and Fiction: A Critical Approach to the French Enlightenment*. Princeton, NJ: Princeton University Press, 1984.

Gehrke, Hans-Joachim. "Die wissenschaftliche Entdeckung des Landes *Hellás*." *Geographia Antiqua* 1 (1992): 15–36; 2 (1993): 3–11.

Gelder, Roelof van. *Het Oost-Indisch avontuur: Duitsers in dienst van de VOC (1600–1800)*. Nijmegen: Uitgeverij SUN, 1997.

Gemelli Careri, Giovanni Francesco. *Giro del mondo*. 6 vols. Naples, 1699–1700.

Gemelli Careri, Giovanni Francesco. "A Voyage round the World." In Churchill and Churchill, *Collection*, vol. 4 (1745), 5–568.

Georgi, Johann Gottlieb. *Bemerkungen einer Reise im Rußischen Reich im Jahre 1772*. 2 vols. Saint Petersburg, 1775.

Georgi, Johann Gottlieb. *Beschreibung aller Nationen des Rußischen Reichs. . . .* 4 vols. Saint Petersburg, 1776–80.

Georgius, Augustinus Antonius. *Alphabetum Tibetanum*. Rome, 1762.

Gerbi, Antonello. *The Dispute of the New World: The History of a Polemic, 1750–1900*. Trans. Jeremy Moyle. Pittsburgh, PA: University of Pittsburgh Press, 1973.

Gervaise, Nicolas. *The Natural and Political History of Siam, A.D. 1688*. Trans. H. St. O'Neill. Bangkok: White Lotus, 1928.

Ghanoonparvar, Mohammad R. *In a Persian Mirror: Images of the West and Westerners in Iranian Fiction*. Austin: University of Texas Press, 1993.

Ghirardini, Giovanni. *Relation du voyage fait à la Chine sur le vaisseau l'Amphitrite, en l'année 1698*. Paris, 1700.

Ghosh, Pranabendra Nath. *Johann Gottfried Herder's Image of India*. Santiniketan: Visva-Bharati Research Publications, 1990.

Giarrizzo, Guiseppe. *Edward Gibbon e la cultura europea del settecento*. Naples: Istituto italiano per gli studi storici, 1954.

Gibbon, Edward. *The History of the Decline and Fall of the Roman Empire*. Ed. David Womersley. 3 vols. London: Penguin, 1994 [1776–88].

Gierl, Martin. *Geschichte als präzisierte Wissenschaft: Johann Christoph Gatterer und die Historiographie des 18. Jahrhunderts im ganzen Umfang*. Stuttgart-Bad Cannstatt: Frommann-Holzboog, 2012.

Gilman, Sander L. *Difference and Pathology: Stereotypes of Sexuality, Race and Madness*. Ithaca, NY: Cornell University Press, 1985.

Glacken, Clarence J. *Traces on the Rhodian Shore: Nature and Culture in Western Thought from Ancient Times to the End of the Eighteenth Century*. Berkeley: University of California Press, 1967.

Gladwin, Francis. *The History of Hindostan during the Reigns of Jahángír, Sháhjehán and Aurungzebe*. Vol. 1. Calcutta, 1788.

Gladwin, Francis, trans. *Ayeen Akbery; or, the Institutes of the Emperor Akbar*. 2 vols. London, 1800.

Gmelin, Johann Georg. *Reise durch Sibirien von dem Jahr 1733 bis 1743*. 4 vols. Göttingen, 1751–52.

Gmelin, Johann Georg. *Expeditionen ins unbekannte Sibirien*. Ed. Dittmar Dahlmann. Sigmaringen: Thorbecke, 1999.

Gmelin, Samuel Georg [Gottlieb]. *Reise durch Rußland zur Untersuchung der drey Natur-Reiche*. 4 vols. Saint Petersburg, 1770–84.

Göçek, Fatma Müge. *East Encounters West: France and the Ottoman Empire in the Eighteenth Century*. New York: Oxford University Press, 1987.

Godlewska, Anne Marie Claire. "Napoleon's Geographers (1797–1815): Imperialism and Soldiers of Modernity." In Anne Godlewska and Neil Smit, eds., *Geography and Empire*, Oxford: Blackwell, 1994, 31–53.

Godlewska, Anne Marie Claire. *Geography Unbound: French Geographic Science from Cassini to Humboldt*. Chicago: University of Chicago Press, 1999.

Godwin, William. *Enquiry Concerning Political Justice*. Ed. K. Codell Carter. Oxford: Clarendon Press, 1971 [1793].

Goerres, Joseph. *Mythengeschichte der asiatischen Welt*. 2 vols. Heidelberg, 1810.

Goethe, Johann Wolfgang. "West-östlicher Divan 1819: Besserem Verständnis." In Goethe, *West-östlicher Divan*. Ed. Hendrik Birus. 2 vols. Frankfurt a.M.: Deutscher Klassiker-Verlag, 2010. Vol. 1, 137–294.

Goldstein, Jürgen. *Georg Forster: Zwischen Freiheit und Naturgewalt*. Berlin: Matthes and Seitz, 2015.

Goldstone, Jack A. *Revolution and Rebellion in the Early Modern World*. Berkeley: University of California Press, 1991.

Gollwitzer, Heinz. *Europabild und Europagedanke: Beiträge zur deutschen Geistesgeschichte des 18. und 19. Jahrhunderts*. 2nd ed. Munich: C. H. Beck, 1964.

Gollwitzer, Heinz. *Geschichte des weltpolitischen Denkens*. 2 vols. Göttingen: Vandenhoeck and Ruprecht, 1972–82.

Golovnin, Vasily Mikhailovich. *Memoirs of a Captivity in Japan during the Years 1811, 1812, and 1813*. 3 vols. London, 1824.

Golvers, Noël. *Libraries of Western Learning for China: Circulation of Western Books between Europe and China in the Jesuit Mission* (ca. 1650–ca. 1750). 3 vols. Leuven: Ferdinand Verbiest Institute, 2012–15.

Gommans, Jos J. L. *The Rise of the Indo-Afghan Empire, c. 1710–1780*. Leiden: Brill, 1995.

Gong, Gerritt W. *The Standard of "Civilization" in International Society*. Oxford: Clarendon Press, 1984.

Goodman, Dana. *The Republic of Letters: A Cultural History of the French Enlightenment*. Ithaca, NY: Cornell University Press, 1994.

Goodman, Grant K. *Japan and the Dutch*. Richmond (Surrey): Curzon Press, 2000.

Goody, Jack. *The East in the West*. Cambridge: Cambridge University Press, 1996.

Goody, Jack. *The Theft of History*. Cambridge: Cambridge University Press, 2006.

Gordon, David, ed. *The Turgot Collection: Writings, Speeches, and Letters of Anne Robert Jacques Turgot, Baron de Laune*. Auburn, AL: Mises Institute, 2011.

Gordon, Stewart. *The Marathas 1600–1818*. Cambridge: Cambridge University Press, 1993.

Goßens, Peter. *Weltliteratur: Modelle transnationaler Literaturwahrnehmung im 19. Jahrhundert*. Stuttgart: Metzler, 2011.

Graaff, Nicolaas de. *Oost-Indise spiegel*. Ed. Marijke Barend-van Haeften and Hetty Plekenpol. Leiden: KITLV Uitgeverij, 2010 [1701].

Grafton, Anthony. *New Worlds and Ancient Texts: The Power of Tradition and the Shock of Discovery*. Cambridge, MA: Harvard University Press, 1993.

Grafton, Anthony. *The Footnote: A Curious History*. London: Faber and Faber, 1997.

Grant, James. *An Inquiry into the Nature of Zemindary Tenures in the Landed Property of Bengal*. 2nd ed. London, 1791.

Grasset de Saint-Sauveur, Jacques. *Encyclopédie des voyages*. 5 vols. Paris, 1796.

Greaves, Rose. "Iranian Relations with Great Britain and British India, 1798–1921." In Avery, Hambly, and Melville, *From Nâdir Shah to the Islamic Republic*, 1991, 374–425.

Green, Nile. *The Love of Strangers: What Six Muslim Students Learned in Jane Austen's London*. Princeton, NJ: Princeton University Press, 2016.

Greenblatt, Stephen. *Marvellous Possessions: The Wonder of the New World*. Oxford: Clarendon Press, 1991.

Gregory, George. *Essays Historical and Moral.* 2nd ed. London, 1788.

Grelot, Guillaume Joseph. *Relation nouvelle d'un voyage de Constantinopel.* Paris, 1680.

Grewal, J. S. *Muslim Rule in India: The Assessments of British Historians.* Calcutta: Oxford University Press, 1970.

Griep, Wolfgang, and Hans-Wolf Jäger, eds. *Reisen im 18. Jahrhundert: Neue Unterhungen.* Heidelberg: Winter, 1986.

Griep, Wolfgang, ed. *Sehen und Beschreiben: Europäische Reisen im 18. und frühen 19. Jahrhundert.* Heide: Westholsteinische Verlagsanstalt Boyens, 1991.

Gronke, Monika. "Am Hofe von Isfahan: Engelbert Kaempfer und das safawidische Persien." In Haberland, *Engelbert Kaempfer,* 2004, 189–98.

Grose, John Henry. *A Voyage to the East Indies.* New ed. 2 vols. London, 1772 [1764].

Grosier, Jean-Baptiste-Gabriel-Alexandre. "Discours préliminaire." In de Mailla, *Histoire générale de la Chine,* 1777–80, vol. 1 (1777), xxi–xlviii.

Grosier, Jean-Baptiste-Gabriel-Alexandre. *Description générale de la Chine, ou Tableau de l'état actuel de cet empire.* Paris, 1785.

Grosier, Jean-Baptiste-Gabriel-Alexandre. *De la Chine, ou Description générale de cet Empire, rédigée d'après les mémoires de la Mission de Pé-kin.* 3rd ed. 7 vols. Paris, 1818–20.

Grosrichard, Alain. *The Sultan's Court: European Fantasies of the East.* Trans. Liz Heron. London: Verso, 1998.

Grotsch, Klaus. "Das Sanskrit und die Ursprache." In Joachim Gessinger and Wolfert von Rahden, eds., *Theorien vom Ursprung der Sprache.* Vol. 2. Berlin, 1989, 85–121.

Grove, Richard. *Green Imperialism: Colonial Scientists, Ecological Crises and the History of Environmental Concern, 1600–1800.* Cambridge: Cambridge University Press, 1995.

Grove, Richard. "Indigenous Knowledge and the Significance of South-West India for Portuguese and Dutch Constructions of Tropical Nature." *Modern Asian Studies* 30 (1996): 121–43.

Grundy, Isobel. *Lady Mary Wortley Montagu.* Oxford: Oxford University Press, 1999.

Grundmann, Johannes. *Die geographischen und völkerkundlichen Quellen und Anschauungen in Herders "Ideen zur Geschichte der Menschheit."* Berlin: Weidmann, 1900.

Guer, Jean Antoine. *Mœurs et usages des Turcs: leur religion, leur gouvernement civil, militaire et politique.* 2 vols. Paris, 1747.

Guha, Ranajit. *A Rule of Property for Bengal: An Essay on the Idea of Permanent Settlement.* Paris: Mouton, 1963.

Guignes, Chrétien Louis Joseph de. *Voyages à Peking, Manille et l'Ile de France, Faits dans l'intervalle des années 1784 à 1801.* 3 vols. Paris, 1808.

Guignes, Joseph de. *Histoire générale des Huns, des Turcs, des Mogols, et des autres Tartares Occidentaux, &c., avant et depuis Jesus-Christ jusqu'a present.* 4 vols. Paris, 1756–58.

Guignes, Joseph de. *Mémoire dans lequel on prouve que les Chinois sont une colonie Égyptienne.* Nouv. éd. Paris, 1759.

Guizot, François. *Histoire de la civilisation en Europe: depuis la chute de l'Empire romain jusqu'à la Révolution française.* Ed. Pierre Rosanvallon. Paris: Hachette, 1985 [1828].

Güldenstädt, Johann Anton. *Reise durch Rußland und ins Caucasische Gebürge.* 2 vols. Saint Petersburg, 1787–91.

Gunn, Geoffrey C. *First Globalization: The Eurasian Exchange, 1500–1800.* Lanham, MD: Rowman and Littlefield, 2003.

Guthke, Karl S. *Goethes Weimar und "Die große Öffnung in die weite Welt."* Wiesbaden: Harrassowitz, 2001.

Guthke, Karl S. *Die Erfindung der Welt*. Tübingen: Francke, 2005.
Guthke, Karl S. *Die Reise ans Ende der Welt: Erkundungen zur Kulturgeschichte der Literatur*. Tübingen: Francke, 2011.
Guthke, Karl S. "At Home in the World: The Savant in the Service of Global Education." In Holenstein, Steinke, and Stuber, *Scholars in Action*, 2013, vol. 2, 569–90.
Guthrie, William. *A New Geographical, Historical, and Commercial Grammar; and Present State of the Several Kingdoms of the World*. 2nd ed. 2 vols. London, 1771.
Guy, Basil. *The French Image of China before and after Voltaire*. Geneva: Institut et Musée Voltaire, 1963.
Haase, Wolfgang, and Meyer Reinhold, eds. *The Classical Tradition and the Americas*. Vol. 1: *European Images of the Americas and the Classical Tradition*. Pt. 1. New York: de Gruyter, 1994.
Haberland, Detlef. *Von Lemgo nach Japan: Das ungewöhnliche Leben des Engelbert Kaempfer, 1651 bis 1716*. Bielefeld: Westfalenverlag, 1990.
Haberland, Detlef, ed. *Engelbert Kaempfer (1651–1716): Ein Gelehrtenleben zwischen Tradition und Innovation*. Wiesbaden: Harrassowitz, 2004.
Haberland, Detlef, ed. *Engelbert Kaempfers "Amoenitates Exoticae" von 1712: Wissenschaftliche Innovation, humanistische Gelehrsamkeit und neulateinische Sprachkunst*. Wiesbaden: Harrassowitz, 2014.
Habesci, Elias. *The Present State of the Ottoman Empire*. London, 1784.
Habib, Irfan, ed. *Confronting Colonialism: Resistance and Modernization under Haidar Ali and Tipu Sultan*. New Delhi: Tulika, 1999.
Hachicho, Mohammed Ali. "English Travel Books about the Arab Near East in the 18th Century." *Die Welt des Islams* 9 (1964): 1–206.
Hager, Johann Georg. *Ausführliche Geographie*. 4th ed. 2 vols. Chemnitz, 1773.
Hakluyt, Richard. *Hakluyt's Edition of the Early Voyages, Travels, and Discoveries of the English Nation*. New ed. 4 vols. London, 1809–12.
Halbfass, Wilhelm. *India and Europe: An Essay in Understanding*. Albany: State University of New York Press, 1988.
Hall, Basil. *Account of a Voyage of Discovery to the West Coast of Corea, and the Great Loo-Choo Island*. London, 1818.
Hall, D.G.E., ed. *Historians of South East Asia*. London: Oxford University Press, 1961.
Hall, John Whitney, ed. *Early Modern Japan*. Cambridge: Cambridge University Press, 1991 (= *The Cambridge History of Japan*, 4).
Hallinger, Johannes Franz. *Das Ende der Chinoiserie: Die Auflösung eines Phänomens der Kunst in der Zeit der Aufklärung*. Munich: Scaneg, 1996.
Hamel, Hendrik. "An Account of the Shipwreck of a Dutch Vessel on the Coast of the Isle of Quelpaert, Together with a Description of the Kingdom of Korea." In Ledyard, *The Dutch Come to Korea*, 1971, 171–226 [1668].
Hamel, Hendrik. *Hamel's Journal and a Description of the Kingdom of Korea, 1653–1666*. Trans. Jean-Paul Buys. Seoul: Royal Asiatic Society, Korea Branch, 1994 [1668].
Hamilton, Alexander. *A New Acccount of the East Indies*. Ed. Sir William Foster. 2 vols. London: Argonaut Press, 1930 [1727].
Hamilton, Charles. *An Historical Relation of the Origin, Progress, and Final Dissolution of the Government of Rohilla Afgans in the North Provincs of Hindostan*. London, 1787.
Hamilton, Francis [Francis Buchanan]. *An Account of the Kingdom of Nepal, and of the Territories Annexed to this Dominion by the House of Gorkha*. Edinburgh, 1819.
Hamilton, Walter. *The East-India Gazetteer*. 2nd ed. 2 vols. London, 1828.

Hammer-Purgstall, Joseph von. *Des osmanischen Reiches Staatsverfassung und Staatsverwaltung. Dargestellt aus den Quellen seiner Grundgesetze.* 2 vols. Vienna, 1815.

Hammer-Purgstall, Joseph von. *Umblick auf einer Reise von Constantinopel nach Brussa und dem Olympos.* Pest, 1818.

Hammer-Purgstall, Joseph von. *Constantinopolis und der Bosporos, örtlich und geschichtlich beschrieben.* 2 vols. Pest, 1822.

Hammer-Purgstall, Joseph von. *Geschichte des Osmanischen Reiches, grosstheils aus bisher unbenützten Handschriften und Archiven.* 10 vols. Pest, 1827–35.

Hammer-Purgstall, Joseph von. *Geschichte der Goldenen Horde in Kiptschak, das ist der Mongolen in Russland.* Pest, 1840.

Hammer-Purgstall, Joseph von. *Geschichte der Chane der Krim unter Osmanischer Herrschaft.* Vienna: Gerold, 1856.

Hammer-Purgstall, Joseph von. *Erinnerungen aus meinem Leben 1774–1852.* Ed. R. Bachofen von Echt. Vienna: Hölder-Pichler-Tempsky, 1940.

Hanway, Jonas. *An Historical Account of the British Trade over the Caspian Sea: With a Journal of Travels from London through Russia and Persia.* 4 vols. London, 1753.

Harbsmeier, Christoph. "La connaissance du Chinois." In Sylvain Auroux, ed., *Histoire des idées linguistiques.* Vol. 2. Liège: Mardaga, 1992, 299–312.

Harbsmeier, Michael. "World Histories before Domestication: Writing Universal Histories, Histories of Mankind and World Histories in 18th-Century Germany." *Culture and History* 5 (1989): 93–131.

Harbsmeier, Michael. "Before Decipherment: Persepolitan Hypotheses in the Late 18th Century." *Culture and History* 11 (1991): 23–59.

Harbsmeier, Michael. "Kadu und Maheine: Entdeckerfreundschaften in deutschen Weltreisen um die Wende zum 19. Jahrhundert." In Griep, *Sehen und Beschreiben,* 1991, 150–78.

Harbsmeier, Michael. *Wilde Völkerkunde: Andere Welten in deutschen Reiseberichten der Frühen Neuzeit.* Frankfurt a.M.: Campus, 1994.

Hardtwig, Wolfgang, ed. *Die Aufklärung und ihre Weltwirkung.* Göttingen: Vandenhoeck and Ruprecht, 2010.

Hardtwig, Wolfgang, and Philipp Müller, eds. *Die Vergangenheit der Weltgeschichte: Universalhistorisches Denken in Berlin 1800–1933.* Göttingen: Vandenhoeck and Ruprecht, 2010.

Harley, J. B., and David Woodward, eds. *The History of Cartography.* Vol. 2, bk. 2: *Cartography in the Traditional East and Southeast Asian Societies.* Chicago: University of Chicago Press, 1994.

Harmer, Thomas. *Observations on Divers Passages of Scripture.* 2nd ed. 4 vols. London. 1786–87.

Harper, James G., ed. *The Turk and Islam in the Western Eye, 1450–1750: Visual Imagery before Orientalism.* Farnham (Surrey): Ashgate, 2011.

Harrington, Jack. *Sir John Malcolm and the Creation of British India.* New York: Palgrave Macmillan, 2010.

Harris, James A. *Hume: An Intellectual Biography.* Cambridge: Cambridge University Press, 2015.

Harris, John. *Sir William Chambers: Knight of the Polar Star.* London: Zwemmer, 1970.

Harris, John / [John Campbell]. *Navigantium atque Itinerantium Bibliotheca or, a Complete Collection of Voyages and Travels.* Rev. ed. 2 vols. London, 1744–48.

Harris, Marvin. *The Rise of Anthropological Theory: A History of Theories of Culture.* London: Routledge and Kegan Paul, 1968.

Harrison, John, and Peter Laslett. *The Library of John Locke*. 2nd ed. Oxford: Clarendon Press, 1971.
Harth, Erica. *Ideology and Culture in Seventeenth-Century France*. Ithaca, NY: Cornell University Press, 1983.
Harvey, David Allen. *The French Enlightenment and Its Others: The Mandarin, the Savage, and the Invention of the Human Sciences*. New York: Palgrave Macmillan, 2012.
Hasan Mushirul, ed. *Westward Bound: Travels of Mirza Abu Taleb*. Trans. Charles Stewart. New Delhi: Oxford University Press, 2005 [1810].
Hassel, Johann Georg Heinrich. *Geographisch-statistisches Handwörterbuch*. 2 vols. Weimar, 1817–18.
Hathaway, Jane. *The Politics of Households in Ottoman Egypt: The Rise of the Qazdaglis*. Cambridge: Cambridge University Press, 1997.
Hauner, Milan. *What Is Asia to Us? Russia's Asian Heartland Yesterday and Today*. Boston: Unwin Hyman, 1990.
Hausberger, Bernd, and Jean-Paul Lehners, eds. *Die Welt im 18. Jahrhundert*. Vienna: Mandelbaum, 2011.
Hausleutner, Philipp Wilhelm Gottlieb. *Geschichte der Araber in Sicilien und Sicilien's unter der Herrschaft der Araber*. 4 vols. Königsberg, 1791–92.
Hayter, Aletha. *Opium and the Romantic Imagination*. London: Faber and Faber, 1968.
Heber, Reginald. *Narrative of a Journey through the Upper Provinces of India, from Calcutta to Bombay, 1824–1825*. 3rd ed. 3 vols. London, 1828.
Heeren, Arnold Hermann Ludwig. *Historische Werke*. 15 vols. Göttingen, 1821–26.
Heeren, Arnold Hermann Ludwig. *Historical Researches into the Politics, Intercourse and Trade of the Principal Nations of Antiquity*. Trans. David Alphonse Talboys et al. 6 vols. London, 1846.
Hegel, Georg Wilhelm Friedrich. *Die orientalische Welt* (= *Vorlesungen über die Philosophie der Weltgeschichte*, vol. 2). Ed. Georg Lasson. Hamburg: Meiner, 1923.
Hegel, Georg Wilhelm Friedrich. *Sämtliche Werke: Jubiläumsausgabe in zwanzig Bänden*. Ed. Hermann Glockner. Stuttgart: Frommann-Holzboog, 1927–40.
Hegel, Georg Wilhelm Friedrich. *Lectures on the Philosophy of World History: Introduction. Reason in History*. Trans. Hugh Barr Nisbet. Cambridge: Cambridge University Press, 1975.
Hegel, Georg Wilhelm Friedrich. *Die Vernunft in der Geschichte* (= *Vorlesungen über die Philosophie der Weltgeschichte*, vol. 1). Ed. Johannes Hoffmeister. 6th ed. Hamburg: Meiner, 1994.
Hegel, Georg Wilhelm Friedrich. *Vorlesungen über die Philosophie der Weltgeschichte: Berlin 1822/1823. Nachschriften von Karl Gustav Julius von Griesheim, Heinrich Gustav Hotho und Friedrich Carl Hermann Victor von Kehler*. Ed. Karl-Heinz Ilting et al. Hamburg: Meiner, 1996.
Hegel, Georg Wilhelm Friedrich. *Die Philosophie der Geschichte: Vorlesungsmitschrift Heimann (Winter 1830/1831)*. Ed. Klaus Vieweg. Munich: Fink, 2005.
Hegel, Georg Wilhelm Friedrich. *Lectures on the Philosophy of World History*. Vol. 1: *Manuscripts of the Introduction and the Lectures of 1822–3*. Ed. and trans. Robert F. Brown and Peter C. Hodgson. Oxford: Clarendon Press, 2011.
Heilbron, Johan. *The Rise of Social Theory*. Oxford: Blackwell, 1995.
Heissig, Walther, ed. *Mongoleireise zur späten Goethezeit: Berichte und Bilder des J. Rehmann und A. Thesleff*. Wiesbaden: Steiner, 1971.

Heniger, Johannes. *Hendrik Adriaan van Reede tot Drakenstein (1636–1691) and Hortus Malabaricus: A Contribution to the History of Dutch Colonial Botany*. Rotterdam: Balkema, 1986.
Henning, Georg. "Die Reiseberichte über Sibirien von Herberstein bis Ides." *Mitteilungen des Vereins für Erdkunde zu Leipzig*, 1905, 241–394.
Hennings, August. *Geschichte des Privathandels und der itzigen Verfaßungen der Dänen in Ostindien*. Copenhagen, 1784.
Hennings, August. *Gegenwärtiger Zustand der Besitzungen der Europäer in Ostindien*. 3 vols. Hamburg (vols. 1–2), Copenhagen (vol. 3), 1784–86.
Hennings, August. *Versuch einer Ostindischen Litteratur-Geschichte*. Hamburg, 1786.
Hentschel, Uwe. "Die Reiseliteratur am Ausgang des 18. Jahrhunderts: Vom gelehrten Bericht zur literarischen Beschreibung." *Internationales Archiv für Sozialgeschichte der deutschen Literatur* 16 (1991): 51–83.
Henze, Dietmar. *Enzyklopädie der Entdecker und Erforscher der Erde*. 5 vols. Graz: Akademische Druck- und Verlagsanstalt, 1978–2004.
Herder, Johann Gottfried. *Outlines of a Philosophy of the History of Man*. Trans. T. Churchill. London, 1800.
Herder, Johann Gottfried. *Ideen zur Philosophie der Geschichte der Menschheit*. Frankfurt a.M.: Deutscher Klassiker-Verlag, 1989 [1784–91] (= *Werke in zehn Bänden*. Ed. Michael Bollacker et al., 6).
Herrmann, Friedrich. *Gemählde von Ostindien in geographischer, naturhistorischer, religiöser, sittlicher, artistischer, merkantilischer und politischer Hinsicht*. Vol. 1. Leipzig, 1799.
Heude, William. *A Voyage up the Persian Gulf, and a Journey Overland from India to England in 1817*. London, 1819.
Hevia, James. *Cherishing Men from Afar: Qing Guest Ritual and the Macartney Embassy of 1793*. Durham, NC: Duke University Press, 1995.
Heydt, Johann Wolfgang. *Allerneuester geographischer und topographischer Schauplatz von Africa und Ost-Indien*. Wilhermsdorf, 1744.
Hill, Aaron. *A Full and Just Account of the Present State of the Ottoman Empire*. London, 1709.
Hintzsche, Wieland, and Thomas Nickol, eds. *Die Große Nordische Expedition: Georg Wilhelm Steller (1709–1746). Ein Lutheraner erforscht Sibirien und Alaska*. Gotha: Perthes, 1996.
Hippocrates. Volume 1 (Loeb Classical Library). Trans. W.H.S. Jones. Cambridge, MA: Harvard University Press, 1923.
Hirschfeld, Christian Cayus Lorenz. *Von der Gastfreundschaft: Eine Apologie für die Menschheit*. Leipzig, 1777.
Hirschfeld, Christian Cayus Lorenz. *Theorie der Gartenkunst*. 5 vols. Leipzig, 1779–85.
Hirschfeld, Christian Cayus Lorenz, ed. *Bibliothek der Geschichte der Menschheit*. 8 vols. Leipzig, 1780–85.
Hirschfeld, Christian Cayus Lorenz. *Von der Gastfreundschaft: Eine Apologie für die Menschheit*. Ed. Maurizio Pirro. Hannover: Wehrhahn, 2015 [1777].
Hoare, Michael E. *The Tactless Philosopher: Johann Reinhold Forster (1729–98)*. Melbourne: Hawthorne Press, 1976.
Hoare, Michael E. "Introduction." In J. R. Forster, *"Resolution" Journal*, 1982, vol. 1, 1–122.
Hobhouse, John C. [Baron Broughton]. *A Journey through Albania and Other Provinces of Turkey in Europe and Asia, to Constantinopel, during the Years 1809 and 1810*. 2nd ed. 2 vols. London, 1813.

Hodgen, Margaret T. *Early Anthropology in the Sixteenth and Seventeenth Centuries*. Philadelphia: University of Pennsylvania Press, 1964.

Hodges, William. *Travels in India during the Years 1780, 1781, 1782 and 1783*. London, 1793.

Hodgson, Marshall G. S. *The Venture of Islam: Conscience and History in a World Civilization*. 3 vols. Chicago: University of Chicago Press, 1974.

Hoffmann, Peter, and V. I. Osipov, eds. *Geographie, Geschichte und Bildungswesen in Rußland und Deutschland im 18. Jahrhundert: Briefwechsel Anton Friedrich Büsching - Gerhard Friedrich Müller 1751 bis 1783*. Berlin: Akademie-Verlag, 1995.

Holberg, Ludwig von. *Vergleichung der Historien und Thaten verschiedener insonderheit Orientalisch- und Indianischer Grosser Helden und Berühmter Männer. Nach Plutarchi Beyspiel*. 2 vols. Vol. 1: n.p., 1754; Vol. 2: Copenhagen, 1748.

Holenstein, André, Hubert Steinke, and Martin Stuber, eds. *Scholars in Action: The Practice of Knowledge and the Figure of the Savant in the 18th Century*. 2 vols. Leiden: Brill, 2013.

Höllmann, Sabine. "Ägyptisches Alltagsleben im Spiegel der Reiseaufzeichnungen von Johann Michael Wansleben (1635–1679)." *Münchner Beiträge zur Völkerkunde* 3 (1990): 81–122.

Holmes, Samuel. *The Journal of Mr. Samuel Holmes, Serjeant-Major of the XIth Light Dragoons, during His Attendance as One of the Guard on Lord Macartney's Embassy to China and Tartary 1792–93*. London, 1798.

Home, Henry: see Kames.

Hoskins, Halford Lancaster. *British Routes to India*. New York: Longmans, Green, and Co., 1928.

Hostetler, Laura. *Qing Colonial Enterprise: Ethnography and Cartography in Early Modern China*. Chicago: University of Chicago Press, 2001.

Hourani, Albert. *Europe and the Middle East*. London: Macmillan, 1980.

Hourani, Albert. *Islam in European Thought*. Cambridge: Cambridge University Press, 1991.

Housley, Norman. *The Later Crusades, 1274–1580*. Oxford: Oxford University Press, 1992.

Hsia, Florence C. *Sojourners in a Strange Land: Jesuits and Their Scientific Missions in Late Imperial China*. Chicago: University of Chicago Press, 2009.

Hsia, Po-chia Ronnie. "The End of the Jesuit Mission in China." In Jeffrey D. Burson and Jonathan Wright, eds., *The Jesuit Suppression in Global Context*. Cambridge: Cambridge University Press, 2015, 100–116.

Hübner, Johann. *Kurtze Fragen aus der Politischen Historia*. 9 vols. Hamburg, 1727–31.

Hüllmann, Karl Dietrich. *Geschichte der Mongolen bis zum Jahre 1206. Ein Beitrag zur Berichtigung der Geschichte und Erdbeschreibung des mittleren Asiens*. Berlin, 1796.

Hüllmann, Karl Dietrich. *Historisch-kritischer Versuch über die Lamaische Religion*. Berlin, 1796.

Hulme, Peter, and Tim Youngs, eds. *The Cambridge Companion to Travel Writing*. Cambridge: Cambridge University Press, 2002.

Humboldt, Alexander von. *Relation historique du voyage aux régions équinoxiales du Nouveau Continent*. 3 vols. Paris, 1814–25.

Humboldt, Alexander von. *Personal Narrative of Travels to the Equinoctial Regions of the New Continent, during the Years 1799–1804*. Trans. Helen Maria Williams. Philadelphia, PA, 1815.

Humboldt, Alexander von. *Essai politique sur le Royaume de la Nouvelle-Espagne*. 2nd ed. 3 vols. Paris, 1825–27 [1808].

Humboldt, Alexander von. *Reise durchs Baltikum nach Rußland und Sibirien 1829*. Ed. Hanno Beck. Stuttgart: Thienemann, 1983.

Humboldt, Alexander von. *Reise auf dem Río Magdalena durch die Anden und Mexico*. Pt. 1: *Texte*. Ed. Margot Faak. Berlin: Akademie-Verlag, 1986 (= *Beiträge zur Alexander von Humboldt-Forschung*, 8).

Humboldt, Alexander von. *Ansichten der Natur*. Ed. Hanno Beck. Darmstadt: Wissenschaftliche Buchgesellschaft, 1987 [1808] (= *Humboldt-Studienausgabe*, 5).

Humboldt, Alexander von. *Briefe aus Russland 1829*. Ed. Eberhard Knobloch, Ingo Schwarz, and Christian Suckow. Berlin: Akademie-Verlag, 2009 (= *Beiträge zur Alexander-von-Humboldt-Forschung*, 30).

Humboldt, Alexander von. *Zentral-Asien: Untersuchungen zu den Gebirgsketten und zur vergleichenden Klimatologie. Das Reisewerk zur Expedition von 1829*. Ed. Oliver Lubrich. Frankfurt a.M.: S. Fischer, 2009.

Humboldt, Alexander von and Carl Ritter. *Briefwechsel*. Ed. Ulrich Päßler. Berlin: Akademie-Verlag, 2010.

Humboldt, Wilhelm von. *Gesammelte Schriften*. Ed. Royal Prussian Academy of Sciences. 17 vols. Berlin, 1903–36.

Hume, David. *The History of England from the Invasion of Julius Caesar to the Revolution of 1688*. 6 vols. Indianapolis: Liberty Fund, 1983 [1754–62].

Hume, David. *Essays Moral, Political, and Literary*. Ed. Eugene F. Miller. Indianapolis: Liberty Fund, 1987 [1741–42].

Hundt, Michael, ed. *Beschreibung der dreijährigen chinesischen Reise: Die russische Gesandtschaft von Moskau nach Peking 1692 bis 1695 in den Darstellungen von Eberhard Isbrand Ides und Adam Brand*. Stuttgart: Steiner, 1999.

Hunt, Lynn, Margaret C. Jacob, and Wijnand Mijnhardt. *The Book that Changed Europe: Picart & Bernard's Religious Ceremonies of the World*. Cambridge, MA: Harvard University Press, 2010.

Hunter, William. *A Concise Account of the Kingdom of Pegu*. Calcutta, 1785.

Huntington, Samuel P. *The Clash of Civilizations and the Remaking of World Order*. New York: Simon and Schuster, 1996.

Husain, Iqbal. *The Ruhela Chieftaincies: The Rise and Fall of Ruhela Power in India in the Eighteenth Century*. Delhi: Oxford University Press, 1994.

Hüttner, Johann Christian. *Nachricht von der britischen Gesandtschaftsreise durch China und einen Teil der Tartarei*. Ed. Sabine Dabringhaus. Sigmaringen: Thorbecke, 1996 [1797].

Ides, Evert Isbrands. *Three Years Travels from Moscow Over-Land to China*. London, 1706.

Imbruglia, Girolamo. "Tra Anquetil-Duperron et 'L'Histoire des deux Indes': Libertà, dispotismo et feudalesimo." *Rivista storica Italiana* 104 (1994): 140–93.

Imbruglia, Girolamo. "Despotisme et féodalité dans 'L'Histoire des deux Indes.'" In Lüsebrink and Strugnell, *L'Histoire des deux Indes*, 1995, 105–17.

Impey, Oliver. *Chinoiserie: The Impact of Oriental Styles on Western Art and Decoration*. London: Oxford University Press, 1977.

Inden, Ronald. *Imagining India*. Oxford: Blackwell, 1990.

Irwin, Robert, ed. *Islamic Cultures and Societies to the End of the Eighteenth Century*. Cambridge: Cambridge University Press, 2010 (= *The New Cambridge History of Islam*, 4).

Israel, Jonathan I. *Radical Enlightenment: Philosophy and the Making of Modernity 1650–1750*. Oxford: Oxford University Press, 2001.

Israel, Jonathan I. *Enlightenment Contested: Philosophy, Modernity, and the Emancipation of Man 1670–1752*. Oxford: Oxford University Press, 2006.

Israel, Jonathan I. *Democratic Enlightenment: Philosophy, Revolution, and Human Rights, 1750–1790*. Oxford: Oxford University Press, 2011.

Jackson, Peter. *The Delhi Sultanate: A Political and Military History*. Cambridge: Cambridge University Press, 1999.

Jackson, Peter, and Laurence Lockhart, eds. *The Timurid and Safavid Periods*. Cambridge: Cambridge University Press, 1986 (= *The Cambridge History of Iran*, 6).

Jacobs, Michael. *The Painted Voyage: Art, Travel and Exploration, 1564–1875*. London: British Museum Press, 1995.

Jacobsen, Stefan Gaarsmand. "Limits to Despotism: Idealizations of Chinese Governance and Legitimizations of Absolutist Europe." *Journal of Early Modern History* 17 (2013): 347–89.

Jäger, Hans-Wolf. "Herder als Leser von Reiseliteratur." In Griep and Jäger, *Reisen im 18. Jahrhundert*, 1986, 181–99.

Jäger, Hans-Wolf, ed. *Europäisches Reisen im Zeitalter der Aufklärung*. Heidelberg: Winter, 1992.

Jain, M. P. *Outlines of Indian Legal History*. 2nd ed. Bombay: Tripathi, 1966.

Jami, Cathérine. *The Emperor's New Mathematics: Western Learning and Imperial Authority during the Kangxi Reign (1662–1722)*. Oxford: Oxford University Press, 2012.

Jancke, Gabriele. *Gastfreundschaft in der frühneuzeitlichen Gesellschaft: Praktiken, Normen und Perspektiven von Gelehrten*. Göttingen: Vandenhoeck and Ruprecht, 2013.

Jasanoff, Maya. *Edge of Empire: Conquest and Collecting in the East 1750–1850*. New York: Vintage, 2005.

Jauß, Hans Robert. *Studien zum Epochenwandel der ästhetischen Moderne*. Frankfurt a.M.: Suhrkamp, 1989.

Jaubert, Amédée. *Voyage en Arménie et en Perse, fait dans les années 1805 et 1806*. Paris, 1821.

Jenour, Matthew. *The Route to India*. London, 1791.

Jeyaraj, Daniel, and Richard Fox Young, eds. and trans. *Hindu-Christian Epistolary Self-Disclosures: "Malabarian Correspondence" between German Pietist Missionaries and South Indian Hindus (1712–1714)*. Wiesbaden: Harrassowitz, 2013.

Jobst, Kerstin S. "Vision und Regime: Die ersten Jahrzehnte russischer Krimherrschaft." In Klein, *Crimean Khanate*, 2012, 211–27.

Johnson, James. *The Oriental Voyager, or Descriptive Sketches and Cursory Remarks on a Voyage to India and China*. London, 1807.

Johnson, John. *A Journey from India to England through Persia, Georgia, Russia, Poland and Prussia, in the Year 1817*. London, 1818.

Johnson, Samuel. "Essay on the 'Description of China' in Two Volumes Folio. From the French of Père Du Halde." *Gentleman's Magazine* 12 (1742): 320–23, 353–57, 484–486.

Johnson, Samuel. *Selected Poetry and Prose*. Ed. Frank Brady and W. K. Wimsatt. Berkeley: University of California Press, 1977.

Joliffe, Thomas Robert. *Letters from Palestine, Descriptive of a Tour through Galilee and Judea, to Which Are Added Letters from Egypt*. 3rd ed. 2 vols. London, 1822 [1820].

Jones, W. R. "The Image of the Barbarian in Medieval Europe." *Comparative Studies in Society and History* 13 (1971): 376–407.

Jones, William. *Histoire de Nader Shah, traduite du Persan par ordre de Sa Majesté le Roi de Dannemark*. London, 1770.

Jones, William. *The Works*. 13 vols. London, 1807.

Jones, William. *The Letters of Sir William Jones*. Ed. Garland Cannon. 2 vols. Oxford: Clarendon Press, 1970.

Joyeux, Frank. *Der Transitweg von Moskau nach Daurien: Sibirische Transport- und Verkehrsprobleme im 17. Jahrhundert*. Unpublished PhD thesis. Cologne, 1981.

Justi, Johann Heinrich Gottlob von. *Vergleichungen der Europäischen mit den Asiatischen und anderen vermeintlich Barbarischen Regierungen*. Berlin, 1762.

Kaempfer, Engelbert. *The History of Japan*. Trans. Johann Caspar Scheuchzer. 2 vols. London, 1727.

Kaempfer, Engelbert. *Geschichte und Beschreibung Japans*. Ed. Christian Wilhelm Dohm. 2 vols. Lemgo, 1777–79.

Kaempfer, Engelbert. *Am Hofe des persischen Großkönigs (1684–1685): Das erste Buch der Amoenitates Exoticae*. Ed. Walther Hinz. Leipzig: Koehler, 1940 [1712].

Kaempfer, Engelbert. *Die Reisetagebücher Engelbert Kaempfers*. Ed. Karl Meier-Lemgo. Wiesbaden: Steiner, 1968.

Kaempfer, Engelbert. *Flora Japonica*. Wiesbaden: Steiner, 1983 [1712].

Kaempfer, Engelbert. *Phoenix Persicus: Die Geschichte der Dattelpalme*. Ed. and trans. Wolfgang Muntschick. Marburg: Basilisken-Presse, 1987 [1712].

Kaempfer, Engelbert. *Kaempfer's Japan: Tokugawa Culture Observed*. Ed., trans., and annotated by Beatrice M. Bodart-Bailey. Honululu: University of Hawaii Press, 1999.

Kaempfer, Engelbert. *Heutiges Japan*. Ed. Wolfgang Michel and Barend J. Terwiel. 2 vols. Munich: Iudicium, 2001 (= *Engelbert Kaempfer Werke*, 1.1 and 1.2).

Kaempfer, Engelbert. *Engelbert Kaempfer in Siam*. Ed. Barend J. Terwiel. Munich: Iudicium, 2003 (= *Engelbert Kaempfer Werke*, 4).

Kaempfer, Engelbert. *Rußlandtagebuch 1683*. Ed. Michael Schippan. Munich: Iudicium, 2003 (= *Engelbert Kaempfer Werke*, 6).

Kaiser, Thomas. "The Evil Empire? The Debate on Turkish Despotism in Eighteenth-Century French Political Culture." *Journal of Modern History* 72 (2000): 6–34.

Kames, Henry Home, Lord. *Sketches of the History of Man*. 2nd ed. 4 vols. Edinburgh, 1778 [1774].

Kant, Immanuel. *Political Writings*. Ed. Hans Reiss, trans. Hugh Barr Nisbet. Cambridge: Cambridge University Press, 1970.

Kant, Immanuel. *Werke in zehn Bänden*. Ed. Wilhelm Weischedel. Darmstadt: Wissenschaftliche Buchgesellschaft, 1970.

Kapitza, Peter. "Engelbert Kaempfer und die europäische Aufklärung: Zur Wirkungsgeschichte seines Japanwerkes im 18. Jahrhundert." In Deutsche Gesellschaft für Natur- und Völkerkunde Ostasiens, ed., *Engelbert Kaempfers Geschichte und Beschreibung von Japan: Beiträge und Kommentar*. Berlin: Springer, 1980, 41–63.

Kapitza, Peter, ed. *Japan in Europa: Texte und Bilddokumente zur europäischen Japankenntnis von Marco Polo bis Wilhelm von Humboldt*. 2 vols. and suppl. Munich: Iudicium, 1990.

Kappeler, Andreas. *The Russian Empire: A Multiethnic History*. Trans. Alfred Clayton. Harlow: Longman, 2001.

Kästner, Hannes. "Das Gespräch des Orientreisenden mit dem heidnischen Herrscher." In Horst Wenzel, ed., *Gespräche—Boten—Briefe: Körpergedächtnis und Schriftgedächtnis im Mittelalter*. Berlin: Erich Schmidt, 1997, 280–95.

Kaukiainen, Yrjö. "Shrinking the World: Improvements in the Speed of Information Transmission, c. 1820–1870." *European Review of Economic History* 5 (2001): 1–28.

Kaye, John William. *The Life and Correspondence of Major-General Sir John Malcolm*. 2 vols. London: Smith, Elder, and Co., 1856.

Keane, John. "Despotism and Democracy: The Origins and Development of the Distinction between Civil Society and the State 1750–1850." In John Keane, ed., *Civil Society and the State*. London: Verso, 1988, 35–71.

Keene, Donald. *The Japanese Discovery of Europe, 1720–1830*. Rev. ed. Stanford, CA: Stanford University Press, 1969.

Keevak, Michael. *The Pretended Asian: George Psalmanazar's Eighteenth-Century Formosan Hoax*. Detroit, MI: Wayne State University Press, 2004.

Keighren, Innes, Charles. W. J. Withers, and Bill Bell. *Travels into Print. Exploration, Writing and Publishing with John Murray, 1773–1853*. Chicago: University of Chicago Press, 2015.

Kejariwal, O. P. *The Asiatic Society of Bengal and the Discovery of India's Past (1784–1838)*. Delhi: Oxford University Press, 1988.

Kerr, James. *A Short Historical Narrative of the Rise and Rapid Advancement of the Mahrattah State*. London, 1782.

Kerr Porter see Porter, Robert Kerr.

Khan, Gulfishan. *Indian Muslim Perceptions of the West during the Eighteenth Century*. Karachi: Oxford University Press, 1998.

Khazanov, Anatolij M. *Nomads and the Outside World*. Trans. Julia Crookenden. Cambridge: Cambridge University Press, 1984.

Khodja, Hamdan. *Le Miroir: aperçu historique et statistique sur la régence d'Alger*. 2nd ed. Ed. Abdelkader Djeghloul. Paris: Sindbad, 2003.

Khurana, Gianeshwar. *British Historiography on the Sikh Power in Punjab*. New Delhi: Allied Publications, 1985.

Kimpel, Dieter, ed. *Mehrsprachigkeit in der deutschen Aufklärung*. Hamburg: Meiner, 1985.

Kindersley, Jemina. *Letters from the Island of Teneriffe, Brazil, the Cape of Good Hope, and the East Indies*. London, 1777.

Kircher, Athanasius. *China monumentis, qua sacris qua profanis . . . illustrata*. Amsterdam, 1667.

Kirkpatrick, William. *An Account of the Kingdom of Nepaul. Being the Substance of Observations Made during a Mission to that Country in the Year 1793*. London, 1811.

Kittsteiner, Heinz Dieter. "Hegels Eurozentrismus in globaler Perspektive." In Hardtwig and Müller, *Die Vergangenheit der Weltgeschichte*, 2010, 51–73.

Klaproth, Julius von. *Reise in den Kaukasus und nach Georgien, unternommen in den Jahren 1807 und 1808*. 2 vols. Halle, 1812–14.

Klaproth, Julius von. *Tableaux historiques de l'Asie, depuis la monarchie de Cyrus jusqu'à nos jours*. Paris, 1826.

Klaproth, Julius von. *Mémoires relatifs à l'Asie, contenant des recherches historiques, géographiques et philologiques sur les peuples de l'Orient*. 3 vols. Paris, 1826–28.

Klaproth, Julius von. *Briefe und Dokumente*. Ed. Hartmut Walravens. Wiesbaden: Harrassowitz, 1999.

Kleemann, Nikolaus Ernst. *Reisen von Wien über Belgrad bis Kilianova . . . in den Jahren 1768, 1769 und 1770: Nebst einem Anhange von den besonderen Merkwürdigkeiten der crimmischen Tartarey*. Vienna, 1771.

Klein, Denise, ed. *The Crimean Khanate between East and West (15th to 19th Century)*. Wiesbaden: Harrassowitz, 2012.

Kleuker, Johann Friedrich. *Anhang zum Zend-Avesta*. 2 vols. in 4 pts. Leipzig, 1781–83.

Klug, Ekkehard. "Das 'asiatische' Rußland: Über die Entstehung eines europäischen Vorurteils." *Historische Zeitschrift* 245 (1987): 265–89.

Knolles, Richard. *The Generall Historie of the Turkes*. London, 1603.

Knolles, Richard. *The Turkish History from the Original of that Nation to the Growth of the Ottoman Empire*. 6th ed. 3 vols. London, 1687–1700.

Knox, Robert. *An Historical Relation of the Island of Ceylon, in the East-Indies*. London, 1681.

Koch, Gerhard, ed. *Imhoff Indienfahrer: Ein Reisebericht aus dem 18. Jahrhundert in Briefen und Bildern*. Göttingen: Wallstein, 2001.

Koch, Manfred. *Weimaraner Weltbewohner. Zur Genese von Goethes Begriff der "Weltliteratur."* Tübingen: Niemeyer, 2002.

Koebner, Richard. "Despot and Despotism: Vicissitudes of a Political Theme." *Journal of the Warburg and Courtauld Institutes* 14 (1951): 275–302.

Kohl, Karl-Heinz. *Entzauberter Blick: Das Bild vom Guten Wilden und die Erfahrung der Zivilisation*. Frankfurt a.M.: Suhrkamp, 1986.

Köhler, Johann Tobias, ed. *Sammlung neuer Reisebeschreibungen aus fremden Sprachen*. 2 vols. Göttingen, 1767–69.

Kolb, Peter. *Caput Bonae Spei Hodiernum: Das ist: Vollständige Beschreibung des Afrikanischen Vorgebürges der Guten Hoffnung*. Nürnberg, 1719.

Kollmann, Nancy Shields. *The Russian Empire 1450–1801*. Oxford: Oxford University Press, 2017.

König, Hans-Joachim, Wolfgang Reinhard, and Reinhardt Wendt, eds. *Der europäische Beobachter außereuropäischer Kulturen: Zur Problematik der Wirklichkeitswahrnehmung*. Berlin: Duncker and Humblot, 1989.

Kontler, László. *Translations, Histories, Enlightenments: William Robertson in Germany, 1760–1795*. Basingstoke: Palgrave Macmillan, 2014.

Kopf, David. *British Orientalism and the Bengal Renaissance: The Dynamics of Indian Modernization 1773–1835*. Berkeley: University of California Press, 1969.

Korshin, Paul J., ed. *The Widening Circle: Essays on the Circulation of Literature in Eighteenth-Century Europe*. Philadelphia: University of Pennsylvania Press, 1976.

Kosegarten, Johann Gottfried Ludwig. *Morgenländische Alterthumskunde oder Beschreibung der Religion, Gesetze, Sitten und Wissenschaften der alten morgenländischen Völker*. Dresden, 1831.

Koselleck, Reinhart. *Futures Past: On the Semantics of Historical Time*. Trans. Keith Tribe. Cambridge, MA: MIT Press, 1985 [1979].

Kotzebue, Otto von. *Entdeckungs-Reise in die Süd-See und nach der Behrings-Straße . . . , unternommen in den Jahren 1815, 1816, 1817 und 1818. . . .* 3 vols. Weimar, 1821.

Krader, Lawrence. *The Asiatic Mode of Production: Sources, Development and Critique in the Writings of Karl Marx*. Assen: Van Gorcum, 1975.

Krahl, Joseph. *China Missions in Crisis: Bishop Laimbeckhoven and His Times, 1738–1787*. Rome: Gregorian University Press, 1964.

Krashenninikov, Stepan Petrovich. *Explorations of Kamchatka: North Pacific Scimitar*. Trans. E.A.P. Crownhart-Vaughan. Portland: Oregon Historical Society, 1972 [1755].

Kraus, Alexander, and Andreas Renner, eds. *Orte eigener Vernunft: Europäische Aufklärung jenseits der Zentren*. Frankfurt a.M.: Campus, 2008.

Krauss, Werner. *Zur Anthropologie des 18. Jahrhunderts: Die Frühgeschichte der Menschheit im Blickpunkt der Aufklärung*. Munich: Hanser, 1979.

Kreiner, Josef. "Das Bild Japans in der europäischen Geistesgeschichte." *Japanstudien* 1 (1990): 13–42.

Kroell, Anne. "Douze Lettres de Jean Chardin." *Journal Asiatique* 270 (1982): 295–337.

Krusenstern, Adam Johann von. *Reise um die Welt in den Jahren 1803, 1804, 1805, 1806 auf Befehl Seiner Kaiserl. Majestät Alexander des Ersten auf den Schiffen Nadeshda und Newa.* 3 vols. Saint Petersburg, 1810–12.

Krusenstern, Adam Johann von. *Voyage round the World in the Years 1803, 1804, 1805, 1806.* Trans. Richard Belgrave Hoppner. 2 vols. London, 1813.

Krusinksi, Judas Thaddæus. *Histoire de la dernière Revolution de Perse.* 2 vols. Paris, 1728.

Krusinski, Judas Thaddæus. *The History of the Revolution in Persia.* Trans. in English by Father Du Cerceau. 2 vols. London, 1728.

Kühn, Arthur. *Die Neugestaltung der deutschen Geographie im 18. Jahrhundert.* Leipzig: Koehler, 1939.

Kumar, Deepak. "The Evolution of Colonial Science in India: Natural History and the East India Company." In MacKenzie, *Imperialism and the Natural World*, 1990, 51–66.

Kupperman, Karen Ordahl, ed. *America in European Consciousness, 1493–1750.* Chapel Hill: University of North Carolina Press, 1995.

Kupperman, Karen Ordahl. "Introduction: The Changing Definitions of America." In ibid. *America in European Consciousness*, 1995, 1–29.

La Bissachère, Pierre-Jacques Lemonnier de. *Etat actuelle du Tunkin, de la Cochinchine, et des Royaumes du Cambodge, Laos et Lac-Tho.* 2 vols. Paris, 1812.

La Loubère, Simon de. *A New Historical Relation of the Kingdom of Siam.* Trans. from the French. 2 vols. London, 1693 [1691].

Lach, Donald F. *Asia in the Making of Europe.* Vol. 2 in 3 bks. *A Century of Wonder.* Chicago: University of Chicago Press, 1970–77.

Lach, Donald F., and Edwin J. Van Kley. *Asia in the Making of Europe.* Vol. 3 in 4 bks. *A Century of Advance.* Chicago: University of Chicago Press, 1993.

Lacouture, Jean. *Champollion: une vie de lumières.* Paris: Grasset, 1988.

Lafitau, Joseph François. *Mémoire concernant la precieuse plante du Gin seng de Tartarie.* Paris, 1718.

Lafitau, Joseph François. *Mœurs des sauvages ameriquains comparées aux moeurs des premiers tems.* 2 vols. Paris, 1724.

Laharpe, Jean François de. *Abrégé de l'Histoire Générale des Voyages.* 29 vols. Paris, 1813–15.

Laissus, Yves. *L'Égypte, une aventure savante 1798–1801.* Paris: Fayard, 1998.

Lamb, Alastair. "British Missions to Cochinchina, 1778–1822." *Journal of the Malayan Branch of the Royal Asiatic Society* 34 (1961): 1–247.

Lamb, Alastair, ed. *Bhutan and Tibet: The Travels of George Bogle and Alexander Hamilton 1774–1777.* Hertingfordbury, Herts.: Roxford Books, 2002.

Landry-Deron, Isabelle. *La preuve par la Chine: La "Description" de J.- B. Du Halde, Jésuite, 1735.* Paris: Éditions de l'École des Hautes Études en Sciences Sociales, 2002.

Landucci, Sergio. *I filosofi e i selvaggi 1580–1780.* Bari: Laterza, 1972.

Lane, Edward William. *An Account of the Manners and Customs of the Modern Egyptians.* London: Gardner, 1895 [1836].

Lange, Lorenz. "Journal du Sieur Lange contenant ses négociations à la Cour de la Chine en 1721 & 1722." In Bernard, *Recueil des voyages au Nord*, vol. 8 (1727), 221–371.

Lange, Lorenz. *Reise nach China.* Ed. Conrad Grau. Berlin: Akademie-Verlag, 1986.

Langlès, Louis Mathieu. *Monuments anciens et modernes de l'Hindoustan.* 2 vols. Paris, 1821.

Langsdorff, Georg Heinrich von. *Bemerkungen auf einer Reise um die Welt in den Jahren 1803 bis 1807.* 2 vols. Frankfurt a.M., 1813.

Laurens, Henry. *Aux sources de l'orientalisme: Le "Bibliothèque Orientale" de Barthélemi de'Herbelot*. Paris: Maisonneuve et Larose, 1978.

Laurens, Henry. *Les origines intellectuelles de l'expédition d'Égypte: l'orientalisme islamisant en France (1698–1798)*. Istanbul: Isis, 1987.

Laurens, Henry. *L'Expédition d'Égypte 1798–1801*. Paris: Colin, 1989.

Lavie, Jean-Charles de. *Des corps politiques et de leur gouvernements*. 2 vols. Lyon, 1764.

Lawrence, Christopher. "Disciplining Disease: Scurvy, the Navy, and Imperial Expansion, 1750–1825." In Miller and Reill, *Visions of Empire*, 1996, 80–106.

Layton, Susan. *Russian Literature and Empire: Conquest of the Caucasus from Pushkin to Tolstoy*. Cambridge: Cambridge University Press, 1994.

Lazzerini, Edward. "The Crimea under Russian Rule: 1783 to the Great Reforms." In Rywkin, ed. *Russian Colonial Expansion*, 1988, 123–38.

Le Comte, Louis. *Nouveaux mémoires sur l'état present de la Chine*. 2 vols. Amsterdam, 1697 [1696].

Le Gentil de la Galaisière, Guillaume-Joseph. *Voyage dans les mers de l'Inde, fait par ordre du Roi*. 2 vols. Paris, 1780–81.

Le Gobien, Charles. *Histoire de l'édit de l'Empereur de la Chine*. Paris, 1698.

Ledyard, Gari. *The Dutch Come to Korea*. Seoul: Royal Asiatic Society, Korea Branch, 1971.

Lee Ki-baik. *A New History of Korea*. Cambridge, MA: Harvard University Press, 1984.

Lee, Peter H., ed. *Sourcebook of Korean Civilization*. Vol. 2: *From the Seventeenth Century to the Modern Period*. New York: Columbia University Press, 1996.

Leezenberg, Michiel. "The Oriental Origins of Orientalism: The Case of Dimitrie Cantemir." In Bod, Maat, and Weststeijn, *The Making of the Humanities*, 2012, 243–63.

Legouix, Susan. *Image of China: William Alexander*. London: Jupiter Books, 1980.

Léguat, François. *Voyage et avantures . . . en deux isles desertes des Indes Orientales*. 2 vols. Amsterdam, 1708.

Lehner, Georg. *China in European Encyclopaedias, 1700–1850*. Leiden: Brill, 2011.

Leibniz, Gottfried Wilhelm. *The Preface to Leibniz' Novissima Sinica*. Trans. Donald F. Lach. Honululu: University of Hawaii Press, 1957 [1697].

Leibniz, Gottfried Wilhelm. *Sämtliche Schriften und Briefe*. Ed. Akademie der Wissenschaften der DDR. Ser. 4: *Politische Schriften*. Vol. 1: *1667–1676*. 3rd ed. Berlin: Akademie-Verlag, 1983.

Leibniz, Gottfried Wilhelm. *Der Briefwechsel mit den Jesuiten in China (1689–1714)*. Ed. Rita Widmaier, trans. Malte-Ludolf Babin. Hamburg: Meiner, 2006.

Leibniz, Gottfried Wilhelm. *Briefe über China (1694–1716): Die Korrespondenz mit Barthélemy des Bosses S. J. und anderen Mitgliedern des Ordens*. Ed. Rita Widmaier and Malte-Ludolf Babin, trans. Malte-Ludolf Babin. Hamburg: Meiner, 2017.

Lemberg, Hans. "Zur Entstehung des Osteuropabegriffs im 19. Jahrhundert: Vom 'Norden' zum 'Osten' Europas." *Jahrbücher für Geschichte Osteuropas* 33 (1985): 48–91.

Lemny, Stefan. *Les Cantemir: l'aventure européenne d'une famille princière au XVIIIe siècle*. Paris: Éditions complexe, 2009.

Lenglet-Dufresnoy, abbé Pierre Nicolas. *A New Method of Studying History*. 2 vols. London, 1728 [1713].

Lenglet-Dufresnoy, abbé Pierre Nicolas. *Méthode pour étudier la géographie*. 3rd ed. Paris, 1741.

Lepenies, Wolf. *Das Ende der Naturgeschichte: Wandel kultureller Selbstverständlichkeiten in den Wissenschaften des 18. und 19. Jahrhunderts*. Munich: Hanser, 1976.

Lequin, Frank. *Isaac Titsingh in China (1794–1796): Het onuitgegeven Journaal van zijn Ambassade naar Peking*. Alphen aan den Rijn: Canaletto, 2005.

Leuze, Reinhard. *Die außerchristlichen Religionen bei Hegel.* Göttingen: Vandenhoeck and Ruprecht, 1975.

Lewis, Bernard. *The Muslim Discovery of Europe.* London: Weidenfeld and Nicolson, 1982.

Lewis, Bernard. "Eurozentrismus." *Merkur* 49 (1995): 644–51.

Lewis, Bernard, and Peter M. Holt, eds. *Historians of the Middle East.* London: Oxford University Press, 1962.

Lewis, Martin G., and Kären E. Wigen. *The Myth of Continents: A Critique of Metageography.* Berkeley: University of California Press, 1997.

Lichtenberg, Georg Christoph. *Schriften und Briefe.* 3 vols. Ed. Wolfgang Promies. Munich: Hanser, 1968–74.

Liebau, Heike. *Die indischen Mitarbeiter der Tranquebarmission (1706–1845): Katecheten, Schulmeister, Übersetzer.* Tübingen: Niemeyer, 2008.

Liebersohn, Harry. *Aristocratic Encounters: European Travelers and North American Indians.* Cambridge: Cambridge University Press, 1998.

Liebersohn, Harry. *The Travelers's World: Europe to the Pacific.* Cambridge, MA : Harvard University Press, 2006.

Lieven, Dominic, ed. *Imperial Russia, 1689–1917.* Cambridge: Cambridge University Press, 2006 (= *The Cambridge History of Russia,* 2).

Lincoln, W. Bruce. *The Conquest of a Continent: Siberia and the Russians.* London: Cape, 1994.

Linguet, Simon-Nicolas-Henri. *Du plus heureux gouvernement ou paralèlle des constitutions politiques de l'Asie avec celles de l'Europe.* 2 vols. London, 1774.

Linguet, Simon-Nicolas-Henri. *Théorie des lois civiles ou principes fondamentaux de la société.* Paris: Fayard, 1984 [1767].

Lisiansky, Urey. *A Voyage round the World in the Years 1803,4,5,&6; By Order of His Imperial Majesty Alexander the First, Emperor of Russia, in the Ship Nera.* London, 1814.

Lloyd, Seton. *Foundations in the Dust: The Story of Mesopotamian Exploration.* Rev. ed. London: Thames and Hudson, 1980.

Lockhart, Laurence. *Nadir Shah: A Critical Study Based Mainly upon Contemporary Sources.* London: Luzac, 1938.

Lockhart, Laurence. *The Fall of the Safavi Dynasty and the Afghan Occupation of Persia.* Cambridge: Cambridge University Press, 1958.

Lockhart, Laurence. "European Contacts with Persia 1350–1736." In Jackson and Lockhart, *Timurid and Safavid Periods,* 1986, 373–409.

Lombard, Denys, ed. *Rêver l'Asie: Exotisme et littérature coloniale aux Indes, en Indochine et au Insulinde.* Paris: Éditions de l' École des Hautes Études en Sciences Sociales, 1993.

Lowe, Lisa. *The Intimacies of Four Continents.* Durham, NC: Duke University Press, 2015.

Lowes, John Livingston. *The Road to Xanadu: A Study in the Ways of the Imagination.* Boston: Houghton Mifflin, 1927.

Lubac, Henri de, S. J. *La rencontre du Bouddhisme et de l'Occident.* Paris: Aubier, 1952.

Lucas, Paul. *Voyage du Sieur Paul Lucas au Levant.* 2 vols. Paris, 1731.

Lueder, August Ferdinand. *Geschichte des Holländischen Handels.* Leipzig, 1788.

Lueder, August Ferdinand. *Geschichte der vornehmsten Völker der alten Welt im Grundrisse.* Brunswick, 1800.

Luhmann, Niklas. *Theory of Society.* Trans. Rhodes Barrett. 2 vols. Stanford, CA: Stanford University Press, 2012–13.

Lunt, James. *Bokhara Burnes*. London: Faber, 1969.
Lüsebrink, Hans-Jürgen, and Anthony Strugnell, eds. *L'Histoire des deux Indes: réécriture et polygraphie*. Oxford: Voltaire Foundation, 1995.
Lynam, Edward, ed. *Richard Hakluyt and His Successors*. London: Hakluyt Society, 1946.
Macdonald, Fraser, and Charles W. J. Withers, eds. *Geography, Technology and Instruments of Exploration*. Farnham (Surrey): Ashgate, 2015.
Macdonald Kinneir, John. *A Geographical Memoir of the Persian Empire*. London, 1813.
Macdonald Kinneir, John. *Journey through Asia Minor, Armenia, and Koordistan, in the Years 1813 and 1814*. London, 1818.
MacKenzie, John M., ed. *Imperialism and the Natural World*. Manchester: Manchester University Press, 1990.
MacKenzie, John M. *Orientalism: History, Theory and the Arts*. Manchester: Manchester University Press, 1995.
Mackerras, Colin. *Western Images of China*. Hong Kong: Oxford University Press, 1989.
Macpherson, David. *The History of the European Commerce with India*. London, 1812.
Maçzak, Antoni, and Hans Jürgen Teuteberg, eds. *Reiseberichte als Quellen europäischer Kulturgeschichte: Aufgaben und Möglichkeiten der historischen Reiseforschung*. Wolfenbüttel: Herzog August Bibliothek, 1982.
Maddison, Angus. *The World Economy: A Millennial Perspective*. Paris: OECD, 2001.
Magalhães, Gabriel de. *A New History of China, Containing a Description of the Most Considerable Particulars of that Vast Empire*. Translated from the French. London, 1688.
Magazin für die Historie und Geographie. Ed. Anton Friedrich Büsching. Vols. 1–22. Halle, 1761–88.
Magazin von merkwürdigen neuen Reisebeschreibungen aus fremden Sprachen übersetzt und mit erläuternden Anmerkungen begleitet. Ed. Johann Reinhold Forster et al. Vols. 1–37. Berlin, 1790–1828.
Mailla, Joseph-Anne-Marie de Moyriac de. *Histoire générale de la Chine, ou Annales de cet Empire*. 12 vols. Paris, 1777–80.
Mailly, Jean-Baptiste. *L'esprit des Croisades*. 2 vols. Dijon, 1780.
Mairan, Jean Jacques Dortous de. *Lettres de M. de Mairan au R.P. Parennin, Missionaire de la Compagnie de Jesus à Pékin, Concernant diverses Questions sur la Chine*. Paris, 1759.
Maistre de la Tour, M. *The History of Ayder Ali Khan, Nabob-Bahadur*. 2 vols. Dublin, 1784 [1783].
Majeed, Javed. *Ungoverned Imaginings: James Mill's "The History of British India" and Orientalism*. Oxford: Clarendon Press, 1992.
Major, Andrea. *Pious Flames: European Encounters with Sati, 1500–1830*. New Delhi: Oxford University Press, 2006.
Major, Andrea, ed. *Sati: A Historical Anthology*. New Delhi: Oxford University Press, 2007.
Makdisi, Saree, and Felicity Nussbaum, eds. *"The Arabian Nights" in Historical Context: between East and West*. Oxford: Oxford University Press, 2008.
Malcolm, John. "Sketch of the Sikhs." *Asiatic Register* 11 (1810): 197–292.
Malcolm, John. *Central India*. 2 vols. London, 1823.
Malcolm, John. *History of Persia*. New ed. 2 vols. London, 1829 [1815].
Malleret, Louis. *Pierre Poivre*. Paris: École Française d'Extrême-Orient, 1974.
Malte-Brun, Conrad. *Précis de la géographie universelle*. 2nd ed. 8 vols. Paris, 1812–29.
Malte-Brun: see also *Annales de voyages*.
Malthus, Thomas Robert. *The Works*. Ed. E. A. Wrigley and David Souden. 8 vols. London: Pickering, 1986.

Mancall, Peter, ed. *Bringing the World to Early Modern Europe: Travel Accounts and Their Audiences*. Leiden: Brill, 2007.

Mandt, Hella. "Tyrannis, Despotie." In Brunner, Conze, and Koselleck, *Geschichtliche Grundbegriffe*, vol. 6 (1990), 651–706.

Mangold, Sabine. *Eine "weltbürgerliche Wissenschaft": Die deutsche Orientalistik im 19. Jahrhundert*. Stuttgart: Steiner, 2004.

Mani, Lata. *Contentious Traditions: The Debate on Sati in Colonial India*. Berkeley: University of California Press, 1998.

Manucci [Manuzzi], Niccolao. *Storia do Mogor, or Mogul India 1653–1708*. Ed. and trans. William Irvine. 4 vols. London: Murray, 1906–8.

Manz, Beatrice Forbes. *The Rise and Rule of Tamerlane*. Cambridge: Cambridge University Press, 1989.

Marazzi, Ugo, ed. *La conoscenza dell'Asia e dell'Africa in Italia nei secoli XVIII e XIX*. 2 vols. Naples: Istituto Universitario Orientale, 1984.

Marchand, Suzanne L. *German Orientalism in the Age of Empire: Religion, Race, and Scholarship*. Cambridge: Cambridge University Press, 2009.

Marcus, Abraham. *The Middle East on the Eve of Modernity: Aleppo in the Eighteenth Century*. New York: Columbia University Press, 1989.

Margat de Tilly, Jean Baptiste. *Histoire de Tamerlan, l'Empereur des Mogols et Conquerant de l'Asie*. 2 vols. Paris, 1739.

Marigny, abbé François Augier de. *Histoire des révolutions de l'empire des Arabes*. 4 vols. Paris, 1750–52.

Markham, Clements R. *Major James Rennell and the Rise of Modern English Geography*. London: Cassell, 1895.

Marsden, William. *The History of Sumatra, Containing an Account of the Government, Laws, Customs, and Manners of the Native Inhabitants*. 3rd ed. London, 1811 [1783].

Marsden, William. *A Grammar of the Malayan Language*. London, 1812.

Marsden, William, ed. and trans. *The Travels of Marco Polo*. London, 1818.

Marsden, William. *A Brief Memoir of the Life and Writings of the Late William Marsden, Written by Himself*. London, 1838.

Marshall, P. J. *The Impeachment of Warren Hastings*. London: Oxford University Press, 1965.

Marshall, P. J., ed. *The British Discovery of Hinduism in the Eighteenth Century*. Cambridge: Cambridge University Press, 1970.

Marshall, P. J. *East India Fortunes: The British in Bengal in the Eighteenth Century*. Oxford: Clarendon Press, 1976.

Marshall, P. J. "Introduction." In Burke, *India: Madras and Bengal*, 1981, 1–27.

Marshall, P. J. *Bengal: The British Bridgehead. Eastern India 1740–1828*. Cambridge: Cambridge University Press, 1988.

Marshall, P. J. "Taming the Exotic: The British and India in the Seventeenth and Eighteenth Centuries." In Rousseau and Porter, *Exoticism in the Enlightenment*, 1990, 46–65.

Marshall, P. J. "Introduction." In Burke, *India: The Launching of the Hastings Impeachment*, 1991, 1–36.

Marshall, P. J. "'Cornwallis Triumphant': War in India and the British Public in the Late Eighteenth Century." In Lawrence Freedman et al., eds., *War, Strategy, and International Politics: Essays in Honour of Sir Michael Howard*. Oxford: Clarendon Press, 1992, 57–74.

Marshall, P. J., and Glyndwr Williams. *The Great Map of Mankind: British Perceptions of the World in the Age of Enlightenment*. London: Dent, 1982.

Martini, Martino. *De bello tartarico historia*. Antwerp, 1654.

Martini, Martino. *Histoire de la Chine*. Traduite du Latin par l'Abbé Le Peletier. 2 vols. Paris, 1692 [1658].

Martino, Pierre. *L'Orient dans la littérature française au XVIIe et au XVIIIe siècle*. Paris: Hachette, 1906.

Mason, George Henry. *The Costume of China*. London, 1800.

Masters, Bruce. *The Origins of Western Economic Dominance in the Middle East: Mercantilism and the Islamic Economy in Aleppo, 1600–1750*. New York: New York University Press, 1988.

Maurice, Thomas. *The Modern History of Hindostan*. 2 vols. and suppl. London, 1802–10.

Maybon, Charles B., ed. *La relation sur le Tonkin et la Cochinchine de M. de La Bissachère, missionnaire français*. Paris: Champion, 1920 [1807].

Mayhew, Henry. *London Labour and the London Poor*. 4 vols. London: Griffin, 1861–62.

Mazlish, Bruce. *Civilization and Its Contents*. Stanford, CA: Stanford University Press, 2004.

McCabe, Ina Baghdiantz. *A History of Global Consumption, 1500–1800*. London: Routledge, 2015.

McDonald, Christie, and Susan Rubin Suleiman, eds. *French Global: A New Approach to Literary History*. New York: Columbia University Press, 2010.

McLaren, Martha. "From Analysis to Prescription: Scottish Concepts of Asian Despotism in Early Nineteenth-Century British India." *International History Review* 15 (1993): 469–501.

McNeill, William H. "The Age of Gunpowder Empires, 1450–1800." In Adas, *Islamic and European Expansion Expansion*, 1993, 103–39.

Medick, Hans. *Naturzustand und Naturgeschichte der bürgerlichen Gesellschaft: Die Ursprünge der bürgerlichen Sozialtheorie als Geschichtsphilosophie und Sozialwissenschaft bei Samuel Pufendorf, John Locke und Adam Smith*. Göttingen: Vandenhoeck and Ruprecht, 1972.

Meek, Roland L. *Social Science and the Ignoble Savage*. Cambridge: Cambridge University Press, 1976.

Mehmed efendi. *Le paradis des infidèles: un ambassadeur ottoman en France sous la Régence*. Ed. Gilles Veinstein. Paris: Maspéro, 1981 [1757].

Meiners, Christoph. *Grundriß der Geschichte der Menschheit*. 2nd ed. Lemgo, 1793 [1765].

Meiners, Christoph. *Betrachtungen über die Fruchtbarkeit, oder Unfruchtbarkeit, über den vormahligen und gegenwärtigen Zustand der vornehmsten Länder in Asien*. 2 vols. Lübeck, 1795–96.

Meiners, Christoph. *History of the Female Sex*. Trans. Frederick Shoberl. 4 vols. London, 1808 [1788–1800].

Melman, Billie. *Women's Orients: English Women and the Middle East, 1718–1918. Sexuality, Religion and Work*. 2nd ed. Basingstoke: Macmillan, 1995.

Mémoires concernant l'histoire, les sciences, les arts, les mœurs, les usages des Chinois. 16 vols. Paris, 1776–1814.

Mendoza, Juan González de. *The History of the Great and Mighty Kingdom of China*. Ed. Sir George T. Staunton. 2 vols. London: Hakluyt Society, 1853–54 [1585].

Merck, Carl Heinrich. *Das sibirisch-amerikanische Tagebuch aus den Jahren 1788–1791*. Ed. Dittmar Dahlmann, Anna Friesen, and Diana Ordubadi. Göttingen: Wallstein, 2009.

Merklein, Johann Jakob. *Reise nach Java, Vorder- und Hinter-Indien, China und Japan 1644–1653*. The Hague: Nijhoff, 1930 [1663] (= Naber, *Reisebeschreibungen*, 3).

Messerschmidt, Daniel Gottlieb. *Forschungsreise durch Sibirien 1720–1727*. Ed. Eduard Winter and N. A. Figurovskij. 5 vols. Berlin: Akademie-Verlag, 1962–77.

Metcalf, Thomas R. *Ideologies of the Raj*. Cambridge: Cambridge University Press, 1994.

Michaelis, Johann David. *Fragen an eine Gesellschaft gelehrter Männer, die auf Befehl Ihro Majestät des Königs von Dännemark nach Arabien reisen*. Frankfurt a.M., 1762.

Michaud, Joseph-François. *Histoire des progrès et de la chûte de l'empire de Mysore, sous les règnes d'Hyder-Aly et Tippoo-Saïb*. 2 vols. Paris, 1801.

Michel, Pierre. *Un mythe romantique: les barbares 1789–1848*. Lyon: Presses universitaires de Lyon, 1981.

Middell, Matthias, ed. *Cultural Transfers, Encounters and Connections in the Global Eighteenth Century*. Leipzig: Leipziger Universitätsverlag, 2014.

Milburn, William. *Oriental Commerce; Containing a Geographical Description of the Principal Places in the East Indies, China and Japan*. 2 vols. London, 1813.

Mill, James. *The History of British India*. 3 vols. London, 1817.

Mill, James. *The History of British India*. 5th ed. with notes and continuation by Horace Hayman Wilson. 10 vols. London: Madden, 1858.

Millar, Ashley E. "Revisiting the Sinophilia / Sinophobia Dichotomy in the European Enlightenment through Adam Smith's 'Duties of Government.'" *Asian Journal of Social Science* 38 (2010): 716–37.

Millar, John. *The Origins of the Distinction of Ranks; or, an Inquiry into the Circumstances Which Give Rise to Influence and Authority, in the Different Members of Society*. Ed. Aaron Garrett. Indianapolis: Liberty Fund, 2006 [1771].

Miller, David, and Peter Hanns Reill, eds. *Visions of Empire: Voyages, Botany and Representations of Nature*. Cambridge: Cambridge University Press, 1996.

Milligan, Barry. *Pleasures and Pains: Opium and the Orient in Nineteenth-Century British Culture*. Charlottesville: University Press of Virginia, 1995.

Mills, Charles. *An History of Muhammedanism*. London, 1817.

Minuti, Rolando. "Proprietà della terra e despotismo orientale: Aspetti di un dibattito sull'India nella seconda metà del settecento." *Materiali per una storia della cultura giuridica* 8 (1978): 29–177.

Minuti, Rolando. *Oriente barbarico e storiografia settecentesca: Rappresentazioni della storia dei Tartari nella cultura francese del XVIII secolo*. Venice: Marsilio, 1994.

Minuti, Rolando. *Una geografia politica della diversità: Studi su Montesquieu*. Naples: Liguori Editore, 2015.

Mitter, Partha. *Much Maligned Monsters: History of European Reactions to Indian Art*. Oxford: Clarendon Press, 1977.

M'Leod, John. *Voyage of His Majesty's Ship Alceste to China, Corea, and the Island of Lewchew*. 3rd ed. London, 1819 [1817].

Modave, Louis-Laurent Dolisy, Comte de. *Voyage en Inde du comte de Modave 1773–1776*. Texte établi et annoté par Jean Deloche. Paris: École Française d'Extrême-Orient, 1971.

Mohnhaupt, Heinz. "Spielarten 'revolutionärer' Entwicklung und ihrer werdenden Begrifflichkeit seit dem Zeitalter der Aufklärung." In Heinz Mohnhaupt, ed., *Revolution, Reform, Restauration: Formen der Veränderung von Recht und Gesellschaft*. Frankfurt a.M.: Klostermann, 1988, 1–36.

Moltke, Helmuth von. *Briefe über Zustände und Begebenheiten in der Türkei aus den Jahren 1835–1839*. Ed. Helmut Arndt. Nördlingen: Greno, 1987 [1841].

Mommsen, Katharina. "Goethe und China in ihren Wechselbeziehungen." In Günther Debon and Adrian Hsia, eds., *Goethe und China, China und Goethe*. Berne: Lang, 1985, 15–33.

Montagu, Lady Mary Wortley. *The Complete Letters of Lady Mary Wortley Montagu*. Ed. Robert Halsband. 3 vols. Oxford: Clarendon Press, 196–67 [1763].

Montesquieu, Charles de Secondat de. *Considerations on the Causes of the Grandeur and Decadence of the Romans*. Trans. Jehu Baker. New York, 1882.

Montesquieu, Charles de Secondat de. *Œuvres complètes*. Ed. Roger Caillois. 2 vols. Paris: Gallimard, 1949–51.

Montesquieu, Charles de Secondat de. *Persian Letters*. Trans. Christopher J. Betts. Harmondsworth: Penguin, 1973.

Montesquieu, Charles de Secondat de. *The Spirit of the Laws*. Ed. and trans. Anne M. Cohler, Basia Carolyn Miller, and Harold Samuel Stone. Cambridge: Cambridge University Press, 1989.

Montesquieu, Charles de Secondat de. *Œuvres complètes de Montesquieu*. Ed. Jean Ehrard and Catherine Volpilhac-Auger. Oxford: Voltaire Foundation, 1998 seq.

Moor, Edward. *The Hindu Pantheon*. London, 1810.

Moorcroft, William, and George Trebeck. *Travels in the Himalayan Provinces of Hindustan and the Panjab from 1819 to 1825*. Prepared for the press from original journals and correspondence by Horace Hayman Wilson. 2 vols. London, 1841.

Moravia, Sergio. *Il pensiero degli Idéologues: Scienza e filosofia in Francia (1780–1815)*. Florence: La nuova Italia, 1974.

Moravia, Sergio. *La scienza dell'uomo nel Settecento*. Rome: Laterza, 1978.

Moravia, Sergio. *Il tramonto dell'illuminismo: Filosofia e politica nella società francese (1770–1810)*. Bari: Laterza, 1986.

Morier, James Justinian. *A Journey through Persia, Armenia, and Asia Minor, to Constantinople, in the Years 1808 and 1809*. London, 1812.

Morier, James Justinian. *A Second Journey through Persia, Armenia and Asia Minor to Constantinopel between the Years 1810 and 1816*. London, 1818.

Morier, James Justinian. *The Adventures of Hajji Baba of Ispahan*. London, 1824.

Morison, Samuel Eliot. *"Old Bruin": Commodore Matthew C. Perry, 1794–1858*. Boston: Little, Brown, 1967.

Morrison, Eliza. *Memoirs of the Life and Labours of Robert Morrison, D. D.* 2 vols. London, 1839.

Morrison, Robert. *A Memoir of Principal Occurences during an Embassy from the British Government to the Court of China in the Year 1819*. London, 1819.

Morse, Hosea Ballou, ed. *The Chronicles of the East India Company Trading to China, 1635–1834*. 5 vols. Oxford: Oxford University Press, 1926–29.

Muhlack, Ulrich. *Geschichtswissenschaft im Humanismus und in der Aufklärung: Die Vorgeschichte des Historismus*. Munich: C. H. Beck, 1991.

Muhlack, Ulrich. "Das Problem der Weltgeschichte bei Leopold Ranke." In Hardtwig and Müller, *Die Vergangenheit der Weltgeschichte*, 2010, 143–71.

Müller, Klaus E. *Geschichte der antiken Ethnographie und ethnologischen Theoriebildung: Von den Anfängen bis auf die byzantinischen Historiographen*. 2 vols. Wiesbaden: Steiner, 1972–80.

Mungello, David E. *Curious Land: Jesuit Accomodation and the Origins of Sinology*. Wiesbaden: Harrassowitz, 1985.

Münkler, Herfried, ed. *Furcht und Faszination: Facetten der Fremdheit*. Berlin: Akademie-Verlag, 1997.

Muntschik, Wolfgang. "Die floristische Erforschung Japans um 1700 und Kaempfers Bedeutung für die Kenntnis japanischer Pflanzen in Europe." In Kaempfer. *Flora Japonica*, 1983, 11–28.

Murphey, Rhoads, with Kristin Stapleton. *A History of Asia*. 7th ed. New York: Routledge, 2016.
Murr, Sylvia. "Les Jésuites et l'Inde au XVIIIe siècle: praxis, utopie et préanthropologie." *Revue de l'Université d'Ottawa* 56 (1986): 9–27.
Murr, Sylvia. *L'indologie du Père Cœurdoux: stratégies, apologétique et scientificité*. Paris: École Française d'Extrême-Orient, 1987.
Murray, Hugh. *Enquiries Historical and Moral Respecting the Character of Nations and the Progress of Society*. Edinburgh, 1808.
Murray, Hugh. *Historical Account of Discoveries and Travels in Asia, from the Earliest Ages to the Present Time*. 3 vols. Edinburgh, 1820.
Muthu, Sankar. *Enlightenment against Empire*. Princeton, NJ: Princeton University Press, 2003.
Naber, S. P. L'Honoré, ed. *Reisebeschreibungen von deutschen Beamten und Kriegsleuten im Dienst der Niederländischen West- und Ost-Indischen Kompagnien 1602–1797*. 13 vols. The Hague: Nijhoff, 1930–32.
Nagel, Tilmann. *Timur der Eroberer und die islamische Welt des späten Mittelalters*. Munich: C. H. Beck, 1993.
Naquin, Susan, and Evelyn S. Rawski. *Chinese Society in the Eighteenth Century*. New Haven, CT: Yale University Press, 1987.
Narasimhan, Sakuntala. *Sati: A Study of Widow Burning in India*. New Delhi: Viking, 1990.
Navarette, Domingo. "An Account of the Empire of China [1676]." In Churchill and Churchill, *Collection*, vol. 1 (1744), 1–311.
Navarette, Domingo. *The Travels and Controversies of Friar Domingo Navarette 1618–1686*. Ed. from manuscript and printed sources by J. S. Cummins. 2 vols. Cambridge: Cambridge University Press, 1962.
Nayar, Pramod K. *English Writing and India, 1600–1920: Colonizing Aesthetics*. London: Routledge, 2008.
Neue Nordische Beyträge zur physikalischen und geographischen Erd- und Völkerbeschreibung, Naturgeschichte und Oekonomie. Vols. 1–7 (1781–96), Saint Petersburg/Leipzig.
Newberry, John ed. *The World Displayed; or, a Curious Collection of Voyages and Travels*. 20 vols. London, 1759–61.
Niebuhr, Barthold Georg. *Carsten Niebuhr's Leben*. Kiel, 1817.
Niebuhr, Barthold Georg. *Lebensnachrichten über Barthold Georg Niebuhr: Aus Briefen desselben und aus Erinnerungen einiger seiner nächsten Freunde*. 3 vols. Gotha, 1838–39.
Niebuhr, Carsten. *Beschreibung von Arabien: Aus eigenen Beobachtungen und im Lande selbst gesammleten Nachrichten*. Copenhagen, 1772.
Niebuhr, Carsten. *Reisebeschreibung nach Arabien und anderen umliegenden Ländern*. 3 vols. Copenhagen and Hamburg, 1774–1837.
Nieuhof, Johan. *An Embassy from the East-India Company of the United Provinces, to the Grand Tartar Cham, Emperour of China*. Trans. John Ogilby. London, 1669 [1665].
Nippel, Wilfried. *Griechen, Barbaren und "Wilde": Alte Geschichte und Sozialanthropologie*. Frankfurt a.M.: Fischer Taschenbuch-Verlag, 1990.
Nørgaard, Anders. *Mission und Obrigkeit: Die Dänisch-hallische Mission in Tranquebar 1706–1845*. Gütersloh: Gütersloher Verlagshaus Mohn, 1988.
Noyes, John K. *Herder: Aesthetics against Imperialism*. Toronto: University of Toronto Press, 2015.
Nussbaum, Felicity A., ed. *The Global Eighteenth Century*. Baltimore, MD: Johns Hopkins University Press, 2003.

O'Brien, Karen. *Narratives of Enlightenment: Cosmopolitan History from Voltaire to Gibbon.* Cambridge: Cambridge University Press, 1997.

Ockley, Simon. *The History of the Saracens.* 3rd ed. 2 vols. Cambridge, 1757 [1708–18].

Oertel, Karl Otto. *Die Naturschilderung bei den deutschen geographischen Reisebeschreibern des 18. Jahrhunderts.* PhD Diss. Leipzig, 1898.

Ogilby, John. *Asia.* London, 1673.

O'Gorman, Frank. *The Long Eighteenth Century: British Political and Social History 1688–1832.* London: Arnold, 1997.

Olearius, Adam. *Vermehrte Newe Beschreibung der Muscowitischen vnd Persischen Reyse.* Schleswig, 1656.

O'Leary, Brendan. *The Asiatic Mode of Production: Orient, Despotism, Historical Materialism and Indian History.* Oxford: Blackwell, 1989.

Oliver, Andrew. *American Travelers on the Nile: Early U.S. Visitors to Egypt, 1774-1839.* Cairo: American University in Cairo, 2014.

Olivier, Guillaume Antoine. *Voyage dans l'Empire Othoman, l'Egypte et la Perse.* 6 vols. Paris, 1804–7.

Olschki, Leonardo. *Marco Polo's Asia.* Berkeley: University of California Press, 1960.

Omont, Henri. *Missions archéologiques françaises en Orient aux XVIIe et XVIIIe siècles.* 2 vols. Paris: Imprimerie nationale, 1902.

Orme, Robert. *History of the Military Transactions of the British Nation in Indostan.* 2 vols. London, 1763–78.

Orme, Robert. *Historic Fragments of the Mogul Empire, of the Morattoes, and of the English Concerns in Hindostan, from the Year MDCLIX.* Ed. J. P. Guha. New Delhi: Associated Publishing House, 1974 [1782].

Osbeck, Peter. *A Voyage to China and the East Indies.* Trans. Johann Reinhold Forster. 2 vols. London, 1771.

Osborne, Thomas, ed. *A Collection of Voyages and Travels. Compiled from the Curious and Valuable Library of the Late Earl of Oxford.* 2 vols. London, 1745.

Osterhammel, Jürgen. *China und die Weltgesellschaft: Vom 18. Jahrhundert bis in unsere Zeit.* Munich: C. H. Beck, 1989.

Osterhammel, Jürgen. "Gastfreiheit und Fremdenabwehr: Interkulturelle Ambivalenzen in der frühen Neuzeit." In Münkler, *Furcht und Faszination,* 1997, 379–435.

Osterhammel, Jürgen. "Wissen als Macht: Deutungen interkulturellen Nichtverstehens bei Tzvetan Todorov und Edward Said." In Auch and Förster, *"Barbaren" und "Weiße Teufel,"* 1997, 145–69.

Osterhammel, Jürgen. "Alexander von Humboldt: Historiker der Gesellschaft, Historiker der Natur." *Archiv für Kulturgeschichte* 80 (1998): 105–31.

Osterhammel, Jürgen. "'Peoples without History' in British and German Historical Thought." In Stuchtey and Wende, *British and German Historiography,* 2000, 265–87.

Osterhammel, Jürgen. *Geschichtswissenschaft jenseits des Nationalstaats: Studien zu Beziehungsgeschichte und Zivilisationsvergleich.* 2nd ed. Göttingen: Vandenhoeck and Ruprecht, 2002.

Osterhammel, Jürgen. *Europe, the "West" and the Civilizing Mission.* London: German Historical Institute, 2006.

Osterhammel, Jürgen. "Globale Horizonte europäischer Kunstmusik." *Geschichte und Gesellschaft* 38 (2012): 86–132.

Osterhammel, Jürgen. *The Transformation of the World: A Global History of the Nineteenth Century.* Trans. Patrick Camiller. Princeton, NJ: Princeton University Press, 2014.

Otter, Jean. *Voyage en Turquie et en Perse. Avec une relation des expéditions de Tahmas Kouli-Khan*. 2 vols. Paris, 1748.
Outram, Dorinda. *The Enlightenment*. 3rd ed. Cambridge: Cambridge University Press, 2013.
Owen, Norman G., ed. *The Emergence of Modern Southeast Asia: A New History*. Honolulu: University of Hawaii Press, 2005.
Pagden, Anthony. *The Fall of Natural Man: The American Indian and the Origins of Comparative Ethnology*. Cambridge: Cambridge University Press, 1982.
Pagden, Anthony, ed. *The Languages of Political Theory in Early Modern Europe*. Cambridge: Cambridge University Press, 1987.
Pagden, Anthony. *European Encounters with the New World: From Renaissance to Romanticism*. New Haven, CT: Yale University Press, 1993.
Pagden, Anthony. *Lords of All the World: Ideologies of Empire in Spain, Britain and France c. 1500–c. 1800*. New Haven CT: Yale University Press, 1995.
Pagden, Anthony. *The Enlightenment: And Why It Still Matters*. New York: Random House, 2013.
Pailin, David A. *Attitudes to Other Religions: Comparative Religion in Seventeenth- and Eighteenth-Century Britain*. Manchester: Manchester University Press, 1984.
Palafox y Mendoza, Juan de. *The History of the Conquest of China by the Tartars*. 2nd ed. London, 1676 [1670].
Pallas, Peter Simon. *Reise durch die verschiedenen Provinzen des Rußischen Reiches*. 4 vols. Saint Petersburg, 1771–76.
Pallas, Peter Simon. *Sammlungen historischer Nachrichten über die Mongolischen Völkerschaften*. Saint Petersburg, 1776–1801.
Pallas, Peter Simon. *Observations sur la formation des montagnes et les changements arrivés au globe. . . .* Saint Petersburg, 1777.
Pallas, Peter Simon. "Geographisch-historische Beschreibung der sinesischen Residenzstadt Peking." *Neue Nordische Beiträge* 2 (1781): 208–32.
Pallas, Peter Simon. *Tagebuch einer Reise, die im Jahr 1781 von der Gränzfestung Mosdok nach dem innern Caucasus unternommen worden*. Saint Petersburg, 1797.
Pallas, Peter Simon. *Bemerkungen auf einer Reise in die südlichen Statthalterschaften des Russischen Reichs in den Jahren 1793 und 1794*. 2 vols. Leipzig, 1799–1801.
Pargiter, Frederick E., ed. *Centenary Volume of the Royal Asiatic Society of Great Britain and Ireland 1823–1923*. London: Royal Asiatic Society of Great Britain and Ireland, 1923.
Parker, Charles H. *Global Interactions in the Early Modern Age, 1400–1800*. Cambridge: Cambridge University Press, 2010.
Parker, Geoffrey. *Global Crisis: War, Climate Change and Catastrophe in the Seventeenth Century*. New Haven, CT: Yale University Press, 2013.
Parker, W. H. "Europe: How Far?" *Geographical Journal* 126 (1960): 278–97.
Parry, John H. *Trade and Dominion: European Overseas Empires in the Eighteenth Century*. London: Hutchinson, 1971.
Parsons, James B. *The Peasant Rebellions of the Late Ming Dynasty*. Tucson: University of Arizona Press, 1970.
Pasley, Rodney. *"Send Malcolm!": The Life of Major-General Sir John Malcolm, 1769–1833*. London: Bacsa, 1982.
Pastoret, Claude Emmanuel de. *Zoroastre, Confucius et Mahomet, Comparés comme Séctaires, Législateurs, et Moralistes*. Paris, 1787.
Pastoret, Claude-Emmanuel de. *Histoire de la législation*. 11 vols. Paris, 1817–37.

Patton, Robert. *The Principles of Asiatic Monarchies, Politically and Historically Investigated, and Contrasted with those of the Monarchies of Europe*. London, 1801.

Paulus, Heinrich Eberhard Gottlob, ed. *Sammlung der merkwürdigsten Reisen in den Orient*. 7 vols. Jena, 1792–1803.

Pauw, Cornelius de. *Recherches philosophiques sur les Egyptiens et les Chinois*. 2 vols. Berlin, 1773.

Peabody, Norbert. "Tod's 'Rajast'han' and Boundaries of Imperial Rule in Nineteenth-Century India." *Modern Asian Studies* 30 (1996): 185–220.

Pearson, M. N. *Before Colonialism: Theories of Asian-European Relations 1500–1750*. Delhi: Oxford University Press, 1988.

Peers, Douglas M. *Between Mars and Mammon: Colonial Armies and the Garrison State in India, 1819–1835*. London: Tauris, 1995.

Peers, Douglas M. "Colonial Knowledge and the Military in India, 1780–1860." *Journal of Imperial and Commonwealth History* 33 (2005): 157–80.

Peirce, Leslie P. *The Imperial Harem: Women and Sovereignty in the Ottoman Empire*. New York: Oxford University Press, 1993.

Penzer, Norman Mosley. *The Harêm: An Account of the Institution as It Existed in the Palace of the Turkish Sultans, with a History of the Grand Seraglio from Its Foundation to Modern Times*. London: Bookplan, 1936.

Percival, Robert. *An Account of the Island of Ceylon*. 2nd ed. London, 1805 [1803].

Percy, Thomas. *Hau Kiou Choaan, or the Pleasing History: A Translation from the Chinese Language*. 4 vols. London, 1761.

Perdue, Peter C. *China Marches West: The Qing Conquest of Central Eurasia*. Cambridge, MA: Harvard University Press, 2005.

Perrin, Jean-Charles. *Voyage dans l'Indostan*. 2 vols. Paris, 1807.

Perry, Charles. *View of the Levant, Particularly of Constantinople, Syria, Egypt and Greece*. London, 1743.

Petech, Luciano, ed. *I missionari italiani nel Tibet e nel Nepal*. Vols. 5–7: *Ippolito Desideri S. I.* Rome: Libreria dello Stato, 1954–56.

Peterson, Willard J., ed. *The Ch'ing Empire to 1800*. Cambridge: Cambridge University Press, 2002 (= *The Cambridge History of China*, 9, pt. 1).

Pétis de la Croix, François, jun., trans. *Histoire de Timur-Bec, connu sous le nom du grand Tamerlan. . . .* Ecrite en Persan par Cherefeddin Ali [Sharaf-al-Din-'Ali]. 4 vols. Delft, 1723.

Petri, Manfred. *Die Urvolkhypothese: Ein Beitrag zum Geschichtsdenken der Spätaufklärung und des deutschen Idealismus*. Berlin: Duncker and Humblot, 1990.

Peyrefitte, Alain. *Images de l'Empire immobile, par William Alexander, peintre-reporter de l'expédition Macartney*. Paris: Fayard, 1990.

Peyrefitte, Alain. *The Immobile Empire*. Trans. Jon Rothschild. New York: Knopf, 1992.

Peyrefitte, Alain. *Un choc de cultures*. Vol. 1: *La vision des Chinois*. Paris: Fayard, 1992.

Peyssonnel, Claude Charles de. *Observations historiques & géographiques, sur les peuples barbares qui ont habité les bords du Danube & du Pont-Euxin*. Paris, 1765.

Peyssonnel, Claude Charles de. *Traité sur le commerce de la Mer Noire*. 2 vols. Paris, 1787.

Peyssonnel, Claude Charles de. *Examen du livre intitulé "Considérations sur la guerre actuelle des turcs," par M. de Volney*. Amsterdam, 1788.

Pfister, Louis. *Notices biographiques et bibliographiques sur les Jésuites de l'ancienne mission de Chine 1552–1773*. Vol 2: *XVIIIe siècle*. Shanghai: Imprimerie de la Mission catholique, 1934.

Philipp, Thomas, and Moshe Perlman, eds. *Abd-al-Rahman al-Jabarti's History of Egypt.* 4 vols. Stuttgart: Steiner, 1994.
Philipp, Thomas, and Ulrich Haarmann, eds. *The Mamluks in Egyptian Politics and Society.* Cambridge: Cambridge University Press, 1998.
Philips, C. H., ed. *Historians of India, Pakistan und Ceylon.* London: Oxford University Press, 1961.
Philliou, Christine M. *Biography of an Empire: Governing Ottomans in an Age of Revolution.* Berkeley: University of California Press, 2011.
Picart, Bernard. *Cérémonies et coutumes religieuses de tous les peuples du monde.* 7 vols. Amsterdam, 1723–37.
Picht, Clemens. *Handel, Politik und Gesellschaft: Zur wirtschaftspolitischen Publizistik Englands im 18. Jahrhundert.* Göttingen: Vandenhoeck and Ruprecht, 1993.
Pigulla, Andreas. *China in der deutschen Weltgeschichtsschreibung vom 18. bis zum 20. Jahrhundert.* Wiesbaden: Harrassowitz, 1996.
Pinkerton, John. *Modern Geography.* New ed. 3 vols. London, 1807.
Pinkerton, John, ed. *A General Collection of the Best und Most Interesting Voyages and Travels in All Parts of the World.* 17 vols. London, 1808–14.
Pinot, Virgile. *La Chine et la formation de l'esprit philosophique en France (1640–1740).* Paris: Geuthner, 1932.
Pirro, Maurizio. "Nachwort." In Hirschfeld, *Von der Gastfreundschaft*, 2015, 99–116.
Pitton de Tournefort, Joseph. *Relation d'un voyage du Levant, fait par ordre du Roy.* 2 vols. Paris, 1717.
Pitts, Jennifer A. *A Turn to Empire: The Rise of Imperial Liberalism in Britain and France.* Princeton, NJ: Princeton University Press, 2005.
Plant, Johann Traugott. *Türkisches Staatslexicon.* Hamburg, 1789.
Plant, Johann Traugott. *Handbuch einer vollständigen Erdbeschreibung und Geschichte Polynesiens oder des fünften Erdtheils.* 2 vols. Leipzig, 1793–99.
Plath, Johann Heinrich. *Geschichte des östlichen Asiens.* Pt. 1: *Chinesische Tartarey.* Sec. 1: *Mandschurey.* 2 vols. Göttingen, 1830–31.
Platteau, Jean-Philippe. *Les économistes classiques et le sous-développement.* 2 vols. Namur: Presses universitaires de Namur, 1978.
Playfair, William. *An Inquiry into the Permanent Causes of the Decline and Fall of Powerful and Wealthy Nations.* London, 1805.
Plewe, Ernst, ed. *Die Carl Ritter Bibliothek.* Wiesbaden: Steiner, 1978.
Pocock, J.G.A. "Gibbon's 'Decline and Fall' and the World View of the Late Enlightenment." *Eighteenth-Century Studies* 10 (1977): 287–303.
Pocock, J.G.A. "Gibbon and the Shepherds: The Stages of Society in the 'Decline and Fall.'" *History of European Ideas* 2 (1981): 193–202.
Pocock, J.G.A. "The Concept of a Language and the 'métier d'historien': Some Considerations on Practice." In Pagden, *Languages of Political Theory*, 1987, 19–38.
Pocock, J.G.A. "Deconstructing Europe." *History of European Ideas* 18 (1994): 329–45.
Pocock, J.G.A. *Barbarism and Religion.* Vol. 2: *Narratives of Civil Government.* Cambridge: Cambridge University Press, 1999.
Pocock, J.G.A. *Barbarism and Religion.* Vol. 4: *Barbarians, Savages and Empires.* Cambridge: Cambridge University Press, 2005.
Pocock, J.G.A. *Barbarism and Religion.* Vol. 6: *Barbarism: Triumph in the West.* Cambridge: Cambridge University Press, 2015.
Pococke, Richard. *A Description of the East and Some Other Countries.* 3 vols. London, 1743–45.

Poivre, Pierre. *Voyages d'un philosophe, ou Observations sur les mœurs & les arts des peuples de l'Afrique, de l'Asie et de l'Amérique*. Yverdon, 1768.

Poivre, Pierre. "Voyage de Pierre Poivre en Cochinchine." *Revue de l'Extrême-Orient* 3 (1885): 81–121, 364–510 [voyage of 1749–50].

Poivre, Pierre. *Un manuscrit inédit de Pierre Poivre: les mémoires d'un voyageur.* Ed. Louis Malleret. Paris: École française d'Extrême-Orient, 1968 [1747?].

Polaschegg, Andrea. *Der andere Orientalismus: Regeln deutsch-morgenländischer Imagination im 19. Jahrhundert.* New York: de Gruyter, 2005.

Poliakov, Léon. *The Aryan Myth: A History of Racist and Nationalist Ideas in Europe.* New York: Basic Books, 1974.

Pomplun, Trent. *Jesuit on the Roof of the World: Ippolito Desideri's Mission to Eighteenth-Century Tibet.* New York: Oxford University Press, 2010.

Porter, David. *The Chinese Taste in Eighteenth-Century England.* Cambridge: Cambridge University Press, 2010.

Porter, Roy, ed. *Eighteenth-Century Science.* Cambridge: Cambridge University Press, 2003 (= *The Cambridge History of Science*, 4).

Porter, Sir James. *Observations on the Religion, Law, Government, and Manners of the Turks.* 2 vols. London, 1768.

Porter, Sir James. *Turkey: Its History and Progress.* 2 Vols. London, 1854.

Porter, Sir Robert Kerr. *Travels in Georgia, Persia, Armenia, Ancient Babylonia, &c., during the Years 1817, 1818, 1819 and 1820.* 2 vols. London, 1821–22.

Posselt, Doris, ed. *Die Große Nordische Expedition von 1733 bis 1743: Aus Berichten der Forschungsreisenden Johann Georg Gmelin und Georg Wilhelm Steller.* Munich: C. H. Beck, 1990.

Potocki, Jean [Jan]. *Voyages.* Introduction et notes de D. Beauvois. 2 vols. Paris: Fayard, 1980.

Pottinger, Henry. *Travels in Belochistan and Sinde; Accompanied by a Geographical and Historical Account of Those Countries.* London, 1816.

Pradt, abbé Dominic-Georges-Frédéric de. *Les trois âges des colonies ou de leur état passé, présent et a venir.* 3 vols. Paris, 1801–2.

Prakash, Om, et al. *Haidar Ali and Tipu Sultan.* New Delhi: Anmol, 2001 (= *Encyclopaedic History of Indian Freedom Movement*, 10).

Pratt, Mary Louise. *Imperial Eyes: Travel Writing and Transculturation.* London: Routledge, 1992.

Prévost, Antoine François. *Histoire générale des voyages, ou Nouvelle collection de toutes les relations de voyages par mer et par terre qui ont été publiées jusqu'à présent dans les différentes langues de toutes les nations connues.* 15 vols. Paris, 1746–59.

Prévost, Antoine François. *Œuvres.* Ed. Jean Sgard et al. Vol. 8. Grenoble: Presses Universitaires de Grenoble, 1986.

Prichard, James Cowles. *Researches into the Physical History of Mankind.* 3rd ed. 5 vols. London, 1836–47.

Psalmanazar, George. *An Historical and Geographical Description of Formosa.* London, 1704.

Pucci, Suzanne Rodin. "The Discrete Charms of the Exotic: Fictions of the Harem in 18th-Century France." In G. S. Rousseau and Porter, *Exoticism in the Enlightenment*, 1990, 145–74.

Pückler-Muskau, Hermann Fürst von. *Aus Mehemed Alis Reich: Ägypten und der Sudan um 1840.* Zurich: Manesse, 1985 [1845].

Pufendorf, Samuel von, et al. *Introduction à l'Histoire moderne, générale et politique de l'Univers*. Nouv. éd. 8 vols. Paris, 1753–59.
Pugh, John. *Remarkable Occurences in the Life of Jonas Hanway, Esq*. London, 1787.
Qaisar, Ahsam Jan. *The Indian Response to European Technology and Culture (AD 1498–1707)*. Delhi: Oxford University Press, 1982.
Quelle, Pithander von der [David Fassmann]. *Herkunft, Leben und Thaten des Persianischen Monarchens Schach Nadyr vormals Kuli-Chan genannt*. Leipzig, 1738.
Quesnay, François. "Despotisme de la Chine." In Auguste Oncken, ed., *Œuvres économiques et philosophiques de F. Quesnay*. Frankfurt a.M.: J. Baer, 1888, 563–659.
Quigley, Declan. *The Interpretation of Caste*. Oxford: Oxford University Press, 1993.
Rabault-Feuerhahn, Pascale. *Archives of Origins: Sanskrit, Philology, Anthropology in 19th-Century Germany*. Wiesbaden: Harrassowitz, 2013.
Raffles, Sir Thomas Stamford. *The History of Java*. 2 vols. London, 1817.
Raffles, Sir Thomas Stamford. *Report on Japan to the Secret Committee of the English East India Company*. Ed. Montague Paske-Smith. Kobe: Thompson, 1929 [1812–16].
Raj, Kapil. *Relocating Modern Science: Circulation and the Construction of Scientific Knowledge in South Asia and Europe: Seventeenth to Nineteenth Centuries*. New Delhi: Permanent Black, 2006.
Raj, Kapil. "The Historical Anatomy of a Contact Zone: Calcutta in the Eighteenth Century." *Indian Economic and Social History Review* 48 (2011): 55–82.
Ramsay, Andrew Michael. *An Essay upon Civil Government*. London, 1732.
Ranke, Leopold von. *Weltgeschichte*. 9 vols. Leipzig: Duncker and Humblot, 1881–88.
Rassem, Mohammed, and Justin Stagl, eds. *Statistik und Staatenbeschreibung in der Neuzeit, vornehmlich im 16.–18. Jahrhundert*. Paderborn: Schöningh, 1980.
Raymond, André. *Artisans et commerçants au Caire au XVIIIe siècle*. 2 vols. Damascus: Institut Français de Damas, 1973.
Raynal, Guillaume Thomas François. *Histoire philosophique et politique des établissement & du Commerce des Européens dans les deux Indes*. 3 vols. Geneva, 1775 [1770].
Rehbinder, Johann A. *Nachrichten und Bemerkungen über den algierischen Staat*. 3 vols. Altona, 1798–1800.
Reichert, Folker. *Begegnungen mit China: Die Entdeckung Ostasiens im Mittelalter*. Sigmaringen: Thorbecke, 1992.
Reid, Anthony. *Southeast Asia in the Age of Commerce, 1450–1680*. 2 vols. New Haven, CT: Yale University Press, 1988–93.
Reineggs, Jacob [= Christian Rudolph Ehlich]. *Allgemeine historisch-topographische Beschreibung des Kaukasus*. 2 vols. Gotha, 1796–97.
Reinhard, Wolfgang, ed. *Empires and Encounters, 1350–1750*. Cambridge, MA: Harvard University Press, 2015.
Reinhard, Wolfgang. *Die Unterwerfung der Welt: Globalgeschichte der europäischen Expansion 1415–2015*. Munich: C. H. Beck, 2016.
Reith, John. *Life of Dr. John Leyden: Poet and Linguist*. London: A. Walker and Son, 1923.
Relation de la Grande Tartarie, dressé sur les mémoires originaux des Suedois Prissoniers en Siberie, Pendant la Guerre de la Suede avec la Russie. Amsterdam, 1737.
Remer, Julius August. *Darstellung der Gestalt der historischen Welt in jedem Zeitraume*. Berlin, 1794.
Renaudot, Eusèbe. *Révolutions des empires, royaumes, républiques, et autres état considérables du monde*. Paris, 1769.
Rennell, James. *Memoir of a Map of Hindoostan; or the Mogul Empire*. 3rd ed. London, 1793.

Rennie, Neil. *Far-Fetched Facts: The Literature of Travel and the Idea of the South Seas.* Oxford: Clarendon Press, 1996.

Renouard de Sainte-Croix, Félix. *Voyage commercial et politique aux Indes Orientales, aux Iles Philippines, à la Chine, avec des notions sur la Cochinchine et le Tonquin, pendant les années 1803, 1804, 1805, 1806 et 1807.* 3 vols. Paris, 1810.

Rich, Claudius James. *Narrative of a Journey to the Site of Babylon in 1811.* London, 1839.

Richard, Francis. *Raphaël du Mans: Missionaire en Perse au XVIIe s.* 2 vols. Paris: L'Harmattan, 1995.

Richard, Jérôme. *Histoire naturelle, civile et politique du Tonquin.* Paris, 1778.

Richards, John F. *The Mughal Empire.* Cambridge: Cambridge University Press, 1993.

Richardson, John. *A Dissertation on the Languages, Literature and Manners of Eastern Nations.* 2 pts. 2nd ed. Oxford, 1778.

Richter, Melvin. "Despotism." In Philip P. Wiener, ed., *Dictionary of the History of Ideas,* vol. 2. New York: Scribner, 1973, 1–18.

Richter, Melvin. *The Political Theory of Montesquieu.* Cambridge: Cambridge University Press, 1977.

Richter, Susan. *Pflug und Steuerruder: Zur Verflechtung von Herrschaft und Landwirtschaft in der Aufklärung.* Cologne: Böhlau, 2015.

Ricklefs, M. C. *A History of Modern Indonesia since c. 1200.* 4th ed. New York: Palgrave Macmillan, 2008.

Riedel, Manfred. "Gesellschaft, Gemeinschaft." In Brunner, Conze, and Koselleck, *Geschichtliche Grundbegriffe,* vol. 2, 1975, 801–62.

Riello, Giorgio. *Cotton: The Fabric that Made the Modern World.* Cambridge: Cambridge University Press, 2013.

Rietbergen, Peter. "Witsen's World: Nicolaas Witsen (1641–1717) between the Dutch East India Company." *Itinerario* 9 (1985): 121–34.

Rietbergen, Peter. *Japan verwoord: Nihon door Nederlandse ogen, 1600–1799.* Amsterdam: Hotei Publishing, 2003.

Rietbergen, Peter. "Ten hove gegaan, ten hove ontvangen: Het shogunale hof in Edo en de VOC." In Elsbeth Locher-Scholten and Peter Rietbergen, eds., *Hof en Handel: Aziatische Vorsten en de VOC 1620–1720.* Leiden: Brill, 2004, 277–303.

Rietbergen, Peter. *Europa's India: Fascinatie en cultureel imperialisme, circa 1750–circa 2000.* Nijmegen: Vantilt, 2007.

Rikord, Pyotr Ivanovich. *Narrative of My Captivity in Japan during the Years 1811, 1812, and 1813.* 2 vols. London 1818 [1816].

Ripa, Matteo. *Memoirs of Father Ripa, during Thirteen Years' Residence at the Court of Peking in the Service of the Emperor of China.* Trans. Fortunato Prandi. London, 1844.

Ritter, Carl. *Die Erdkunde im Verhältniß zur Natur und zur Geschichte des Menschen oder allgemeine vergleichende Geographie als sichere Grundlage des Studiums und Unterrichts in physicalischen und historischen Wissenschaften.* 2nd ed. 8 vols. in 10 pts. Berlin, 1832–47.

Ritter, Paul. *Leibniz' Ägyptischer Plan.* Darmstadt: Reichl, 1930.

Robel, Gert. "Der Wandel des deutschen Sibirienbildes im 18. Jahrhundert." *Canadian-American Slavonic Studies* 14 (1980): 407–26.

Robel, Gert. "Bemerkungen zu deutschen Reisebeschreibungen über das Rußland der Epoche Katharinas II." In Jäger, *Europäisches Reisen im Zeitalter der Aufklärung,* 1992, 223–41.

Robertson, William. *An Historical Disquisition Concerning the Knowledge which the Ancients Had of India.* London, 1812 [1791] (= *Works,* 12).

Robertson, William. *Works*. 12 vols. London, 1812.

Robertson, William. *The Progress of Society in Europe: An Historical Outline from the Subversion of the Roman Empire to the Beginning of the Sixteenth Century*. Ed. Felix Gilbert. Chicago: University of Chicago Press, 1972 [1769].

Robinet, Jean Baptiste René. *Vue philosophique de la gradation naturelle des formes de l'être*. Amsterdam, 1768.

Robson, Francis. *The Life of Hyder Ally*. London, 1786.

Roche, Daniel. *La France des Lumières*. Paris: Fayard, 1993.

Roche, Daniel. *Humeurs vagabondes: de la circulation des hommes et de l'utilité des voyages*. Paris: Fayard, 2003.

Roche, Daniel. *Les circulations dans l'Europe moderne, XVIIe–XVIIIe siècle*. Paris: Fayard, 2011.

Rochemonteix, Camille de, S. J. *Joseph Amiot et les derniers survivants de la mission française à Pékin (1750–1795)*. Paris: Picard et fils, 1915.

Rocher, Rosane. *Orientalism, Poetry, and the Millenium: The Checkered Life of Nathaniel Brassey Halhed 1751–1830*. Delhi: Motilal Banarsidass, 1983.

Rocher, Rosane. "British Orientalism in the Eighteenth Century: The Dialectics of Knowledge and Government." In Breckenridge and Van der Veer, *Orientalism and the Postcolonial Predicament*, 1993, 215–49.

Rocher, Rosane, and Ludo Rocher. *The Making of Western Indology: Henry Thomas Colebrooke and the East India Company*. London and New York: Routledge, 2012.

Rochon, abbé Alexis Marie. *Voyage à Madagascar et aux Indes Orientales*. Paris, 1791.

Roemer, Hans Robert. *Persien auf dem Weg in die Neuzeit: Iranische Geschichte von 1350–1750*. Darmstadt: Wissenschaftliche Buchgesellschaft, 1989.

Roger, Jacques. *Les sciences de la vie dans la pensée française du XVIIIe siècle*. Paris: Colin, 1963.

Roque, Jean de la. *Voyage de l'Arabie Heureuse*. Paris, 1715.

Rosselli, John. *Lord William Bentinck: The Making of a Liberal Imperialist, 1774–1839*. London: Chatto and Windus, 1974.

Rossi, Paolo. *The Dark Abyss of Time: The History of the Earth and the History of Nations from Hooke to Vico*. Trans. Lydia G. Cochran. Chicago: University of Chicago Press, 1984.

Röttgers, Kurt. *Kants Kollege und seine ungeschriebene Schrift über die Zigeuner*. Heidelberg: Manutius, 1993.

Roubaud, Pierre Joseph André. *Histoire générale de l'Asie, de l'Afrique et de l'Amérique*. 4 vols. Paris, 1770–72.

Rougemont, Frédéric de. *Précis d'ethnographie, de statistique et de géographie historique, ou Essai d'une géographie de l'homme*. 2 vols. Neuchâtel, 1835–37.

Rouse, Charles William Boughton. *Dissertation Concerning the Landed Property of Bengal*. London, 1791.

Rousseau, G. S., and Roy Porter, eds. *Exoticism in the Enlightenment*. Manchester: Manchester University Press, 1990.

Rousseau, G. S., and Roy Porter. "Introduction: Approaching Enlightenment Exoticism." In ibid., *Exoticism in the Enlightenment*, 1990, 1–22.

Rousseau, Jean-Baptiste-Louis. *Description du Pachalik de Bagdad*. Paris, 1809.

Rousseau, Jean-Jacques. *Œuvres complètes*. 5 vols. Paris: Gallimard, 1959–95.

Rousseau, Jean-Jacques. *Basic Political Writings*. Ed. and trans. Donald A. Cress. Indianapolis, IN: Liberty Fund, 1987.

Rowe, William T. *China's Last Empire: The Great Qing*. Cambridge, MA: Harvard University Press, 2009.

Ruangsilp, Bhawan. *Dutch East India Company Merchants at the Court of Ayutthaya: Dutch Perceptions of the Thai Kingdom, c. 1604–1765*. Leiden: Brill, 2007.

Rubiés, Joan-Pau. "Oriental Despotism and European Orientalism: Botero to Montesquieu." *Journal of Early Modern History* 9 (2005): 109–80.

Rubiés, Joan-Pau. "Travel Writing and Humanistic Culture: A Blunted Impact?" In Mancall, *Bringing the World to Early Modern Europe*, 2007, 131–68.

Rubiés, Joan-Pau. *Travellers and Cosmographers: Studies in the History of Early Modern Travel and Ethnology*. Aldershot: Ashgate, 2007.

Rubiés, Joan-Pau, and Manel Ollé. "The Comparative History of a Genre: The Production and Circulation of Books on Travel and Ethnographies in Early Modern Europe and China." *Modern Asian Studies* 50 (2016): 259–309.

Russell, Alexander. *The Natural History of Aleppo. Containing a Description of the City, and the Principal Natural Productions of Its Neighbourhood. Together with an Account of the Climate, Inhabitants, and Diseases, Particularly the Plague*. 2nd ed. 2 vols. London, 1794.

Ryan, Michael T. "Assimilating New Worlds in the Sixteenth and Seventeenth Centuries." *Comparative Studies in Society and History* 23 (1981): 519–38.

Rycaut, Sir Paul. *The Present State of the Ottoman Empire*. London, 1668.

Rycaut, Sir Paul. *The History of the Turkish Empire*. London, 1680.

Rywkin, Michael, ed. *Russian Colonial Expansion to 1917*. London: Mansell, 1988.

Sacy, Jacques Silvestre de. *Henri Bertin dans le sillage de la Chine, 1720–1792*. Paris: Éditions Cathasia, Les Belles Lettres, 1970.

Said, Edward W. *Orientalism*. New York: Pantheon, 1978.

Said, Edward W. *Culture and Imperialism*. London: Chatto and Windus, 1993.

Salaberry, Charles-Marie Comte de. *Histoire de l'Empire Ottoman, depuis sa fondation jusqu'à la Paix d'Yassi, en 1792*. 4 vols. Paris, 1813.

Sale, George. "Preliminary Discourse." In *The Koran, Commonly Called the Alcoran of Mohammed*. Trans. George Sale. 2 vols. London, 1764. Vol. 1, 1–248.

Salmon, Thomas. *The Universal Traveller; or, a Compleat Description of the Several Nations of the World*. 2 vols. London, 1752–53.

Salvucci, Pasquale. *Adam Ferguson: Sociologia e filosofia politica*. Urbino: Argalìa, 1972.

San Bartolomeo, Fra Paolino da. *Viaggio alle Indie orientale*. Rome, 1796.

Sangermano, Vincentius. *A Description of the Burmese Empire*. Compiled chiefly from Burmese documents. Trans. from his manuscript by W. Tandy. 2nd ed. London: Oriental Translation Fund of Great Britain, 1885 [1833].

Savary, Claude-Etienne. *Le Coran*. Paris, 1783.

Savary, Claude Etienne. *Lettres sur l'Égypte*. 3 vols. Paris, 1785–86.

Savory, Roger. *Iran under the Safavids*. Cambridge: Cambridge University Press, 1980.

Schäbler, Birgit. "Ulrich Jasper Seetzen (1767–1811). Jeveraner Patriot, aufgeklärter Kosmopolit und Orientreisender." In *Ulrich Jasper Seetzen (1767–1811). Leben und Werk. Die arabischen Länder und die Nahostforschung im napoleonischen Zeitalter*. Gotha: Forschungs- und Landesbibliothek, 1995, 113–34.

Schaffer, Simon, et al., eds. *The Brokered World: Go-Betweens and Global Intelligence, 1770–1820*. Sagamore Beach, MA: Science History Publications, 2009.

Schefer, Charles. "Introduction." In Du Mans, *Estat de la Perse en 1660*, 1890, I–CXV.

Schiller, Friedrich. *Sämtliche Werke*. Ed. Gerhard Fricke and Herbert G. Göpfert. 5 vols. 4th ed. Munich: Hanser, 1966.

Schiller, Friedrich. "The Nature and Value of Universal History: An Inaugural Lecture [1789]." *History and Theory* 11 (1972): 321–34.

Schlegel, Friedrich. “On the Indian Language, Literature, and Philosophy.” In *The Aesthetic and Miscellaneous Works of Frederick von Schlegel*. Trans. E. J. Millington. London 1849 (Reprint Cambridge 2014), 425–526.

Schlegel, Friedrich. “Philosophie der Geschichte. In achtzehn Vorlesungen gehalten zu Wien im Jahre 1828.” (*Kritische Friedrich-Schlegel-Ausgabe*. Sec. 1, vol. 9.) Ed. Jean-Jacques Anstett. Munich: Schöningh, 1971.

Schlegel, Friedrich. “Über die Sprache und Weisheit der Indier [1808].” (*Kritische Friedrich-Schlegel-Ausgabe*. Sec. 1, vol. 8.) Ed. Ernst Behler. Munich: Schöningh, 1975, 205–367.

Schleier, Hans. *Geschichte der deutschen Kulturgeschichtsschreibung*. 2 vols. Waltrop: Spener, 2003.

Schlereth, Thomas J. *The Cosmopolitan Ideal in Enlightenment Thought: Its Form and Function in the Ideas of Franklin, Hume, and Voltaire, 1694–1790*. Notre Dame, IN: Universityof Notre Dame Press, 1977.

Schlözer, August Ludwig. *Vorstellung seiner Universal-Historie*, 2 vols. Göttingen, 1772–73.

Schlözer, August Ludwig. *Vorbereitung zur Weltgeschichte für Kinder: Ein Buch für Kinderlehrer*. Ed. Marko Demantowsky and Susanne Popp. Göttingen: Vandenhoeck and Ruprecht, 2011 [1779].

Schlözer, August Ludwig. *WeltGeschichte nach ihren HauptTheilen im Auszug und Zusammenhange*. 2 vols. Göttingen, 1785–89.

Schlözer, August Ludwig. *Vorlesungen über Land- und Seereisen*. Nach dem Kollegheft des stud. jur. E. F. Haupt (Wintersemester 1795/96). Ed. Wilhelm Ebel. Göttingen: Vandenhoeck and Ruprecht, 1962.

Schmidt, Benjamin. *Inventing Exoticism: Geography, Globalism, and Europe's Early Modern World*. Philadelphia: University of Pennsylvania Press, 2015.

Schmidt-Biggemann, Wilhelm. *Topica Universalis: Eine Modellgeschichte humanistischer und barocker Wissenschaft*. Hamburg: Meiner, 1983.

Schmidt, Isaac Jacob. *Forschungen im Gebiete der älteren religiösen, politischen und literärischen Bildungsgeschichte der Völker Mittel-Asiens, vorzüglich der Mongolen und Tibeter*. Saint Petersburg, 1824.

Schneider, Ulrich Johannes, ed. *Kulturen des Wissens im 18. Jahrhundert*. Berlin: de Gruyter, 2008.

Schneiders, Werner. “Einleitung: Das Zeitalter der Aufklärung.” In ibid., ed., *Lexikon der Aufklärung: Deutschland und Europa*. Munich: C.H. Beck, 1995, 9–23.

Schröder, Iris. *Das Wissen von der ganzen Welt: Globale Geographien und räumliche Ordnungen Afrikas und Europas 1790–1870*. Paderborn: Schöningh, 2011.

Schrödter, Joseph. *See- und Landreise nach Ostindien und Aegypten in den Jahren 1795–1799*. Leipzig, 1800.

Schroeder, Paul W. *The Transformation of European Politics 1763–1848*. Oxford: Clarendon Press, 1994.

Schulin, Ernst. *Die weltgeschichtliche Erfassung des Orients bei Hegel und Ranke*. Göttingen: Vandenhoeck and Ruprecht, 1958.

Schultz, Arthur R. “Goethe and the Literature of Travel.” *Journal of English and Germanic Philology* 48 (1949): 445–68.

Schumann, Hans-Gerd. *Edmund Burkes Anschauungen vom Gleichgewicht in Staat und Staatensystem*. Meisenheim: Hain, 1964.

Schwab, Raymond. *Vie d'Anquetil-Duperron*. Paris: Presses universitaires de France, 1934.

Schwab, Raymond. *The Oriental Renaissance: Europe's Rediscovery of India and the East, 1680–1880.* New York: Columbia University Press, 1984 [1950].
Schwabe, Johann Joachim, ed. *Allgemeine Historie aller merckwürdigen Reisen, zu Wasser und zu Lande.* 21 vols. Basle, 1747–74.
Schwartz, Stuart B., ed. *Implicit Understandings: Observing, Reporting and Reflecting on the Encounters between Europeans and Other Peoples in the Early Modern Era.* Cambridge: Cambridge University Press, 1994.
Scott, Hamish M. *The Birth of a Great Power System, 1740–1815.* Harlow: Longman, 2006.
Scott, Jonathan. *An Historical and Political View of the Deccan.* London, 1791.
Scott Waring, Edward. *A Tour to Sheeraz.* London, 1807.
Sebastiani, Silvia. "Storia universale e teoria stadiale negli 'Sketches of the History of Man' di Lord Kames." *Studi storici* 39 (1998): 113–36.
Sebastiani, Silvia. *The Scottish Enlightenment: Race, Gender, and the Limits of Progress.* Basingstoke: Palgrave Macmillan, 2012.
Seetzen, Ulrich Jasper. *Reisen durch Syrien, Palästina, Phönicien, die Transjordan-Länder, Arabia Petraea und Unter-Aegypten.* 4 vols. Berlin: Reimer, 1854–59.
Seetzen, Ulrich Jasper. *Tagebuch des Aufenthalts in Aleppo 1803–1805.* Ed. Judith Zepter et al. Hildesheim: Olms, 2011.
Seifert, Arno. "Von der heiligen zur philosophischen Geschichte: Die Rationalisierung der universalhistorischen Erkenntnis im Zeitalter der Aufklärung." *Archiv für Kulturgeschichte* 68 (1986): 81–116.
Semedo, Alvarez. *The History of that Great and Renowned Monarchy of China.* London 1655 [1642].
Sestini, Domenico. *Voyage de Constantinopel à Bassora en 1781.* Paris, 1797.
Shackleton, Robert. *Montesquieu: A Critical Biography.* London: Oxford University Press, 1961.
Shackleton, Robert. *Essays on Montesquieu and on the Enlightenment.* Ed. D. Gilson and M. Smith. Oxford: Voltaire Foundation, 1988.
Shapin, Stephen. *A Social History of Truth: Civility and Science in Seventeenth-Century England.* Chicago: University of Chicago Press, 1994.
Shaw, Stanford J. *Between Old and New: The Ottoman Empire under Sultan Selim III, 1789–1807.* Cambridge, MA: Harvard University Press, 1971.
Shaw, Thomas. *Travels or Observations Relating to Several Parts of Barbary and the Levant.* 3rd ed. 2 vols. Edinburgh, 1808 [1738].
Shellim, Maurice. *Oil Paintings of India and the East by Thomas Daniell 1749–1840 and William Daniell 1769–1837.* London: Inchcape, 1979.
Shelvocke, George. *A Voyage round the World by Way of the Great South Sea Perform'd in the Years 1719, 20, 21, 22, in the "Speedwell" of London.* London, 1726.
Silhouette, Étienne de. *Idée générale du gouvernement et de la morale des Chinois. Tirée particulièrement des Ouvrages de Confucius.* Paris, 1731.
Silva, K. M. de. *A History of Sri Lanka.* London: Hurst, 1981.
Simms, Brendan, and D.J.B. Trim, eds. *Humanitarian Intervention: A History.* Cambridge: Cambridge University Press, 2011.
Singh, O. P. *Surat and Its Trade in the Second Half of the 17th Century.* Delhi: University of Delhi, 1977.
Slezkine, Yuri. *Arctic Mirros: Russia and the Small Peoples of the North.* Ithaca, NY: Cornell University Press, 1994.

Slotkin, J. S., ed. *Readings in Early Anthropology.* Chicago: University of Chicago Press, 1965.
Smith, Adam. *An Inquiry into the Nature and Causes of the Wealth of Nations.* Ed. R. H. Campbell and A. S. Skinner. 2 vols. Oxford: Clarendon Press, 1976 [1776] (= *Glasgow Edition of the Works and Correspondence of Adam Smith,* 2).
Smith, Adam. *The Correspondence of Adam Smith.* Ed. Ernest Campbell Mossner and Ian Simpson Ross. Oxford: Clarendon Press, 1977 (= *Glasgow Edition of the Works and Correspondence of Adam Smith,* 6).
Smith, Adam. *Lectures on Jurisprudence.* Ed. Ronald L. Meek, David D. Raphael, and Philip G. Stein. Oxford: Clarendon Press, 1978 [1762–66] (= *Glasgow Edition of the Works and Correspondence of Adam Smith,* 5).
Smith, Andrew. *Journal of His Expedition into the Interior of South Africa, 1834–36.* Ed. W. F. Lye. Cape Town: Balkema, 1975.
Smith, Bernard. *European Vision and the South Pacific: A Study in the History of Art and Ideas.* 2nd ed. New Haven, CT: Yale University Press, 1985.
Smith, Bernard. *Imagining the Pacific: In the Wake of the Cook Voyages.* New Haven, CT: Yale University Press, 1992.
Smith, Blake. "Myths of South Asian Stasis." *Journal of the Economic and Social History of the Orient* 59 (2016): 499–530.
Sobel, Dava. *Longitude: The True Story of a Lone Genius Who Solved the Greatest Scientific Problem of His Time.* London: Fourth Estate, 1996.
Societas Jesu. *Lettres édifiantes et curieuses écrites des Missions etrangères par quelques Missionaires de la Compagnie de Jesus.* Paris, 1702–1776.
Societas Jesu. *Lettres édifiantes et curieuses écrites des Missions etrangères par quelques Missionaires de la Compagnie de Jesus.* New ed. 26 vols. Paris, 1780–83.
Societas Jesu. *Nouvelles lettres édifiantes des missions de la Chine et des Indes Orientales.* 5 vols. Paris, 1818–20.
Société Asiatique. *Le Livre du centenaire, 1822–1922.* Paris: Geuthner, 1922.
Sommer, Johann Gottfried. *Neuestes Gemälde von Asien.* 2nd ed. 4 vols. Vienna, 1834.
Sonnerat, Pierre. *Voyages aux Indes Orientales et à la Chine, Fait par ordre du Roi, depuis 1774 jusqu'en 1781.* 2 vols. Paris, 1782.
Sonnini, Charles S. *Voyage dans la haute et basse Égypte, fait par ordre de l'ancien gouvernement.* 3 vols. Paris, 1799.
Sörlin, Sverker. "Scientific Travel: The Linnean Tradition." In Frängsmyr, *Science in Sweden,* 1989, 96–123.
Spate, Oscar H. K. *Paradise Found and Lost.* London: Croom Helm, 1988 (= *The Pacific since Magellan,* 3).
Spence, Jonathan D. *The Question of Hu.* New York: Knopf, 1988.
Spence, Jonathan D. *The Chan's Great Continent: China in Western Minds.* New York: Norton, 1998.
Spittler, Ludwig Timotheus. *Entwurf der Geschichte der europäischen Staaten.* 2 vols. Berlin, 1793–94.
Sprengel, Matthias Christian. *Vom Ursprung des Negerhandels: Ein Antrittsprogramm.* Halle, 1779.
Sprengel, Matthias Christian. *Geschichte der wichtigsten geographischen Entdeckungen durch Reisen.* Halle, 1783.
Sprengel, Matthias Christian. *Über den Krieg der Engländer in Ostindien.* Halle, 1783.
Sprengel, Matthias Christian. *Geschichte der Maratten bis auf den letzten Frieden mit England den 17. May 1782.* Frankenthal, 1791.

Sprengel, Matthias Christian, ed. *Auswahl der besten ausländischen geographischen und statistischen Nachrichten zur Aufklärung der Völker- und Länderkunde*. 14 vols. Halle, 1794–1800.

Sprengel, Matthias Christian. *Über die Fortschritte des Handels zwischen Großbrittannien und China seit 1784*. Halle, 1795.

Sprengel, Matthias Christian. *Gegenwärtiger Zustand der Ostindischen Handels-Gesellschaft in den Vereinigten Niederlanden*. Lübeck, 1797.

Sprengel, Matthias Christian. *Hyder Aly und Tippo Saheb oder historisch-geographische Übersicht des Mysorischen Reichs, nebst dessen Entstehung und Zertheilung*. Weimar, 1801.

Springborg, Patricia. *Western Republicanism and the Oriental Prince*. Cambridge: Polity Press, 1992.

Stafford, Barbara Maria. *Voyage into Substance: Art, Science, Nature, and the Illustrated Travel Account, 1760–1840*. Cambridge, MA: Harvard University Press, 1984.

Stagl, Justin. "Die Methodisierung des Reisens im 16. Jahrhundert." In Brenner, *Reisebericht*, 1989, 140–77.

Stagl, Justin. *A History of Curiosity: The Theory of Travel 1550–1800*. Chur: Harwood Academic Publishers, 1995.

Standaert, Nicolas, ed. *Handbook of Christianity in China*. Leiden: Brill, 2001 (= *Handbook of Oriental Studies*, 4/15.1).

Standaert, Nicolas. "Jesuits in China." In Thomas Worcester, ed., *The Cambridge Companion to the Jesuits*. Cambridge: Cambridge University Press, 2008, 169–85.

Starkey, Janet C. M. "No Myopic Mirage: Alexander and Patrick Russell in Aleppo." *History and Anthropology* 13 (2002): 257–73.

Staunton, Sir George Leonard. *An Authentic Account of an Embassy from the King of Great Britain to the Emperor of China*. 2 vols. with atlas. London, 1797.

Staunton, Sir George Thomas. *Ta Tsing Leu Lee; Being the Fundamental Laws, and a Selection from the Supplementary Statutes, of the Penal Code of China*. Translated from the Chinese. London, 1810.

Staunton, Sir George Thomas. *Memoirs of the Chief Incidents of the Public Life of Sir George Thomas Staunton, Bart*. London: L. Booth, 1856.

Stavorinus, Jan Splinter. *Reise nach dem Vorgebirge der Guten Hoffnung, Java und Bengalen in den Jahren 1768 bis 1771*. A. d. Holl. frey übers. u. mit Anm. begl. v. Professor Lueder in Braunschweig, Berlin, 1796 [1793].

Steadman, John M. *The Myth of Asia*. London: Macmillan, 1970.

Steeb, Johann Gottlieb. *Versuch einer allgemeinen Beschreibung von dem Zustand der ungesitteten und gesitteten Voelker nach ihrer moralischen und physicalischen Beschaffenheit*. Karlsruhe, 1766.

Stein, Burton. *Thomas Munro: The Origins of the Colonial State and His Vision of Empire*. Delhi: Oxford University Press, 1989.

Steller, Georg Wilhelm. *Beschreibung von dem Lande Kamtschatka, dessen Einwohnern, deren Sitten, Nahmen, Lebensart und verschiedenen Gewohnheiten*. Frankfurt a.M., 1774.

Steller, Georg Wilhelm. *Briefe und Dokumente 1740*. Ed. Wieland Hintzsche, Thomas Nickol, and Ol'ga Vladimirovna Novochatko. Halle a.d.S.: Franckesche Stiftungen, 2000.

Steller, Georg Wilhelm, Stepan Krašeninnikov, and Johann Eberhard Fischer. *Reisetagebücher 1735 bis 1743*. Ed. Wieland Hintzsche. Halle a.d.S.: Franckesche Stiftungen, 2000.

Stewart, Dugald. *Collected Works*. Ed. Sir William Hamilton. 10 vols. and suppl. Edinburgh: Thomas Constable, 1854–60.

Stewart, Gordon T. *Journeys to Empire: Enlightenment, Imperialism, and the British Encounter with Tibet, 1774–1904*. Cambridge: Cambridge University Press, 2009.

Stifler, Susan Reed. "The Language Students of the East India Company's Canton Factory." *Journal of the North China Branch of the Royal Asiatic Society* 69 (1938): 46–82.

Still, Judith. *Enlightenment Hospitality: Cannibals, Harems and Adoption*. Oxford: Voltaire Foundation, 2011.

Stocking, Jr., George W. *Victorian Anthropology*. New York: Free Press, 1987.

Stokes, Eric. *The English Utilitarians and India*. Oxford: Oxford University Press, 1959.

Strahlenberg, Philipp Johann von. *Das Nord- und Ostliche Theil von Europa und Asia in so weit solches das gantze Rußische Reich mit Sibirien und der grossen Tartarey in sich begreiffet* . . . . Stockholm, 1730.

Stuchtey, Benedikt, and Peter Wende, eds. *British and German Historiography: Traditions and Transfers*. Oxford: Oxford University Press, 2000.

Stuurman, Siep. "Cosmopolitan Egalitarianism in the Enlightenment: Anquetil Duperron on India and America." *Journal of the History of Ideas* 68 (2007): 255–78.

Subrahmanyam, Sanjay. "Connected Histories: Notes towards a Reconfiguration of Early Modern Eurasia." *Modern Asian Studies* 31 (1997): 735–62.

Subrahmanyam, Sanjay. *Explorations in Connected History: Mughals and Franks*. Oxford: Oxford University Press, 2005.

Subrahmanyam, Sanjay. *Three Ways to Be Alien: Travails and Encounters in the Early Modern World*. Waltham, MA: Brandeis University Press, 2011.

Subrahmanyam, Sanjay. "One Asia, or Many? Reflections from Connected History." *Modern Asian Studies* 50 (2016): 5–43.

Subrahmanyam, Sanjay. *Europe's India: Words, People, Empires, 1500–1800*. Cambridge, MA: Harvard University Press, 2017.

Swiderski, Richard M. *The False Formosan: George Psalmanazer and the Eighteenth-Century Experiment of Identity*. San Francisco, CA: Mellen Research University Press, 1991.

Symes, Michael. *An Account of an Embassy to the Kingdom of Ava, Sent by the Governor-General of India, in the Year 1795*. London, 1800.

Symes, Michael. *Journal of his Second Embassy to the Court of Ava in 1802*. Ed. D.G.E. Hall. London: George Allen and Unwin, 1955.

Syndram, Dirk. *Der Thron des Großmoguls: Johann Melchior Dinglingers goldener Traum vom Fernen Osten*. Leipzig: Seemann, 1996.

Tacitus. *Germania*. Trans. J. B. Rives. Oxford: Oxford University Press, 1999.

Tafazoli, Hamid. *Der deutsche Persien-Diskurs: Zur Verwissenschaftlichung und Literarisierung des Persien-Bildes im deutschen Schrifttum: Von der frühen Neuzeit bis in das neunzehnte Jahrhundert*. Bielefeld: Transcript, 2007.

Tahtāwi, Rifā'a al-. *An Imam in Paris: Al-Tahtawi's Visit to France 1826–1831*. Trans. Daniel L. Newman. London: Saqi Books, 2004.

Tavernier, Jean-Baptiste. *Nouvelle relation de l'interieur du Serraill du Grand Seigneur*. Paris, 1675.

Tavernier, Jean-Baptiste. *Travels in India*. Trans. Valentine Ball. Ed. William Crooke. 2 vols. London: Macmillan, 1889 [1676].

Taylor, Jean Gelman. *The Social World of Batavia: European and Eurasian in Dutch Asia*. 2nd ed. Madison: University of Wisconsin Press, 2009.

Teltscher, Kate. *India Inscribed: European and British Writing on India 1600–1800*. Delhi: Oxford University Press, 1995.

Temple, Sir William. *Works*. New ed. 4 vols. London, 1814.

Teng Ssu-yü. "Chinese Influence on the Western Examination System." *Harvard Journal of Asiatic Studies* 7 (1942–43): 267–312.

Tennant, William. *Indian Recreations; Consisting Chiefly of Strictures on the Domestic and Rural Economy of the Mahommedans & Hindoos*. 2 vols. Edinburgh, 1803.

Tennant, William. *Thoughts on the Effects of the British Government on the State of India*. Edinburgh, 1807.

Thackeray, William. *Vanity Fair*. Harmondsworth: Penguin, 2001 [1848].

Theolin, Sture, et al. *The Torch of the Empire: Ignatius Mouradgea d'Ohsson and the "Tableau général of the Ottoman Empire" in the Eighteenth Century*. Istabul: Yapı Kredi Yayınları, 2002.

Thévenot, Jean de. *The Travels of Monsieur de Thevenot into the Levant*. Translated from the French. 3 vols. London, 1687 [1664–84].

Thom, Martin. *Republics, Nations and Tribes*. London: Verso, 1995.

Thomas, Nicholas. *Entangled Objects: Exchange, Material Culture, and Colonialism in the Pacific*. Cambridge, MA: Harvard University Press, 1991.

Thomaz de Bossière, Mme. Yves de. *Jean-François Gerbillon, S .J. (1654–1707): Mathematicien de Louis XIV, premier supérieur général de la Mission française de Chine*. Louvain: F. Verbiest Foundation, 1994.

Thompson, Jason. "Osman Effendi: A Scottish Convert to Islam in Early Nineteenth-Century Egypt." *Journal of World History* 5 (1994): 99–123.

Thompson, Jason. *Wonderful Things: A History of Egyptology*. Vol. 1: *From Antiquity to 1881*. Cairo: American University Press, 2015.

Thomson, Ann. *Barbary and Enlightenment: European Attitudes towards the Maghreb in the Eighteenth Century*. Leiden: Brill, 1987.

Thornton, Thomas. *The Present State of Turkey; or Description of the Political, Civil and Religious Constitution, Government, and Laws of the Ottoman Empire*. 2nd ed. London, 1809 [1807].

Thunberg, Carl Peter. *Reisen in Afrika und Asien, vorzüglich in Japan, während der Jahre 1772 bis 1779*. Auszugsweise übers. v. K. Sprengel . . . u. mit Anm. begl. v. J. R. Forster, Berlin 1792 [Swedish, 1788–93].

Thunberg, Carl Peter. *Reise durch einen Theil von Europa, Afrika und Asien, hauptsächlich in Japan, in den Jahren 1770 bis 1779*. Trans. from Swedish by C. H. Großkurd. 2 vols. Berlin, 1794.

Thunberg, Carl Peter. *Voyages de C. P. Thunberg au Japon, par le Cap de Bonne-Espérance, les Isles de la Sonde, &c*. Traduits, rédigés et augmentés de notes . . . par Louis Mathieu Langlès. 2 vols. Paris, 1796.

Tidrick, Kathryn. *Heart-Beguiling Araby: The English Romance with Arabia*. 2nd ed. London: Tauris, 1989.

Tieffenthaler: see Bernoulli.

Tillotson, Giles. *Artificial Empire: The Indian Landscapes of William Hodges*. Richmond: Curzon, 2000.

Timkovski, George. *Voyage à Pekin, a travers la Mongolie en 1820 et 1821*. Ed. Julius von Klaproth. 2 vols. Paris, 1827.

Tissanier, Joseph. *Relation du Voyage du P. Joseph Tissanier de la Compagnie de Iesus. Depuis la France, iusqu'au Royaume de Tunquin*. Paris, 1663.

Titsingh, Isaac. *Mémoires et anecdotes sur la dynastie régnante des Djogouns, souverains du Japon. . . .* Publié par M. Abel-Rémusat. Paris, 1820.
Titsingh, Isaac. *The Private Correspondence of Isaac Titsingh.* Ed. Frank Lequin. 2 vols. Amsterdam: Gieben, 1990–92.
Titsingh, Isaac. *Secret Memoirs of the Shoguns: Isaac Titsingh and Japan, 1779–1822.* Annotated and introduced by Timon Screech. London: Routledge, 2006.
Tocqueville, Alexis de. *Œuvres complètes.* Vol. 3 in 2 pts. *Ecrits et discours politiques.* Paris: Gallimard, 1962.
Tod, James. *Annals and Antiquities of Rajasthan or the Central and Western Rajput States of India.* Ed. William Crooke. 3 vols. London: Humphrey Milford, Oxford University Press, 1920 [1829–32].
Tombe, Charles François. *Voyage aux Indes Orientales pendant les années 1802, 1803, 1804, 1805 et 1806.* 2 vols. and atlas. Paris, 1810.
Tone, William Henry. "Illustrations of Some Institutions of the Mahratta People." *Asiatic Annual Register,* 1798–99, 124–51.
Toreen, Olof. "A *Voyage* to Surate, China, &c., from the 1st of April, 1750, to the 26th of June, 1752, in a Series of Letters to Doctor Linnaeus." In Osbeck, *Voyage,* vol. 2, 1771, 153–266.
Tortarolo, Edoardo. *L'illuminismo: ragioni e dubbi della modernità.* 3rd ed. Rome: Carocci, 2007.
Totman, Conrad. *Early Modern Japan.* Berkeley: University of California Press, 1993.
Tott, Baron François de. *Memoirs of Baron de Tott; Containing the State of the Turkish Empire and the Crimea during the Late War with Russia.* 2nd ed. 2 vols. London, 1786 [1785].
Tournefort: see Pitton de Tournefort.
Trakulhun, Sven. *Asiatische Revolutionen: Europa und der Aufstieg und Fall asiatischer Imperien (1600–1830).* Frankfurt a.M.: Campus, 2017.
Travels of the Jesuits into Various Parts of the World, Compiled from Their Letters. London, 1743.
Tucker, Ernest S. *Nadir Shah's Quest for Legitimacy in Post-Safavid Iran.* Gainesville: University Press of Florida, 2006.
Turgot, Anne Robert Jacques. *Œuvres.* Ed. Gustave Schelle. 5 vols. Paris: Alcan, 1913–23.
Turner, Samuel. *Account of an Embassy to the Court of the Teshoo Lama in Tibet.* London, 1800.
Turner, William. *Journal of a Tour in the Levant.* 3 vols. London, 1820.
Turpin, François René. *Histoire civile et naturelle du royaume de Siam. Et des Révolutions qui ont bouleversée cet Empire jusqu'en 1770.* 2 vols. Paris, 1771.
Tzoref-Ashkenazi, Chen. "Romantic Attitudes toward Oriental Despotism." *Journal of Modern History* 85 (2013): 280–320.
Universal History. An Universal History, from the Earliest Account of Time. 7 vols. London, 1736–44.
Universal History. The Modern Part of an Universal History from the Earliest Account of Time; Compiled from Original Authors by the Authors of the Ancient Part. 44 vols. and 16 vols. in folio. London, 1759–66.
Universal History. New ed. 60 vols. London, 1779–84.
Unverzagt, Georg Johann. *Die Gesandtschaft Ihrer Kayserlichen Majestät von Groß-Rußland an den Sinesischen Kayser.* Lübeck, 1727.
Valensi, Lucette. *Venise et la Sublime Porte: La naissance du despote.* Paris: Hachette, 1987.

Valensi, Lucette. "The Making of a Political Paradigm: The Ottoman State and Oriental Despotism." In Anthony Grafton and Ann Blair, eds., *The Transmission of Culture in Early Modern Europe*. Pittsburgh, PA: University of Pittsburgh Press, 1990, 173–203.

Valentia, George Viscount. *Voyages and Travels to India, Ceylon, the Red Sea, Abyssinia, and Egypt, in the Years 1802, 1803, 1804, 1805, and 1806*. 4 vols. London, 1809.

Valentia, George Viscount. *Reisen nach Indien. . . .* Aus dem Engl. im Auszuge übers. v. Friedrich Rühs. 2 vols. Weimar, 1811.

Valentyn, François. *Oud en nieuw Ooost-Indien*. 5 vols. Dordrecht, 1724–26.

Valentyn, François. *Description of Ceylon*. Trans. and ed. S. Arasaratnam. London: Hakluyt Society, 1978.

Valéry, Paul. *Œuvres*. Ed. Jean Hytier. 2 vols. Paris: Gallimard, 1957–60.

Van Aalst, Frank Daigh. "The British View of India, 1750 to 1785." PhD thesis, University of Pennsylvania, 1970.

Van der Brug, Peter Harmen. *Malaria en malaise: De VOC in Batavia in de achttiende eeuw*. Amsterdam: De Bataafsche Leeuw, 1994.

Van der Cruysse, Dirk. *Louis XIV et le Siam*. Paris: Fayard, 1991.

Van Kley, Edwin J. "Europe's 'Discovery' of China and the Writing of World History." *American Historical Review* 76 (1971): 358–85.

Van Kley, Edwin J. "News from China: Seventeenth-Century European Notices of the Manchu Conquest." *Journal of Modern History* 45 (1973): 561–82.

Varenius, Bernhardus. *Descriptio Regni Japoniae / Beschreibung des japanischen Reiches*. Ed. Martin Schwind and Horst Hammitzsch, trans. E.- C. Volkmann. Darmstadt: Wissenschaftliche Buchgesellschaft, 1974 [1649].

Venturi, Franco. *L'antichità svelata e l'idea del progresso in N.A. Boulanger (1722–1759)*. Bari: Laterza, 1947.

Venturi, Franco. "Oriental Despotism." *Journal of the History of Ideas* 24 (1963): 133–42.

Venturi, Franco. *Europe des Lumières: Recherches sur le 18e siècle*. Paris: Mouton, 1971.

Verbiest, Ferdinand. "Voyage de l'Empereur de la Chine dans la Tartarie." In Bernard, *Recueil des voyages au nord*, vol. 4 (nouv. éd., 1732), 414–55 [1682].

Verelst, Harry. *A View of the Rise, Progress, and Present State of the English Government in Bengal*. London, 1772.

Vicziany, Marika. "Imperialism, Botany and Statistics in Early Nineteenth-Century India: The Surveys of Francis Buchanan." *Modern Asian Studies* 20 (1986): 625–60.

Villiers, Patrick, and Jean-Pierre Duteil. *L'Europe, la mer et les colonies, XVIIe–XVIIIe siècle*. Paris: Hachette, 1997.

Virey, Julien Joseph. *Histoire naturelle du genre humain*. Nouv. éd. 3 vols. Paris, 1824.

Visdelou, Claude. "Histoire abregée de la Tartarie . . . ." In d'Herbelot, *Bibliothèque Orientale*, vol. 4 (1779), 46–294.

Voegelin, Eric. *Anamnesis: Zur Theorie der Geschichte und Politik*. Munich: Piper, 1966.

Vogel, Johann Wilhelm. *Zehn-Jährige, Jetzo auffs neue revidirt und vermehrte Ost-Indianische Reise-Beschreibung*. Altenburg, 1716.

Volney, Constantin François de. *Considérations sur la guerre actuelle des Turcs*. Paris, 1788.

Volney, Constantin François de. *Les ruines, ou Méditation sur les révolutions des empires*. Paris, 1826 [1791].

Volney, Constantin François de. *The Ruins, or a Survey of the Revolutions of Empires*. London, 1849 [1791].

Volney, Constantin François de. *Voyage en Égypte et en Syrie*. Ed. Jean Gaulmier. Paris: Mouton, 1959 [1787].

Volney, Constantin François de. *Œuvres*. Ed. Anne and Henry Deneys. 3 vols. Paris: Fayard, 1989–98.

Voltaire. *The Works of M. de Voltaire*. Trans. Tobias Smollett et al. 25 vols. London, 1761–65.

Voltaire. *The History of Peter the Great, Emperor of Russia*. Trans. Tobias Smollett. 2 vols. New York, 1848.

Voltaire. *Les œuvres complètes de Voltaire*. Oxford: Voltaire Foundation, 1968*ff*–.

Vyverberg, Henry. *Human Nature, Cultural Diversity, and the French Enlightenment*. New York, 1989.

Wahl, Samuel Friedrich Günther. *Allgemeine Geschichte der morgenländischen Sprachen und Litteratur*. Leipzig, 1784.

Wahl, Samuel Friedrich Günther. *Der Geist und die Geschichte des Schach-Spiels bei den Indern, Persern, Arabern, Türken, Sinesen und übrigen Morgenländern, Deutschen und anderen Europäern*. Halle, 1798.

Wahl, Samuel Friedrich Günther. *Erdbeschreibung von Ostindien, nemlich Hindostan und Dekan, nebst den Inseln Lakdiven, Maldiven und Ceylon*. Hamburg, 1805.

Wakefield, Priscilla. *The Traveller in Asia; or, a Visit to the Most Celebrated Parts of the East Indies and China. For the Instruction and Entertainment of Young Persons*. London, 1817.

Walckenaer, Charles Athanase. *Essai sur l'histoire de l'espèce humaine*. Paris, 1798.

Walckenaer, Charles Athanas, ed. *Histoire générale des voyages, ou Nouvelle collection des relations de voyages par mer et par terre*. 21 vols. Paris, 1826–31.

Walckenaer, Charles Athanase. *Vies de plusieurs personnages célèbres des temps anciens et modernes*. 2 vols. Laon, 1830.

Wallace, Jennifer. *Shelley and Greece: Rethinking Romantic Hellenism*. Basingstoke: Macmillan, 1997.

Wallace, Robert. *A Dissertation on the Numbers of Mankind in Ancient and Modern Times*. Edinburgh, 1809 [1753].

Waller, Derek. *The Pundits: British Exploration of Tibet and Central Asia*. Rev. ed. Lexington, KY: University Press of Kentucky, 2004.

Walpole, Robert, ed. *Travels in Various Countries of the East*. London, 1820.

Walravens, Hartmut. *Julius Klaproth (1738–1835): Leben und Werk*. Wiesbaden: Harrassowitz, 1999.

Walter, Richard, and Benjamin Robins. *A Voyage round the World in the Years MDCCXL, I, II, III, IV. By George Anson*. Ed. Glyndwr Williams. London: Oxford University Press, 1974 [1749].

Walter, Xavier. *John Barrow, un Anglais en Chine au XVIIIe siècle*. Paris: Payot, 1994.

Walvin, James. *Fruits of Empire: Exotic Produce and British Taste, 1660–1800*. Basingstoke: Macmillan, 1997.

Wang Mei-chu. *Die Rezeption des chinesischen Ton-, Zahl- und Denksystems in der westlichen Musiktheorie und Ästhetik*. Frankfurt a.M.: Lang, 1985.

Wansleb, Johann Michael. "Beschreibung von Aegypten im Jahre 1664." In Paulus, *Sammlung der merkwürdigsten Reisen in den Orient*, vol. 3, 1794, 1–122.

Wansleb, Johann Michael. "Neue Beschreibung einer Reise nach Aegypten in den Jahren 1672, 1673." In Paulus, *Sammlung der merkwürdigsten Reisen in den Orient*, vol. 3, 1794, 123–412.

Ward, William. *A View of the History, Literature, and Religion of the Hindoos*. 3rd ed. 4 vols. London, 1817–20.

Wathen, James. *Journal of a Voyage in 1811 and 1812 to Madras and China*. London, 1814.

Weber, Friedrich Christian. *Das veränderte Rußland*. 3 pts. Frankfurt a.M. and Leipzig (pt. 1, new ed.), Hannover (pts. 2 and 3), 1738–39.

Weber, Max. *Die Wirtschaftsethik der Weltreligionen. Konfuzianismus und Taoismus. Schriften 1915–1920*. Ed. Helwig Schmidt-Glintzer and Petra Kolonko. Tübingen: Mohr (Siebeck), 1989 (= *Max Weber Gesamtausgabe*, 1/19).

Weißhaupt, Winfried. *Europa sieht sich mit fremdem Blick. Werke nach dem Schema der "Lettres persanes" in der europäischen, insbesondere der deutschen Literatur des 18. Jahrhunderts*. 3 vols. Frankfurt a.M.: Lang, 1979.

Wendland, Folkwart. "Das Russische Reich am Vorabend der Großen Nordischen Expedition, der sogenannten zweiten Kamtschatka-Expedition." In Posselt, *Große Nordische Expedition*, 1990, 332–84.

Wendland, Folkwart. *Peter Simon Pallas (1741–1811): Materialien einer Biographie*. 2 vols. Berlin: de Gruyter, 1992.

Wessels, Cornelius. *Early Jesuit Travellers in Central Asia 1603–1721*. The Hague: Nijhoff, 1924.

Whelan, Frederick G. *Edmund Burke and India: Political Morality and Empire*. Pittsburgh, PA: University of Pittsburgh Press, 1996.

Whelan, Frederick G. "Oriental Despotism: Anquetil-Duperron's Response to Montesquieu." *History of Political Thought* 22 (2001): 619–47.

Whelan, Frederick G. *Enlightenment Political Thought and Non-Western Societies: Sultans and Savages*. New York: Routledge, 2009.

White, John. *A Voyage to Cochin China*. London, 1824.

White, Joseph. *Institutes Political and Military Written Originally in the Mogul Language, by the Great Timour, Improperly Called Tamerlane*. Oxford, 1783.

Wieser, Friedrich von. *Recht und Macht*. Leipzig: Duncker and Humblot, 1910.

Wilks, Mark. *Historical Sketches of the South of India*. 3 vols. London, 1810–17.

Williams, Glyndwr. *The Great South Sea: English Voyages and Encounters 1570–1750*. New Haven, CT: Yale University Press, 1997.

Wills, John E., Jr. "Maritime Asia, 1500–1800: The Interactive Emergence of European Dominance." *American Historical Review* 98 (1993): 83–105.

Wills, John E., Jr. *1688: A Global History*. New York: Norton, 2001.

Wills, John E., Jr. *The World from 1450 to 1700*. Oxford: Oxford University Press, 2009.

Wills, John E., Jr. "What's New? Studies of Revolutions and Divergences, 1770–1840." *Journal of World History* 25 (2014): 127–86.

Willson, A. Leslie. *A Mythical Image: The Ideal of India in German Romanticism*. Durham, NC: Duke University Press, 1964.

Wilson, Jon. *India Conquered: Britain's Raj and the Chaos of Empire*. London: Simon and Schuster, 2016.

Winch, Donald. *Classical Political Economy and Colonies*. Cambridge, MA: Harvard University Press, 1965.

Winckelmann, Johann Joachim. *History of the Art of Antiquity*. Trans. Harry Francis Mallgrave. Los Angeles: Getty Research Institute, 2006 [1764].

Windisch, Ernst. *Geschichte der Sanskrit-Philologie und der Indischen Altertumskunde*. 2 vols. Strassbourg: Trübner, 1917–20.

Winterbotham, William. *An Historical, Geographical, and Philosophical View of the Chinese Empire*. London, 1795.

Wintle, Michael. *The Image of Europe: Visualizing Europe in Cartography and Iconography throughout the Ages*. Cambridge: Cambridge University Press, 2009.

Wisotzki, Emil. *Zeitströmungen in der Geographie*. Leipzig: Duncker and Humblot, 1897.

Withers, Charles W. J. *Placing the Enlightenment: Thinking Geographically about the Age of Reason*. Chicago: University of Chicago Press, 2007.

Withers, Charles W. J. "On Enlightenment's Margins: Geography, Imperialism and Mapping in Central Asia, c. 1798–c. 1838." *Journal of Historical Geography* 39 (2013): 3–18.

Witsen, Nicolaas. *Noord en Oost Tartarye*. 2 vols. Amsterdam, 1705 [1692].

Wittman, William. *Travels in Turkey, Asia Minor, Syria and across the Desert to Egypt during the Years 1799, 1800, and 1801*. London, 1803.

Wolf, Johann Christoph. *Reise nach Zeilan*. 2 vols. Berlin, 1781–84.

Wolff, Larry. *Inventing Eastern Europe: The Map of Civilization on the Mind of the Enlightenment*. Stanford, CA : Stanford University Press, 1994.

Wolff, Larry, and Marco Cipolloni, eds. *The Anthropology of the Enlightenment*. Stanford, CA: Stanford University Press, 2007.

Wollmann, Therese. *Scheich Ibrahim: Die Reisen des Johann Ludwig Burckhardt 1784–1817*. Basle: Reinhardt, 1984.

Wood, Robert. *The Ruins of Palmyra*. London, 1753.

Wood, Robert. *The Ruins of Balbec*. London, 1757.

Woodhead, Christine. "'The Present Terrour of the World?' Contemporary Views of the Ottoman Empire." *History* 72 (1987): 20–37.

Woodhouselee, Lord Alexander Fraser Tytler. *Elements of General History, Ancient and Modern*. 9th ed. 2 vols. London, 1825 [1801].

Woolf, Harry. *The Transits of Venus: A Study of Eighteenth-Century Science*. Princeton, NJ: Princeton University Press, 1959.

Woolf, Stuart. "The Construction of a European World View in the Revolutionary-Napoleonic Years." *Past and Present*, no. 137 (1992): 72–101.

Wright, Denis. *The Persians amongst the English: Episodes in Anglo-Persian History*. London: Tauris, 1985.

Wurtzburg, Charles Edward. *Raffles of the Eastern Isles*. London: Hodder and Stoughton, 1954.

Wyatt, David K. *Thailand: A Short History*. New Haven, CT: Yale University Press, 1982.

Yakovaki, Nassia. "'Ancient and Modern Greeks' in the Late 18th Century: A Comparative Approach from a European Perspective." In Evangelos Konstantinou, ed., *Ausdrucksformen des europäischen und internationalen Philhellenismus vom 17. -19. Jahrhundert*. Frankfurt a.M.: Lang, 2007, 199–209.

Yapp, Malcolm E. "Europe in the Turkish Mirror." *Past and Present*, no. 137 (1992): 34–55.

Yerasimos, Stéphane. *Les voyageurs dans l'Empire Ottoman (XIV–XVIe siècles)*. Ankara: Société Turque d'Histoire, 1991.

Young, David. "Montesquieu's View of Despotism and His Use of Travel Literature." *Review of Politics* 40 (1978): 392–405.

Yule, Henry, and A. C. Burnell. *Hobson-Jobson: A Glossary of Colloquial Anglo-Indian Words and Phrases*. London: Murray, 1886.

Zaidi, S. Inayat A. "European Mercenaries in the Indian Armies, AD 1750–1803." *Studies in History* 27 (2011): 55–83.

Zammito, John H. *Kant, Herder, and the Birth of Anthropology*. Chicago: University of Chicago Press, 2002.

Zastoupil, Lynn. *John Stuart Mill and India*. Stanford, CA: Stanford University Press, 1994.

Zedler, Johann Friedrich et al., eds. *Grosses vollständiges Universal-Lexicon aller Wissenschaften und Künste, Welche bißhero durch menschlichen Verstand und Witz erfunden und verbessert wurden. . . .* 64 vols. Halle, 1732–50.

Zheng Yangwen. *China on the Sea: How the Maritime World Shaped Modern China.* Leiden: Brill, 2012.

Ziegenbalg, Bartholomäus. *Malabarisches Heidenthum.* Ed. Willem Caland. Amsterdam: Koninklijke Akademie van Wetenschappen, 1926 [1711].

Ziegenbalg, Bartholomäus, and Johann Ernst Gründler. "Malabarische Correspondenz." In *Der königl. dänischen Missionarien aus Ost-Indien eingesandte ausführliche Berichte.* Halle. [Pt. 1]: *Siebende Continuation . . .* (1714), 337–504; [Pt. 2]: *Elfte Continuation . . .* (1717), 871–959.

Zilfi, Madeline C., ed. *Women in the Ottoman Empire: Middle Eastern Women in the Early Modern Era.* Leiden: Brill, 1997.

Zimmermann, Eberhardt August Wilhelm von. *Geographische Geschichte des Menschen und der allgemein verbreiteten vierfüßigen Thiere.* 3 vols. Leipzig, 1778–83.

Zimmermann, Eberhardt August Wilhelm von. *Ueber die Verbreitung und Ausartung des Menschengeschlechts.* Leipzig, 1778.

Zimmermann, Eberhardt August Wilhelm von. *Versuch einer Anwendung der zoologischen Geographie auf die Geschichte der Erde.* Leipzig, 1783.

Zimmermann, Eberhardt August Wilhelm von. *Annalen der Geographie und Statistik.* 3 vols. Braunschweig, 1790–92.

Zimmermann, Eberhardt August Wilhelm von. *Die Erde und ihre Bewohner nach den neuesten Entdekkungen.* 5 vols. Leipzig, 1810–14.

Zoli, Sergio. "Le polemiche sulla Cina nella cultura storica, filosofica, letteraria italiana della prima metà del settecento." *Archivio storico italiano* 130 (1972): 409–67.

Zoli, Sergio. *La Cina e la cultura italiana: Dal 1500 al 1700.* Bologna: Pàtron, 1973.

Zoli, Sergio. *La Cina e l'età dell'illuminismo in Italia.* Bologna: Pàtron, 1974.

Züge, Christian Gottlob. *Der russische Colonist oder Christian Gottlob Züge's Leben in Russland, nebst einer Schilderung der Sitten und Gebräuche der Russen vornehmlich in den asiatischen Provinzen.* Ed. Gert Robel. Bremen: Edition Temmen, 1988 [1802].

Index